Dictionary of

Banking
and Finance

fourth edition

B L O O M S B U R Y
LONDON • NEW DELHI • NEW YORK • SYDNEY

First published in Great Britain by Peter Collin Publishing in 1991
Second edition published 1999
Third edition published 2003
Reprinted 2005, 2009, 2010

Bloomsbury Publishing Plc
50 Bedford Square
London
WC1B 3DP

www.bloomsbury.com

Bloomsbury is a trade mark of Bloomsbury Publishing Plc

Bloomsbury Publishing, London, New Delhi, New York and Sydney

A CIP catalogue record for this book is available from the British Library

ISBN 978 071367 7393 (paperback edition)
ISBN 978 1408 198117 (ebook edition)

10 9 8 7 6 5 4 3 2 1

Typeset by Hewer Text UK Ltd, Edinburgh

Preface

This dictionary provides a basic vocabulary of terms used in the fields of banking, investment, the Stock Exchange, and general finance. It covers both British and American usage.

The main words and phrases are defined in simple English, and many examples are given to show how the words may be used in context. In some cases, the definitions are expanded by explanatory comments. We also give quotations from newspapers and financial magazines from various parts of the world.

The supplements at the back of the book offer additional information.

At the same time, to make the dictionary more useful to students, we now give phonetic transcriptions for all the headwords.

Pronunciation Guide

The following symbols have been used to show the pronunciation of the main words in the dictionary.

Stress is indicated by a main stress mark (') and a secondary stress mark (,). Note that these are only guides, as the stress of the word changes according to its position in the sentence.

Vowels		*Consonants*	
æ	back	b	buck
ɑː	harm	d	dead
ɒ	stop	ð	other
aɪ	type	dʒ	jump
aʊ	how	f	fare
aɪə	hire	g	gold
aʊə	hour	h	head
ɔː	course	j	yellow
ɔɪ	annoy	k	cab
e	head	l	leave
eə	fair	m	mix
eɪ	make	n	nil
eʊ	go	ŋ	sing
ɜː	word	p	print
iː	keep	r	rest
i	happy	s	save
ə	about	ʃ	shop
ɪ	fit	t	take
ɪə	near	tʃ	change
u	annual	θ	theft
uː	pool	v	value
ʊ	book	w	work
ʊə	tour	x	loch
ʌ	shut	ʒ	measure
		z	zone

A

A /eɪ/, **AA** /ˌdʌb(ə)l 'eɪ/, **AAA** /ˌtrɪp(ə)l 'eɪ/, *noun* letters that show how reliable a particular share, bond or company is considered to be ○ *These bonds have a AAA rating.*

'…the rating concern lowered its rating to single-A from double-A, and its senior debt rating to triple-B from single-A' [*Wall Street Journal*]

COMMENT: The AAA rating is given by Standard & Poor's or by Moody's, and indicates a very high level of reliability for a corporate or municipal bond in the US

A1 /ˌeɪ 'wʌn/ *adjective* □ **ship which is A1 at Lloyd's** a ship which is in the best possible condition according to Lloyd's Register

AAD *abbreviation* Arab accounting dinar

ABA *abbreviation* American Bankers Association

abandonment /ə'bændənmənt/ *noun* an act of giving up voluntarily something that you own, such as an option or the right to a property

abatement /ə'beɪtmənt/ *noun* **1.** an act of reducing **2.** a reduction in a payment, e.g., if a company's or individual's total assets are insufficient to cover their debts or legacies

ABA transit number /ˌeɪ biː eɪ 'trænzɪt ˌnʌmbə/ *noun* a number allocated to an American financial institution, such as a bank (NOTE: The number appears on US cheques in the top right-hand corner, above the 'check routing symbol'.)

abbreviated accounts /əˌbriːviːeɪtɪd ə'kaʊnts/ *plural noun* a shortened version of a company's annual accounts that a small or medium sized company can file with the Registrar of Companies, instead of a full version

ABI *abbreviation* Association of British Insurers

above par /əˌbʌv 'pɑː/ *adjective* referring to a share with a market price higher than its face value

above-the-line /əˌbʌv ðə 'laɪn/ *adjective, adverb* **1.** used to describe entries in a company's profit and loss accounts that appear above the line which separates entries showing the origin of the funds that have contributed to the profit or loss from those that relate to its distribution. Exceptional and extraordinary items appear above the line. ○ *Exceptional items are noted above the line in company accounts.* ◊ **below-the-line 2.** relating to revenue items in a government budget

absolute /'æbsəluːt/ *adjective* complete or total

absolute monopoly /ˌæbsəluːt mə'nɒpəli/ *noun* a situation where only one producer produces or only one supplier supplies something ○ *The company has an absolute monopoly of imports of French wine.* ○ *The supplier's absolute monopoly of the product meant that customers had to accept her terms.*

absolute title /ˌæbsəluːt 'taɪt(ə)l/ *noun* a form of ownership of a piece of land in which the owner's right is guaranteed by being registered with the Land Registry (NOTE: Absolute title also exists to leasehold land, giving the proprietor a guaranteed valid lease.)

absorb /əb'zɔːb/ *verb* to take in a small item so that it forms part of a larger one □ **overheads have absorbed all our profits** all our profits have gone in paying overhead expenses □ **to absorb a loss by a subsidiary** to include a subsidiary company's loss in the group accounts □ **a business which has been absorbed by a competitor** a small business which has been made part of a larger one

absorption /əb'zɔːpʃən/ *noun* the process of making a smaller business part of a larger one, so that the smaller company in effect no longer exists

absorption costing /əb'zɔːpʃən ˌkɒstɪŋ/ *noun* a form of costing for a product that includes both the direct costs of production and the indirect overhead costs as well

absorption rate /əb'zɔːpʃən ˌreɪt/ *noun* a rate at which overhead costs are absorbed into each unit of production

abstract /'æbstrækt/ *noun* a short form of a report or document ○ *to make an abstract of the company accounts*

a/c, **acc** *abbreviation* account

ACAS /'eɪkæs/ *abbreviation* Advisory, Conciliation and Arbitration Service

accelerate /ək'seləreɪt/ *verb* **1.** to make something go faster **2.** to reduce the amount of time before a maturity date

accelerated cost recovery system /æk,selrəreɪtɪd 'kɒst rɪ ˌkʌvəri ˌsɪstəm/ *noun* a system used in the United States for calculating depreciation in a way that reduces tax liability

accelerated depreciation /ək ˌseləreɪtɪd dɪpriːʃɪ'eɪʃ(ə)n/ *noun* a system of depreciation which reduces the value of assets at a high rate in the early years to encourage companies, as a result of tax advantages, to invest in new equipment

COMMENT: This applied in the UK until 1984; until then companies could depreciate new equipment at 100% in the first year of purchase.

acceleration /ək,selə'reɪʃ(ə)n/ *noun* the act of making an unpaid balance or bond repayment become payable immediately

accept /ək'sept/ *verb* **1.** to take something which is being offered □ **to accept delivery of a shipment** to take goods into the warehouse officially when they are delivered **2.** to say 'yes' or to agree to something ○ *She accepted the offer of a job in Australia.* ○ *He accepted $2,000 instead of one week's notice.* ○ *60% of shareholders have accepted the offer.*

acceptable /ək'septəb(ə)l/ *adjective* easily accepted ○ *Both parties found the offer acceptable.* ○ *The terms of the contract of employment are not acceptable to the candidate.* ○ *The offer is not acceptable to the shareholders.*

acceptance /ək'septəns/ *noun* **1.** the act of signing a bill of exchange to show that you agree to pay it □ **to present a bill for acceptance** to present a bill for payment by the person who has accepted it **2.** □ **acceptance of an offer** the act of agreeing to an offer □ **to give an offer a conditional acceptance** to accept an offer provided that specific things happen or that specific terms apply □ **we have their letter of acceptance** we have received a letter from them accepting the offer **3.** a bill which has been accepted **4.** the act of accepting an offer of new shares for which you have applied

acceptance credit /ək'septəns ˌkredɪt/ *noun* an arrangement of credit from a bank, where the bank accepts bills of exchange drawn on the bank by the debtor: the bank then discounts the bills and is responsible for paying them when they mature. The debtor owes the bank for the bills but these are covered by letters of credit.

acceptance sampling /ək'septəns ˌsɑːmplɪŋ/ *noun* the process of testing a small sample of a batch to see if the whole batch is good enough to be accepted

accepting house /ək'septɪŋ 'haʊs/, **acceptance house** /ək'septəns haʊs/ *noun* a firm, usually a merchant bank, which accepts bills of exchange at a discount, in return for immediate payment to the issuer, in this case the Bank of England

Accepting Houses Committee /ək ˌseptɪŋ ˌhaʊzɪz kə'mɪti/ *noun* the main London merchant banks, which organise the lending of money with the Bank of England. They receive slightly better discount rates from the Bank.

acceptor /ək'septə/ *noun* a person who accepts a bill of exchange by signing it, thus making a commitment to pay it by a specified date

access /'ækses/ *noun* □ **to have access to something** a way of obtaining or reaching something ○ *She has access to large amounts of venture capital.* ■ *verb* to call up data which is stored in a computer ○ *She accessed the address file on the computer.*

Access /ˈækses/ *noun* a credit card system formerly operated by some British banks, part of the MasterCard network

access fee /ˈækses fiː/ *noun* a fee charged to bank customers for using online services

access time /ˈækses taɪm/ *noun* the time taken by a computer to find data stored in it

accident insurance /ˌæksɪd(ə)nt ɪnˈʃʊərəns/ *noun* insurance which will pay the insured person when an accident takes place

accident policy /ˌæksɪd(ə)nt ˈpɒlɪsi/ *noun* an insurance contract which provides a person with accident insurance

accommodation /əˌkɒməˈdeɪʃ(ə)n/ *noun* **1.** money lent for a short time **2.** □ **to reach an accommodation with creditors** to agree terms for settlement with creditors

'…any non-resident private landlord can let furnished or unfurnished accommodation to a tenant' [*Times*]

accommodation address /əˌkɒmə ˈdeɪʃ(ə)n əˌdres/ *noun* an address used for receiving messages, but which is not the real address of the company

accommodation bill /əˌkɒmə ˈdeɪʃ(ə)n ˌbɪl/ *noun* a bill of exchange where the person signing (the 'drawee') is helping another company (the 'drawer') to raise a loan

accordance /əˈkɔːd(ə)ns/ *noun* □ **in accordance with** in agreement or conformity with, as a result of what someone has said should be done ○ *In accordance with your instructions we have deposited the money in your current account.* ○ *I am submitting the claim for damages in accordance with the advice of our legal advisers.*

accord and satisfaction /əˌkɔːd ən sætɪsˈfækʃən/ *noun* the payment by a debtor of (part of) a debt

accordingly /əˈkɔːdɪŋli/ *adverb* in agreement with what has been decided ○ *We have received your letter and have altered the contract accordingly.*

according to /əˈkɔːdɪŋ tuː/ *preposition* **1.** in accordance with ○ *The*

computer was installed according to the manufacturer's instructions.* ○ *The shares were bought according to written instructions from the client.* **2.** as stated or shown by someone

'…the budget targets for employment and growth are within reach according to the latest figures' [*Australian Financial Review*]

account /əˈkaʊnt/ *noun* **1.** a record of financial transactions over a period of time, such as money paid, received, borrowed or owed ○ *Please send me your account or a detailed or an itemised account.* **2.** (*in a shop*) an arrangement in which a customer acquires goods and pays for them at a later date, usually the end of the month ○ *to have an account or a credit account with Harrods* ○ *Put it on my account or charge it to my account.* ○ *They are one of our largest accounts.* □ **to open an account** (*of a customer*) to ask a shop to supply goods which you will pay for at a later date □ **to open an account, to close an account** (*of a shop*) to start or to stop supplying a customer on credit □ **to settle an account** to pay all the money owed on an account □ **to stop an account** to stop supplying a customer until payment has been made for goods supplied **3.** □ **on account** as part of a total bill □ **to pay money on account** to pay to settle part of a bill □ **advance on account** money paid as a part payment **4.** a customer who does a large amount of business with a firm and has an account with it ○ *Smith Brothers is one of our largest accounts.* ○ *Our sales people call on their best accounts twice a month.* **5.** □ **to keep the accounts** to write each sum of money in the account book ○ *The bookkeeper's job is to keep the accounts.* **6.** □ **overdrawn account** an account where you have taken out more money than you have put in, i.e. the bank is effectively lending you money □ **to open an account** to start an account by putting money in ○ *She opened an account with Santander.* □ **to close an account** to take all money out of a bank account and stop the account ○ *We closed our account with Lloyds.* **7.** a period during which shares are traded for credit, and at the end of which the shares bought must be paid for (NOTE: On the London Stock Exchange, there are twenty-four accounts during the year, each running usually for ten working days.) **8.** a notice □ **to take account of inflation, to take inflation into account** to assume that there will be a specific percentage of inflation when making calculations ■ *verb* □ **to account for** to explain and record a money transaction ○ *to account for a loss* or *a discrepancy* ○ *The reps have to account for all their expenses to the sales manager.*

account aggregation /əˈkaʊnt ægrəˌgeɪʃ(ə)n/ *noun* a service for online banking customers, which allows them to group various accounts, including credit card accounts, together

accountancy /əˈkaʊntənsi/ *noun* the work of an accountant ○ *They are studying accountancy* or *They are accountancy students.*

accountant /əˈkaʊntənt/ *noun* a person who keeps a company's accounts or deals with an individual person's tax affairs ○ *The chief accountant of a manufacturing group.* ○ *The accountant has shown that there is a sharp variance in our labour costs.* ○ *I send all my income tax queries to my accountant.*

accountants' opinion /əˌkaʊntənts əˈpɪnjən/ *noun* a report of the audit of a company's books, carried out by a certified public accountant (NOTE: The US term is **audit opinion**.)

account book /əˈkaʊnt bʊk/ *noun* a book with printed columns which is used to record sales and purchases

account day /əˈkaʊnt deɪ/ *noun* a day on which shares which have been bought must be paid for, usually a Monday ten days after the end of an account. Also called **settlement day**

account end /əˌkaʊnt ˈend/ *noun* the end of an accounting period

account executive /əˈkaʊnt ɪɡˌzekjʊtɪv/ *noun* **1.** an employee who looks after customers or who is the link between customers and the company **2.** an employee of an organisation such as a bank, public relations firm or advertising agency who is responsible for looking after particular clients and handling their business with the organisation

accounting /əˈkaʊntɪŋ/ *noun* the work of recording money paid, received, borrowed, or owed ○ *accounting methods*

○ *accounting procedures* ○ *an accounting machine* ○ *The auditors have introduced a new accounting system.*

'…applicants will be professionally qualified and have a degree in Commerce or Accounting'
[*Australian Financial Review*]

accounting noise /əˈkaʊntɪŋ ˌnɔɪz/ *noun* the distortion of a company's financial statements due to accounting rules and regulations that must be followed but which make it difficult for investors to know a company's true financial condition ○ *Reading the small print can help an investor cut through the accounting noise and get the real story.*

accounting period /əˈkaʊntɪŋ ˌpɪəriəd/ *noun* a period of time at the end of which the firm's accounts are made up

Accounting Standards Board /əˌkaʊntɪŋ ˈstændədz bɔːd/ *noun* a committee set up by British accounting institutions to monitor methods used in accounting. Abbreviation **ASB**

account number /əˈkaʊnt ˌnʌmbə/ *noun* a special number given to an account, either a bank account (in which case it appears on cheques) or a customer account

account reconcilement /əˌkaʊnt ˌrekənˈsaɪlmənt/ *noun* same as **bank reconciliation**

accounts department /əˈkaʊnts dɪˌpɑːtmənt/ *noun* a department in a company which deals with money paid, received, borrowed, or owed

accounts manager /əˈkaʊnts ˌmænɪdʒə/ *noun* the manager of an accounts department

accounts payable /əˌkaʊnts ˈpeɪəb(ə)l/ *plural noun* money owed by a company. Abbreviation **AP**

accounts receivable /əˌkaʊnts rɪˈsiːvəb(ə)l/ *plural noun* money owed to a company. Abbreviation **AR**

account statement /əˈkaʊnt ˌsteɪtmənt/ *noun* a written document from a bank showing the balance of an account at the end of a period

account trading /əˈkaʊnt ˌtreɪdɪŋ/ *noun* the process of buying shares and selling the same shares during an account, which means that the dealer has only to pay the difference between the price of the shares bought and the price obtained for them when they are sold

accrete /əˈkriːt/ *verb* **1.** (*of a fund*) to have interest added to it **2.** (*of assets*) to grow as a result of mergers, expansion or the acquisition of other interests

accretion /əˈkriːʃ(ə)n/ *noun* the process of adding interest to a fund over a period of time

accrual /əˈkruːəl/ *noun* a gradual increase by addition □ **accrual of interest** the automatic addition of interest to capital

accrual basis /əˈkruːəl ˌbeɪsɪs/ *noun* an accounting method in which receipts and payments are accounted for when they are entered in the books, whether or not the money has actually been received or paid out

accrual bond /əˈkruːəl ˌbɒnd/ *noun* a fixed-interest bond that is issued at its face value and repaid at the end of the maturity period together with the accrued interest

accruals basis /əˈkruːəl ˌbeɪsɪs/, **accruals concept** /əˈkruːəlz ˌkɒnsept/ *noun* a method of preparing accounts in which revenues and costs are both reported during the period to which they refer and not during the period when payments are received or made

accrue /əˈkruː/ *verb* to increase and be due for payment at a later date ○ *Interest accrues from the beginning of the month.*

accrued dividend /əˌkruːd ˈdɪvɪdend/ *noun* a dividend earned since the last dividend was paid

accrued interest /əˌkruːd ˈɪntrəst/ *noun* interest which has been earned by an interest-bearing investment ○ *Accrued interest is added quarterly.*

acct *abbreviation* account

accumulate /əˈkjuːmjʊleɪt/ *verb* to grow in quantity by being added to, or to get more of something over a period of time ○ *We allow dividends to accumulate in the fund.*

accumulated depreciation /əˌkjuː mjʊleɪtɪd dɪˌpriːʃiˈeɪʃ(ə)n/ *noun* the total amount by which an asset has been depreciated since it was purchased

accumulated profit /əˌkjuːmjʊ leɪtɪd ˈprɒfɪt/ *noun* a profit which is not

paid as dividend but is taken over into the accounts of the following year

accumulated reserves /əˌkjuːmjʊ leɪtɪd rɪˈzɜːvz/ *plural noun* reserves which a company has put aside over a period of years

accumulation /əˌkjuːmjʊˈleɪʃ(ə)n/ *noun* the process of growing larger by being added to, or of getting more and more of something

accumulation unit /əˌkjuːmjʊ ˈleɪʃ(ə)n ˌjuːnɪt/ *noun* a type of unit in a unit trust, which produces dividends which are used to form more units (as opposed to an income unit, which produces dividends which the investor receives as income)

ACD /ˌeɪ siː ˈdiː/ *abbreviation* authorised corporate director

ACH *abbreviation US* Automated Clearing House

achieve /əˈtʃiːv/ *verb* to succeed in doing something, to do something successfully ○ *The company has achieved great success in the Far East.* ○ *We achieved all our objectives in 2009.*

'...the company expects to move to profits of FFr 2m next year and achieve equally rapid growth in following years' [*Financial Times*]

acid test ratio /ˌæsɪd ˈtest ˌreɪʃiəʊ/ *noun* same as **liquidity ratio**

ACP state /ˌeɪ siː ˈpiː steɪt/ *noun* an African, Caribbean and Pacific state which is linked to the European Community through the Lomé Convention (1985)

acquire /əˈkwaɪə/ *verb* to buy ○ *to acquire a company* ○ *We have acquired a new office building in the centre of town.*

acquirer /əˈkwaɪərə/ *noun* a person or company which buys something

acquisition /ˌækwɪˈzɪʃ(ə)n/ *noun* something bought ○ *The chocolate factory is our latest acquisition.* ○ *The company has a record of making profitable acquisitions of traders in the retail sector.*

acquisition accounting /ˌækwɪ ˈzɪʃ(ə)n əˌkaʊntɪŋ/ *noun* a full consolidation, where the assets of a subsidiary company which has been purchased are included in the parent company's balance sheet, and the premium paid for the goodwill is written off against the year's earnings

acquisition indigestion /ˌækwɪˈzɪʃ(ə)n ɪndɪˌdʒestʃən/ *noun* (*informal*) **1.** an acquisition or merger in which the companies involved have trouble integrating with one another **2.** a situation in which the purchasing company has difficulty making the most of a takeover

across-the-board /əˌkrɒs ðə ˈbɔːd/ *adjective* applying to everything or everyone ○ *an across-the-board price increase* or *wage increase*

across-the-board tariff increase /əˌkrɒs ðiː bɔːd ˈtærɪf ˌɪnkriːs/ *noun* an increase in duty which applies to a whole range of items

act /ækt/ *noun* a law passed by parliament which must be obeyed by the people ■ *verb* **1.** to work ○ *He has agreed to act as an agent for an American company.* ○ *The solicitor is acting for us* or *on our behalf.* **2.** to do something ○ *The board will have to act quickly if the company's losses are going to be reduced.* □ **to act on something** to do what you have been asked to do by someone ○ *to act on a letter* ○ *The lawyers are acting on our instructions.*

ACT *abbreviation* Advance Corporation Tax

action /ˈækʃən/ *noun* **1.** a thing which has been done □ **to take action** to do something ○ *You must take action if you want to stop people cheating you.* **2.** □ **to take industrial action** to do something (usually to go on strike) to show that you are not happy with conditions at work **3.** a case in a law court where a person or company sues another person or company □ **to take legal action** to sue someone ○ *an action for libel* or *a libel action* ○ *an action for damages* ○ *She brought an action for wrongful dismissal against her former employer.*

active /ˈæktɪv/ *adjective* involving many transactions or activities ○ *an active demand for oil shares* ○ *an active day on the stock exchange* ○ *Computer shares are very active.*

active account /ˌæktɪv əˈkaʊnt/ *noun* an account, such as a bank account or investment account, which is used to deposit and withdraw money frequently

active partner /ˌæktɪv ˈpɑːtnə/ *noun* a partner who works in a company that is a partnership

activity /ækˈtɪvɪti/ *noun* the fact of being active or busy ○ *a low level of business activity* ○ *There was a lot of activity on the stock exchange.* □ **monthly activity report** a report by a department on what has been done during the past month

'…preliminary indications of the level of business investment and activity during the March quarter will provide a good picture of economic activity in the year' [*Australian Financial Review*]

activity chart /ækˈtɪvɪti tʃɑːt/ *noun* a plan showing work which has been done, made so that it can be compared to a previous plan showing how much work should be done

act of God /ˌækt əv ˈɡɒd/ *noun* something you do not expect to happen and which cannot be avoided, e.g. a storm or a flood (NOTE: Acts of God are not usually covered by insurance policies.)

actual /ˈæktʃuəl/ *adjective* real or correct ○ *What is the actual cost of one unit?* ○ *The actual figures for directors' expenses are not shown to the shareholders.* ■ *noun* a physical commodity which is ready for delivery (as opposed to futures)

actual price /ˌæktʃuəl ˈpraɪs/ *noun* a price for a commodity which is for immediate delivery

actuals /ˈæktʃuəlz/ *plural noun* real figures ○ *These figures are the actuals for last year.*

actuarial /ˌæktʃuˈeəriəl/ *adjective* calculated by an actuary ○ *The premiums are worked out according to actuarial calculations.*

actuarial tables /ˌæktʃueəriəl ˈteɪb(ə)lz/ *plural noun* lists showing how long people are likely to live, used to calculate life assurance premiums and annuities

actuary /ˈæktʃuəri/ *noun* a person employed by an insurance company or other organisation to calculate the risk involved in an insurance, and therefore the premiums payable by people taking out insurance

COMMENT: In the UK, actuaries are qualified after passing the examinations of the Institute of Actuaries.

ACU /ˌeɪ siː ˈjuː/ *abbreviation* Asian Currency Unit

adaptable /əˈdæptəb(ə)l/ *adjective* able to change or be changed

adaptation /ˌædæpˈteɪʃ(ə)n/ *noun* the process of changing something, or of being changed, to fit new conditions ○ *adaptation to new surroundings*

ADB *abbreviation* **1.** African Development Bank **2.** Asian Development Bank

add /æd/ *verb* to put figures together to make a total ○ *If you add the interest to the capital you will get quite a large sum.* ○ *Interest is added monthly.*

add up /ˌæd ˈʌp/ *phrasal verb* **1.** to put several figures together to make a total ○ *He made a mistake in adding up the column of figures.* □ **the figures do not add up** the total given is not correct **2.** to make sense ○ *The complaints in the letter just do not add up.*

add up to /ˌæd ˈʌp tʊ/ *phrasal verb* to make a total of ○ *The total expenditure adds up to more than £1,000.*

added value /ˌædɪd ˈvæljuː/ *noun* an amount added to the value of a product or service, equal to the difference between its cost and the amount received when it is sold. Wages, taxes, etc. are deducted from the added value to give the profit. ◊ **VAT**

addition /əˈdɪʃ(ə)n/ *noun* an arithmetical operation consisting of adding together two or more numbers to make a sum ○ *You don't need a calculator to do simple addition.*

additional /əˈdɪʃ(ə)nəl/ *adjective* extra which is added ○ *additional costs* ○ *They sent us a list of additional charges.* ○ *Some additional clauses were added to the contract.* ○ *Additional duty will have to be paid.*

additional borrowing /əˌdɪʃ(ə)n(ə)l ˈbɒrəʊɪŋ/ *noun* extra borrowing in addition to money already borrowed

additional premium /əˌdɪʃ(ə)nəl ˈpriːmiəm/ *noun* a payment made to cover extra items in an existing insurance

additional voluntary contributions /əˌdɪʃ(ə)n(ə)l ˌvɒlənt(ə)ri ˌkɒntrɪˈbjuːʃ(ə)nz/ *plural noun* extra payments made voluntarily by an employee to a pension scheme on top of the normal contributions. Abbreviation **AVCs**

address /əˈdres/ *noun* the details of number, street and town where an office is located or a person lives ○ *My business address and phone number are printed on the card.* ■ *verb* **1.** to write the details of an address on an envelope or package ○ *a letter addressed to the managing director* ○ *an incorrectly addressed package* ○ *Please address your enquiries to the manager.* **2.** to say something to someone ○ *The chairman addressed the meeting.*

addressee /ˌædreˈsiː/ *noun* a person to whom a letter or package is addressed

address list /əˈdres lɪst/ *noun* a list of names and addresses of people and companies

adequacy /ˈædɪkwəsi/ *noun* the fact of being large enough or good enough for something

adequate /ˈædɪkwət/ *adjective* large or good enough □ **to operate without adequate cover** to act without being completely protected by insurance

adjudicate /əˈdʒuːdɪkeɪt/ *verb* to give a judgment between two parties in law or to decide a legal problem ○ *to adjudicate a claim* ○ *to adjudicate in a dispute* □ **he was adjudicated bankrupt** he was declared legally bankrupt

adjudication /əˌdʒuːdɪˈkeɪʃ(ə)n/ *noun* the act of giving a judgment or of deciding a legal problem

adjudication of bankruptcy /əˌdʒuːdɪkeɪʃ(ə)n əv ˈbæŋkrʌptsi/ *noun* a legal order making someone bankrupt

adjudication tribunal /əˌdʒuːdɪˈkeɪʃ(ə)n traɪˌbjuːn(ə)l/ *noun* a group which adjudicates in industrial disputes

adjudicator /əˈdʒuːdɪkeɪtə/ *noun* a person who gives a decision on a problem ○ *an adjudicator in an industrial dispute*

adjust /əˈdʒʌst/ *verb* to change something to fit new conditions ○ *Prices are adjusted for inflation.*

'…inflation-adjusted GNP moved up at a 1.3% annual rate' [*Fortune*]

'Saudi Arabia will no longer adjust its production to match short-term supply with demand' [*Economist*]

'…on a seasonally-adjusted basis, output of trucks, electric power, steel and paper decreased' [*Business Week*]

adjustable /əˈdʒʌstəb(ə)l/ *adjective*
easily adjusted

adjustable peg /əˈdʒʌstəb(ə)l peg/
noun a method of pegging one currency
to another, which allows the exchange
rate to be adjusted from time to time

adjustable rate mortgage /ə
ˌdʒʌstəb(ə)l reɪt ˈmɔːgɪdʒ/ *noun* a
mortgage where the interest rate changes
according to the current market rates.
Abbreviation **ARM**

adjustable rate preferred stock /ə
ˌdʒʌstəb(ə)l reɪt prɪˌfɜːd ˈstɒk/ *noun*
preference shares on which dividends are
paid in line with the interest rate on
Treasury bills. Abbreviation **ARPS**

adjusted balance /əˌdʒʌstɪd
ˈbæləns/ *noun* a balance in a bank
account which is adjusted to take account
of debits and credits during a period. This
balance can then be used as a basis for
calculating bank charges.

adjusted gross income /əˌdʒʌstɪd
grəʊs ˈɪnkʌm/ *noun US* a person's total
annual income less expenses, pension
contributions, capital losses, etc., used as
a basis to calculate federal income tax.
Abbreviation **AGI**

adjuster /əˈdʒʌstə/ *noun* a person who
calculates losses for an insurance
company

adjustment /əˈdʒʌstmənt/ *noun* **1.**
the act of adjusting ○ *to make an adjustment to salaries* ○ *an adjustment of prices
to take account of rising costs* **2.** a slight
change ○ *Details of tax adjustments are
set out in the enclosed document.* **3.** an
entry in accounts which does not represent a receipt or payment, but which is
made to make the accounts correct **4.** a
change in the exchange rates, made to
correct a balance of payment deficit

adjustment credit /əˈdʒʌstmənt
ˌkredɪt/ *noun* a short-term loan from the
Federal Reserve to a commercial bank

adjustment trigger /əˈdʒʌstmənt
ˌtrɪgə/ *noun* a factor such as inflation
which triggers an adjustment in exchange
rates

adjustor /əˈdʒʌstə/ *noun* same as
adjuster

administer /ədˈmɪnɪstə/ *verb* to
organise, manage or direct the whole of
an organisation or part of one ○ *She
administers a large pension fund.*

administered price /ədˈmɪnɪstəd
praɪs/ *noun US* a price fixed by a manufacturer which cannot be varied by a
retailer (NOTE: The UK term is **resale
price maintenance**.)

administration /ədˌmɪnɪˈstreɪʃ(ə)n/
noun **1.** the action of organising, controlling or managing a company **2.** a person
or group of people who manage or direct
an organisation ○ *It is up to the administration to solve the problem, not the
government.* **3.** an appointment by a court
of a person to manage the affairs of a
company

administration costs /ədˌmɪnɪ
ˈstreɪʃ(ə)n ˌkɒsts/, **administration
expenses** /ədˌmɪnɪˈstreɪʃ(ə)n ɪk
ˌspensɪz/ *plural noun* the costs of
management, not including production,
marketing or distribution costs

administration order /ədˌmɪnɪ
ˈstreɪʃ(ə)n ˌɔːdə/ *noun* **1.** an order by a
court, by which a debtor repays his debts
in instalments **2.** an order by a court to
appoint an administrator for a company

administrative receiver /əd
ˌmɪnɪstrətɪv rɪˈsiːvə/ *noun* a person
appointed by a court to administer the
affairs of a company

administrator /ədˈmɪnɪstreɪtə/ *noun*
1. a person who directs the work of other
employees in a business ○ *After several
years as a college teacher, she hopes to
become an administrator.* **2.** a person
appointed by a court to manage the affairs
of someone who dies without leaving a
will

ADR *abbreviation* American Depositary
Receipt

ad valorem duty /ˌæd vəˈlɔːrəm
ˌdjuːti/ *noun* the duty calculated on the
sales value of the goods

ad valorem tax /ˌæd vəˈlɔːrem tæks/
noun a tax calculated according to the
value of the goods taxed

advance /ədˈvɑːns/ *noun* **1.** money
paid as a loan or as a part of a payment to
be made later ○ *She asked if she could
have a cash advance.* ○ *We paid her an
advance on account.* **2.** an increase **3.** □ **in
advance** early, before something happens
○ *freight payable in advance* ○ *prices
fixed in advance* ■ *adjective* early, or
taking place before something else
happens ○ *advance payment* ○ *Advance*

holiday bookings are up on last year. ○ *You must give seven days' advance notice of withdrawals from the account.* ■ *verb*
1. to pay an amount of money to someone as a loan or as a part of a payment to be made later ○ *The bank advanced him $100,000 against the security of his house.* **2.** to increase ○ *Prices generally advanced on the stock market.* **3.** to make something happen earlier ○ *The date of the shipping has been advanced to May 10th.* ○ *The meeting with the German distributors has been advanced from 11.00 to 9.30.*

Advance Corporation Tax /əd ˌvɑːns ˌkɔːpəˈreɪʃ(ə)n tæks/ *noun* a tax which was abolished in 1999, paid by a company in advance of its main corporation tax payments. It was paid when dividends were paid to shareholders and was deducted from the main tax payment when that fell due. It appeared on the tax voucher attached to a dividend warrant. Abbreviation **ACT**

adverse /ˈædvɜːs/ *adjective* unfavourable □ **adverse balance of trade** a situation in which a country imports more than it exports □ **adverse trading conditions** bad conditions for trade

adverse action /ˌædvɜːs ˈækʃən/ *noun* a decision which has unfavourable consequences for employees ○ *The new bonus system was considered adverse action by underachievers in the organisation.*

advice /ədˈvaɪs/ *noun* an opinion as to what action to take ○ *The accountant's advice was to send the documents to the police.* □ **to take legal advice** to ask a lawyer to say what should be done ◇ **as per advice 1.** according to what is written on the advice note **2.** advising that a bill of exchange has been drawn

advice note /ədˈvaɪs nəʊt/ *noun* the written notice to a customer giving details of goods ordered and shipped but not yet delivered. Also called **letter of advice**

advise /ədˈvaɪz/ *verb* **1.** to tell someone what has happened ○ *We have been advised that the shipment will arrive next week.* **2.** to suggest to someone what should be done ○ *The lawyer advised us to send the documents to the police.*

advise against /ədˌvaɪz əˈɡenst/ *phrasal verb* to suggest that something should not be done ○ *The HR manager*

advised against dismissing the staff without notice.

adviser /ədˈvaɪzə/, **advisor** *noun* a person who suggests what should be done ○ *He is consulting the company's legal adviser.*

advisory /ədˈvaɪz(ə)ri/ *adjective* as an adviser ○ *She is acting in an advisory capacity.*

Advisory, Conciliation and Arbitration Service /əd ˌvaɪz(ə)ri kənsɪli ˌeɪʃ(ə)n ənd ˌɑːbɪˈtreɪʃ(ə)n ˌsɜːvɪs/ *noun* a British government service which arbitrates in disputes between management and employees. Abbreviation **ACAS**

advisory board /ədˈvaɪz(ə)ri ˌbɔːd/ *noun* a group of advisers

advisory funds /ədˈvaɪz(ə)ri ˌfʌndz/ *plural noun* funds placed with a financial institution to invest on behalf of a client, the institution investing them at its own discretion

AER *abbreviation* Annual Equivalent Rate

AEX *abbreviation* Amsterdam Stock Exchange

AFBD *abbreviation* Association of Futures Brokers and Dealers

Affärsvärlden General Index /ɔː ˌfæʃværldən ˌdʒen(ə)rəl ˈɪndeks/ an index of prices on the Stockholm Stock Exchange

affect /əˈfekt/ *verb* to cause some change in something, especially to have a bad effect on something ○ *The new government regulations do not affect us.*

affiliate /əˈfɪlieɪt/ *noun* a company which partly owns another company, or is partly owned by the same holding company as another

affiliated /əˈfɪlieɪtɪd/ *adjective* connected with or owned by another company ○ *Smiths Ltd is one of our affiliated companies.*

affinity card /əˈfɪnɪti kɑːd/ *noun* a credit card where a percentage of each purchase made is given by the credit card company to a stated charity

affluent /ˈæfluənt/ *adjective* rich ○ *Our more affluent clients prefer the luxury model.* □ **the affluent** rich people □ **the mass affluent** people with more than £50,000 in liquid assets

affluent society /ˌæfluənt səˈsaɪəti/ *noun* a type of society where most people are rich

affluenza /ˌæfluˈenzə/ *noun* **1.** a term used by critics of capitalism and consumerism to describe the unfulfilled feeling that results from an effort to 'keep up with the Joneses' ○ *There is an affluenza epidemic throughout the world.* **2.** an unsustainable addiction to economic growth

afford /əˈfɔːd/ *verb* to be able to pay for or buy something ○ *We could not afford the cost of two telephones.* ○ *The company cannot afford the time to train new staff.* (NOTE: Only used after **can, cannot, could, could not, able to**)

afghani /æfˈgɑːni/ a unit of currency used in Afghanistan

African Development Bank /ˌæfrɪkən dɪˈveləpmənt/ *noun* a bank set up by African countries to provide long-term loans to help agricultural development and improvement of the infrastructure. Abbreviation **ADB** (NOTE: The bank now has non-African members.)

afterdate /ˈɑːftədeɪt/ *noun* a bill of exchange payable at a date later than that on the bill

aftermarket /ˈɑːftəˌmɑːkɪt/ *noun* a market in new shares, which starts immediately after trading in the shares begins

after tax /ˌɑːftər ˈtæks/ *adverb* after tax has been paid

after-tax profit /ˌɑːftə ˈtæks ˌprɒfɪt/ *noun* a profit after tax has been deducted

AG *abbreviation* Aktiengesellschaft

against /əˈgenst/ *preposition* **1.** in view of the fact that something else is owed or has been pledged ○ *Can I have an advance against next month's salary?* ○ *The bank advanced him £10,000 against the security of his house.* **2.** compared with

'…investment can be written off against the marginal rate of tax' [*Investors Chronicle*]

aged debtors analysis /ˌeɪdʒd ˈdetəz əˌnæləsɪs/, **ageing schedule** /ˈeɪdʒɪŋ ˌʃedjuːl/ *noun* a list which analyses a company's debtors, showing the number of days their payments are outstanding

COMMENT: An ageing schedule shows all the debtors of a company and lists (usually in descending order of age) all the debts that are outstanding. The debtors will be shown as: £X at 30 days, £Y at 60 days, £Z at 90 days, etc.

agency /ˈeɪdʒənsi/ *noun* **1.** an office or job of representing another company in an area ○ *They signed an agency agreement* or *an agency contract.* **2.** an office or business which arranges things for other companies **3.** *US* a security issued by a government agency

agency bank /ˈeɪdʒənsi bæŋk/ *noun* a bank which does not accept deposits, but acts as an agent for another, usually foreign, bank

agency bill /ˈeɪdʒənsi bɪl/ *noun* a bill of exchange drawn on the local branch of a foreign bank

agency broker /ˈeɪdʒənsi ˌbrəʊkə/ *noun* a dealer who acts as the agent for an investor, buying and selling for a commission

agent /ˈeɪdʒənt/ *noun* **1.** a person who represents a company or another person in an area ○ *to be the agent for BMW cars* **2.** a person in charge of an agency ○ *an advertising agent* ○ *The estate agent sent me a list of properties for sale.* ○ *Our trip was organised through our local travel agent.* **3.** □ (business) **agent** *US* the chief local official of a trade union ○ *Management would only discuss the new payment scheme with agents officially representing the workers.*

agent bank /ˈeɪdʒənt bæŋk/ *noun* a bank which uses the credit card system set up by another bank

agent de change *noun* the French word for **stockbroker**

agente de cambio y bolsa *noun* the Spanish word for **stockbroker**

agente di cambio *noun* the Italian word for **stockbroker**

agent's commission /ˌeɪdʒənts kəˈmɪʃ(ə)n/ *noun* money, often a percentage of sales, paid to an agent

aggregate /ˈægrɪgət/ *adjective* total, with everything added together ○ *aggregate output*

aggregate demand /ˌægrɪgət dɪˈmɑːnd/ *noun* the total demand for goods and services from all sectors of the economy including individuals, companies and the government ○ *Economists are studying the recent fall in aggregate demand.* ○ *As incomes have risen, so has aggregate demand.*

aggregate risk /ˌægrɪgət ˈrɪsk/ *noun* the risk which a bank runs in lending to a customer

aggregate supply /ˌægrɪgət səˈplaɪ/ *noun* all goods and services on the market ○ *Is aggregate supply meeting aggregate demand?*

AGI *abbreviation* **1.** *US* adjusted gross income **2.** annual gross income

agio /ˈædʒɪəʊ/ *noun* **1.** a charge made for changing money of one currency into another, or for changing banknotes into cash **2.** the difference between two values, such as between the interest charged on loans made by a bank and the interest paid by the bank on deposits, or the difference between the values of two currencies

AGM *abbreviation* Annual General Meeting

agree /əˈɡriː/ *verb* **1.** to decide and approve something together with another person or other people ○ *The figures were agreed between the two parties.* ○ *We have agreed the budgets for next year.* ○ *He has agreed your prices.* ○ *The terms of the contract are still to be agreed.* **2.** □ **to agree on something** to come to a decision that is acceptable to everyone about something ○ *We all agreed on the need for action.* **3.** □ **to agree to something** to say that you accept something that is suggested ○ *After some discussion he agreed to our plan.* □ **to agree to do something** to say that you will do something ○ *She agreed to be chairman.* ○ *Will the finance director agree to resign?*

agree with /əˈɡriː wɪð/ *phrasal verb* **1.** to say that your opinions are the same as someone else's ○ *I agree with the chairman that the figures are lower than normal.* **2.** to be the same as ○ *The auditors' figures do not agree with those of the accounts department.*

agreed /əˈɡriːd/ *adjective* having been accepted by everyone ○ *We pay an agreed amount each month.* ○ *The agreed terms of employment are laid down in the contract.*

agreed price /əˈɡriːd ˈpraɪs/ *noun* a price which has been accepted by both the buyer and seller

agreed takeover bid /əˈɡriːd ˈteɪkəʊvə bɪd/ *noun* a takeover bid which is accepted by the target company and recommended by its directors to its shareholders

agreement /əˈɡriːmənt/ *noun* a spoken or written contract between people or groups which explains how they will act ○ *a written agreement* ○ *an unwritten* or *verbal agreement* ○ *to draw up* or *to draft an agreement* ○ *to break an agreement* ○ *to sign an agreement* ○ *to reach an agreement* or *to come to an agreement on something* ○ *a collective wage agreement*

'…after three days of tough negotiations the company has reached agreement with its 1,200 unionized workers' [*Toronto Star*]

agreement among underwriters /əˌɡriːmənt əˌmʌŋ ˈʌndəraɪtəz/ *noun* a document which forms a syndicate of underwriters, linking them to the issuer of a new share issue

AICPA *abbreviation* American Institute of Certified Public Accountants

AIM *abbreviation* Alternative Investment Market

AIMA *abbreviation* Alternative Investment Management Association

air carrier /ˈeə ˌkæriə/ *noun* a company which sends cargo or passengers by air

air forwarding /ˈeə ˌfɔːwədɪŋ/ *noun* the process of arranging for goods to be shipped by air

air freight /ˈeə freɪt/ *noun* the transportation of goods in aircraft, or goods sent by air ○ *to send a shipment by air freight* ○ *Air freight tariffs are rising.*

airmail /ˈeəmeɪl/ *noun* a postal service which sends letters or parcels by air ○ *to send a package by airmail* ○ *Airmail charges have risen by 15%.* ■ *verb* to send letters or parcels by air ○ *We airmailed the document to New York.*

airmail transfer /ˈeəmeɪl ˌtrænsfɜː/ *noun* an act of sending money from one bank to another by airmail

air pocket stock /ˈeə ˌpɒkɪt ˌstɒk/ *noun US* a share that experiences a sudden drop, similar to a plane hitting an air pocket. Air pocket shares are usually caused by shareholders selling because of unexpected bad news.

airport tax /'eəpɔːt tæks/ *noun* a tax added to the price of an air ticket to cover the cost of running an airport

Aktie *noun* the German word for **share**

Aktiengesellschaft *noun* the German word for **public limited company**. Abbreviation **AG**

alien corporation /ˌeɪliən ˌkɔːpə'reɪʃ(ə)n/ *noun US* a company which is incorporated in a foreign country

A list /'eɪ lɪst/ *noun* a list of members of a company at the time it is wound up who may be liable for the company's unpaid debts

alligator property /'ælɪɡeɪtə ˌprɒpəti/ *noun* a situation where the cost of mortgage payments, property taxes, insurance and maintenance on a rental property is greater than the income it brings in, eventually reducing the owner's profit and leaving him or her with negative cash flow

all-in policy /ˌɔːl ɪn 'pɒlɪsi/ *noun* an insurance policy which covers all risks

all-in rate /ˌɔːl ɪn 'reɪt/ *noun* **1.** a price which covers all the costs connected with a purchase, such as delivery, tax and insurance, as well as the cost of the goods themselves **2.** a wage which includes all extra payments such as bonuses and merit pay

allocate /'æləkeɪt/ *verb* **1.** to provide a particular amount from a total sum of money for a particular purpose ○ *We allocate 10% of revenue to publicity.* ○ *$2,500 was allocated to office furniture.* **2.** to divide something in various ways and share it out ○ *How are we going to allocate the available office space?*

allocation /ˌælə'keɪʃ(ə)n/ *noun* the process of providing sums of money for particular purposes, or a sum provided for a purpose ○ *the allocation of funds to a project*

allocation rate /ˌælə'keɪʃ(ə)n reɪt/ *noun* the percentage of a payment that is actually invested in a fund after initial charges have been taken into account

allonge /æ'lɒnʒ/ *noun* a piece of paper attached to a bill of exchange, so that more endorsements can be written on it

All Ordinaries Index /ˌɔːl 'ɔːd(ə)n(ə)riz ˌɪndeks/ *noun* the index of prices on the Australian Stock Exchange. Abbreviation **AO Index, AO**

all or none /ˌɔːl ɔː 'nʌn/ *noun* a buying order which stipulates that the whole order has to be bought at a certain price and no parts of the order can be executed separately. Abbreviation **AON**

allot /ə'lɒt/ *verb* to share out (NOTE: **allotting – allotted**) □ **to allot shares** to give a certain number of shares to people who have applied for them

allotment /ə'lɒtmənt/ *noun* **1.** the process of sharing out something, especially money between various departments, projects or people ○ *The allotment of funds to each project is the responsibility of the finance director.* **2.** the act of giving shares in a new company to people who have applied for them ○ *share allotment* ○ *payment in full on allotment*

allow /ə'laʊ/ *verb* **1.** to say that someone can do something ○ *Junior members of staff are not allowed to use the chairman's lift.* ○ *The company allows all members of staff to take six days' holiday at Christmas.* **2.** to give ○ *to allow 5% discount to members of staff* **3.** to agree to or accept legally ○ *to allow a claim* or *an appeal*

allow for /ə'laʊ fɔː/ *phrasal verb* **1.** to give a discount for something, or to add an extra sum to cover something ○ *to allow for money paid in advance* ○ *Add on an extra 10% to allow for postage and packing.* □ **delivery is not allowed for** delivery charges are not included **2.** to include something in your calculations □ **allow 28 days for delivery** calculate that delivery will take up to 28 days

allowable /ə'laʊəb(ə)l/ *adjective* legally accepted

allowable expenses /əˌlaʊəb(ə)l 'spensɪz/ *plural noun* business expenses which can be claimed against tax

allowance /ə'laʊəns/ *noun* **1.** money which is given for a special reason ○ *a travel allowance* or *a travelling allowance* **2.** a part of an income which is not taxed ○ *allowances against tax* or *tax allowances* ○ *personal allowances* (NOTE: The US term is **exemption**) **3.** money removed in the form of a discount

○ *an allowance for depreciation* ○ *an allowance for exchange loss*

'…the compensation plan includes base, incentive and car allowance totalling $50,000+' [*Globe and Mail (Toronto)*]

allowance for bad debt /əˌlaʊəns fə bæd 'det/ *noun* a provision made in a company's accounts for debts which may never be paid

all-risks policy /ˌɔːl 'rɪsks ˌpɒlɪsi/ *noun* an insurance policy which covers risks of any kind, with no exclusions

All-Share Index /ɔːl 'ʃeə ˌɪndeks/ *noun* an index based on the market price of about 700 companies listed on the London Stock Exchange (NOTE: The full name is the **Financial Times Actuaries All-Share Index**.)

alpha /'ælfə/ *noun* **1.** an anticipated performance of a share, compared to the market in general **2.** a rate of return on a unit trust or mutual fund, compared with typical returns for that category of trust. ◊ **beta**

alpha shares /'ælfə ʃeəz/, **alpha securities** /'ælfə sɪˌkjʊərɪtiz/, **alpha stocks** /'ælfə stɒks/ *plural noun* shares in the main companies listed on the London Stock Exchange (about 130 companies, whose shares are frequently traded, normally in parcels of 1,000 shares) (NOTE: Transactions in alpha stocks are listed on SEAQ.)

alternate account /ɔːlˌtɜːnət ə'kaʊnt/ *noun* a bank account where several signatories can each sign cheques without asking another to validate their signature

alternative /ɔːl'tɜːnətɪv/ *adjective* other, which can take the place of something □ **to find someone alternative employment** to find someone another job

alternative cost /ɔːl'tɜːnətɪv kɒst/ *noun* same as **opportunity cost**

alternative investment /ɔːlˌtɜːnətɪv ɪn'vestmənt/ *noun* an investment that is not one of the three traditional asset types (shares, bonds and cash), that are held mostly by high-net-worth individuals and include hedge funds, managed futures, real estate, commodities and derivatives contracts

Alternative Investment Market /ɔːl ˌtɜːnətɪv ɪn'vestmənt ˌmɑːkɪt/ *noun* a London stock market, regulated by the London Stock Exchange, dealing in shares in smaller companies which are not listed on the main London Stock Exchange. Abbreviation **AIM** (NOTE: The **AIM** is a way in which smaller companies can sell shares to the investing public without going to the expense of obtaining a full share listing.)

alternative minimum tax /ɔːl ˌtɜːnətɪv ˌmɪnɪməm 'tæks/ *noun US* a way of calculating US income tax that is intended to ensure that wealthy individuals, corporations, trusts, and estates pay at least some tax regardless of deductions, but that is increasingly targeting the middle class. Abbreviation **AMT**

alternative order /ɔːl'tɜːnətɪv ˌɔːdə/ *noun* an order to do one of two things (such as buy or sell stock at certain prices)

aluminium /ˌæljə'mɪniəm/ *noun* a metal which is frequently traded on commodity exchanges such as the London Metal Exchange (NOTE: The US spelling is **aluminum**.)

a.m. /ˌeɪ 'em/ *adverb* in the morning, before 12 midday ○ *The flight leaves at 9.20 a.m.* ○ *Telephone calls before 6 a.m. are charged at the cheap rate.* (NOTE: The US spelling is **A.M.**)

American Bankers Association /ə ˌmerɪkən 'bæŋkəz əˌsəʊsieɪʃ(ə)n/ *noun* an association that represents US banks and promotes good practice. Abbreviation **ABA**

American Depositary Receipt /ə ˌmerɪkən dɪ'pɒzɪtri rɪˌsiːt/ *noun* a document issued by an American bank to US citizens, making them unregistered shareholders of companies in foreign countries. The document allows them to receive dividends from their investments, and ADRs can themselves be bought or sold. Abbreviation **ADR**

COMMENT: Buying and selling ADRs is easier for American investors than buying or selling the actual shares themselves, as it avoids stamp duty and can be carried out in dollars without incurring exchange costs.

American Express /əˌmerɪkən ɪk 'spres/ *noun* full form of **AmEx**

American Institute of Banking /ə ˌmerɪkən ˌɪnstɪtjuːt əv 'bæŋkɪŋ/ *noun* part of the ABA which organises training for bank staff. Abbreviation **AIB**

American Institute of Certified Public Accountants /ə,merɪkən ,ɪnstɪtjuːt əv ,sɜːtɪfaɪd ,pʌblɪk ə'kaʊntənts/ *noun* the national association for certified public accountants in the US. Abbreviation **AICPA**

American Stock Exchange /ə ,merɪkən 'stɒk ɪks,tʃeɪndʒ/ *noun* the smaller of the two stock exchanges based in New York (the other is the New York Stock Exchange or NYSE). Abbreviation **Amex** (NOTE: Also called **Curb Exchange** or **Little Board**, as opposed to the **Big Board**, or **NYSE**.)

Amex /'æmeks/ *abbreviation* American Stock Exchange (*informal*)

AmEx /'æmeks/ *abbreviation* American Express

amortisable /,æmɔː'taɪzəb(ə)l/ *adjective* being possible to amortise ○ *The capital cost is amortisable over a period of ten years.*

amortisation /ə,mɔːtaɪ'zeɪʃ(ə)n/ *noun* an act of amortising ○ *amortisation of a debt*

amortise /ə'mɔːtaɪz/, **amortize** *verb* **1.** to repay a loan by regular payments, most of which pay off the interest on the loan at first, and then reduce the principal as the repayment period progresses ○ *The capital cost is amortised over five years.* **2.** to depreciate or to write down the capital value of an asset over a period of time in a company's accounts

amount /ə'maʊnt/ *noun* a quantity of money ○ *A small amount has been deducted to cover our costs.* ○ *A large amount is still owing.* ○ *What is the amount to be written off?* ○ *She has a small amount invested in gilt-edged stock.*

amount to /ə'maʊnt tʊ/ *phrasal verb* to make a total of ○ *Their debts amount to over £1m.*

amount paid up /ə,maʊnt peɪd 'ʌp/ *noun* an amount paid for a new issue of shares, either the total payment or the first instalment, if the shares are offered with instalment payments

Amsterdam Stock Exchange /,æmstədæm 'stɒk ɪks,tʃeɪndʒ/ *noun* the main stock exchange in the Netherlands. Business is transacted by 'hoekmen' (marketmakers) or directly between banks on the Amsterdam Inter-

professional Market (AIM). Abbreviation **AEX**

analogue computer /,ænəlɒg kəm'pjuːtə/ *noun* a computer which works on the basis of electrical impulses representing numbers

analyse /'ænəlaɪz/, **analyze** *verb* to examine someone or something in detail ○ *to analyse a statement of account* ○ *to analyse the market potential*

analysis /ə'næləsɪs/ *noun* a detailed examination and report ○ *a job analysis* ○ *market analysis* ○ *Her job is to produce a regular sales analysis.* (NOTE: The plural is **analyses**.)

analyst /'ænəlɪst/ *noun* a person who analyses ○ *a market analyst* ○ *a systems analyst*

angel /'eɪndʒəl/ *noun* a person who provides backing for a stage performance, such as a play or musical, and receives a percentage dividend when the start-up costs have been covered

angel network /'eɪndʒəl ,netwɜːk/ *noun* a network of backers, organised through a central office which keeps a database of suitable investors and puts them in touch with entrepreneurs who need financial backing

announce /ə'naʊns/ *verb* to tell something to the public ○ *to announce the first year's trading results* ○ *The director has announced a programme of investment.*

announcement /ə'naʊnsmənt/ *noun* an act of telling something in public ○ *the announcement of a cutback in expenditure* ○ *the announcement of the appointment of a new managing director* ○ *The managing director made an announcement to the staff.*

annual /'ænjuəl/ *adjective* for one year ○ *an annual statement of income* ○ *They have six weeks' annual leave.* ○ *The company has an annual growth of 5%.* ○ *We get an annual bonus.* □ **on an annual basis** each year ○ *The figures are revised on an annual basis.*

'…real wages have risen at an annual rate of only 1% in the last two years' [*Sunday Times*]

'…the remuneration package will include an attractive salary, profit sharing and a company car together with four weeks' annual holiday' [*Times*]

annual accounts /ˌænjuəl əˈkaʊnts/ plural noun the accounts prepared at the end of a financial year ○ *The annual accounts have been sent to the shareholders.*

annual depreciation /ˌænjuəl dɪˌpriːʃiˈeɪʃ(ə)n/ noun a reduction in the book value of an asset at a particular rate per year. ◊ **straight line depreciation**

Annual Equivalent Rate /ˌænjuəl ɪˌkwɪvələnt ˈreɪt/ noun a figure which shows what the interest rate on an account would be if interest was paid for a full year and compounded. Abbreviation **AER**

Annual General Meeting /ˌænjuəl ˌdʒen(ə)rəl ˈmiːtɪŋ/ noun an annual meeting of all shareholders of a company, when the company's financial situation is presented by and discussed with the directors, when the accounts for the past year are approved and when dividends are declared and audited. Abbreviation **AGM** (NOTE: The US term is **annual meeting** or **annual stockholders' meeting**.)

annual gross income /ˌænjuəl grəʊs ˈɪnkʌm/ noun total annual income before any deductions or exclusions. Abbreviation **AGI**

annual income /ˌænjuəl ˈɪnkʌm/ noun money received during a calendar year

annualised /ˈænjuəlaɪzd/, **annualized** adjective shown on an annual basis '…he believes this may have caused the economy to grow at an annualized rate of almost 5 per cent in the final quarter of last year' [*Investors Chronicle*]

annualised percentage rate /ˌænjuəlaɪzd pəˈsentɪdʒ ˌreɪt/ noun a yearly percentage rate, calculated by multiplying the monthly rate by twelve. Abbreviation **APR** (NOTE: The annualised percentage rate is not as accurate as the Annual Percentage Rate (APR), which includes fees and other charges.)

annually /ˈænjuəli/ adverb each year ○ *The figures are updated annually.*

annual management charge /ˌænjuəl ˈmænɪdʒmənt tʃɑːdʒ/ noun a charge made by the financial institution which is managing an account

annual management fee /ˌænjuəl ˈmænɪdʒmənt fiː/ noun an annual charge made for running a fund, usually

calculated as a percentage of the amount invested

annual meeting /ˌænjuəl ˈmiːtɪŋ/ noun US same as **Annual General Meeting**

Annual Percentage Rate /ˌænjuəl pəˈsentɪdʒ ˌreɪt/ noun a rate of interest (such as on a hire-purchase agreement) shown on an annual compound basis, and including fees and charges. Abbreviation **APR**

COMMENT: Because hire purchase agreements quote a flat rate of interest covering the whole amount borrowed or a monthly repayment figure, the Consumer Credit Act, 1974, forces lenders to show the APR on documentation concerning hire purchase agreements, so as to give an accurate figure of the real rate of interest as opposed to the nominal rate. The APR includes various fees charged (such as the valuation of a house for mortgage). It may also vary according to the sum borrowed – a credit card company will quote a lower APR if the borrower's credit limit is low.

annual percentage yield /ˌænjuəl pəˌsentɪdʒ ˈjiːld/ noun the annual rate of compound interest earned by an account. Abbreviation **APY**

annual report /ˌænjuəl rɪˈpɔːt/ noun a report of a company's financial situation at the end of a year, sent to all the shareholders

annual rest system /ˌænjuəl ˈrest ˌsɪstəm/ noun a system by which extra payments or overpayments made to reduce the amount borrowed on a mortgage are credited to the account only once a year

annual return /ˌænjuəl rɪˈtɜːn/ noun an official report which a registered company has to make each year to the Registrar of Companies

annuitant /əˈnjuːɪtənt/ noun a person who receives an annuity

annuity /əˈnjuːɪti/ noun money paid each year to a retired person, usually in return for a lump-sum payment. The value of the annuity depends on how long the person lives, as it usually cannot be passed on to another person. Annuities are fixed payments, and lose their value with inflation, whereas a pension can be index-linked. ○ *to buy* or *to take out an annuity* ○ *She has a government annuity* or *an annuity from the government.*

COMMENT: When a person retires, he or she is required by law to purchase a 'compulsory purchase annuity' with the funds accumulated in his or her pension fund. This provides a taxable income for the rest of his or her life, but usually it is a fixed income which does not change with inflation.

annuity certain /əˌnjuːɪti ˈsɜːtən/ noun an annuity that provides payments for a specific number of years, regardless of life or death of the annuitant

antedate /ˌæntɪˈdeɪt/ verb to put an earlier date on a document ○ *The invoice was antedated to 1st January.*

anti- /ænti/ prefix against

anticipate /ænˈtɪsɪpeɪt/ verb to expect something to happen

anticipated balance /ænˌtɪsɪpeɪtɪd ˈbæləns/ noun a balance which is forecast from a deposit when it matures

anti-dumping /ˌænti ˈdʌmpɪŋ/ adjective protecting a country against dumping ○ *anti-dumping legislation*

'…just days before the Department of Commerce decides on anti-dumping duties for Chinese wooden bedroom furniture.' [Forbes]

anti-dumping duty /ˌænti ˈdʌmpɪŋ ˌdjuːti/ noun same as **countervailing duty**

anti-inflationary /ˌænti ɪn ˈfleɪʃ(ə)n(ə)ri/ adjective restricting or trying to restrict inflation ○ *anti-inflationary measures*

anti-trust /ˌænti ˈtrʌst/ adjective attacking monopolies and encouraging competition ○ *anti-trust measures*

antitrust law /ˈæntitrʌst lɔː/ noun US a law that promotes or maintains market competition by regulating anti-competitive behaviour

anti-trust laws /ˌænti ˈtrʌst ˌlɔːz/, **anti-trust legislation** /ˌænti ˈtrʌst ledʒɪˌsleɪʃ(ə)n/ plural noun laws in the US which prevent the formation of monopolies

AO abbreviation All Ordinaries Index

AOB abbreviation any other business

AON abbreviation all or none

APACS abbreviation Association for Payment Clearing Services

applicant /ˈæplɪkənt/ noun a person who applies for something ○ *an applicant for a job* or *a job applicant* ○ *an applicant* to an industrial tribunal ○ *There were thousands of applicants for shares in the new company.*

application /ˌæplɪˈkeɪʃ(ə)n/ noun **1.** the act of asking for something, usually in writing, or a document in which someone asks for something, e.g. a job ○ *shares payable on application* ○ *She sent off six applications for job* or *six job applications.* **2.** effort or diligence ○ *She has shown great application in her work on the project.*

application form /ˌæplɪˈkeɪʃ(ə)n ˌfɔːm/ noun a form to be filled in when applying for a new issue of shares or for a job

apply /əˈplaɪ/ verb **1.** to ask for something, usually in writing ○ *to apply in writing* ○ *to apply in person* ○ *The more ambitious of the employees will apply for the management trainee programme.* ○ *About fifty people have applied for the job, but there is only one vacancy.* **2.** to affect or to relate to ○ *This clause applies only to deals outside the EU.* (NOTE: [all senses] **applies – applying – applied**)

appoint /əˈpɔɪnt/ verb to choose someone for a job ○ *We have appointed a new distribution manager.* ○ *They've appointed Janet Smith (to the post of) manager.* (NOTE: You appoint a person **to** a job.)

appointment /əˈpɔɪntmənt/ noun the act of being appointed to a job, or of appointing someone to a job □ **on his appointment as manager** when he was made manager

apportion /əˈpɔːʃ(ə)n/ verb to share out something, e.g. costs, funds or blame ○ *Costs are apportioned according to projected revenue.*

apportionment /əˈpɔːʃ(ə)nmənt/ noun the sharing out of costs

appraisal /əˈpreɪz(ə)l/ noun a calculation of the value of someone or something

'…we are now reaching a stage in industry and commerce where appraisals are becoming part of the management culture. Most managers now take it for granted that they will appraise and be appraised' [*Personnel Management*]

appraise /əˈpreɪz/ verb to assess or to calculate the value of something or someone

appraisee /əpreɪˈziː/ *noun* an employee who is being appraised by his or her manager in an appraisal interview

appreciate /əˈpriːʃieɪt/ *verb* **1.** to notice how good something is ○ *The customer always appreciates efficient service.* **2.** (*of currency, shares, etc.*) to increase in value

appreciation /əˌpriːʃiˈeɪʃ(ə)n/ *noun* **1.** an increase in value ○ *the appreciation of the dollar against the euro* Also called **capital appreciation 2.** the act of valuing something highly ○ *She was given a pay rise in appreciation of her excellent work.*

appro /ˈæprəʊ/ *noun* same as **approval** (*informal*) □ **to buy something on appro** to buy something which you will only pay for if it is satisfactory

appropriate *adjective* /əˈprəʊpriət/ suitable ○ *I leave it to you to take appropriate action.* ■ *verb* /əˈprəʊprieɪt/ to put a sum of money aside for a special purpose ○ *to appropriate a sum of money for a capital project*

appropriation /əˌprəʊpriˈeɪʃ(ə)n/ *noun* the act of putting money aside for a special purpose ○ *appropriation of funds to the reserve*

appropriation account /əˌprəʊpri ˈeɪʃ(ə)n əˌkaʊnt/ *noun* the part of a profit and loss account which shows how the profit has been dealt with, e.g., how much has been given to the shareholders as dividends and how much is being put into the reserves

approval /əˈpruːv(ə)l/ *noun* **1.** the act of saying or thinking that something is good ○ *to submit a budget for approval* **2.** □ **on approval** in order to be able to use something for a period of time and check that it is satisfactory before paying for it ○ *to buy a photocopier on approval*

approve /əˈpruːv/ *verb* **1.** □ **to approve of something** to think something is good ○ *The chairman approves of the new company letter heading.* ○ *The sales staff do not approve of interference from the accounts division.* **2.** to agree to something officially ○ *to approve the terms of a contract* ○ *The proposal was approved by the board.*

approved securities /əˌpruːvd sɪ ˈkjʊərɪtiz/ *plural noun* state bonds which can be held by banks to form part of their reserves (NOTE: The list of these bonds is the 'approved list'.)

approximate /əˈprɒksɪmət/ *adjective* not exact, but almost correct ○ *The sales division has made an approximate forecast of expenditure.*

approximately /əˈprɒksɪmətli/ *adverb* not quite exactly, but close to the figure shown ○ *Expenditure on marketing is approximately 10% down on the previous quarter.*

approximation /əˌprɒksɪˈmeɪʃ(ə)n/ *noun* a rough calculation ○ *Each department has been asked to provide an approximation of expenditure for next year.* ○ *The final figure is only an approximation.*

APR *abbreviation* **1.** Annual Percentage Rate **2.** annualised percentage rate

APY *abbreviation* annual percentage yield

Arab accounting dinar /ˌærəb ə ˈkaʊntɪŋ ˌdiːnɑː/ *noun* a unit used for accounting purposes between member countries of the Arab Monetary Fund. Abbreviation **AAD**

arb *abbreviation* arbitrageur (*informal*)

arbitrage /ˈɑːbɪˌtrɑːʒ/ *noun* the business of making a profit from the difference in value of various assets, e.g. by selling foreign currencies or commodities on one market and buying on another at almost the same time to profit from different exchange rates, or by buying currencies forward and selling them forward at a later date, to benefit from a difference in prices

arbitrage fund /ˈɑːbɪtrɑːʒ fʌnd/ *noun* a fund which tries to take advantage of price discrepancies for the same asset in different markets

arbitrage syndicate /ˈɑːbɪtrɑːʒ ˌsɪndɪkət/ *noun* a group of people who together raise the capital to invest in arbitrage deals

arbitrageur /ˈɑːbɪtreɪdʒə/, **arbitrager** /ˌɑːbɪtrɑːˈʒɜː/ *noun* an investor who tries to profit from price inefficiencies in the market by making simultaneous trades that offset each other and capturing risk-free profits ○ *As an arbitrageur he made a profit by selling in New York and buying in London.*

COMMENT: Arbitrageurs buy shares in companies which are potential takeover targets, either to force up the price of the shares before the takeover bid, or simply as a position while waiting for the takeover bid to take place. They also sell shares in the company which is expected to make the takeover bid, since one of the consequences of a takeover bid is usually that the price of the target company rises while that of the bidding company falls. Arbitrageurs may then sell the shares in the target company at a profit, either to one of the parties making the takeover bid, or back to the company itself.

arbitration /ˌɑːbɪˈtreɪʃ(ə)n/ *noun* the settling of a dispute by an outside party agreed on by both sides ○ *to take a dispute to arbitration* or *to go to arbitration* ○ *arbitration in an industrial dispute* ○ *The two sides decided to submit the dispute to arbitration* or *to refer the question to arbitration.*

area manager /ˌeəriə ˈmænɪdʒə/ *noun* a manager who is responsible for a company's work in a specific part of the country

arithmetic average /ˌærɪθmetɪk ˈæv(ə)rɪdʒ/ *noun* same as **average**

ARM *abbreviation* adjustable rate mortgage

arm's length /ˌɑːmz ˈleŋθ/ *adjective* □ **arm's length transaction** a transaction which is carried out by two parties with no connection between them (resulting in a fair market value for the item sold) □ **to deal with someone at arm's length** to deal as if there were no financial link between the two parties (as when a company buys a service from one of its own subsidiaries)

around /əˈraʊnd/ *preposition* **1.** approximately ○ *The office costs around £2,000 a year to heat.* ○ *Her salary is around $85,000.* **2.** with a premium or discount □ **5 points around** with a 5-point premium and a 5-point discount, both calculated on the spot price

ARPS *abbreviation* adjustable rate preferred stock

arrangement fee /əˈreɪndʒmənt fiː/ *noun* a charge made by a bank to a client for arranging credit facilities

arrears /əˈrɪəz/ *plural noun* **1.** money which is owed, but which has not been paid at the right time ○ *a salary with arrears effective from 1st January* ○ *We are pressing the company to pay arrears of interest.* ○ *You must not allow the mort-*

gage payments to fall into arrears. **2.** □ **in arrears** owing money which should have been paid earlier ○ *The payments are six months in arrears.* ○ *He is six weeks in arrears with his rent.*

arrive /əˈraɪv/ *verb* to reach a place ○ *The consignment has still not arrived.* ○ *The shipment arrived without any documentation.* ○ *The plane arrives in Sydney at 04.00.* ○ *The train leaves Paris at 09.20 and arrives at Bordeaux two hours later.* (NOTE: You arrive **at** *or* **in** a place or town, but only **in** a country.)

arrive at /əˈraɪv ət/ *phrasal verb* to work out and agree on something ○ *They very quickly arrived at an acceptable price.* ○ *After some discussion we arrived at a compromise.*

article /ˈɑːtɪk(ə)l/ *noun* **1.** a product or thing for sale ○ *to launch a new article on the market* ○ *a black market in luxury articles* **2.** a section of a legal agreement such as a contract or treaty ○ *See article 8 of the contract.*

article 8 currency /ˌɑːtɪk(ə)l ˈeɪt ˌkʌrənsi/ *noun* a strong convertible currency according to the IMF

articled clerk /ˌɑːtɪk(ə)ld ˈklɑːk/ *noun uk* a clerk who is bound by contract to work in a solicitor's office for some years to learn the law (NOTE: Such as person is now officially called a **trainee solicitor**, though the old term is still used)

articles of association /ˌɑːtɪk(ə)lz əv əˌsəʊsiˈeɪʃ(ə)n/ *plural noun* a document which lays down the rules for a company regarding such matters as the issue of shares, the conduct of meetings and the appointment of directors ○ *This procedure is not allowed under the articles of association of the company.* (NOTE: The US term is **bylaws**)

articles of incorporation /ˌɑːtɪk(ə)lz əv ɪnˌkɔːpəˈreɪʃ(ə)n/ *plural noun US* same as **memorandum and articles of association**

articles of partnership /ˌɑːtɪk(ə)lz əv ˈpɑːtnəʃɪp/ *plural noun* same as **partnership agreement**

asap /ˌeɪ es eɪ ˈpiː, ˈeɪsæp/, **ASAP** *abbreviation* as soon as possible

ascending tops /əˌsendɪŋ ˈtɒps/ *noun* a term used by chartists to refer to an upward trend in the market, where each peak is higher than the preceding one

ASEAN *abbreviation* Association of Southeast Asian Nations

A shares /ˈeɪ ˌʃeəz/ *plural noun* ordinary shares with limited voting rights or no voting rights at all

COMMENT: A company may be set up with two classes of share: 'A' shares, which are available to the general investor, and 'B' shares which are only bought by certain individuals, such as the founder and his family. Such division of shares is becoming less usual nowadays.

Asian Currency Unit /ˌeɪʒ(ə)n ˈkʌrənsi ˌjuːnɪt/ *noun* a unit of account for dollar deposits held in Singapore and other Asian markets. Abbreviation **ACU**

Asian Development Bank /ˌeɪʒ(ə)n dɪˈveləpmənt bæŋk/ *noun* a bank set up by various Asian countries, with other outside members, to assist countries in the region with money and technical advice. Abbreviation **ADB**

Asian dollar /ˌeɪʒ(ə)n ˈdɒlə/ *noun* an American dollar deposited in Singapore and other Asian markets, and traded in Singapore

Asian dollar bonds /ˌeɪʒ(ə)n ˈdɒlə bɒndz/ *plural noun* bonds issued in Asian dollars

Asian monetary unit /ˌeɪʒ(ə)n ˈmʌnɪt(ə)ri ˌjuːnɪt/ *noun* a unit used in financial dealings between members of the Asian Clearing Union

ask /ɑːsk/ *verb* **1.** to put a question to someone ○ *He asked the information office for details of companies exhibiting at the motor show.* ○ *Ask the salesclerk if the bill includes VAT.* **2.** to tell someone to do something ○ *He asked the switchboard operator to get him a number in Germany.* ○ *She asked her secretary to fetch a file from the managing director's office.* ○ *Customs officials asked him to open his case.*

ask for /ˈɑːsk fɔː/ *phrasal verb* **1.** to say that you want or need something ○ *They asked for more time to repay the loan.* **2.** to put a price on something for sale ○ *They are asking £24,000 for the car.*

asked price /ˈɑːskt praɪs/ *noun* a price at which a commodity or stock is offered for sale by a seller, also called 'offer price' in the UK

asking price /ˈɑːskɪŋ ˌpraɪs/ *noun* a price which the seller is hoping will be paid for the item being sold ○ *the asking price is $24,000*

as per /ˌæz ˈpɜː/ ♦ **per**

assay mark /ˈæseɪ mɑːk/ *noun* a mark put on gold, silver or platinum items to show that the metal is of the correct quality

assess /əˈses/ *verb* to calculate the value of something or someone ○ *to assess damages at £1,000* ○ *to assess a property for the purposes of insurance*

assessment /əˈsesmənt/ *noun* a calculation of value ○ *a property assessment* ○ *a tax assessment* ○ *They made a complete assessment of each employee's contribution to the organisation.*

assessor /əˈsesə/ *noun* a person who advises a tribunal

asset /ˈæset/ *noun* something which belongs to a company or person, and which has a value ○ *Her assets are only $640 as against liabilities of $24,000.*

COMMENT: A company's balance sheet will show assets in various forms: current assets, fixed assets, intangible assets, etc.

asset allocation /ˈæset æləˌkeɪʃ(ə)n/ *noun* the work of deciding how much money should be spent on the purchase of different types of investment, such as growth units or income units, depending on the particular needs of the individual investor

asset-backed securities /ˌæset bækt sɪˈkjʊərɪtiz/ *plural noun* bonds secured against specific assets

asset backing /ˈæset ˌbækɪŋ/ *noun* a support for a share price provided by the value of the company's assets

asset management account /ˌæset ˈmænɪdʒmənt əˌkaʊnt/ *noun* an account with a stockbroker which also acts as a bank account, and has credit card facilities as well. Also called **central assets account**

asset play /ˈæset pleɪ/ *noun* a share which seems to be undervalued based on its asset value and so is an attractive buy

assets /ˈæsets/ *plural noun* all items of property that contribute to the value of an organisation, including tangible items such as cash, stock and real estate, as well as intangible items such as goodwill

asset stripper /'æset ˌstrɪpə/ *noun* a person who buys a company to sell its assets

asset stripping /'æset ˌstrɪpɪŋ/ *noun* the practice of buying a company at a lower price than its asset value, and then selling its assets

asset value /'æset ˌvæljuː/ *noun* the value of a company calculated by adding together all its assets

assign /ə'saɪn/ *verb* **1.** to give something to someone by means of an official legal transfer ○ *to assign a right to someone* ○ *to assign shares to someone* **2.** to give someone a job of work to do and make him or her responsible for doing it ○ *She was assigned the task of checking the sales figures.*

assignation /ˌæsɪg'neɪʃ(ə)n/ *noun* a legal transfer ○ *the assignation of shares to someone* ○ *the assignation of a patent*

assignee /ˌæsaɪ'niː/ *noun* a person who receives something which has been assigned to him or her

assignment /ə'saɪnmənt/ *noun* **1.** the legal transfer of a property or right ○ *the assignment of a patent* or *of a copyright* ○ *to sign a deed of assignment* **2.** a particular task given to someone ○ *Her first assignment was to improve the company's image.* ○ *The oil team is on an assignment in the North Sea.*

assignor /ˌæsaɪ'nɔː/ *noun* a person who assigns something to someone

assigns /ə'saɪnz/ *plural noun* people to whom property has been assigned □ **his heirs and assigns** the people who have inherited his property and had it transferred to them

associate /ə'səʊsiət/ *adjective* linked ■ *noun* **1.** a person who works in the same business as someone ○ *She is a business associate of mine.* **2.** a person or company linked to another in a takeover bid **3.** same as **associate company**

associate bank /ə,səʊsiət 'bæŋk/ *noun* a bank which is part of a group such as Visa or MasterCard

associate company /ə,səʊsiət 'kʌmp(ə)ni/ *noun* a company which is partly owned by another company

associated company /ə,səʊsieɪtɪd 'kʌmp(ə)ni/ *noun* a company which is partly owned by another company (though less than 50%), which exerts some management control over it or has a close trading relationship with it ○ *Smith Ltd and its associated company, Jones Brothers*

associate director /ə,səʊsiət daɪ'rektə/ *noun* a director who attends board meetings, but has not been elected by the shareholders

association /ə,səʊsi'eɪʃ(ə)n/ *noun* a group of people or companies with the same interest ○ *an employers' association* ○ *Our company has applied to join the trade association.* ○ *The manufacturers' association has sent a letter to the minister.*

Association for Payment Clearing Services /ə,səʊsieɪʃ(ə)n fə 'peɪmənt ˌklɪərɪŋ ˌsɜːvɪsɪz/ *noun* an organisation which deals with the clearing of payments in the UK. Abbreviation **APACS**

Association of British Insurers /ə,səʊsieɪʃ(ə)n əv ˌbrɪtɪʃ ɪn'ʃʊərəz/ *noun* an organisation representing British companies which are authorised to transact insurance business. Abbreviation **ABI**

Association of Chartered Certified Accountants /ə,səʊsieɪʃ(ə)n əv ˌtʃɑːtəd ˌsɜːtɪfaɪd ə'kaʊntənts/ *noun* an organisation whose members are certified accountants. Abbreviation **ACCA**

Association of Futures Brokers and Dealers /ə,səʊsieɪʃ(ə)n əv 'fjuːtʃəz ˌbrəʊkəz ən ˌdiːləz/ *noun* a self-regulating organisation which oversees the activities of dealers in futures and options. Abbreviation **AFBD**

Association of Southeast Asian Nations /ə,səʊsieɪʃ(ə)n əv ˌsaʊθiːst ˌeɪʒ(ə)n 'neɪʃ(ə)nz/ *noun* an organisation formed originally in 1967 to promote economic growth, social and educational development and general stability in Southeast Asia. Abbreviation **ASEAN** (NOTE: The current members are: Brunei, Indonesia, Laos, Malaysia, Myanmar, Philippines, Singapore, Thailand and Vietnam.)

assumable mortgage /ə ˌsjuːməb(ə)l 'mɔːgɪdʒ/ *noun US* a mortgage which can be passed to another person

assume /ə'sjuːm/ *verb* to take for yourself ○ *He has assumed responsibility for* *marketing.* ○ *The company will assume all risks.*

assumption /ə'sʌmpʃ(ə)n/ *noun* **1.** the act of taking for yourself ○ *assumption of risks* **2.** the transfer of the rest of a mortgage to someone

assurance /ə'ʃʊərəns/ *noun* a type of insurance which pays compensation for an event that is certain to happen at some time, especially for the death of the insured person. Also called **life assurance, life insurance**

assure /ə'ʃʊə/ *verb* to insure someone, or someone's life, so that the insurance company will pay compensation when that person dies ○ *He has paid the premiums to have his wife's life assured.* (NOTE: **Assure, assurer** and **assurance** are used in Britain for insurance policies relating to something which will certainly happen (such as death); for other types of policy (i.e. those against something which may or may not happen, such as an accident) use the terms **insure, insurer** and **insurance.** In the US **insure, insurer** and **insurance** are used for both.)

assurer /ə'ʃʊərə/, **assuror** *noun* an insurer or a company which insures

AST *abbreviation* Automated Screen Trading

ASX *abbreviation* Australian Stock Exchange

at best /ˌæt 'best/ *adverb* □ **buy at best** an instruction to a stockbroker to buy securities at the best price available, even if it is high □ **sell at best** an instruction to a stockbroker to sell securities at the best price possible

at call /ˌæt 'kɔːl/ *adverb* immediately available

ATM /ˌeɪ tiː 'em/ *abbreviation* automated teller machine

'…the major supermarket operator is planning a new type of bank that would earn 90% of its revenue from fees on automated teller machine transactions. With the bank setting up ATMs at 7,000 group outlets nationwide, it would have a branch network at least 20 times larger than any of the major banks' [*Nikkei Weekly*]

ATM alliance /ˌeɪ tiː 'em ə,laɪəns/ *noun* a group of banks whose cards can be used at the same ATMs

at par /ˌæt 'pɑː/ *phrase* equal to the face value

ATS *abbreviation* automatic transfer service

at sight /ˌæt 'saɪt/ *adverb* immediately, when it is presented ○ *a bill of exchange payable at sight*

attachment order /ə'tætʃmənt ,ɔːdə/ *noun* an order from a court to hold a debtor's property to prevent it being sold until debts are paid

attract /ə'trækt/ *verb* to make someone want to join or come to something ○ *The company is offering free holidays in Spain to attract buyers.* ○ *We have difficulty in attracting skilled staff to this part of the country.*

attractive /ə'træktɪv/ *adjective* attracting something or someone □ **attractive prices** prices which are cheap enough to make buyers want to buy □ **attractive salary** a good salary to make high-quality applicants apply for the job

attributable profit /ə,trɪbjʊtəb(ə)l 'prɒfɪt/ *noun* a profit which can be shown to come from a particular area of the company's operations

auction /'ɔːkʃən/ *noun* **1.** a method of selling goods where people who want to buy compete with each other by saying how much they will offer for something, and the item is sold to the person who makes the highest offer ○ *Their furniture will be sold in the auction rooms next week.* ○ *They announced a sale by auction of the fire-damaged stock.* ○ *The equipment was sold by auction* or *at auction.* □ **to put an item up for auction** to offer an item for sale at an auction **2.** a method of selling government stock, where all stock on issue will be sold, and the highest price offered will be accepted, as opposed to tendering ■ *verb* to sell something at an auction ○ *The factory was closed and the machinery was auctioned off.*

auctioneer /ˌɔːkʃə'nɪə/ *noun* the person who conducts an auction

auction system /'ɔːkʃən ,sɪstəm/ *noun* a system where prices are agreed as the result of marketmakers offering stock for sale on the trading floor (as opposed to a quote system, where prices are quoted on a computerised screen)

audit /'ɔːdɪt/ *noun* **1.** the examination of the books and accounts of a company ○ *to carry out the annual audit* **2.** a detailed examination of something in order to assess it ○ *A thorough job audit was needed for job evaluation.* ○ *A manpower audit showed up a desperate lack of talent.* ■ *verb* to examine the books and accounts of a company ○ *Messrs Smith have been asked to audit the accounts.* ○ *The books have not yet been audited.*

auditing /'ɔːdɪtɪŋ/ *noun* the work of examining the books and accounts of a company

auditor /'ɔːdɪtə/ *noun* a person who audits

COMMENT: Auditors are appointed by the company's directors and voted for by the AGM. In the US, audited accounts are only required by corporations which are registered with the SEC, but in the UK all limited companies with a turnover over a certain limit must provide audited annual accounts.

auditors' fees /'ɔːdɪtəz fiːz/ *plural noun* fees paid to a company's auditors, which are approved by the shareholders at an AGM

auditors' qualification /ˌɔːdɪtəz ˌkwɒlɪfɪ'keɪʃ(ə)n/ *noun* a form of words in a report from the auditors of a company's accounts, stating that in their opinion the accounts are not a true reflection of the company's financial position. Also called **qualification of accounts**

auditors' report /'ɔːdɪtəz rɪˌpɔːt/ *noun* a report written by a company's auditors after they have examined the accounts of the company. Also called **audit report** (NOTE: If the auditors are satisfied, the report certifies that, in their opinion, the accounts give a 'true and fair' view of the company's financial position.)

audit report /'ɔːdɪt rɪˌpɔːt/ *noun* same as **auditors' report**

audit trail /'ɔːdɪt treɪl/ *noun* the records that show all the stages of a transaction, e.g. a purchase, a sale or a customer complaint, in the order in which they happened (NOTE: An audit trail can be a useful tool for problem-solving and, in financial markets, may be used to ensure that the dealers have been fair and accurate in their proceedings.)

'…provides real-time fax monitoring and audit trail to safeguard information privacy and accuracy' [Forbes]

austral /'ɔːstr(ə)l/ *noun* a unit of currency used in Argentina

Australian Stock Exchange /ɒˌstreɪliən 'stɒk ɪkˌstʃeɪndʒ/ *noun* the national stock exchange of Australia, made up of six exchanges (in Adelaide, Brisbane, Hobart, Melbourne, Perth and Sydney). Abbreviation **ASX**

AUT *abbreviation* authorised unit trust

authenticate /ɔː'θentɪkeɪt/ *verb* to say that something is true or genuine, especially to state that gold is of a correct quality

authentication /ɔːˌθentɪ'keɪʃ(ə)n/ *noun* **1.** an action of checking that something is true, such as an instruction sent to a bank by email **2.** a method of proving the identity of a person or company

COMMENT: Authentication is particularly important on the Internet where you do not actually see the person or premises of a company when making a purchase. If CompanyX wants to prove to Internet customers that they are really CompanyX and not a fraudster, they must ask an independent authenticator to issue them with a unique certificate of authentication. A visitor to the CompanyX website can ask to see this certificate and will be shown the unique number supplied by the trustworthy independent authenticator. Authentication is normally only used on commercial web sites that are selling goods.

authorisation /ˌɔːθəraɪ'zeɪʃ(ə)n/, **authorization** *noun* permission or power to do something ○ *Do you have authorisation for this expenditure?* ○ *He has not been given authorisation to act on our behalf.*

authorise /'ɔːθəraɪz/, **authorize** *verb* **1.** to give permission for something to be done ○ *to authorise payment of £10,000* **2.** to give someone the authority to do something ○ *to authorise someone to act on the company's behalf*

authorised /'ɔːθəraɪzd/, **authorized** *adjective* permitted

authorised capital /ˌɔːθəraɪzd 'kæpɪt(ə)l/ *noun* the amount of capital which a company is allowed to have, as stated in the memorandum of association

authorised corporate director /ˌɔːθəraɪzd ˌkɔːp(ə)rət daɪ'rektə/ *noun* the person who is in charge of an open-ended investment company. Abbreviation **ACD**

authorised dealer /ˌɔːθəraɪzd ˈdiːlə/ *noun* a person or company (such as a bank) that is allowed by the country's central bank to buy and sell foreign currency

authorised share capital /ˌɔːθəraɪzd ˈʃeə ˌkæpɪt(ə)l/ *noun* the amount of capital that a company is authorised to issue in the form of shares

authorised unit trust /ˌɔːθəraɪzd ˈjuːnɪt trʌst/ *noun* the official name for a unit trust which has to be managed according to EU directives. Abbreviation **AUT**

authority /ɔːˈθɒrɪti/ *noun* the power to do something ○ *a manager with authority to sign cheques* ○ *He has no authority to act on our behalf.* ○ *Only senior managers have the authority to initiate these changes.*

authority to purchase /ɔːˌθɒrɪti tə ˈpɜːtʃɪs/ *noun* a bill drawn up and presented with shipping documentation to the purchaser's bank, allowing the bank to purchase the bill

authorized stock /ˌɔːθəraɪzd ˈstɒk/ *noun US* same as **authorised capital**

automaker /ˈɔːtəʊmeɪkə/ *noun US* a company that manufactures cars (NOTE: The UK term is **car maker**.)

automated /ˈɔːtəmeɪtɪd/ *adjective* worked automatically by machines ○ *a fully automated car assembly plant*

Automated Clearing House /ˌɔːtəmeɪtɪd ˈklɪərɪŋ haʊs/ *noun US* an organisation set up by the federal authorities to settle transactions carried out by computer, such as automatic mortgage payments and trade payments between businesses. Abbreviation **ACH**

Automated Screen Trading /ˌɔːtəmeɪtɪd ˈskriːn ˌtreɪdɪŋ/ *noun* a system where securities are bought, sold and matched automatically by computer. Abbreviation **AST**

automated teller machine /ˌɔːtəmeɪtɪd ˈtelə məˌʃiːn/ *noun US* same as **cash dispenser**

automatic /ˌɔːtəˈmætɪk/ *adjective* working or taking place without any person making it happen ○ *There is an automatic increase in salaries on 1st January.*

automatically /ˌɔːtəˈmætɪkli/ *adverb* without a person giving instructions ○ *The invoices are sent out automatically.* ○ *Addresses are typed in automatically.* ○ *A demand note is sent automatically when the invoice is overdue.*

automatic data processing /ˌɔːtəmætɪk ˈdeɪtə ˌprəʊsesɪŋ/ *noun* data processing done by a computer. Abbreviation **ADP**

automatic transfer service /ˌɔːtəmætɪk ˈtrænsfə ˌsɜːvɪs/ *noun US* a service by which money can be transferred automatically from a customer's savings account to cover an overdraft in a current account. Abbreviation **ATS**

automation /ˌɔːtəˈmeɪʃ(ə)n/ *noun* the use of machines to do work with very little supervision by people

availability /əˌveɪləˈbɪlɪti/ *noun* the fact of being easy to obtain □ **offer subject to availability** the offer is valid only if the goods are available

availability float /əˌveɪləˈbɪlɪti fləʊt/ *noun* 1. a time between the moment a cheque is deposited and the time the money will have cleared 2. the amount of money in an account represented by deposits which have not yet cleared

available /əˈveɪləb(ə)l/ *adjective* able to be obtained or bought ○ *an item which is no longer available* ○ *funds which are made available for investment in small businesses* ○ *This product is available in all branches.*

available capital /əˌveɪləb(ə)l ˈkæpɪt(ə)l/ *noun* capital which is ready to be used

available funds /əˌveɪləb(ə)l ˈfʌndz/ *plural noun* funds held by a bank which it can use for loans or other investments

aval /əˈvɑːl/ *noun* a term used in Europe to refer to a bill or promissory note which is guaranteed by a third party

AVC /ˌeɪ viː ˈsiː/ *abbreviation* average variable cost

average /ˈæv(ə)rɪdʒ/ *noun* 1. a number calculated by adding several figures together and dividing by the number of figures added ○ *the average for the last three months* or *the last three months' average* ○ *sales average* or *average of sales* 2. □ **on average, on an average** in general ○ *On average, $15 worth of goods are stolen every day.* 3. the sharing of the cost of damage or loss of a ship between the insurers and the owners ■ *adjective* equal to the average of a set of figures ○ *the average increase in salaries* ○ *The average cost per unit is too high.* ○ *The average sales per representative are rising.* ■ *verb* **1.** to amount to something when the average of a set of figures is worked out ○ *Price increases have averaged 10% per annum.* ○ *Days lost through sickness have averaged twenty-two over the last four years.* **2.** to work out an average figure for something

'…a share with an average rating might yield 5 per cent and have a PER of about 10' [*Investors Chronicle*]

'…the average price per kilogram for this season to the end of April has been 300 cents' [*Australian Financial Review*]

average out /ˌæv(ə)rɪdʒ 'aʊt/ *phrasal verb* to come to a figure as an average ○ *It averages out at 10% per annum.* ○ *Sales increases have averaged out at 15%.*

average adjuster /ˌæv(ə)rɪdʒ ə 'dʒʌstə/ *noun* a person who calculates how much of a maritime insurance is to be paid by the insurer against a claim

average adjustment /ˌæv(ə)rɪdʒ ə 'dʒʌstmənt/ *noun* a calculation of the share of the cost of damage or loss of a ship that an insurer has to pay

average balance /ˌæv(ə)rɪdʒ 'bæləns/ *noun* the balance in an account calculated over a period

average cost of capital /ˌævərɪdʒ kɒst əv 'kæpɪt(ə)l/ *noun* an average figure for the cost of borrowing or the capital raised by selling shares

average daily balance /ˌæv(ə)rɪdʒ ˌdeɪli 'bæləns/ *noun* the balance in an account calculated by taking the final balances for each day, and averaging them (NOTE: The average daily balance is used for the purpose of calculating interest or bank charges.)

average due date /ˌæv(ə)rɪdʒ 'djuː ˌdeɪt/ *noun* the average date when several different payments fall due

averager /ˈævərɪdʒə/ *noun* a person who buys the same share at various times and at various prices to get an average value

average-sized /ˌævərɪdʒ 'saɪzd/ *adjective* of a similar size to most others,

not very large or very small ○ *They are an average-sized company.* ○ *She has an average-sized office.*

averaging /ˈævərɪdʒɪŋ/ *noun* the buying or selling of shares at different times and at different prices to establish an average price

avoid /ə'vɔɪd/ *verb* to try not to do something ○ *My aim is to avoid paying too much tax.* ○ *We want to avoid direct competition with Smith Ltd.* ○ *The company is struggling to avoid bankruptcy.* (NOTE: You avoid something or avoid **doing** something.)

avoidance /ə'vɔɪd(ə)ns/ *noun* the act of trying not to do something or not to pay something ○ *tax avoidance*

avoirdupois /ˌævədə'pɔɪz/ *noun* a non-metric system of weights used in the UK, the US and other countries, whose basic units are the ounce, the pound, the hundredweight and the ton (NOTE: The system is now no longer officially used in the UK)

COMMENT: Avoirdupois weight is divided into drams (16 drams = 1 ounce); ounces (14 ounces = one pound); pounds (100 pounds = 1 hundredweight); hundredweight (20 hundredweight = 1 ton). Avoirdupois weights are slightly heavier than troy weights with the same names: the avoirdupois pound equals 0.45kg, whereas the troy pound equals 0.37kg. See also TROY.

award /ə'wɔːd/ *noun* something given by a court, tribunal or other official body, especially when settling a dispute or claim ○ *an award by an industrial tribunal* ○ *The arbitrator's award was set aside on appeal.* ○ *The latest pay award has been announced.* ■ *verb* to decide the amount of money to be given to someone ○ *to award someone a salary increase* ○ *He was awarded £10,000 damages in the libel case.* ○ *The judge awarded costs to the defendant.* □ **to award a contract to someone** to decide that someone will be given the contract

away /ə'weɪ/ *adverb* not here, somewhere else ○ *The company is moving away from its down-market image.* □ **the bid is away from the market** *US* the bid is lower than the quoted market level

ax /æks/ *noun US* the financial adviser who is the current expert on a particular stock or market sector (*informal*)

B

B2B /ˌbiː tə 'biː/ *adjective* referring to products or services that are aimed at other businesses rather than at consumers (NOTE: The word is most commonly used of business-to-business dealings conducted over the Internet.)

'…rather than opening markets to greater competition, B2B exchanges could become powerful monopolistic tools' [*Economist*]

B2C /ˌbiː tə 'siː/ *adjective* referring to products or services that are aimed at consumers rather than at other businesses (NOTE: The word is most commonly used of business-to-consumer dealings conducted over the Internet.)

'While B2C companies were the target of choice last May, this spring they ranked fourth: The leaders were B2B outfits, e-marketplaces, and online service companies' [*BusinessWeek*]

Baby Bills /'beɪbi bɪlz/ *noun US* a nickname given to the hypothetical companies that would have formed if the Microsoft Corporation had been broken up by the Justice Department (*informal*)

baby bonds /'beɪbi bɒndz/ *plural noun US* bonds in small denominations which the small investor can afford to buy

back /bæk/ *noun* the opposite side to the front ○ *Write your address on the back of the envelope.* ○ *Please endorse the cheque on the back.* ■ *adjective* referring to the past ○ *a back payment* ■ *adverb* so as to make things as they were before ○ *He will pay back the money in monthly instalments.* ○ *The store sent back the cheque because the date was wrong.* ○ *The company went back on its agreement to supply at £1.50 a unit.* ■ *verb* **1.** to help someone, especially financially ○ *The bank is backing us to the tune of $10,000.*

○ *She is looking for someone to back her project.* **2.** □ **to back a bill** to sign a bill promising to pay it if the person it is addressed to is not able to do so

'…the businesses we back range from start-up ventures to established companies in need of further capital for expansion' [*Times*]

back out /ˌbæk 'aʊt/ *phrasal verb* to stop being part of a deal or an agreement ○ *The bank backed out of the contract.* ○ *We had to cancel the project when our German partners backed out.*

back up /ˌbæk 'ʌp/ *phrasal verb* **1.** to support or help ○ *She brought along a file of documents to back up his claim.* ○ *The finance director said the managing director had refused to back her up in her argument.* **2.** to go into reverse **3.** □ **to back up a portfolio** to sell long-term bonds and replace them with short-term bonds

back and filling /ˌbæk ən 'fɪlɪŋ/ *adjective* referring to a market where prices rise and fall slightly

backdate /bæk'deɪt/ *verb* **1.** to put an earlier date on a document such as a cheque or an invoice ○ *Backdate your invoice to 1st April.* **2.** to make something effective from an earlier date than the current date ○ *The pay increase is back-dated to 1st January.*

back door /ˌbæk 'dɔː/ *noun* □ **by the back door** by buying a listed company on order to acquire a listing on a stock exchange (which is cheaper than applying for a new listing)

back-end load /ˌbæk end 'ləʊd/ *noun* a management charge or commission which is levied when the investor sells out of the fund

back-end loaded /ˌbæk end ˈləʊdɪd/ *adjective* referring to an insurance or investment scheme where commission is charged when the investor withdraws his or her money from the scheme. Compare **front-end loaded**

backer /ˈbækə/ *noun* **1.** a person or company that backs someone ○ *One of the company's backers has withdrawn.* **2.** □ **the backer of a bill** the person who backs a bill

backhander /ˈbækˌhændə/ *noun* a bribe or money given to persuade someone to do something for you (*informal*) ○ *He was accused of taking backhanders from the company's suppliers.*

backing /ˈbækɪŋ/ *noun* support, especially financial support ○ *She has the backing of an Australian bank.* ○ *The company will succeed only if it has sufficient backing.* ○ *She gave her backing to the proposal.*

'…the company has received the backing of a number of oil companies who are willing to pay for the results of the survey' [*Lloyd's List*]

back interest /ˈbæk ˌɪntrəst/ *noun* interest which has not yet been paid

backlog /ˈbæklɒg/ *noun* an amount of work, or of items such as orders or letters, which should have been dealt with earlier but is still waiting to be done ○ *The warehouse is trying to cope with a backlog of orders.* ○ *We're finding it hard to cope with the backlog of paperwork.*

back office /ˌbæk ˈɒfɪs/ *noun* **1.** the part of a broking firm where the paperwork involved in buying and selling shares is processed **2.** *US* the part of a bank where cheques are processed, statements of account drawn up and other administrative tasks are done **3.** *US* general administration department of a company

back orders /ˈbæk ˌɔːdəz/ *plural noun* orders received and not yet fulfilled, usually because the item is out of stock ○ *It took the factory six weeks to clear all the accumulated back orders.*

back pay /ˈbæk peɪ/ *noun* a salary which has not been paid ○ *I am owed £500 in back pay.*

back payment /ˈbæk ˌpeɪmənt/ *noun* **1.** a payment which is due but has not yet been paid **2.** the act of paying money which is owed

back rent /ˈbæk rent/ *noun* a rent due but not paid ○ *The company owes £100,000 in back rent.*

back tax /ˈbæk tæks/ *noun* tax which is owed

back-to-back credit /ˌbæk tə ˌbæk ˈkredɪt/ *noun* **1.** credit facilities for the purchase of goods, where the credit is asked for by the purchaser, but is granted to a middleman, who buys the goods, then sells them on to the final purchaser, and uses the credit as a basis for obtaining further credit facilities **2.** credit in a currency allowed to a foreign trader on the basis of credit which has been granted by a bank in the trader's own country

back-to-back loan /ˌbæk tə ˌbæk ˈləʊn/ *noun* a loan from one company to another in one currency arranged against a loan from the second company to the first in another currency. Also called **parallel loan** (NOTE: Back-to-back loans are used by international companies to get round exchange controls.)

backup /ˈbækʌp/ *adjective* supporting or helping ○ *We offer a free backup service to customers.* ○ *After a series of sales tours by representatives, the sales director sends backup letters to all the contacts.*

backup copy /ˈbækʌp ˌkɒpi/ *noun* a copy of a computer file to be kept in case the original file is damaged

backup credit /ˈbækʌp ˌkredɪt/ *noun* credit provided by banks for a eurocurrency note

backup line /ˈbækʌp laɪn/ *noun* credit provided by banks against the security of commercial bills of exchange which are about to mature

backup withholding /ˈbækʌp wɪθ ˌhəʊldɪŋ/ *noun US* a tax retained from investment income so that the IRS is sure of getting the tax due

back wages /ˌbæk ˈweɪdʒɪz/ *plural noun* same as **back pay**

backwardation /ˌbækwəˈdeɪʃ(ə)n/ *noun* **1.** a penalty paid by the seller when postponing delivery of shares to the buyer **2.** a situation in which the cash price is higher than the forward price. Opposite **forwardation 3.** the difference between the spot and futures prices

backward integration /ˌbækwəd ˌɪntɪˈɡreɪʃ(ə)n/ *noun* a process of expansion in which a business that deals with the later stages in the production and sale of a product acquires a business that deals with an earlier stage in the same process, usually a supplier ○ *Buying up rubber plantations is part of the tyre company's backward integration policy.* ○ *Backward integration will ensure cheap supplies but forward integration would bring us nearer to the market.* Also called **vertical integration**. Opposite **forward integration**

BACS /bæks/ *noun* a company set up to organise the payment of direct debits, standing orders, salary cheques and other payments generated by computers. It operates for all the British clearing banks and several building societies; it forms part of APACS. Compare **CHAPS**. Full form **Bankers' Automated Clearing Services**

bad /bæd/ *adjective* not good

bad bargain /ˌbæd ˈbɑːɡɪn/ *noun* an item which is not worth the price asked

bad buy /ˌbæd ˈbaɪ/ *noun* a thing bought which was not worth the money paid for it

bad cheque /ˌbæd ˈtʃek/ *noun* a cheque which is returned to the drawer for any reason

bad debt /ˌbæd ˈdet/ *noun* a debt which will not be paid, usually because the debtor has gone out of business, and which has to be written off in the accounts ○ *The company has written off $30,000 in bad debts.*

bad debt provision /ˌbæd ˈdet prəˌvɪʒ(ə)n/ *noun* money put aside in accounts to cover potential bad debts

bag holder /ˈbæɡ ˌhəʊldə/ *noun US* a shareholder left holding worthless shares because of corporate bankruptcy or accounting scandal or due to falling for email scams or tricks used by touts to drive up the price of worthless shares (*informal*)

baht /bɑːt/ *noun* a unit of currency used in Thailand

bail out /ˌbeɪl ˈaʊt/ *phrasal verb* **1.** to rescue a company which is in financial difficulties **2.** □ **to bail someone out** to pay money to a court as a guarantee that

someone will return to face charges ○ *She paid $3,000 to bail him out.*

'…the government has decided to bail out the bank which has suffered losses to the extent that its capital has been wiped out' [*South China Morning Post*]

bailee /ˌbeɪˈliː/ *noun* a person who receives property by way of bailment

bailment /ˈbeɪlmənt/ *noun* a transfer of goods by someone (the 'bailor') to someone (the 'bailee') who then holds them until they have to be returned to the bailor (NOTE: Putting jewels in a bank's safe deposit box is an example of bailment.)

bailor /ˌbeɪˈlɔː/ *noun* a person who transfers property by way of bailment

bail-out /ˈbeɪl aʊt/ *noun* a rescue of a company in financial difficulties

balance /ˈbæləns/ *noun* **1.** the amount which has to be put in one of the columns of an account to make the total debits and credits equal □ **balance in hand** cash held to pay small debts □ **balance brought down** *or* **forward** the closing balance of the previous period used as the opening balance of the current period □ **balance carried down** *or* **forward** the closing balance of the current period **2.** the rest of an amount owed ○ *You can pay £100 deposit and the balance within 60 days.* □ **balance due to us** the amount owed to us which is due to be paid ■ *verb* **1.** to be equal, i.e. the assets owned must always equal the total liabilities plus capital □ **the February accounts do not balance** the two sides are not equal □ **to balance off the accounts** to make the two sides of an account balance at the end of an accounting period, by entering a debit balance in the credit side or a credit balance in the debit side, and carrying the balance forward into the next period **2.** to calculate the amount needed to make the two sides of an account equal ○ *I have finished balancing the accounts for March.* **3.** to plan a budget so that expenditure and income are equal ○ *The president is planning for a balanced budget.*

balance certificate /ˈbæləns sɜː ˌtɪfɪkət/ *noun* a share certificate given to an investor who has sold part of his or her shareholding and shows the number of shares which he or she has retained

balanced budget /ˌbælənst ˈbʌdʒɪt/ *noun* a budget where expenditure and income are equal

balance of payments /ˌbæləns əv ˈpeɪmənts/ *noun* a comparison between total receipts and payments arising from a country's international trade in goods, services and financial transactions. Abbreviation **BOP**

balance of payments deficit /ˌbæləns əv ˈpeɪmənts ˌdefɪsɪt/ *noun* a situation in which a country imports more than it exports

balance of payments surplus /ˌbæləns əv ˈpeɪmənts ˌsɜːpləs/ *noun* a situation in which a country exports more than it imports

balance of trade /ˌbæləns əv ˈtreɪd/ *noun* a record of the international trading position of a country in merchandise, excluding invisible trade. Also called **trade balance**

balance sheet /ˈbæləns ʃiːt/ *noun* a statement of the financial position of a company at a particular time, such as the end of the financial year or the end of a quarter, showing the company's assets and liabilities ○ *Our accountant has prepared the balance sheet for the first half-year.* ○ *The company balance sheet for the last financial year shows a worse position than for the previous year.* ○ *The company balance sheet for 2009 shows a substantial loss.*

COMMENT: The balance sheet shows the state of a company's finances at a certain date. The profit and loss account shows the movements which have taken place since the end of the previous accounting period. A balance sheet must balance, with the basic equation that assets (i.e. what the company owns, including money owed to the company) must equal liabilities (i.e. what the company owes to its creditors) plus capital (i.e. what it owes to its shareholders). A balance sheet can be drawn up either in the horizontal form, with (in the UK) liabilities and capital on the left-hand side of the page (in the US, it is the reverse) or in the vertical form, with assets at the top of the page, followed by liabilities, and capital at the bottom. Most are usually drawn up in the vertical format, as opposed to the more old-fashioned horizontal style.

balancing item /ˈbælənsɪŋ ˌaɪtəm/, **balancing figure** /ˈbælənsɪŋ ˌfɪɡə/ *noun* an item introduced into a balance sheet to make the two sides balance

balboa /bælˈbəʊə/ *noun* a unit of currency used in Panama

balloon /bəˈluːn/ *noun* a loan where the last repayment is larger than the others

balloon mortgage /bəˈluːn ˌmɔːɡɪdʒ/ *noun* a mortgage in which the final payment (called a 'balloon payment') is larger than the others

ballot /ˈbælət/ *noun* **1.** an election where people vote for someone by marking a cross on a paper with a list of names ○ *Six names were put forward for three vacancies on the committee so a ballot was held.* **2.** a selection made by taking papers at random out of a box ○ *The share issue was oversubscribed, so there was a ballot for the shares.* ■ *verb* to take a vote by ballot ○ *The union is balloting for the post of president.*

ballot box /ˈbælət bɒks/ *noun* a sealed box into which ballot papers are put

ballot paper /ˈbælət ˌpeɪpə/ *noun* a paper on which the voter marks a cross to show who they want to vote for

Baltic Futures Exchange /ˌbɔːltɪk ˈfjuːtʃəz ɪksˌtʃeɪndʒ/ *noun* an institution in London specialising in the chartering of shipping for sea freight and planes for airfreight, and also in commodity futures, such as wheat, barley, potatoes and pigs. Abbreviation **BFE**

banca *noun* the Italian word for **bank**

Banca d'Italia *noun* the central bank of Italy

bancassurer /ˈbæŋkəˌsjʊərə/ *noun* a bank offering a range of financial services to its customers, including insurance from a subsidiary insurance company

banco *noun* the word for **bank** in Spanish and Portuguese

Banco de España *noun* the central bank of Spain

Banco de Portugal *noun* the central bank of Portugal

band /bænd/ *noun* a range of figures with an upper and a lower limit, to which something, e.g. the amount of someone's salary or the exchange value of a currency, is restricted but within which it can move ○ *a salary band*

bank /bæŋk/ *noun* a business which holds money for its clients, lends money at interest, and trades generally in money ○ *the First National Bank* ○ *the Royal*

Bank of Scotland ○ *She put all her earnings into the bank.* ○ *I have had a letter from my bank telling me my account is overdrawn.* ■ *verb* to deposit money into a bank or to have an account with a bank ○ *He banked the cheque as soon as he received it.* ○ *I bank at* or *with Barclays.* □ **where do you bank?** where do you have a bank account?

bank on /ˈbæŋk ɒn/ *phrasal verb* to feel sure that something will happen ○ *He is banking on getting a loan from his father to set up in business.* ○ *Do not bank on the sale of your house.*

Bank *noun* the German word for **bank**

bankable /ˈbæŋkəb(ə)l/ *adjective* acceptable by a bank as security for a loan

bankable paper /ˌbæŋkəb(ə)l ˈpeɪpə/ *noun* a document which a bank will accept as security for a loan

bank account /ˈbæŋk əˌkaʊnt/ *noun* an account which a customer has with a bank, where the customer can deposit and withdraw money ○ *to open a bank account* ○ *to close a bank account* ○ *How much money do you have in your bank account?* ○ *If you let the balance in your bank account fall below $1,000, you have to pay bank charges.*

bank advance /ˈbæŋk ədˌvɑːns/ *noun* same as **bank loan** ○ *She asked for a bank advance to start her business.*

bank balance /ˈbæŋk ˌbæləns/ *noun* the state of a bank account at any particular time ○ *Our bank balance went into the red last month.*

bank base rate /ˌbæŋk ˈbeɪs ˌreɪt/ *noun* a basic rate of interest, on which the actual rate a bank charges on loans to its customers is calculated. Also called **base rate**

bank bill /ˈbæŋk bɪl/ *noun* **1.** a bill of exchange by one bank telling another bank, usually in another country, to pay money to someone **2.** same as **banker's bill 3.** *US* same as **banknote**

bank book /ˈbæŋk bʊk/ *noun* a book given by a bank or building society which shows money which you deposit or withdraw from your savings account or building society account. Also called **passbook**

bank borrowing /ˌbæŋk ˈbɒrəʊɪŋ/ *noun* money borrowed from a bank ○ *The*

new factory was financed by bank borrowing.

bank card /ˈbæŋk kɑːd/ *noun* a credit card or debit card issued to a customer by a bank for use instead of cash when buying goods or services (NOTE: There are internationally recognised rules that govern the authorisation of the use of bank cards and the clearing and settlement of transactions in which they are used.)

bank certificate /ˈbæŋk səˌtɪfɪkət/ *noun* a document, often requested during an audit, that is signed by a bank official and confirms the balances due to or from a company on a specific date

bank charge /ˈbæŋk tʃɑːdʒ/ *noun* same as **service charge**

bank charter /ˌbæŋk ˈtʃɑːtə/ *noun* an official government document allowing the establishment of a bank

bank cheque /ˈbæŋk tʃek/ *noun* a bank's own cheque, drawn on itself and signed by a bank official

bank clerk /ˈbæŋk klɑːk/ *noun* a person who works in a bank, but is not a manager

bank collapse /ˈbæŋk kəˌlæps/ *noun* a financial crisis in 2007 that resulted in the collapse of large financial institutions, the bailout of banks by national governments and downturns in stock markets around the world

bank confirmation /ˈbæŋk ˌkɒnfə meɪʃ(ə)n/ *noun* verification of a company's balances requested by an auditor from a bank

bank credit /ˈbæŋk ˌkredɪt/ *noun* loans or overdrafts from a bank to a customer

bank deposits /ˈbæŋk dɪˌpɒzɪts/ *plural noun* all money placed in banks by private or corporate customers

bank discount rate /bæŋk ˈdɪskaʊnt reɪt/ *noun* a rate charged by a bank for a loan where the interest charges are deducted when the loan is made

bank draft /ˈbæŋk drɑːft/ *noun* an order by one bank telling another bank, usually in another country, to pay money to someone

banker /ˈbæŋkə/ *noun* **1.** a person who is in an important position in a bank **2.** a bank ○ *the company's banker is Barclays*

banker's acceptance /ˌbæŋkəz ək
'septəns/ *noun* a bill of exchange guaranteed by a bank

**Bankers' Automated Clearing
Services** /ˌbæŋkəz ˌɔːtəmeɪtɪd
'klɪərɪŋ ˌsɜːvɪsɪz/ *plural noun* full form
of **BACS**

banker's bill /ˈbæŋkəz bɪl/ *noun* an
order by one bank telling another bank,
usually in another country, to pay money
to someone. Also called **bank bill**

banker's credit card /ˌbæŋkəz
ˈkredɪt ˌkɑːd/ *noun* a credit card issued
by a bank, as opposed to cards issued by
stores. Typical such cards are Visa, Egg or
Barclaycard.

banker's draft /ˌbæŋkəz ˈdrɑːft/
noun a draft payable by a bank in cash on
presentation. Abbreviation **B/D**

banker's lien /ˌbæŋkəz ˈliːn/ *noun* the
right of a bank to hold some property of a
customer as security against payment of a
debt

banker's order /ˈbæŋkəz ˌɔːdə/ *noun*
an order written by a customer asking a
bank to make a regular payment ○ *He
pays his subscription by banker's order.*

banker's reference /ˌbæŋkəz
ˈref(ə)rəns/ *noun* **1.** details of a
company's bank, account number, etc.,
supplied so that a client can check if the
company is a risk **2.** a written report
issued by a bank regarding a particular
customer's creditworthiness

Bank Examiner /ˈbæŋk ɪgˌzæmɪnə/
noun US an official of one of the Federal
Reserve Banks who examines the
working of companies who apply to
become banks, and who supervises the
running of banks within the Reserve
Bank's district

Bank for International Settlements /ˌbæŋk fə ɪntəˌnæʃ(ə)nəl
ˈset(ə)lmənts/ *noun* a bank (based in
Basle) which acts as the clearing bank for
the central banks of various countries
through which they settle their currency
transactions, and which also acts on
behalf of the IMF. Abbreviation **BIS**

bank giro /ˈbæŋk ˌdʒaɪrəʊ/ *noun* a
method used by clearing banks to transfer
money rapidly from one account to
another

bank giro credit /bæŋk ˌdʒaɪrəʊ
ˈkredɪt/ *noun* a cash or cheque payment

to an organisation or person which
usually takes three working days to
process. Abbreviation **BGC**

bank holiday /ˌbæŋk ˈhɒlɪdeɪ/ *noun* a
weekday which is a public holiday when
the banks are closed ○ *New Year's Day is
a bank holiday.* ○ *Are we paid for bank
holidays in this job?*

bank identification number /ˌbæŋk
aɪdentɪfɪˈkeɪʃ(ə)n ˌnʌmbə/ *noun* an
internationally organised six-digit
number which identifies a bank for charge
card purposes. Abbreviation **BIN**

banking /ˈbæŋkɪŋ/ *noun* the business
of banks ○ *He is studying banking.* ○ *She
has gone into banking.* □ **a banking crisis**
a crisis affecting the banks

banking account /ˈbæŋkɪŋ əˌkaʊnt/
noun US an account which a customer
has with a bank

Banking Code /ˈbæŋkɪŋ kəʊd/ *noun*
a voluntary code of practice adopted by
banks and building societies in their dealings with their customers

banking covenants /ˈbæŋkɪŋ
ˌkʌvənənts/ *plural noun* a set of conditions imposed by a bank when it lends an
institution a large amount of money

banking hours /ˈbæŋkɪŋ ˌaʊəz/ *plural
noun* the hours when a bank is open for its
customers ○ *You cannot get money out of
the bank after banking hours.*

banking products /ˈbæŋkɪŋ
ˈprɒdʌkts/ *plural noun* goods and services produced by banks for customers,
e.g. statements, direct debits

banking service /ˈbæŋkɪŋ ˌsɜːvɪs/
noun the various ways in which a bank
can help a customer, such as operating
accounts, making transfers, paying
standing orders and selling foreign
currency

bank line /ˈbæŋk laɪn/ *noun* same as
line of credit

bank loan /ˈbæŋk ləʊn/ *noun* a loan
made by a bank to a customer, usually
against the security of a property or asset
○ *She asked for a bank loan to start her
business.* Also called **bank advance**

bank manager /ˈbæŋk ˌmænɪdʒə/
noun the person in charge of a branch of
a bank ○ *They asked their bank manager
for a loan.*

bank mandate /ˈbæŋk ˌmændeɪt/ noun a written order to a bank, asking it to open an account and allow someone to sign cheques on behalf of the account holder, and giving specimen signatures and relevant information

banknote /ˈbæŋk nəʊt/ noun **1.** a piece of printed paper money ○ a counterfeit £20 banknote (NOTE: The US term is **bill**.) **2.** US a non-interest bearing note, issued by a Federal Reserve Bank, which can be used as cash

Bank of England /ˌbæŋk əv ˈɪŋglənd/ noun the UK central bank, owned by the state, which, together with the Treasury, regulates the nation's finances

COMMENT: The Bank of England issues banknotes which carry the signatures of its officials. It is the lender of last resort to commercial banks and supervises banking institutions in the UK Its Monetary Policy Committee is independent of the government and sets interest rates. The Governor of the Bank of England is appointed by the government.

Bank of Japan /ˌbæŋk əv dʒəˈpæn/ noun the central bank of Japan. Abbreviation **BOJ**

bank rate /ˈbæŋk ˈreɪt/ noun **1.** the discount rate of a central bank **2.** formerly, the rate at which the Bank of England lent to other banks (then also called the Minimum Lending Rate (MLR), and now called the bank base rate)

bank reconciliation /ˌbæŋk ˌrekənsɪliˈeɪʃ(ə)n/ noun the act of making sure that the bank statements agree with the company's ledgers

bank reference /ˈbæŋk ˌref(ə)rəns/ noun same as **banker's reference**

bank release /ˈbæŋk rɪˌliːs/ noun same as **release note**

bank reserves /ˈbæŋk rɪˌzɜːvz/ plural noun cash and securities held by a bank to cover deposits

bank return /ˈbæŋk rɪˌtɜːn/ noun a regular report from a bank on its financial position

bankroll /ˈbæŋkrəʊl/ verb to provide the money that enables something or someone to survive (informal) ○ How long can he go on bankrolling his daughter's art gallery?

bankrupt /ˈbæŋkrʌpt/ noun, adjective (a person) who has been declared by a court not to be capable of paying his or her debts and whose affairs are put into the hands of a receiver ○ a bankrupt property developer ○ She was adjudicated or declared bankrupt. ○ He went bankrupt after two years in business. ■ verb to make someone become bankrupt ○ The recession bankrupted my father.

bankruptcy /ˈbæŋkrʌptsi/ noun the state of being bankrupt ○ The recession has caused thousands of bankruptcies. (NOTE: The plural is **bankruptcies**.)

COMMENT: In the UK, bankruptcy is applied only to individual persons, but in the US the term is also applied to corporations. In the UK, a bankrupt cannot hold public office (for example, they cannot be elected an MP) and cannot be the director of a company. They also cannot borrow money. In the US, there are two types of bankruptcy: involuntary, where the creditors ask for a person or corporation to be made bankrupt; and voluntary, where a person or corporation applies to be made bankrupt (in the UK, this is called voluntary liquidation).

bankruptcy order /ˈbæŋkrʌptsi ˌɔːdə/ noun same as **declaration of bankruptcy**

bankruptcy petition /ˈbæŋkrʌptsi pəˌtɪʃ(ə)n/ noun an application to a court asking for an order making someone bankrupt

bankruptcy proceedings /ˈbæŋk rʌptsi prəˌsiːdɪŋz/ plural noun a court case to make someone bankrupt

bank statement /ˈbæŋk ˌsteɪtmənt/ noun a written statement from a bank showing the balance of an account at a specific date

bank syndicate /ˈbæŋk ˌsɪndɪkət/ noun a group of major international banks which group together to underwrite a very large loan

bank transfer /ˈbæŋk ˌtrænsfɜː/ noun an act of moving money from a bank account to another account

Bankwire /ˈbæŋkwaɪə/ noun US a system operated by a group of banks to pass information among member banks

banque noun the French word for **bank**

banque d'affaires noun the French word for **merchant bank**

Banque de France noun the Central Bank of France

bar /bɑː/ *noun* **1.** a thing which stops you doing something ○ *Government legislation is a bar to foreign trade.* **2. the Bar** the profession of barrister

bar-bell /'bɑː bel/ *noun US* a portfolio which concentrates on very long-term and very short-term bonds only. Compare **ladder**

bar chart /'bɑː tʃɑːt/ *noun* a chart where values or quantities are shown as columns of different heights set on a base line, the different lengths expressing the quantity of the item or unit. Also called **bar graph, histogram**

Barclays Index /'bɑːkliːz ˌɪndeks/ *noun* an index of prices on the New Zealand Stock Exchange

barefoot pilgrim /ˌbeəfʊt 'pɪlgrɪm/ *noun* an unsophisticated investor who loses all of his or her wealth by trading equities in the stock market (*informal*)

bargain /'bɑːgɪn/ *noun* **1.** an agreement on the price of something ○ *to strike a bargain* or *to make a bargain* □ **to drive a hard bargain** to be a difficult person to negotiate with **2.** something which is cheaper than usual ○ *That car is a (real) bargain at $500.* **3.** a sale and purchase of one lot of shares on the stock exchange ■ *verb* to try to reach agreement about something, especially a price, usually with each person or group involved putting forward suggestions or offers which are discussed until a compromise is arrived at ○ *You will have to bargain with the dealer if you want a discount.* ○ *They spent two hours bargaining about or over the price.* (NOTE: You bargain **with** someone **over** or **about** or **for** something.)

bargain hunter /'bɑːgɪn ˌhʌntə/ *noun* a person who looks for cheap deals

bargain hunting /'bɑːgɪn ˌhʌntɪŋ/ *noun* looking for cheap goods or shares, which no one has noticed

bargaining /'bɑːgɪnɪŋ/ *noun* the act of trying to reach agreement about something, e.g. a price or a wage increase for workers

bargaining position /'bɑːgɪnɪŋ pə ˌzɪʃ(ə)n/ *noun* the offers or demands made by one group during negotiations

bargaining power /'bɑːgɪnɪŋ ˌpaʊə/ *noun* the strength of one person or group when discussing prices or wage settlements

bargain offer /ˌbɑːgɪn 'ɒfə/ *noun* the sale of a particular type of goods at a cheap price ○ *This week's bargain offer – 30% off all carpet prices.*

bargain price /ˌbɑːgɪn 'praɪs/ *noun* a cheap price ○ *These carpets are for sale at a bargain price.*

bargain sale /ˌbɑːgɪn 'seɪl/ *noun* the sale of all goods in a store at cheap prices

bargains done /ˌbɑːgɪnz 'dʌn/ *plural noun* the number of deals made on the stock exchange during a day

bar graph /'bɑː grɑːf/ *noun* same as **bar chart**

barrels per day /ˌbærəlz pə 'deɪ/ *plural noun* a figure used to show the output of an oilfield

barren /'bærən/ *adjective* referring to money which is not earning any interest

barrier /'bæriə/ *noun* anything which makes it difficult for someone to do something, especially to send goods from one place to another □ **to impose trade barriers on certain goods** to restrict import of some goods by charging high duty ○ *They considered imposing trade barriers on some food products.* □ **to lift trade barriers from imports** to remove restrictions on imports ○ *The government has lifted trade barriers on foreign cars.*

'…a senior European Community official has denounced Japanese trade barriers, saying they cost European producers $3 billion a year' [*Times*]

'…to create a single market out of the EC member states, physical, technical and tax barriers to free movement of trade between member states had to be removed. Imposing VAT on importation of goods from other member states was seen as one such tax barrier' [*Accountancy*]

barrier to entry /ˌbæriə tʊ 'entri/ *noun* a factor that makes it impossible or unprofitable for a company to try to start selling its products in a particular market (NOTE: Barriers to entry may be created, for example, when companies already in a market have patents that prevent their goods from being copied, when the cost of the advertising needed to gain a market share is too high, or when an existing product commands very strong brand loyalty.)

barter /'bɑːtə/ noun **1.** a system in which goods are exchanged for other goods and not sold for money **2.** a system in which advertising space or time is exchanged for goods from the advertiser ■ *verb* to exchange goods for other goods and not for money ○ *They agreed a deal to barter tractors for barrels of wine.*

'…under the barter agreements, Nigeria will export 175,000 barrels a day of crude oil in exchange for trucks, food, planes and chemicals' [*Wall Street Journal*]

barter agreement /ˌbɑːtə ə'griːmənt/ *noun* an agreement to exchange goods by barter ○ *The company has agreed a barter deal with Bulgaria.*

bartering /'bɑːtərɪŋ/ *noun* the act of exchanging goods for other goods and not for money

base /beɪs/ *noun* **1.** the lowest or first position ○ *Turnover increased by 200%, but started from a low base.* **2.** a place where a company has its main office or factory, or a place where a business person's office is located ○ *The company has its base in London and branches throughout Europe.* ○ *She has an office in Madrid which she uses as a base while travelling overseas.* ■ *verb* **1.** □ **to base something on something** to calculate something using something as your starting point or basic material for the calculation ○ *We based our calculations on the forecast turnover.* □ **based on** calculating from ○ *based on last year's figures* ○ *based on population forecasts* **2.** to set up a company or a person in a place ○ *The European manager is based in our London office.* ○ *Our overseas branch is based in the Bahamas.* ■ *adjective* lowest or first, and used for calculating others

'…the base lending rate, or prime rate, is the rate at which banks lend to their top corporate borrowers' [*Wall Street Journal*]

'…other investments include a large stake in the Chicago-based insurance company' [*Lloyd's List*]

base currency /'beɪs ˌkʌrənsi/ *noun* a currency against which exchange rates of other currencies are quoted

base metals /beɪs 'met(ə)lz/ *plural noun* ordinary metals used in industry, such as aluminium and lead

base rate /'beɪs reɪt/ *noun* same as **bank base rate**

base-weighted index /ˌbeɪs ˌweɪtɪd 'ɪndeks/ *noun* an index which is weighted according to the base year

base year /'beɪs jɪə/ *noun* the first year of an index, against which changes occurring in later years are measured

basic /'beɪsɪk/ *adjective* **1.** normal **2.** most important **3.** simple, or from which everything starts ○ *She has a basic knowledge of the market.* ○ *To work at the cash desk, you need a basic qualification in maths.*

basic balance /ˌbeɪsɪk 'bæləns/ *noun* the balance of current account and long-term capital accounts in a country's balance of payments

basic banking service /ˌbeɪsɪk 'bæŋkɪŋ ˌsɜːvɪs/ *noun* basic service offered by banks to their customers, in connection with operating their accounts

basic commodities /ˌbeɪsɪk kə'mɒdɪtiz/ *plural noun* ordinary farm produce, produced in large quantities, e.g. corn, rice or sugar

basic discount /ˌbeɪsɪk 'dɪskaʊnt/ *noun* a normal discount without extra percentages ○ *Our basic discount is 20%, but we offer 5% extra for rapid settlement.*

basic industry /ˌbeɪsɪk 'ɪndəstri/ *noun* the most important industry of a country, e.g. coal, steel or agriculture

basic pay /ˌbeɪsɪk 'peɪ/ *noun* a normal salary without extra payments

basic product /ˌbeɪsɪk 'prɒdʌkt/ *noun* the main product made from a raw material

basic rate tax /'beɪsɪk reɪt ˌtæks/ *noun* the lowest rate of income tax

basics /'beɪsɪks/ *plural noun* simple and important facts or principles ○ *She has studied the basics of foreign exchange dealing.* □ **to get back to basics** to consider the main facts or principles again

basic salary /ˌbeɪsɪk 'sæləri/ *noun* same as **basic pay**

basic wage /ˌbeɪsɪk 'weɪdʒ/ *noun* same as **basic pay** ○ *The basic wage is*

£110 a week, but you can expect to earn more than that with overtime.

basis /'beɪsɪs/ *noun* **1.** a point or number from which calculations are made ○ *We forecast the turnover on the basis of a 6% price increase.* (NOTE: The plural is **bases.**) **2.** the general terms of agreement or general principles on which something is decided or done ○ *This document should form the basis for an agreement.* ○ *We have three people working on a freelance basis.* (NOTE: The plural is **bases.**) □ **on a short-term** *or* **long-term basis** for a short or long period ○ *He has been appointed on a short-term basis.*

basis point /'beɪsɪs pɔɪnt/ *noun* one hundredth of a percentage point (0.01%), the basic unit used in measuring market movements or interest rates

basis price /'beɪsɪs praɪs/ *noun* **1.** the price agreed between buyer and seller on the over-the-counter market **2.** the price of a bond shown as its annual percentage yield to maturity

basis swap /'beɪsɪs swɒp/ *noun* the exchange of two financial instruments, each with a variable interest calculated on a different rate

basket /'bɑːskɪt/ *noun* **1.** a container made of thin pieces of wood, metal, plastic, etc. ○ *a basket of apples* **2.** a group of prices or currencies taken as a standard ○ *the price of the average shopping basket* ○ *The pound has fallen against a basket of European currencies.* ○ *The market basket has risen by 6%.*

'…the weekly adjusted average total basket price of £37.89 was just 3p more than the week before Christmas' [*The Grocer*]

basket of currencies /ˌbɑːskɪt əv ˈkʌrənsiz/ *noun* same as **currency basket**

batch /bætʃ/ *noun* **1.** a group of items which are made at one time ○ *This batch of shoes has the serial number 25–02.* **2.** a group of documents which are processed at the same time ○ *Today's batch of invoices is ready to be mailed.* ○ *The accountant signed a batch of cheques.* ○ *We deal with the orders in batches of fifty at a time.* ■ *verb* to put items together in groups ○ *to batch invoices or cheques*

batch number /'bætʃ ˌnʌmbə/ *noun* a number attached to a batch ○ *When making a complaint always quote the batch number on the packet.*

batch processing /'bætʃ ˌprəʊsesɪŋ/ *noun* a system of data processing where information is collected into batches before being loaded on to the computer

batch production /'bætʃ prəˌdʌkʃən/ *noun* production in batches

BBA *abbreviation* British Bankers' Association

bear /beə/ *noun* a person who sells shares, commodities or currency because he or she thinks their price will fall and it will be possible to buy them again more cheaply later. Opposite **bull** □ **taking a bear position** acting on the assumption that the market is likely to fall ■ *verb* **1.** to give interest ○ *government bonds which bear 5% interest* **2.** to have something, especially to have something written on it ○ *an envelope which bears a London postmark* ○ *a letter bearing yesterday's date* ○ *The cheque bears the signature of the company secretary.* ○ *The share certificate bears his name.* **3.** to pay costs ○ *The costs of the exhibition will be borne by the company.* ○ *The company bore the legal costs of both parties.* (NOTE: **bearing – bore – has borne**)

bear covering /'beə ˌkʌvərɪŋ/ *noun* a point in a market where dealers who sold stock short, now buy back at lower prices to cover their positions

bearer /'beərə/ *noun* a person who holds a cheque or certificate □ **the cheque is payable to bearer** the cheque will be paid to the person who holds it, not to any particular name written on it

bearer bond /'beərə bɒnd/, **bearer security** /'beərə sɪˌkjʊərɪti/ *noun* a bond which is payable to the bearer and does not have a name written on it

bear hug /'beə hʌg/ *noun* an offer made by one company to buy the shares of another for a much higher per-share price than what that company is worth, usually made when there is doubt that the target company's management will be willing to sell ○ *The bear hug often comes before a full hostile bid.*

bearing /ˈbeərɪŋ/ *adjective* producing ○ *certificates bearing interest at 5%* ○ *interest-bearing deposits*

bearish /ˈbeərɪʃ/ *adjective* referring to a factor which tends to make market prices fall

bear market /ˈbeə ˌmɑːkɪt/ *noun* a period when share prices fall because shareholders are selling since they believe the market will fall further. Opposite **bull market**

bear position /ˈbeə pəˌzɪʃ(ə)n/ *noun* a short position, i.e., selling shares which you do not own with the intention of buying them back later at a lower price, so as to be able to settle

bear raid /ˈbeə reɪd/ *noun* the act of selling large numbers of shares to try to bring down prices

bear squeeze /ˈbeə skwiːz/ *noun* **1.** an action by banks to raise exchange rates, forcing currency bear sellers to buy back currency at a loss (i.e., at a higher price) **2.** an operation by marketmakers to increase the price of shares, so as to force bears to buy at higher prices than they intended

bed-pepping /ˈbed ˌpepɪŋ/ *noun* arrangement by which you sell existing investments and put the resulting cash into a PEP. This establishes any gains on the investments, so that you can calculate whether you should pay capital gains tax.

beginning inventory /bɪˈɡɪnɪŋ ˌɪnvənt(ə)ri/ *noun US* same as **opening stock**

behavioural finance /bɪˌheɪvjərəl ˈfaɪnæns/ *noun* a psychological view of the way people take financial decisions

Beige Book /beɪʒ ˈbʊk/ *noun US* a report on the financial position prepared by the district banks for the Federal Reserve Board. ◊ **Blue Book**, **Green Book**

bellwether /ˈbelweðə/ *noun* a leading share which is thought of as an indicator of market trends as a whole, e.g. Lloyds in the UK

belly up /ˌbeli ˈʌp/ *adverb* □ **to go belly up** to fail or to go into liquidation (*informal*)

below par /bɪˌləʊ ˈpɑː/ *adjective* referring to a share with a market price lower than its par value

below-the-line /bɪˌləʊ ðə ˈlaɪn/ *adjective, adverb* used to describe entries in a company's profit and loss account that show how the profit is distributed, or where the funds to finance the loss originate. ◊ **above-the-line 1**

below-the-line expenditure /bɪˌləʊ ðə laɪn ɪkˈspendɪtʃə/ *noun* **1.** payments which do not arise from a company's usual activities, e.g. redundancy payments **2.** extraordinary items which are shown in the profit and loss account below net profit after taxation, as opposed to exceptional items which are included in the figure for profit before taxation

belt and braces /ˌbelt ən ˈbreɪsɪz/, **belt and suspenders** /ˌbelt ən səs ˈpendəz/ *noun* □ **a belt and braces person** a very cautious lender, one who asks for extra collateral as well as guarantees for a loan

benchmark /ˈbentʃmɑːk/ *noun* a point in an index which is important, and can be used to compare with other figures

beneficial interest /ˌbenɪfɪʃ(ə)l ˈɪntrəst/ *noun* a situation where someone is allowed to occupy or receive rent from a house without owning it

beneficial occupier /ˌbenɪfɪʃ(ə)l ˈɒkjʊpaɪə/ *noun* a person who occupies a property but does not own it fully

beneficial owner /ˌbenɪfɪʃ(ə)l ˈəʊnə/ *noun* a person who owns a property which is being used by someone else

beneficiary /ˌbenɪˈfɪʃəri/ *noun* a person who gains money from something ○ *the beneficiaries of a will*

benefit /ˈbenɪfɪt/ *noun* **1.** payments which are made to someone under a national or private insurance scheme ○ *She receives £75 a week as unemployment benefit.* ○ *Sickness benefit is paid monthly.* ○ *The insurance office sends out benefit cheques each week.* **2.** something of value given to an employee in addition to their salary ■ *verb* **1.** to make better or to improve ○ *A fall in inflation benefits the exchange rate.* **2.** □ **to benefit from** or **by something** to be improved by something, to gain more money because of something ○ *Exports have benefited from the fall in the exchange rate.* ○ *The employees have benefited from the profit-sharing scheme.*

'…the retail sector will also benefit from the expected influx of tourists' [*Australian Financial Review*]

benefit-cost analysis /ˌbenɪfɪt ˈkɒst əˌnælɪsɪs/ *noun* same as **cost-benefit analysis**

benefit in kind /ˌbenɪfɪt ɪn ˈkaɪnd/ *noun* a benefit other than money received by an employee as part of his or her total compensation package, e.g. a company car or private health insurance. Such benefits are usually subject to tax.

bequest /bɪˈkwest/ *noun* something such as property or money (but not freehold land), given to someone in a will ○ *He made several bequests to his staff.*

berhad *noun* a Malay word meaning 'private', used to describe a limited company in Malaysia. Abbreviation **Bhd**. ◊ **Sdn**

best practice /ˌbest ˈpræktɪs/ *noun* the most effective and efficient way to do something or to achieve a particular aim (NOTE: In business, best practice is often determined by benchmarking, that is by comparing the method one organisation uses to carry out a task with the methods used by other similar organisations and determining which method is most efficient and effective.)

'For the past 25 years, managers have been taught that the best practice for valuing assets…is to use a discounted-cash-flow (DCF) methodology.' [*Harvard Business Review*]

best-selling /ˌbest ˈselɪŋ/ *adjective* selling better than any other ○ *These computer disks are our best-selling line.*

bet /bet/ *noun* an amount deposited when you risk money on the result of a race or of a game ■ *verb* to risk money on the result of something ○ *He bet £100 on the result of the election.* ○ *I bet you £25 the dollar will rise against the pound.*

beta /ˈbiːtə/ *noun* a measurement of the return on investment in a stock compared against a one percentage point return on the stock market in general: it shows the volatility in the price of the share compared to the FTSE All-Share Index

beta shares /ˈbiːtə ʃeəz/, **beta securities** /ˈbiːtə sɪˌkjʊərɪtiz/, **beta stocks** /ˈbiːtə stɒks/ *plural noun* a group of about 500 shares which are traded on the London Stock Exchange, but not as frequently as the alpha shares (NOTE: Prices of beta shares are quoted on SEAQ, but not the share transactions.)

betting tax /ˈbetɪŋ tæks/ *noun* a tax levied on betting on horses, dogs, etc. (NOTE: **betting – bet – has bet**)

b/f *abbreviation* brought forward

BFE *abbreviation* Baltic Futures Exchange

BGC *abbreviation* bank giro credit

Bhd *abbreviation* berhad

bi- /baɪ/ *prefix* twice □ **bi-monthly** twice a month □ **bi-annually** twice a year

bid /bɪd/ *noun* **1.** an offer to buy something at a specific price. ◊ **takeover bid** □ **to make a bid for something** to offer to buy something ○ *We made a bid for the house.* ○ *The company made a bid for its rival.* □ **to make a cash bid** to offer to pay cash for something □ **to put in** *or* **enter a bid for something** to offer to buy something, usually in writing **2.** an offer to sell something or do a piece of work at a specific price ○ *She made the lowest bid for the job.* ○ *They asked for bids for the supply of spare parts.* ■ *verb* to offer to buy (NOTE: **bidding – bid – has bid**) □ **to bid for something** (*at an auction*) to offer to buy something □ **he bid £1,000 for the jewels** he offered to pay £1,000 for the jewels

bid basis /ˈbɪd ˌbeɪsɪs/ *noun* the pricing of unit trusts at a lower bid price to encourage buyers

bidder /ˈbɪdə/ *noun* a person who makes a bid, usually at an auction ○ *Several bidders made offers for the house.* □ **the property was sold to the highest bidder** to the person who had made the highest bid or who offered the most money □ **the tender will go to the lowest bidder** to the person who offers the best terms or the lowest price for services

bidding /ˈbɪdɪŋ/ *noun* the act of making offers to buy, usually at an auction □ **the bidding started at £1,000** the first and lowest bid was £1,000 □ **the bidding stopped at £250,000** the last bid, i.e. the successful bid, was for £250,000 □ **the auctioneer started the bidding at £100** the auctioneer suggested that the first bid should be £100

bid market /ˈbɪd ˌmɑːkɪt/ *noun* a market where there are more bids to buy than offers to sell. Opposite **offered market**

bid-offer price /ˌbɪd ˈɒfə praɪs/ *noun* a price charged by unit trusts to buyers and sellers of units, based on the bid-offer spread

bid-offer spread /ˌbɪd ˈɒfə spred/ *noun* the difference between buying and selling prices (i.e. between the bid and offer prices)

bid price /ˈbɪd praɪs/ *noun* a price at which investors sell shares or units in a unit trust (NOTE: The opposite, i.e. the buying price, is called the **offer price**; the difference between the two is **spread**.)

bid rate /ˈbɪd reɪt/ *noun* a rate of interest offered on deposits

bid whacking /ˈbɪd ˌwækɪŋ/ *noun* selling shares at or below the bid price instead of settling for a price between the bid and ask quotes ○ *Bid whacking temporarily drives down the market price of a security.*

Big Bang /ˌbɪg ˈbæŋ/ *noun* **1.** the change in practices on the London Stock Exchange, with the introduction of electronic trading on October 27th 1986 **2.** a similar change in financial practices in another country

COMMENT: The changes included the abolition of stock jobbers and the removal of the system of fixed commissions. The stock exchange trading floor closed and deals are now done by phone or computer or on the Internet.

Big Blue /ˌbɪg ˈbluː/ *noun* IBM (*informal*)

Big Board /ˈbɪg ˈbɔːd/ *noun* US same as **New York Stock Exchange** (*informal*)

'…at the close, the Dow Jones Industrial Average was up 24.25 at 2,559.65, while New York S.E. volume totalled 180m shares. Away from the Big Board, the American S.E. Composite climbed 2.31 to 297.87' [*Financial Times*]

big business /ˌbɪg ˈbɪznɪs/ *noun* very large commercial firms

Big Four /ˌbɪg ˈfɔː/ *noun* **1.** the four large British commercial banks: Barclays, LloydsTSB, HSBC and Natwest, now joined by several former building societies that have become banks **2.** the four largest Japanese securities

houses: Daiwa, Nikko, Nomura and Yamaichi

Big Mac Index /ˌbɪg ˈmæk ˌɪndeks/ *noun* an informal way of measuring the purchasing power parity between two currencies and tests the extent to which market exchange rates result in goods costing the same in different countries ○ *The Big Mac Index aims to make exchange-rate theory more digestible.*

Big Three /bɪg ˈθriː/ *noun US* a name for the three big car makers in Detroit, i.e., General Motors (GM), Chrysler and Ford (*informal*)

bilateral /baɪˈlæt(ə)rəl/ *adjective* between two parties or countries ○ *The minister signed a bilateral trade agreement.*

bilateral clearing /baɪˌlæt(ə)rəl ˈklɪərɪŋ/ *noun* the system of annual settlements of accounts between some countries, where accounts are settled by the central banks

bilateral credit /baɪˌlæt(ə)rəl ˈkredɪt/ *noun* credit allowed by banks to other banks in a clearing system, to cover the period while cheques are being cleared

bilateral netting /baɪˌlæt(ə)rəl ˈnetɪŋ/ *noun* the settlement of contracts between two banks to give a new position

bill /bɪl/ *noun* **1.** a written list of charges to be paid ○ *The bill is made out to Smith Ltd* ○ *The sales assistant wrote out the bill.* ○ *Does the bill include VAT?* ○ *The builder sent in his bill.* ○ *She left the country without paying her bills.* **2.** a list of charges in a restaurant ○ *Can I have the bill please?* ○ *The bill comes to £20 including service.* **3.** a written paper promising to pay money □ **due bills** which are owed but not yet paid. ◊ **bill of exchange 4.** *US* same as **banknote** ○ *a $5 bill* **5.** a draft of a new law which will be discussed in Parliament **6.** a small poster □ **'stick no bills'** the unauthorised putting up of posters is prohibited ■ *verb* to present a bill to someone so that it can be paid ○ *The plumbers billed us for the repairs.*

bill broker /ˈbɪl ˌbrəʊkə/ *noun* a discount house, a firm which buys and sells bills of exchange for a fee

billing /ˈbɪlɪŋ/ *noun* the work of writing invoices or bills

billing error /'bɪlɪŋ ˌerə/ *noun* a mistake in charging a sum to a credit card

billion /'bɪljən/ *noun* one thousand million (NOTE: In the US, it has always meant one thousand million, but in UK English it formerly meant one million million, and it is still sometimes used with this meaning. With figures it is usually written **bn: $5bn** say 'five billion dollars'.)

'…gross wool receipts for the selling season to end June 30 appear likely to top $2 billion' [*Australian Financial Review*]

'…at its last traded price the bank was capitalized at around $1.05 billion' [*South China Morning Post*]

bill of exchange /ˌbɪl əv ɪks't ʃeɪndʒ/ *noun* a document, signed by the person authorising it, which tells another person or a financial institution to pay money unconditionally to a named person on a specific date (NOTE: Bills of exchange are usually used for payments in foreign currency.) □ **to accept a bill** to sign a bill of exchange to show that you promise to pay it □ **to discount a bill** to buy or sell a bill of exchange at a lower price than that written on it in order to cash it later

COMMENT: A bill of exchange is a document raised by a seller and signed by a purchaser, stating that the purchaser accepts that he owes the seller money, and promises to pay it at a later date. The person raising the bill is the 'drawer'; the person who accepts it is the 'drawee'. The seller can then sell the bill at a discount to raise cash. This is called a 'trade bill'. A bill can also be accepted (i.e. guaranteed) by a bank, and in this case it is called a 'bank bill'.

bill of lading /ˌbɪl əv 'leɪdɪŋ/ *noun* a document listing goods that have been shipped, sent by the transporter to the seller and entered in the seller's accounts as money owed but not yet paid, and therefore as an asset

bill of sale /ˌbɪl əv 'seɪl/ *noun* a document which the seller gives to the buyer to show that the sale has taken place

bills payable /ˌbɪlz 'peɪəb(ə)l/ *plural noun* bills, especially bills of exchange, which a company will have to pay to its creditors. Abbreviation **B/P**

bills receivable /ˌbɪlz rɪ'siːvəb(ə)l/ *plural noun* bills, especially bills of exchange, which are due to be paid by a company's debtors. Abbreviation **B/R**

BIN *abbreviation* bank identification number

bind /baɪnd/ *verb* **1.** to tie or to attach **2.** to make it a legal duty for someone or something to act in a particular way ○ *The company is bound by its articles of association.* ○ *He does not consider himself bound by the agreement which was signed by his predecessor.* (NOTE: [all senses] **binding – bound**)

binder /'baɪndə/ *noun* **1.** a stiff cardboard cover for papers **2.** *US* a temporary agreement for insurance sent before the insurance policy is issued (NOTE: The UK term is **cover note**.)

binding /'baɪndɪŋ/ *adjective* being a legal requirement that someone does something ○ *a binding contract* ○ *This document is not legally binding.* □ **the agreement is binding on all parties** all parties signing it must do what is agreed

birr /bɜː/ *noun* a unit of currency used in Ethiopia

birth rate /'bɜːθ reɪt/ *noun* the number of children born per 1,000 of the population

BIS *abbreviation* Bank for International Settlements

BlackBerry /'blækbəri/ a trade name for a portable handheld device that combines functions such as email, web browsing, text messaging, scheduling and a mobile phone ○ *She kept up to date with her emails on her BlackBerry.*

black economy /ˌblæk ɪ'kɒnəmi/ *noun* goods and services which are paid for in cash, and therefore not declared for tax. Also called **hidden economy**, **parallel economy**, **shadow economy**

Black Friday /ˌblæk 'fraɪdeɪ/ *noun* a sudden collapse on a stock market (NOTE: Called after the first major collapse of the US stock market on 24th September, 1869.)

black list /'blæk lɪst/ *noun* **1.** a list of goods which are forbidden, or people or companies with which trade is forbidden **2.** a list of people considered by an employer to be too dangerous or disruptive to employ

blacklist /'blæklɪst/ *verb* to put goods, people, or a company on a black list ○ *Their firm was blacklisted by the government.*

black market /ˌblæk ˈmɑːkɪt/ *noun* the buying and selling of goods or currency in a way which is not allowed by law ○ *There is a flourishing black market in spare parts for cars.* ○ *You can buy gold coins on the black market.* □ **to pay black market prices** to pay high prices to get items which are not easily available

Black Monday /ˌblæk ˈmʌndeɪ/ *noun* Monday, 19th October, 1987, when world stock markets crashed

Black Tuesday /ˌblæk ˈtjuːzdeɪ/ *noun* Tuesday, 29th October, 1929, when the US stock market crashed

Black Wednesday /ˌblæk ˈwenzdeɪ/ *noun* Wednesday, 16th September, 1992, when the pound sterling left the European Exchange Rate Mechanism and was devalued against other currencies

COMMENT: Not always seen as 'black', since some people believe it was a good thing that the pound left the ERM.

blank /blæŋk/ *adjective* with nothing written on it ■ *noun* a space on a form which has to be completed ○ *Fill in the blanks and return the form to your local office.*

blank cheque /ˌblæŋk ˈtʃek/ *noun* a cheque with the amount of money and the payee left blank, but signed by the drawer

blank endorsement /blæŋk ɪnˈdɔːsmənt/ *noun* an endorsement which consists of a signature, and no other details

blanket agreement /ˌblæŋkɪt əˈɡriːmənt/ *noun* an agreement which covers many different items

blanket lien /ˌblæŋkɪt ˈliːn/ *noun US* a lien on a person's property, including personal effects

blind trust /ˌblaɪnd ˈtrʌst/ *noun* a trust set up to run a person's affairs without the details of any transaction being known to the person concerned (NOTE: Blind trusts are set up by politicians to avoid potential conflicts of interest.)

blip /blɪp/ *noun* bad economic figures (a higher inflation rate, lower exports, etc.), which only have a short-term effect

'…whether these pressures are just a cyclical blip in a low inflation era, or whether the UK is drifting back to the bad old days will be one of the crucial questions for the stock market this year' [*Financial Times*]

block /blɒk/ *noun* **1.** a series of items grouped together **2.** a series of buildings forming a square with streets on all sides ○ *They want to redevelop a block in the centre of the town.* □ **a block of offices, an office block** a large building which only contains offices ■ *verb* to stop something taking place ○ *He used his casting vote to block the motion.* ○ *The planning committee blocked the redevelopment plan.*

block booking /ˌblɒk ˈbʊkɪŋ/ *noun* an act of booking of several seats or rooms at the same time ○ *The company has a block booking for twenty seats on the plane* or *for ten rooms at the hotel.*

blocked account /ˌblɒkt əˈkaʊnt/ *noun* a bank account which cannot be used, usually because a government has forbidden its use

blocked currency /ˌblɒkt ˈkʌrənsi/ *noun* a currency which cannot be taken out of a country because of government exchange controls

block trading /ˌblɒk ˈtreɪdɪŋ/ *noun* trading in very large numbers of shares

blowout /ˈbləʊaʊt/ *noun US* a rapid sale of the whole of a new stock issue (*informal*)

Blue Book /ˌbluː ˈbʊk/ *noun* **1.** an annual publication of national statistics of personal incomes and spending patterns **2.** *US* a document reviewing monetary policy, prepared for the Federal Reserve

blue chip /ˈbluː tʃɪp/ *noun* a very safe investment, a risk-free share in a good company

blue-chip investments /ˌbluː tʃɪp ɪnˈvestmənts/, **blue-chip shares** /ˌbluː tʃɪp ˈseəz/, **blue-chips** /ˈbluː tʃɪps/ *plural noun* low-risk shares in good companies

blue-collar union /bluː ˈkɒlə ˌjuːnjən/ *noun* a trade union formed mainly of blue-collar workers

blue-collar worker /bluː ˈkɒlə ˌwɜːkə/ *noun* a manual worker in a factory

Blue list /ˈbluː lɪst/ *noun US* a daily list of municipal bonds and their ratings, issued by Standard & Poor's

blue sky laws /ˌbluː ˈskaɪ ˌlɔːz/ *plural noun US* state laws to protect investors against fraudulent traders in securities

bn /'bɪljən/ *abbreviation* billion

board /bɔːd/ *noun* **1.** same as **board of directors** ○ *He sits on the board as a representative of the bank.* ○ *Two directors were removed from the board at the AGM.* **2.** a group of people who run an organisation, trust or society **3.** □ **on board** on a ship, plane or train **4.** a screen on which share prices are posted (on the wall of the trading floor in a stock exchange) ■ *verb* to go on to a ship, plane or train ○ *Customs officials boarded the ship in the harbour.*

'CEOs, with their wealth of practical experience, are in great demand and can pick and choose the boards they want to serve on' [*Duns Business Month*]

board meeting /'bɔːd ˌmiːtɪŋ/ *noun* a meeting of the directors of a company

board of directors /ˌbɔːd əv daɪˈrektəz/ *noun* **1.** a group of directors elected by the shareholders to run a company ○ *The bank has two representatives on the board of directors.* **2.** *US* a group of people elected by the shareholders to draw up company policy and to appoint the president and other executive officers who are responsible for managing the company

'…a proxy is the written authorization an investor sends to a stockholder meeting conveying his vote on a corporate resolution or the election of a company's board of directors' [*Barrons*]

COMMENT: Directors are elected by shareholders at the AGM, though they are usually chosen by the chairman or chief executive. A board will consist of a chairman (who may be non-executive), a chief executive or managing director, and a series of specialist directors in charge of various activities of the company (such as production director or sales director). The company secretary will attend board meetings, but is not a director. Apart from the executive directors, who are in fact employees of the company, there may be several non-executive directors, appointed either for their expertise and contacts, or as representatives of important shareholders such as banks. These non-executive directors are paid fees. The board of an American company may be made up of a large number of non-executive directors and only one or two executive officers; a British board has more executive directors.

board order /'bɔːd ˌɔːdə/ *noun* an order to a stockbroker to buy or sell at a particular price

boardroom /'bɔːdruːm/ *noun* a room where the directors of a company meet

boardroom battle /ˌbɔːdruːm ˈbæt(ə)l/ *noun* an argument between directors

boiler room /'bɔɪlə ˈrʊm/ *noun* a room in which telephone sales executives try to sell securities to potential investors

BOJ *abbreviation* Bank of Japan

bolivar /'bɒlɪvɑː/ *noun* the unit of currency used in Venezuela

boliviano /bəˌlɪviˈɑːnəʊ/ *noun* a unit of currency used in Bolivia (NOTE: Also called the **Bolivian peso**.)

bolsa *noun* the Spanish word for stock exchange

Bombay Stock Exchange /ˌbɒmbeɪ ˈstɒk ɪksˌtʃeɪndʒ/ *noun* the main stock exchange in India. Abbreviation **BSE**

bona fide /ˌbəʊnə ˈfaɪdi/ *adjective* trustworthy, which can be trusted □ **a bona fide offer** an offer which is made honestly

bonanza /bəˈnænzə/ *noun* great wealth, or a source of great wealth ○ *The oil well was a bonanza for the company.* ○ *Last year was a bonanza year for the electronics industry.*

bona vacantia /ˌbəʊnə vəˈkæntiə/ *noun* a property with no owner, or which does not have an obvious owner, and which usually passes to the Crown

bond /bɒnd/ *noun* **1.** a contract document promising to repay money borrowed by a company or by the government on a specific date, and paying interest at regular intervals **2.** □ **goods (held) in bond** goods held by customs until duty has been paid □ **entry of goods under bond** bringing goods into a country in bond □ **to take goods out of bond** to pay duty on goods so that they can be released by customs **3.** a form of insurance fund which is linked to a unit trust, but where there is no yield because the income is automatically added to the fund

COMMENT: Bonds are in effect another form of long-term borrowing by a company or government. They can carry a fixed interest or a floating interest, but the yield varies according to the price at which they are bought; bond prices go up and down in the same way as share prices.

bond discount /'bɒnd ˌdɪskaʊnt/ *noun* the difference between the face value of a bond and the lower price at which it is issued

bonded /ˈbɒndɪd/ *adjective* held in bond

bonded warehouse /ˌbɒndɪd ˈweəhaʊs/ *noun* a warehouse where goods are stored until excise duty has been paid

bond fund /ˈbɒnd fʌnd/ *noun* a unit trust in which investments are made in the form of bonds

bondholder /ˈbɒndˌhəʊldə/ *noun* a person who holds government bonds

bond indenture /ˈbɒnd ɪnˌdentʃə/ *noun* a document that details the terms of a bond

bondised /ˈbɒndaɪzd/, **bondized** *adjective* referring to an insurance fund linked to a unit trust

bond market /ˈbɒnd ˌmɑːkɪt/ *noun* a market in which government or municipal bonds are traded

bond premium /ˈbɒnd ˌpriːmiəm/ *noun* the difference between the face value of a bond and a higher price at which it is issued

bond rating /ˈbɒnd ˌreɪtɪŋ/ *noun* a rating of the reliability of a company or government or local authority which has issued a bond

bond-washing /ˈbɒnd ˌwɒʃɪŋ/ *noun* the act of selling securities cum dividend and buying them back later ex dividend, or selling US Treasury bonds with the interest coupon, and buying them back ex coupon, so as to reduce tax

bond yield /ˈbɒnd jiːld/ *noun* income produced by a bond, shown as a percentage of its purchase price

bonus /ˈbəʊnəs/ *noun* an extra payment in addition to a normal payment

bonus issue /ˌbəʊnəs ˈɪʃuː/ *noun* a scrip issue or capitalisation issue, in which a company transfers money from reserves to share capital and issues free extra shares to the shareholders. The value of the company remains the same, and the total market value of shareholders' shares remains the same, the market price being adjusted to account for the new shares. Also called **share split** (NOTE: The US term is **stock split**.)

bonus share /ˈbəʊnəs ʃeə/ *noun* an extra share given to an existing shareholder

book /bʊk/ *noun* **1.** a set of sheets of paper attached together □ **a company's books** the financial records of a company **2.** a statement of a dealer's exposure to the market, i.e. the amount which he or she is due to pay or has borrowed □ **to make a book** to have a list of shares which he or she is prepared to buy or sell on behalf of clients

COMMENT: The books of account record a company's financial transactions. These are: sales (sales day book and sales returns book); purchases (purchases day book and purchases returns book); cash payments and receipts (cash book) and adjustments (journal). These books are commonly known as the 'books of prime entry', but in addition, a company's accounting records usually include the ledger accounts (nominal ledger, sales ledger and purchase ledger) which may also be referred to as 'books of account'.

book debts /ˈbʊk dets/ *plural noun* trade debts as recorded in a company's accounts

bookkeeper /ˈbʊkˌkiːpə/ *noun* a person who keeps the financial records of a company or an organisation

bookkeeping /ˈbʊkˌkiːpɪŋ/ *noun* the work of keeping the financial records of a company or an organisation

bookkeeping transaction /ˈbʊk kiːpɪŋ trænˌzækʃən/ *noun* a transaction which involves changes to a company's books of accounts, but does not alter the value of the company in any way, e.g. the issue of bonus shares

book sales /ˈbʊk seɪlz/ *plural noun* sales as recorded in the sales book

book-squaring /ˈbʊk ˌskweərɪŋ/ *noun* the process of reducing the dealer's exposure to the market to nil

book value /ˈbʊk ˌvæljuː/ *noun* the value of an asset as recorded in the company's balance sheet

book value per share /ˈbʊk ˌvæljuː pə ˌʃeə/ *noun* a company's own assessment of the value of its shares, which may differ considerably from the market value

bookwork /ˈbʊkwɜːk/ *noun* the keeping of financial records

boom /buːm/ *noun* **1.** a time when sales, production or business activity are increasing ○ *a period of economic boom* ○ *the boom of the 1990s* □ **the boom years** years when there is an economic boom **2.** a time when anything is increasing ■ *verb* to expand or to become prosperous ○ *Business is booming* or *Sales are booming.*

boom industry /ˈbuːm ˌɪndəstri/ *noun* an industry which is expanding rapidly

booming /ˈbuːmɪŋ/ *adjective* expanding or becoming prosperous ○ *a booming industry* or *company* ○ *Technology is a booming sector of the economy.*

boom share /ˈbuːm ʃeə/ *noun* a share in a company which is expanding

boost /buːst/ *noun* help given to increase something ○ *This publicity will give sales a boost.* ○ *The government hopes to give a boost to industrial development.* ■ *verb* to make something increase ○ *We expect our publicity campaign to boost sales by 25%.* ○ *The company hopes to boost its market share.* ○ *Incentive schemes are boosting production.*

'…the company expects to boost turnover this year to FFr 16bn from FFr 13.6bn last year' [*Financial Times*]

BOP *abbreviation* balance of payments

border /ˈbɔːdə/ *noun* a frontier between two countries

borderline case /ˌbɔːdəlaɪn ˈkeɪs/ *noun* a worker who may or may not be recommended for a particular type of treatment, such as for promotion or dismissal

border tax adjustment /ˈbɔːdə tæks əˌdʒʌstmənt/ *noun* a deduction of indirect tax paid on goods being exported or imposition of local indirect tax on goods being imported

borrow /ˈbɒrəʊ/ *verb* **1.** to take money from someone for a time, possibly paying interest for it, and repaying it at the end of the period ○ *She borrowed £1,000 from the bank.* ○ *The company had to borrow heavily to repay its debts.* ○ *They borrowed £25,000 against the security of the factory.* **2.** to buy at spot prices and sell forward at the same time

borrow short /ˌbɒrəʊ ˈʃɔːt/ *phrasal verb* to borrow for a short period

borrower /ˈbɒrəʊə/ *noun* a person who borrows ○ *Borrowers from the bank pay 12% interest.*

borrowing /ˈbɒrəʊɪŋ/ *noun* the act of borrowing money ○ *The new factory was financed by bank borrowing.*

'…we tend to think of building societies as having the best borrowing rates and indeed many do offer excellent terms' [*Financial Times*]

borrowing costs /ˈbɒrəʊɪŋ kɒsts/ *plural noun* the interest and other charges paid on money borrowed

borrowing power /ˈbɒrəʊɪŋ ˌpaʊə/ *noun* the amount of money which a company can borrow

borrowings /ˈbɒrəʊɪŋz/ *plural noun* money borrowed ○ *The company's borrowings have doubled.*

COMMENT: Borrowings are sometimes shown as a percentage of shareholders' funds (i.e. capital and money in reserves); this gives a percentage which is the 'gearing' of the company.

borsa *noun* the Italian word for stock exchange

Börse *noun* the German word for stock exchange

bottom /ˈbɒtəm/ *noun* the lowest part or point □ **sales have reached rock bottom** the very lowest point of all □ **the bottom has fallen out of the market** sales have fallen below what previously seemed to be the lowest point □ **rock-bottom price** the lowest price of all □ **to go bottom up** to crash or to go into liquidation ■ *verb* to reach the lowest point

bottom feeder /ˌbɒtəm ˈfiːdə/ *noun* a someone who tries to buy shares when they are falling or have fallen substantially, in the hope that they will rise again (*informal*)

bottom fishing /ˈbɒtəm ˌfɪʃɪŋ/ *noun* the act of buying shares when they are falling or have fallen substantially, in the hope that they will rise again (*informal*)

bottom line /ˌbɒtəm ˈlaɪn/ *noun* **1.** the last line on a balance sheet indicating profit or loss **2.** the final decision on a matter ○ *The bottom line was that the work had to completed within budget.*

bought /bɔːt/ ♦ buy

bought deal /bɔːt ˈdiːl/ *noun* a method of selling shares in a new company or selling an issue of new shares in an existing company, where securities houses guarantee to buy all the shares on offer at a fixed price

bought ledger /ˈbɔːt ˌledʒə/ noun a book in which purchases are recorded

bought ledger clerk /ˌbɔːt ˈledʒə ˌklɑːk/ noun an office employee who deals with the bought ledger or the sales ledger

bounce /baʊns/ verb (of a cheque) to be returned by the bank to the person who has tried to cash it, because there is not enough money in the payer's account to pay it ○ She paid for the car with a cheque that bounced.

bourse noun 1. the French word for stock exchange (NOTE: In English, the word is often used of European stock exchanges in general.) 2. a small financial institution offering specialist advice or services

boycott /ˈbɔɪkɒt/ noun a refusal to buy or to deal in certain products ○ The union organised a boycott against or of imported cars. ■ verb to refuse to buy or deal in a product ○ We are boycotting all imports from that country. □ the management has boycotted the meeting the management has refused to attend the meeting

B/P abbreviation bills payable

B/R abbreviation bills receivable

bracket /ˈbrækɪt/ noun a group of items or people taken together □ **people in the middle-income bracket** people with average incomes, not high or low □ **she is in the top tax bracket** she pays the highest level of tax

bracket together /ˌbrækɪt təˈgeðə/ phrasal verb to treat several items together in the same way ○ In the sales reports, all the European countries are bracketed together.

branch /brɑːntʃ/ noun the local office of a bank or large business, or a local shop which is part of a large chain

branch manager /ˌbrɑːntʃ ˈmænɪdʒə/ noun a person in charge of a branch of a company

'...a leading manufacturer of business, industrial and commercial products requires a branch manager to head up its mid-western Canada operations based in Winnipeg' [Globe and Mail (Toronto)]

branch office /ˌbrɑːntʃ ˈɒfɪs/ noun a less important office, usually in a different town or country from the main office

brand loyalty /ˌbrænd ˈlɔɪəlti/ noun the feeling of trust and satisfaction that makes a customer always buy the same brand of product

brand name /ˈbrænd neɪm/ noun a name of a particular make of product

breach /briːtʃ/ noun a failure to carry out the terms of an agreement □ **the company is in breach of contract** it has failed to carry out the duties of the contract

breach of contract /ˌbriːtʃ əv ˈkɒntrækt/ noun the failure to do something which has been agreed in a contract □ **the company is in breach of contract** the company has failed to do what was agreed in the contract

breach of trust /ˌbriːtʃ əv ˈtrʌst/ noun a situation where a person does not act correctly or honestly when people expect him or her to

breach of warranty /ˌbriːtʃ əv ˈwɒrənti/ noun 1. the act of supplying goods which do not meet the standards of the warranty applied to them 2. a failure to do something which is a part of a contract

break /breɪk/ noun 1. a sharp fall in share prices 2. a lucky deal or good opportunity ■ verb 1. □ **to break even** to balance costs and receipts, but not make a profit ○ Last year the company only just broke even. ○ We broke even in our first two months of trading. (NOTE: **breaking – broke – has broken**) 2. to fail to carry out the duties of a contract ○ The company has broken the contract or the agreement by selling at a lower price. (NOTE: **breaking – broke – has broken**) □ **to break an engagement to do something** not to do what has been agreed 3. to cancel a contract ○ The company is hoping to be able to break the contract. (NOTE: **breaking – broke – has broken**)

break down /ˌbreɪk ˈdaʊn/ phrasal verb 1. to stop working because of mechanical failure ○ The fax machine has broken down. 2. to stop ○ Negotiations broke down after six hours. 3. to show all the items in a total list of costs or expenditure ○ We broke the expendi-

ture down into fixed and variable costs.

break up /ˌbreɪk ˈʌp/ *phrasal verb* to split something large into small sections ○ *The company was broken up and separate divisions sold off.*

breakdown /ˈbreɪkdaʊn/ *noun* **1.** an act of stopping working because of mechanical failure ○ *We cannot communicate with our Nigerian office because of the breakdown of the telephone lines.* **2.** an act of stopping talking ○ *a breakdown in wage negotiations* **3.** an act of showing details item by item ○ *Give me a breakdown of investment costs.*

break-even point /ˈbreɪkˌiːv(ə)n ˌpɔɪnt/ *noun* the point or level of financial activity at which expenditure equals income, or the value of an investment equals its cost so that the result is neither a profit nor a loss. Abbreviation **BEP**

break-out /ˈbreɪk aʊt/ *noun* a movement of a share price above or below its previous trading level

breakpoint /ˈbreɪkpɔɪnt/ *noun* a level of deposits in an account that triggers a new higher level of interest

break-up value /ˈbreɪk ʌp ˌvæljuː/ *noun* **1.** the value of the material of a fixed asset ○ *What would the break-up value of our old machinery be?* ○ *Scrap merchants were asked to estimate the tractors' break-up value.* **2.** the value of various parts of a company taken separately

Bretton Woods Agreement *noun* an international agreement reached in 1944, setting up the International Monetary Fund and the World Bank, and a system of fixed exchange rates between currencies

bribe /braɪb/ *noun* money given secretly and usually illegally to someone in authority to get them to help ○ *The minister was dismissed for taking a bribe.* ■ *verb* to pay someone money secretly and usually illegally to get them to do something for you

bricks-and-mortar /ˌbrɪks ən ˈmɔːtə/ *adjective* **1.** conducting business in the traditional way in buildings such as shops and warehouses and not being involved in e-commerce. Compare **clicks-and-mortar** **2.** referring to the fixed assets of a company, especially its buildings

bridge finance /ˈbrɪdʒ ˌfaɪnæns/ *noun* loans to cover short-term needs

bridging loan /ˈbrɪdʒɪŋ ləʊn/ *noun* **1.** a short-term loan to help someone buy a new house when the old one has not yet been sold **2.** a short-term loan made to a company, e.g. to help in a cash-flow crisis or to fund company restructuring (NOTE: [all senses] The US term is **bridge loan**.)

bring /brɪŋ/ *verb* to come to a place with someone or something ○ *He brought his documents with him.* ○ *The finance director brought her assistant to take notes of the meeting.* (NOTE: **bringing – brought**) □ **to bring a lawsuit against someone** to tell someone to appear in court to settle an argument

bring down /ˌbrɪŋ ˈdaʊn/ *phrasal verb* **1.** to reduce ○ *Petrol companies have brought down the price of oil.* **2.** same as **bring forward 2**

bring forward /ˌbrɪŋ ˈfɔːwəd/ *phrasal verb* **1.** to make something take place earlier ○ *to bring forward the date of repayment* ○ *The date of the next meeting has been brought forward to March.* **2.** to take an account balance from the end of the previous period as the starting point for the current period ○ *Balance brought forward: £365.15*

bring in /ˌbrɪŋ ˈɪn/ *phrasal verb* to earn an amount of interest ○ *The shares bring in a small amount.*

brisk /brɪsk/ *adjective* characterised by a lot of activity ○ *sales are brisk* ○ *a brisk market in technology shares* ○ *The market in oil shares is particularly brisk.*

British Bankers' Association /ˌbrɪtɪʃ ˈbæŋkəz əˌsəʊsieɪʃ(ə)n/ *noun* an organisation representing British banks. Abbreviation **BBA**

broad tape /brɔːd ˈteɪp/ *noun* US a news service giving general information about securities and commodities

broker /ˈbrəʊkə/ *noun* **1.** a dealer who acts as a middleman between a buyer and a seller **2.** □ **(stock)broker** a person or firm that buys and sells shares or bonds on behalf of clients

brokerage /ˈbrəʊkərɪdʒ/ *noun* **1.** same as **broker's commission** **2.** same as **broking**

brokerage firm /ˈbrəʊkərɪdʒ fɜːm/, **brokerage house** /ˈbrəʊkərɪdʒ haʊs/

noun a firm which buys and sells shares for clients

brokerage rebates /'brəʊkərɪdʒ ˌriːbeɪts/ *plural noun* the percentage of the commission paid to a broker which is returned to the customer as an incentive to do more business

broker-dealer /ˌbrəʊkə 'diːlə/ *noun* a dealer who buys shares and holds them for resale, and also deals on behalf of investor clients

broker's commission /ˌbrəʊkəz kə 'mɪʃ(ə)n/ *noun* the payment to a broker for a deal which he or she has carried out. Also called **brokerage** (NOTE: Formerly, the commission charged by brokers on the London Stock Exchange was fixed, but since 1986, commissions have been variable.)

broking /'brəʊkɪŋ/ *noun* the business of dealing in stocks and shares

brought down /ˌbrɔːt 'daʊn/, **brought forward** /ˌbrɔːt 'fɔːwəd/ *adjective* used to describe the balance in an account from the previous period when it is taken as the starting point for the current period ○ *balance brought down* or *forward: £365.15* Abbreviation **b/d**, **b/f**

BSA *abbreviation* Building Societies Association

BSE Index /ˌbiː es 'iː ˌɪndeks/ *noun* an index of prices on the Indian Stock Exchange. Full form **Bombay Stock Exchange Index**

B shares /'biː ʃeəz/ *plural noun* ordinary shares with special voting rights, often owned by the founder of a company and his or her family. See Comment at **A shares**

bubble /'bʌb(ə)l/ *noun* a continued rise in the value of an asset, such as a share price, which is caused by people thinking that the price will continue to rise. Also called **speculative bubble**

buck /bʌk/ *noun US* a dollar (*informal*) □ **to make a quick buck** to make a profit very quickly ■ *verb* □ **to buck the trend** to go against the trend

bucket shop /'bʌkɪt ʃɒp/ *noun* **1.** *US* a dishonest stockbroking firm where customers' orders to buy and sell stock are treated as bets on the rise and fall of prices **2.** a firm of brokers or dealers that sells shares that may be worthless **3.** a

brokerage firm which tries to push the sale of some securities more than others

'…at last something is being done about the thousands of bucket shops across the nation that sell investment scams by phone' [*Forbes Magazine*]

budget /'bʌdʒɪt/ *noun* **1.** a plan of expected spending and income for a period of time ○ *to draw up a budget for salaries for the coming year* ○ *We have agreed on the budgets for next year.* **2.** □ **the Budget** the annual plan of taxes and government spending. In the US the Office of Management and Budget prepares the budget based on requests for funds by the various agencies. The President then submits the budget to Congress, which passes legislation to appropriate and authorise the funds. In the UK the budget is proposed by a finance minister and drawn up by the Chancellor of the Exchequer. ○ *The minister put forward a budget aimed at boosting the economy.* □ **to balance the budget** to plan income and expenditure so that they balance ○ *The president is planning for a balanced budget.* ■ *adjective* cheap □ **budget prices** low prices ■ *verb* to plan probable income and expenditure ○ *We are budgeting for $10,000 of sales next year.*

'…he budgeted for further growth of 150,000 jobs (or 2.5 per cent) in the current financial year' [*Sydney Morning Herald*]

'…the Federal government's budget targets for employment and growth are within reach according to the latest figures' [*Australian Financial Review*]

budget account /'bʌdʒɪt əˌkaʊnt/ *noun* a bank account where you plan income and expenditure to allow for periods when expenditure is high, by paying a set amount each month

budgetary /'bʌdʒɪt(ə)ri/ *adjective* referring to a budget

budgetary control /ˌbʌdʒɪt(ə)ri kən 'trəʊl/ *noun* controlled spending according to a planned budget

budgetary policy /ˌbʌdʒɪt(ə)ri 'pɒlɪsi/ *noun* the policy of planning income and expenditure

budgetary requirements /ˌbʌdʒɪt(ə)ri rɪ'kwaɪəməntz/ *plural noun* the rate of spending or income required to meet the budget forecasts

budget deficit /ˈbʌdʒɪt ˌdefɪsɪt/ *noun*
1. a deficit in a country's planned budget, where income from taxation will not be sufficient to pay for the government's expenditure **2.** a deficit in personal finances where a household will borrow to finance large purchases which cannot be made out of income alone

budget department /ˈbʌdʒɪt dɪˌpɑːtmənt/ *noun* a department in a large store which sells cheaper goods

budgeting /ˈbʌdʒɪtɪŋ/ *noun* the preparation of budgets to help plan expenditure and income

budget surplus /ˌbʌdʒɪt ˈsɜːpləs/ *noun* a situation where there is more revenue than was planned for in the budget

budget variance /ˈbʌdʒɪt ˌveəriəns/ *noun* the difference between the cost as estimated for a budget and the actual cost

buffer stocks /ˈbʌfə stɒks/ *plural noun* stocks of a commodity bought by an international body when prices are low and held for resale at a time when prices have risen, with the intention of reducing sharp fluctuations in world prices of the commodity

    build into /ˈbɪld ˌɪntuː/ *phrasal verb* to include something in something which is being set up ○ *You must build all the forecasts into the budget.* □ **we have built 10% for contingencies into our cost forecast** we have added 10% to our basic forecast to allow for items which may appear suddenly

    build up /ˌbɪld ˈʌp/ *phrasal verb* **1.** to create something by adding pieces together ○ *She bought several shoe shops and gradually built up a chain.* **2.** to expand something gradually ○ *to build up a profitable business*

building and loan association /ˌbɪldɪŋ ən ˈləʊn əˌsəʊsieɪʃ(ə)n/ *noun US* same as **building society**

Building Societies Association /ˈbɪldɪŋ səˌsaɪətiz əˌsəʊsieɪʃ(ə)n/ *noun* an organisation representing building societies. Abbreviation **BSA**

building society /ˈbɪldɪŋ səˌsaɪəti/ *noun* a financial institution which accepts and pays interest on deposits, and lends money to people who are buying property against the security of the property which is being bought ○ *We put our savings into*

a building society or *into a building society account.* ○ *I have an account with the Nationwide Building Society.* ○ *I saw the building society manager to ask for a mortgage.* (NOTE: The US term is **savings and loan**.)

COMMENT: Building societies mainly invest the money deposited with them as mortgages on properties, but a percentage is invested in government securities. Societies can now offer a range of banking services, such as cheque books, standing orders, overdrafts, etc., and now operate in much the same way as banks. Indeed, many building societies have changed from 'mutual status', where the owners of the society are its investors and borrowers, to become publicly-owned banks whose shares are bought and sold on the stock exchange. The comparable US institutions are the savings & loan associations, or 'thrifts'.

buildup /ˈbɪldʌp/ *noun* a gradual increase ○ *a buildup in sales* or *a sales buildup* ○ *There will be a big publicity buildup before the launch of the new model.* ○ *There has been a buildup of complaints about customer service.*

bulk buying /ˌbʌlk ˈbaɪɪŋ/ *noun* the act of buying large quantities of goods at low prices

bulk carrier /ˌbʌlk ˈkæriə/ *noun* a ship which carries large quantities of loose goods such as corn or coal

bulk purchase /ˌbʌlk ˈpɜːtʃɪs/ *noun* an act of buying a large quantity of goods at low prices

bull /bʊl/ *noun* a person who believes the market will rise, and therefore buys shares, commodities, or currency to sell at a higher price later. Opposite **bear**

'…lower interest rates are always a bull factor for the stock market' [*Financial Times*]

bulldog bond /ˈbʊldɒg bɒnd/ *noun* a bond issued in sterling in the UK market by a non-British corporation. Compare **samurai bond**, **Yankee bond**

bullet /ˈbʊlɪt/ *noun US* a repayment of the capital of a loan when it matures

bullet bond /ˈbʊlɪt bɒnd/ *noun US* a Eurobond which is only redeemed when it is mature (NOTE: Bullet bonds are used in payments between central banks and also act as currency backing.)

bullet loan /ˈbʊlɪt ləʊn/ *noun US* a loan which is repaid in a single payment

bullion /ˈbʊliən/ *noun* gold or silver in the form of bars ○ *A shipment of gold bullion was stolen from the security van.* ○ *The price of bullion is fixed daily.*

bullion bank /ˈbʊliən bæŋk/ *noun* a bank which holds bullion for customers

bullish /ˈbʊlɪʃ/ *adjective* optimistic, feeling that prices of shares will rise

'…another factor behind the currency market's bullish mood may be the growing realisation that Japan stands to benefit from the current combination of high domestic interest rates and a steadily rising exchange rate' [*Far Eastern Economic Review*]

'…currency traders chose to ignore better unemployment statistics from France, preferring to focus on the bullish outlook for the dollar' [*Times*]

bull market /ˈbʊl ˌmɑːkɪt/ *noun* a period when share prices rise because people are optimistic and buy shares. Opposite **bear market**

bull position /ˈbʊl pəˌzɪʃ(ə)n/ *noun* a strategy of buying shares in the hope that they will rise

bumping /ˈbʌmpɪŋ/ *noun* **1.** *US* a lay-off procedure that allows an employee with greater seniority to displace a more junior employee ○ *The economic recession led to extensive bumping in companies where only the most qualified were retained for some jobs.* **2.** the situation where a senior employee takes the place of a junior (in a restaurant)

Bund *noun* a German government bond

Bundesobligation *noun* a German medium-term note, which cannot be bought by non-German buyers

bundle /ˈbʌnd(ə)l/ *noun* □ **to make a bundle** to make a lot of money (*informal*)

bundling /ˈbʌndlɪŋ/ *noun* the action of selling various financial services together as a package, such as a mortgage and house insurance

buoyant /ˈbɔɪənt/ *adjective* referring to a market where share prices are rising continuously

bureau de change /ˌbjʊərəʊ də ˈʃɒnʒ/ *noun* an office where you can change foreign currency

business /ˈbɪznɪs/ *noun* **1.** work in buying, selling, or doing other things to make a profit ○ *We do a lot of business*

with Japan. ○ *Business is expanding.* ○ *Business is slow.* ○ *We did more business in the week before Christmas than we usually do in a month.* ○ *What's your line of business?* □ **to be in business** to run a commercial firm □ **on business** doing commercial work ○ *She had to go abroad on business.* ○ *The chairman is in Holland on business.* **2.** a commercial company ○ *She runs a business from her home.* ○ *I set up in business as an insurance broker.* **3.** the affairs discussed ○ *The main business of the meeting was finished by 3 p.m.*

business address /ˈbɪznɪs əˌdres/ *noun* the details of number, street, and city or town where a company is located

business agent /ˈbɪznɪs ˌeɪdʒənt/ *noun US* the chief local official of a trade union

business call /ˈbɪznɪs kɔːl/ *noun* a visit to talk to someone about business

business card /ˈbɪznɪs kɑːd/ *noun* a card showing a businessperson's name and the name and address of the company he or she works for

business centre /ˈbɪznɪs ˌsentə/ *noun* the part of a town where the main banks, shops and offices are located

business computer /ˈbɪznɪs kəmˌpjuːtə/ *noun* a powerful small computer that runs software written to manage a business

business correspondence /ˈbɪznɪs kɒrɪˌspɒndəns/ *noun* letters concerned with a business

business correspondent /ˈbɪznɪs kɒrɪˌspɒndənt/ *noun* a journalist who writes articles on business news for newspapers

business customer /ˈbɪznɪs ˌkʌstəmə/ *noun* company which has an account with a bank

business cycle /ˈbɪznɪs ˌsaɪk(ə)l/ *noun* the period during which trade expands, slows down and then expands again. Also called **trade cycle**

business day /ˈbɪznɪs deɪ/ *noun* a weekday when banks and stock exchanges are open for business

business expenses /ˈbɪznɪs ɪkˌspensɪz/ *plural noun* money spent on running a business, not on stock or assets

business hours /ˈbɪznɪs ˌaʊəz/ *plural noun* the time when a business is open, usually 9.00 a.m. to 5.30 p.m.

business magazine /ˈbɪznɪs ˌmægəziːn/ *noun* a magazine dealing with business affairs

businessman /ˈbɪznɪsmæn/ *noun* a man engaged in business

business plan /ˈbɪznɪs plæn/ *noun* a document drawn up to show how a business is planned to work, with cash flow forecasts, sales forecasts, etc., often used when trying to raise a loan, or when setting up a new business

business rate /ˈbɪznɪs reɪt/ *noun* a tax levied on business property (NOTE: The US term is **local property tax**.)

business ratepayer /ˈbɪznɪs ˌreɪt peɪə/ *noun* a business which pays local taxes on a shop, office, factory, etc.

business-to-business /ˌbɪznɪs tə ˈbɪznɪs/ *adjective* full form of **B2B**

business-to-consumer /ˌbɪznɪs tə kənˈsjuːmə/ *adjective* full form of **B2C**

business transaction /ˈbɪznɪs trænˌzækʃən/ *noun* an act of buying or selling

businesswoman /ˈbɪznɪsmæn/ *noun* a woman engaged in business

busted bonds /ˈbʌstɪd bɒndz/ *noun* old shares or bonds which are no longer marketable, though the certificates may still have a value as collectors' items

butterfly spread /ˈbʌtəflaɪ spred/ *noun* an act of buying two call options and selling two call options, with different dates and prices, all at the same time

buy /baɪ/ *verb* to get something by paying money ○ *to buy wholesale and sell retail* ○ *to buy for cash* ○ *She bought 10,000 shares.* ○ *The company has been bought by its leading supplier.* (NOTE: **buying – bought**) □ **to buy at best** to buy securities at the best price available, even if it is high

buy back /ˌbaɪ ˈbæk/ *phrasal verb* **1.** to buy something which you sold earlier ○ *She sold the shop last year and is now trying to buy it back.* **2.** to buy its own shares

buy forward /ˌbaɪ ˈfɔːwəd/ *phrasal verb* to buy foreign currency before you need it, in order to be sure of the exchange rate

buy in /ˌbaɪ ˈɪn/ *phrasal verb* **1.** (*of a seller at an auction*) to buy the thing which you are trying to sell because no one will pay the price you want **2.** to buy stock to cover a position **3.** (*of a company*) to buy its own shares

buyback /ˈbaɪbæk/ *noun* **1.** a type of loan agreement to repurchase bonds or securities at a later date for the same price as they are being sold **2.** an international trading agreement where a company builds a factory in a foreign country and agrees to buy all its production **3.** the continuation of a life assurance cover after a claim has been paid on critical illness under a policy that provides cover against both critical illness and death

'…the corporate sector also continued to return cash to shareholders in the form of buy-backs, while raising little money in the form of new or rights issues' [*Financial Times*]

buydown /ˈbaɪdaʊn/ *noun US* the action of paying extra money to a mortgage in order to get a better rate in the future

buyer /ˈbaɪə/ *noun* **1.** a person who buys □ **there were no buyers** no one wanted to buy **2.** a person who buys stock on behalf of a trading organisation for resale or for use in production

buyer's market /ˈbaɪəz ˌmɑːkɪt/ *noun* a market where products are sold cheaply because there are few people who want to buy them. Opposite **seller's market**

buying /ˈbaɪɪŋ/ *noun* the act of getting something for money

buying department /ˈbaɪɪŋ dɪ ˌpɑːtmənt/ *noun* the department in a company which buys raw materials or goods for use in the company (NOTE: The US term is **purchasing department**.)

buying power /ˈbaɪɪŋ ˌpaʊə/ *noun* an assessment of an individual's or organisation's disposable income regarded as conferring the power to make purchases ○ *The buying power of the dollar has fallen over the last five years.*

buyout /ˈbaɪaʊt/ *noun* the purchase of a controlling interest in a company

'…we also invest in companies whose growth and profitability could be improved by a management buyout' [*Times*]

'…in a normal leveraged buyout, the acquirer raises money by borrowing against the assets or cash flow of the target company' [*Fortune*]

buy to let /ˌbaɪ tə ˈlet/ *verb* a situation where a property is bought as an investment to rent out rather than live in

BV *noun* a Dutch public limited company. Full form **besloten venootschap**

bylaw /ˈbaɪlɔː/ *noun* US a rule governing the internal running of a corporation, such as the number of meetings, the appointment of officers (NOTE: In the UK, these are called **Articles of Association**.)

by-product /ˈbaɪ ˌprɒdʌkt/ *noun* a secondary product made as a result of manufacturing a main product which can be sold for profit

C

CA *abbreviation* chartered accountant

cable /'keɪb(ə)l/ *noun* **1.** a telegram, a message sent by telegraph ○ *He sent a cable to his office asking for more money.* **2.** a spot exchange rate for the dollar and sterling ■ *verb* to send a message or money by telegraph ○ *He cabled his office to ask them to send more money.* ○ *The office cabled him £1,000 to cover his expenses.* ○ *The money was cabled to the Spanish bank.*

cable address /'keɪb(ə)l ə,dres/ *noun* a short address for sending cables

cable transfer /'keɪb(ə)l ,trænsfɜː/ *noun* a transfer of money by telegraph

CAC 40 /,siː eɪ siː 'fɔːti/, **CAC 40 index** *noun* an index of prices on the Paris Stock Exchange, based on the prices of forty leading shares

CAD /kæd/ *abbreviation* cash against documents

cage /keɪdʒ/ *noun US* **1.** the part of a broking firm where the paperwork involved in buying and selling shares is processed (NOTE: The UK term is **back office**.) **2.** a section of a bank where a teller works, surrounded by glass windows

caisse d'épargne *noun* the French word for **savings bank**

caja popular *noun* the Spanish word for **savings bank**

calculate /'kælkjʊleɪt/ *verb* **1.** to find the answer to a problem using numbers ○ *The bank clerk calculated the rate of exchange for the dollar.* **2.** to estimate ○ *I calculate that we have six months' stock left.*

calculating machine /'kælkjʊleɪtɪŋ mə,ʃiːn/ *noun* same as **calculator** ○ *She added up the sales figures on the calculating machine next to the typewriter.*

calculation /,kælkjʊ'leɪʃ(ə)n/ *noun* the answer to a problem in mathematics ○ *According to my calculations, we have six months' stock left.* □ **we are £20,000 out in our calculations** we have made a mistake in our calculations and arrived at a figure which is £20,000 too much or too little

calculator /'kælkjʊleɪtə/ *noun* an electronic machine which does calculations such as adding, subtracting and multiplying ○ *He worked out the discount on his calculator.*

calendar /'kælɪndə/ *noun* **1.** a book or set of sheets of paper showing the days and months in a year, often attached to pictures **2.** a list of dates, especially a list of dates of new share issues

calendar month /'kælɪndə mʌnθ/ *noun* a whole month as on a calendar, from the 1st to the 30th or 31st ○ *Ninety days' credit is almost three calendar months.*

calendar year /,kælɪndə 'jɪə/ *noun* a year from the 1st January to 31st December

call /kɔːl/ *noun* **1.** a conversation on the telephone □ **to make a call** to dial and speak to someone on the telephone □ **to take a call** to answer the telephone □ **to log calls** to note all details of telephone calls made **2.** a demand for repayment of a loan by a lender **3.** a demand to pay for new shares which then become paid up **4.** a price established during a trading session **5.** same as **call option** ■ *verb* **1.** to ask for a loan to be repaid immediately **2.** to telephone someone ○ *I'll call you at your office tomorrow.* **3.** □ **to call on someone** to visit someone ○ *Our sales-people call on their best accounts twice a month.* **4.** to ask for or order something to be done ○ *to call a meeting* □ **the union**

called a strike the union told its members to go on strike

call in /ˌkɔːl ˈɪn/ *phrasal verb* to ask for a debt to be paid

call up /ˌkɔːl ˈʌp/ *phrasal verb* to ask for share capital to be paid

callable bond /ˌkɔːləb(ə)l ˈbɒnd/ *noun* a bond which can be redeemed before it matures

callable capital /ˌkɔːləb(ə)l ˈkæpɪt(ə)l/ *noun* the part of a company's capital which has not been called up

call-back pay /ˈkɔːl bæk ˌpeɪ/ *noun* pay given to an employee who has been called back to work after his or her usual working hours

called up capital /ˌkɔːld ʌp ˈkæpɪt(ə)l/ *noun* share capital in a company which has been called up. The share capital becomes fully paid when all the authorised shares have been called up.

'…a circular to shareholders highlights that the company's net assets as at August 1, amounted to £47.9 million – less than half the company's called-up share capital of £96.8 million. Accordingly, an EGM has been called for October 7' [*Times*]

call loan /ˈkɔːl ləʊn/ *noun* a bank loan repayable at call

call money /ˈkɔːl ˌmʌni/ *noun* money loaned for which repayment can be demanded without notice. Also called **money at call**, **money on call**

call option /ˈkɔːl ˌɒpʃən/ *noun* an option to buy shares at a future date and at a specific price. Also called **call**. Opposite **put option**

call-over price /ˌkɔːl ˈəʊvə praɪs/ *noun* a price which is applied when selling is conducted by a chairman, and not by open outcry

call price /ˈkɔːl praɪs/ *noun* a price to be paid on redemption of a US bond

call purchase /ˈkɔːl ˌpɜːtʃɪs/, **call sale** /ˈkɔːl seɪl/ *noun* a transaction where the seller or purchaser can fix the price for future delivery

call rate /ˈkɔːl reɪt/ *noun* **1.** the number of calls per day or per week which a salesperson makes on customers **2.** a rate of interest on money at call

call rule /ˈkɔːl ruːl/ *noun* a price fixed on a stock exchange at the end of a day's

trading and which remains valid until trading starts again the next day

calm /kɑːm/ *adjective* quiet, not excited ○ *The markets were calmer after the government statement on the exchange rate.*

cambio *noun* the Spanish word for **foreign exchange**

cambiste *noun* the French word for a **foreign exchange broker**

cancel /ˈkæns(ə)l/ *verb* **1.** to stop something which has been agreed or planned ○ *to cancel an appointment* or *a meeting* ○ *The government has cancelled the order for a fleet of buses.* ○ *The manager is still ill, so the interviews planned for this week have been cancelled.* (NOTE: **cancelling – cancelled**. The US spelling is **canceling – canceled**.) **2.** □ **to cancel a cheque** to stop payment of a cheque which has been signed (NOTE: UK English is **cancelling – cancelled**, but the US spelling is **canceling – canceled**.)

cancel out /ˌkæns(ə)l ˈaʊt/ *phrasal verb* (*of two things*) to balance each other or act against each other so that there is no change in the existing situation ○ *The two clauses cancel each other out.* ○ *Higher costs have cancelled out the increased sales revenue.*

cancellation /ˌkænsəˈleɪʃ(ə)n/ *noun* the act of stopping something which has been agreed or planned ○ *the cancellation of an appointment* ○ *the cancellation of an agreement*

cancellation clause /ˌkænsə ˈleɪʃ(ə)n klɔːz/ *noun* a clause in a contract which states the terms on which the contract may be cancelled

candlestick chart /ˈkænd(ə)lstɪk tʃɑːt/ *noun* a chart similar to a bar chart, but showing the opening and close as well as the high and low figures for a particular period. These are shown as lines standing up on top of the body of the chart or hanging down beneath it, so that they look a little like the wick on a candle.

cap /kæp/ *noun* **1.** an upper limit placed on something, such as an interest rate. The opposite, i.e. a lower limit, is a 'floor'). **2.** same as **capitalisation** (*informal*) ○ *Last year the total market cap of all the world's gold companies fell from $71 billion to $46 billion.* ■ *verb* to place an upper limit on something ○ *to cap a local authority's budget* ○ *to cap a department's budget* (NOTE: **capping – capped**)

capacity /kəˈpæsɪti/ *noun* **1.** the amount which can be produced, or the amount of work which can be done ○ *industrial* or *manufacturing* or *production capacity* □ **to work at full capacity** to do as much work as possible **2.** the amount of space **3.** ability ○ *She has a particular capacity for detailed business deals with overseas companies.* **4.** (*of a borrower*) the ability to pay back a loan **5.** □ **speaking in an official capacity** speaking officially

'…analysts are increasingly convinced that the industry simply has too much capacity' [*Fortune*]

capacity utilisation /kəˌpæsəti ˌjuːtɪlaɪˈzeɪʃ(ə)n/ *noun* a measurement that shows how much of the plant and equipment of a company or industry is actually being used to produce goods or services. It is usually expressed as a ratio between actual output over a particular period and the maximum output the plant or equipment designed to produce during the same period.

cap and collar /ˌkæp ən ˈkɒlə/ *noun* an agreement giving both an upper and a lower limit to a loan

capita /ˈkæpɪtə/ ♦ **per capita**

capital /ˈkæpɪt(ə)l/ *noun* **1.** the money, property, and assets used in a business ○ *a company with $10,000 capital* or *with a capital of $10,000* **2.** money owned by individuals or companies, which they use for investment □ **flight of capital** the rapid movement of capital out of one country because of lack of confidence in that country's economic future

capital account /ˈkæpɪt(ə)l əˌkaʊnt/ *noun* **1.** an account that states the value of funds and assets invested in a business by the owners or shareholders **2.** the portion of a country's balance of payments that refers to investments, rather than to the buying and selling of merchandise **3.** a statement of the net worth of an organisation at a given time

capital adequacy /ˌkæpɪt(ə)l ˈædɪkwəsi/, **capital adequacy ratio** /ˌkæpɪt(ə)l ˈædɪkwəsi ˌreɪʃəʊ/ *noun* the amount of money which a bank has to have in the form of shareholders' capital, shown as a percentage of its assets. Also called **capital-to-asset ratio** (NOTE: The amount is internationally agreed at 8%.)

capital allowances /ˌkæpɪt(ə)l əˈlaʊənsɪz/ *plural noun* the allowances based on the value of fixed assets which may be deducted from a company's profits and so reduce its tax liability

COMMENT: Under current UK law, depreciation is not allowable for tax on profits, whereas capital allowances, based on the value of fixed assets owned by the company, are tax-allowable.

capital appreciation /ˌkæpɪt(ə)l əˌpriːʃiˈeɪʃ(ə)n/ *noun* same as **appreciation**

capital asset pricing model /ˌkæpɪt(ə)l ˌæset ˈpraɪsɪŋ ˌmɒd(ə)l/ *noun* an equation that shows the relationship between expected risk and expected return on an investment and serves as a model for valuing risky securities. Abbreviation **CAPM**

capital assets /ˌkæpɪt(ə)l ˈæsets/ *plural noun* the property, machines, and other assets which a company owns and uses but which it does not buy and sell as part of its regular trade. Also called **fixed assets**

capital base /ˈkæpɪt(ə)l beɪs/ *noun* the capital structure of a company (shareholders' capital plus loans and retained profits) used as a way of assessing the company's worth

capital bonus /ˌkæpɪt(ə)l ˈbəʊnəs/ *noun* an extra payment by an insurance company which is produced by a capital gain

capital city /ˌkæpɪt(ə)l ˈsɪti/ *noun* the main city in a country, where the government is located

capital commitments /ˌkæpɪt(ə)l kə ˈmɪtmənts/ *plural noun* expenditure on assets which has been authorised by directors, but not yet spent at the end of a financial period

capital employed /ˌkæpɪt(ə)l ɪm ˈplɔɪd/ *noun* an amount of capital consisting of shareholders' funds plus the long-term debts of a business. ♢ **return on assets**

capital equipment /ˌkæpɪt(ə)l ɪ ˈkwɪpmənt/ *noun* equipment which a factory or office uses to work

capital expenditure /ˌkæpɪt(ə)l ɪk ˈspendɪtʃə/ *noun* money spent on fixed assets such as property, machines and furniture. Also called **capital investment, capital outlay**. Abbreviation **CAPEX**

capital exports /ˌkæpɪt(ə)l ˈekspɔːts/ *plural noun* the movement of capital out of a country into overseas investments, or into loans to overseas countries

capital flow /ˌkæpɪt(ə)l ˈfləʊ/ *noun* the movement of investment capital from one country to another. Also called **capital movement, movement of capital**

capital gain /ˌkæpɪt(ə)l ˈɡeɪn/ *noun* an amount of money made by selling a fixed asset. Opposite **capital loss**

capital gains tax /ˌkæpɪt(ə)l ˈɡeɪnz tæks/ *noun* a tax on the difference between the gross acquisition cost and the net proceeds when an asset is sold. In the UK, this tax also applies when assets are given or exchanged, although each individual has an annual capital gains tax allowance that exempts gains within that tax year below a stated level. In addition, certain assets may be exempt, e.g., a person's principal private residence and transfers of assets between spouses. Abbreviation **CGT**

capital goods /ˈkæpɪt(ə)l ɡʊdz/ *plural noun* machinery, buildings, and raw materials which are used to make other goods

capital-intensive industry /ˌkæpɪt(ə)l ɪnˈtensɪv ˌɪndəstri/ *noun* an industry which needs a large amount of capital investment in plant to make it work

capital investment /ˌkæpɪt(ə)l ɪnˈvestmənt/ *noun* same as **capital expenditure**

capitalisation/ˌkæpɪt(ə)laɪˈzeɪʃ(ə)n/, **capitalization** *noun* the value of a company calculated by multiplying the price of its shares on the stock exchange by the number of shares issued. Also called **market capitalisation**

'…she aimed to double the company's market capitalization' [*Fortune*]

capitalisation issue /ˌkæpɪtəlaɪ ˈzeɪʃ(ə)n ˌɪʃuː/ *noun* same as **bonus issue**

capitalisation of reserves /ˌkæpɪt(ə)laɪzeɪʃ(ə)n əv rɪˈzɜːvz/ *noun* the issuing of free bonus shares to shareholders

capitalise /ˈkæpɪt(ə)laɪz/, **capitalize** *verb* **1.** to invest money in a working company □ **the company is capitalised at £10,000** the company has a working capital of £10,000 **2.** to convert reserves or assets into capital

'…at its last traded price the bank was capitalized at around $1.05 billion with 60 per cent in the hands of the family' [*South China Morning Post*]

capitalise on *phrasal verb* to make a profit from ○ *We are seeking to capitalise on our market position.*

capitalism /ˈkæpɪt(ə)lɪz(ə)m/ *noun* the economic system in which each person has the right to invest money, to work in business and to buy and sell, with no restrictions from the state

capitalist /ˈkæpɪt(ə)lɪst/ *adjective* working according to the principles of capitalism ○ *the capitalist system* ○ *the capitalist countries* or *world* ■ *noun* a person who invests capital in business enterprises

capitalist economy /ˌkæpɪt(ə)lɪst ɪ ˈkɒnəmi/ *noun* an economy in which each person has the right to invest money, to work in business and to buy and sell, with no restrictions from the state

capital levy /ˌkæpɪt(ə)l ˈlevi/ *noun* a tax on the value of a person's property and possessions

capital loss /ˌkæpɪt(ə)l ˈlɒs/ *noun* a loss made by selling assets. Opposite **capital gain**

capital market /ˌkæpɪt(ə)l ˈmɑːkɪt/ *noun* an international market where money can be raised for investment in a business

capital movement /ˌkæpɪt(ə)l ˈmuːvmənt/ *noun* same as **capital flow**

capital outlay /ˌkæpɪt(ə)l ˈaʊtleɪ/ *noun* same as **capital expenditure**

capital profit /ˌkæpɪt(ə)l ˈprɒfɪt/ *noun* a profit made by selling an asset

capital-protected fund /ˌkæpɪt(ə)l prəˈtektɪd fʌnd/ *noun* a fund which guarantees the investor's capital and at the same time gives some growth

capital ratio /'kæpɪt(ə)l ˌreɪʃiəʊ/ *noun* same as **capital adequacy**

capital requirements /ˌkæpɪt(ə)l rɪ'kwaɪəmənts/ *plural noun* **1.** the amount of capital which a firm needs to operate normally **2.** the amount of liquid assets needed by a bank to fulfil its obligations

capital reserves /ˌkæpɪt(ə)l rɪ'zɜːvz/ *plural noun* **1.** money from profits, which forms part of the capital of a company and can be used for distribution to shareholders only when a company is wound up. Also called **undistributable reserves 2.** the share capital of a company which comes from selling assets and not from their usual trading

capital shares /ˌkæpɪt(ə)l 'ʃeəz/ *plural noun* (*on the stock exchange*) shares in a unit trust which rise in value as the capital value of the units rises, but do not receive any income (NOTE: The other form of shares in a split-level investment trust are income shares, which receive income from the investments, but do not rise in value.)

capital stock /'kæpɪt(ə)l stɒk/ *noun* the amount of money raised by a company through the sale of shares, entitling holders to dividends, some rights of ownership and other benefits

capital structure /ˌkæpɪt(ə)l 'strʌktʃə/ *noun* the relative proportions of equity capital and debt capital within a company's balance sheet

capital-to-asset ratio /ˌkæpɪt(ə)l tʊ 'æset ˌreɪʃiəʊ/, **capital/asset ratio** *noun* same as **capital adequacy**

capital transfer tax /ˌkæpɪt(ə)l 'trænsfɜː ˌtæks/ *noun* in the UK, a tax on the transfer of assets that was replaced in 1986 by inheritance tax

CAPM *abbreviation* capital asset pricing model

capped floating rate note /ˌkæpt 'fləʊtɪŋ reɪt ˌnəʊt/ *noun* a floating rate note which has an agreed maximum rate

capped rate /ˌkæpt 'reɪt/ *verb* a mortgage rate which is guaranteed not to go above a certain level for a set period of time, although it can move downwards

captive market /ˌkæptɪv 'mɑːkɪt/ *noun* a market where one supplier has a monopoly and the buyer has no choice over the product which he or she must purchase

capture /'kæptʃə/ *verb* to take or get control of something □ **to capture 10% of the market** to sell hard, and so take a 10% market share □ **to capture 20% of a company's shares** to buy shares in a company rapidly and so own 20% of it

carat /'kærət/ *noun* **1.** a measure of the quality of gold (pure gold being 24 carat) ○ *a 22-carat gold ring* **2.** a measure of the weight of precious stones ○ *a 5-carat diamond*

COMMENT: Pure gold is 24 carats and is too soft to make jewellery. Most jewellery and other items made from gold are not pure, but between 19 and 22 carats. Twenty-two carat gold has 22 parts of gold to two parts of alloy.

cardholder /'kɑːdˌhəʊldə/ *noun* a person who holds a credit card or bank cash card

carpetbagger /'kɑːpɪtˌbægə/ *noun* a person who invests in a building society or pension fund, hoping to benefit from eventual windfall payments if the society is demutualised or the fund is bought

carriage /'kærɪdʒ/ *noun* the transporting of goods from one place to another ○ *to pay for carriage*

carriage forward /ˌkærɪdʒ 'fɔːwəd/ *noun* a deal where the customer pays for transporting the goods

carriage free /ˌkærɪdʒ 'friː/ *noun* a deal where the customer does not pay for the shipping

carriage paid /ˌkærɪdʒ 'peɪd/ *noun* a deal where the seller has paid for the shipping

carrier /'kærɪə/ *noun* **1.** a company that transports goods ○ *We only use reputable carriers.* **2.** a vehicle or ship that transports goods

carry /'kæri/ *verb* **1.** to take from one place to another ○ *a tanker carrying oil from the Gulf* ○ *The truck was carrying goods to the supermarket.* (NOTE: **carries – carrying – carried**) **2.** to vote to approve (NOTE: **carries – carrying – carried**) □ **the motion was carried** the motion was accepted after a vote **3.** to produce ○ *The bonds carry interest at 10%.* (NOTE: **carries – carrying – carried**) ■ *noun* the cost of borrowing to finance a deal

carry forward /ˌkæri 'fɔːwəd/ *phrasal verb* to take an account balance at the end of the current period or page as the starting point for the next period or page

carry over /ˌkæri ˈəʊvə/ *phrasal verb* **1.** □ **to carry over a balance** to take a balance from the end of one page or period to the beginning of the next **2.** □ **to carry over stock** to hold stock from the end of one stocktaking period to the beginning of the next

carry-over /ˈkæri ˌəʊvə/ *noun* **1.** the stock of a commodity held at the beginning of a new financial year **2.** the fact of not paying an account on settlement day, but later. Also called **contango**

carryover day /ˈkæriˌəʊvə deɪ/ *noun* the first day of trading on a new account on the London Stock Exchange

cartel /kɑːˈtel/ *noun* **1.** a group of companies which try to fix the price or to regulate the supply of a product so that they can make more profit **2.** reasons for doing something ○ *The negotiators put forward the union's case for a pay rise.*

cash /kæʃ/ *noun* money in the form of coins or notes □ **settlement in cash**, **cash settlement** paying a bill in cash ■ *verb* □ **to cash a cheque** to exchange a cheque for cash

cash in /ˌkæʃ ˈɪn/ *phrasal verb* to sell shares or other property for cash

cash in on /ˌkæʃ ˈɪn ˌɒn/ *phrasal verb* to profit from ○ *The company is cashing in on the interest in computer games.*

cash out *phrasal verb US* same as **cash up**

cash up /ˌkæʃ ˈʌp/ *phrasal verb* to add up the cash in a shop at the end of the day

cashable /ˈkæʃəb(ə)l/ *adjective* able to be cashed ○ *A crossed cheque is not cashable at any bank.*

cash account /ˈkæʃ əˌkaʊnt/ *noun* an account which records the money which is received and spent

cash advance /ˌkæʃ ədˈvɑːns/ *noun* a loan in cash against a future payment

cash against documents /ˌkæʃ əgenst ˈdɒkjʊmənts/ *noun* a system whereby a buyer receives documents for the goods on payment of a bill of exchange

cash and carry /ˌkæʃ ən ˈkæri/ *noun* **1.** a large store selling goods at low prices, where the customer pays cash and takes the goods away immediately ○ *We*

get our supplies every morning from the cash and carry. **2.** the activity of buying a commodity for cash and selling the same commodity on the futures market

'…the small independent retailer who stocks up using cash and carries could be hit hard by the loss of footfall associated with any increase in smuggled goods' [*The Grocer*]

cash balance /ˈkæʃ ˌbæləns/ *noun* a balance that represents cash alone, as distinct from a balance that includes money owed but as yet unpaid

cash basis /ˈkæʃ ˌbeɪsɪs/ *noun* a method of preparing the accounts of a business, where receipts and payments are shown at the time when they are made, as opposed to showing debts or credits which are outstanding at the end of the accounting period. Also called **receipts and payments basis**

cash book /ˈkæʃ bʊk/ *noun* a book in which all cash payments and receipts are recorded. In a double-entry bookkeeping system, the balance at the end of a given period is included in the trial balance and then transferred to the balance sheet itself.

cash box /ˈkæʃ bɒks/ *noun* metal box for keeping cash

cash budget /ˈkæʃ ˌbʌdʒɪt/ *noun* a plan of cash income and expenditure. Also called **cash-flow budget**

cash card /ˈkæʃ kɑːd/ *noun* a plastic card used to obtain money from a cash dispenser

cash cow /ˈkæʃ kaʊ/ *noun* a product or subsidiary company that consistently generates good profits but does not provide growth

cash crop /ˈkæʃ krɒp/ *noun* an agricultural crop grown for sale to other buyers or to other countries, rather than for domestic consumption

cash deal /ˌkæʃ ˈdiːl/ *noun* a sale done for cash

cash desk /ˈkæʃ desk/ *noun* the place in a store where you pay for the goods bought

cash discount /ˌkæʃ ˈdɪskaʊnt/ *noun* a discount given for payment in cash. Also called **discount for cash**

cash dispenser /ˈkæʃ dɪˌspensə/ *noun* a machine which gives out money when a special card is inserted and instructions given

cash dividend /ˌkæʃ ˈdɪvɪdend/ *noun* a dividend paid in cash, as opposed to a dividend in the form of bonus shares

cash economy /ˌkæʃ ɪˈkɒnəmi/ *noun* a black economy, where goods and services are paid for in cash, and therefore not declared for tax

cash float /ˈkæʃ fləʊt/ *noun* cash put into the cash box at the beginning of the day or week to allow change to be given to customers

cash flow /ˈkæʃ fləʊ/ *noun* cash which comes into a company from sales (cash inflow) or the money which goes out in purchases or overhead expenditure (cash outflow) □ **the company is suffering from cash flow problems** cash income is not coming in fast enough to pay the expenditure going out

cash-flow budget /ˈkæʃ fləʊ ˌbʌdʒɪt/ *noun* same as **cash budget**

cash-flow forecast /ˈkæʃ fləʊ ˌfɔːkɑːst/ *noun* a forecast of when cash will be received or paid out

cash-flow statement /ˈkæʃ fləʊ ˌsteɪtmənt/ *noun* a record of a company's cash inflows and cash outflows over a specific period of time, typically a year

cashier /kæˈʃɪə/ *noun* **1.** a person who takes money from customers in a shop or who deals with the money that has been paid **2.** a person who deals with customers in a bank and takes or gives cash at the counter

cashier's check /kæˌʃɪəz ˈtʃek/ *noun* US a bank's own cheque, drawn on itself and signed by a cashier or other bank official

cash in hand /ˌkæʃ ɪn ˈhænd/ *noun* money and notes, kept to pay small amounts but not deposited in the bank

cash in transit /ˌkæʃ ɪn ˈtrænzɪt/ *noun* cash being moved from one bank or business to another ○ *Cash-in-transit services are an easy target for robbers.*

cash items /ˈkæʃ ˌaɪtəmz/ *plural noun* goods sold for cash

cashless society /ˌkæʃləs səˈsaɪəti/ *noun* a society where no one uses cash, all purchases being made by credit cards,

charge cards, cheques or direct transfer from one account to another

cash limit /ˈkæʃ ˌlɪmɪt/ *noun* **1.** a fixed amount of money which can be spent during some period **2.** a maximum amount someone can withdraw from an ATM using a cash card

cash market /ˌkæʃ ˈmɑːkɪt/ *noun* the gilt-edged securities market where purchases are paid for almost immediately, as opposed to the futures market

cash offer /ˈkæʃ ˌɒfə/ *noun* an offer to pay in cash, especially an offer to pay cash when buying shares in a takeover bid

cash payment /ˈkæʃ ˌpeɪmənt/ *noun* payment in cash

cash position /ˈkæʃ pəˌzɪʃ(ə)n/ *noun* a state of the cash which a company currently has available

cash positive /kæʃ ˈpɒzɪtɪv/ *adjective* having cash in hand, as opposed to having debts and overdrafts

'…as the group's shares are already widely held, the listing will be via an introduction. It will also be accompanied by a deeply discounted £25m rights issue, leaving the company cash positive' [*Sunday Times*]

cash price /ˈkæʃ praɪs/ *noun* a lower price or better terms which apply if the customer pays cash

cash purchase /ˈkæʃ ˌpɜːtʃɪs/ *noun* a purchase made for cash

cash register /ˈkæʃ ˌredʒɪstə/ *noun* a machine which shows and adds the prices of items bought, with a drawer for keeping the cash received

cash reserves /ˈkæʃ rɪˌzɜːvz/ *plural noun* a company's reserves in cash deposits or bills kept in case of urgent need ○ *The company was forced to fall back on its cash reserves.*

cash sale /ˈkæʃ seɪl/ *noun* a transaction paid for in cash

cash-strapped /ˈkæʃ stræpt/ *adjective* short of money

cash terms /ˈkæʃ tɜːmz/ *plural noun* lower terms which apply if the customer pays cash

cash till /ˈkæʃ tɪl/ *noun* same as **cash register**

cash transaction /ˈkæʃ trænˌzækʃən/ *noun* a transaction paid for in cash, as distinct from a transaction paid for by means of a transfer of a financial instrument

cash transfer hatch /kæʃ 'trænsfɜː hætʃ/ *noun* a small door in an outside wall, allowing cash to be passed through (as from a supermarket to a security van)

cash voucher /'kæʃ ˌvaʊtʃə/ *noun* a piece of paper which can be exchanged for cash ○ *With every $20 of purchases, the customer gets a cash voucher to the value of $2.*

Cashwire /'kæʃwaɪə/ *noun US* a system operated by a group of banks to clear payments between member banks

cash with order /ˌkæʃ wɪð 'ɔːdə/ *noun* terms of sale showing the payment has to be made in cash when the order is placed. Abbreviation **CWO**

casting vote /ˌkɑːstɪŋ 'vəʊt/ *noun* a vote used by the chairman in the case where the votes for and against a proposal are equal ○ *The chairman has the casting vote.* ○ *She used her casting vote to block the motion.*

casual /'kæʒuəl/ *adjective* not permanent, or not regular

casual labour /ˌkæʒuəl 'leɪbə/ *noun* workers who are hired for a short period

casual work /'kæʒuəl wɜːk/ *noun* work where the employees are hired only for a short period

casual worker /ˌkæʒuəl 'wɜːkə/ *noun* an employee who can be hired for a short period

cat /kæt/ ♦ **fat cat**, **dead-cat bounce**

catalogue price /'kæt(ə)lɒg praɪs/ *noun* a price as marked in a catalogue or list

catastrophe /kə'tæstrəfi/ *noun* a sudden disaster

catastrophe bond /kə'tæstrəfi bɒnd/ *noun* a bond with very high interest rate but, which may be worth less, or give a lower rate of interest, if a disaster such as an earthquake occurs

CAT standards /'kæt ˌstændədz/ *plural noun* standards introduced by the government as an incentive to offer savers an even better deal, and to make it easier to spot the best investment value

caveat /'kæviæt/ *noun* warning □ **to enter a caveat** to warn someone legally that you have an interest in a case, and

that no steps can be taken without your permission

caveat emptor /ˌkæviæt 'emptɔː/ *phrase* a Latin phrase meaning 'let the buyer beware', which indicates that the buyer is responsible for checking that what he or she buys is in good order

'…the idea that buyers at a car boot sale should have any rights at all is laughable. Even those who do not understand Latin know that caveat emptor is the rule' [*Times*]

caveat venditor /ˌkæviæt ven'diːtɔː/ *phrase* a Latin phrase meaning 'let the seller beware', which indicates that the seller is legally bound to make sure that the goods he sells are in good order

CBOT *abbreviation* Chicago Board of Trade

CBS All-Share /ˌsiː biː es 'ɔːl ʃeə/ *noun* an index of prices on the Amsterdam Stock Exchange (NOTE: The CBS Tendency also lists Amsterdam share prices.)

CCA *abbreviation* current cost accounting

CD /ˌsiː 'diː/ *abbreviation* certificate of deposit

cedi /'siːdi/ *noun* a unit of currency used in Ghana

ceiling /'siːlɪŋ/ *noun* the highest point that something can reach, e.g. the highest rate of a pay increase ○ *to fix a ceiling for a budget* ○ *There is a ceiling of $100,000 on deposits.* ○ *Output reached its ceiling in June and has since fallen back.* ○ *What ceiling has the government put on wage increases this year?*

ceiling price /'siːlɪŋ praɪs/ *noun* the highest price that can be reached

cent /sent/ *noun* a small coin, one hundredth of a dollar ○ *The stores are only a 25-cent bus ride away.* ○ *They sell oranges at 99 cents each.* (NOTE: **Cent** is usually written **¢** in prices: **25¢,** but not when a dollar price is mentioned: **$1.25.**)

central /'sentrəl/ *adjective* organised from one main point

central assets account /ˌsentrəl 'æsets əˌkaʊnt/ *noun* same as **asset management account**

central bank /ˌsentrəl 'bæŋk/ *noun* the main government-controlled bank in a country, which controls that country's financial affairs by fixing main interest rates, issuing currency, supervising the commercial banks and trying to control the foreign exchange rate

central bank discount rate /ˌsentrəl bæŋk 'dɪskaʊnt reɪt/ *noun* the rate at which a central bank discounts bills such as Treasury bills

central bank intervention /ˌsentrəl bæŋk ˌɪntə'venʃ(ə)n/ *noun* an action by a central bank to change base interest rates, to impose exchange controls or to buy or sell the country's own currency in an attempt to influence international money markets

central government /ˌsentrəl 'ɡʌv(ə)nmənt/ *noun* the main government of a country as opposed to municipal, local, provincial or state governments

centralisation /ˌsentrəlaɪ'zeɪʃ(ə)n/, **centralization** *noun* the organisation of everything from a central point

centralise /'sentrəlaɪz/ *verb* to organise from a central point ○ *All purchasing has been centralised in our main office.* ○ *The company has become very centralised, and far more staff work at headquarters.*

central office /ˌsentrəl 'ɒfɪs/ *noun* the main office which controls all smaller offices

central purchasing /ˌsentrəl 'pɜːtʃɪsɪŋ/ *noun* purchasing organised by a central office for all branches of a company

central rate /'sentrəl reɪt/ *noun* an exchange rate of a currency against the US dollar according to IMF rules

centre /'sentə/ *noun* **1.** an important town ○ *Sheffield is a major industrial centre.* ○ *Nottingham is the centre for the shoe industry.* **2.** a department, area or function to which costs and/or revenues are charged (NOTE: [all senses] The US spelling is **center**.)

CEO *abbreviation* chief executive officer

certain annuity /ˌsɜːt(ə)n ə'njuːɪti/ *noun* an annuity which will be paid for a specific number of years only

certificate /sə'tɪfɪkət/ *noun* an official document which shows that something is owned by someone or that something is true

certificated bankrupt /sə,tɪfɪkeɪtɪd 'bæŋkrʌpt/ *noun* a bankrupt who has been discharged from bankruptcy with a certificate to show that he or she was not at fault

certificate of approval /sə,tɪfɪkət əv ə'pruːv(ə)l/ *noun* a document showing that an item has been approved officially

certificate of authentication /sə,tɪfɪkət əv ɔː,θentɪ'keɪʃ(ə)n/ *noun* a unique number supplied to a company by an independent source (an 'authenticator') to prove that the company is who they claim to be

certificate of authority /sə,tɪfɪkət əv ɔː'θɒrəti/ *noun* a certificate showing that someone has the authority to do something, such as sign a cheque

certificate of deposit /sə,tɪfɪkət əv dɪ'pɒzɪt/ *noun* a document from a bank showing that money has been deposited at a guaranteed interest rate for a certain period of time. Abbreviation **CD**

'…interest rates on certificates of deposit may have little room to decline in August as demand for funds from major city banks is likely to remain strong. After delaying for months, banks are now expected to issue a large volume of CDs. If banks issue more CDs on the assumption that the official discount rate reduction will be delayed, it is very likely that CD rates will be pegged for a longer period than expected' [*Nikkei Weekly*]

COMMENT: A CD is a bearer instrument, which can be sold by the bearer. It can be sold at a discount to the value, so that the yield on CDs varies.

certificate of incorporation /sə,tɪfɪkət əv ɪn,kɔːpə'reɪʃ(ə)n/ *noun* a document issued by Companies House to show that a company has been legally set up and officially registered

certificate of origin /sə,tɪfɪkət əv 'ɒrɪdʒɪn/ *noun* a document showing where imported goods come from or were made

certificate of quality /sə,tɪfɪkət əv 'kwɒlɪti/ *noun* a certificate showing the grade of a soft commodity

certificate of registration /sə,tɪfɪkət əv ,redʒɪ'streɪʃ(ə)n/ *noun* a document showing that an item has been registered

certificate of tax deducted /səˌtɪfɪkət əv tæks dɪˈdʌktɪd/ *noun* a document issued by a financial institution showing that tax has been deducted from interest payments on an account

certified accountant /ˌsɜːtɪfaɪd əˈkaʊntənt/ *noun* an accountant who has passed the professional examinations and is a member of the Association of Certified Chartered Accountants (ACCA). ◊ **chartered accountant**

certified cheque /ˌsɜːtɪfaɪd ˈtʃek/, **certified check** *noun* a cheque which a bank says is good and will be paid out of money put aside from the payer's bank account

certified public accountant /ˌsɜːtɪfaɪd ˌpʌblɪk əˈkaʊntənt/ *noun* US same as **chartered accountant**

certify /ˈsɜːtɪfaɪ/ *verb* to make an official declaration in writing ○ *I certify that this is a true copy.* ○ *The document is certified as a true copy.* (NOTE: **certifies – certifying – certified**)

cession /ˈseʃ(ə)n/ *noun* the act of giving up property to someone, especially a creditor

c/f *abbreviation* carried forward

CFA *abbreviation* Communauté française africaine

CFA franc /ˌsiː ef eɪ ˈfræŋk/ *noun* a franc with a fixed exchange rate against the euro, used in African countries which were formerly French colonies (Benin, Burkina Faso, Cameroon, the Central African Republic, Chad, Congo, Equatorial Guinea, Gabon, Ivory Coast, Mali, Niger, Senegal and Togo)

CFO *abbreviation* chief financial officer

CFP *abbreviation* Communauté française pacifique

CFP franc /ˌsiː ef piː ˈfræŋk/ *noun* a franc with a fixed exchange rate against the euro, used in French territories in the Pacific

CGT *abbreviation* capital gains tax

chairman /ˈtʃeəmən/ *noun* a person who presides over the board meetings of a company ○ *the chairman of the board* or *the company chairman* (NOTE: Note also that in a UK company, the chairman is less important than the managing director, although one person can combine both posts. In the US, a

company president is less important than the chairman of the board. The plural is **chairmen**.) □ **the chairman's report**, **the chairman's statement** an annual report from the chairman of a company to the shareholders

'…the corporation's entrepreneurial chairman seeks a dedicated but part-time president. The new president will work a three-day week' [*Globe and Mail (Toronto)*]

COMMENT: Note that in a UK company, the chairman is less important than the managing director, although one person can combine both posts. In the US, a company president is less important than the chairman of the board.

chairman and managing director /ˌtʃeəmən ən ˌmænɪdʒɪŋ daɪˈrektə/ *noun* a managing director who is also chairman of the board of directors

Chamber of Commerce /ˌtʃeɪmbər əv ˈkɒmɜːs/ *noun* an organisation of local business people who work together to promote and protect common interest in trade

champagne stock /ʃæmˈpeɪn stɒk/ *noun* a share that has doubled or tripled its value in a relatively short period of time, making shareholders a great deal of money. The term is used because individuals who hold such shares will often order an expensive bottle of champagne to celebrate their good fortune.

Chancellor of the Exchequer /ˌtʃɑːnsələr əv ði ɪksˈtʃekə/ *noun* the chief finance minister in the British government (NOTE: The US term is **Secretary of the Treasury**.)

change /tʃeɪndʒ/ *noun* **1.** money in coins or small notes. ◊ **exchange** □ **to give someone change for £10** to give someone coins or notes in exchange for a ten pound note **2.** money given back by the seller, when the buyer can pay only with a larger note or coin than the amount asked ○ *She gave me the wrong change.* ○ *You paid the £5.75 bill with a £10 note, so you should have £4.25 change.* □ **keep the change** keep it as a tip (said to e.g. waiters, taxi-drivers) ■ *verb* **1.** □ **to change a £20 note** to give someone smaller notes or coins in place of a £20 note **2.** to give one type of currency for another ○ *to change £1,000 into dollars* ○ *We want to change some traveller's* *cheques.* **3.** □ **to change hands** (*of a business, property, etc.*) to be sold to a new owner ○ *The shop changed hands for £100,000.*

change machine /'tʃeɪndʒ məˌʃiːn/ *noun* a machine which gives small change for a note or larger coin

changer /'tʃeɪndʒə/ *noun* a person who changes money

channel /'tʃæn(ə)l/ *verb* to send in some direction ○ *They are channelling their research funds into developing European communication systems.* (NOTE: **channelling – channelled**. The US spelling is **channeling – channeled**.)

channel of distribution /ˌtʃæn(ə)l əv ˌdɪstrɪ'bjuːʃ(ə)n/ *noun* same as **distribution channel**

CHAPS /tʃæps/ *noun* an electronic, bank-to-bank payment system that guarantees same-day payment. Compare **BACS**. Full form **Clearing House Automated Payments System**

chapter /'tʃæptə/ *noun US* a section of an Act of Congress

'…the company filed under Chapter 11 of the federal bankruptcy code, the largest failure ever in the steel industry' [*Fortune*]

'…the firm, whose trademark dates back to 1871, has been desperately trying to cut costs to compete with manufacturers in cheaper countries, but has also been hit by management problems. It said the filing for Chapter 11 protection should have little impact on customers and employees and would allow it to restructure' [*Times*]

Chapter 7 /ˌtʃæptə 'sev(ə)n/ *noun* a section of the US Bankruptcy Reform Act 1978, which sets out the rules for liquidation, a choice available to individuals, partnerships and corporations

Chapter 11 /ˌtʃæptə 'ten/ *noun* a section of the US Bankruptcy Reform Act 1978, which allows a corporation to be protected from demands made by its creditors for a period of time, while it is reorganised with a view to paying its debts

charge /tʃɑːdʒ/ *noun* **1.** money which must be paid, or the price of a service ○ *to make no charge for delivery* ○ *to make a small charge for rental* ○ *There is no charge for this service* or *No charge is made for this service.* □ **free of charge** free, with no payment to be made **2.** a

debit on an account ○ *It appears as a charge on the accounts.* **3.** a guarantee of security for a loan, for which assets are pledged **4.** a formal accusation in a court ○ *He appeared in court on a charge of embezzling* or *on an embezzlement charge.* ■ *verb* **1.** to ask for money to be paid ○ *to charge $5 for delivery* ○ *How much does he charge?* □ **he charges £16 an hour** he asks to be paid £16 for an hour's work **2.** to pay for something by putting it on a charge account ○ *Can you charge the meal to my room?* ○ *I want to charge these purchases to the company account.* **3.** to take something as guarantee for a loan **4.** to accuse someone formally of having committed a crime ○ *He was charged with embezzling his clients' money.*

chargeable /'tʃɑːdʒəb(ə)l/ *adjective* able to be charged ○ *repairs chargeable to the occupier*

chargeable asset /ˌtʃɑːdʒəb(ə)l 'æset/ *noun* an asset which will produce a capital gain when sold. Assets which are not chargeable include your family home, cars, and some types of investments such as government stocks.

chargeable gains /ˌtʃɑːdʒəb(ə)l 'ɡeɪnz/ *plural noun* gains made by selling an asset such as shares, on which capital gains will be charged

charge account /'tʃɑːdʒ əˌkaʊnt/ *noun US* same as **credit account** (NOTE: The customer will make regular monthly payments into the account and is allowed credit of a multiple of those payments.)

charge card /'tʃɑːdʒ kɑːd/ *noun* a card issued to customers by a shop, bank or other organisation, used to charge purchases to an account for later payment. ◊ **credit card**

chargee /tʃɑː'dʒiː/ *noun* a person who has the right to force a debtor to pay

charges forward /ˌtʃɑːdʒɪz 'fɔːwəd/ *plural noun* charges which will be paid by the customer

charging period /'tʃɑːdʒɪŋ ˌpɪəriəd/ *noun* a period of time during which charges are made to a credit card before they are charged to the cardholder

chart /tʃɑːt/ *noun* a diagram displaying information as a series of lines, blocks, etc.

charter /'tʃɑːtə/ *noun* the action or business of hiring transport for a special purpose ■ *verb* to hire for a special purpose ○ *to charter a plane* or *a boat* or *a bus*

chartered /'tʃɑːtəd/ *adjective* **1.** in the UK, used to describe a company which has been set up by charter, and not registered under the Companies Act ○ *a chartered bank* **2.** □ **a chartered ship** *or* **bus** *or* **plane** a ship, bus or plane which has been hired for a special purpose

chartered accountant /,tʃɑːtəd ə'kaʊntənt/ *noun* an accountant who has passed the necessary professional examinations and is a member of the Institute of Chartered Accountants. Abbreviation **CA**

Chartered Association of Certified Accountants /,tʃɑːtəd ə,səʊsieɪʃ(ə)n əv ,sɜːtɪfaɪd ə'kaʊntənts/ *noun* the former name of the Association of Chartered Certified Accountants

chartered bank /,tʃɑːtəd 'bæŋk/ *noun* a bank which has been set up by government charter, formerly used in England, but now only done in the USA and Canada

Chartered Institute of Bankers /,tʃɑːtəd ,ɪnstɪtjuːt əv 'bæŋkəz/ *noun* formerly, a professional association of bankers, providing training, professional examinations and qualifications which are recognised worldwide. Abbreviation **CIB**

charter value /'tʃɑːtə ,væljuː/ *noun* the value of a bank's being able to continue do business in the future, reflected as part of its share price

charting /'tʃɑːtɪŋ/ *noun* the work of using charts to analyse information such as stock market trends and forecast future rises or falls

chartist /'tʃɑːtɪst/ *noun* a person who studies stock market trends and forecasts future rises or falls

chattel mortgage /'tʃæt(ə)l ,mɔːgɪdʒ/ *noun* money lent against the security of an item purchased, but not against real estate

chattels /'tʃæt(ə)lz/ *plural noun* goods, movable property but not real estate

cheap /tʃiːp/ *adjective, adverb* not costing a lot of money or not expensive □ **to buy something cheap** at a low price ○

He bought two companies cheap and sold them again at a profit. □ **they work out cheaper by the box** these items are cheaper per unit if you buy a box of them

cheap labour /,tʃiːp 'leɪbə/ *noun* workers who do not earn much money

cheaply /'tʃiːpli/ *adverb* without paying much money ○ *The salesman was living cheaply at home and claiming an enormous hotel bill on expenses.*

cheap money /,tʃiːp 'mʌni/ *noun* money which can be borrowed at a low rate of interest

cheapness /'tʃiːpnəs/ *noun* the fact of being cheap ○ *The cheapness of the pound means that many more tourists will come to London.*

cheap rate /'tʃiːp reɪt/ *noun* a rate which is not expensive ○ *Cheap rate phone calls start at 8 p.m.*

cheat /tʃiːt/ *verb* to trick someone so that he or she loses money ○ *He cheated the Inland Revenue out of thousands of pounds.* ○ *She was accused of cheating clients who came to ask her for advice.*

check /tʃek/ *noun* **1.** a sudden stop □ **to put a check on imports** to stop some imports coming into a country **2.** investigation or examination ○ *a routine check of the fire equipment* ○ *The auditors carried out checks on the petty cash book.* **3.** *US* (*in a restaurant*) a bill **4.** same as **cheque 5.** *US* a mark on paper to show that something is correct ○ *Make a check in the box marked 'R'.* (NOTE: The UK term is **tick**.) ■ *verb* **1.** to stop or delay something ○ *to check the entry of contraband into the country* ○ *to check the flow of money out of a country* **2.** to examine or to investigate something ○ *to check that an invoice is correct* ○ *to check and sign for goods* □ **she checked the computer printout against the invoices** she examined the printout and the invoices to see if the figures were the same **3.** *US* to mark something with a sign to show that it is correct ○ *check the box marked 'R'* (NOTE: The UK term is **tick**.)

check out /,tʃek 'aʊt/ *phrasal verb* to go through a checkout and pay for the goods bought

checkable /'tʃekəb(ə)l/ *adjective US* referring to a deposit account on which checks can be drawn

check card /'tʃek kɑːd/ *noun US* same as **cheque card**

check digit /'tʃek ˌdɪdʒɪt/ *noun* the last digit of a string of computerised reference numbers, used to validate the transaction

checking account /'tʃekɪŋ əˌkaʊnt/ *noun US* same as **current account 1**

checkoff /'tʃekɒf/ *noun US* a system where union dues are automatically deducted by the employer from an employee's pay cheque ○ *Checkoffs are seen by most employees as worthwhile as long as their interests are well represented by the union.* ○ *After checkoffs and tax deductions the employees' pay had been reduced by one third.*

check routing symbol /'tʃek ˌruːtɪŋ ˌsɪmbəl/ *noun US* a number shown on a US cheque which identifies the Federal Reserve district through which the cheque will be cleared, similar to the UK 'bank sort code'

check sample /'tʃek ˌsɑːmp(ə)l/ *noun* a sample to be used to see if a consignment is acceptable

cheque /tʃek/ *noun* a note to a bank asking them to pay money from your account to the account of the person whose name is written on the note ○ *a cheque for £10* or *a £10 cheque* (NOTE: The US spelling is **check**.) □ **to cash a cheque** to exchange a cheque for cash □ **to endorse a cheque** to sign a cheque on the back to show that you accept it □ **to make out a cheque to someone** to write someone's name on a cheque ○ *Who shall I make the cheque out to?* □ **to pay by cheque** to pay by writing a cheque, and not using cash or a credit card □ **to pay a cheque into your account** to deposit a cheque □ **the bank referred the cheque to the drawer** the bank returned the cheque to the person who wrote it because there was not enough money in the account to pay it □ **to sign a cheque** to sign on the front of a cheque to show that you authorise the bank to pay the money from your account □ **to stop a cheque** to ask a bank not to pay a cheque which has been signed and sent

cheque account /'tʃek əˌkaʊnt/ *noun* same as **current account**

cheque book /'tʃek bʊk/ *noun* a booklet with new blank cheques (NOTE: The usual US term is **checkbook**.)

cheque card /'tʃek kɑːd/, **cheque guarantee card** /ˌtʃek ˌgærən'tiː kɑːd/ *noun* a plastic card from a bank which guarantees payment of a cheque up to some amount, even if the user has no money in his account

cheque requisition /'tʃek ˌrekwɪzɪʃ(ə)n/ *noun* an official note from a department to the company accounts staff asking for a cheque to be written

cheque stub /'tʃek stʌb/ *noun* a piece of paper left in a cheque book after a cheque has been written and taken out

cheque to bearer /ˌtʃek tə 'beərə/ *noun* a cheque with no name written on it, so that the person who holds it can cash it

Chicago Board of Trade /ʃɪˌkɑːgəʊ bɔːd əv 'treɪd/ *noun* a commodity market based in Chicago, trading in metals, soft commodities and financial futures. Abbreviation **CBOT**

Chicago Mercantile Exchange /ʃɪˌkɑːgəʊ 'mɜːkəntaɪl ɪksˌtʃeɪndʒ/ *noun* a commodity market based in Chicago, trading in livestock futures, and in financial futures on the IMM. Abbreviation **CME**

Chicago School /ʃɪ'kɑːgəʊ skuːl/ *noun* a school of monetarists, based at the University of Chicago, led by Professor Milton Friedman

chickenfeed /'tʃɪkɪnˌfiːd/ *noun* a small amount of money (*informal*)

chief /tʃiːf/ *adjective* most important ○ *He is the chief accountant of an industrial group.* ○ *She is the chief buyer for a department store.*

chief cashier /ˌtʃiːf kæ'ʃɪə/ *noun* a main cashier in a bank

chief executive /ˌtʃiːf ɪg'zekjʊtɪv/, **chief executive officer** /ˌtʃiːf ɪg ˌzekjʊtɪv 'ɒfɪsə/ *noun* the most important director in charge of a company. Abbreviation **CEO**

chief financial officer /ˌtʃiːf faɪ 'nænʃəl ˌɒfɪsə/ *noun* an executive in charge of a company's financial operations, reporting to the CEO. Abbreviation **CFO**

chief operating officer /tʃiːf ˈɒpəreɪtɪŋ ˌɒfɪsə/ *noun* a director in charge of all a company's operations (same as a 'managing director'). Abbreviation **COO**

Chief Secretary to the Treasury /ˌtʃiːf ˌsekrətri tə ðə ˈtreʒ(ə)ri/ *noun* a government minister responsible to the Chancellor of the Exchequer for the control of public expenditure (NOTE: In the USA, this is the responsibility of the **Director of the Budget**.)

Chinese walls /ˌtʃaɪniːz ˈwɔːlz/ *plural noun* imaginary barriers between departments in the same organisation, set up to avoid insider dealing or conflict of interest. For example, if a merchant bank is advising on a planned takeover bid, its investment department should not know that the bid is taking place, or they would advise their clients to invest in the company being taken over.

chip and pin /ˌtʃɪp ən ˈpɪn/ *noun* a government-backed initiative in the UK where credit/debit cards contain an embedded microchip and are authenticated automatically using the customer's PIN. ◊ **PIN**

chip card /ˌtʃɪp ˈkɑːd/ *noun* same as **smart card**

CHIPS *noun* the computerised clearing bank system used in the US. Full form **Clearing House Interbank Payments System**

chop /tʃɒp/ *noun* a mark made on a document to show that it has been agreed, acknowledged, paid or that payment has been received

chronological order /ˌkrɒnəlɒdʒɪk(ə)l ˈɔːdə/ *noun* the arrangement of records such as files and invoices in order of their dates

churning /ˈtʃɜːnɪŋ/ *noun* 1. a practice employed by stockbrokers, where they buy and sell on a client's discretionary account in order to earn their commission. The deals are frequently of no advantage to the client. 2. a practice employed by insurance salesmen where the salesman suggests that a client should change his or her insurance policy solely in order to earn the salesman a commission

'…more small investors lose money through churning than almost any other abuse, yet most people have never heard of it. Churning involves brokers generating income simply by buying and selling investments on behalf of their clients. Constant and needless churning earns them hefty commissions which bites into the investment portfolio' [*Guardian*]

CIB *abbreviation* Chartered Institute of Bankers

CIF /ˌsiː aɪ ˈef/, **c.i.f.** *abbreviation* 1. cost, insurance, and freight 2. *US* customer identification file

circular /ˈsɜːkjʊlə/ *adjective* sent to many people ■ *noun* 1. a leaflet or letter sent to many people ○ *They sent out a circular offering a 10% discount.* ○ *Senior management sent out a circular to all the employees explaining the changes in the payment scheme.* 2. a leaflet sent by a broker to clients, with information about companies and shares

circularise /ˈsɜːkjʊləraɪz/, **circularize** *verb* to send a circular to ○ *The committee has agreed to circularise the members of the society.* ○ *They circularised all their customers with a new list of prices.*

circular letter /ˌsɜːkjʊlə ˈletə/ *noun* a letter sent to many people

circular letter of credit /ˌsɜːkjʊlə ˌletər əv ˈkredɪt/ *noun* a letter of credit sent to all branches of the bank which issues it

circulate /ˈsɜːkjʊleɪt/ *verb* 1. □ **to circulate freely** (*of money*) to move about without restriction by the government 2. to send or to give out without restrictions □ **to circulate money** to issue money, to make money available to the public and industry 3. to send information to ○ *They circulated a new list of prices to all their customers.* ○ *They circulated information about job vacancies to all colleges in the area.*

circulating capital /ˌsɜːkjʊleɪtɪŋ ˈkæpɪt(ə)l/ *noun* capital in the form of cash or debtors, raw materials, finished products and work in progress which a company requires to carry on its business

circulation /ˌsɜːkjʊˈleɪʃ(ə)n/ *noun* movement □ **to put money into circulation** to issue new notes to business and the public ○ *The amount of money in circulation increased more than was expected.*

circulation of capital /ˌsɜːkjʊ leɪʃ(ə)n əv ˈkæpɪt(ə)l/ *noun* a movement of capital from one investment to another

circumstances /ˈsɜːkəmstænsɪz/ *plural noun* a general situation, especially insofar as it influences what a person can do or the way in which something happens. ◊ **financial**

City /ˈsɪti/, **City of London** *noun* **1.** a large town ○ *The largest cities in Europe are linked by hourly flights.* **2.** □ **the City (of London)** the old centre of London, where banks and large companies have their main offices; the British financial centre ○ *He works in the City or He is in the City.*

City analyst /ˌsɪti ˈænəlɪst/ *noun* a person who studies the London stock market

City desk /ˈsɪti desk/ *noun* the department in a British newspaper which deals with business news

City editor /ˈsɪti ˌedɪtə/ *noun* the business and finance editor of a British newspaper

civil /ˈsɪv(ə)l/ *adjective* relating to ordinary people

civil action /ˌsɪv(ə)l ˈækʃən/ *noun* a court case brought by a person or a company against someone who has done them wrong

civil law /ˌsɪv(ə)l ˈlɔː/ *noun* laws relating to people's rights and to agreements between individuals

civil servant /ˌsɪv(ə)l ˈsɜːvənt/ *noun* a person who works in the civil service

civil service /ˌsɪv(ə)l ˈsɜːvɪs/ *noun* the organisation and personnel which administer a country ○ *You have to pass an examination to get a job in the civil service or to get a civil service job.*

claim /kleɪm/ *noun* **1.** an act of asking for something that you feel you have a right to □ **the union put in a 6% wage claim** the union asked for a 6% increase in wages for its members **2.** an act of stating that something is a fact ○ *Her claim that she had been authorised to take the money was demonstrably false.* **3.** an act of asking for money from an insurance company when something you insured against has taken place □ **to put in a claim** to ask the insurance company officially to pay damages ○ *to put in a claim* for repairs to the car ○ *She put in a claim for £250,000 damages against the driver of the other car.* □ **to settle a claim** to agree to pay what is asked for ○ *The insurance company refused to settle his claim for storm damage.* ■ *verb* **1.** to ask for money, especially from an insurance company ○ *He claimed £100,000 damages against the cleaning firm.* ○ *She claimed for repairs to the car against her insurance policy.* **2.** to say that you have a right to something or that something is your property ○ *She is claiming possession of the house.* ○ *No one claimed the umbrella found in my office.* **3.** to state that something is a fact ○ *He claims he never received the goods.* ○ *She claims that the shares are her property.*

claim back /ˌkleɪm ˈbæk/ *phrasal verb* to ask for money to be paid back

claimant /ˈkleɪmənt/ *noun* a person who makes a claim against someone in the civil courts (NOTE: This term has now replaced **plaintiff**. The other side in a case is the **defendant**.)

claimer /ˈkleɪmə/ *noun* same as **claimant**

claim form /ˈkleɪm fɔːm/ *noun* a form which has to be filled in when making an insurance claim

claims department /ˈkleɪmz dɪ ˌpɑːtmənt/ *noun* a department of an insurance company which deals with claims

claims manager /ˈkleɪmz ˌmænɪdʒə/ *noun* the manager of a claims department

claims reserve /ˈkleɪmz rɪˌzɜːv/ *noun* money set aside by an insurance company to meet costs of claims incurred but not yet settled

class /klɑːs/ *noun* **1.** a category or group into which things are classified **2.** *US* a type of common stock (NOTE: Class **A** stock is similar to the British **A** shares.)

classified advertisements /ˌklæsɪfaɪd ədˈvɜːtɪsmənts/, **classified ads** /ˈklæsɪfaɪd ædz/ *plural noun* advertisements listed in a newspaper under special headings such as 'property for sale' or 'jobs wanted' ○ *Look in the small ads to see if anyone has a filing cabinet for sale.*

classified directory /ˌklæsɪfaɪd daɪ ˈrekt(ə)ri/ *noun* a list of businesses grouped under various headings such as computer shops or newsagents

classify /ˈklæsɪfaɪ/ *verb* to put into classes or categories according to specific characteristics (NOTE: **classifies – classifying – classified**)

clause /klɔːz/ *noun* a section of a contract ○ *There are ten clauses in the contract of employment.* ○ *There is a clause in this contract concerning the employer's right to dismiss an employee.* ○ *According to clause six, payments will not be due until next year.* ■ *verb* to list details of the relevant parties to a bill of exchange

claw back /ˌklɔː ˈbæk/ *verb* to take back money which has been allocated ○ *Income tax claws back 25% of pensions paid out by the government.* ○ *Of the £1m allocated to the project, the government clawed back £100,000 in taxes.*

clawback /ˈklɔːbæk/ *noun* **1.** money taken back, especially money taken back by the government from grants or tax concessions which had previously been made **2.** the allocation of new shares to existing shareholders, so as to maintain the value of their holdings

clean /kliːn/ *adjective* with no problems or no record of offences

clean bill of lading /ˌkliːn bɪl əv ˈleɪdɪŋ/ *noun* a bill of lading with no note to say the shipment is faulty or damaged

clean float /ˈkliːn fləʊt/ *noun* an act of floating a currency freely on the international markets, without any interference from the government

clear /klɪə/ *adjective* (*of a period of time*) free, total □ **three clear days** three whole working days ○ *Allow three clear days for the cheque to be paid into your account.* ■ *verb* **1.** to sell something cheaply in order to get rid of stock ○ *'Demonstration models to clear'* **2.** □ **to clear goods through customs** to have all documentation passed by customs so that goods can enter or leave the country **3.** □ **we cleared only our expenses** the sales revenue only paid for the costs and expenses without making any profit **4.** □ **to clear a cheque** to pass a cheque through the banking system, so that the money is transferred from the payer's account to another ○ *the cheque took ten days to clear* or *the bank took ten days to clear the cheque*

clear off /ˌklɪər ˈɒf/ *phrasal verb* □ **to clear off a debt** to pay all of a debt

clearance /ˈklɪərəns/ *noun* **1.** □ **to effect customs clearance** to clear goods through customs **2.** □ **clearance of a cheque** the passing of a cheque through the banking system, transferring money from one account to another ○ *You should allow six days for cheque clearance.*

clearance certificate /ˈklɪərəns səˌtɪfɪkət/ *noun* a document showing that goods have been passed by customs

clearance sale /ˈklɪərəns seɪl/ *noun* a sale of items at low prices to get rid of stock

cleared date /ˈklɪəd deɪt/ *noun* a date on which a cheque has cleared and funds have been removed from the account

clearing /ˈklɪərɪŋ/ *noun* **1.** □ **clearing of goods through customs** passing of goods through customs **2.** □ **clearing of a debt** paying all of a debt **3.** an act of passing of a cheque through the banking system, transferring money from one account to another

clearing bank /ˈklɪərɪŋ bæŋk/ *noun* a bank which clears cheques, especially one of the major UK High Street banks, specialising in usual banking business for ordinary customers, such as loans, cheques, overdrafts and interest-bearing deposits

clearing house /ˈklɪərɪŋ haʊs/ *noun* a central office where clearing banks exchange cheques, or where stock exchange or commodity exchange transactions are settled

Clearing House Automated Payments System /ˌklɪərɪŋ haʊs ˌɔːtəmeɪtɪd ˈpeɪmənts ˌsɪstəm/ *noun* full form of **CHAPS**

clearing house funds /ˈklɪərɪŋ haʊs ˌfʌndz/ *plural noun* funds which are in the process of passing through the clearing house system

Clearing House Interbank Payments System /ˌklɪərɪŋ haʊs ˌɪntəbæŋk ˈpeɪmənts ˌsɪstəm/ *noun* a computerised system for clearing cheques organised by the banks in the USA. Abbreviation **CHIPS**

clearing member /ˈklɪərɪŋ ˌmembə/ *noun* a member firm of a stock exchange which is also a member of the stock exchange clearing house

clear profit /ˌklɪə ˈprɒfɪt/ *noun* a profit after all expenses have been paid ○ *We made $6,000 clear profit on the deal.*

clear title /klɪə ˈtaɪt(ə)l/ *noun* title to property without any charges or other encumbrances

clerical error /ˌklerɪk(ə)l ˈerə/ *noun* a mistake made by someone doing office work

clerical work /ˈklerɪk(ə)l wɜːk/ *noun* work done in an office

clerical worker /ˈklerɪk(ə)l ˌwɜːkə/ *noun* a person who works in an office

clerk /klɑːk/ *noun* a person who works in an office

clicks-and-mortar /ˌklɪks ən ˈmɔːtə/ *adjective* conducting business both through e-commerce and also in the traditional way in buildings such as stores and warehouses. Compare **bricks-and-mortar**

'…there may be a silver lining for 'clicks-and-mortar' stores that have both an online and a high street presence. Many of these are accepting returns of goods purchased online at their traditional stores. This is a service that may make them more popular as consumers become more experienced online shoppers' [*Financial Times*]

client /ˈklaɪənt/ *noun* a person with whom business is done or who pays for a service ○ *One of our major clients has defaulted on her payments.*

clientele /ˌkliːɒnˈtel/ *noun* all the clients of a business or all the customers of a shop

clients' account /ˌklaɪənts əˈkaʊnt/ *noun* an account with a bank for clients of a solicitor

climb /klaɪm/ *verb* to go up ○ *The company has climbed to the No. 1 position in the market.* ○ *Profits climbed rapidly as the new management cut costs.*

close *noun* /kləʊz/ the end of a day's trading on the stock exchange ○ *At the close shares had fallen 20%.* ■ *adjective* /kləʊs/ □ **close to** very near, almost ○ *The company was close to bankruptcy.* ○ *We are close to meeting our sales targets.* ■ *verb* /kləʊz/ **1.** □ **to close a position** to arrange your affairs so that you no longer have any liability to pay (e.g. by selling all your securities or when a purchaser of

a futures contract takes on a sales contract for the same amount to offset the risk) □ **to close the accounts** to come to the end of an accounting period and make up the profit and loss account **2.** to bring something to an end □ **she closed her building society account** she took all the money out and stopped using the account **3.** □ **the shares closed at $15** at the end of the day's trading the price of the shares was $15

close down /ˌkləʊz ˈdaʊn/ *phrasal verb* **1.** to shut a shop, factory, or service for a long period or for ever ○ *The company is closing down its London office.* ○ *The accident closed down the station for a period.* **2.** (*of a shop, factory, or service*) to stop doing business or operating

'…the best thing would be to have a few more plants close down and bring supply more in line with current demand' [*Fortune*]

close off /ˌkləʊz ˈɒf/ *phrasal verb* to come to the end of an accounting period and make up the profit and loss account

close out /ˌkləʊz ˈaʊt/ *phrasal verb* to end a futures contract by selling the relevant commodity or financial instrument

close company /ˌkləʊs ˈkʌmp(ə)ni/ *noun* a privately owned company controlled by a few shareholders (in the UK, fewer than five) where the public may own a small number of the shares (NOTE: The US term is **close corporation** or **closed corporation**.)

closed /kləʊzd/ *adjective* **1.** not open for business, or not doing business ○ *The office is closed on Mondays.* ○ *These warehouses are usually closed to the public.* ○ *All the banks are closed on Christmas Day.* **2.** restricted

closed economy /ˌkləʊzd ɪˈkɒnəmi/ *noun* a type of economy where trade and financial dealings are tightly controlled by the government

closed-end mortgage /ˌkləʊzd end ˈmɔːɡɪdʒ/ *noun* a mortgage where the borrower cannot use the property as security for other borrowings, such as a second mortgage, and cannot repay the mortgage early either

closed fund /ˌkləʊzd ˈfʌnd/ *noun* a fund, such as an investment trust, where the investor buys shares in the trust and receives dividends. This is as opposed to an open-ended trust, such as a unit trust, where the investor buys units, and the investment is used to purchase further securities for the trust.

closed market /ˌkləʊzd 'mɑːkɪt/ noun a market where a supplier deals only with one agent or distributor and does not supply any others direct ○ *They signed a closed-market agreement with an Egyptian company.*

closed shop /ˌkləʊzd 'ʃɒp/ noun a system where a company agrees to employ only union members for specific jobs ○ *The union is asking the management to agree to a closed shop.*

COMMENT: Closed shops are illegal in many countries.

close-ended /ˌkləʊs 'endɪd/, **closed-end** /'kləʊzd end/ adjective referring to an investment which has a fixed capital, such as an investment trust

closely held /ˌkləʊsli 'held/ adjective referring to shares in a company which are controlled by only a few shareholders

closing /'kləʊzɪŋ/ adjective **1.** final or coming at the end **2.** at the end of an accounting period ○ *At the end of the quarter the bookkeeper has to calculate the closing balance.* ■ noun **1.** □ **the closing of an account** the act of stopping supply to a customer on credit **2.** the action of finalising a deal

closing bell /'kləʊzɪŋ bel/ noun a bell which is rung when a stock exchange closes for business

closing bid /'kləʊzɪŋ bɪd/ noun the last bid at an auction, the bid which is successful

closing costs /'kləʊzɪŋ kɒsts/ plural noun US the costs involved in finalising a deal, especially a mortgage or other bank loan

closing date /'kləʊzɪŋ deɪt/ noun the last date ○ *The closing date for tenders to be received is May 1st.*

closing out /ˌkləʊzɪŋ 'aʊt/ noun the ending of a futures contract by selling the relevant commodity

closing price /'kləʊzɪŋ praɪs/ noun the price of a share at the end of a day's trading

closing statement /ˌkləʊzɪŋ 'steɪtmənt/ noun a statement of all charges and fees involved in a mortgage, made just before the mortgage is signed

closing stock /ˌkləʊzɪŋ 'stɒk/ noun a business's remaining stock at the end of an accounting period. It includes finished products, raw materials, or work in progress and is deducted from the period's costs in the balance sheets. ○ *At the end of the month the closing stock was 10% higher than at the end of the previous month.*

closing time /'kləʊzɪŋ taɪm/ noun the time when a shop or office stops work

closure /'kləʊʒə/ noun the act of closing

CM abbreviation US compounding method

CMBS abbreviation commercial mortgage-backed securities

CME abbreviation Chicago Mercantile Exchange

CML abbreviation Council of Mortgage Lenders

C/N abbreviation credit note

Co. abbreviation company ○ *J. Smith & Co.*

co- /kəʊ/ prefix working or acting together

c/o abbreviation care of

coattail investing /'kəʊteɪl ɪnˌvestɪŋ/ noun an investment strategy in which investors copy the trades of well known and historically successful investors

COB abbreviation Commission des Opérations de Bourse

co-creditor /ˌkəʊ 'kredɪtə/ noun a person who is a creditor of the same company as you are

code /kəʊd/ noun **1.** a system of signs, numbers, or letters which mean something **2.** a set of rules

code of practice /ˌkəʊd əv 'præktɪs/ noun **1.** rules drawn up by an association which the members must follow when doing business **2.** the formally established ways in which members of a profession agree to work ○ *Advertisers have agreed to abide by the code of practice set out by the advertising council.*

co-director /ˌkəʊ daɪˌrektə/ noun a person who is a director of the same company as you

co-financing /ˌkəʊ ˈfaɪnænsɪŋ/ *noun* the act of arranging finance for a project from a series of sources

cohabit /kəʊˈhæbɪt/ *verb* to live together when not married ○ *A woman who cohabits may lose out financially if her partner dies.*

cohabitant /kəʊˈhæbɪtənt/ *noun* a person who lives with another

cohabitation /kəʊˌhæbɪˈteɪʃ(ə)n/ *noun* living together, when not married ○ *Most public-sector pension schemes do not recognise cohabitation.*

coin /kɔɪn/ *noun* a piece of metal money ○ *He gave me two 10-cent coins in my change.* ○ *I need some 10p coins for the telephone.* □ **coins of the realm** the coins which are legal tender in the UK These are: 1p, 2p, 5p, 10p, 20p, 50p, £1 and £2

coincident indicator /kəʊˈɪnsɪd(ə)ns ˌɪndɪkeɪtə/ *noun* an indicator which coincides with economic activity (as opposed to leading indicators and lagging indicators)

co-insurance /ˌkəʊ ɪnˈʃʊərəns/ *noun* an insurance policy where the risk is shared among several insurers

COLA *abbreviation US* cost-of-living allowance

cold /kəʊld/ *adjective* without being prepared

'...the board is considering the introduction of a set of common provisions on unsolicited calls to investors. The board is aiming to permit the cold calling of customer agreements for the provision of services relating to listed securities. Cold calling would be allowed when the investor is not a private investor' [*Accountancy*]

cold call /ˌkəʊld ˈkɔːl/ *noun* a telephone call or sales visit where the salesperson has no appointment and the client is not an established customer ■ *verb* to make a cold call

cold caller /ˌkəʊld ˈkɔːlə/ *noun* a salesman who makes cold calls

cold calling /ˌkəʊld ˈkɔːlɪŋ/ *noun* the act of making cold calls on potential customers

cold start /ˌkəʊld ˈstɑːt/ *noun* the act of beginning a new business or opening a new shop with no previous turnover to base it on

collapse /kəˈlæps/ *noun* **1.** a sudden fall in price ○ *the collapse of the market in silver* ○ *the collapse of the dollar on the foreign exchange markets* **2.** a sudden failure ○ *the collapse of the pay negotiations* ○ *Investors lost thousands of pounds in the collapse of the company.* ■ *verb* **1.** to fall suddenly ○ *The market in silver collapsed.* ○ *The yen collapsed on the foreign exchange markets.* **2.** to fail suddenly ○ *The company collapsed with £250,000 in debts.* ○ *Talks between management and unions collapsed last night.*

collar /ˈkɒlə/ *noun* purchasing fixed minimum and maximum rates ('floors' and 'caps') of interest, dividends or repayments at the same time

COMMENT: If a company has money in variable rate investments and wants to protect its income, it will buy a floor; instead of paying the premium for this purchase it will simultaneously sell a cap, so effectively creating a 'collar' round its investments.

collateral /kəˈlæt(ə)rəl/ *adjective* used to provide a guarantee for a loan ■ *noun* a security, such as negotiable instruments, shares or goods, used to provide a guarantee for a loan

'...examiners have come to inspect the collateral that thrifts may use in borrowing from the Fed' [*Wall Street Journal*]

collateralise /kəˈlæt(ə)rəlaɪz/, **collateralize** *verb* to secure a debt by means of a collateral

collateral loan /kəˈlæt(ə)rəl ləʊn/ *noun* a loan secured on assets

collect /kəˈlekt/ *verb* **1.** to get money which is owed to you by making the person who owes it pay □ **to collect a debt** to go and make someone pay a debt **2.** to take things away from a place ○ *We have to collect the stock from the warehouse.* ■ *adverb, adjective* used to describe a phone call which the person receiving the call agrees to pay for

collectables /kəˈlektɪb(ə)lz/ *plural noun* items which people collect, e.g. stamps, playing cards, or matchboxes

collecting agency /kəˈlektɪŋ ˌeɪdʒənsi/ *noun* an agency which collects money owed to other companies for a commission

collecting bank /kəˈlektɪŋ bæŋk/ *noun* a bank into which a person has deposited a cheque, and which has the duty to collect the money from the account of the writer of the cheque

collection /kə'lekʃən/ *noun* **1.** the act of getting money together, or of making someone pay money which is owed ○ *tax collection* or *collection of tax* □ **bills for collection** bills where payment is due **2.** the fetching of goods ○ *The stock is in the warehouse awaiting collection.* □ **to hand something in for collection** to leave something for someone to come and collect

collection charge /kə'lekʃən ˌtʃɑːdʒɪz/, **collection rate** /kə'lekʃən reɪt/ *noun* a charge for collecting something

collections /kə'lekʃənz/ *plural noun* money which has been collected

collective investment /kə,lektɪv ɪn'vestmənt/ *noun* the practice of investing money with other individuals or organisations in order to share costs and risk

collector /kə'lektə/ *noun* a person who makes people pay money which is owed ○ *He works as a debt collector.*

colon /'kəʊlɒn/ *noun* a unit of currency used in Costa Rica and El Salvador

column /'kɒləm/ *noun* a series of numbers arranged one underneath the other ○ *to add up a column of figures* ○ *Put the total at the bottom of the column.*

combine /'kɒmbaɪn/ *noun* a large financial or commercial group ○ *a German industrial combine*

COMECON /'kɒmikɒn/ *noun* formerly, an economic alliance of countries in Eastern Europe, including Bulgaria, Czechoslovakia, Hungary, Poland, Romania and the USSR, and also including Cuba, Vietnam and Mongolia. Full form **Council for Mutual Economic Assistance**

COMEX *abbreviation* New York Commodity Exchange

COMIT index *noun* the index of prices on the Milan Stock Exchange

command economy /kə,mɑːnd ɪ'kɒnəmi/ *noun* same as **planned economy**

commerce /'kɒmɜːs/ *noun* the buying and selling of goods and services

commercial /kə'mɜːʃ(ə)l/ *adjective* **1.** referring to business **2.** profitable □ **not a**

commercial proposition not likely to make a profit

commercial aircraft /kə,mɜːʃ(ə)l 'eəkrɑːft/ *noun* an aircraft used to carry cargo or passengers for payment

commercial attaché /kə'mɜːʃ(ə)l ə,tæʃeɪ/ *noun* a diplomat whose job is to promote the commercial interests of his or her country

commercial bank /kə'mɜːʃ(ə)l bæŋk/ *noun* a bank which offers banking services to the public, as opposed to a merchant bank

commercial bill /kə,mɜːʃ(ə)l 'bɪl/ *noun* a bill of exchange issued by a company (a **trade bill**) or accepted by a bank (a **bank bill**), as opposed to a **Treasury bill**, which is issued by the government

commercial directory /kə'mɜːʃ(ə)l daɪ,rekt(ə)ri/ *noun* a book which lists all the businesses and business people in a town

commercial district /kə'mɜːʃ(ə)l ,dɪstrɪkt/ *noun* the part of a town where offices and shops are located

commercial failure /kə,mɜːʃ(ə)l 'feɪljə/ *noun* financial collapse or bankruptcy

commercialisation /kə,mɜːʃ(ə)laɪ 'zeɪʃ(ə)n/, **commercialization** *noun* the act of making something into a business run for profit ○ *the commercialisation of museums*

commercialise /kə'mɜːʃəlaɪz/, **commercialize** *verb* to make something into a business ○ *The holiday town has become unpleasantly commercialised.*

commercial law /kə,mɜːʃ(ə)l 'lɔː/ *noun* the laws regarding the conduct of businesses

commercial lawyer /kə,mɜːʃ(ə)l 'lɔːjə/ *noun* a person who specialises in company law or who advises companies on legal problems

commercially /kə'mɜːʃ(ə)li/ *adverb* **1.** for the purpose of making a profit □ **not commercially viable** not likely to make a profit **2.** in the operation of a business

commercial mortgage /kə,mɜːʃ(ə)l 'mɔːgɪdʒ/ *noun* a mortgage on commercial property, such as offices, shops and factories

commercial mortgage-backed securities /kə,mɜːʃ(ə)l ,mɔːɡɪdʒ bækt sɪ'kjʊərɪtiz/ *plural noun* shares which are backed by the security of a commercial mortgage. Abbreviation **CMBS**

commercial paper /kə,mɜːʃ(ə)l 'peɪpə/ *noun* an IOU issued by a company to raise a short-term loan. Abbreviation **CP**

commercial port /kə,mɜːʃ(ə)l 'pɔːt/ *noun* a port which has only goods traffic and no passengers

commercial property /kə,mɜːʃ(ə)l 'prɒpəti/ *noun* a building, or buildings, used as offices or shops

commercial value /kə,mɜːʃ(ə)l 'væljuː/ *noun* the value that a thing would have if it were offered for sale □ **'sample only – of no commercial value'** these goods are intended only as a sample and would not be worth anything if sold

commingling /kə'mɪŋɡlɪŋ/ *noun US* the action of mixing financial information from different sources so that no single source can be identified, as when the difference between personal financial information and company financial information is blurred

commission /kə'mɪʃ(ə)n/ *noun* **1.** money paid to a salesperson or agent, usually a percentage of the sales made ○ *She gets 10% commission on everything she sells.* ○ *He is paid on a commission basis.* □ **he charges 10% commission** he asks for 10% of sales as his payment **2.** a group of people officially appointed to examine some problem ○ *He is the chairman of the government commission on export subsidies.* ○ *The government has appointed a commission of inquiry to look into the problems of small exporters.*

commission agent /kə'mɪʃ(ə)n ,eɪdʒənt/ *noun* an agent who is paid a percentage of sales

commission broker /kə'mɪʃ(ə)n ,brəʊkə/ *noun* a stockbroker who works for a commission

Commission des Opérations de Bourse *noun* the body which supervises the French Stock Exchanges (the equivalent of the British SIB or the American SEC). Abbreviation **COB**

commissioner /kə'mɪʃ(ə)nə/ *noun* an important official appointed by a government or other authority, or a member of a commission

Commissioner of Inland Revenue /kə,mɪʃ(ə)nə əv ,ɪnlənd 'revənjuː/ *noun* formerly, a person appointed officially to supervise the collection of taxes, including income tax, capital gains tax and corporation tax, but not VAT. ◊ **Special Commissioner**

commission house /kə'mɪʃ(ə)n haʊs/ *noun* a firm which buys or sells for clients, and charges a commission for this service

Commission of the European Community /kə,mɪʃ(ə)n əv ðiː ,jʊərəpiːən kə'mjuːnɪti/ *noun* same as **European Commission**

commission rep /kə'mɪʃ(ə)n rep/ *noun* a representative who is not paid a salary but receives a commission on sales

commission sale /kə'mɪʃ(ə)n seɪl/ *noun* a sale where the salesperson is paid a commission

commit /kə'mɪt/ *verb* □ **to commit yourself to** to guarantee something, especially a loan issue, or to guarantee to do something

commitment /kə'mɪtmənt/ *noun* an agreement by an underwriting syndicate to underwrite a Note Issuance Facility

commitment fee /kə'mɪtmənt fiː/ *noun* a fee paid to a bank which has arranged a line of credit which has not been fully used

commodity /kə'mɒdɪti/ *noun* something sold in very large quantities, especially a raw material such as a metal or a food such as wheat

COMMENT: Commodities are either traded for immediate delivery (as 'actuals' or 'physicals'), or for delivery in the future (as 'futures'). Commodity markets deal either in metals (aluminium, copper, lead, nickel, silver and zinc) or in 'soft' items, such as cocoa, coffee, sugar and oil.

commodity exchange /kə'mɒdɪti ɪks,tʃeɪndʒ/ *noun* a place where commodities are bought and sold

commodity futures /kə,mɒdɪti 'fjuːtʃəz/ *plural noun* commodities traded for delivery at a later date ○ *Silver rose 5% on the commodity futures market yesterday.*

commodity market /kə'mɒdɪti ˌmɑːkɪt/ *noun* a place where people buy and sell commodities

commodity trader /kə'mɒdɪti ˌtreɪdə/ *noun* a person whose business is buying and selling commodities

common /'kɒmən/ *adjective* belonging to several different people or to everyone

common carrier /ˌkɒmən 'kæriə/ *noun* a firm which carries goods or passengers, and which anyone can use

common dividend /ˌkɒmən 'dɪvɪdend/ *noun* a dividend payable on common stock

common equity /ˌkɒmən 'ekwɪti/ *noun* ordinary shares in a company

common law /ˌkɒmən 'lɔː/ *noun* a law as laid down in decisions of courts, rather than by statute

common ownership /ˌkɒmən 'əʊnəʃɪp/ *noun* a situation where a business is owned by the employees who work in it

common pricing /ˌkɒmən 'praɪsɪŋ/ *noun* the illegal fixing of prices by several businesses so that they all charge the same price

common seal /ˌkɒmən 'siːl/, **company's seal** /ˌkʌmp(ə)niz 'siːl/ *noun* a metal stamp for stamping documents with the name of the company to show that they have been approved officially ○ *to attach the company's seal to a document*

common stock /ˌkɒmən 'stɒk/ *noun* US same as **ordinary shares**

Communauté française africaine full form of **CFA**

Communauté française pacifique full form of **CFP**

commutation factors /ˌkɒmjʊ 'teɪʃ(ə)n ˌfæktəz/ *plural noun* factors used to calculate the amount of pension to be given up in exchange for a lump sum

commute /kə'mjuːt/ *verb* 1. to travel to work from home each day ○ *He commutes from the country to his office in the centre of town.* ○ *She spends two hours a day commuting to and from work.* ○ *We have bought a house within commuting distance of London.* 2. to change a right into cash

'Commuting is never business use. A trip to work is personal and not deductible.

And making a business phone call or holding a business meeting in your car while you drive will not change that fact' [*Nation's Business*]

Companies Act /'kʌmp(ə)niz ækt/ *noun* an Act of Parliament which regulates the workings of companies, stating the legal limits within which companies may do their business

Companies Registration Office /ˌkʌmp(ə)niz ˌredʒɪ'streɪʃ(ə)n ˌɒfɪs/ *noun* an office of the Registrar of Companies, the official organisation where the records of companies must be deposited, so that they can be inspected by the public. Abbreviation **CRO**. Also called **Companies House**

company /'kʌmp(ə)ni/ *noun* a business organisation, a group of people organised to buy, sell, or provide a service, usually for profit □ **to put a company into liquidation** to close a company by selling its assets for cash □ **to set up a company** to start a company legally

COMMENT: A company can be incorporated (with memorandum and articles of association) as a private limited company, and adds the initials 'Ltd' after its name, or as a public limited company, when its name must end in 'Plc'. Unincorporated companies are partnerships such as firms of solicitors, architects, accountants, etc., and they add the initials 'Co'. after their name.

company car /ˌkʌmp(ə)ni 'kɑː/ *noun* a car which belongs to a company and is lent to an employee to use for business or other purposes

company director /ˌkʌmp(ə)ni daɪ 'rektə/ *noun* a person appointed by the shareholders to help run a company

company doctor /ˌkʌmp(ə)ni 'dɒktə/ *noun* 1. a doctor who works for a company and looks after sick workers ○ *The staff are all sent to see the company doctor once a year.* 2. a specialist businessperson who rescues businesses which are in difficulties

company law /ˌkʌmp(ə)ni 'lɔː/ *noun* laws which refer to the way companies work

company pension scheme /ˌkʌmp(ə)ni 'penʃən skiːm/ *noun* same as **occupational pension scheme** ○ *She decided to join the company's pension scheme.*

company promoter /ˌkʌmp(ə)ni prə
'məʊtə/ *noun* a person who organises the
setting up of a new company

company registrar /ˌkʌmp(ə)ni
'redʒɪstrɑː/ *noun* the person who keeps
the share register of a company

company reserves /ˌkʌmp(ə)ni rɪ
'zɜːvz/ *plural noun* same as **revenue
reserves**

company secretary /ˌkʌmp(ə)ni
'sekrɪt(ə)ri/ *noun* a person who is
responsible for a company's legal and
financial affairs

comparable /'kɒmp(ə)rəb(ə)l/ *adjective* possible to compare ○ *The two sets of
figures are not comparable.* □ **which is
the nearest company comparable to
this one in size?** which company is most
similar in size to this one? □ **on a compa-
rable-store basis** when comparing
similar stores belonging to different
companies

compare with /kəm'peə wɪð/ *phrasal
verb* to examine two things to see where
they are the same and where they differ
○ *How do the sales this year compare
with last year's?* ○ *Compared with the
previous month, last month was terrific.*

compensate /'kɒmpənseɪt/ *verb* to
give someone money to make up for a
loss or injury ○ *In this case we will
compensate a manager for loss of
commission.* ○ *The company will
compensate the employee for the burns
suffered in the accident.* (NOTE: You
compensate someone **for** something.)

compensating balance
/ˌkɒmpənseɪtɪŋ 'bæləns/ *noun* the
amount of money which a customer has to
keep in a bank account in order to get free
services from the bank

compensation /ˌkɒmpən'seɪʃ(ə)n/
noun **1.** □ **compensation for damage**
payment for damage done □ **compensation for loss of office** payment to a
director who is asked to leave a company
before their contract ends □ **compensation for loss of earnings** payment to
someone who has stopped earning money
or who is not able to earn money **2.** *US* a
salary

'…compensation can also be via the
magistrates courts for relatively minor
injuries' [*Personnel Management*]

compensation deal /ˌkɒmpən
'seɪʃ(ə)n diːl/ *noun* a deal where an
exporter is paid (at least in part) in goods
from the country to which he or she is
exporting

compensation fund /ˌkɒmpən
'seɪʃ(ə)n fʌnd/ *noun* a fund operated by
the stock exchange to compensate investors for losses suffered when members of
the stock exchange default

compensation package /ˌkɒmpən
'seɪʃ(ə)n ˌpækɪdʒ/ *noun* the salary,
pension and other benefits offered with a
job

'…golden parachutes are liberal compensation packages given to executives
leaving a company' [*Publishers Weekly*]

compensatory /ˌkɒmpən'seɪt(ə)ri/
adjective which compensates for something

compensatory financing
/ˌkɒmpənseɪt(ə)ri 'faɪnænsɪŋ/ *noun*
finance from the IMF to help a country in
difficulty

compete /kəm'piːt/ *verb* □ **to compete
with someone** *or* **with a company** to try
to do better than another person or
another company ○ *We have to compete
with cheap imports from the Far East.* ○
*They were competing unsuccessfully with
local companies on their home territory.*
□ **the two companies are competing for
a market share** *or* **for a contract** each
company is trying to win a larger part of
the market, trying to win the contract

competence framework
/'kɒmpɪt(ə)ns ˌfreɪmwɜːk/ *noun* the set
of duties or tasks performed as part of a
job with the standards which should be
achieved in these duties

competing /kəm'piːtɪŋ/ *adjective*
which competes □ **competing firms**
firms which compete with each other □
competing products products from
different companies which have the same
use and are sold in the same markets at
similar prices

competition /ˌkɒmpə'tɪʃ(ə)n/ *noun* **1.**
a situation where companies or individuals are trying to do better than others,
e.g. trying to win a larger share of the
market, or to produce a better or cheaper
product or to control the use of resources
□ **keen competition** strong competition
○ *We are facing keen competition from*

European manufacturers. **2.** □ **the competition** companies which are trying to compete with your product (*singular, but can take a plural verb in this sense*) ○ *We have lowered our prices to beat the competition.* ○ *The competition have brought out a new range of products.*

'…profit margins in the industries most exposed to foreign competition are worse than usual' [*Sunday Times*]

'…competition is steadily increasing and could affect profit margins as the company tries to retain its market share' [*Citizen (Ottawa)*]

competition law /ˌkɒmpəˈtɪʃ(ə)n ˌlɔː/ *noun* a law that promotes or maintains market competition by regulating anti-competitive behaviour

competitive /kəmˈpetɪtɪv/ *adjective* **1.** involving competition **2.** intended to compete with others, usually by being cheaper or better □ **competitive price** a low price aimed to compete with a rival product □ **competitive product** a product made or priced to compete with existing products

'…the company blamed fiercely competitive market conditions in Europe for a £14m operating loss last year' [*Financial Times*]

competitive bid /kəmˌpetɪtɪv ˈbɪd/ *noun* a method of auctioning new securities, where various underwriters offer the stock at competing prices

competitive devaluation /kəm ˌpetɪtɪv ˌdiːvæljuˈeɪʃ(ə)n/ *noun* a devaluation of a currency to make a country's goods more competitive on the international markets

competitively /kəmˈpetɪtɪvli/ *adverb* □ **competitively priced** sold at a low price which competes with the price of similar products from other companies

competitiveness /kəmˈpetɪtɪvnəs/ *noun* the fact of being competitive

'…farmers are increasingly worried by the growing lack of competitiveness for their products on world markets' [*Australian Financial Review*]

competitive pricing /kəmˌpetɪtɪv ˈpraɪsɪŋ/ *noun* the practice of putting low prices on goods so as to compete with other products

competitive products /kəmˌpetɪtɪv ˈprɒdʌkts/ *plural noun* products made to compete with existing products

competitor /kəmˈpetɪtə/ *noun* a person or company that is competing with another ○ *Two German firms are our main competitors.*

'…sterling labour costs continue to rise between 3% and 5% a year faster than in most of our competitor countries' [*Sunday Times*]

complete /kəmˈpliːt/ *verb* to sign a contract for the sale of a property and to exchange it with the other party, so making it legal

completion /kəmˈpliːʃ(ə)n/ *noun* the act of finishing something □ **completion of a contract** the act of signing a contract for the sale of a property whereby the buyer pays and the seller transfers ownership to the buyer

completion date /kəmˈpliːʃ(ə)n deɪt/ *noun* a date when something will be finished

compliance /kəmˈplaɪəns/ *noun* agreement to do what is ordered

compliance department /kəm ˈplaɪəns dɪˌpɑːtmənt/ *noun* a department in a stockbroking firm which makes sure that the stock exchange rules are followed and that confidentiality is maintained in cases where the same firm represents rival clients

compliance officer /kəmˈplaɪəns ˌɒfɪsə/ *noun* an employee of a financial organisation whose job is to make sure that the organisation complies with the regulations governing its business

comply /kəmˈplaɪ/ *verb* to agree to do what is ordered (NOTE: **complies – complying – complied**) □ **to comply with a court order** to obey an order given by a court

composite /ˈkɒmpəzɪt/ *adjective* made up a various parts joined together

composite index /ˌkɒmpəzɪt ˈɪndeks/ *noun* an index made from various indices

composition /ˌkɒmpəˈzɪʃ(ə)n/ *noun* an agreement between a debtor and creditors, where the debtor settles a debt by repaying only part of it

compound /kəmˈpaʊnd/ *verb* **1.** to agree with creditors to settle a debt by paying part of what is owed **2.** to add to ○ *The interest is compounded daily.*

compounded /kəm'paʊndɪd/ *adjective* added together

compounded annual return /kəm ˌpaʊndɪd ˌænjuəl rɪ'tɜːn/ *noun* a net return on an investment, calculated after adding interest and deducting tax

compounded interest rate /kəm ˌpaʊndɪd 'ɪntrəst reɪt/ *noun* an interest rate showing the effect of adding the interest to the capital

compounding method /kəm 'paʊndɪŋ ˌmeθəd/ *noun* the method used when compounding interest (daily, monthly, quarterly or annually). Abbreviation **CM**

compound interest /ˌkɒmpaʊnd 'ɪntrəst/ *noun* interest which is added to the capital and then earns interest itself

comprehensive insurance /ˌkɒmprɪhensɪv ɪn'ʃʊərəns/, **comprehensive policy** /ˌkɒmprɪhensɪv 'pɒlɪsi/ *noun* an insurance policy which covers you against all risks which are likely to happen

compromise /'kɒmprəmaɪz/ *noun* an agreement between two sides, where each side gives way a little ○ *Management offered £5 an hour, the union asked for £9, and a compromise of £7.50 was reached.* ■ *verb* to reach an agreement by giving way a little ○ *She asked £15 for it, I offered £7 and we compromised on £10.*

comptroller /kən'trəʊlə/ *noun* a financial controller

Comptroller of the Currency /kən ˌtrəʊlə əv ðə 'kʌrənsi/ *noun* an official of the US government responsible for the regulation of US national banks (that is, banks which are members of the Federal Reserve)

compulsory /kəm'pʌlsəri/ *adjective* which is forced or ordered

compulsory liquidation /kəm ˌpʌlsəri ˌlɪkwɪ'deɪʃ(ə)n/ *noun* liquidation which is ordered by a court

compulsory purchase /kəmˌpʌlsəri 'pɜːtʃɪs/ *noun* the purchase of an annuity with the fund built up in a personal pension scheme

compulsory winding up /kəm ˌpʌlsəri ˌwaɪndɪŋ 'ʌp/ *noun* liquidation which is ordered by a court

computable /kəm'pjuːtəb(ə)l/ *adjective* possible to calculate

computation /ˌkɒmpjʊ'teɪʃ(ə)n/ *noun* a calculation

computational error /ˌkɒmpjʊteɪʃ(ə)nəl 'erə/ *noun* a mistake made in calculating

compute /kəm'pjuːt/ *verb* to calculate, to do calculations

computer /kəm'pjuːtə/ *noun* an electronic machine which calculates or stores information and processes it automatically

computerise /kəm'pjuːtəraɪz/, **computerize** *verb* to change something from a manual system to one using computers ○ *We have computerised all our records.* ○ *Stock control is now completely computerised.*

concealment of assets /kən ˌsiːlmənt əv 'æsets/ *noun* the act of hiding assets so that creditors do not know they exist

concentration /ˌkɒnsən'treɪʃ(ə)n/ *noun* **1.** the action of grouping a large number of things together. Also called **market concentration 2.** the action of a bank in lending too much to one single sector of the economy (NOTE: It is generally thought that banks should not make more than 10% of their loans to a single sector.)

concern /kən'sɜːn/ *noun* a business or company □ **sold as a going concern** sold as an actively trading company

concert /'kɒnsət/ *noun* □ **to act in concert** (*of several people*) to work together to achieve an aim. This is illegal if the aim is to influence a share price by all selling or buying together.

concert party /'kɒnsət ˌpɑːti/ *noun* an arrangement where several people or companies work together in secret, usually to acquire another company through a takeover bid

concession /kən'seʃ(ə)n/ *noun* **1.** the right to use someone else's property for business purposes **2.** the right to be the only seller of a product in a place ○ *She runs a jewellery concession in a department store.* **3.** an allowance, e.g. a reduction of tax or price

concessionaire /kənˌseʃə'neə/ *noun* a person or business that has the right to be the only seller of a product in a place

concessionary fare /kən,seʃ(ə)nəri ˈfeə/ *noun* a reduced fare for some types of passenger such as pensioners, students or employees of a transport company

conciliation /kən,sɪliˈeɪʃ(ə)n/ *noun* the practice of bringing together the parties in a dispute with an independent third party, so that the dispute can be settled through a series of negotiations

condition /kənˈdɪʃ(ə)n/ *noun* **1.** something which has to be carried out as part of a contract or which has to be agreed before a contract becomes valid □ **on condition that** provided that ○ *They were granted the lease on condition that they paid the legal costs.* **2.** a general state or the general way of life in a place ○ *item sold in good condition* ○ *The union has complained of the bad working conditions in the factory.* ○ *What was the condition of the car when it was sold?* ○ *Adverse trading conditions affected our profits.*

conditional /kənˈdɪʃ(ə)n(ə)l/ *adjective* provided that specific conditions are taken into account □ **to give a conditional acceptance** to accept, provided that specific things happen or that specific terms apply

conditionality /kən,dɪʃ(ə)ˈnælɪti/ *noun* the fact of having conditions attached

conditional offer /kən,dɪʃ(ə)nəl ˈɒfə/ *noun* an offer to buy provided that specific terms apply

conditions of employment /kən,dɪʃ(ə)nz əv ɪmˈplɔɪmənt/ *plural noun* the terms of a contract of employment

conditions of sale /kən,dɪʃ(ə)nz əv ˈseɪl/ *plural noun* special features that apply to a particular sale, e.g. discounts or credit terms

conference proceedings /ˈkɒnf(ə)rəns prə,siːdɪŋz/ *plural noun* a written report of what has taken place at a conference

confidential report /,kɒnfɪdenʃəl rɪˈpɔːt/ *noun* a secret document which must not be shown to other people

confirm /kənˈfɜːm/ *verb* **1.** to say again that something agreed before is correct ○ *to confirm a hotel reservation* or *a ticket* or *an agreement* or *a booking* ○ *They wrote to confirm the details of the contract.* **2.** to say that letters of credit

from foreign purchasers are agreed, and that the sellers will be paid for orders placed

confirmation /,kɒnfəˈmeɪʃən/ *noun* **1.** the act of writing to confirm the details of a transaction or agreement **2.** an agreement that orders from foreign purchasers will be paid

confiscation /,kɒnfɪsˈkeɪʃ(ə)n/ *noun* the act of taking away someone's possessions as a punishment

conflict of interest /,kɒnflɪkt əv ˈɪntrəst/ *noun* a situation where a person or firm may profit personally from decisions taken in an official capacity

conglomerate /kənˈglɒmərət/ *noun* a group of subsidiary companies linked together and forming a group, each making very different types of products

consensus /kənˈsensəs/ *noun* an opinion which most people agree on ○ *management by consensus* □ **the Wall Street consensus** the general opinion among analysts on Wall Street

consequential /,kɒnsɪˈkwenʃəl/ *adjective* which follows as a consequence

consequential loss /,kɒnsɪkwenʃəl ˈlɒs/ *noun* loss which occurs as the result of some other loss. Also called **indirect loss**

conservative /kənˈsɜːvətɪv/ *adjective* careful, not overestimating ○ *His forecast of expenditure was very conservative* or *She made a conservative forecast of expenditure.* □ **a conservative estimate** a calculation which probably underestimates the final figure ○ *Their turnover has risen by at least 20% in the last year, and that is probably a conservative estimate.*

'…we are calculating our next budget income at an oil price of $15 per barrel. We know it is a conservative projection, but we do not want to come in for a shock should prices dive at any time during the year' [*Lloyd's List*]

conservatively /kənˈsɜːvətɪvli/ *adverb* not overestimating ○ *The total sales are conservatively estimated at £2.3m.*

conservator /kənˈsɜːvətər/ *noun US* an official appointed by a court to manage a person's affairs

consider /kənˈsɪdə/ *verb* to think seriously about something □ **to consider the**

terms of a contract to examine a contract and discuss whether the terms are acceptable

consideration /kənˌsɪdəˈreɪʃ(ə)n/ noun **1.** serious thought ○ *We are giving consideration to moving the head office to Scotland.* **2.** something valuable exchanged as part of a contract

consign /kənˈsaɪn/ verb □ **to consign goods to someone** to send goods to someone for them to use or to sell for you

consignation /ˌkɒnsaɪˈneɪʃ(ə)n/ noun the act of consigning

consignee /ˌkɒnsaɪˈniː/ noun a person who receives goods from someone for their own use or to sell for the sender

consignment /kənˈsaɪnmənt/ noun **1.** the sending of goods to someone who will sell them for you □ **goods on consignment** goods kept for another company to be sold on their behalf for a commission **2.** a group of goods sent for sale ○ *A consignment of goods has arrived.* ○ *We are expecting a consignment of cars from Japan.*

'…some of the most prominent stores are gradually moving away from the traditional consignment system, under which manufacturers agree to repurchase any unsold goods, and in return dictate prices and sales strategies and even dispatch staff to sell the products' [*Nikkei Weekly*]

consignment note /kənˈsaɪnmənt nəʊt/ noun a note saying that goods have been sent

consignor /kənˈsaɪnə/ noun a person who consigns goods to someone

COMMENT: The goods remain the property of the consignor until the consignee sells or pays for them.

consolidate /kənˈsɒlɪdeɪt/ verb **1.** to include the accounts of several subsidiary companies as well as the holding company in a single set of accounts **2.** to group goods together for shipping **3.** to remain at the same level for some time, before moving up again

consolidated accounts /kənˌsɒlɪdeɪtɪd əˈkaʊnts/ plural noun accounts where the financial position of several different companies, i.e. a holding company and its subsidiaries, are recorded together

consolidated balance sheet /kənˌsɒlɪdeɪtɪd ˈbæləns ʃiːt/ noun the balance sheets of subsidiary companies grouped together into the balance sheet of the parent company. Also called **group balance sheet**

consolidated fund /kənˌsɒlɪdeɪtɪd ˈfʌnd/ noun money in the Exchequer which comes from tax revenues and is used to pay for government expenditure

consolidated profit and loss account /kənˌsɒlɪdeɪtɪd ˌprɒfɪt ən ˈlɒs əˌkaʊnt/ noun profit and loss accounts of the holding company and its subsidiary companies, grouped together into a single profit and loss account (NOTE: The US term is **profit and loss statement** or **income statement**.)

consolidated shipment /kənˌsɒlɪdeɪtɪd ˈʃɪpmənt/ noun a single shipment of goods from different companies grouped together

consolidated stock /kənˌsɒlɪdeɪtɪd ˈstɒk/ noun full form of **consols**

consolidation /kənˌsɒlɪˈdeɪʃ(ə)n/ noun **1.** the grouping together of goods for shipping **2.** the act of taking profits from speculative investments and investing them safely in blue-chip companies

consols /ˈkɒnsɒlz/ plural noun government bonds which pay interest but do not have a maturity date

consortium /kənˈsɔːtiəm/ noun a group of companies which work together ○ *A consortium of Canadian companies* or *A Canadian consortium has tendered for the job.* (NOTE: The plural is **consortia**.)

'…the consortium was one of only four bidders for the £2 billion contract to run the lines, seen as potentially the most difficult contract because of the need for huge investment' [*Times*]

constructive notice /kənˌstrʌktɪv ˈnəʊtɪs/ noun **1.** knowledge which the law says a person has of something (whether or not the person actually has it) because certain information is available to him if he makes reasonable inquiry **2.** *US* a printed notice published in a newspaper to inform the public that something has taken place

consular invoice /ˌkɒnsjʊlə ˈɪnvɔɪs/ noun an invoice stamped by a consul to show that goods being imported have correct documentation and are being shipped legally

consult /kən'sʌlt/ *verb* to ask an expert for advice ○ *We consulted our accountant about our tax.*

consultancy /kən'sʌltənsi/ *noun* the act of giving specialist advice ○ *a consultancy firm* ○ *She offers a consultancy service.*

consultant /kən'sʌltənt/ *noun* a specialist who gives advice ○ *an engineering consultant* ○ *a management consultant* ○ *a tax consultant*

consulting /kən'sʌltɪŋ/ *adjective* giving specialist advice ○ *a consulting engineer*

consulting actuary /kən,sʌltɪŋ 'æktjuəri/ *noun* an independent actuary who advises large pension funds

consumable goods /kən,sjuːməb(ə)l 'gʊdz/ *plural noun* goods which are bought by members of the public and not by companies. Also called **consumer goods**, **consumables**

consumer /kən'sjuːmə/ *noun* a person or company that buys and uses goods and services ○ *Gas consumers are protesting at the increase in prices.* ○ *The factory is a heavy consumer of water.*

consumer bank /kən,sjuːmə 'bæŋk/ *noun* same as **retail bank**

consumer council /kən,sjuːmə 'kaʊns(ə)l/ *noun* a group representing the interests of consumers

consumer credit /kən,sjuːmə 'kredɪt/ *noun* credit given by shops, banks and other financial institutions to consumers so that they can buy goods (NOTE: Lenders have to be licensed under the Consumer Credit Act, 1974.)

Consumer Credit Act, 1974 /kən,sjuːmə 'kredɪt ækt/ *noun* an Act of Parliament which licenses lenders, and requires them to state clearly the full terms of loans which they make, including the APR

Consumer Credit Counselling Service /kən,sjuːmə ,kredɪt 'kaʊnsəlɪŋ ,sɜːvɪs/ *noun* a service which advises people about problems with items bought on credit

consumer durables /kən,sjuːmə 'djʊərəb(ə)lz/ *plural noun* items which are bought and used by the public, e.g.

washing machines, refrigerators or cookers

consumer goods /kən,sjuːmə 'gʊdz/ *plural noun* same as **consumable goods**

consumer lease /kən,sjuːmə 'liːs/ *noun* a lease for the use or purchase of an item of equipment to be used in the home

consumer panel /kən'sjuːmə ,pæn(ə)l/ *noun* a group of consumers who report on products they have used so that the manufacturers can improve them or use what the panel says about them in advertising

Consumer Price Index /kən,sjuːmə 'praɪs ,ɪndeks/ *noun* a US index showing how prices of consumer goods have risen over a period of time, used as a way of measuring inflation and the cost of living. Abbreviation **CPI** (NOTE: The UK term is **retail price index**.)

'…analysis of the consumer price index for the first half of the year shows that the rate of inflation went down by about 12.9 per cent' [*Business Times (Lagos)*]

consumer protection /kən,sjuːmə prə'tekʃən/ *noun* the activity of protecting consumers against unfair or illegal traders

consumer research /kən,sjuːmə rɪ 'sɜːtʃ/ *noun* research into why consumers buy goods and what goods they may want to buy

consumer resistance /kən,sjuːmə rɪ'zɪstəns/ *noun* a lack of interest by consumers in buying a new product ○ *The new product met no consumer resistance even though the price was high.*

consumer society /kən,sjuːmə sə 'saɪəti/ *noun* a type of society where consumers are encouraged to buy goods

consumer spending /kən,sjuːmə 'spendɪŋ/ *noun* spending by private households on goods and services

'…companies selling in the UK market are worried about reduced consumer spending as a consequence of higher interest rates and inflation' [*Business*]

contango /kən'tæŋgəʊ/ *noun* **1.** the payment of interest by a stockbroker for permission to carry payment for shares from one account to the next (NOTE: Contango is no longer applied on the London Stock Exchange because of the rolling account system, but it is still applied on some other exchanges.) **2.** a cash price which is lower than the forward price

contango day /kən'tæŋɡəʊ deɪ/ *noun* formerly, the day when the rate of contango payments was fixed

contested takeover /kən,testɪd 'teɪkəʊvə/ *noun* a takeover bid where the board of the target company does not recommend it to the shareholders and tries to fight it. Also called **hostile bid**

contingency /kən'tɪndʒənsi/ *noun* a possible state of emergency when decisions will have to be taken quickly □ **to add on 10% to provide for contingencies** to provide for further expenditure which may be incurred

contingency fund /kən'tɪndʒənsi fʌnd/ *noun* money set aside in case it is needed urgently

contingency plan /kən'tɪndʒənsi plæn/ *noun* a plan which will be put into action if something unexpected happens

contingent expenses /kən,tɪndʒənt ɪk'spensɪz/ *plural noun* expenses which will be incurred only if something happens

contingent liability /kən,tɪndʒənt ,laɪə'bɪlɪti/ *noun* a liability which may or may not occur, but for which provision is made in a company's accounts, as opposed to 'provisions', where money is set aside for an anticipated expenditure

contingent policy /kən,tɪndʒənt 'pɒlɪsi/ *noun* an insurance policy which pays out only if something happens, such as if a person named in the policy dies before the person due to benefit

contingent reserves /kən,tɪndʒənt rɪ'zɜːvz/ *plural noun* money set aside to cover unexpected payments

continuous compounding /kən,tɪnjuəs kəm'paʊndɪŋ/ *noun* a system where interest is calculated all the time and added to the principal

contra /'kɒntrə/ *verb* □ **to contra an entry** to enter a similar amount in the opposite side of an account

contra account /'kɒntrə ə,kaʊnt/ *noun* an account which offsets another account, e.g. where a company's supplier is not only a creditor in that company's books but also a debtor because it has purchased goods on credit

contract *noun* /'kɒntrækt/ **1.** a legal agreement between two parties ○ *to draw up a contract* ○ *to draft a contract* ○ *to sign a contract* □ **the contract is binding on both parties** both parties signing the contract must do what is agreed □ **under contract** bound by the terms of a contract ○ *The firm is under contract to deliver the goods by November.* □ **to void a contract** to make a contract invalid **2.** □ **by private contract** by private legal agreement **3.** an agreement for the supply of a service or goods ○ *to enter into a contract to supply spare parts* ○ *to sign a contract for $10,000 worth of spare parts* □ **to put work out to contract** to decide that work should be done by another company on a contract, rather than by employing members of staff to do it □ **to award a contract to a company, to place a contract with a company** to decide that a company shall have the contract to do work for you □ **to tender for a contract** to put forward an estimate of cost for work under contract □ **the company is in breach of contract** the company has failed to do what was agreed in the contract **4.** (*stock exchange*) a deal to buy or sell shares, or an agreement to purchase options or futures ■ *verb* /kən'trækt/ to agree to do some work on the basis of a legally binding contract ○ *to contract to supply spare parts* or *to contract for the supply of spare parts* □ **the supply of spare parts was contracted out to Smith Ltd** Smith Ltd was given the contract for supplying spare parts □ **to contract out of an agreement** to withdraw from an agreement with the written permission of the other party

COMMENT: A contract is an agreement between two or more parties which creates legal obligations between them. Some contracts are made 'under seal', i.e. they are signed and sealed by the parties; most contracts are made orally or in writing. The essential elements of a contract are: (a) that an offer made by one party should be accepted by the other; (b) consideration (i.e. payment of money); (c) the intention to create legal relations. The terms of a contract may be express or implied. A breach of contract by one party entitles the other party to sue for damages or to ask for something to be done.

contracted in /kən,træktɪd 'ɪn/ *adjective* referring to a member of an occupational or personal pension scheme who is also a member of SERPS

contracted out /kən,træktɪd 'aʊt/ *adjective* referring to a member of an occupational or personal pension scheme who is not a member of SERPS

contract for deed /,kɒntrækt fə 'diːd/ *noun US* a written agreement showing the terms of the sale of a property, where the title is only transferred to the purchaser after he has made a stated number of monthly payments

contracting party /kən,træktɪŋ 'pɑːti/ *noun* a person or company that signs a contract

contractionary fiscal policy *noun* also called **deflationary fiscal policy**

contractionary monetary policy *noun* also called **deflationary monetary policy**

contract law /'kɒntrækt lɔː/ *noun* laws relating to private agreements

contract note /'kɒntrækt nəʊt/ *noun* a note showing that shares have been bought or sold but not yet paid for, also including the commission

contract of employment /,kɒntrækt əv ɪm'plɔɪmənt/ *noun* a contract between an employer and an employee stating all the conditions of work. Also called **employment contract**

contractor /kən'træktə/ *noun* a person or company that does work according to a written agreement

contractual /kən'træktʃʊəl/ *adjective* according to a contract ○ *contractual conditions*

contractual liability /kən,træktʃʊəl ,laɪə'bɪlɪti/ *noun* a legal responsibility for something as stated in a contract

contractually /kən'træktjuəli/ *adverb* according to a contract ○ *The company is contractually bound to pay our expenses.*

contractual obligation /kən,træktʃʊəl ,ɒblɪ'geɪʃ(ə)n/ *noun* something that a person is legally forced to do through having signed a contract to do ○ **to fulfil your contractual obligations** to do what you have agreed to do in a contract ○ **he is under no contractual obligation to buy** he has signed no agreement to buy

contractual savings /kən,træktʃʊəl 'seɪvɪŋs/ *plural noun* savings in the form of regular payments into long-term investments such as pension schemes

contract work /'kɒntrækt wɜːk/ *noun* work done according to a written agreement

contra entry /'kɒntrə ,entri/ *noun* an entry made in the opposite side of an account to make an earlier entry worthless, i.e. a debit against a credit

contrarian /kɒn'treəriən/ *adjective* going against a trend

contrarian research /kɒn,treəriən rɪ'sɜːtʃ/ *noun* research that shows you should buy shares against the current trend

contrarian stockpicking /kɒn,treəriən 'stɒkpɪkɪŋ/ *noun* choosing stocks and shares against the trend of the market

contribute /kən'trɪbjuːt/ *verb* to give money or add to money ○ *We agreed to contribute 10% of the profits.* ○ *They had contributed to the pension fund for 10 years.*

contribution /,kɒntrɪ'bjuːʃ(ə)n/ *noun* money paid to add to a sum

contribution of capital /kɒntrɪ,bjuːʃ(ə)n əv 'kæpɪt(ə)l/ *noun* money paid to a company as additional capital

contributor /kən'trɪbjʊtə/ *noun* a person who gives money

contributor of capital /kən,trɪbjʊtər əv 'kæpɪt(ə)l/ *noun* a person who contributes capital

contributory /kən'trɪbjʊt(ə)ri/ *adjective* causing or helping to cause ○ *Falling exchange rates have been a contributory factor in the company's loss of profits.*

control /kən'trəʊl/ *noun* **1.** the power or ability to direct something ○ *The company is under the control of three shareholders.* ○ *Top management exercises tight control over spending.* □ **to gain control of a business** to buy more than 50% of the shares so that you can direct the business **2.** the act of restricting or checking something or making sure that something is kept in check □ **under control** kept in check ○ *Expenses are kept under tight control.* ○ *The company is trying to bring its overheads back under control.* □ **out of control** not kept in check ○ *Costs have got out of control.*

■ *verb* **1.** □ **to control a company** to be able to direct the business of a company, because you own more than 50% of the shares ○ *The business is controlled by a company based in Luxembourg.* ○ *The company is controlled by the majority shareholder.* **2.** to make sure that something is kept in check or is not allowed to develop ○ *The government is fighting to control inflation* or *to control the rise in the cost of living.* (NOTE: **controlling – controlled**)

control key /kənˈtrəʊl kiː/ *noun* a key on a computer which works part of a program

controlled /kənˈtrəʊld/ *adjective* ruled or kept in check

controlled economy /kənˌtrəʊld ɪˈkɒnəmi/ *noun* an economy where most business activity is directed by orders from the government

controller /kənˈtrəʊlə/ *noun* **1.** a person who controls something, especially the finances of a company **2.** *US* the chief accountant in a company

controlling interest /kənˌtrəʊlɪŋ ˈɪntrəst/ *noun* □ **to have a controlling interest in a company** to own more than 50% of the shares so that you can direct how the company is run

convergence /kənˈvɜːdʒəns/ *noun* **1.** a situation where the economic factors applying in two countries move closer together, e.g. when basic interest rates, or budget deficits become more and more similar **2.** a situation where the price of a commodity on the futures market moves towards the spot price as settlement date approaches

conversion /kənˈvɜːʃ(ə)n/ *noun* **1.** a change **2.** the action of changing convertible loan stock into ordinary shares

conversion discount /kənˈvɜːʃ(ə)n ˌdɪskaʊnt/, **conversion premium** /kənˈvɜːʃ(ə)n ˌpriːmiəm/ *noun* the difference between the price of convertible stock and the ordinary shares into which they are to be converted (NOTE: If the convertible stock is cheaper, the difference is a **conversion premium**; if the stock is dearer, the difference is a **conversion discount**.)

conversion issue /kənˈvɜːʃ(ə)n ˌɪʃuː/ *noun* an issue of new bonds, or 'conversion bonds', timed to coincide

with the date of maturity of older bonds, with the intention of persuading investors to reinvest

conversion of funds /kənˌvɜːʃ(ə)n əv ˈfʌndz/ *noun* the act of using money which does not belong to you for a purpose for which it is not supposed to be used

conversion period /kənˈvɜːʃ(ə)n ˌpɪəriəd/ *noun* a time during which convertible loan stock may be changed into ordinary shares

conversion price /kənˈvɜːʃ(ə)n praɪs/, **conversion rate** /kənˈvɜːʃ(ə)n reɪt/ *noun* **1.** a price at which preference shares are converted into ordinary shares **2.** a rate at which a currency is changed into a foreign currency

conversion value /kənˈvɜːʃ(ə)n ˌvæljuː/ *noun* a value of convertible stock, including the extra value of the ordinary shares into which they may be converted

convert /kənˈvɜːt/ *verb* **1.** to change money of one country for money of another ○ *We converted our pounds into Swiss francs.* **2.** □ **to convert funds to your own use** to use someone else's money for yourself

convertibility /kənˌvɜːtəˈbɪləti/ *noun* the ability of a currency to be exchanged for another easily

convertible ARM /kənˌvɜːtəb(ə)l eɪ ɑːr ˈem/ *noun US* an adjustable rate mortgage that can converted to a fixed rate mortgage

convertible currency /kənˌvɜːtəb(ə)l ˈkʌrənsi/ *noun* a currency which can easily be exchanged for another

convertible debenture /kənˌvɜːtəb(ə)l dɪˈbentʃə/ *noun* a debenture or loan stock which can be exchanged for ordinary shares at a later date

convertible loan stock /kənˌvɜːtəb(ə)l ˈləʊn stɒk/ *noun* money lent to a company which can be converted into shares at a later date

convertibles /kənˈvɜːtəb(ə)lz/ *plural noun* corporate bonds or preference shares which can be converted into ordinary shares at a set price on set dates

conveyance /kənˈveɪəns/ *noun* a legal document which transfers a property from the seller to the buyer

conveyancer /kən'veɪənsə/ *noun* a person who draws up a conveyance

conveyancing /kən'veɪənsɪŋ/ *noun* the work of legally transferring a property from a seller to a buyer

COO *abbreviation* chief operating officer

cooling-off period /ˌkuːlɪŋ 'ɒf ˌpɪəriəd/ *noun* (*during an industrial dispute*) a period when negotiations have to be carried on and no action can be taken by either side

cooperative /kəʊ'ɒp(ə)rətɪv/ *adjective* used to describe a business in which the profits are shared among the workers

cooperative bank /kəʊ'ɒp(ə)rətɪv bæŋk/ *noun* a bank which is owned by its members, who deposit money or who borrow money as loans

cooperative society /kəʊ'ɒp(ə)rətɪv sə,saɪəti/ *noun* an organisation where customers and employees are partners and share the profits

copper /'kɒpə/ *noun* a metal which is traded on commodity exchanges such as the London Metal Exchange

coproperty /kəʊ'prɒpəti/ *noun* the ownership of property by two or more people together

coproprietor /ˌkəʊprə'praɪətə/ *noun* a person who owns a property with another person or several other people

copyright /'kɒpiraɪt/ *noun* a legal right which protects the creative work of writers and artists and prevents others from copying or using it without authorisation, and which also applies to such things as company logos and brand names

cordoba /'kɔːdəbə/ *noun* a unit of currency used in Nicaragua

corner /'kɔːnə/ *noun* **1.** a place where two streets or two walls join ○ *The Post Office is on the corner of the High Street and London Road.* **2.** a situation where one person or a group controls the supply of a certain commodity ○ *The syndicate tried to create a corner in the silver market.* ■ *verb* □ **to corner the market** to own most or all of the supply of a commodity and so control the price ○ *The syndicate tried to corner the market in silver.*

corp *abbreviation US* corporation

corporate /'kɔːp(ə)rət/ *adjective* **1.** referring to corporations or companies, or to a particular company as a whole **2.** referring to business in general ○ *corporate America* ○ *corporate Britain*

'…the prime rate is the rate at which banks lend to their top corporate borrowers' [*Wall Street Journal*]

'…if corporate forecasts are met, sales will exceed $50 million next year' [*Citizen (Ottawa)*]

corporate bond /'kɔːp(ə)rət bɒnd/ *noun* a loan stock officially issued by a company to raise capital, usually against the security of some of its assets (NOTE: The company promises to pay an amount of interest on a set date every year until the redemption date, when it repays the loan.)

corporate finance /ˌkɔːp(ə)rət 'faɪnæns/ *noun* the financial affairs of companies

corporate governance /ˌkɔːp(ə)rət 'gʌv(ə)nəns/ *noun* the way a company or other organisation is run, including the powers of the board of directors, audit committees, ethics, environmental impact, treatment of workers, directors' salaries and internal control

corporate image /ˌkɔːp(ə)rət 'ɪmɪdʒ/ *noun* an idea which a company would like the public to have of it

corporate loan /ˌkɔːp(ə)rət 'ləʊn/ *noun* a loan issued by a corporation

corporate name /ˌkɔːp(ə)rət 'neɪm/ *noun* the name of a large corporation

corporate plan /ˌkɔːp(ə)rət 'plæn/ *noun* a plan for the future work of a whole company

corporate planning /ˌkɔːp(ə)rət 'plænɪŋ/ *noun* **1.** the process of planning the future work of a whole company **2.** planning the future financial state of a group of companies

corporate profits /ˌkɔːp(ə)rət 'prɒfɪts/ *plural noun* the profits of a corporation

'…corporate profits for the first quarter showed a 4 per cent drop from last year' [*Financial Times*]

corporate raider /ˌkɔːp(ə)rət 'reɪdə/ *noun* a person or company which buys a stake in another company before making a hostile takeover bid

corporate resolution /ˌkɔːp(ə)rət ˌrezəˈluːʃ(ə)n/ *noun* a document signed by the officers of a corporation, naming those persons who can sign cheques, withdraw cash and have access to the corporation's bank account

corporate secretary /ˌkɔːp(ə)rət ˈsekrət(ə)ri/ *noun* a person responsible for the corporation's legal and financial affairs

corporate spinoffs /ˌkɔːp(ə)rət ˈspɪnɒfs/ *plural noun* small companies which have been split off from larger organisations

corporate taxpayers /ˌkɔːp(ə)rət ˈtækspeɪəz/ *plural noun* companies that pay tax

corporation /ˌkɔːpəˈreɪʃ(ə)n/ *noun* **1.** a large company **2.** *US* a company which is incorporated in the US **3.** a municipal authority

COMMENT: A corporation is formed by registration with the Registrar of Companies under the Companies Act (in the case of public and private companies) or other Acts of Parliament (in the case of building societies and charities).

corporation income tax /ˌkɔːpəreɪʃ(ə)n ˈɪnkʌm tæks/ *noun* a tax on profits made by incorporated companies

corporation loan /ˌkɔːpəˈreɪʃ(ə)n ləʊn/ *noun* a loan issued by a local authority

corporation tax /ˌkɔːpəˈreɪʃ(ə)n tæks/ *noun* a tax on profits and capital gains made by companies, calculated before dividends are paid. Abbreviation **CT**

correction /kəˈrekʃ(ə)n/ *noun* **1.** an act of making something correct ○ *She made some corrections to the text of the speech.* **2.** a change in the valuation of something that is thought to be overvalued or undervalued which results in its being more realistically valued

'…there were fears in October that shares were overvalued and bears were ready to enter the market. This only proved to be a small correction' [*Investors Chronicle*]

correspondent bank /ˌkɒrɪˈspɒndənt bæŋk/ *noun* a bank which acts as an agent for a foreign bank

cost /kɒst/ *noun* **1.** the amount of money paid to acquire, produce or main-

tain something, e.g. the money paid for materials, labour and overheads in the manufacture of a product produced and sold by a business ○ *What is the cost of a first class ticket to New York?* ○ *Computer costs are falling each year.* ○ *We cannot afford the cost of two cars.* □ **to cover costs** to produce enough money in sales to pay for the costs of production ○ *The sales revenue barely covers the costs of advertising* or *the advertising costs.* □ **to sell at cost** to sell at a price which is the same as the cost of manufacture or the wholesale cost **2.** □ **cost of borrowing** Same as **borrowing costs** ■ *verb* **1.** to have as its price ○ *How much does the machine cost?* ○ *This cloth costs $10 a metre.* (NOTE: **costing – cost**) **2.** to cause money to be spent or lost (NOTE: **costing – cost**) **3.** to determine the cost of something (NOTE: **costing – cost**) □ **to cost a product** to calculate how much money will be needed to make a product, and so work out its selling price

cost, insurance, and freight /ˌkɒst ɪnˌʃʊərəns ən ˈfreɪt/ *noun* the estimate of a price, which includes the cost of the goods, the insurance, and the transport charges. Abbreviation **CIF, c.i.f.**

cost accountant /ˈkɒst əˌkaʊntənt/ *noun* an accountant who gives managers information about their business costs

cost accounting /ˈkɒst əˌkaʊntɪŋ/ *noun* the process of preparing special accounts of manufacturing and sales costs

cost analysis /ˈkɒst əˌnæləsɪs/ *noun* the process of calculating in advance what a new product will cost

cost-benefit analysis /ˌkɒst ˈbenɪfɪt əˌnæləsɪs/ *noun* **1.** the process of comparing the costs and benefits of various possible ways of using available resources. Also called **benefit-cost analysis 2.** the process of weighing the total expected costs against the total expected benefits of a project or proposal in order to choose the most profitable option ○ *The research was used in a cost-benefit analysis to see if the project was viable.* ◊ **cost-benefit ratio 3.** an informal approach to making economic decisions of any kind

cost-benefit ratio /ˌkɒst ˈbenəfɪt ˌreɪʃiəʊ/ *noun* an indicator that attempts to summarise the overall value for money of a project or proposal

cost centre /ˈkɒst ˌsentə/ *noun* **1.** a person or group whose costs can be itemised and to which costs can be allocated in accounts **2.** a unit, a process or an individual that provides a service needed by another part of an organisation and whose cost is therefore accepted as an overhead of the business

cost-cutting /ˈkɒst ˌkʌtɪŋ/ *adjective* intended to reduce costs ○ *We have taken out the second telephone line as a cost-cutting exercise.* ■ *noun* the process of reducing costs ○ *As a result of cost-cutting, we have had to make three staff redundant.*

cost-effective /ˌkɒstɪ ˈfektɪv/ *adjective* giving good value when compared with the original cost ○ *We find advertising in the Sunday newspapers very cost-effective.*

cost-effectiveness /ˌkɒst ɪ ˈfektɪvnəs/, **cost efficiency** /ˌkɒst ɪ ˈfɪʃənsi/ *noun* the quality of being cost-effective ○ *Can we calculate the cost-effectiveness of air freight against shipping by sea?*

cost factor /ˈkɒst ˌfæktə/ *noun* any activity or item of material, equipment or personnel that incurs a cost

cost-income ratio /ˌkɒst ˈɪnkʌm ˌreɪʃiəʊ/ *noun* a ratio between the costs involved in running a business and the income the business produces

cost inflation /kɒst ɪnˈfleɪʃ(ə)n/ *noun* same as **cost-push inflation**

costing /ˈkɒstɪŋ/ *noun* a calculation of the manufacturing costs, and so the selling price, of a product ○ *The costings give us a retail price of $2.95.* ○ *We cannot do the costing until we have details of all the production expenditure.*

costly /ˈkɒstli/ *adjective* costing a lot of money, or costing too much money ○ *Defending the court case was a costly process.* ○ *The mistakes were time-consuming and costly.*

cost of capital /ˌkɒst əv ˈkæpɪt(ə)l/ *noun* interest paid on the capital used in operating a business

cost of goods sold /ˌkɒst əv ˌɡʊdz ˈsəʊld/ *noun* same as **cost of sales**

cost of living /ˌkɒst əv ˈlɪvɪŋ/ *noun* money which has to be paid for basic items such as food, heating or rent ○ *to allow for the cost of living in the salary adjustments*

cost-of-living allowance /ˌkɒst əv ˈlɪvɪŋ əˌlaʊəns/ *noun* an addition to normal salary to cover increases in the cost of living

cost-of-living bonus /ˌkɒst əv ˈlɪvɪŋ ˌbəʊnəs/ *noun* money paid to meet an increase in the cost of living

cost-of-living increase /ˌkɒst əv ˈlɪvɪŋ ˌɪnkriːs/ *noun* an increase in salary to allow it to keep up with the increased cost of living

cost-of-living index /ˌkɒst əv ˈlɪvɪŋ ˌɪndeks/ *noun* a way of measuring the cost of living which is shown as a percentage increase on the figure for the previous year. It is similar to the consumer price index, but includes other items such as the interest on mortgages.

cost of sales /ˌkɒst əv ˈseɪlz/ *noun* all the costs of a product sold, including manufacturing costs and the staff costs of the production department, before general overheads are calculated. Also called **cost of goods sold**

cost plus /ˌkɒst ˈplʌs/ *noun* a system of calculating a price, by taking the cost of production of goods or services and adding a percentage to cover the supplier's overheads and margin ○ *We are charging for the work on a cost plus basis.*

cost price /ˈkɒst praɪs/ *noun* a selling price that is the same as the price paid by the seller, which results in no profit being made

cost-push inflation /ˌkɒst ˈpʊʃ ɪn ˌfleɪʃ(ə)n/ *noun* inflation caused by increased wage demands and increased raw materials costs, which lead to higher prices, which in turn lead to further wage demands. Also called **cost inflation**

costs /kɒsts/ *plural noun* the expenses involved in a court case ○ *The judge awarded costs to the defendant.* ○ *Costs of the case will be borne by the prosecution.* □ **to pay costs** to pay the expenses of a court case

council /ˈkaʊnsəl/ *noun* an official group chosen to run something or to advise on a problem

Council of Mortgage Lenders /ˌkaʊnsəl əv ˈmɔːɡɪdʒ ˌlendəz/ *noun* an organisation which represents companies which provide mortgage lending to the residential market

counselling /'kaʊnsəlɪŋ/ *noun* the act of giving professional advice to others on personal matters ○ *An office is being set up for counselling employees who have professional or social problems.* ○ *Counselling helps employees get accustomed to their new environment, by offering advice and guidance.* (NOTE: The US spelling is **counseling**.)

count /kaʊnt/ *verb* **1.** to add figures together to make a total ○ *She counted up the sales for the six months to December.* **2.** to include something ○ *Did you count my trip to New York as part of my sales expenses?*

count on *phrasal verb* to expect something to happen or to be given to you ○ *They are counting on getting a good response from the TV advertising.* ○ *Do not count on a bank loan to start your business.*

counter- /kaʊntə/ *prefix* against

counterbid /'kaʊntəbɪd/ *noun* a higher bid in reply to a previous bid ○ *When I bid $20 she put in a counterbid of $25.*

counter-claim /'kaʊntə kleɪm/ *noun* a claim for damages made in reply to a previous claim ○ *Jones claimed £25,000 in damages against Smith, and Smith entered a counter-claim of £50,000 for loss of office.* ■ *verb* to put in a counter-claim for something ○ *Jones claimed £25,000 in damages and Smith counter-claimed £50,000 for loss of office.*

counterfeit /'kaʊntəfɪt/ *adjective* referring to false or imitation money ○ *Shops in the area have been asked to look out for counterfeit £20 notes.* ■ *verb* to make imitation money

counterfoil /'kaʊntəfɔɪl/ *noun* a slip of paper kept after writing a cheque, an invoice or a receipt, as a record of the deal which has taken place

countermand /ˌkaʊntə'mɑːnd/ *verb* to say that an order must not be carried out ○ *to countermand an order*

counter-offer /'kaʊntər ˌɒfə/ *noun* a higher or lower offer made in reply to another offer ○ *Smith Ltd made an offer of $1m for the property, and Blacks replied with a counter-offer of $1.4m.*

'…the company set about paring costs and improving the design of its product. It came up with a price cut of 14%, but its counter-offer – for an order that was to have provided 8% of its workload next year – was too late and too expensive' [*Wall Street Journal*]

counterparty /'kaʊntəpɑːti/ *noun* each of the other parties to a contract, considered from the viewpoint of a particular party

counterpurchase /'kaʊntəpɜːtʃɪs/ *noun* an international trading deal, where a company agrees to use money received on a sale to purchase goods in the country where the sale was made

countersign /'kaʊntəsaɪn/ *verb* to sign a document which has already been signed by someone else ○ *All our cheques have to be countersigned by the finance director.* ○ *The sales director countersigns all my orders.*

countertrade /'kaʊntətreɪd/ *noun* a trade which does not involve payment of money, but something such as a barter or a buy-back deal instead

countervailing duty /'kaʊntəveɪlɪŋ ˌdjuːti/ *noun* a duty imposed by a country on imported goods, where the price of the goods includes a subsidy from the government in the country of origin. Also called **anti-dumping duty**

counting house /'kaʊntɪŋ haʊs/ *noun* a department dealing with cash (*dated*)

country bank /ˌkʌntri 'bæŋk/ *noun* US a bank based in a town which has no office of the Federal Reserve

country broker /ˌkʌntri 'brəʊkə/ *noun* a broking firm which is not based in London (NOTE: Country brokers are often independently run and charge lower commission than larger London firms.)

coupon /'kuːpɒn/ *noun* **1.** a piece of paper used in place of money **2.** a piece of paper which replaces an order form **3.** a slip of paper attached to a government bond certificate which can be cashed to provide the annual interest

coupon rate /'kuːpɒn reɪt/ *noun* the percentage fixed interest rate on a government bond or a debenture

coupon security /'kuːpɒn sɪˌkjʊərɪti/ *noun* a government security which carries a coupon and pays interest, as opposed to one which pays no interest but is sold at a discount to its face value

covenant /ˈkʌvənənt/ *noun* a legal contract ■ *verb* to agree to pay annually a specified sum of money to a person or organisation by contract. When payments are made under covenant to a charity, the charity can reclaim the tax paid by the donee. ○ *to covenant to pay £10 per annum*

cover /ˈkʌvə/ *noun* **1.** the proportion of a target audience reached by advertising **2.** the protection guaranteed by insurance □ **to operate without adequate cover** to operate without being protected by enough insurance □ **to ask for additional cover** to ask the insurance company to increase the amount for which you are insured **3.** an amount of money large enough to guarantee that something can be paid for ○ *Do you have sufficient cover for this loan?* ■ *verb* **1.** to provide protection by insurance against something ○ *The insurance covers fire, theft and loss of work.* □ **the damage was covered by the insurance** the damage was of a kind that the insurance policy protects against or the insurance company paid enough money to enable the damage to be repaired □ **to be fully covered** to have insurance against all risks **2.** to have, earn or provide enough money to pay for something ○ *We do not make enough sales to cover the expense of running the shop.* ○ *Breakeven point is reached when sales cover all costs.* □ **to cover a position** to have enough money to be able to pay for a forward purchase **3.** to ask for security against a loan which you are making

'…three export credit agencies have agreed to provide cover for large projects in Nigeria' [*Business Times (Lagos)*]

coverage /ˈkʌv(ə)rɪdʒ/ *noun* *US* protection guaranteed by insurance ○ *Do you have coverage against fire damage?*

covered bear /ˌkʌvəd ˈbeə/ *noun* a bear who holds the stock which he or she is selling

covering letter /ˌkʌvərɪŋ ˈletə/, **covering note** /ˌkʌvərɪŋ ˈnəʊt/ *noun* a letter sent with documents to say why they are being sent

cover note /ˈkʌvə nəʊt/ *noun* a letter from an insurance company giving details

of an insurance policy and confirming that the policy exists

CP *abbreviation* commercial paper

CPI *abbreviation* Consumer Price Index

crash /kræʃ/ *noun* a financial collapse ○ *The financial crash caused several bankruptcies.* ○ *He lost all his money in the crash of 1929.* ■ *verb* to collapse financially ○ *The company crashed with debts of over £1 million.*

crawling peg /ˈkrɔːlɪŋ peg/ *noun* a method of controlling exchange rates, allowing them to move up or down slowly

create /kriˈeɪt/ *verb* to make something new ○ *By acquiring small unprofitable companies he soon created a large manufacturing group.* ○ *The government scheme aims at creating new jobs for young people.*

'…he insisted that the tax advantages he directed towards small businesses will help create jobs and reduce the unemployment rate' [*Toronto Star*]

creation /kriˈeɪʃ(ə)n/ *noun* the process of making something

creative /kriˈeɪtɪv/ *noun* someone who works in the conceptual or artistic side of a business

'…agencies are being called on to produce great creative work and at the same time deliver value for money' [*Marketing Week*]

creative accountancy /kriˌeɪtɪv əˈkaʊntənsi/, **creative accounting** /kriˌeɪtɪv əˈkaʊntɪŋ/ *noun* an adaptation of a company's figures to present a better picture than is correct, usually intended to make a company more attractive to a potential buyer, or done for some other reason which may not be strictly legal

COMMENT: Creative accounting is the term used to cover a number of accounting practices which, although legal, may be used to mislead banks, investors, and shareholders about the profitability or liquidity of a business.

creative financing /kriˌeɪtɪv ˈfaɪnænsɪŋ/ *noun* finding methods of financing a commercial project that are different from the usual methods of raising money

credere /ˈkreɪdəri/ *noun* ♦ **del credere agent**

credit /ˈkredɪt/ *noun* **1.** a period of time allowed before a customer has to pay a debt incurred for goods or services ○ *to give someone six months' credit* ○ *to sell on good credit terms* □ **on credit** without paying immediately ○ *to live on credit* ○ *We buy everything on sixty days' credit.* ○ *The company exists on credit from its suppliers.* **2.** an amount entered in accounts to show a decrease in assets or expenses or an increase in liabilities, revenue or capital. In accounts, credits are entered in the right-hand column. ○ *to enter $100 to someone's credit* ○ *to pay in $100 to the credit of Mr Smith* Compare **debit** □ **account in credit** an account where the credits are higher than the debits ■ *verb* to put money into someone's account, or to note money received in an account ○ *to credit an account with £100* or *to credit £100 to an account*

credit account /'kredɪt ə,kaʊnt/ *noun* an account which a customer has with a shop which allows him or her to buy goods and pay for them later

credit agency /'kredɪt ,eɪdʒənsi/ *noun* a company which reports on the creditworthiness of customers to show whether they should be allowed credit. Also called **credit bureau**

credit balance /'kredɪt ,bæləns/ *noun* a balance in an account showing that more money has been received than is owed ○ *The account has a credit balance of £100.*

credit bank /'kredɪt bæŋk/ *noun* a bank which lends money

credit bureau /'kredɪt ,bjʊərəʊ/ *noun* US same as **credit agency**

credit card /'kredɪt kɑːd/ *noun* a plastic card which allows someone to borrow money and to buy goods up to a certain limit without paying for them immediately, but only after a period of grace of about 25–30 days. ♢ **charge card**

credit card holder /'kredɪt kɑːd ,həʊldə/ *noun* **1.** a person who has a credit card **2.** a plastic wallet for keeping credit cards

credit card issuer /'kredɪt kɑːd ,ɪʃuə/ *noun* a bank or other financial institution that issues credit cards

credit card sale /'kredɪt kɑːd ,seɪl/ *noun* the act of selling where the buyer uses a credit card to pay

credit column /'kredɪt ,kɒləm/ *noun* the right-hand column in accounts showing money received

credit control /'kredɪt kən,trəʊl/ *noun* a check that customers pay on time and do not owe more than their credit limit

credit crunch /'kredɪt krʌntʃ/, **credit crisis** /'kredɪt ,kraɪsɪs/, **credit squeeze** /'kredɪt skwiːz/ *noun* a reduction in the general availability of loans or credit or a tightening on conditions required to obtain a loan from the banks ○ *Small businesses have been worst hit by the credit crunch.* ○ *We've had to tighten our belts because of the credit crunch.*

credit crunch lunch /'kredɪt krʌntʃ ,lʌntʃ/ *noun* **1.** an expression used during the financial crisis of 2008–9 to describe a homemade packed lunch brought to work by employees **2.** a special offer by restaurants for discounted meals to attract more customers during the credit crunch of 2008–9

credit entry /'kredɪt ,entri/ *noun* an entry on the credit side of an account

credit facilities /'kredɪt fə,sɪlɪtiz/ *plural noun* an arrangement with a bank or supplier to have credit so as to buy goods

credit freeze /'kredɪt friːz/ *noun* a period when lending by banks is restricted by the government

credit history /'kredɪt ,hɪst(ə)ri/ *noun* a record of how a potential borrower has repaid his or her previous debts

'…failed to consider numerous factors, such as an applicant's credit history and ability to repay based on income.' [*Economist*]

credit limit /'kredɪt ,lɪmɪt/ *noun* the largest amount of money which a customer can borrow □ **he has exceeded his credit limit** he has borrowed more money than he is allowed to

credit line /'kredɪt laɪn/ *noun* an overdraft, the amount by which a person can draw money from an account with no funds, with the agreement of the bank □ **to open a credit line** *or* **line of credit** to make credit available to someone

credit note /'kredɪt nəʊt/ *noun* a note showing that money is owed to a customer ○ *The company sent the wrong* *order and so had to issue a credit note.* Abbreviation **C/N**

creditor /'kredɪtə/ *noun* a person or company that is owed money, i.e. a company's creditors are its liabilities

creditor nation /ˌkredɪtə 'neɪʃ(ə)n/ *noun* a country which has lent money to another. Compare **debtor nation**

creditors' committee /'kredɪtəz kə ˌmɪti/ *noun* a group of creditors of a corporation which is being reorganised under Chapter 11, who meet officials of the corporation to discuss the progress of the reorganisation

creditors' meeting /'kredɪtəz ˌmiːtɪŋ/ *noun* a meeting of all the people to whom an insolvent company owes money, to decide how to obtain the money owed

credit rating /'kredɪt ˌreɪtɪŋ/ *noun* an amount which a credit agency feels a customer will be able to repay

credit rationing /'kredɪt ˌræʃ(ə)nɪŋ/ *noun* a situation in which lenders are unwilling to advance additional funds to borrowers at the prevailing market interest rate

credit-reference agency /'kredɪt ˌrefər(ə)ns ˌeɪdʒənsi/ *noun* same as **credit agency**

credit references /'kredɪt ˌrefər(ə)nsɪz/ *plural noun* details of persons, companies or banks who have given credit to a person or company in the past, supplied as references when opening a credit account with a new supplier

credit refusal /'kredɪt rɪˌfjuːz(ə)l/ *noun* a decision not to give someone credit (NOTE: Anyone who has been refused credit can ask to see the reasons for the decision.)

credit risk /'kredɪt rɪsk/ *noun* a risk that a borrower may not be able to repay a loan

credit scoring /'kredɪt ˌskɔːrɪŋ/ *noun* a calculation made when assessing the creditworthiness of someone or something

credit-shelter trust /ˌkredɪt ˌʃeltə 'trʌst/ *noun* money put in trust in order to escape federal estate tax

COMMENT: This type of trust is where someone leaves half his estate to his wife and puts the other half into a trust. After his death, his wife can continue to enjoy the

income from the trust, and when she dies her estate and also the trust pass to her heirs tax free.

credit side /'kredɪt saɪd/ *noun* the right-hand column of accounts showing money received

credit squeeze /'kredɪt skwiːz/ *noun* **1.** a period when lending by the banks is restricted by the government **2.** same as **credit crunch**

Crédit Suisse Index /ˌkredɪt 'swiːs ˌɪndeks/ *noun* an index of prices on the Zurich Stock Exchange

credit threshold /'kredɪt ˌθreʃhəʊld/ *noun* a limit for credit allowed to a customer

credit transfer /'kredɪt ˌtrænsfɜː/ *noun* an act of moving money from one account to another

credit union /'kredɪt ˌjuːnjən/ *noun* a group of people who pay in regular deposits or subscriptions which earn interest and are used to make loans to other members of the group

creditworthiness /'kredɪtˌwɜːðinəs/ *noun* the extent to which an individual or organisation is creditworthy

creditworthy /'kredɪtwɜːði/ *adjective* judged as likely to be able to repay money borrowed, either, in the case of an individual, by a credit reference agency, or, in the case of an organisation, by a credit rating agency ○ *We will do some checks on her to see if she is creditworthy.*

criminal action /ˌkrɪmɪn(ə)l 'ækʃən/ *noun* a court case brought by the state against someone who is charged with a crime

criminal record /ˌkrɪmɪn(ə)l 'rekɔːd/ *noun* same as **police record**

crisis /'kraɪsɪs/ *noun* a serious economic situation where decisions have to be taken rapidly ○ *a banking crisis* ○ *The government stepped in to try to resolve the international crisis.* ○ *Withdrawals from the bank have reached crisis level.* □ **to take crisis measures** to take severe measures rapidly to stop a crisis developing

crisis management /'kraɪsɪs ˌmænɪdʒmənt/ *noun* **1.** management of a business or a country's economy during a period of crisis **2.** actions taken by an organisation to protect itself when unexpected events or situations occur that could threaten its success or continued operation (NOTE: Crisis situations may result from external factors such as the development of a new product by a competitor or changes in legislation, or from internal factors such as a product failure or faulty decision-making, and often involve the need to make quick decisions on the basis of uncertain or incomplete information.)

CRO abbreviation Companies Registration Office

crore /krɔː/ noun (in India) ten million (NOTE: One crore equals 100 lakh.)

'…the company clocked a sales turnover of Rs.7.09 crore and earned a profit after tax of Rs.10.39 lakh on an equity base of Rs.14 lakh' [Business India]

'…the turnover for the nine months ended December 31 registered a 6.26 per cent increase to Rs. 87.91 crores from Rs. 82.73 crores in the corresponding period last year' [The Hindu]

cross /krɒs/ verb □ **to cross a cheque** to write two lines across a cheque to show that it has to be paid into a bank

COMMENT: Crossed cheques have the words 'A/C payee' printed in the space between the two vertical lines: all British cheques are now printed in this way. This means that the cheque can only be paid into a bank, and only into the account of the person whose name is written on it – it cannot be endorsed to a third party.

cross out phrasal verb to put a line through something which has been written ○ She crossed out £250 and put in £500.

cross-border /ˌkrɒs ˈbɔːdə/ adjective from one country to another, covering several countries

cross-border capital flows /ˌkrɒs ˌbɔːdə ˈkæpɪt(ə)l fləʊz/ plural noun movements of capital from one country to another

cross-border listing /ˌkrɒs ˌbɔːdə ˈlɪstɪŋ/ noun the listing of a security on stock exchanges in more than one country

crossed cheque /ˌkrɒst ˈtʃek/ noun a cheque with two lines across it showing that it can only be deposited at a bank and not exchanged for cash

cross holdings /ˈkrɒs ˌhəʊldɪŋz/ plural noun a situation where two companies own shares in each other in order to stop either from being taken over ○ The

two companies have protected themselves from takeover by a system of cross holdings.

cross rate /ˈkrɒs reɪt/ noun an exchange rate between two currencies expressed in a third currency

cross rates /krɒs reɪts/ plural noun same as **exchange cross rates**

cross-selling /ˌkrɒs ˈselɪŋ/ noun the act of selling insurance or other financial services at the same time as a mortgage

crowding out /ˌkraʊdɪŋ ˈaʊt/ noun a situation where there is little money for private companies to borrow, because the government's borrowings are very heavy

crown /kraʊn/ noun a word used in English to refer to the units of currency of several countries such as the Czech Republic, Denmark, Norway and Sweden

crown jewels /ˌkraʊn ˈdʒuːəlz/ plural noun the most valuable assets of a company, the reason why other companies may want to make takeover bids

crude petroleum /ˌkruːd pə ˈtrəʊliəm/ noun raw petroleum which has not been processed

cum /kʌm/ preposition with

cum all /ˌkʌm ˈɔːl/ adverb including all entitlements

cum coupon /ˌkʌm ˈkuːpɒn/ adverb with a coupon attached or before interest due on a security is paid

cum dividend /ˌkʌm ˈdɪvɪdend/, **cum div** adverb including the next dividend still to be paid

cum rights /ˌkʌm ˈraɪts/ adverb sold with the right to purchase new shares in a rights issue

cumulative /ˈkjuːmjʊlətɪv/ adjective added to regularly over a period of time

cumulative interest /ˌkjuːmjʊlətɪv ˈɪntrəst/ noun the total amount of interest that has been charged on a loan up to a given point

cumulative preference share /ˌkjuːmjʊlətɪv ˈpref(ə)rəns ʃeə/ noun a preference share which will have the dividend paid at a later date even if the company is not able to pay a dividend in the current year (NOTE: The US term is **cumulative preferred stock**.)

curb exchange /ˈkɜːb ɪksˌtʃeɪndʒ/ same as **American Stock Exchange**

currency /ˈkʌrənsi/ *noun* **1.** money in coins and notes which is used in a particular country **2.** foreign currency, the currency of another country (NOTE: **Currency** has no plural when it refers to the money of one country: *He was arrested trying to take currency out of the country.*)

'…today's wide daily variations in exchange rates show the instability of a system based on a single currency, namely the dollar' [*Economist*]

'…the level of currency in circulation increased to N4.9 billion in the month of August' [*Business Times (Lagos)*]

currency backing /ˈkʌrənsi ˌbækɪŋ/ *noun* gold or government securities which maintain the strength of a currency

currency band /ˈkʌrənsi bænd/ *noun* the exchange rate levels between which a currency is allowed to move without full devaluation

currency basket /ˈkʌrənsi ˌbɑːskɪt/ *noun* a group of currencies, each of which is weighted, calculated together as a single unit against which another currency can be measured

currency clause /ˈkʌrənsi klɔːz/ *noun* a clause in a contract which avoids problems of payment caused by changes in exchange rates, by fixing the exchange rate for the various transactions covered by the contract

currency conversion systems /ˈkʌrənsi kənˌvɜːʃ(ə)n ˌsɪstəmz/ *plural noun* computer software used to convert accounts from one currency to another automatically

currency futures /ˈkʌrənsi ˌfjuːtʃəz/ *plural noun* purchases of foreign currency for delivery at a future date

currency movements /ˈkʌrənsi ˌmuːvmənts/ *plural noun* fluctuations in the value of the world's currencies that occur as they are traded

currency note /ˈkʌrənsi nəʊt/ *noun* a bank note

currency reserves /ˈkʌrənsi rɪˌzɜːvz/ *plural noun* foreign money held by a government to support its own currency and to pay its debts

currency swap /ˈkʌrənsi swɒp/ *noun* an agreement to use a certain currency for payments under a contract in exchange for another currency (the two companies involved can each buy one of the currencies at a more favourable rate than the other)

current /ˈkʌrənt/ *adjective* referring to the present time ○ *the current round of wage negotiations*

'…crude oil output plunged during the past month and is likely to remain at its current level for the near future' [*Wall Street Journal*]

current account /ˈkʌrənt əˌkaʊnt/ *noun* **1.** an account in an bank from which the customer can withdraw money when he or she wants. Current accounts do not always pay interest. ○ *to pay money into a current account* Also called **cheque account** (NOTE: The US term is **checking account**.) **2.** an account of the balance of payments of a country relating to the sale or purchase of raw materials, goods and invisibles □ **current account balance of payments** a record of imports and exports, payments for services, and invisibles, etc.

current assets /ˌkʌrənt ˈæsets/ *plural noun* the assets used by a company in its ordinary work, e.g. materials, finished goods, cash and monies due, which are held for a short time only

current balance /ˌkʌrənt ˈbæləns/ *noun* the balance in an account at the start of a day's trading. Also called **ledger account**

current cost accounting /ˌkʌrənt ˈkɒst əˌkaʊntɪŋ/ *noun* a method of accounting in which assets are valued at the amount it would cost to replace them, rather than at the original cost. Abbreviation **CCA**. Also called **replacement cost accounting**

current liabilities /ˌkʌrənt ˌlaɪə ˈbɪlɪtiz/ *plural noun* the debts which a company has to pay within the next accounting period. In a company's annual accounts, these would be debts which must be paid within the year and are usually payments for goods or services received.

current price /ˌkʌrənt ˈpraɪs/ *noun* today's price

current rate of exchange /ˌkʌrənt reɪt əv ɪksˈtʃeɪndʒ/ *noun* today's rate of exchange

current yield /ˌkʌrənt ˈjiːld/ *noun* a dividend calculated as a percentage of the current price of a share on the stock market

curve /kɜːv/ *noun* a line which is not straight, e.g. a line on a graph ○ *The graph shows an upward curve.*

cushion /'kuʃ(ə)n/ *noun* money which allows a company to pay interest on its borrowings or to survive a loss ○ *We have sums on deposit which are a useful cushion when cash flow is tight.*

custodial /kʌ'stəʊdiəl/ *adjective* referring to custody, to holding valuable items for someone

custodial account /kʌ'stəʊdiəl ə ˌkaʊnt/ *noun* an account in which money is held for someone, usually a child, by a custodian

custodian /kʌ'stəʊdiən/ *noun* a person or company that looks after valuable items for someone, in particular money or other assets belonging to a child

custody /'kʌstədi/ *noun* control of a thing under the law, as when holding valuables or share certificates in safe-keeping for someone

custom /'kʌstəm/ *noun* **1.** the use of a shop by regular shoppers □ **to lose someone's custom** to do something which makes a regular customer go to another shop **2.** a thing which is usually done ○ *It is the custom of the book trade to allow unlimited returns for credit.* □ **the customs of the trade** the general way of working in a trade

custom-built /'kʌstəm bɪlt/ *adjective* made specially for one customer ○ *He drives a custom-built Rolls Royce.*

customer /'kʌstəmə/ *noun* a person or company that buys goods ○ *The shop was full of customers.* ○ *Can you serve this customer first please?* ○ *She's a regular customer of ours.* (NOTE: The customer may not be the consumer or end user of the product.)

'...unless advertising and promotion is done in the context of an overall customer orientation, it cannot seriously be thought of as marketing' [*Quarterly Review of Marketing*]

customer appeal /'kʌstəmər əˌpiːl/ *noun* what attracts customers to a product

customer identification file /ˌkʌstəmər ˌaɪdentɪfɪ'keɪʃ(ə)n faɪl/ *noun US* a computer record which a bank keeps on each customer, containing information about the customer's credit rating. Abbreviation **CIF**

customer service department /ˌkʌstəmə 'sɜːvɪs dɪˌpɑːtmənt/ *noun* a department which deals with customers and their complaints and orders

customise /'kʌstəmaɪz/, **customize** *verb* to change something to fit the special needs of a customer ○ *We use customised computer terminals.*

customs /'kʌstəmz/ *plural noun* the government department which organises the collection of taxes on imports, or an office of this department at a port or airport ○ *He was stopped by customs.* ○ *Her car was searched by customs.* □ **to go through customs** to pass through the area of a port or airport where customs officials examine goods □ **to take something through customs** to carry something illegal through a customs area without declaring it □ **the crates had to go through a customs examination** the crates had to be examined by customs officials

customs barrier /'kʌstəmz ˌbæriə/ *noun* any provision intended to make trade more difficult, e.g. a high level of duty

customs broker /'kʌstəmz ˌbrəʊkə/ *noun* a person or company that takes goods through customs for a shipping company

customs clearance /'kʌstəmz ˌklɪərəns/ *noun* **1.** the act of passing goods through customs so that they can enter or leave the country **2.** a document given by customs to a shipper to show that customs duty has been paid and the goods can be shipped ○ *to wait for customs clearance*

customs declaration /'kʌstəmz dekləˌreɪʃ(ə)n/ *noun* a statement showing goods being imported on which duty will have to be paid ○ *to fill in a customs declaration form*

customs duty /'kʌstəmz ˌdjuːti/ *noun* a tax on goods imported into a country

customs entry point /ˌkʌstəmz 'entri pɔɪnt/ *noun* a place at a border between two countries where goods are declared to customs

customs examination /'kʌstəmz ɪg
ˌzæmɪneɪʃ(ə)n/ *noun* the inspection of
goods or baggage by customs officials

customs formalities /'kʌstəmz fɔː
ˌmælɪtiz/ *plural noun* a declaration of
goods by the shipper and examination of
them by customs

customs officer /'kʌstəm ˌɒfɪsə/
noun a person working for the customs
department of a country

customs official /'kʌstəmz əˌfɪʃ(ə)l/
noun a person working for the Customs
and Excise Department

customs seal /'kʌstəmz siːl/ *noun* a
seal attached by a customs officer to a
box, to show that the contents have not
passed through customs

customs tariff /'kʌstəmz ˌtærɪf/
noun a list of taxes to be paid on imported
goods

customs union /'kʌstəmz ˌjuːnjən/
noun an agreement between several
countries that goods can travel between
them, without paying duty, while goods
from other countries have to pay special
duties

cut /kʌt/ *noun* **1.** the sudden lowering of
a price, salary or the number of jobs ○
price cuts or *cuts in prices* □ he took a
cut in salary, he took a salary cut he
accepted a lower salary **2.** a share in a
payment ○ *She introduces new customers
and gets a cut of the sales rep's commission.* ■ *verb* **1.** to lower something
suddenly ○ *We are cutting prices on all
our models.* ○ *We have taken out the
second telephone line in order to try to cut
costs.* (NOTE: **cutting – cut – has cut**) □
to cut (back) production to reduce the
quantity of products made **2.** to reduce the
number of something (NOTE: **cutting –
cut – has cut**) □ **to cut jobs** to reduce the
number of jobs by making people redundant □ **he cut his losses** he stopped doing
something which was creating a loss

'...state-owned banks cut their prime rates
a percentage point to 11%' [*Wall Street
Journal*]

'...the US bank announced a cut in its
prime from 10½ per cent to 10 per cent'
[*Financial Times*]

cut in *phrasal verb* □ **to cut someone
in on a deal** to give someone a share in
the profits of a deal (*informal*)

cut down (on) *phrasal verb* to reduce
suddenly the amount of something used
○ *The government is cutting down on
welfare expenditure.* ○ *The office is
trying to cut down on electricity
consumption.* ○ *We have installed
networked computers to cut down on
paperwork.*

cutback /'kʌtbæk/ *noun* a reduction ○
cutbacks in government spending

cutoff date /'kʌtɒf deɪt/ *noun* a date
when something is stopped, such as the
final date for receiving applications for
shares, or the date when the current
trading account ends and the next account
begins

cut-price /ˌkʌt 'praɪs/ *adjective* sold at
a cheaper price than usual ○ *He made his
money selling cut-price goods in the local
market.* ○ *You can get cut-price petrol in
some petrol stations near the border.*

cut-throat competition /ˌkʌt θrəʊt
ˌkɒmpə'tɪʃ(ə)n/ *noun* sharp competition
which cuts prices and offers high
discounts

CWO *abbreviation* cash with order

cycle /'saɪk(ə)l/ *noun* a period of time
during which something leaves its original position and then returns to it

cyclical /'sɪklɪk(ə)l/ *adjective*
happening in cycles

cyclical factors /ˌsɪklɪk(ə)l 'fæktəz/
plural noun the way in which a trade
cycle affects businesses

cyclical stocks /ˌsɪklɪk(ə)l 'stɒks/
plural noun shares in companies which
move in a regular pattern (such as shares
in a turkey producer might rise in the
period before Christmas)

D

daily /'deɪli/ *adjective* done every day □
daily interest, **interest calculated daily**
or **on a daily basis** a rate of interest calculated each day and added to the principal

daily consumption /ˌdeɪli kən
'sʌmpʃən/ *noun* an amount used each
day

daily sales returns /ˌdeɪli 'seɪlz rɪ
ˌtɜːnz/ *plural noun* reports of sales made
each day

Daimyo bond /'daɪmjəʊ bɒnd/ *noun*
a Japanese bearer bond which can be
cleared through European clearing houses

dalasi /dəˈlɑːsi/ *noun* a unit of currency
used in the Gambia

damp down *phrasal verb* to reduce ○
*to damp down demand for domestic
consumption of oil*

danger money /'deɪndʒə ˌmʌni/
noun extra money paid to employees in
dangerous jobs ○ *The workforce has
stopped work and asked for danger
money.* ○ *He decided to go to work on an
oil rig because of the danger money
offered as an incentive.*

data /'deɪtə/ *noun* information available
on computer, e.g. letters or figures ○ *All
important data on employees was fed into
the computer.* ○ *To calculate the weekly
wages, you need data on hours worked
and rates of pay.* (NOTE: takes a singular
or plural verb)

data acquisition /'deɪtə
ˌækwɪzɪʃ(ə)n/ *noun* the act of gathering
information about a subject

data bank /'deɪtə bæŋk/ *noun* a store
of information in a computer

database /'deɪtəbeɪs/ *noun* a set of
data stored in an organised way in a
computer system ○ *We can extract the
lists of potential customers from our database.*

data capture /'deɪtə ˌkæptʃə/, **data
entry** /ˌdeɪtə 'entri/ *noun* same as **data
acquisition**

data mining /'deɪtə ˌmaɪnɪŋ/ *noun* the
use of advanced software to search online
databases and identify statistical patterns
or relationships in the data that may be
commercially useful

'…it used decision-science-based analyt-
ical tools and database marketing. This
deep data mining has succeeded because
Harrah's has simultaneously maintained
its focus on satisfying its customers.'
[*Harvard Business Review*]

data processing /'deɪtə ˌprəʊsesɪŋ/
noun the act of selecting and examining
data in a computer to produce information
in a special form

Datastream /'deɪtəstriːm/ *noun* a data
system available online, giving information about securities, prices, stock
exchange transactions, etc.

date /deɪt/ *noun* **1.** the number of the
day, month, and year ○ *I have received
your letter of yesterday's date.* □ **date of
receipt** the date when something is
received **2.** □ **to date** up to now □ **interest
to date** interest up to the present time ■
verb to put a date on a document ○ *The
cheque was dated March 24th.* ○ *You
forgot to date the cheque.* □ **to date a
cheque forward** to put a later date than
the present one on a cheque. In the US,
this would be **predate a check**.

dated /'deɪtɪd/ *adjective* **1.** with a date
written on it ○ *Thank you for your letter
dated June 15th.* **2.** out-of-date ○ *The
unions have criticised management for its
dated ideas.*

date draft /'deɪt drɑːft/ *noun* a draft
which has a certain maturity date

date of bill /ˌdeɪt əv ˈbɪl/ *noun* a date when a bill will mature

date of maturity /ˌdeɪt əv məˈtjʊərɪti/ *noun* same as **maturity date**

date of record /ˌdeɪt əv ˈrekɔːd/ *noun* the date when a shareholder must be registered to qualify for a dividend

date stamp /ˈdeɪt stæmp/ *noun* a stamp with rubber figures which can be moved, used for marking the date on documents

dawn raid /dɔːn ˈreɪd/ *noun* a sudden planned purchase of a large number of a company's shares at the beginning of a day's trading (NOTE: Up to 15% of a company's shares may be bought in this way, and the purchaser must wait for seven days before purchasing any more shares. Sometimes a dawn raid is the first step towards a takeover of the target company.)

DAX index *noun* an index of prices on the Frankfurt Stock Exchange. Full form **Deutsche Aktien index**

day /deɪ/ *noun* **1.** a period of 24 hours ○ *There are thirty days in June.* ○ *The first day of the month is a public holiday.* □ **days of grace** the time given to a debtor to repay a loan, to pay the amount purchased using a credit card, or to pay an insurance premium ○ *Let's send the cheque at once since we have only five days of grace left.* ○ *Because the shopowner has so little cash available, we will have to allow him additional days of grace.* □ **three clear days** three whole working days ○ *to give ten clear days' notice* ○ *Allow four clear days for the cheque to be paid into the bank.* **2.** a period of work from morning to night □ **she took two days off** she did not come to work for two days □ **she works three days on, two days off** she works for three days, then has two days' holiday □ **to work an eight-hour day** to spend eight hours at work each day **3.** one of the days of the week

day book /ˈdeɪ bʊk/ *noun* a book with an account of sales and purchases made each day

day order /ˈdeɪ ˌɔːdə/ *noun* an order to a stockbroker to buy or sell on a specific day

day shift /ˈdeɪ ʃɪft/ *noun* a shift worked during the daylight hours

day trader /ˈdeɪ ˌtreɪdə/ *noun* a person who buys shares and sells them within the same day

day work /ˈdeɪ wɜːk/ *noun* work done during a day

DCF *abbreviation* discounted cash flow

dead /ded/ *adjective* not working

dead account /ˌded əˈkaʊnt/ *noun* an account which is no longer used

dead-cat bounce /ˌded kæt ˈbaʊns/ *noun* a slight rise in a share price after a sharp fall, showing that some investors are still interested in buying the share at the lower price, although further sharp falls will follow

COMMENT: Called this because when dropped from a great height even a dead cat will bounce a little!

deadline /ˈdedlaɪn/ *noun* the date by which something has to be done □ **to meet a deadline** to finish something in time □ **to miss a deadline** to finish something later than it was planned ○ *We've missed our October 1st deadline.*

deadlock /ˈdedlɒk/ *noun* a point where two sides in a dispute cannot agree ○ *The negotiations have reached deadlock or a deadlock.* □ **to break a deadlock** to find a way to start discussions again after being at a point where no agreement was possible ■ *verb* to be unable to agree to continue negotiations □ **talks have been deadlocked for ten days** after ten days the talks have not produced any agreement

dead loss /ˌded ˈlɒs/ *noun* a total loss ○ *The car was written off as a dead loss.*

deal /diːl/ *noun* a business agreement, affair or contract ○ *The sales director set up a deal with a Russian bank.* ○ *The deal will be signed tomorrow.* ○ *They did a deal with an American airline.* □ **to call off a deal** to stop an agreement ○ *When the chairman heard about the deal he called it off.* ■ *verb* **1.** □ **to deal with** to organise something ○ *Leave it to the filing clerk – he'll deal with it.* □ **to deal with an order** to work to supply an order **2.** to buy and sell (NOTE: **dealing – dealt**) □ **to deal with someone** to do business with someone □ **to deal in leather** *or* **options** to buy and sell leather or options □ **he deals on the stock exchange** his work involves buying and selling shares on the stock exchange for clients

dealer /'di:lə/ *noun* **1.** a person who buys and sells ○ *a used-car dealer* **2.** a person or firm that buys or sells on their own account, not on behalf of clients

dealer bank /'di:lər bæŋk/ *noun* a bank which deals on the stock exchange or which deals in government securities

dealing /'di:lɪŋ/ *noun* **1.** the business of buying and selling on the stock exchange, commodity markets or currency markets □ **dealing for** *or* **within the account** buying shares and selling the same shares during an account, which means that the dealer has only to pay the difference between the price of the shares bought and the price obtained for them when they are sold **2.** the business of buying and selling goods □ **to have dealings with someone** to do business with someone

dealing floor /'di:lɪŋ flɔː/ *noun* **1.** an area of a brokerage firm where dealing in securities is carried out by phone, using monitors to display current prices and stock exchange transactions **2.** a part of a stock exchange where dealers trade in securities

dealing-only broker /ˌdi:lɪŋ 'əʊnli ˌbrəʊkə/ *noun* a broker who buys and sells shares for clients, but does not provide any advice and does not manage portfolios (as opposed to a full-service broker)

dear /dɪə/ *adjective* expensive, costing a lot of money ○ *Property is very dear in this area.*

dear money /'dɪə ˌmʌni/ *noun* money which has to be borrowed at a high interest rate, and so restricts expenditure by companies. Also called **tight money**

death benefit /'deθ ˌbenɪfɪt/ *noun* insurance benefit paid to the family of someone who dies in an accident at work

death duty /'deθ ˌdjuːti/ *noun* same as **inheritance tax**

death in service /ˌdeθ ɪn 'sɜːvɪs/ *noun* an insurance benefit or pension paid when someone dies while employed by a company

death tax /'deθ tæks/ *noun* same as **inheritance tax**

debenture /dɪ'bentʃə/ *noun* agreement to repay a debt with fixed interest using the company's assets as security ○ *The bank holds a debenture on the company.*

COMMENT: In the UK, debentures are always secured on the company's assets. In the US, debenture bonds are not secured.

debenture bond /dɪ'bentʃə bɒnd/ *noun US* **1.** a certificate showing that a debenture has been issued **2.** an unsecured loan

debenture capital /dɪ'bentʃə ˌkæpɪt(ə)l/ *noun* capital borrowed by a company, using its fixed assets as security

debenture holder /dɪ'bentʃə ˌhəʊldə/ *noun* a person who holds a debenture for money lent

debenture stock /dɪ'bentʃə stɒk/ *noun* a form of debt instrument in which a company guarantees payments on a fixed schedule or at a fixed rate of interest

debit /'debɪt/ *noun* an amount entered in accounts which shows an increase in assets or expenses or a decrease in liabilities, revenue or capital. In accounts, debits are entered in the left-hand column. Compare **credit** ■ *verb* □ **to debit an account** to charge an account with a cost ○ *His account was debited with the sum of £25.*

debitable /'debɪtəb(ə)l/ *adjective* able to be debited

debit balance /'debɪt ˌbæləns/ *noun* a balance in an account showing that more money is owed than has been received ○ *Because of large payments to suppliers, the account has a debit balance of £1,000.*

debit bureau /'debɪt ˌbjʊərəʊ/ *noun* a centralised system for checking a customer's credit rating when he or she presents a cheque as payment

debit card /'debɪt kɑːd/ *noun* a plastic card, similar to a credit card, but which debits the holder's account immediately through an EPOS system

debit column /'debɪt ˌkɒləm/ *noun* the left-hand column in accounts showing the money paid or owed to others

debit entry /'debɪt ˌentri/ *noun* an entry on the debit side of an account

debit interest /'debɪt ˌɪntrəst/ *noun* an interest on debts, such as overdrafts

debit note /'debɪt nəʊt/ *noun* a note showing that a customer owes money ○ *We undercharged Mr Smith and had to send him a debit note for the extra amount.*

debits and credits /ˌdebɪts ən 'kredɪts/ *plural noun* money which a company owes and money it receives, or figures which are entered in the accounts to record increases or decreases in assets, expenses, liabilities, revenue or capital

debit side /'debɪt saɪd/ *noun* a left-hand column of accounts showing money owed or paid to others

debt /det/ *noun* money owed for goods or services ○ *The company stopped trading with debts of over £1 million.* □ **to be in debt** to owe money □ **he is in debt to the tune of £250,000** he owes £250,000 □ **to get into debt** to start to borrow more money than you can pay back □ **the company is out of debt** the company does not owe money any more □ **to pay back a debt** to pay all the money owed □ **to pay off a debt** to finish paying money owed □ **to reschedule a debt** to arrange for the repayment of a debt to be put off to a later date □ **to service a debt** to pay interest on a debt ○ *The company is having problems in servicing its debts.* □ **debts due** money owed which is due for repayment

debt collection /'det kə,lekʃən/ *noun* the act of collecting money which is owed

debt collection agency /'det kə,lekʃən ,eɪdʒənsi/ *noun* a company which collects debts for other companies for a commission

debt collector /'det kə,lektə/ *noun* a person who collects debts

debt-convertible bond /,det kən,vɜːtɪb(ə)l 'bɒnd/ *noun* a floating-rate bond which can be converted to a fixed rate of interest. ◊ **droplock bond**

debt counselling /'det ,kaʊnsəlɪŋ/ *noun* the work of advising people who are in debt of the best ways to arrange their finances so as to pay off their debts

debt instrument /'det ,ɪnstrʊmənt/ *noun* a document by which someone promises to repay a debt (NOTE: Debt instruments include such things as IOUs, CDs and bank notes.)

debtor /'detə/ *noun* a person who owes money

debtor nation /'detə ,neɪʃ(ə)n/ *noun* a country whose foreign debts are larger than money owed to it by other countries

'...the United States is now a debtor nation for the first time since 1914, owing more to foreigners than it is owed itself' [*Economist*]

debtor side /'detə saɪd/ *noun* the debit side of an account

debtors ledger /'detəz ,ledʒə/ *noun* same as **sales ledger**

debtors turnover ratio /,detəz 'tɜːnəʊvə ,reɪʃiəʊ/ *noun* the average time which debtors take to pay

debt ratio /'det ,reɪʃiəʊ/ *noun* the debts of a company shown as a percentage of its equity plus loan capital

debt rescheduling /'det riː ,ʃedjuːlɪŋ/ *noun* the process of reorganising the way in which debts are repaid. Debt rescheduling may be necessary if a company is unable to pay its debts and may involve postponing debt payments, postponing payment of interest, or negotiating a new loan.

debt-service ratio /,det 'sɜːvɪs ,reɪʃiəʊ/ *noun* the debts of a company shown as a percentage of its equity

debt servicing /'det ,sɜːvɪsɪŋ/ *noun* the payment of interest on a debt

debt swap /'det swɒp/ *noun* a method of reducing exposure to a long-term Third World debt by selling it at a discount to another bank

decelerate /diː'seləreɪt/ *verb* to slow down

deciding factor /dɪ,saɪdɪŋ 'fæktə/ *noun* the most important factor which influences a decision ○ *A deciding factor in marketing our range of sports goods in the country was the rising standard of living there.*

decile /'desaɪl/ *noun* one of a series of nine figures below which one tenth or several tenths of the total fall

decimal /'desɪm(ə)l/ *noun* □ **correct to three places of decimals** correct to three figures after the decimal point (e.g. 3.485)

decimalisation /,desɪm(ə)laɪ 'zeɪʃ(ə)n/, **decimalization** *noun* the process of changing to a decimal system

decimalise /'desɪm(ə)laɪz/, **decimalize** *verb* to change something to a decimal system

decimal point /,desɪm(ə)l 'pɔɪnt/ *noun* a dot which indicates the division between the whole unit and its smaller parts, e.g. 4.75

COMMENT: The decimal point is used in the UK and US In most European countries a comma is used to indicate a decimal, so

4,75% in Germany means 4.75% in the UK and the US

decimal system /ˈdesɪm(ə)l ˌsɪstəm/ *noun* a system of mathematics based on the number 10

decision-maker /dɪˈsɪʒ(ə)n ˌmeɪkə/ *noun* a person who takes decisions

declaration /ˌdekləˈreɪʃ(ə)n/ *noun* an official statement

declaration of bankruptcy /ˌdeklə reɪʃ(ə)n əv ˈbæŋkrʌptsi/ *noun* an official statement that someone is bankrupt

declaration of income /ˌdeklə reɪʃ(ə)n əv ˈɪnkʌm/ *noun* same as **income tax return**

declare /dɪˈkleə/ *verb* to make an official statement of something, or announce something to the public ○ *to declare someone bankrupt* ○ *The company declared an interim dividend of 10p per share.* □ **to declare goods to customs** to state that you are importing goods which are liable to duty ○ *Customs officials asked him if he had anything to declare.* □ **to declare an interest** to state in public that you own shares in a company being discussed or that you are related to someone who can benefit from your contacts

declared /dɪˈkleəd/ *adjective* having been made public or officially stated

declared value /dɪˌkleəd ˈvæljuː/ *noun* the value of goods entered on a customs declaration

decline /dɪˈklaɪn/ *noun* **1.** a gradual fall ○ *the decline in the value of the dollar* ○ *a decline in buying power* ○ *The last year has seen a decline in real wages.* **2.** the final stage in the life cycle of a product when the sales and profitability are falling off and the product is no longer worth investing in ■ *verb* to fall slowly or decrease ○ *Shares declined in a weak market.* ○ *New job applications have declined over the last year.* ○ *The economy declined during the last government.* ○ *The purchasing power of the pound declined over the decade.*

'Saudi oil production has declined by three quarters to around 2.5m barrels a day' [*Economist*]

'…this gives an average monthly decline of 2.15 per cent during the period' [*Business Times (Lagos)*]

'…share prices disclosed a weak tendency right from the onset of business and declined further, showing losses over a broad front' [*The Hindu*]

declining balance method /dɪ ˌklaɪnɪŋ ˈbæləns ˌmeθəd/ *noun US* same as **reducing balance method**

decrease *noun* /ˈdiːkriːs/ a fall or reduction ○ *The decrease in the prices of consumer goods is reflected in the fall in the cost of living.* ○ *Exports have registered a decrease.* ○ *Sales show a 10% decrease on last year.* ■ *verb* /dɪˈkriːs/ to fall or to become less ○ *Imports are decreasing.* ○ *The value of the pound has decreased by 5%.*

deduct /dɪˈdʌkt/ *verb* to take money away from a total ○ *to deduct £3 from the price* ○ *to deduct a sum for expenses* ○ *After deducting costs the gross margin is only 23%.* ○ *Expenses are still to be deducted.* □ **tax deducted at source** tax which is removed from a salary, interest payment or dividend payment on shares before the money is paid

deductible /dɪˈdʌktɪb(ə)l/ *adjective* possible to deduct □ **these expenses are not tax-deductible** tax has to be paid on these expenses

deduction /dɪˈdʌkʃən/ *noun* the removing of money from a total, or the amount of money removed from a total ○ *Net salary is salary after deduction of tax and social security.* ○ *The deduction from her wages represented the cost of repairing the damage she had caused to the machinery.* □ **deductions from salary, salary deductions, deductions at source** money which a company removes from salaries to give to the government as tax, National Insurance contributions, etc.

deed /diːd/ *noun* a legal document or written agreement

deed of assignment /ˌdiːd əv ə ˈsaɪnmənt/ *noun* a document which legally transfers a property from a debtor to a creditor

deed of covenant /ˌdiːd əv ˈkʌvənənt/ *noun* a legal document in which a person or organisation promises to pay a third party a sum of money on an annual basis. In certain countries this arrangement may have tax advantages. For example, in the UK, it is often used for making regular payments to a charity.

deed of partnership /ˌdiːd əv ˈpɑːtnəʃɪp/ *noun* agreement which sets up a partnership

deed of transfer /ˌdiːd əv ˈtrænsfɜː/ *noun* a document which transfers the ownership of shares

deep discount /ˌdiːp ˈdɪskaʊnt/ *noun* a very large discount

'…when it needed to make its financial results look good, it shipped a lot of inventory. It did this by offering deep discounts to distributors' [*Forbes*]

deep discounted bonds /diːp ˌdɪskaʊntɪd ˈbɒndz/ *plural noun* Eurobonds which are issued at a very large discount but which do not produce any interest

deep discounted rights issue /diːp dɪsˈkaʊntɪd raɪts/ *noun* rights issue where the new shares are priced at a very low price compared to their current market value

'…as the group's shares are already widely held, the listing will be via an introduction. It will also be accompanied by a deeply discounted £25m rights issue, leaving the company cash positive' [*Sunday Times*]

defalcation /ˌdiːfælˈkeɪʃ(ə)n/ *noun* the illegal use of money by someone who is not the owner but who has been trusted to look after it

default /dɪˈfɔːlt/ *noun* **1.** a failure to carry out the terms of a contract, especially failure to pay back a debt □ **in default of payment** with no payment made □ **the company is in default** the company has failed to carry out the terms of the contract **2.** □ **by default** because no one else will act □ **he was elected by default** he was elected because all the other candidates withdrew ■ *verb* to fail to carry out the terms of a contract, especially to fail to pay back a debt ○ *There was a major financial crisis when the bank defaulted.* □ **to default on payments** not to make payments which are due under the terms of a contract

defaulter /dɪˈfɔːltə/ *noun* a person who defaults

defeasance /dɪˈfiːz(ə)ns/ *noun* a clause (in a collateral deed) which says that a contract or bond or recognisance will be revoked if something happens or if some act is performed

defence /dɪˈfens/ *noun* **1.** the action of protecting someone or something against attack ○ *The merchant bank is organising the company's defence against the takeover bid.* **2.** the act of fighting a lawsuit on behalf of a defendant (NOTE: [all senses] The US spelling is **defense**.)

defence counsel /dɪˈfens ˌkaʊnsəl/ *noun* a lawyer who represents the defendant in a lawsuit

defence document /dɪˈfens ˌdɒkjʊmənt/ *noun* a document published by a company which is the subject of a takeover bid, saying why the bid should be rejected

defend /dɪˈfend/ *verb* to fight to protect someone or something that is being attacked ○ *The company is defending itself against the takeover bid.* ○ *They hired the best lawyers to defend them against the tax authorities.* □ **to defend a lawsuit** to appear in court to state your case when accused of something

defendant /dɪˈfendənt/ *noun* a person against whom a legal action is taken or who is accused of doing something to harm someone (NOTE: The other side in a case is the **claimant**.)

defended takeover /dɪˌfendɪd ˈteɪkəʊvə/ *noun* same as **contested takeover**

defensive shares /dɪˈfensɪv ʃeəz/, **defensive stocks** /dɪˈfensɪv stɒks/ *plural noun* shares which are not likely to fall in value because they are in stable market sectors, and which are therefore bought as protection against potential losses in more speculative investments

defer /dɪˈfɜː/ *verb* to put back to a later date, to postpone ○ *We will have to defer payment until January.* ○ *The decision has been deferred until the next meeting.* (NOTE: **deferring – deferred**)

deferment /dɪˈfɜːmənt/ *noun* the act of leaving until a later date ○ *deferment of payment* ○ *deferment of a decision*

deferral /dɪˈfɜːrəl/ *noun* a postponement, a putting back to a later date ○ *tax deferral*

deferred /dɪˈfɜːd/ *adjective* put back to a later date

deferred coupon note /dɪˌfɜːd ˈkuːpɒn nəʊt/ *noun* a bond where the interest is not paid immediately, but only after a specific date

deferred creditor /dɪˌfɜːd ˈkredɪtə/ noun a person who is owed money by a bankrupt but who is paid only after all other creditors

deferred equity /dɪˌfɜːd ˈekwɪti/ noun a share ownership at a later date, i.e. as part of convertible loan stock

deferred interest bond /dɪˌfɜːd ˈɪntrəst bɒnd/ noun same as **deferred coupon note**

deferred payment /dɪˌfɜːd ˈpeɪmənt/ noun **1.** money paid later than the agreed date **2.** payment for goods by instalments over a long period

deferred shares /dɪˌfɜːd ˈʃeəz/, **deferred stock** /dɪˌfɜːd ˈstɒk/ noun shares that receive a dividend only after all other dividends have been paid

deferred tax /dɪˌfɜːd ˈtæks/ noun a tax which may become payable at some later date

deficiency /dɪˈfɪʃ(ə)nsi/ noun a lack of something, or the amount by which something, e.g. a sum of money, is less than it should be ○ *There is a £10 deficiency in the petty cash.* □ **to make up a deficiency** to put money into an account to balance it

deficit /ˈdefɪsɪt/ noun the amount by which spending is higher than income □ **the accounts show a deficit** the accounts show a loss □ **to make good a deficit** to put money into an account to balance it

deficit financing /ˈdefɪsɪt ˌfaɪnænsɪŋ/ noun a type of financial planning by a government in which it borrows money to cover the difference between its tax income and its expenditure

defined /dɪˈfaɪnd/ adjective with specific aims

defined benefit plan /dɪˌfaɪnd ˈbenɪfɪt ˌplæn/, **defined contribution plan** /dɪˌfaɪnd ˌkɒntrɪˈbjuːʃ(ə)n plæn/ noun US a pension plan set up by corporations for their employees

deflate /diːˈfleɪt/ verb □ **to deflate the economy** to reduce activity in the economy by cutting the supply of money

deflation /diːˈfleɪʃ(ə)n/ noun a general reduction in economic activity as a result of a reduced supply of money and credit, leading to lower prices ○ *The oil crisis resulted in worldwide deflation.* Opposite **inflation**

'…the reluctance of people to spend is one of the main reasons behind 26 consecutive months of price deflation, a key economic ill that has led to price wars, depressed the profit margins of state enterprises and hit incomes among the rural population' [*Financial Times*]

deflationary /diːˈfleɪʃ(ə)n(ə)ri/ adjective causing deflation ○ *The government has introduced some deflationary measures in the budget.*

deflator /diːˈfleɪtə/ noun the amount by which a country's GNP is reduced to take inflation into account

defray /dɪˈfreɪ/ verb to provide money to pay costs ○ *The company agreed to defray the costs of the exhibition.*

degearing /diːˈɡɪərɪŋ/ noun a reduction in gearing, reducing a company's loan capital in relation to the value of its ordinary shares

del credere /ˌdel ˈkreɪdəri/ noun an amount added to a charge to cover the possibility of not being paid

del credere agent /ˌdel ˈkreɪdəri ˌeɪdʒənt/ noun an agent who receives a high commission because he or she guarantees payment by customers

delinquency /dɪˈlɪŋkwənsi/ noun US the fact of being overdue in payment of an account, an interest payment, etc.

delinquent /dɪˈlɪŋkwənt/ adjective US referring to an account or payment of tax which is overdue

delist /diːˈlɪst/ verb to remove a company from a stock exchange listing (as when a company is 'taken private' when an individual investor buys all the shares)

delisting /diːˈlɪstɪŋ/ noun an action of removing a company from a stock exchange listing

deliver /dɪˈlɪvə/ verb to transport goods to a customer □ **goods delivered free** or **free delivered goods** goods transported to the customer's address at a price which includes transport costs □ **goods delivered on board** goods transported free to the ship or plane but not to the customer's warehouse

delivered price /dɪˈlɪvəd praɪs/ noun a price which includes packing and transport

delivery /dɪˈlɪv(ə)ri/ noun **1.** the transporting of goods to a customer ○ *allow 28* *days for delivery* ○ *parcels awaiting delivery* ○ *free delivery* or *delivery free* ○ *a delivery date* ○ *Delivery is not allowed for* or *is not included.* ○ *We have a pallet of parcels awaiting delivery.* □ **to take delivery of goods** to accept goods when they are delivered ○ *We took delivery of the stock into our warehouse on the 25th.* **2.** a consignment of goods being delivered ○ *We take in three deliveries a day.* ○ *There were four items missing in the last delivery.* **3.** the transport of a commodity to a purchaser **4.** the transfer of a bill of exchange or other negotiable instrument to the bank which is due to make payment

delivery month /dɪ'lɪv(ə)ri mʌnθ/ *noun* a month in a futures contract when actual delivery will take place

delivery note /dɪ'lɪv(ə)ri nəʊt/ *noun* a list of goods being delivered, given to the customer with the goods

delivery of goods /dɪˌlɪv(ə)ri əv 'ɡʊdz/ *noun* the transport of goods to a customer's address

delivery order /dɪ'lɪv(ə)ri ˌɔːdə/ *noun* the instructions given by the customer to the person holding her goods, to tell her where and when to deliver them

delivery service /dɪ'lɪv(ə)ri ˌsɜːvɪs/ *noun* a transport service organised by a supplier or a shop to take goods to customers

delivery time /dɪ'lɪv(ə)ri taɪm/ *noun* the number of days before something will be delivered

delta shares /'deltə ʃeəz/, **delta securities** /'deltə sɪˌkjʊərɪtiz/, **delta stocks** /'deltə stɒks/ *noun* shares in about 120 companies listed on the London Stock Exchange, but not on the SEAQ system because they are very rarely traded

demand /dɪ'mɑːnd/ *noun* an act of asking for payment □ **payable on demand** which must be paid when payment is asked for ■ *verb* **1.** the need that customers have for a product or their eagerness to buy it ○ *There was an active demand for oil shares on the stock market.* ○ *The factory had to cut production when demand slackened.* ○ *The office cleaning company cannot keep up with the demand for its services.* □ **there is not much demand for this item** not many

people want to buy it □ **this book is in great demand** or **there is a great demand for this book** many people want to buy it □ **to meet** or **fill a demand** to supply what is needed ○ *The factory had to increase production to meet the extra demand.* **2.** to ask for something and expect to get it ○ *She demanded a refund.* ○ *The suppliers are demanding immediate payment of their outstanding invoices.* ○ *The shop stewards demanded an urgent meeting with the managing director.*

'…spot prices are now relatively stable in the run-up to the winter's peak demand' [*Economist*]

'…the demand for the company's products remained strong throughout the first six months of the year with production and sales showing significant increases' [*Business Times (Lagos)*]

'…growth in demand is still coming from the private rather than the public sector' [*Lloyd's List*]

demand bill /dɪ'mɑːnd bɪl/ *noun* a bill of exchange which must be paid when payment is asked for

demand deposit /dɪ'mɑːnd dɪˌpɒzɪt/ *noun US* money in a deposit account which can be taken out when you want it by writing a cheque

demand draft /dɪ'mɑːnd drɑːft/ *noun* a draft which is to be paid immediately

demand-led inflation /dɪˌmɑːnd led ɪn'fleɪʃ(ə)n/, **demand-pull inflation** /dɪ ˌmɑːnd pʊl ɪn'fleɪʃ(ə)n/ *noun* inflation caused by rising demand which cannot be met

demand note /dɪ'mɑːnd nəʊt/ *noun* a promissory note which must be paid when it is presented

demand price /dɪ'mɑːnd praɪs/ *noun* the price at which a quantity of goods will be bought

demerge /diː'mɜːdʒ/ *verb* to separate a company into several separate parts

demerger /diː'mɜːdʒə/ *noun* the separation of a company into several separate parts, especially used of companies which have grown by acquisition

demise /dɪ'maɪz/ *noun* **1.** a death ○ *On his demise the estate passed to his daughter.* **2.** the act of granting a property on a lease

demonetisation /diːˌmʌnɪtaɪˈzeɪʃ(ə)n/, **demonetization** *noun* the act of stopping a coin or note being used as money

demonetise /diːˈmʌnɪtaɪz/, **demonetize** *verb* to stop a coin or note being used as money

demurrage /dɪˈmʌrɪdʒ/ *noun* money paid to a customer when a shipment is delayed at a port or by customs

demutualisation /diːˌmjuːtjuəlaɪˈzeɪʃ(ə)n/, **demutualization** *noun* the process by which a mutual society, such as a building society, becomes a publicly owned corporation

demutualise /diːˈmjuːtjuəlaɪz/, **demutualize** /diːˈmjuːtʃuəˌlaɪz/ *verb* to stop having mutual status and become a publicly owned corporation by selling shares to the general public on the stock market

COMMENT: Building societies, insurance companies, etc., have mutual status, that is they belong to their members, the people who have deposits with them, who invest in their pensions funds, or who borrow money from them. By floating on the stock exchange and becoming Plcs, they can act like any large company and borrow money to fund development or to acquire other companies. However, when a mutual society becomes a Plc or is bought by a Plc, its structure has to change. Its members become shareholders, and value is returned to them in the form of cash windfalls, free shares, etc.

denomination /dɪˌnɒmɪˈneɪʃ(ə)n/ *noun* a unit of money on a coin, banknote or stamp ○ *We collect coins of all denominations for charity.* ○ *Small denomination notes are not often counterfeited.*

department /dɪˈpɑːtmənt/ *noun* **1.** a specialised section of a large organisation ○ *Trainee managers work for a while in each department to get an idea of the organisation as a whole.* **2.** a section of a large store selling one type of product ○ *You will find beds in the furniture department.* **3.** a section of the British government containing several ministries

departmental /ˌdiːpɑːtˈment(ə)l/ *adjective* referring to a department

departmental manager /ˌdiːpɑːtˈment(ə)l ˈmænɪdʒə/ *noun* the manager of a department

Department for Business, Innovation and Skills /dɪˌpɑːtmənt fə ˌbɪznəs ˌɪnəveɪʃ(ə)n ən ˈskɪlz/ *noun* a British government department which deals with areas such as commerce, international trade and the stock exchange. Abbreviation **BIS**

Department for Work and Pensions /dɪˌpɑːtmənt fə ˌwɜːk ən ˈpenʃənz/ *noun* a British government department responsible for services to people of working age, pensioners and families. Abbreviation **DWP**

department store /dɪˈpɑːtmənt stɔː/ *noun* a large store with separate sections for different types of goods

deposit /dɪˈpɒzɪt/ *noun* **1.** money placed in a bank for safe keeping or to earn interest □ **deposit at 7 days' notice** money deposited which you can withdraw by giving seven days' notice **2.** money given in advance so that the thing which you want to buy will not be sold to someone else ○ *to pay a deposit on a watch* ○ *to leave £10 as deposit* ■ *verb* **1.** to put documents somewhere for safe keeping ○ *to deposit shares with a bank* ○ *We have deposited the deeds of the house with the bank.* ○ *He deposited his will with his solicitor.* **2.** to put money into a bank account ○ *to deposit £100 in a current account*

deposit account /dɪˈpɒzɪt əˌkaʊnt/ *noun* a bank account which pays interest but on which notice has to be given to withdraw money. Abbreviation **D/A**

depositary /dɪˈpɒzɪtəri/ *noun US* a person or corporation which can place money or documents for safekeeping with a depository. ◊ **American Depositary Receipt** (NOTE: Do not confuse with **depository**.)

deposit multiplier /dɪˈpɒzɪt ˌmʌltɪplaɪə/ *noun* a factor by which a bank can increase deposits as a ratio of its reserves

depositor /dɪˈpɒzɪtə/ *noun* a person who deposits money in a bank, building society, etc.

depository /dɪˈpɒzɪt(ə)ri/ *noun* a person or company with whom money or documents can be deposited (NOTE: Do not confuse with **depositary**.)

deposit slip /dɪˈpɒzɪt slɪp/ *noun US* same as **paying-in slip**

deposit-taking institution /dɪˌpɒzɪt ˌteɪkɪŋ ˌɪnstɪˈtjuːʃ(ə)n/, **depository institution** /dɪˌpɒzɪt(ə)ri ˌɪnstɪ 'tjuːʃ(ə)n/ *noun* an institution which is licensed to receive money on deposit from private individuals and to pay interest on it, e.g. a building society, bank or friendly society

depreciate /dɪ'priːʃieɪt/ *verb* **1.** to make an allowance in accounts for the loss of value of an asset over time ○ *We depreciate our company cars over three years.* **2.** to lose value ○ *a share that has depreciated by 10% over the year* ○ *The pound has depreciated by 5% against the dollar.*

COMMENT: Various methods of depreciating assets are used, such as the 'straight line method', where the asset is depreciated at a constant percentage of its cost each year and the 'reducing balance method', where the asset is depreciated at a constant percentage which is applied to the cost of the asset after each of the previous years' depreciation has been deducted.

depreciation /dɪˌpriːʃi'eɪʃ(ə)n/ *noun* **1.** a loss of value ○ *a share that has shown a depreciation of 10% over the year* ○ *the depreciation of the pound against the dollar* **2.** the loss of value of an asset over time, which is recorded in accounts as an expense

depreciation rate /dɪˌpriːʃi'eɪʃ(ə)n reɪt/ *noun* the rate at which an asset is depreciated each year in the company accounts

depress /dɪ'pres/ *verb* to reduce something ○ *Reducing the money supply has the effect of depressing demand for consumer goods.*

depressed area /dɪˌprest 'eəriə/ *noun* a part of a country suffering from depression

depressed market /dɪˌprest 'mɑːkɪt/ *noun* a market where there are more goods than customers

depression /dɪ'preʃ(ə)n/ *noun* a period of economic crisis with high unemployment and loss of trade ○ *The country entered a period of economic depression.*

dept *abbreviation* department

deregulate /diː'regjʊleɪt/ *verb* to remove government controls from an industry ○ *The US government deregulated the banking sector in the 1980s.*

deregulation /diːˌregjʊ'leɪʃ(ə)n/ *noun* the reduction of government control over an industry ○ *the deregulation of the airlines*

'…after the slump in receipts last year that followed liner shipping deregulation in the US, carriers are probably still losing money on their transatlantic services. But with a possible contraction in capacity and healthy trade growth, this year has begun in a much more promising fashion than last' [*Lloyd's List*]

derivative instruments /dɪˌrɪvətɪv 'ɪnstrʊmənts/, **derivatives** /dɪ'rɪvətɪvz/ *plural noun* any forms of traded security such as option contracts, which are derived from ordinary bonds and shares, exchange rates or stock market indices

COMMENT: Derivatives traded on stock exchanges or futures exchanges include options on futures or exchange rates or interest rates. While they can be seen as a way of hedging against possible swings in exchange rates or commodity prices, they can also produce huge losses if the market goes against the trader.

descending tops /dɪˌsendɪŋ 'tɒps/ *plural noun* a term used by chartists to refer to a falling market, where each peak is lower than the one before

designate *adjective* /'dezɪgnət/ appointed to a job but not yet working ○ *the chairman designate* (NOTE: always follows a noun) ■ *verb* /'dezɪgneɪt/ to appoint someone to a post

designer /dɪ'zaɪnə/ *adjective* expensive and fashionable ○ *designer jeans*

destabilise /diː'steɪbɪlaɪz/, **destabilize** *verb* to make something less stable ○ *The comments by the speculators were aimed at destabilising the country's economy.*

destabilising /diː'steɪbɪlaɪzɪŋ/, **destabilizing** *adjective* which makes something less stable

detailed account /ˌdiːteɪld ə'kaʊnt/ *noun* an account which lists every item

determine /dɪ'tɜːmɪn/ *verb* to fix, arrange or decide ○ *to determine prices* or *quantities* ○ *conditions still to be determined*

Deutsches Bundesbank *noun* the German central bank, based in Frankfurt

Deutschmark /'dɔɪtʃmɑːk/ *noun* a unit of currency used before the euro in Germany

devaluation /ˌdiːvæljuˈeɪʃ(ə)n/ *noun* a reduction in the value of a currency against other currencies ○ *the devaluation of the rand*

devalue /diːˈvæljuː/ *verb* to reduce the value of a currency against other currencies ○ *The pound has been devalued by 7%.*

develop /dɪˈveləp/ *verb* **1.** to plan and produce ○ *to develop a new product* **2.** to plan and build an area ○ *to develop an industrial estate*

developing country /dɪˌveləpɪŋ ˈkʌntri/, **developing nation** /dɪ ˌveləpɪŋ ˈneɪʃ(ə)n/ *noun* a country which is not fully industrialised

development /dɪˈveləpmənt/ *noun* the work of planning the production of a new product and constructing the first prototypes ○ *We spend a great deal on research and development.*

development area /dɪˈveləpmənt ˌeəriə/, **development zone** /dɪ ˈveləpmənt zəʊn/ *noun* an area which has been given special help from a government to encourage businesses and factories to be set up there

deviate /ˈdiːvieɪt/ *verb* to turn away from what is normal or usual

deviation /ˌdiːviˈeɪʃ(ə)n/ *noun* a change of route or strategy ○ *Advertising in the tabloids will mean a deviation from our normal marketing strategy.*

devise /dɪˈvaɪz/ *noun* the act of giving freehold land to someone in a will

COMMENT: Giving of other types of property is a **bequest**.

dial /ˈdaɪəl/ *verb* to call a telephone number on a telephone ○ *to dial a number* ○ *to dial the operator* (NOTE: **dialling – dialled**. The UK spelling is **dialling – dialled**.) □ **to dial direct** to contact a phone number without asking the operator to do it for you ○ *You can dial New York direct from London.*

differential /ˌdɪfəˈrenʃəl/ *adjective* showing a difference ■ *noun* □ **to erode wage differentials** to reduce differences in salary gradually

differential tariffs /ˌdɪfərenʃəl ˈtærɪfs/ *plural noun* different tariffs for different classes of goods as, e.g., when imports from some countries are taxed more heavily than similar imports from other countries

difficulty /ˈdɪfɪk(ə)lti/ *noun* a problem, or trouble in doing something ○ *They had a lot of difficulty selling into the European market.* ○ *We have had some difficulties with customs over the export of computers.*

digit /ˈdɪdʒɪt/ *noun* a single number ○ *a seven-digit phone number*

digital /ˈdɪdʒɪt(ə)l/ *adjective* converted into a form that can be processed by computers and accurately reproduced

digital cash /ˌdɪdʒɪt(ə)l ˈkæʃ/ *noun* a form of digital money that can be used like physical cash to make online purchases and is anonymous because there is no way of obtaining information about the buyer when it is used

digital money /ˌdɪdʒɪt(ə)l ˈmʌni/ *noun* a series of numbers that has a value equivalent to a sum of money in a physical currency

digital wallet /ˌdɪdʒɪt(ə)l ˈwɒlɪt/ *noun* a piece of personalised software on the hard drive of a user's computer that contains, in coded form, such items as credit card information, digital cash, a digital identity certificate, and standardised shipping information, and can be used when paying for a transaction electronically. Also called **e-purse**, **electronic purse**

diligence /ˈdɪlɪdʒəns/ *noun* ♦ **due diligence**

dilute /daɪˈluːt/ *verb* to make less valuable ○ *Conversion of the loan stock will dilute the assets per share by 5%.*

dilution levy /daɪˈluːʃ(ə)n ˌlevi/ *noun* an extra charge levied by fund managers on investors buying or selling units in a fund, to offset any potential effect on the value of the fund of such sales or purchases

dilution of shareholding /daɪ ˌluːʃ(ə)n əv ˈʃeəhəʊldɪŋ/ *noun* a situation where the ordinary share capital of a company has been increased, but without an increase in the assets so that each share is worth less than before

dime /daɪm/ *noun US* a ten cent coin (*informal*)

diminish /dɪˈmɪnɪʃ/ *verb* to become smaller ○ *Our share of the market has diminished over the last few years.*

dinar /ˈdiːnɑː/ *noun* a unit of currency used in some European countries (including Bosnia, Macedonia and Serbia) and in many Arabic countries: Algeria, Bahrain, Iraq, Jordan, Kuwait, Libya, Tunisia, South Yemen and Sudan

dip /dɪp/ *noun* a sudden small fall ○ *Last year saw a dip in the company's performance.* ■ *verb* to fall in price ○ *Shares dipped sharply in yesterday's trading.* (NOTE: **dipping – dipped**)

direct /daɪˈrekt/ *verb* to manage or organise something ○ *He directs our South-East Asian operations.* ○ *She was directing the development unit until last year.* ■ *adjective* straight or without interference ■ *adverb* with no third party involved ○ *We pay income tax direct to the government.*

direct action /daɪˌrekt ˈækʃən/ *noun* a strike or go-slow by a workforce

direct business /daɪˌrekt ˈbɪznɪs/ *noun* insurance business transacted between an insurance company and the person taking out the insurance without going through a broker

direct cost /daɪˌrekt ˈkɒst/ *noun* a cost which can be directly related to the making of a product, i.e. its production cost

direct debit /daɪˌrekt ˈdebɪt/ *noun* a system where a customer allows a company to charge costs to his or her bank account automatically and where the amount charged can be increased or decreased with the agreement of the customer ○ *I pay my electricity bill by direct debit.* Abbreviation **DD**

direction /daɪˈrekʃən/ *noun* **1.** the process of organising or managing ○ *He took over the direction of a multinational group.* **2.** □ **directions for use** instructions showing how to use something

directive /daɪˈrektɪv/ *noun* an order or command to someone to do something ○ *The Commission issued a directive on food prices.* (NOTE: Directives from the European Union are binding, but member states can implement them as they wish. A directive is binding as to the result to be achieved, but leaves to the national authorities the choice of form and method.)

directly /daɪˈrektli/ *adverb* with no third party involved ○ *We deal directly with the manufacturer, without using a wholesaler.*

direct mail /daɪˌrekt ˈmeɪl/ *noun* the practice of selling a product by sending publicity material to possible buyers through the post ○ *These calculators are only sold by direct mail.* ○ *The company runs a successful direct-mail operation.*

'…all of those who had used direct marketing techniques had used direct mail, 79% had used some kind of telephone technique and 63% had tried off-the-page selling' [*Precision marketing*]

direct-mail advertising /daɪˌrekt ˈmeɪl ˌædvətaɪzɪŋ/ *noun* advertising by sending leaflets to people through the post

direct mailing /daɪˌrekt ˈmeɪlɪŋ/ *noun* the sending of publicity material by post to possible buyers

director /daɪˈrektə/ *noun* **1.** a senior employee appointed by the shareholders to help run a company, who is usually in charge of one or other of its main functions, e.g. sales or human relations, and usually, but not always, a member of the board of directors □ **directors' salaries** salaries of directors (which have to be listed in the company's profit and loss account) **2.** the person who is in charge of a project, an official institute, or other organisation ○ *the director of the government research institute* ○ *She was appointed director of the trade association.*

'…the research director will manage and direct a team of business analysts reporting on the latest developments in retail distribution throughout the UK' [*Times*]

COMMENT: Directors are elected by shareholders at the AGM, though they are usually chosen by the chairman or chief executive. A board will consist of a chairman (who may be non-executive), a chief executive or managing director and a series of specialist directors in charge of various activities of the company (such as a finance director, production director or sales director). The company secretary will attend board meetings, but need not be a director. Apart from the executive directors, who are in fact employees of the company, there may be several non-executive directors, appointed either for their expertise and contacts, or as representatives of important shareholders such as banks. The board of an American company may be made up of a large number of non-executive directors and only one or two executive officers. A British board has more executive directors.

directorate /daɪ'rekt(ə)rət/ *noun* a group of directors

Director of the Budget /daɪˌrektər əv ðə 'bʌdʒɪt/ *noun* the member of a government in charge of the preparation of the budget

director's fees /daɪ'rektəz fiːz/ *plural noun* money paid to a director for attendance at board meetings

directorship /daɪ'rektəʃɪp/ *noun* the post of director ○ *She was offered a directorship with Smith Ltd*

directors' report /daɪ'rektəz rɪˌpɔːt/ *noun* the annual report from the board of directors to the shareholders

directory /daɪ'rekt(ə)ri/ *noun* **1.** a reference book containing information on companies and their products **2.** a list of people or businesses with information about their addresses and telephone numbers

direct paper /daɪˌrekt 'peɪpə/ *noun* a financial paper sold direct to investors

direct placement /daɪˌrekt 'pleɪsmənt/ *noun US* the act of placing new shares directly with purchasers, without going through a broker

direct selling /daɪˌrekt 'selɪŋ/ *noun* the work of selling a product direct to the customer without going through a shop

direct sends /daɪˌrekt 'sendz/ *plural noun US* cheques sent directly to a drawee bank to be cleared, without going through the clearing house process

direct share ownership /daɪˌrekt 'ʃeə ˌəʊnəʃɪp/ *noun* the ownership of shares by private individuals, buying or selling through brokers, and not via holdings in unit trusts

direct tax /daɪˌrekt 'tæks/ *noun* a tax that is paid directly to the government, e.g. income tax, as distinct from a tax such as VAT that is paid indirectly

direct taxation /daɪˌrekt tæk 'seɪʃ(ə)n/ *noun* the process in which a government raises revenue in the form of direct taxes ○ *The government raises more money by direct taxation than by indirect.*

dirham /'dɪəræm/ *noun* a unit of currency used in Morocco and the United Arab Emirates

dirty float /'dɜːti fləʊt/ *noun* the process of floating a currency, in which

the government intervenes to regulate the exchange rate

disallow /ˌdɪsə'laʊ/ *verb* not to accept a claim for insurance ○ *She claimed £2,000 for fire damage, but the claim was disallowed.*

disburse /dɪs'bɜːs/ *verb* to pay money

disbursement /dɪs'bɜːsmənt/ *noun* the payment of money

discharge *noun* /'dɪstʃɑːdʒ/ **1.** the act of paying a debt □ **in full discharge of a debt** as full payment of a debt **2.** □ **in discharge of her duties as director** while carrying out her duties as director ■ *verb* **1.** to pay a debt □ **to discharge a bankrupt** to release someone from bankruptcy because they have has paid their debts **2.** to dismiss an employee ○ *to discharge an employee for negligence*

discharged bankrupt /dɪsˌtʃɑːdʒd 'bæŋkrʌpt/ *noun* a person who has been released from being bankrupt because his or her debts have been paid

discharge in bankruptcy /ˌdɪstʃɑːdʒ ɪn 'bæŋkrʌptsi/, **discharge of bankruptcy** *noun* the legal process of being released from bankruptcy after paying your debts

disciplinary procedure /ˌdɪsɪ 'plɪnəri prəˌsiːdʒə/ *noun* a way of warning a worker officially that he or she is breaking rules or is working badly

disclaimer /dɪs'kleɪmə/ *noun* a legal refusal to accept responsibility

disclose /dɪs'kləʊz/ *verb* to tell something that was previously unknown to other people or secret ○ *The bank has no right to disclose details of my account to the tax office.*

disclosure /dɪs'kləʊʒə/ *noun* the act of telling something that was previously unknown to other people or secret ○ *The disclosure of the takeover bid raised the price of the shares.*

disclosure of shareholding /dɪs ˌkləʊʒər əv 'ʃeəhəʊldɪŋ/ *noun* the act of making public the fact that someone owns shares in a company

discount *noun* /'dɪskaʊnt/ **1.** the percentage by which the seller reduces the full price for the buyer ○ *to give a discount on bulk purchases* □ **to sell goods at a discount** *or* **at a discount price** to sell goods below the normal price

◻ **10% discount for cash**, **10% cash discount** you pay 10% less if you pay in cash **2.** the amount by which something is sold for less than its value ◻ **currency at a discount** a currency whose future value is less than its spot value ◻ **shares at a discount** shares which are lower in price than their asset value or their par value ■ *verb* /dɪsˈkaʊnt/ **1.** to reduce prices to increase sales **2.** ◻ **to discount bills of exchange** to buy or sell bills of exchange for less than the value written on them in order to cash them later **3.** to react to something which may happen in the future, such as a possible takeover bid or currency devaluation ◻ **shares are discounting a rise in the dollar** shares have risen in advance of a rise in the dollar price

discountable /ˈdɪskaʊntəb(ə)l/ *adjective* possible to discount ○ *These bills are not discountable.*

discount broker /ˈdɪskaʊnt ˌbrəʊkə/ *noun* a broker who charges a lower commission than other brokers

discounted cash flow /ˌdɪskaʊntɪd ˈkæʃ fləʊ/ *noun* the calculation of the forecast return on capital investment by discounting future cash flows from the investment, usually at a rate equivalent to the company's minimum required rate of return. Abbreviation **DCF**

COMMENT: Discounting is necessary because it is generally accepted that money held today is worth more than money to be received in the future. The effect of discounting is to reduce future income or expenses to their 'present value'. Once discounted, future cash flows can be compared directly with the initial cost of a capital investment which is already stated in present value terms. If the present value of income is greater than the present value of costs, the investment can be said to be worthwhile.

discounted value /ˌdɪskaʊntɪd ˈvæljuː/ *noun* the difference between the face value of a share and its lower market price

discounter /ˈdɪskaʊntə/ *noun* a person or company that discounts bills or invoices, or sells goods at a discount

discount for cash /ˌdɪskaʊnt fə ˈkæʃ/ *noun* same as **cash discount**

discount house /ˈdɪskaʊnt haʊs/ *noun* **1.** a financial company which specialises in discounting bills **2.** a shop which specialises in selling cheap goods bought at a high discount

discount market /ˈdɪskaʊnt ˌmɑːkɪt/ *noun* a market for borrowing and lending money, through Treasury bills, certificates of deposit, etc.

discount points /ˈdɪskaʊnt pɔɪnts/ *plural noun US* extra payments made to a lender to produce a reduction in the interest rate on a mortgage

discount price /ˈdɪskaʊnt praɪs/ *noun* the full price less a discount

discount rate /ˈdɪskaʊnt reɪt/ *noun* the rate charged by a central bank on any loans it makes to other banks

discount store /ˈdɪskaʊnt stɔː/ *noun* a shop which specialises in cheap goods bought at a high discount

discount window /ˈdɪskaʊnt ˌwɪndəʊ/ *noun US* a way in which the Federal Reserve grants loans to a bank by giving advances on the security of Treasury bills which the bank is holding

discrepancy /dɪˈskrepənsi/ *noun* a lack of agreement between figures in invoices or accounts

discrete compounding /dɪˌskriːt ˈkɒmpaʊndɪŋ/ *noun* a system where interest is calculated at certain times, such as the end of a month or year, and then added to the principal

discretion /dɪˈskreʃ(ə)n/ *noun* the ability to decide what should be done ◻ **I leave it to your discretion** I leave it for you to decide what to do ◻ **at the discretion of someone** according to what someone decides ○ *Membership is at the discretion of the committee.*

discretionary /dɪˈskreʃ(ə)n(ə)ri/ *adjective* possible if someone wants ◻ **the governor's discretionary powers** powers which the governor could use if he or she thought it necessary ◻ **on a discretionary basis** referring to a way of managing a client's funds, where the fund manager uses his discretion to do as he wants, without the client giving him any specific instructions

discretionary account /dɪˌskreʃ(ə)n(ə)ri əˈkaʊnt/ *noun* a client's account with a stockbroker, where the broker invests and sells at his or her own discretion without the client needing to give him specific instructions

discretionary client /dɪˌskreʃ(ə)n(ə)ri ˈklaɪənt/ *noun* a client whose funds are managed on a discretionary basis

discretionary funds /dɪˌskreʃ(ə)n(ə)ri ˈfʌndz/ *plural noun* funds managed on a discretionary basis

diseconomies of scale /dɪsɪˌkɒnəmiz əv ˈskeɪl/ *plural noun* a situation where increased production leads to a higher production cost per unit or average production cost

COMMENT: After having increased production using the existing workforce and machinery, giving economies of scale, the company finds that in order to increase production further it has to employ more workers and buy more machinery, leading to an increase in unit cost.

disenfranchise /ˌdɪsɪnˈfræntʃaɪz/ *verb* to take away someone's right to vote ○ *The company has tried to disenfranchise the ordinary shareholders.*

disequilibrium /ˌdɪsiːkwɪˈlɪbriəm/ *noun* an imbalance in the economy when supply does not equal demand or a country's balance of payments is in deficit

dishonour /dɪsˈɒnə/ *verb* □ **to dishonour a bill** not to pay a bill (NOTE: The US spelling is **dishonor**.)

dishonoured cheque /dɪsˌɒnəd ˈtʃek/ *noun* a cheque which the bank will not pay because there is not enough money in the account to pay it

disinflation /ˌdɪsɪnˈfleɪʃ(ə)n/ *noun* the process of reducing inflation in the economy by increasing tax and reducing the level of money supply. Compare **deflation**

disinflationary /ˌdɪsɪnˈfleɪʃ(ə)n(ə)ri/ *adjective* which reduces the level of inflation in the economy

disintermediation /dɪsˌɪntəmiːdiˈeɪʃ(ə)n/ *noun* **1.** the removal of any intermediaries from a process so that, e.g., lenders lend money direct to borrowers **2.** a situation where investors remove their money from deposit accounts and invest directly in the stock market

disinvest /ˌdɪsɪnˈvest/ *verb* **1.** to reduce investment by not replacing capital assets when they wear out **2.** to reduce investment by selling shares

disinvestment /ˌdɪsɪnˈvestmənt/ *noun* **1.** a reduction in capital assets by not replacing them when they wear out **2.** a process of reducing investments by selling shares

dismissal procedures /dɪsˈmɪs(ə)l prəˌsiːdʒəz/ *plural noun* the correct way to dismiss someone, following the rules in the contract of employment

dispatch note /dɪˈspætʃ nəʊt/ *noun* a note saying that goods have been sent

disposable personal income /dɪˌspəʊzəb(ə)l ˌpɜːs(ə)nəl ˈɪnkʌm/ *noun* the income left after tax and National Insurance have been deducted. Also called **take-home pay**

disposal /dɪˈspəʊz(ə)l/ *noun* a sale ○ *a disposal of securities* ○ *The company has started a systematic disposal of its property portfolio.* □ **lease or business for disposal** a lease or business for sale

dispose /dɪˈspəʊz/ *verb* □ **to dispose of** to get rid of or to sell, especially cheaply ○ *to dispose of excess stock* ○ *to dispose of excess equipment* ○ *He is planning to dispose of his business in the new year.*

disqualification /dɪsˌkwɒlɪfɪˈkeɪʃ(ə)n/ *noun* the act of making someone disqualified to do something

'Even 'administrative offences' can result in disqualification. A person may be disqualified for up to five years following persistent breach of company legislation in terms of failing to file returns, accounts and other documents with the Registrar' [*Accountancy*]

disqualify /dɪsˈkwɒlɪfaɪ/ *verb* to make a person unqualified to do something, such as to be a director of a company

dissolution /ˌdɪsəˈluːʃ(ə)n/ *noun* the ending of a partnership

dissolve /dɪˈzɒlv/ *verb* to bring to an end ○ *to dissolve a partnership*

distrain /dɪˈstreɪn/ *verb* to seize goods to pay for debts

distress /dɪˈstres/ *noun* the act of taking someone's goods to pay for debts

distressed /dɪˈstrest/ *adjective* experiencing economic or financial difficulties

distressed companies /dɪˌstrest ˈkʌmp(ə)niz/ *plural noun* companies which may go into liquidation, and whose shares are seen as a speculative buy

distress merchandise /dɪˈstres ˌmɜːtʃəndaɪs/ *noun US* goods sold cheaply to pay a company's debts

distress sale /dɪˈstres seɪl/ *noun* a sale of goods at low prices to pay a company's debts

distress securities fund /dɪˌstres sɪ ˈkjʊərɪtiz fʌnd/ *noun* a type of fund which invests in companies where there may be a major problems

distributable profits /dɪs ˌtrɪbjʊtəb(ə)l ˈprɒfɪts/ *plural noun* profits which can be distributed to shareholders as dividends if the directors decide to do so

distribute /dɪˈstrɪbjuːt/ *verb* **1.** to share out dividends ○ *Profits were distributed among the shareholders.* **2.** to send out goods from a manufacturer's warehouse to retail shops ○ *Smith Ltd distributes for several smaller companies.* ○ *All orders are distributed from our warehouse near Oxford.*

distributed profits /dɪˌstrɪbjʊtɪd ˈprɒfɪts/ *plural noun* profits passed to shareholders in the form of dividends

distribution /ˌdɪstrɪˈbjuːʃ(ə)n/ *noun* the act of sending goods from the manufacturer to the wholesaler and then to retailers ○ *Stock is held in a distribution centre which deals with all order processing.* ○ *Distribution costs have risen sharply over the last 18 months.* ○ *She has several years' experience as distribution manager.*

'British distribution companies are poised to capture a major share of the European market' [*Management News*]

distribution channel /ˌdɪstrɪ ˈbjuːʃ(ə)n ˌtʃæn(ə)l/ *noun* the route by which a product or service reaches a customer after it leaves the producer or supplier (NOTE: A distribution channel usually consists of a chain of intermediaries, for example wholesalers and retailers, that is designed to move goods from the point of production to the point of consumption in the most efficient way.)

'…there is evidence that distribution channels are supply driven' [*Quarterly Review of Marketing*]

distribution network /ˌdɪstrɪ ˈbjuːʃ(ə)n ˌnetwɜːk/ *noun* a series of

points or small warehouses from which goods are sent all over a country

distribution of income /ˌdɪstrɪ bjuːʃ(ə)n əv ˈɪnkʌm/ *noun* the payment of dividends to shareholders

distribution slip /ˌdɪstrɪˈbjuːʃ(ə)n slɪp/ *noun* a paper attached to a document or to a magazine, showing all the people in an office who should read it

distributive trades /dɪˈstrɪbjʊtɪv ˌtreɪdz/ *plural noun* all businesses involved in the distribution of goods

distributor /dɪˈstrɪbjʊtə/ *noun* a company which sells goods for another company which makes them □ **a network of distributors** a number of distributors spread all over a country

distributorship /dɪˈstrɪbjʊtəʃɪp/ *noun* the position of being a distributor for a company

diversification /daɪˌvɜːsɪfɪˈkeɪʃ(ə)n/ *noun* the process in which a company begins to engage in a new and different type of business

diversify /daɪˈvɜːsɪfaɪ/ *verb* **1.** to add new types of business to existing ones ○ *The company is planning to diversify into new products.* **2.** to invest in different types of shares or savings so as to spread the risk of loss

divest /daɪˈvest/ *verb* □ **to divest oneself of something** to get rid of something ○ *The company had divested itself of its US interests.*

divestiture /daɪˈvestɪtʃə/ *noun* the sale of an asset

dividend /ˈdɪvɪdend/ *noun* a percentage of profits paid to shareholders □ **to raise** *or* **increase the dividend** to pay out a higher dividend than in the previous year □ **to maintain the dividend** to keep the same dividend as in the previous year □ **to omit** *or* **pass the dividend** to pay no dividend □ **the dividend is covered four times** the profits are four times the dividend □ **the shares are quoted ex dividend** the share price does not include the right to the dividend

COMMENT: The dividend is calculated as the proportion of profits a company can pay to its shareholders after tax has been paid, always keeping some of the profit back to reinvest in the company's products or activities. Large companies usually pay dividends twice a year, once after the half-year results have been declared (called the 'interim dividend') and gain when the final results are published.

dividend check /'dɪvɪdend tʃek/ *noun US* same as **dividend warrant**

dividend cover /'dɪvɪdend ˌkʌvə/ *noun* the ratio of profits to dividends paid to shareholders

dividend forecast /'dɪvɪdend ˌfɔːkɑːst/ *noun* a forecast of the amount of an expected dividend

dividend payout /'dɪvɪdend ˌpeɪaʊt/ *noun* money paid as dividends to shareholders

dividend per share /ˌdɪvɪdend pə 'ʃeə/ *noun* an amount of money paid as dividend for each share held

dividend warrant /'dɪvɪdend ˌwɒrənt/ *noun* a cheque which makes payment of a dividend (NOTE: The US term is **dividend check**.)

dividend yield /'dɪvɪdend jiːld/ *noun* a dividend expressed as a percentage of the current market price of a share

divisional headquarters /dɪˌvɪʒ(ə)nəl hedˈkwɔːtəz/ *plural noun* the main office of a division of a company

DJIA *abbreviation* Dow Jones Industrial Average

DM, D-mark *abbreviation* Deutschmark

dock dues /'dɒk djuːz/ *plural noun* a payment which a ship makes to the harbour authorities for the right to use the harbour

document /'dɒkjʊmənt/ *noun* a paper, especially an official paper, with written information on it ○ *He left a file of documents in the taxi.* ○ *She asked to see the documents relating to the case.*

documentary /ˌdɒkjʊ'ment(ə)ri/ *adjective* in the form of documents ○ *documentary evidence*

documentary credit /ˌdɒkjʊment(ə)ri 'kredɪt/ *noun* a credit document used in export trade, when a bank issues a letter of credit against shipping documents

documentary proof /ˌdɒkjʊment(ə)ri 'pruːf/ *noun* a proof in the form of a document

documentation /ˌdɒkjʊmen'teɪʃ(ə)n/ *noun* all the documents referring to something ○ *Please send me the complete documentation concerning the sale.*

document image processing /ˌdɒkjʊmənt 'ɪmɪdʒ ˌprəʊsesɪŋ/ *noun* a system for scanning documents, such as cheques, and storing the information in a retrieval system

documents against acceptance /ˌdɒkjʊmənts əˌgenst ək'septəns/ *noun* **1.** an arrangement whereby buyers receive documents for the goods on their acceptance of a bill of exchange **2.** a note to a bank to instruct it that documents attached to a draft should be given to the drawee when the draft is accepted

do-it-yourself conveyancing /ˌduːɪt jəˌself kən'veɪənsɪŋ/ *noun* the drawing up of a legal conveyance by the person selling a property, without the help of a lawyer

dollar /'dɒlə/ *noun* a unit of currency used in the US and other countries such as Australia, Bahamas, Barbados, Bermuda, Brunei, Canada, Fiji, Hong Kong, Jamaica, New Zealand, Singapore and Zimbabwe ○ *The US dollar rose 2%.* ○ *They sent a cheque for fifty Canadian dollars.* ○ *It costs six Australian dollars.* □ **a five dollar bill** a banknote for five dollars

dollar area /'dɒlər ˌeəriə/ *noun* an area of the world where the US dollar is the main trading currency

dollar balances /'dɒlə ˌbælənsɪz/ *plural noun* a country's trade balances expressed in US dollars

dollar-cost averaging /ˌdɒlər kɒst 'æv(ə)rɪdʒɪŋ/ *noun* ♦ **pound-cost averaging**

dollar crisis /'dɒlə ˌkraɪsɪs/ *noun* a fall in the exchange rate for the US dollar

dollar gap /ˌdɒlə 'gæp/ *noun* a situation where the supply of US dollars is not enough to satisfy the demand for them from overseas buyers

dollar millionaire /ˌdɒlə ˌmɪljə'neə/ *noun* a person who has more than one million dollars

dollar stocks /ˌdɒlə 'stɒks/ *plural noun* shares in US companies

domestic /də'mestɪk/ *adjective* referring to the home market or the market of the country where the business is situated ○ *Domestic sales have increased over the last six months.*

domestic consumption /dəˌmestɪk kən'sʌmpʃən/ *noun* use in the home country ○ *Domestic consumption of oil has fallen sharply.*

domestic demand deflator /də,mestɪk dɪ,mɑːnd diːˈfleɪtə/ *noun* a figure used to remove inflation from the calculations for domestic demand

domestic interest rates /də,mestɪk ˈɪntrəst reɪts/ *plural noun* interest rates payable in a local currency on deposits placed in that country

domestic market /də,mestɪk ˈmɑːkɪt/ *noun* the market in the country where a company is based ○ *They produce goods for the domestic market.*

domestic production /də,mestɪk prəˈdʌkʃən/ *noun* the production of goods for use in the home country

domestic sales /dəˈmestɪk seɪlz/ *noun* sales in the home country

domicile /ˈdɒmɪsaɪl/ *noun* the country where someone lives or where a company's office is registered ■ *verb* □ **she is domiciled in Denmark** she lives in Denmark officially □ **bills domiciled in France** bills of exchange which have to be paid in France

dong /dɒŋ/ *noun* a unit of currency used in Vietnam

donor /ˈdəʊnə/ *noun* a person who gives, especially someone who gives money

dormant /ˈdɔːmənt/ *adjective* no longer active or no longer operating

dormant account /,dɔːmənt əˈkaʊnt/ *noun* **1.** a bank account which is no longer used **2.** a past customer who is no longer buying ○ *Let's re-establish contact with some of our dormant accounts.* ○ *All the old reports on dormant accounts have been filed away.*

dot.com /,dɒt ˈkɒm/, **dot-com** /,dɒt ˈkɒm/ *noun* a business that markets its products through the Internet, rather than by using traditional marketing channels

double /ˈdʌb(ə)l/ *adjective* twice as large or two times the size ○ *Their turnover is double ours.* □ **to be on double time** to earn twice the usual wages for working on Sundays or other holidays □ **in double figures** with two figures, from 10 to 99 ○ *Inflation is in double figures.* ○ *We have had double-figure inflation for some years.* ■ *verb* to become twice as big, or make something twice as big ○ *We have doubled our profits this year* or *our*

profits have doubled this year. ○ *The company's borrowings have doubled.*

double-digit /,dʌb(ə)l ˈdɪdʒɪt/ *adjective* more than 10 and less than 100 ○ *double-digit inflation*

double-entry bookkeeping /,dʌb(ə)l ,entri ˈbʊkkiːpɪŋ/ *noun* the most commonly used system of bookkeeping, based on the principle that every financial transaction is accounted for on both the credit and debit side of an account

double option /,dʌb(ə)l ˈɒpʃ(ə)n/ *noun* an option to buy or sell at an agreed price in the future, a combination of call and put options

double taxation /,dʌb(ə)l tæk ˈseɪʃ(ə)n/ *noun* the act of taxing the same income twice

doubtful /ˈdaʊtf(ə)l/ *adjective* □ **doubtful debt** a debt which may never be paid □ **doubtful loan** a loan which may never be repaid

Dow □ **the Dow** Same as **Dow Jones Index** □ **the Dow 30** Same as **Dow Jones Industrial Average** □ **Dogs of the Dow** the ten highest-yielding stocks from the Dow 30 that are supposed to do well over long periods

Dow 30 /,daʊ ˈθɜːti/ *noun* same as **Dow Jones Industrial Average**

Dow Jones Average /,daʊ ˈdʒəʊnz ,æv(ə)rɪdʒ/ *noun* same as **Dow Jones Industrial Average**

Dow Jones Index /daʊ ˈdʒəʊnz ,ɪndeks/ *noun* any of a number of indexes published by the Dow Jones Co., based on prices on the New York Stock Exchange.

COMMENT: The main index is the Dow Jones Industrial Average (see below). Other Dow Jones indexes are the Dow Jones 20 Transportation Average; Dow Jones 15 Utility Average; Dow Jones 65 Composite Average (formed of the Industrial average the Transportation Average and the Utility Average taken together and averaged); also the Dow Jones Global-US Index is a capitalisation weighted index based on 30 June 1982 = 100. A new European-based index is the Dow Jones Euro Stoxx 50 Index, comprising fifty blue-chip companies from various European countries.

Dow Jones Industrial Average

/daʊ ,dʒəʊnz ɪnˈdʌstrɪəl ,æv(ə)rɪdʒ/ *noun* an index of share prices on the New York Stock Exchange, based on a group of thirty major corporations ○ *The Dow Jones Average rose ten points.* ○ *General optimism showed in the rise on the Dow Jones Average.* Abbreviation **DJIA**

down /daʊn/ *adverb, preposition* in a lower position or to a lower position ○ *The inflation rate is gradually coming down.* ○ *Shares are slightly down on the day.* ○ *The price of petrol has gone down.* □ **to pay money down** to pay a deposit ○ *They paid £50 down and the rest in monthly instalments.*

downgrade /ˈdaʊngreɪd/ *verb* to revise an earlier assessment of a company's future financial position, or of the return on an investment, to give a less favourable likely outcome

down market /ˈdaʊn ˌmɑːkɪt/ *noun* a stock market which is falling or is at its lowest level

downmarket /ˌdaʊnˈmɑːkɪt/ *adverb, adjective* cheaper or appealing to a less wealthy section of the population ○ *The company has adopted a downmarket image.*

down payment /ˌdaʊn ˈpeɪmənt/ *noun* part of a total payment made in advance ○ *We made a down payment of $100.*

downside factor /ˈdaʊnsaɪd ˌfæktə/, **downside potential** /ˌdaʊnsaɪd pəˈtenʃ(ə)l/ *noun* the possibility of making a loss in an investment

downside risk /ˈdaʊnsaɪd rɪsk/ *noun* the risk that an investment will fall in value. Opposite **upside potential**

downstream /ˈdaʊnstriːm/ *adjective* referring to the operations of a company at the end of a process (such as selling petrol through garages considered as an operation of a petroleum company). Compare **upstream**

downswing /ˈdaʊnswɪŋ/ *noun* a downward movement of share prices (NOTE: The opposite is **upswing**.)

downtick /ˈdaʊntɪk/ *noun US* a price of stock sold which is lower than the price of the previous sale

down time /ˈdaʊn taɪm/ *noun* 1. the time when a machine is not working or not available because it is broken or being mended 2. time when a worker cannot work because machines have broken down or because components are not available

downtown /ˈdaʊntaʊn/ *adjective, adverb, noun* (in) the central business district of a town ○ *His office is in downtown New York.* ○ *She works in a downtown store.* ○ *They established a business downtown.*

down trend /ˈdaʊn trend/ *noun* a falling trend in prices ○ *The price per chip has been in a long-term down trend.*

downturn /ˈdaʊntɜːn/ *noun* a downward trend in sales or profits ○ *a downturn in the market price* ○ *The last quarter saw a downturn in the economy.*

dozen /ˈdʌz(ə)n/ *noun* a twelve ○ *to sell in sets of one dozen* □ **cheaper by the dozen** the product is cheaper if you buy twelve at a time

Dr *abbreviation* drachma

drachma /ˈdrækmə/ *noun* a unit of currency in Greece before the euro

draft /drɑːft/ *noun* 1. an order for money to be paid by a bank ○ *We asked for payment by banker's draft.* □ **to make a draft on a bank** to ask a bank to pay money for you 2. a first rough plan or document which has not been finished ○ *The finance depart* ○ *A draft of the contract* or *The draft contract is waiting for the MD's comments.* ○ *He drew up the draft agreement on the back of an envelope.* ■ *verb* to make a first rough plan of a document ○ *to draft a letter* ○ *to draft a contract* ○ *The contract is still being drafted* or *is still in the drafting stage.*

drafter /ˈdrɑːftə/ *noun* a person who makes a draft ○ *the drafter of the agreement*

drafting /ˈdrɑːftɪŋ/ *noun* an act of preparing the draft of a document ○ *The drafting of the contract took six weeks.*

drain /dreɪn/ *noun* a gradual loss of money flowing away ○ *The costs of the London office are a continual drain on our resources.* ■ *verb* to remove something gradually ○ *The expansion plan has drained all our profits.* ○ *The company's capital resources have drained away.*

draw /drɔː/ *verb* 1. to take money away ○ *to draw money out of an account* □ **to draw a salary** to have a salary paid by the company ○ *The chairman does not draw a salary.* 2. to write a cheque ○ *She paid the invoice with a cheque drawn on an Egyptian bank.* (NOTE: **drawing – drew – has drawn**)

draw down *phrasal verb* to draw money which is available under a credit agreement

draw up *phrasal verb* to write a legal document ○ *to draw up a contract* or *an agreement* ○ *to draw up a company's articles of association*

drawback /'drɔːbæk/ *noun* **1.** something which is not convenient or which is likely to cause problems ○ *One of the main drawbacks of the scheme is that it will take six years to complete.* **2.** a rebate on customs duty for imported goods when these are then used in producing exports

drawdown /'drɔːdaʊn/ *noun* the act of drawing money which is available under a credit agreement

drawee /drɔː'iː/ *noun* the person or bank asked to make a payment by a drawer

drawer /'drɔːə/ *noun* the person who writes a cheque or a bill asking a drawee to pay money to a payee □ **the bank returned the cheque to drawer** the bank would not pay the cheque because the person who wrote it did not have enough money in the account to pay it

drawing account /'drɔːɪŋ əˌkaʊnt/ *noun* a current account, or any account from which the customer may take money when he or she wants

drawing rights /'drɔːɪŋ raɪts/ *noun* a right of a member country of the IMF to borrow money from the fund in a foreign currency. ◊ **special drawing rights**

dressing up /ˌdresɪŋ 'ʌp/ *noun US* same as **window dressing 2**

drift /drɪft/ *noun* gradual movement without any control ■ *verb* to move gradually in a particular direction ○ *Shares drifted lower in a dull market.* ○ *Strikers are drifting back to work.*

drive /draɪv/ *noun* an energetic way of doing things ■ *verb* □ **to drive a company out of business** to force a company into liquidation ○ *The company was almost driven out of business a few years ago.*

driver /'draɪvə/ *noun* something or someone that provides an impetus for something to happen

drop /drɒp/ *noun* a fall ○ *a drop in sales* ○ *Sales show a drop of 10%.* ○ *The drop in prices resulted in no significant increase in sales.* ■ *verb* to fall ○ *Sales have dropped by 10%* or *have dropped*

10%. ○ *The pound dropped three points against the dollar.*

'…while unemployment dropped by 1.6 per cent in the rural areas, it rose by 1.9 per cent in urban areas during the period under review' [*Business Times (Lagos)*]

'…corporate profits for the first quarter showed a 4 per cent drop from last year's final three months' [*Financial Times*]

'…since last summer American interest rates have dropped by between three and four percentage points' [*Sunday Times*]

drop ship *phrasal verb* to deliver a large order direct to a customer

droplock bond /'drɒplɒk bɒnd/ *noun* a floating rate bond which will convert to a fixed rate of interest if interest rates fall to some level. ◊ **debt-convertible bond**

drop shipment /'drɒp ˌʃɪpmənt/ *noun* the delivery of a large order from the manufacturer direct to a customer's shop or warehouse without going through an agent or wholesaler

dry goods /ˌdraɪ 'ɡʊdz/ *plural noun* cloth, clothes and household goods

dual /'djuːəl/ *adjective* referring to two things at the same time

dual control /ˌdjuːəl kən'trəʊl/ *noun* a system where two people have to sign a cheque, or validate a transaction, or have keys to a safe, etc.

dual currency bond /ˌdjuːəl 'kʌrənsi bɒnd/ *noun* a bond which is paid for in one currency but which is repayable in another on redemption

dual listing /ˌdjuːəl 'lɪstɪŋ/ *noun* the listing of a share on two stock exchanges

dual pricing /ˌdjuːəl 'praɪsɪŋ/ *noun* the practice of setting different prices for a given product in the different market in which it is sold

duck /dʌk/ ◊ **lame duck**

dud /dʌd/ *noun, adjective* referring to a coin or banknote that is false or not good, or something that does not do what it is supposed to do (*informal*) ○ *The £50 note was a dud.*

dud cheque /ˌdʌd 'tʃek/ *noun* a cheque which cannot be cashed because the person writing it does not have enough money in the account to pay it

due /djuː/ *adjective* **1.** owed ○ *a sum due from a debtor* □ **to fall** or **become due** to be ready for payment □ **bill due on**

May 1st a bill which has to be paid on May 1st □ **balance due to us** the amount owed to us which should be paid **2.** correct and appropriate in the situation □ **in due form** written in the correct legal form ○ *a receipt in due form* ○ *a contract drawn up in due form* □ **after due consideration of the problem** after thinking seriously about the problem

'...many expect the US economic indicators for April, due out this Thursday, to show faster economic growth' [*Australian Financial Review*]

due diligence /ˌdjuː ˈdɪlɪdʒəns/ *noun* **1.** the examination of a company's accounts prior to a potential takeover by another organisation. This assessment is often undertaken by an independent third party. **2.** the duty of an official such as a bank manager not to act in an irresponsible way

dues /djuːz/ *plural noun* orders taken but not supplied until new stock arrives □ **to release dues** to send off orders which had been piling up while a product was out of stock ○ *We have recorded thousands of dues for that item and our supplier cannot supply it.*

dull market /ˌdʌl ˈmɑːkɪt/ *noun* a market where little business is done

dullness /ˈdʌlnəs/ *noun* the fact of being dull ○ *the dullness of the market*

dump /dʌmp/ *verb* □ **to dump goods on a market** to get rid of large quantities of excess goods cheaply in an overseas market

'...a serious threat lies in the 400,000 tonnes of subsidized beef in European cold stores. If dumped, this meat will have disastrous effects in Pacific Basin markets' [*Australian Financial Review*]

dumping /ˈdʌmpɪŋ/ *noun* the act of getting rid of excess goods cheaply in an overseas market ○ *The government has passed anti-dumping legislation.* ○ *Dumping of goods on the European market is banned.* □ **panic dumping of sterling** a rush to sell sterling at any price because of possible devaluation

Dun & Bradstreet /ˌdʌn ən ˈbrædstriːt/ *noun* an organisation which produces reports on the financial rating of companies, and also acts as a debt collection agency. Abbreviation **D&B**

duplicate *noun* /ˈdjuːplɪkət/ a copy ○ *He sent me the duplicate of the contract.* □ **in duplicate** with a copy ○ *to print an invoice in duplicate* □ **receipt in duplicate** two copies of a receipt ■ *verb* /ˈdjuːplɪkeɪt/ **1.** □ **to duplicate with another** (*of a bookkeeping entry*) to repeat another entry or to be the same as another entry **2.** □ **to duplicate a letter** to make a copy of a letter

duplication /ˌdjuːplɪˈkeɪʃ(ə)n/ *noun* the act of doing something that is already being done in the same way by somebody else, copying □ **duplication of work** the fact of doing the same thing twice unnecessarily

Dutch /dʌtʃ/ *adjective* referring to the Netherlands

go Dutch *phrasal verb* to share the bill in a restaurant

Dutch auction /ˌdʌtʃ ˈɔːkʃən/ *noun* an auction in which the auctioneer offers an item for sale at a high price and then gradually reduces the price until someone makes a bid

dutiable goods /ˌdjuːtiəb(ə)l ˈgʊdz/ *plural noun* goods on which a customs duty has to be paid

duty /ˈdjuːti/ *noun* **1.** a tax that has to be paid ○ *Traders are asking the government to take the duty off alcohol* or *to put a duty on cigarettes.* □ **goods which are liable to duty** goods on which customs or excise tax has to be paid **2.** work which has to be done

'Canadian and European negotiators agreed to a deal under which Canada could lower its import duties on $150 million worth of European goods' [*Globe and Mail (Toronto)*]

'...the Department of Customs and Excise collected a total of N79m under the new advance duty payment scheme' [*Business Times (Lagos)*]

duty-free /ˌdjuːti ˈfriː/ *adjective, adverb* sold with no duty to be paid ○ *She bought duty-free perfume at the airport.* ○ *He bought the watch duty-free.*

duty of care /ˌdjuːti əv ˈkeə/ *noun* a duty which every person has not to act in a negligent way

duty-paid goods /ˌdjuːti ˈpeɪd gʊdz/ *plural noun* goods where the duty has been paid

E

e. & o.e. *abbreviation* errors and omissions excepted

early /ˈɜːlɪ/ *adjective, adverb* before the usual time ○ *The mail arrived early.* □ **to take early retirement** to retire from work before the usual age ■ *adjective* at the beginning of a period of time ○ *He took an early flight to Paris.*

early closing day /ˌɜːlɪ ˈkləʊzɪŋ deɪ/ *noun* a weekday, usually Wednesday or Thursday, when some shops close in the afternoon

early withdrawal /ˌɜːlɪ wɪðˈdrɔːəl/ *noun* the act of withdrawing money from a deposit account before the due date ○ *Early withdrawal usually incurs a penalty.*

early withdrawal penalty /ˌɜːlɪ wɪð ˈdrɔːəl ˌpenəltɪ/ *noun* a penalty which a depositor pays for withdrawing money early from an account

earmark /ˈɪəmɑːk/ *verb* **1.** to reserve for a special purpose ○ *to earmark funds for a project* ○ *The grant is earmarked for computer systems development.* **2.** to link a tax to a particular service, such as earmarking road taxes for the upkeep of roads

earn /ɜːn/ *verb* **1.** to be paid money for working ○ *to earn £100 a day* ○ *Our agent in Paris certainly does not earn his commission.* ○ *Her new job is more of a transfer than a promotion, since she doesn't earn any more.* ○ *How much do you earn in your new job?* **2.** to produce interest or dividends ○ *a building society account which earns interest at 10%* ○ *What level of dividend do these shares earn?*

earned income /ˌɜːnd ˈɪnkʌm/ *noun* income from wages, salaries, pensions,

fees, rental income, etc., as opposed to 'unearned' income from investments

earner /ˈɜːnə/ *noun* a person who earns money □ **a nice little earner** a business that produces a good income

earnest /ˈɜːnɪst/ *noun* money paid as an initial payment by a buyer to a seller, to show commitment to the contract of sale

earning capacity /ˈɜːnɪŋ kəˌpæsɪtɪ/, **earning power** /ˈɜːnɪŋ ˌpaʊə/ *noun* the amount of money someone should be able to earn

earning potential /ˈɜːnɪŋ pəˌtenʃəl/ *noun* **1.** the amount of money a person should be able to earn in his or her professional capacity **2.** the amount of dividend which a share is capable of earning

earning power /ˈɜːnɪŋ ˌpaʊə/ *noun* the amount of money someone should be able to earn ○ *She is such a fine designer that her earning power is very large.*

earnings /ˈɜːnɪŋz/ *plural noun* **1.** salary, wages, dividends or interest received ○ *High earnings in top management reflect the heavy responsibilities involved.* ○ *The calculation is based on average earnings over three years.* □ **compensation for loss of earnings** payment to someone who has stopped earning money or who is not able to earn money **2.** money which is earned in interest or dividend **3.** the profit made by a company

'…the US now accounts for more than half of our world-wide sales. It has made a huge contribution to our earnings turna-round' [*Duns Business Month*]

'…last fiscal year the chain reported a 116% jump in earnings, to $6.4 million or $1.10 a share' [*Barrons*]

earnings before interest, taxes, depreciation and amortisation /ˌɜːnɪŋz bɪˌfɔː ˌɪntrəst ˌtæksɪz dɪ ˌpriːʃieɪʃ(ə)n ənd əˌmɔːtaɪˈzeɪʃ(ə)n/ *plural noun* the earnings generated by a business's fundamental operating performance, frequently used in accounting ratios for comparison with other companies. Interest on borrowings, tax payable on those profits, depreciation, and amortisation are excluded on the basis that they can distort the underlying performance. Abbreviation **EBITDA**

earnings before interest and tax /ˌɜːnɪŋz bɪˌfɔː ˈɪntrəst ən tæks/ *noun* the amount earned by a business before deductions are made for tax and interest payments. Abbreviation **EBIT**

earnings cap /ˈɜːnɪŋz kæp/ *noun* the upper limit on the amount of salary that can be taken into account when calculating pensions

earnings credit /ˈɜːnɪŋz ˌkredɪt/ *noun* an allowance which reduces bank charges on checking accounts

earnings drift /ˈɜːnɪŋz drɪft/ *noun* a situation where an increase in pay is greater than that of officially negotiated rates ○ *The earnings drift is caused by a sudden increased demand for a certain class of employee.* Also called **salary drift**, **wage drift**

earnings growth /ˈɜːnɪŋz grəʊθ/ *noun* an increase in profit per share

earnings number /ˈɜːnɪŋz ˌnʌmbə/ *noun* profits expressed as a percentage

earnings performance /ˈɜːnɪŋz pəˌfɔːməns/ *noun* a way in which shares earn dividends

earnings per share /ˌɜːnɪŋz pə ˈʃeə/ *plural noun* the money earned in dividends per share, shown as a percentage of the market price of one share. Abbreviation **EPS**

earnings projection /ˈɜːnɪŋz prəˌdʒekʃən/ *noun* a forecast of earnings per share

earnings-related contributions /ˌɜːnɪŋz rɪˌleɪtɪd ˌkɒntrɪˈbjuːʃ(ə)nz/ *plural noun* contributions to social security which rise as the employee's earnings rise

earnings-related pension /ˌɜːnɪŋz rɪˌleɪtɪd ˈpenʃən/ *noun* a pension which is linked to the size of a person's salary

earnings season /ˈɜːnɪŋz ˌsiːz(ə)n/ *noun* the time of year when major companies declare their results for the previous period ○ *the quarterly ritual known as earnings season*

earnings yield /ˈɜːnɪŋz jiːld/ *noun* the money earned in dividends per share as a percentage of the current market price of the share

EASDAQ *noun* an independent European stock market, based in Brussels and London, trading in companies with European-wide interests

ease /iːz/ *verb* to fall a little ○ *The share index eased slightly today.* ■ *noun* a slight fall in prices

East Caribbean dollar /iːst ˌkærɪbiən ˈdɒlə/ *noun* a unit of currency used in Antigua, Dominica, Grenada, Montserrat, St Lucia and St Vincent

easy /ˈiːzi/ *adjective* **1.** not difficult **2.** referring to a market where few people are buying, so prices are lower than they were before ○ *The stock exchange was easy yesterday.* □ **share prices are easier** prices have fallen slightly

easy money /ˌiːzi ˈmʌni/ *noun* **1.** money which can be earned with no difficulty **2.** a loan available on easy repayment terms

easy money policy /ˌiːzi ˈmʌni ˌpɒlɪsi/ *noun* a government policy of expanding the economy by making money more easily available, e.g. through lower interest rates and easy access to credit

easy terms /ˌiːzi ˈtɜːmz/ *plural noun* financial terms which are not difficult to accept ○ *The shop is let on very easy terms.*

EBA *abbreviation* Euro Banking Association

EBIT /ˈiːbɪt/ *abbreviation* earnings before interest and tax

EBITDA /ˈiːbɪtˌdɑː/ *abbreviation* earnings before interest, taxes, depreciation and amortisation

EBRD *abbreviation* European Bank for Reconstruction and Development

e-business /ˈiː ˌbɪznɪs/ *noun* a general term that refers to any type of business activity on the Internet, including marketing, branding and research ○ *E-business is a rising part of the economy.*

'...the enormous potential of e-business is that it can automate the link between suppliers and customers' [*Investors Chronicle*]

EC *abbreviation* European Community (NOTE: now called the **European Union**)

e-cash /'iː kæʃ/ *noun* same as **digital cash**

ECB *abbreviation* European Central Bank

ECGD *abbreviation* Export Credit Guarantee Department

e-cheque /'iː tʃek/, **echeque** *noun* same as **electronic cheque**

e-commerce /ˌiː 'kɒmɜːs/ *noun* a general term that is usually used to refer to the process of buying and selling goods over the Internet

'...the problem is that if e-commerce takes just a 3 per cent slice of the market that would be enough to reduce margins to ribbons' [*Investors Chronicle*]

'...the new economy requires new company structures. He believes that other blue-chip organizations are going to find that new set-ups would be needed to attract and retain the best talent for e-commerce' [*Times*]

econometrics /ɪˌkɒnə'metrɪks/ *noun* the study of the statistics of economics, using computers to analyse these statistics and make forecasts using mathematical models

economic /ˌiːkə'nɒmɪk/ *adjective* **1.** providing enough money to make a profit ○ *The flat is let at an economic rent.* ○ *It is hardly economic for the company to run its own warehouse.* **2.** referring to the financial state of a country ○ *economic planning* ○ *economic trends* ○ *Economic planners are expecting a consumer-led boom.* ○ *The government's economic policy is in ruins after the devaluation.* ○ *The economic situation is getting worse.* ○ *The country's economic system needs more regulation.*

'...each of the major issues on the agenda at this week's meeting is important to the government's success in overall economic management'
[*Australian Financial Review*]

economical /ˌiːkə'nɒmɪk(ə)l/ *adjective* saving money or materials or being less expensive ○ *This car is very economical.* □ **economical car** a car which does

not use much petrol □ **an economical use of resources** the fact of using resources as carefully as possible

Economic and Monetary Union /ˌiːkənɒmɪk ən ˌmʌnɪt(ə)ri 'juːnjən/ *noun* same as **European Monetary Union**

economic crisis /ˌiːkənɒmɪk 'kraɪsɪs/, **economic depression** /ˌiːkənɒmɪk dɪ'preʃ(ə)n/ *noun* a situation where a country is in financial collapse ○ *The government has introduced import controls to solve the current economic crisis.*

economic cycle /ˌiːkənɒmɪk 'saɪk(ə)l/ *noun* a period during which trade expands, then slows down and then expands again

economic development /ˌiːkə nɒmɪk dɪ'veləpmənt/ *noun* improvements in the living standards and wealth of the citizens of a country ○ *The government has offered tax incentives to speed up the economic development of the region.* ○ *Economic development has been relatively slow in the north, compared with the rest of the country.*

economic environment /ˌiːkənɒmɪk ɪn'vaɪrənmənt/ *noun* the general situation in the economy

economic forecaster /ˌiːkənɒmɪk 'fɔːkɑːstə/ *noun* a person who says how he or she thinks a country's economy will perform in the future

economic growth /ˌiːkənɒmɪk 'grəʊθ/ *noun* the rate at which a country's national income grows

economic indicator /ˌiːkənɒmɪk 'ɪndɪkeɪtəz/ *noun* various statistics, e.g. for the unemployment rate or overseas trade, which show how the economy is going to perform in the short or long term

economic model /ˌiːkənɒmɪk 'mɒd(ə)l/ *noun* a computerised plan of a country's economic system, used for forecasting economic trends

economic planning /ˌiːkənɒmɪk 'plænɪŋ/ *noun* plans made by a government for the future financial state of a country

economics /ˌiːkə'nɒmɪks/ *noun* the study of the production, distribution, selling and use of goods and services ■ *plural noun* the study of financial structures to show how a product or service is costed and what returns it produces ○ *I do not understand the economics of the coal industry.* (NOTE: [all senses] takes a singular verb)

economic sanctions /ˌiːkənɒmɪk 'sæŋkʃ(ə)nz/ *plural noun* restrictions on trade that foreign governments impose with the aim of influencing the political situation of a country ○ *to impose economic sanctions on a country*

economic slowdown /ˌiːkənɒmɪk 'sləʊdaʊn/ *noun* a general reduction in a country's economic activity

economic stagnation /ˌiːkənɒmɪk stæg'neɪʃ(ə)n/ *noun* a lack of expansion in the economy

economic value added /ˌiːkənɒmɪk ˌvæljuː 'ædɪd/ *noun* the difference between a company's profit and the cost of its capital. A company does not have simply to make a profit from its business – it has to make enough profit to cover the cost of its capital, including equity invested by shareholders. Abbreviation **EVA**

economies of scale /ɪˌkɒnəmiz əv 'skeɪl/ *plural noun* the cost advantages of a company producing a product in larger quantities so that each unit costs less to make. Compare **diseconomies of scale**

economist /ɪ'kɒnəmɪst/ *noun* a person who specialises in the study of economics ○ *Government economists are forecasting a growth rate of 3% next year.* ○ *An agricultural economist studies the economics of the agriculture industry.*

economy /ɪ'kɒnəmi/ *noun* **1.** an action which is intended to stop money or materials from being wasted, or the quality of being careful not to waste money or materials □ **to introduce economies** *or* **economy measures into the system** to start using methods to save money or materials **2.** the financial state of a country, or the way in which a country makes and uses its money ○ *The country's economy is in ruins.*

economy car /ɪ'kɒnəmi kɑː/ *noun* a car which does not use much petrol

economy class /ɪ'kɒnəmi klɑːs/ *noun* a lower-quality, less expensive way of travelling ○ *I travel economy class because it is cheaper.* ○ *I always travels first class because economy class is too uncomfortable.*

economy drive /ɪ'kɒnəmi draɪv/ *noun* a vigorous effort to save money or materials

economy measure /ɪ'kɒnəmi ˌmeʒə/ *noun* an action to save money or materials

economy size /ɪ'kɒnəmi saɪz/ *noun* a large size or large packet which is cheaper than usual

ECP *abbreviation* Eurocommercial paper

ecu /'ekjuː/, **ECU** *abbreviation* European Currency Unit

COMMENT: The ECU is used for internal accounting purposes within the EU, and for settlements between banks. The value of the ECU is calculated as a composite of various European currencies: currently, it is 0.719DM + 1.31FFr + 3.71BFr + 140L + 0.256fl + 0.14LuxFr + £0.0378 + I£0.00871 + 0.217DKr + dr1.15. These values remain the same, but the actual value of each currency may fluctuate slightly within set limits in the Exchange Rate Mechanism.

EDI /ˌiː diː 'aɪ/ *abbreviation* electronic data interchange

Education IRA /ˌedjʊ'keɪʃ(ə)n ˌaɪrə/ *noun US* an account in which people can contribute up to $500 annually for the education of a child or a grandchild under the age of 18. These contributions are not tax-deductible but can grow tax-free. There is no tax on withdrawals as long as the child uses them (by the time he or she is 30) to pay for higher education. Full form **Education Individual Retirement Account**

EEA *abbreviation* European Economic Area

EEC *abbreviation* European Economic Community (NOTE: now called the **European Union (EU)**)

effect /ɪ'fekt/ *noun* **1.** a result ○ *The effect of the pay increase was to raise productivity levels.* **2.** an operation □ **terms of a contract which take effect** *or* **come into effect from 1st January** terms which start to operate on 1st January □ **prices are increased 10% with effect from 1st January** new prices will apply from 1st January □ **to remain in effect** to continue to be applied **3.** meaning □ **a clause to the effect that** a clause which means that □ **we have made provision to this effect** we have put into the contract terms which will make this work ■ *verb* to carry out □ **to effect a payment** to make a payment □ **to effect customs clearance** to clear something through customs □ **to effect a settlement between two parties** to bring two parties together and make them agree to a settlement

effective /ɪˈfektɪv/ *adjective* **1.** actual, as opposed to theoretical **2.** □ **a clause effective as from 1st January** a clause which starts to be applied on 1st January

effective annual rate /ɪˌfektɪv ˌænjuəl ˈreɪt/ *noun* the average interest rate paid on a deposit for a period of a year. It is the total interest received over 12 months expressed as a percentage of the principal at the beginning of the period.

effective control /ɪˌfektɪv kənˈtrəʊl/ *noun* a situation where someone owns a large number of shares in a company, but less than 50%, and so in effect controls the company because no other single shareholder can outvote him or her

effective date /ɪˈfektɪv deɪt/ *noun* the date on which a rule or contract starts to be applied, or on which a transaction takes place

effective demand /ɪˌfektɪv dɪ ˈmɑːnd/ *noun* demand for a product made by individuals and institutions with sufficient wealth pay for it

effective exchange rate /ɪˌfektɪv ɪksˈtʃeɪndʒ ˌreɪt/ *noun* a rate of exchange for a currency calculated against a basket of currencies

effectiveness /ɪˈfektɪvnəs/ *noun* the quality of working successfully or producing results ○ *I doubt the effectiveness of television advertising.* ○ *Her effectiveness as a manager was due to her quick grasp of detail.* ♢ **cost-effectiveness**

effective price /ɪˌfektɪv ˈpraɪs/ *noun* a share price which has been adjusted to allow for a rights issue

effective rate /ɪˌfektɪv ˈreɪt/ *noun* the real interest rate on a loan or deposit, i.e., the APR

effective tax rate /ɪˌfektɪv ˈtæks ˌreɪt/ *noun* the average tax rate applicable to a given transaction, whether it is income from work undertaken, the sale of an asset, or a gift, taking into account personal allowances and scales of tax. It is

the amount of money generated by the transaction divided by the additional tax payable because of it.

effective yield /ɪˌfektɪv ˈjiːld/ *noun* actual yield shown as a percentage of the price paid after adjustments have been made

effectual /ɪˈfektʃuəl/ *adjective* which produces a correct result

efficiency /ɪˈfɪʃ(ə)nsi/ *noun* the ability to work well or to produce the right result or the right work quickly ○ *a business efficiency exhibition* ○ *The bus system is run with a high degree of efficiency.* ○ *We called in an efficiency expert to report on ways of increasing profitability.*

'…increased control means improved efficiency in purchasing, shipping, sales and delivery' [*Duns Business Month*]

efficient /ɪˈfɪʃ(ə)nt/ *adjective* able to work well or to produce the right result quickly ○ *the efficient working of a system* ○ *An efficient assistant is invaluable.* ○ *An efficient new machine would save time.*

efficiently /ɪˈfɪʃ(ə)ntli/ *adverb* in an efficient way ○ *She organised the sales conference very efficiently.*

efficient-market theory /ɪˌfɪʃ(ə)nt ˈmɑːkɪt ˌθɪəri/ *noun* a theory that the prices operating in a certain market reflect all known information about the market and therefore make it impossible for abnormal profits to be made ○ *the efficient working of a system* ○ *he needs an efficient secretary to look after him*

efflux /ˈeflʌks/ *noun* the act of flowing out ○ *the efflux of capital to North America*

EFT /ˌiː ef ˈtiː/ *abbreviation* electronic funds transfer

EFTA *abbreviation* European Free Trade Association

EFTPOS /ˈeftpɒz/ *abbreviation* electronic funds transfer at point of sale

EGM *abbreviation* Extraordinary General Meeting

EIB *abbreviation* European Investment Bank

eighty/twenty law /ˌeɪti ˈtwenti ruːl/, **80/20 law** *noun* the rule that a small percentage of customers may account for a large percentage of sales. ♢ **Pareto's Law**

EIRIS *abbreviation* Ethical Investment Research Service

EIS /ˌiː aɪ 'es/ *abbreviation* Enterprise Investment Scheme

elastic /ɪ'læstɪk/ *adjective* able to expand or contract easily because of small changes in price

elasticity /ˌɪlæ'stɪsɪti/ *noun* the ability to change easily in response to a change in circumstances □ **elasticity of supply and demand** changes in supply and demand of an item depending on its market price

elect /ɪ'lekt/ *verb* to choose someone by a vote ○ *to elect the officers of an association* ○ *She was elected president of the staff club.*

-elect /ɪlekt/ *suffix* referring to a person who has been elected but has not yet started the term of office

election /ɪ'lekʃən/ *noun* the act of electing someone ○ *the election of officers of an association* ○ *the election of directors by the shareholders*

electric utility stocks /ɪˌlektrɪk juː 'tɪlɪti stɒks/ *plural noun* shares in electricity companies

electronic /ˌelek'trɒnɪk/ *adjective* referring to computers and electronics

electronic banking /ˌelektrɒnɪk 'bæŋkɪŋ/ *noun* the use of computers to carry out banking transactions such as withdrawals through cash dispensers or transfer of funds at point of sale

electronic business /ˌelektrɒnɪk 'bɪznɪs/ *noun* same as **e-business**

electronic cash /ˌelektrɒnɪk 'kæʃ/ *noun* same as **digital cash**

electronic cheque /ˌelektrɒnɪk 'tʃek/ *noun* a system that transfers money electronically from the buyer's current account to the seller's bank account

electronic commerce /ˌelektrɒnɪk 'kɒmɜːs/ *noun* same as **e-commerce**

electronic data interchange /ˌelektrɒnɪk 'deɪtə ˌɪntətʃeɪndʒ/ *noun* a standard format used when business documents such as invoices and purchase orders are exchanged over electronic networks such as the Internet. Abbreviation **EDI**

electronic funds transfer /ˌelektrɒnɪk 'fʌndz ˌtrænsfɜː/ *noun* the system used by banking organisations for the movement of funds between accounts and for the provision of services to the customer. Abbreviation **EFT**

electronic funds transfer at point of sale /ˌelektrɒnɪk ˌfʌndz ˌtrænsfɜː ət ˌpɔɪnt əv 'seɪl/ *noun* the payment for goods or services by a bank customer using a card that is swiped through an electronic reader on the till, thereby transferring the cash from the customer's account to the retailer's or service provider's account. Abbreviation **EFTPOS**

electronic mail /ˌelektrɒnɪk 'meɪl/ *noun* same as **email** *noun* 1

electronic payment system /ˌelektrɒnɪk 'peɪmənt ˌsɪstəm/ *noun* a means of making payments over an electronic network such as the Internet

electronic point of sale /ˌelektrɒnɪk pɔɪnt əv 'seɪl/ *noun* a system where sales are charged automatically to a customer's credit card and stock is controlled by the shop's computer. Abbreviation **EPOS**

electronic purse /ˌelektrɒnɪk 'pɜːs/ *noun* same as **digital wallet**

electronics /ˌelek'trɒnɪks/ *plural noun* the scientific study of systems worked by a flow of electrons which are used in manufactured products, such as computers, calculators or telephones ○ *the electronics industry* ○ *an electronics specialist* or *expert* ○ *an electronics engineer* (NOTE: takes a singular verb)

element /'elɪmənt/ *noun* a basic part or the smallest unit into which something can be divided ○ *the elements of a settlement* ○ *Work study resulted in a standard time for each job element.*

elevator pitch /'eləveɪtə ˌpɪtʃ/ *noun* a very concise description of a business model, often delivered to a potential investor ○ *He delivered his elevator pitch to the venture capitalist who was interested in investing in his business idea.* (NOTE: The idea here is that the description should take no longer than the time it takes to ride a lift between floors.)

eligibility /ˌelɪdʒɪ'bɪlɪti/ *noun* the fact of being eligible ○ *The chairman questioned her eligibility to stand for re-election.*

eligibility date /ˌelɪdʒɪˈbɪlɪti deɪt/ noun the date at which someone becomes eligible for benefits

eligible /ˈelɪdʒɪb(ə)l/ adjective possible to choose ○ She is eligible for re-election.

eligible liabilities /ˌelɪdʒɪb(ə)l ˌlaɪəˈbɪlɪtiz/ plural noun liabilities which go into the calculation of a bank's reserves

eliminate /ɪˈlɪmɪneɪt/ verb to remove ○ to eliminate defects in the system ○ Using a computer should eliminate all possibility of error. ○ We have decided to eliminate this series of old products from our range. ○ Most of the candidates were eliminated after the first batch of tests.

elite /ɪˈliːt/ noun a group of the best people

elite stock /ɪˌliːt ˈstɒk/ noun a top-quality share

email /ˈiːmeɪl/, **e-mail** /ˈiː meɪl/ noun **1.** a system of sending messages from one computer terminal to another, using a modem and telephone lines ○ You can contact me by phone or email if you want. **2.** a message sent electronically ○ I had six emails from him today. ■ verb to send a message from one computer to another, using a modem and telephone lines ○ She emailed her order to the warehouse. ○ I emailed him about the meeting.

embargo /ɪmˈbɑːɡəʊ/ noun a government order which stops a type of trade, such as exports to or other commercial activity with another country □ **to impose** or **put an embargo on trade with a country** to say that trade with a country must not take place ○ The government has put an embargo on the export of computer equipment. □ **to lift an embargo** to allow trade to start again ○ The government has lifted the embargo on the export of computers. □ **to be under an embargo** to be forbidden ■ verb to stop trade, or not to allow something to be traded ○ The government has embargoed trade with countries that are in breach of international agreements.

embezzle /ɪmˈbez(ə)l/ verb to use illegally money which is not yours, or which you are looking after for someone ○ He was sent to prison for six months for embezzling his clients' money.

embezzlement /ɪmˈbez(ə)lmənt/ noun the act of embezzling ○ He was sent to prison for six months for embezzlement.

embezzler /ɪmˈbez(ə)lə/ noun a person who embezzles

emergency /ɪˈmɜːdʒənsi/ noun a dangerous situation where decisions have to be taken quickly

emergency credit /ɪˌmɜːdʒənsi ˈkredɪt/ noun credit given by the Federal Reserve to an organisation which has no other means of borrowing

emerging /ɪˈmɜːdʒɪŋ/ adjective which is beginning to appear and grow

emerging country /ɪˌmɜːdʒɪŋ ˈkʌntri/ noun a country which is developing rapidly

emerging growth fund /ɪˌmɜːdʒɪŋ ˈɡrəʊθ fʌnd/ noun growth fund that invests in emerging markets

emerging market /ɪˌmɜːdʒɪŋ ˈmɑːkɪt/ noun a new market, as in South-East Asia or Eastern Europe, which is developing fast and is seen as potentially profitable to fund managers

emoluments /ɪˈmɒljʊmənts/ plural noun pay, salary or fees, or the earnings of directors who are not employees (NOTE: US English uses the singular **emolument**.)

e-money /ˈiː ˌmʌni/ noun same as **digital money**

COMMENT: This normally refers to either credit card payments or virtual tokens or a virtual credit card or a micropayment.

employ /ɪmˈplɔɪ/ verb to give someone regular paid work □ **to employ twenty staff** to have twenty people working for you □ **to employ twenty new staff** to give work to twenty new people

'70 per cent of Australia's labour force was employed in service activity' [Australian Financial Review]

employed /ɪmˈplɔɪd/ adjective **1.** in regular paid work □ **he is not gainfully employed** he has no regular paid work **2.** referring to money used profitably ■ plural noun people who are working ○ the employers and the employed □ **the self-employed** people who work for themselves

employee /ɪmˈplɔɪiː/ noun a person employed by another ○ Employees of the firm are eligible to join a profit-sharing scheme. ○ Relations between manage-

ment and employees are good. ○ *The company has decided to take on new employees.*

'…companies introducing robotics think it important to involve individual employees in planning their introduction' [*Economist*]

employee buyout /ɪmˌplɔɪiː ˈbaɪaʊt/ *noun* a purchase of a company by its employees

employee share ownership plan /ɪmˌplɔɪiː ˈʃeər ˌəʊnəʃɪp ˌplæn/, **employee share ownership programme** /ɪmˌplɔɪiː ˈʃeər ˌəʊnəʃɪp ˌprəʊɡræm/, **employee share scheme** /ɪmˌplɔɪiː ˈʃeə ˌskiːm/ *noun* a plan which allows employees to obtain shares in the company for which they work, though tax may be payable if the shares are sold to employees at a price which is lower than the current market price. Abbreviation **ESOP**

employer /ɪmˈplɔɪə/ *noun* a person or company that has regular employees and pays them

employer's contribution /ɪmˌplɔɪəz ˌkɒntrɪˈbjuːʃ(ə)n/ *noun* money paid by an employer towards an employee's pension

employers' liability insurance /ɪmˌplɔɪəz ˌlaɪəˈbɪlɪti ɪnˌʃʊərəns/ *noun* insurance to cover accidents which may happen at work, and for which the company may be responsible

employment /ɪmˈplɔɪmənt/ *noun* regular paid work □ **to be without employment** to have no work □ **to find someone alternative employment** to find another job for someone

'…the blue-collar unions are the people who stand to lose most in terms of employment growth' [*Sydney Morning Herald*]

employment agency /ɪmˈplɔɪmənt ˌeɪdʒənsi/, **employment bureau** /ɪmˈplɔɪmənt ˌbjʊərəʊ/ *noun* an office or company that finds jobs for people

employment contract /ɪmˌplɔɪmənt ˈkɒntrækt/ *noun* same as **contract of employment**

employment office /ɪmˈplɔɪmənt ˌɒfɪs/ *noun* an office which finds jobs for people

employment tribunal /ɪmˈplɔɪmənt traɪˌbjuːnəl/ *noun* a government body in

the UK that is responsible for dealing with disputes between employees and employers

empower /ɪmˈpaʊə/ *verb* to give someone the power to do something ○ *She was empowered by the company to sign the contract.* ○ *Her new position empowers her to hire and fire at will.*

EMS /ˌiː em ˈes/ *abbreviation* European Monetary System

EMU *abbreviation* **1.** Economic and Monetary Union **2.** European Monetary Union

encash /ɪnˈkæʃ/ *verb* to cash a cheque, to exchange a cheque for cash

encashable /ɪnˈkæʃəb(ə)l/ *adjective* possible to cash

encashment /ɪnˈkæʃmənt/ *noun* an act of exchanging something for cash

encryption /ɪnˈkrɪpʃən/ *noun* a conversion of plain text to a secure coded form by means of a cipher system

encumbrance /ɪnˈkʌmbrəns/ *noun* a liability which is attached usually to a property or land, e.g. a mortgage or charge

end /end/ *noun* the final point or last part ○ *at the end of the contract period* □ **at the end of six months** after six months have passed ■ *verb* to finish ○ *The distribution agreement ends in July.* ○ *The chairman ended the discussion by getting up and walking out of the room.*

endorse /ɪnˈdɔːs/ *verb* to say that a product is good □ **to endorse a bill** *or* **a cheque** to sign a bill or cheque on the back to show that you accept it

COMMENT: By endorsing a cheque (i.e., signing it on the back), a person whose name is on the front of the cheque is passing ownership of it to another party, such as the bank, which can then accept it and pay him cash for it. If a cheque is deposited in an account, it does not need to be endorsed. Cheques can also be endorsed to another person: a cheque made payable to Mr A. Smith can be endorsed by Mr Smith on the back, with the words: 'Pay to Brown Ltd', and then his signature. This has the effect of making the cheque payable to Brown Ltd, and to no one else. Most cheques are now printed as crossed cheques with the words 'A/C Payee' printed in the space between the two vertical lines. These cheques can only be paid to the person whose name is written on the cheque and cannot be endorsed.

endorsee /ˌendɔːˈsiː/ *noun* a person whose name is written on a bill or cheque as having the right to cash it

endorsement /ɪnˈdɔːsmənt/ *noun* **1.** the act of endorsing **2.** a signature on a document which endorses it **3.** a note on an insurance policy which adds conditions to the policy

endorser /ɪnˈdɔːsə/ *noun* a person who endorses a bill or cheque which is then paid to him or her

endowment /ɪnˈdaʊmənt/ *noun* the act of giving money to provide a regular income

endowment assurance /ɪn ˈdaʊmənt əˌʃʊərəns/, **endowment insurance** /ɪnˈdaʊmənt ɪnˌʃʊərəns/ *noun* an insurance policy where a sum of money is paid to the insured person on a specific date or to his heirs if he dies before that date

endowment mortgage /ɪnˈdaʊmənt ˌmɔːgɪdʒ/ *noun* a mortgage in which the initial sum borrowed is repaid at the end of the loan term by the proceeds of an insurance policy linked to it

COMMENT: The borrower pays interest on the mortgage in the usual way, but does not repay the capital. Instead, he or she takes out an endowment assurance (a life insurance) policy, which is intended to cover the total capital sum borrowed. When the assurance matures, the capital is in theory paid off, though this depends on the performance of the investments made by the company providing the endowment assurance and the actual yield of the policy may be less or more than the sum required. A mortgage where the borrower repays both interest and capital is called a 'repayment mortgage'.

endowment policy /ɪnˈdaʊmənt ˌpɒlɪsi/ *noun* same as **endowment assurance**

end product /ˌend ˈprɒdʌkt/ *noun* a manufactured product resulting from a production process

end user /ˌend ˈjuːzə/ *noun* a person who actually uses a product

energy /ˈenədʒi/ *noun* power produced from electricity, petrol or a similar source ○ *We try to save energy by switching off the lights when the rooms are empty.* ○ *If you reduce the room temperature to eighteen degrees, you will save energy.*

energy shares /ˈenədʒi ʃeəz/ *plural noun* shares in companies which provide energy

enforce /ɪnˈfɔːs/ *verb* to make sure something is done or that a rule is obeyed ○ *to enforce the terms of a contract*

enforcement /ɪnˈfɔːsmənt/ *noun* the act of making sure that something is obeyed ○ *enforcement of the terms of a contract*

engage /ɪnˈgeɪdʒ/ *verb* **1.** to arrange to employ employees or advisors ○ *If we increase production we will need to engage more machinists.* ○ *She was engaged as a temporary replacement for the marketing manager who was ill.* ○ *The company has engaged twenty new sales representatives.* □ **to engage someone to do something** to make someone do something legally ○ *The contract engages us to a minimum annual purchase.* **2.** □ **to be engaged in** to be busy with ○ *He is engaged in work on computers.* ○ *The company is engaged in trade with Africa.*

engagement /ɪnˈgeɪdʒmənt/ *noun* an agreement to do something □ **to break an engagement to do something** not to do what you have legally agreed ○ *Our agents broke their engagement not to sell our rivals' products.*

Enron /ˈenrɒn/ *noun* a US energy trading and utilities company that housed one of the biggest accounting frauds in history

entail /ɪnˈteɪl/ *noun* a legal condition which passes ownership of a property only to some specific persons ■ *verb* to involve ○ *Itemising the sales figures will entail about ten days' work.*

enter /ˈentə/ *verb* to write ○ *to enter a name on a list* ○ *The clerk entered the interest in my bank book.* ○ *She entered a competition for a holiday in Greece.* ○ *They entered the sum in the ledger.* □ **to enter a bid for something** to offer (usually in writing) to buy something □ **to enter a caveat** to warn legally that you have an interest in a case, and that no steps can be taken without your permission

enter into *phrasal verb* to begin ○ *to enter into relations with someone* ○ *to enter into negotiations with a foreign government* ○ *to enter into a partner-*

ship with a friend ○ *The company does not want to enter into any long-term agreement.*

entering /'entərɪŋ/ *noun* the act of writing items in a record

enterprise /'entəpraɪz/ *noun* **1.** a system of carrying on a business **2.** a business

Enterprise Investment Scheme /ˌentəpraɪz ɪn'vestmənt skiːm/ *noun* a scheme which provides income and capital gains tax relief for people prepared to risk investing in a single unquoted or AIM-listed trading company. Abbreviation **EIS**

enterprise zone /'entəpraɪz zəʊn/ *noun* an area of the country where businesses are encouraged to develop by offering special conditions such as easy planning permission for buildings or a reduction in the business rate

entertain /ˌentə'teɪn/ *verb* to offer such things as meals, hotel accommodation and theatre tickets for the comfort and enjoyment of business visitors

entertainment /ˌentə'teɪnmənt/ *noun* the practice of offering meals or other recreation to business visitors

entertainment allowance /ˌentə'teɪnmənt əˌlaʊəns/ *noun* an amount of money set aside by a company for entertaining clients and visitors

entertainment expenses /ˌentə'teɪnmənt ɪkˌspensɪz/ *plural noun* money spent on giving meals to business visitors

entitle /ɪn'taɪt(ə)l/ *verb* to give the right to someone to have something ○ *After one year's service the employee is entitled to four weeks' holiday.* □ **he is entitled to a discount** he has the right to be given a discount

entitlement /ɪn'taɪt(ə)lmənt/ *noun* a person's right to something

entitlement issue /ɪn'taɪt(ə)lmənt ˌɪʃuː/ *noun* a rights issue

entrepot port /'ɒntrəpəʊ pɔːt/ *noun* a town with a large international commercial port dealing in re-exports

entrepot trade /'ɒntrəpəʊ treɪd/ *noun* the exporting of imported goods

entrepreneur /ˌɒntrəprə'nɜː/ *noun* a person who is willing to take commercial

risks by starting or financing commercial enterprises

entrepreneurial /ˌɒntrəprə'nɜːriəl/ *adjective* taking commercial risks ○ *an entrepreneurial decision*

entry /'entri/ *noun* **1.** an item of written information put in an accounts ledger (NOTE: The plural is **entries**.) □ **to make an entry in a ledger** to write in details of a transaction □ **to contra an entry** to enter a similar amount on the opposite side of the account **2.** an act of going in or the place where you can go in ○ *to pass a customs entry point* ○ *entry of goods under bond*

environmental shares /ɪnˌvaɪrənmənt(ə)l 'ʃeəz/ *plural noun* shares in companies which are seen to be active in the environmental field (stores which sell 'green' produce, waste disposal companies, etc.)

epos /'iːpɒs/, **EPOS, EPoS** *abbreviation* electronic point of sale

EPS *abbreviation* earnings per share

e-purse /'iː pɜːs/ *noun* same as **digital wallet**

equal /'iːkwəl/ *adjective* exactly the same ○ *Male and female employees have equal pay.* ■ *verb* to be the same as ○ *Production this month has equalled our best month ever.* (NOTE: **equalling – equalled**. The US spelling is **equaling – equaled**.)

equalise /'iːkwəlaɪz/, **equalize** *verb* to make equal ○ *to equalise dividends*

equally /'iːkwəli/ *adverb* so that each has or pays the same, or to the same degree ○ *Costs will be shared equally between the two parties.* ○ *They were both equally responsible for the disastrous launch.*

equal opportunities programme /ˌiːkwəl ɒpə'tjuːnɪtiz ˌprəʊgræm/ *noun* a programme to avoid discrimination in employment (NOTE: The US term is **affirmative action**.)

equate /ɪ'kweɪt/ *verb* to reduce to a standard value

equation /ɪ'kweɪʒ(ə)n/ *noun* a set of mathematical rules applied to solve a problem ○ *The basic accounting equation is that assets equal liabilities plus equity.*

equilibrium /ˌiːkwɪ'lɪbriəm/ *noun* the state of balance in the economy where supply equals demand or a country's balance of payments is neither in deficit nor in excess

equities /'ekwɪtiz/ *plural noun* ordinary shares

'…in the past three years commercial property has seriously underperformed equities and dropped out of favour as a result' [*Investors Chronicle*]

equity /'ekwɪti/ *noun* **1.** the ordinary shares in a company **2.** the value of a company that is the property of its shareholders, calculated as the value of the company's assets minus the value of its liabilities, not including the ordinary share capital **3.** the value of an asset minus any loans outstanding on it

COMMENT: 'Equity' (also called 'capital' or 'shareholders' equity' or 'shareholders' capital' or 'shareholders' funds') is the current net value of the company including the nominal value of the shares in issue. After several years a company would expect to increase its net worth above the value of the starting capital. 'Equity capital' on the other hand is only the nominal value of the shares in issue.

equity accounting /'ekwɪti ə,kaʊntɪŋ/ *noun* a method of accounting which puts part of the profits of a subsidiary into the parent company's books

equity capital /'ekwɪti ,kæpɪt(ə)l/ *noun* the nominal value of the shares owned by the ordinary shareholders of a company (NOTE: Preference shares are not equity capital. If the company were wound up, none of the equity capital would be distributed to preference shareholders.)

equity earnings /'ekwɪti ,ɜːnɪŋz/ *plural noun* profits after tax, which are available for distribution to shareholders in the form of dividends, or which can be retained in the company for future development

equity finance /'ekwɪti ,faɪnæns/ *noun* finance for a company in the form of ordinary shares paid for by shareholders

equity fund /'ekwɪti fʌnd/ *noun* a fund which is invested in equities, not in government securities or other funds

equity gearing /'ekwɪti ,ɡɪərɪŋ/ *noun* the ratio between a company's borrowings at interest and its ordinary share capital

equity growth fund /,ekwɪti 'ɡrəʊθ fʌnd/ *noun* a fund invested in equities, aiming to provide capital growth

equity investment fund /,ekwɪti ɪn'vestmənt ,fʌnd/ *noun* same as **equity fund**

equity kicker /'ekwɪti ,kɪkə/ *noun US* an incentive given to people to lend a company money, in the form of a warrant to share in future earnings (NOTE: The UK term is **equity sweetener**.)

equity of redemption /,ekwɪti əv rɪ'dempʃən/ *noun* a right of a mortgagor to redeem the estate by paying off the principal and interest

equity REIT /,ekwɪti 'raɪt/ *noun* a trust which invests in rented property. Full form **equity real estate investment trust**

equity release /'ekwɪti rɪ,liːs/ *noun* the act of remortgaging a property on which there is currently no mortgage, in order to use it as security for new borrowing

equity risk premium /,ekwɪti 'rɪsk ,priːmiəm/ *noun* an extra return on equities over the return on bonds, because of the risk involved in investing in equities

equity sweetener /'ekwɪti ,swiːt(ə)nə/ *noun* an incentive to encourage people to lend a company money, in the form of a warrant giving the right to buy shares at a later date and at an agreed price

equivalence /ɪ'kwɪvələns/ *noun* the condition of having the same value or of being the same

equivalent /ɪ'kwɪvələnt/ *adjective* □ **to be equivalent to** to have the same value as or to be the same as ○ *The total dividend paid is equivalent to one quarter of the pretax profits.* ○ *Our managing director's salary is equivalent to that of far less experienced employees in other organisations.* ■ *noun* a person who is the equal of someone else

ERDF *abbreviation* European Regional Development Fund

ERM *abbreviation* exchange rate mechanism

erode /ɪ'rəʊd/ *verb* to wear away gradually □ **to erode wage differentials** to reduce gradually differences in salary between different grades

error /'erə/ *noun* a mistake ○ *He made an error in calculating the total.* ○ *Someone must have made a keyboarding error.*

error rate /'erə reɪt/ *noun* the number of mistakes per thousand entries or per page

errors and omissions excepted /ˌerəz ənd əʊˌmɪʃ(ə)nz ɪkˈseptɪd/ *phrase* words written on an invoice to show that the company has no responsibility for mistakes in the invoice. Abbreviation **e. & o.e.**

escalate /'eskəleɪt/ *verb* to increase steadily

escalation /ˌeskəˈleɪʃ(ə)n/ *noun* a steady increase ○ *an escalation of wage demands* ○ *The union has threatened an escalation in strike action.* □ **escalation of prices** a steady increase in prices

escalation clause /ˌeskəˈleɪʃ(ə)n klɔːz/ *noun* same as **escalator clause**

escalator /'eskəleɪtə/ *noun* a moving staircase

escalator bond /'eskəleɪtə bɒnd/ *noun* a fixed-rate bond where the rate rises each year

escalator clause /'eskəleɪtə klɔːz/ *noun* a clause in a contract allowing for regular price increases because of increased costs, or regular wage increases because of the increased cost of living

escape /ɪˈskeɪp/ *noun* an act of getting away from a difficult situation

escape clause /ɪˈskeɪp klɔːz/ *noun* a clause in a contract which allows one of the parties to avoid carrying out the terms of the contract under conditions

ESCB *abbreviation* European System of Central Banks

escrow /'eskrəʊ/ *noun US* an agreement between two parties that something should be held by a third party until conditions are fulfilled □ **in escrow** held in safe keeping by a third party □ **document held in escrow** a document given to a third party to keep and to pass on to someone when money has been paid

escrow account /'eskrəʊ əˌkaʊnt/ *noun US* an account where money is held in escrow until a contract is signed or until goods are delivered

escudo /esˈkjuːdəʊ/ *noun* a unit of currency in Portugal before the euro

ESOP *abbreviation* employee share ownership plan

establish /ɪˈstæblɪʃ/ *verb* to set up or to open ○ *The company has established a branch in Australia.* ○ *The business was established in Scotland in 1823.* ○ *It is still a young company, having been established for only four years.* □ **to establish oneself in business** to become successful in a new business

establishment /ɪˈstæblɪʃmənt/ *noun* **1.** a commercial business ○ *He runs an important printing establishment.* **2.** the number of people working in a company □ **to be on the establishment** to be a full-time employee □ **office with an establishment of fifteen** an office with a budgeted staff of fifteen

establishment charges /ɪˈstæblɪʃ mənt ˌtʃɑːdʒɪz/ *plural noun* the cost of people and property in a company's accounts

estate /ɪˈsteɪt/ *noun* property left by a dead person

estate agency /ɪˈsteɪt ˌeɪdʒənsi/ *noun* an office which arranges for the sale of properties

estate agent /ɪˈsteɪt ˌeɪdʒənt/ *noun* a person in charge of an estate agency

estate duty /ɪˈsteɪt ˌdjuːti/ *noun* a tax paid on the property left by a dead person (NOTE: now called **inheritance tax**)

estate tax /ɪˈsteɪt tæks/ *noun US* a tax paid on the right to pass property on to heirs, based on the value of the property and paid before it is passed to the heirs

estimate *noun* /'estɪmət/ **1.** a calculation of the probable cost, size or time of something ○ *Can you give me an estimate of how much time was spent on the job?* □ **at a conservative estimate** probably underestimating the final figure ○ *Their turnover has risen by at least 20% in the last year, at a conservative estimate.* □ **these figures are only an estimate** these are not the final accurate figures **2.** a calculation by a contractor or seller of a service of how much something is likely to cost, given to a client in advance of an order ○ *You should ask for an estimate before committing yourselves.* ○ *Before we can give the grant we must have an estimate of the total costs involved.* ○ *Unfortunately the final bill was quite different from the estimate.* □ **to put in an**

estimate to give someone a written calculation of the probable costs of carrying out a job ○ *Three firms put in estimates for the job.* ■ *verb* /ˈestɪmeɪt/ **1.** to calculate the probable cost, size, or time of something ○ *to estimate that it will cost £1m* or *to estimate costs at £1m* ○ *We estimate current sales at only 60% of last year.* **2.** □ **to estimate for a job** to state in writing the future costs of carrying out a piece of work so that a client can make an order ○ *Three firms estimated for the refitting of the offices.*

estimated /ˈestɪmeɪtɪd/ *adjective* calculated approximately ○ *estimated sales* ○ *Costs were slightly more than the estimated figure.*

estimation /ˌestɪˈmeɪʃ(ə)n/ *noun* an approximate calculation

estimator /ˈestɪmeɪtə/ *noun* a person whose job is to calculate estimates for carrying out work

estoppel /ɪˈstɒp(ə)l/ *noun* a rule of evidence whereby someone is prevented from denying or asserting a fact in legal proceedings

ethical /ˈeθɪk(ə)l/ *adjective* morally right

ethical criteria /ˌeθɪk(ə)l kraɪˈtɪəriə/ *plural noun* standards used to judge if something is morally right or not

ethical fund /ˈeθɪk(ə)l fʌnd/ *noun* a fund which invests in companies which follow certain moral standards, e.g. companies which do not manufacture weapons, or which do not trade with certain countries or which only use environmentally acceptable sources of raw materials

ethical index /ˈeθɪk(ə)l ˌɪndeks/ *noun* an index of shares in companies which follow certain moral standards

ethical investment /ˌeθɪk(ə)l ɪnˈvestmənt/ *noun* an investment in companies that follow certain moral standards

Ethical Investment Research Service /ˌeθɪk(ə)l ɪnˌvestmənt rɪˈsɜːtʃ ˌsɜːvɪs/ *noun* an organisation which does research into companies and recommends those which follow certain standards. Abbreviation **EIRIS**

ethical screening /ˌeθɪk(ə)l ˈskriːnɪŋ/ *noun* the process of checking companies against certain moral standards, and removing those which do not conform

EU *abbreviation* European Union ○ *EU ministers met today in Brussels.* ○ *The US is increasing its trade with the EU.*

Eurex /ˈjʊəreks/ *noun* a European derivatives market developed by combining the German Terminbörse and the Swiss Soffex

EURIBOR *abbreviation* European Interbank Offered Rate

euro /ˈjʊərəʊ/ *noun* a unit of currency adopted by several European countries for electronic payments in 1999 and then as legal tender from 1st January, 2002 ○ *Many articles are priced in euros.* ○ *What's the exchange rate for the euro?* (NOTE: The plural is **euro** or **euros**. Written € before numbers: €250: say: 'two hundred and fifty euros'.)

'…cross-border mergers in the European Union have shot up since the introduction of the euro' [*Investors Chronicle*]

COMMENT: The countries which are joined together in the European Monetary Union and adopted the euro as their common currency in 1999 are: Austria, Belgium, Finland, France, Germany, Ireland, Italy, Luxembourg, the Netherlands, Portugal, and Spain. The conversion of these currencies to the euro was fixed on 1st January 1999 at the following rates: Austrian schilling: 13.7603; Belgian & Luxembourg franc: 40.3399; Finnish Markka: 5.94573; French franc: 6.55957; German mark: 1.95583; Irish punt: 0.787564; Italian lira: 1936.27; Dutch guilder: 2.20371; Portuguese escudo: 200.482; Spanish peseta: 166.386. The CFA franc and CFP franc were pegged to the euro at the same time.

Euro- /ˈjʊərəʊ/ *prefix* referring to Europe or the European Union

euro account /ˈjʊərəʊ əˌkaʊnt/ *noun* a bank account in euros

Eurobond /ˈjʊərəʊbɒnd/ *noun* a long-term bearer bond issued by an international corporation or government outside its country of origin and sold to purchasers who pay in a Eurocurrency, sold on the Eurobond market

Eurocard /ˈjʊərəʊkɑːd/ a cheque card used when writing Eurocheques

Eurocheque /ˈjʊərəʊtʃek/ *noun* a cheque which can be cashed in any European bank. The Eurocheque system is based in Brussels.

Eurocommercial paper /ˌjʊərəʊ kəmɜːʃ(ə)l ˈpeɪpə/ *noun* a form of short-term borrowing in Eurocurrencies. Abbreviation **ECP**

eurocredit /ˈjʊərəʊˌkredɪt/ *noun* a large bank loan in a Eurocurrency, usually provided by a group of banks to a large commercial undertaking

Eurocurrency /ˈjʊərəʊkʌrənsi/ *noun* any currency used for trade within Europe but outside its country of origin, the Eurodollar being the most important ○ *a Eurocurrency loan* ○ *the Eurocurrency market*

eurodeposit /ˈjʊərəʊdɪˌpɒzɪt/ *noun* a deposit of Eurodollars in a bank outside the US

Eurodollar /ˈjʊərəʊdɒlə/ *noun* a US dollar deposited in a bank outside the US, used mainly for trade within Europe ○ *a Eurodollar loan* ○ *the Eurodollar markets*

euroequity /ˈjʊərəʊˌekwɪti/ *noun* a share in an international company traded on European stock markets outside its country of origin

Euroland /ˈjʊərəʊlænd/ *noun* same as **Eurozone**

Euromarket /ˈjʊərəʊmaːkɪt/ *noun* **1.** the European Union seen as a potential market for sales **2.** the Eurocurrency market, the international market for lending or borrowing in Eurocurrencies

euronote /ˈjʊərəʊˌnəʊt/ *noun* a short-term Eurocurrency bearer note

euro-option /ˈjʊərəʊ ˌɒpʃ(ə)n/ *noun* an option to buy European bonds at a later date

Europe /ˈjʊərəp/ *noun* **1.** the continent of Europe, the part of the world to the west of Asia, from Russia to Ireland ○ *Most of the countries of Western Europe are members of the EU.* ○ *Poland is in eastern Europe, and Greece, Spain and Portugal are in southern Europe.* **2.** the European Union, including the UK ○ *Canadian exports to Europe have risen by 25%.*

European /ˌjʊərəˈpiːən/ *adjective* referring to Europe ○ *They do business with several European countries.*

European Bank for Reconstruction and Development /ˌjʊərəpiːən bæŋk fə riːkənˌstrʌktʃ(ə)n ən dɪ ˈveləpmənt/ *noun* a bank, based in London, which channels aid from the EU

to Eastern European and Central Asian countries. Abbreviation **EBRD**

European Central Bank /ˌjʊərəpiːən ˌsentrəl ˈbæŋk/ *noun* the central bank for most of the countries in the European Union, those which have accepted European Monetary Union and have the euro as their common currency. Abbreviation **ECB**

'…the ECB begins with some $300 billion of foreign exchange reserves, far more than any other central bank' [*Investors Chronicle*]

'…any change in the European bank's statutes must be agreed and ratified by all EU member nations' [*The Times*]

European Commercial Paper /ˌjʊərəpiːən kəˌmɜːʃ(ə)l ˈpeɪpə/ *noun* a commercial paper issued in a eurocurrency. Abbreviation **ECP**

European Commission /ˌjʊərəpiːən kəˈmɪʃ(ə)n/ *noun* the main executive body of the EU, made up of members nominated by each member state. Also called **Commission of the European Community**

European Common Market /ˌjʊərəpiːən ˌkɒmən ˈmaːkɪt/ *noun* formerly, the name for the European Community, an organisation which links several European countries for the purposes of trade

European Community /ˌjʊərəpiːən kəˈmjuːnɪti/ *noun* formerly, the name of the European Union. Abbreviation **EC**

European Currency Unit /ˌjʊərəpiːən ˈkʌrənsi ˈjuːnɪt/ *noun* the official monetary unit of the European Union from 1979 to 1999. Abbreviation **ECU**

European Economic Area /ˌjʊərəpiːən ˌiːkənɒmɪk ˈeərɪə/ an area comprising the countries of the EU and the members of EFTA, formed by an agreement on trade between the two organisations. Abbreviation **EEA**

European Economic Community /ˌjʊərəpiːən ˌiːkənɒmɪk kəˈmjuːnɪti/ *noun* a grouping of European countries which later became the European Union. Abbreviation **EEC**. Also called **European Community**

European Free Trade Association /ˌjʊərəpiːən friː ˈtreɪd əˌsəʊsieɪʃ(ə)n/ *noun* a group of countries

(Iceland, Liechtenstein, Norway and Switzerland) formed to encourage freedom of trade between its members, and linked with the EU in the European Economic Area. Abbreviation **EFTA**

European Interbank Offered Rate /ˌjʊərəpiːən ˌɪntəbæŋk ˌɒfəd 'reɪt/ *noun* rate at which European banks offer to lend funds to other banks

European Investment Bank /ˌjʊərəpiːən ɪn'vestmənt bæŋk/ *noun* a financial institution whose main task is to facilitate regional development within the EU by financing capital projects, modernising or converting undertakings, and developing new activities. Abbreviation **EIB**

European Monetary System /ˌjʊərəpiːən 'mʌnɪt(ə)ri ˌsɪstəm/ *noun* the first stage of economic and monetary union of the EU, which came into force in March 1979, giving stable, but adjustable, exchange rates. Abbreviation **EMS**

COMMENT: The EMS now only applies to countries such as Greece which are members of the EU but not part of the EMU.

European Monetary Union /ˌjʊərəpiːən 'mʌnɪt(ə)ri ˌjuːnjən/ *noun* the process by which some of the member states of the EU joined together to adopt the euro as their common currency on 1st January 1999. The euro became legal tender for these member states from 2002. Abbreviation **EMU**

European options /ˌjʊərə'piːən ˌɒpʃənz/ *plural noun* an American term for options which can only be exercised on their expiration date

European Parliament /ˌjʊərəpiːən 'pɑːləmənt/ *noun* the parliament with members (MEPs) from each country of the EU

European Regional Development Fund /ˌjʊərəpiːən ˌriːdʒ(ə)nəl dɪ'veləpmənt fʌnd/ *noun* a fund set up to provide grants to underdeveloped parts of Europe. Abbreviation **ERDF**

European Social Charter /ˌjʊərəpiːən ˌsəʊʃ(ə)l 'tʃɑːtə/ *noun* a charter for employees, drawn up by the EU in 1989, by which employees have the right to a fair wage, and to equal treatment for men and women, a safe work environment, training, freedom of association and collective bargaining, provision for

disabled workers, freedom of movement from country to country, guaranteed standards of living both for the working population and for retired people. Abbreviation **ESC**. Also called **Social Charter**

European Union /ˌjʊərəpiːən 'juːnjən/ *noun* a group of European countries linked together by the Treaty of Rome. Abbreviation **EU**

COMMENT: The European Community was set up in 1957 and changed its name to the European Union when it adopted the single market. It has now grown to include twenty-seven member states. These are: Austria, Belgium, Bulgaria, Cyprus, the Czech Republic, Denmark, Estonia, Finland, France, Germany, Greece, Hungary, Ireland, Italy, Latvia, Lithuania, Luxembourg, Malta, the Netherlands, Poland, Portugal, Romania, Slovakia, Slovenia, Spain, Sweden and the UK. The member states of the EU are linked together by the Treaty of Rome in such a way that trade is more free, that money can be moved from one country to another freely, that people can move from one country to another more freely and that people can work more freely in other countries of the group (the four fundamental freedoms).

euroyen /'jʊərəʊˌjen/ *noun* a Japanese yen deposited in a European bank and used for trade within Europe

Eurozone /'jʊərəʊzəʊn/ *noun* the European countries which use the euro as a common currency, seen as a group. Also called **Euroland**

'…the European Central Bank left the door open yesterday for a cut in Eurozone interest rates' [*Financial Times*]

'…a sustained recovery in the euro will require either a sharp slowdown in US growth or a rise in inflation and interest rates in the Eurozone beyond that already discounted' [*Investors Chronicle*]

EVA *abbreviation* economic value added

evade /ɪ'veɪd/ *verb* to try to avoid something □ **to evade tax** to try illegally to avoid paying tax

evaluate /ɪ'væljueɪt/ *verb* to calculate a value for something ○ *to evaluate costs* ○ *We will evaluate jobs on the basis of their contribution to the organisation as a whole.* ○ *We need to evaluate the experience and qualifications of all the candidates.*

evaluation /ɪˌvæljuˈeɪʃ(ə)n/ *noun* the process of calculating the value of an asset

evasion /ɪ'veɪʒ(ə)n/ *noun* the act of avoiding something

event-driven /ɪ'vent ˌdrɪv(ə)n/ *adjective* activated by, and designed to profit from, a certain event, such as a merger, bankruptcy or takeover

ex /eks/ *prefix* out of or from ■ *adverb* without

ex- /eks/ *prefix* former ○ *an ex-director of the company*

exact /ɪg'zækt/ *adjective* strictly correct, not varying in any way from, e.g. not any more or less than, what is stated ○ *The exact time is 10.27.* ○ *The salesgirl asked me if I had the exact sum, since the shop had no change.*

exact interest /ɪgˌzækt 'ɪntrəst/ *noun* annual interest calculated on the basis of 365 days, as opposed to ordinary interest which is calculated on 360 days

exactly /ɪg'zæktli/ *adverb* not varying in any way from, e.g. not any more or less than, what is stated ○ *The total cost was exactly £6,500.*

ex-all /ˌeks 'ɔːl/ *adjective* referring to a share price where the share is sold without the dividend, rights issue or any other current issue. Abbreviation **xa**

examination /ɪgˌzæmɪ'neɪʃ(ə)n/ *noun* **1.** an act of looking at something very carefully to see if it is acceptable **2.** a written or oral test to see if someone has passed a course ○ *He passed his accountancy examinations.* ○ *She came first in the final examination for the course.* ○ *Examinations are given to candidates to test their mathematical ability.*

examine /ɪg'zæmɪn/ *verb* to look at someone or something very carefully ○ *Customs officials asked to examine the inside of the car.* ○ *The police are examining the papers from the managing director's safe.*

examiner /ɪg'zæmɪnə/ *noun* **1.** a person who examines something to see if it is correct **2.** a court-appointed administrator for a company

ex-capitalisation /eks ˌkæpɪt(ə)laɪ'zeɪʃ(ə)n/, **ex cap** /eks 'kæp/ *adjective* referring to a share price where the share is sold without a recent scrip issue. Abbreviation **xc**

exceed /ɪk'siːd/ *verb* to be more than ○ *a discount not exceeding 15%* ○ *Last year costs exceeded 20% of income for the first*

time. □ **he has exceeded his credit limit** he has borrowed more money than he is allowed

except /ɪk'sept/ *preposition, conjunction* not including ○ *VAT is levied on all goods and services except books, newspapers and children's clothes.* ○ *Sales are rising in all markets except the Far East.*

excepted /ɪk'septɪd/ *adverb* not including

exceptional /ɪk'sepʃ(ə)l/ *adjective* different or not usual

exceptional items /ɪkˌsepʃ(ə)l 'aɪtəmz/ *plural noun* **1.** items which arise from normal trading but which are unusual because of their size or nature (NOTE: Such items are shown separately in a note to the company's accounts but not on the face of the P & L account unless they are profits or losses on the sale or termination of an operation, or costs of a fundamental reorganisation or restructuring which have a material effect on the nature and focus of the reporting entity's operations, or profits or losses on the disposal of fixed assets.) **2.** items in a balance sheet which do not appear there each year and which are included in the accounts before the pre-tax profit is calculated, as opposed to extraordinary items which are calculated after the pre-tax profit

excess /'ekses/; /ɪk'ses/ *noun, adjective* an amount which is more than what is allowed ○ *an excess of expenditure over revenue* ○ *Excess costs have caused us considerable problems.*

excess capacity /ˌekses kə'pæsɪti/ *noun* spare capacity which is not being used

excessive /ɪk'sesɪv/ *adjective* too large ○ *Excessive production costs made the product uneconomic.*

excess liquidity /ˌekses lɪ'kwɪdɪti/ *noun* cash held by a bank above the usual requirement for that bank

excess profit /ˌekses 'prɒfɪt/ *noun* a level of profit that is higher than a level regarded as normal

excess profits tax /ˌekses 'prɒfɪts tæks/ *noun* a tax on excess profit

exchange /ɪks'tʃeɪndʒ/ *noun* **1.** the act of giving one thing for another **2.** a market for shares, commodities, futures, etc. ■ *verb* **1.** □ **to exchange something**

(**for something else**) to give one thing in place of something else ○ *He exchanged his motorcycle for a car.* ○ *Goods can be exchanged only on production of the sales slip.* **2.** □ **to exchange contracts** to sign a contract when buying a property, carried out by both buyer and seller at the same time **3.** to change money of one country for money of another ○ *to exchange euros for pounds*

'…under the barter agreements, Nigeria will export crude oil in exchange for trucks, food, planes and chemicals' [*Wall Street Journal*]

exchangeable /ɪksˈtʃeɪndʒəb(ə)l/ *adjective* possible to exchange

exchange control /ɪksˈtʃeɪndʒ kənˌtrəʊl/ *noun* the control by a government of the way in which its currency may be exchanged for foreign currencies

exchange controls /ɪksˈtʃeɪndʒ kənˌtrəʊlz/ *plural noun* government restrictions on changing the local currency into foreign currency ○ *The government had to impose exchange controls to stop the rush to buy dollars.* ○ *They say the government is going to lift exchange controls.*

exchange cross rates /ɪksˌtʃeɪndʒ ˈkrɒs reɪts/ *plural noun* rates of exchange for two currencies, shown against each other, but in terms of a third currency, often the US dollar. Also called **cross rates**

exchange dealer /ɪksˈtʃeɪndʒ ˌdiːlə/ *noun* a person who buys and sells foreign currency

exchange dealings /ɪksˈtʃeɪndʒ ˌdiːlɪŋz/ *plural noun* the buying and selling of foreign currency

Exchange Equalisation Account /ɪksˌtʃeɪndʒ ˌiːkwəlaɪˈzeɪʃ(ə)n əˌkaʊnt/ *noun* an account with the Bank of England used by the government when buying or selling foreign currency to influence the sterling exchange rate

exchange of contracts /ɪksˌtʃeɪndʒ əv ˈkɒntrækts/ *noun* the point in the sale of property when the buyer and the seller both sign the contract of sale, which then becomes binding

exchange premium /ɪksˈtʃeɪndʒ ˌpriːmiəm/ *noun* an extra cost above the usual rate for buying a foreign currency

exchanger /ɪksˈtʃeɪndʒə/ *noun* a person who buys and sells foreign currency

exchange rate /ɪksˈtʃeɪndʒ reɪt/ *noun* **1.** a rate at which one currency is exchanged for another. Also called **rate of exchange 2.** a figure that expresses how much a unit of one country's currency is worth in terms of the currency of another country

exchange rate mechanism /ɪks ˈtʃeɪndʒ reɪt ˌmekənɪz(ə)m/ *noun* a method of stabilising exchange rates within the European Monetary System, where currencies could only move up or down within a narrow band (usually 2.25% either way, but for certain currencies widened to 6%) without involving a realignment of all the currencies in the system. Abbreviation **ERM**

Exchequer /ɪksˈtʃekə/ ◇ **the Exchequer 1.** the fund of all money received by the government of the UK from taxes and other revenues **2.** the British government's account with the Bank of England **3.** the British government department dealing with public revenue

Exchequer stocks /ɪksˈtʃekə stɒks/ *plural noun* same as **Treasury stocks**

excise duty /ˈeksaɪz ˌdjuːti/ *noun* a tax on goods such as alcohol and petrol which are produced in the country

exciseman /ˈeksaɪzmæn/ *noun* a person who works in the Excise Department

exclude /ɪkˈskluːd/ *verb* to keep out, or not to include ○ *The interest charges have been excluded from the document.* ○ *Damage by fire is excluded from the policy.*

exclusion /ɪkˈskluːʒ(ə)n/ *noun* **1.** the act of not including something **2.** an item reported on the tax return but on which no tax is payable

exclusion clause /ɪkˈskluːʒ(ə)n klɔːz/ *noun* a clause in an insurance policy or warranty which says which items or events are not covered

exclusive /ɪkˈskluːsɪv/ *adjective* **1.** limited to one person or group □ **to have exclusive right to market a product** to be the only person who has the right to market a product **2.** □ **exclusive of** not including ○ *The invoice is exclusive of VAT.*

exclusive agreement /ɪkˌskluːsɪv ə ˈgriːmənt/ *noun* an agreement where a person is made sole agent for a product in a market

exclusive of tax /ɪkˌskluːsɪv əv ˈtæks/ *adjective* not including tax ○ *All payments are exclusive of tax.*

exclusivity /ˌekskluːˈsɪvɪti/ *noun* the exclusive right to market a product

ex coupon /ˌeks ˈkuːpɒn/ *adverb* without the interest coupons or after interest has been paid

ex dividend /ˌeks ˈdɪvɪdend/, **ex div** /ˌeks ˈdɪv/ *adjective* used to describe a share that does not have the right to receive the next dividend ○ *The shares went ex dividend yesterday.* Abbreviation **xd**

execute /ˈeksɪkjuːt/ *verb* to carry out an order ○ *Failure to execute orders may lead to dismissal.* ○ *There were many practical difficulties in executing the managing director's instructions.*

execution /ˌeksɪˈkjuːʃ(ə)n/ *noun* **1.** the carrying out of a commercial order or contract **2.** the carrying out of a legal order or contract

execution-only broker /ˌeksɪk juːʃ(ə)n ˈəʊnli ˌbrəʊkə/ *noun* same as **dealing-only broker**

execution-only service /ˌeksɪk juːʃ(ə)n ˈəʊnli ˌsɜːvɪs/ *noun* a service which buys and sells shares for clients, but does not provide any advice and does not manage portfolios

executive /ɪɡˈzekjʊtɪv/ *adjective* putting decisions into action ■ *noun* a person in a business who takes decisions, a manager or director ○ *sales executives* ○ *a senior or junior executive*

'…one in ten students commented on the long hours which executives worked' [*Employment Gazette*]

'…our executives are motivated by a desire to carry out a project to the best of their ability' [*British Business*]

executive committee /ɪɡˌzekjʊtɪv kəˈmɪti/ *noun* a committee which runs a society or a club

executive director /ɪɡˌzekjʊtɪv daɪ ˈrektə/ *noun* a director who works full-

time in the company. Compare **non-executive director**

executive powers /ɪɡˌzekjʊtɪv ˈpaʊəz/ *plural noun* the right to act as director or to put decisions into action ○ *She was made managing director with full executive powers over the European operation.*

executive share option scheme /ɪɡˌzekjʊtɪv ˈʃeər ɒpʃən ˌskiːm/ *noun* a scheme under which senior managers are given the opportunity to buy shares in their company at a preferential fixed price at a later date

executor /ɪɡˈzekjʊtə/ *noun* a person or firm that sees that the terms of a will are carried out ○ *She was named executor of her brother's will.*

exempt /ɪɡˈzempt/ *adjective* not forced to do something, especially not forced to obey a particular law or rule, or not forced to pay something ○ *Anyone over 65 is exempt from charges* ○ *He was exempt from military service in his country.* □ **exempt from tax** not required to pay tax ○ *As a non-profit-making organisation we are exempt from tax.* ■ *verb* **1.** ○ *Non-profit-making organisations are exempted from tax.* ○ *The government exempted trusts from tax.* □ **to exempt something from tax** to free something from having tax paid on it ○ *Food is exempted from sales tax.* **2.** □ **to exempt someone or something from something** to allow someone or something not to do something that others are forced to do

'Companies with sales under $500,000 a year will be exempt from the minimum-wage requirements' [*Nation's Business*]

exemption /ɪɡˈzempʃ(ə)n/ *noun* the act of exempting something from a contract or from a tax □ **exemption from tax**, **tax exemption** the fact of being free from having to pay tax ○ *As a non-profit-making organisation you can claim tax exemption.*

exempt securities /ɪɡˌzempt sɪ ˈkjʊərɪtiz/ *plural noun* securities, such as municipal bonds, which do not need to be registered with the SEC

exercise /ˈeksəsaɪz/ *noun* **1.** the use of something □ **exercise of an option** using an option, putting an option into action **2.** a financial year ○ *during the current exercise* ■ *verb* to use ○ *The chairwoman* *exercised her veto to block the motion.* □ **to exercise an option** to put an option into action ○ *He exercised his option to acquire sole marketing rights for the product.*

exercise date /ˈeksəsaɪz deɪt/ *noun* the date when an option can be put into effect

exercise price /ˈeksəsaɪz praɪs/ *noun* the price at which an option will be put into effect

ex gratia /ˌeks ˈɡreɪʃə/ *adjective* as an act of favour, without obligation

ex gratia payment /eks ˌɡreɪʃə ˈpeɪmənt/ *noun* a payment made as a gift, with no other obligations

exit /ˈeksɪt/ *noun* the act of going out or leaving

exit charge /ˈeksɪt tʃɑːdʒ/, **exit fee** /ˈeksɪt fiː/ *noun* a charge sometimes made by a trust when selling units in a unit trust or when selling out of an investment such as an ISA

ex officio /ˌeks əˈfɪʃiəʊ/ *adjective, adverb* because of an office held ○ *The treasurer is ex officio a member* or *an ex officio member of the finance committee.*

expand /ɪkˈspænd/ *verb* to get bigger, or make something bigger ○ *an expanding economy* ○ *The company is expanding fast.* ○ *We have had to expand our sales force.*

expansion /ɪkˈspænʃən/ *noun* an increase in size ○ *The expansion of the domestic market.* ○ *The company had difficulty in financing its current expansion programme.*

'…inflation-adjusted GNP moved up at a 1.3% annual rate, its worst performance since the economic expansion began' [*Fortune*]

'…the businesses we back range from start-up ventures to established businesses in need of further capital for expansion' [*Times*]

'…the group is undergoing a period of rapid expansion and this has created an exciting opportunity for a qualified accountant' [*Financial Times*]

expect /ɪkˈspekt/ *verb* to hope that something is going to happen ○ *We are expecting him to arrive at 10:45.* ○ *They are expecting a cheque from their agent next week.* ○ *The house was sold for more than the expected price.*

'…he observed that he expected exports to grow faster than imports in the coming year' [*Sydney Morning Herald*]

'American business as a whole has seen profits well above the levels normally expected at this stage of the cycle' [*Sunday Times*]

expenditure /ɪkˈspendɪtʃə/ *noun* the amount of money spent (NOTE: There is no plural in UK English, but US English often uses **expenditures**.) □ **the company's current expenditure programme** the company's spending according to the current plan □ **heavy expenditure on equipment** spending large sums of money on equipment

expense /ɪkˈspens/ *noun* money spent ○ *It is not worth the expense.* ○ *The expense is too much for my bank balance.* ○ *The likely profits do not justify the expense of setting up the project.* ○ *It was well worth the expense to get really high-quality equipment.* □ **at great expense** having spent a lot of money □ **he furnished the office regardless of expense** without thinking how much it cost

expense account /ɪkˈspens əˌkaʊnt/ *noun* an allowance of money which a business pays for an employee to spend on travelling and entertaining clients in connection with that business ○ *I'll put this lunch on my expense account.*

expenses /ɪkˈspensɪz/ *plural noun* money paid to cover the costs incurred by someone when doing something ○ *The salary offered is £10,000 plus expenses.* ○ *She has a high salary and all her travel expenses are paid by the company.* □ **all expenses paid** with all costs paid by the company ○ *The company sent him to San Francisco all expenses paid.* □ **to cut down on expenses** to reduce spending □ **legal expenses** money spent on fees paid to lawyers

expiration /ˌekspəˈreɪʃ(ə)n/ *noun* the act of coming to an end ○ *the expiration of an insurance policy* ○ *to repay before the expiration of the stated period* □ **on expiration of the lease** when the lease comes to an end

expiration date /ˌekspəˈreɪʃ(ə)n deɪt/ *noun US* same as **expiry date**

expire /ɪkˈspaɪə/ *verb* to come to an end ○ *The lease expires in 2010.* ○ *The option* *expired last Tuesday.* □ **his passport has expired** his passport is no longer valid

expiry /ɪkˈspaɪəri/ *noun* the act of coming to an end ○ *the expiry of an insurance policy*

expiry date /ɪkˈspaɪəri deɪt/ *noun* **1.** a date when something will end **2.** the last date on which a credit card can be used

export *noun* /ˈekspɔːt/ the practice or business of sending goods to foreign countries to be sold ○ *50% of the company's profits come from the export trade* or *the export market.* ◊ **exports** ■ *verb* /ɪkˈspɔːt/ to send goods to foreign countries for sale ○ *50% of our production is exported.* ○ *The company imports raw materials and exports the finished products.*

exportation /ˌekspɔːˈteɪʃ(ə)n/ *noun* the act of sending goods to foreign countries for sale

Export Credit Guarantee Department /ˌekspɔːt ˌkredɪt ˌɡærənˈtiː dɪˌpɑːtmənt/ *noun* a British government department which insures sellers of exports sold on credit against the possibility of non-payment by the purchasers. Abbreviation **ECGD**

export department /ˈekspɔːt dɪˌpɑːtmənt/ *noun* the section of a company which deals in sales to foreign countries

export duty /ˈekspɔːt ˌdjuːti/ *noun* a tax paid on goods sent out of a country for sale

exporter /ɪkˈspɔːtə/ *noun* a person, company, or country that sells goods in foreign countries ○ *a major furniture exporter* ○ *Canada is an important exporter of oil* or *an important oil exporter.*

export house /ˈekspɔːt haʊs/ *noun* a company which specialises in the export of goods manufactured by other companies

exporting /ekˈspɔːtɪŋ/ *adjective* sending goods out of a country

export licence /ˈekspɔːt ˌlaɪs(ə)ns/ *noun* a government permit allowing something to be exported ○ *The government has refused an export licence for computer parts.*

export manager /ˈekspɔːt ˌmænɪdʒə/ *noun* the person in charge of an export department in a company ○ *The*

export manager planned to set up a sales force in Southern Europe. ○ *Sales managers from all export markets report to our export manager.*

export restitution /ˌekspɔːt ˌrestɪˈtjuːʃ(ə)n/ *noun* (*in the EU*) subsidies to European food exporters

exports /ˈekspɔːts/ *plural noun* goods sent to a foreign country to be sold ○ *Exports to Africa have increased by 25%.* ◊ **export** (NOTE: Usually used in the plural, but the singular form is used before a noun.)

expose /ɪkˈspəʊz/ *verb* □ **to be exposed to something** to be in a position where something might harm you ○ *The banks are highly exposed to bad debts in Asia.*

exposure /ɪkˈspəʊʒə/ *noun* the amount of risk which a lender or investor runs ○ *He is trying to limit his exposure in the property market.*

'…it attributed the poor result to the bank's high exposure to residential mortgages, which showed a significant slowdown in the past few months' [*South China Morning Post*]

COMMENT: Exposure can be the amount of money lent to a customer (a bank's exposure to a foreign country) or the amount of money which an investor may lose if his investments collapse (his or her exposure in the stock market).

express /ɪkˈspres/ *adjective* **1.** rapid or very fast ○ *an express letter* **2.** clearly shown in words ○ *The contract has an express condition forbidding sale in Africa.* ■ *verb* **1.** to put into words or diagrams ○ *This chart shows home sales expressed as a percentage of total turnover.* **2.** to send something very fast ○ *We expressed the order to the customer's warehouse.*

express delivery /ɪkˌspres dɪˈlɪv(ə)ri/ *noun* a very fast delivery

expressly /ɪkˈspresli/ *adverb* clearly in words ○ *The contract expressly forbids sales to the US*

express money transfer /ɪkˌspres ˈmʌni ˌtrænsfɜː/ *noun* a foreign currency payment to an individual or organisation delivered electronically to a bank

ex-rights /ˌeks ˈraɪts/ *adjective* referring to a share price where the share is sold without a recent rights issue. Abbreviation **xr**

extend /ɪk'stend/ *verb* **1.** to offer something ○ *to extend credit to a customer* **2.** to make something longer ○ *Her contract of employment was extended for two years.* ○ *We have extended the deadline for making the appointment by two weeks.*

extended credit /ɪk‚stendɪd 'kredɪt/ *noun* **1.** credit allowing the borrower a very long time to pay ○ *We sell to Australia on extended credit.* **2.** *US* an extra long credit used by commercial banks borrowing from the Federal Reserve

extension /ɪk'stenʃən/ *noun* **1.** an additional period of time allowed for something, e.g. the repayment of a debt □ **to get an extension of credit** to get more time to pay back □ **extension of a contract** the continuing of a contract for a further period **2.** (*in an office*) an individual telephone linked to the main switchboard ○ *The sales manager is on extension 53.* ○ *Can you get me extension 21?* ○ *Extension 21 is engaged.*

extensive /ɪk'stensɪv/ *adjective* very large or covering a wide area ○ *an extensive network of sales outlets* ○ *an extensive recruitment drive*

external /ɪk'stɜːn(ə)l/ *adjective* **1.** outside a country. Opposite **internal 2.** outside a company

external account /ɪk‚stɜːn(ə)l ə 'kaʊnt/ *noun* an account in a British bank belonging to someone who is living in another country

external audit /ɪk‚stɜːn(ə)l 'ɔːdɪt/ *noun* **1.** an audit carried out by an independent auditor who is not employed by the company **2.** an evaluation of the effec-

tiveness of a company's public relations carried out by an outside agency

external auditor /ɪk‚stɜːn(ə)l 'ɔːdɪtə/ *noun* an independent person who audits the company's accounts

external debt /ɪk‚stɜːn(ə)l 'det/ *noun* money which a company has borrowed from outside sources such as a bank, as opposed to money raised from shareholders. Also called **external funds**

external funds /ɪk‚stɜːn(ə)l 'fʌndz/ *plural noun* same as **external debt**

external growth /ɪk‚stɜːn(ə)l 'grəʊθ/ *noun* the growth of a firm by buying other companies, rather than by expanding existing sales or products. Opposite **internal growth**

external trade /ɪk‚stɜːn(ə)l 'treɪd/ *noun* trade with foreign countries. Opposite **internal trade**

extract /'ekstrækt/ *noun* a printed document which is part of a larger document ○ *He sent me an extract of the accounts.*

extraordinary /ɪk'strɔːd(ə)n(ə)ri/ *adjective* different from normal

Extraordinary General Meeting /ɪk‚strɔːd(ə)n(ə)ri ‚dʒen(ə)rəl 'miːtɪŋ/ *noun* a special meeting of shareholders to discuss an important matter (such as a change in the company's articles of association) which cannot wait until the next AGM ○ *to call an Extraordinary General Meeting* Abbreviation **EGM**

extraordinary item /ɪk 'strɔːd(ə)n(ə)ri ‚aɪtəm/ *noun* a large item of income or expenditure entered into accounts that is unusual in nature and also occurs very infrequently

F

face value /ˌfeɪs ˈvæljuː/ *noun* the value written on a coin, banknote or share certificate

'…travellers cheques cost 1% of their face value – some banks charge more for small amounts' [*Sunday Times*]

facility /fəˈsɪlɪti/ *noun* **1.** something that allows something to be done something easily ○ *We offer facilities for payment.* **2.** the total amount of credit which a lender will allow a borrower

facility fee /fəˈsɪlɪti fiː/ *noun* a charge made to a borrower by a bank for arranging credit facilities

factor /ˈfæktə/ *noun* **1.** something which is important, or which is taken into account when making a decision ○ *The drop in sales is an important factor in the company's lower profits.* ○ *Motivation was an important factor in drawing up the new pay scheme.* **2.** a number used in multiplication to produce another number □ **by a factor of ten** ten times **3.** a person or company which is responsible for collecting debts for companies, by buying debts at a discount on their face value **4.** a person who sells for a business or another person and earns a commission ■ *verb* to buy debts from a company at a discount

'…factors 'buy' invoices from a company, which then gets an immediate cash advance representing most of their value. The balance is paid when the debt is met. The client company is charged a fee as well as interest on the cash advanced' [*Times*]

COMMENT: A factor collects a company's debts when due, and pays the creditor in advance part of the sum to be collected, so 'buying' the debt.

factor in /ˌfæktər ˈɪn/ *verb* to add a factor when making calculations

factoring /ˈfæktərɪŋ/ *noun* the business of buying debts from a firm at a discount and then enforcing the payment of the debt

factoring charges /ˈfæktərɪŋ ˌtʃɑːdʒɪz/ *plural noun* the cost of selling debts to a factor for a commission

factors of production /ˌfæktəz əv prəˈdʌkʃən/ *plural noun* land, labour and capital, i.e. the three things needed to produce a product

factory floor /ˌfækt(ə)ri ˈflɔː/ *noun* the main works of a factory

factory gate price /ˌfækt(ə)ri ˈgeɪt praɪs/ *noun* the actual cost of manufacturing goods before any mark-up is added to give profit (NOTE: The factory gate price includes direct costs such as labour, raw materials and energy, and indirect costs such as interest on loans, plant maintenance or rent.)

factory inspectorate /ˈfækt(ə)ri ɪnˌspekt(ə)rət/ *noun* all inspectors of factories

factory price /ˈfækt(ə)ri praɪs/ *noun* a price not including transport from the maker's factory

factory worker /ˈfækt(ə)ri ˌwɜːkə/ *noun* a person who works in a factory

fail /feɪl/ *verb* **1.** not to do something which you were trying to do ○ *The company failed to notify the tax office of its change of address.* ○ *They failed to agree on an agenda for the meeting.* ○ *Negotiations continued until midnight but the two sides failed to come to an agreement.* **2.** to be unsuccessful ○ *The prototype failed its first test.* □ **the company failed** the company went bankrupt ○ *He lost all his money when the bank failed.*

failure /'feɪljə/ *noun* the fact of not doing something which you promised to do □ **failure to pay a bill** not paying a bill

fair /feə/ *noun* same as **trade fair** ○ *The computer fair runs from 1st to 6th April.* ■ *adjective* reasonable, with equal treatment

fair deal /ˌfeə 'diːl/ *noun* an arrangement where both parties are treated equally ○ *The employees feel they did not get a fair deal from the management.*

fair dealing /ˌfeə 'diːlɪŋ/ *noun* the legal buying and selling of shares

fairly /'feəli/ *adverb* reasonably or equally ○ *The union representatives put the employees' side of the case fairly and without argument.*

fair price /ˌfeə 'praɪs/ *noun* a good price for both buyer and seller

fair trade /ˌfeə 'treɪd/ *noun* an international business system where countries agree not to charge import duties on some items imported from their trading partners

fair trading /ˌfeə 'treɪdɪŋ/ *noun* **1.** a way of doing business which is reasonable and does not harm the consumer **2.** a legal trade in shares or the legal buying and selling of shares

fair value /ˌfeə 'væljuː/ *noun* a price paid by a buyer who knows the value of what he or she is buying, to a seller who also knows the value of what is being sold, i.e., neither is cheating the other

fair wear and tear /ˌfeə weər ən 'teə/ *noun* acceptable damage caused by normal use ○ *The insurance policy covers most damage but not fair wear and tear to the machine.*

faith /feɪθ/ *noun* □ **to buy something in good faith** to buy something thinking that is of good quality, that it has not been stolen or that it is not an imitation

fall /fɔːl/ *noun* a sudden reduction or loss of value ○ *a fall in the exchange rate* ○ *a fall in the price of gold* ○ *a fall on the stock exchange* ○ *Profits showed a 10% fall.* ■ *verb* **1.** to be reduced suddenly to a lower price or value ○ *Shares fell on the market today.* ○ *Gold shares fell 10% or fell 45 cents on the stock exchange.* ○ *The price of gold fell for the second day running.* ○ *The pound fell against the euro.* (NOTE: **falling – fell – has fallen**) **2.** to happen or to take place ○ *The public*

holiday falls on a Tuesday. (NOTE: **falling – fell – has fallen**) □ **payments which fall due** payments which are now due to be made

'…market analysts described the falls in the second half of last week as a technical correction to the market' [*Australian Financial Review*]

'…for the first time since mortgage rates began falling in March a financial institution has raised charges on homeowner loans' [*Globe and Mail (Toronto)*]

'…interest rates were still falling as late as June, and underlying inflation remains below the government's target of 2.5 per cent' [*Financial Times*]

fall away *phrasal verb* to become less ○ *Hotel bookings have fallen away since the tourist season ended.*

fall back *phrasal verb* to become lower or cheaper after rising in price ○ *Shares fell back in light trading.*

fall back on *phrasal verb* to have to use something kept for emergencies ○ *to fall back on cash reserves* ○ *The management fell back on the usual old excuses.*

fall behind *phrasal verb* to be late in doing something ○ *They fell behind with their mortgage repayments.*

fall off *phrasal verb* to become lower, cheaper, or less ○ *Sales have fallen off since the tourist season ended.*

fall out *phrasal verb* □ **the bottom has fallen out of the market** sales have fallen below what previously seemed to be their lowest point

fallen angel /ˌfɔːlən 'eɪndʒəl/ *noun* **1.** a share that was once in favour, but whose attraction has slipped and whose share price is on the way down **2.** a bond that was once investment grade but has fallen substantially from its all time highs

falling /'fɔːlɪŋ/ *adjective* becoming smaller or dropping in price

'…falling profitability means falling share prices' [*Investors Chronicle*]

falling pound /ˌfɔːlɪŋ 'paʊnd/ *noun* the pound when it is losing its value against other currencies

fallout /'fɔːlaʊt/ *noun* a bad result or collapse

false /fɔːls/ *adjective* not true or not correct ○ *to make a false claim for a* product ○ *to make a false entry in the balance sheet*

false market /ˌfɔːls ˈmɑːkɪt/ *noun* a market in shares caused by persons or companies conspiring to buy or sell and so influence the share price to their advantage

false pretences /ˌfɔːls prɪˈtensɪz/ *plural noun* doing or saying something to cheat someone ○ *He was sent to prison for obtaining money by false pretences.*

false weight /ˌfɔːls ˈweɪt/ *noun* a weight as measured on a shop scales which is wrong and so cheats customers

falsification /ˌfɔːlsɪfɪˈkeɪʃ(ə)n/ *noun* the act of making false entries in accounts

falsify /ˈfɔːlsɪfaɪ/ *verb* to change something to make it wrong ○ *They were accused of falsifying the accounts.*

family /ˈfæm(ə)li/ *noun* a group of people, formed of parents and children

family company /ˈfæm(ə)li ˌkʌmp(ə)ni/ *noun* a company in which most of the shares are owned by members of a family

family firm /ˌfæm(ə)li ˈfɜːm/, **family-run firm** /ˌfæm(ə)li rʌn ˈfɜːm/ *noun* a firm where the shareholders and directors are members of the same family

Fannie Mae /ˌfæni ˈmeɪ/ *noun* same as **Federal National Mortgage Association**

FAQ /fæk, ˌef eɪ ˈkjuː/ *noun* an item on a menu which gives answers to questions which people often ask about the website, service or product. Full form **frequently asked question**

FAS *abbreviation* Federal Accounting Standards

FASIT *abbreviation* Financial Asset Securitisation Investment Trust

fat cat /ˌfæt ˈkæt/ *noun* a businessman who earns an enormous salary and bonus (*informal*)

favourable /ˈfeɪv(ə)rəb(ə)l/ *adjective* giving an advantage (NOTE: The US spelling is **favorable**.) □ **on favourable terms** on especially good terms ○ *The shop is let on very favourable terms.*

favourable balance of trade /ˌfeɪv(ə)rəb(ə)l ˌbæləns əv ˈtreɪd/, **favourable trade balance** /ˌfeɪv(ə)rəb(ə)l ˈtreɪd ˌbæləns/ *noun* a

situation where a country's exports are larger than its imports

fax /fæks/ *noun* a system for sending the exact copy of a document via telephone lines ○ *Can you confirm the booking by fax?* ■ *verb* to send a message by fax ○ *The details of the offer were faxed to the brokers this morning.* ○ *I've faxed the documents to our New York office.*

COMMENT: Banks will not accept fax messages as binding instructions (as for example, a faxed order for money to be transferred from one account to another).

FAZ index *noun* a daily index of leading industrial shares on the Frankfurt Stock Exchange (published in the Frankfurter Allgemeine Zeitung)

FD *abbreviation* financial director

FDI *abbreviation* foreign direct investment

FDIC *abbreviation* Federal Deposit Insurance Corporation

feasibility report /ˌfiːzəˈbɪlɪti rɪˌpɔːt/ *noun* a document which says if it is worth undertaking something

Fed /fed/ *noun* US same as **Federal Reserve Board** (*informal*)

'…indications of weakness in the US economy were contained in figures from the Fed on industrial production for April' [*Financial Times*]

'…the half-point discount rate move gives the Fed room to reduce the federal funds rate further if economic weakness persists. The Fed sets the discount rate directly, but controls the federal funds rate by buying and selling Treasury securities' [*Wall Street Journal*]

federal /ˈfed(ə)rəl/ *adjective* **1.** referring to a system of government where a group of states are linked together in a federation **2.** referring to the central government of the US ○ *Most federal offices are in Washington.*

'…federal examiners will determine which of the privately-insured savings and loans qualify for federal insurance' [*Wall Street Journal*]

'…since 1978 America has freed many of its industries from federal rules that set prices and controlled the entry of new companies' [*Economist*]

Federal Accounting Standards /ˌfed(ə)rəl əˈkaʊntɪŋ ˌstændədz/ *noun* US the US regulations governing accounting procedures. Abbreviation **FAS**

federal credit agencies /ˌfed(ə)rəl ˈkredɪt/, **federal agencies** /ˌfed(ə)rəl ˈeɪdʒənsiz/ *plural noun* agencies such as the Federal Home Loan Banks which provide credit to individual borrowers and are backed by the federal government

Federal Deposit Insurance Corporation /ˌfed(ə)rəl dɪˌpɒzɪt ɪnˈʃʊərəns ˌkɔːpəreɪʃ(ə)n/ *noun* federal agency which manages insurance funds that insure deposits in commercial banks and in savings and loans associations. Abbreviation **FDIC**

Federal Funds /ˌfed(ə)rəl ˈfʌndz/ *plural noun* deposits by commercial banks with the Federal Reserve Banks, which can be used for short-term loans to other banks

Federal Home Loan Banks /ˌfed(ə)rəl həʊm ləʊn ˈbæŋks/ *plural noun US* a group of twelve banks which lend to savings and loans associations, and to other institutions which lend money to homeowners against mortgages

Federal Home Loan Mortgage Corporation /ˌfed(ə)rəl həʊm ləʊn ˈmɔːgɪdʒ kɔːpəˌreɪʃ(ə)n/ *noun US* a federal organisation which backs mortgages issued by the Savings and Loans Associations. Abbreviation **FHLMC, Freddie Mac**

Federal National Mortgage Association /ˌfed(ə)rəl ˌnæʃ(ə)nəl ˈmɔːgɪdʒ əˌsəʊsieɪʃ(ə)n/ *noun* a privately owned US organisation which regulates mortgages and helps offer mortgages backed by federal funds. Abbreviation **FNMA**. Also called **Fannie Mae**

Federal Reserve /ˌfed(ə)rəl rɪˈzɜːv/, **Federal Reserve System** /ˌfed(ə)rəl rɪˈzɜːv ˌsɪstəm/ *noun* the system of federal government control of the US banks, where the Federal Reserve Board regulates money supply, prints money, fixes the discount rate and issues government bonds

COMMENT: The Federal Reserve system is the central bank of the US The system is run by the Federal Reserve Board, under a chairman and seven committee members (or 'governors') who are all appointed by the President. The twelve Federal Reserve Banks act as lenders of last resort to local commercial banks. Although the board is appointed by the president, the whole

system is relatively independent of the US government.

Federal Reserve Bank /ˌfed(ə)rəl rɪˈzɜːv ˌbæŋk/ *noun* any one of the twelve federally-owned regional banks in the US, which are directed by the Federal Reserve Board. Abbreviation **FRB**

Federal Reserve Board /ˌfed(ə)rəl rɪˈzɜːv bɔːd/ *noun* a government organisation which runs the central banks in the US. Abbreviation **FRB**

'…pressure on the Federal Reserve Board to ease monetary policy mounted yesterday with the release of a set of pessimistic economic statistics' [*Financial Times*]

Federal Reserve Wire System /ˌfed(ə)rəl rɪˌzɜːv ˈwaɪə ˌsɪstəm/ *noun* a computerised communications system which links the Federal Reserve Board, its banks and the US Treasury

Federal Trade Commission /ˌfed(ə)rəl ˈtreɪd kəˌmɪʃ(ə)n/ *noun* a federal agency established to keep business competition free and fair

federation /ˌfedəˈreɪʃ(ə)n/ *noun* a group of societies, companies or organisations which have a central organisation which represents them and looks after their common interests ○ *a federation of trades unions* ○ *the employers' federation*

Fed Funds /ˈfed fʌndz/ *plural noun US* same as **Federal Funds** (*informal*)

fed funds rate /ˈfed fʌndz ˌreɪt/ *noun* the rate charged by banks for lending money deposited with the Federal Reserve to other banks

Fedwire /ˈfedwaɪə/, **FedWire** *noun US* same as **Federal Reserve Wire System** (*informal*)

fee /fiː/ *noun* **1.** money paid for work carried out by a professional person such as an accountant, a doctor or a lawyer ○ *We charge a small fee for our services.* ○ *The consultant's fee was much higher than we expected.* □ **director's fees** money paid to a director as a lump sum, not a salary **2.** money paid for something ○ *an entrance fee* or *admission fee* ○ *a registration fee*

few /fjuː/ *adjective, noun* **1.** not many **2.** □ **a few** some

FHFB *abbreviation* Federal Housing Finance Board

FHLBB *abbreviation* Federal Home Loan Bank Board

FHLBS *abbreviation* Federal Home Loan Bank System

FHLMC *abbreviation* Federal Home Loan Mortgage Corporation

fiat money /ˈfiːæt ˌmʌni/ *noun* coins or notes which are not worth much as paper or metal, but are said by the government to have a value and are recognised as legal tender

FIBOR *abbreviation* Frankfurt Interbank Offered Rate

fictitious assets /fɪkˌtɪʃəs ˈæsets/ *plural noun* assets which do not really exist, but are entered as assets to balance the accounts

fiddle /ˈfɪd(ə)l/ *noun* an act of cheating (*informal*) ○ *It's all a fiddle.* □ **he's on the fiddle** he is trying to cheat ■ *verb* to cheat (*informal*) ○ *He tried to fiddle his tax returns.* ○ *The salesman was caught fiddling his expense account.*

fide ♦ bona fide

fiduciary /fɪˈdjuːʃjəri/ *noun, adjective* (a person) in a position of trust ○ *Directors have fiduciary duty to act in the best interests of the company.*

fiduciary deposits /fɪˌdjuːʃəri dɪ ˈpɒzɪtz/ *plural noun* bank deposits which are managed for the depositor by the bank

FIFO /ˈfaɪfəʊ/ *abbreviation* first in first out

fifty-fifty /ˌfɪfti ˈfɪfti/ *adjective, adverb* half □ **he has a fifty-fifty chance of making a profit** he has an equal chance of making a profit or a loss

go fifty-fifty *phrasal verb* to share the costs equally

figure /ˈfɪɡə/ *noun* **1.** a number, or a cost written in numbers ○ *The figure in the accounts for heating is very high.* □ **he put a very low figure on the value of the lease** he calculated the value of the lease as very low **2.** □ **to work out the figures** to calculate something □ **his income runs into six figures** *or* **he has a six-figure income** his income is more than £100,000 □ **in round figures** not totally accurate, but correct to the nearest 10 or 100 ○ *They have a workforce of 2,500 in round figures.*

figures /ˈfɪɡəz/ *plural noun* **1.** written numbers **2.** the results for a company ○

the figures for last year or *last year's figures*

file /faɪl/ *noun* **1.** a cardboard holder for documents, which can fit in the drawer of a filing cabinet ○ *Put these letters in the customer file.* ○ *Look in the file marked 'Scottish sales'.* **2.** documents kept for reference □ **to place something on file** to keep a record of something □ **to keep someone's name on file** to keep someone's name on a list for reference **3.** a section of data on a computer, e.g. payroll, address list, customer accounts ○ *How can we protect our computer files?* ■ *verb* **1.** ○ *You will find the salary scales filed by department.* ○ *The correspondence is filed under 'complaints'.* □ **to file documents** to put documents in order so that they can be found easily ○ *The correspondence is filed under 'complaints'.* **2.** to make an official request □ **to file a petition in bankruptcy** *or* **to file for bankruptcy** to ask officially to be made bankrupt or to ask officially for someone else to be made bankrupt **3.** to register something officially ○ *to file an application for a patent* ○ *to file a return to the tax office* □ **to file a return to the tax office** *US* to fill in and send a tax return ○ **to file jointly** to make a joint tax declaration □ **to file separately** to file two separate tax returns, one for the husband and one for the wife ◇ **to file a petition in bankruptcy, to file for bankruptcy 1.** to ask officially to be made bankrupt **2.** to ask officially for someone else to be made bankrupt

file copy /ˈfaɪl ˌkɒpi/ *noun* a copy of a document which is kept for reference in an office

filer /ˈfaɪlə/ *noun US* a person who files an income tax return

fill /fɪl/ *verb* to carry out a client's instructions to buy or sell

fill or kill /ˌfɪl ɔː ˈkɪl/ *verb US* to carry out a client's order immediately or else the order is cancelled. Abbreviation **FOK**

FIMBRA *abbreviation* Financial Intermediaries, Managers and Brokers Association

final /ˈfaɪn(ə)l/ *adjective* last, coming at the end of a period ○ *to pay the final instalment* ○ *to make the final payment* ○ *to put the final details on a document* □ **final date for payment** last date by which payment should be made

final closing date /ˌfaɪn(ə)l ˈkləʊzɪŋ deɪt/ *noun* the last date for acceptance of a takeover bid, when the bidder has to announce how many shareholders have accepted his or her offer

final demand /ˌfaɪn(ə)l dɪˈmɑːnd/ *noun* a last reminder that payment of a debt is due, after which a supplier normally sues for payment

final discharge /ˌfaɪn(ə)l ˈdɪstʃɑːdʒ/ *noun* a final payment the completes the repayment of a debt

final dividend /ˌfaɪn(ə)l ˈdɪvɪdend/ *noun* a dividend paid at the end of a year's trading, which has to be approved by the shareholders at an AGM

finalise /ˈfaɪnəlaɪz/, **finalize** *verb* to agree final details ○ *We hope to finalise the agreement tomorrow.* ○ *After six weeks of negotiations the loan was finalised yesterday.*

final product /ˌfaɪn(ə)l ˈprɒdʌkt/ *noun* a manufactured product, made at the end of a production process

final salary scheme /ˌfaɪn(ə)l ˈsæləri skiːm/ *noun* a form of pension scheme where the benefit is based on the final salary of the member and his or her years of service

finance /ˈfaɪnæns/ *noun* **1.** money used by a company, provided by the shareholders or by loans ○ *Where will they get the necessary finance for the project?* (NOTE: The US term is **financing**) **2.** money (used by a club, local authority, etc.) ○ *She is the secretary of the local authority finance committee.* **3.** the business of managing money ■ *verb* to provide money to pay for something ○ *They plan to finance the operation with short-term loans.*

'…an official said that the company began to experience a sharp increase in demand for longer-term mortgages at a time when the flow of money used to finance these loans diminished' [*Globe and Mail*]

Finance Act /ˈfaɪnæns ækt/ *noun* an annual Act of Parliament which gives the government the power to obtain money from taxes as proposed in the Budget

Finance and Leasing Association /ˌfaɪnæns ən ˈliːsɪŋ əˌsəʊsieɪʃ(ə)n/ *noun* an organisation representing firms engaged in business finance and the leasing of equipment and cars. Abbreviation **FLA**

Finance and Tax Tribunals /ˌfaɪnæns ən ˈtæks ˌtraɪbjuːn(ə)lz/ *plural noun* a collective name for four tribunals established in 2006 to hear appeals against decisions of HM Customs and Excise and the Inland Revenue and to adjudicate on matters relating to certain decisions of the Financial Services Authority and the Pensions Regulator

Finance Bill /ˈfaɪnæns bɪl/ *noun* **1.** a bill that lists the proposals in a Chancellor's budget and that is debated before being voted into law as the Finance Act **2.** *US* a short-term bill of exchange which provides credit for a corporation so that it can continue trading

finance charge /ˈfaɪnæns tʃɑːdʒ/ *noun* **1.** the cost of borrowing money **2.** an additional charge made to a customer who asks for extended credit

finance company /ˈfaɪnæns ˌkʌmp(ə)ni/, **finance corporation** /ˈfaɪnæns ˌkɔːpəreɪʃ(ə)n/, **finance house** *noun* a company, usually part of a commercial bank, that provides money for hire-purchase

finance controller /ˈfaɪnæns kən ˌtrəʊlə/ *noun* an accountant whose main task is to manage the company's monetary resources

Finance Corporation for Industry /ˌfaɪnæns ˌkɔːpəˈreɪʃ(ə)n fə/ *noun* abbreviation **FCI**

finance house /ˈfaɪnæns haʊs/ *noun* same as **finance company**

finance house deposits /ˈfaɪnæns haʊs dɪˌpɒzɪts/ *plural noun* amounts of money deposited by banks with finance houses and used by them to provide hire-purchase loans to clients

finance market /ˈfaɪnæns ˌmɑːkɪt/ *noun* a place where large sums of money can be lent or borrowed

Finance Ministry /ˈfaɪnæns ˌmɪnɪstri/ *noun* a government department dealing with a country's finance

COMMENT: In most countries, the government department dealing with finance is called the Finance Ministry, with a Finance Minister in charge. Both in the UK and the US, the department is called the Treasury, and the minister in charge is the Chancellor of the Exchequer in the UK, and the Treasury Secretary in the US

finances /ˈfaɪnænsɪz/ *plural noun* money or cash which is available ○ *the bad state of the company's finances*

financial /faɪˈnænʃəl/ *adjective* relating to money □ **financial circumstances** the state of someone's finances ○ *The more you tell us about your full financial circumstances, the more we may be able to help.* □ **financial difficulties** a bad state of someone's finances ○ *If you find yourself in financial difficulties go to your bank manager for advice.*

Financial Accountant /faɪˌnænʃ(ə)l əˈkaʊntənt/ *noun* a qualified accountant, a member of the Institute of Financial Accountants, who advises on accounting matters or who works as the financial director of a company

financial adviser /faɪˌnænʃəl əd ˈvaɪzə/ *noun* a person or company that gives financial advice to clients for a fee

Financial Asset Securitisation Investment Trust /ˌfaɪnænʃəl ˌæset sɪˌkjʊərɪtaɪzeɪʃ(ə)n ɪnˈvestmənt trʌst/ *noun US* an investment trust that combines various loans, money outstanding on credit card purchases, etc., into one single fund for an individual. Abbreviation **FASIT**

financial assistance /faɪˌnænʃəl əˈsɪstəns/ *noun* help in the form of money

financial calendar /faɪˌnænʃəl ˈkælɪndə/ *noun* a list of significant events and dates in a company's financial reporting year

financial centre /faɪˌnænʃəl ˈsentə/ *noun* a town or part of a town where the main banks and financial institutions are located

financial correspondent /faɪ ˌnænʃəl ˌkɒrɪsˈpɒndənt/ *noun* a journalist who writes articles on money matters for a newspaper

financial crisis /faɪˈnænʃəl ˌkraɪsɪs/ *noun* a situation where financial institutions or assets suddenly lose a large part of their value

financial director /faɪˈnænʃəl daɪ ˌrektə/ *noun* the member of a board of directors who is responsible for a company's financial operations. Abbreviation **FD**

financial futures /faɪˌnænʃəl ˈfjuːtʃəz/, **financial futures contract** /faɪˌnænʃəl ˈfjuːtʃəz ˌkɒntrækt/ *noun* a contract for the purchase of gilt-edged securities for delivery at a date in the future. Also called **financials**

financial futures market /faɪ ˌnænʃəl ˈfjuːtʃəz ˌmɑːkɪt/ *noun* the market in gilt-edged securities for delivery at a date in the future

financial information system /faɪ ˌnænʃəl ˌɪnfəˈmeɪʃ(ə)n ˌsɪstəm/ *noun* a computer-based system that analyses and gathers financial information for use in running a business

financial institution /faɪˌnænʃəl ˌɪnstɪˈtjuːʃ(ə)n/ *noun* a bank, investment trust or insurance company whose work involves lending or investing large sums of money

financial instrument /faɪˌnænʃəl ˈɪnstrʊmənt/ *noun* **1.** a document showing that money has been lent or borrowed, invested or passed from one account to another, e.g. a bill of exchange, share certificate, certificate of deposit or IOU **2.** any form of investment in the stock market or in other financial markets, e.g. shares, government stocks, certificates of deposit or bills of exchange

Financial Intermediaries, Managers and Brokers Regulatory Association *noun* abbreviation **FIMBRA**

financial intermediary /faɪˌnænʃəl ˌɪntəˈmiːdiəri/ *noun* an institution which takes deposits or loans from individuals and lends money to clients

financially /fɪˈnænʃəli/ *adverb* regarding money □ **a company which is financially sound** a company which is profitable and has strong assets

Financial Ombudsman Service /faɪˌnænʃ(ə)l ˈɒmbʊdzmən ˌsɜːvɪs/ *noun* an independent body which investigates complaints by the public against banks, financial advisors, building societies, pension funds, or insurance companies

financial position /faɪˌnænʃəl pə ˈzɪʃ(ə)n/ *noun* the state of a person's or company's bank balance in terms of assets and debts

financial report /faɪˌnænʃəl rɪˈpɔːt/ *noun* a document which gives the financial position of a company or of a club, etc.

Financial Reporting Council /faɪ
ˌnænʃ(ə)l rɪˈpɔːtɪŋ ˌkaʊns(ə)l/ *noun* the
UK's independent regulator for corporate
reporting and governance

financial resources /faɪˌnænʃəl rɪ
ˈzɔːsɪz/ *plural noun* the supply of money
for something ○ *a company with strong
financial resources*

financial review /faɪˌnænʃəl rɪˈvjuː/
noun an examination of an organisation's
finances

financial risk /faɪˌnænʃəl ˈrɪsk/ *noun*
the possibility of losing money ○ *The
company is taking a considerable financial risk in manufacturing 25 million
units without doing any market research.*
○ *There is always some financial risk in
selling on credit.*

financials /faɪˈnænʃəlz/ *plural noun*
same as **financial futures**

**Financial Secretary to the
Treasury** /faɪˌnænʃəl ˌsekrət(ə)ri tə
ðə ˈtreʒəri/ *noun* a minister of state in
charge of the Treasury, under the Chancellor of the Exchequer. ◊ **Chief Secretary to the Treasury**

financial services /faɪˌnænʃəl
ˈsɜːvɪsɪz/ *plural noun* services such as
banking and insurance the main business
of which is the management and transfer
of money

Financial Services Act /faɪˌnænʃəl
ˈsɜːvɪsɪz ækt/ *noun* an Act of the British
Parliament which regulates the offering
of financial services to the general public
and to private investors

Financial Services Authority /faɪ
ˌnænʃəl ˈsɜːvɪsɪz ɔːˌθɒrəti/ *noun* an
independent non-governmental body
formed in 1997 as a result of reforms in
the regulation of financial services in the
United Kingdom. The Securities and
Investments Board (SIB) became responsible for the supervision of banking and
investment services and changed its name
to become the Financial Services
Authority. The FSA's four statutory
objectives were specified by the Financial
Services and Markets Act 2000: maintaining market confidence; increasing
public knowledge of the finance system;
ensuring appropriate protection for
consumers; and reducing financial crime.
Abbreviation **FSA**

'...the FSA has set up an independent
ombudsman scheme covering all areas of
financial services' [*Times*]

financial statement /faɪˌnænʃəl
ˈsteɪtmənt/ *noun* a document which
shows the financial situation of a
company ○ *The accounts department has
prepared a financial statement for the
shareholders.* □ **the Financial Statement**
a document which sets out the details of
the budget presented by the Chancellor of
the Exchequer and is published on Budget
Day

financial supermarket /faɪˌnænʃəl
ˈsuːpəmɑːkɪt/ *noun* a company which
offers a range of financial services, e.g. a
bank offering loans, mortgages, pensions
and insurance as well as the usual
personal banking services

Financial Times /faɪˌnænʃ(ə)l
ˈtaɪmz/ *noun* an important British financial daily newspaper (printed on pink
paper). Abbreviation **FT**

Financial Times Index /faɪˌnænʃəl
ˈtaɪmz ɪnˌdeks/, **Financial Times Ordinary Index** /faɪˌnænʃəl taɪmz ˈɔːdɪnəri
ˌɪndeks/ *noun* an index based on the
market prices of thirty blue-chip companies (this index is the oldest of the FT
indices, and is now considered too narrow
to have much relevance)

financial year /faɪˌnænʃəl ˈjɪə/ *noun*
the twelve-month period for which a
company produces accounts. A financial
year is not necessarily the same as a
calendar year.

financier /faɪˈnænsiə/ *noun* a person
who lends large amounts of money to
companies or who buys shares in companies as an investment

financing /ˈfaɪnænsɪŋ/ *noun* the act of
providing money for a project ○ *The
financing of the project was done by two
international banks.*

finder's fee /ˈfaɪndəz fiː/ *noun* **1.** a fee
paid to a person who finds a client for
another, e.g., someone who introduces a
client to a stockbroking firm **2.** a fee paid
to a person who arranges a loan for
someone, finds a property for someone to
buy, etc.

fine /faɪn/ *noun* money paid because of
something wrong which has been done ○
She was asked to pay a $25,000 fine. ○ *We
had to pay a £50 parking fine.* ■ *verb* to

punish someone by making him or her pay money ○ *to fine someone £2,500 for obtaining money by false pretences* ■ *adverb* very thin or very small □ **we are cutting our margins very fine** we are reducing our margins to the smallest possible amount ■ *adjective* □ **fine rate of discount** the lowest rate of discount on offer

fine-tune /ˌfaɪn ˈtjuːn/ *verb* to make small adjustments to a plan or the economy so that it works better

fine-tuning /ˌfaɪn ˈtjuːnɪŋ/ *noun* the act of making small adjustments in areas such as interest rates, tax bands or the money supply, to improve a nation's economy

finish /ˈfɪnɪʃ/ *noun* an end of a day's trading on the stock exchange ○ *Oil shares rallied at the finish.* ■ *verb* to come to an end ○ *The contract is due to finish next month.* ○ *The market finished the day on a stronger note.*

finished goods /ˌfɪnɪʃt ˈgʊdz/ *plural noun* manufactured goods which are ready to be sold

Finnmark /ˈfɪnmɑːk/ *noun* a name for the currency used before the euro in Finland

fire insurance /ˈfaɪər ɪnˌʃʊərəns/ *noun* insurance against damage by fire

fireproof safe /ˈfaɪəˌpruːf seɪf/ *noun* a safe which cannot be harmed by fire

fire sale /ˈfaɪə seɪl/ *noun* 1. a sale of fire-damaged goods 2. a sale of anything at a very low price

firewalls /ˈfaɪəwɔːlz/ *plural noun US* same as **Chinese walls**

firm /fɜːm/ *noun* a company, business or partnership ○ *a manufacturing firm* ○ *an important publishing firm* ○ *She is a partner in a law firm.* ■ *adjective* 1. unchangeable ○ *to make a firm offer for something* ○ *to place a firm order for two aircraft* 2. not dropping in price and possibly going to rise ○ *Sterling was firmer on the foreign exchange markets.* ○ *Shares remained firm.* ■ *verb* to remain at a price and seem likely to rise ○ *The shares firmed at £1.50.*

'…some profit-taking was noted, but underlying sentiment remained firm' [*Financial Times*]

COMMENT: Strictly speaking, a 'firm' is a partnership or other trading organisation

which is not a limited company. In practice, it is better to use the term for unincorporated businesses such as 'a firm of accountants' or 'a firm of stockbrokers', rather than for 'a major aircraft construction firm' which is likely to be a plc.

firm up *phrasal verb* to agree on the final details of something ○ *We expect to firm up the deal at the next trade fair.*

firmness /ˈfɜːmnəs/ *noun* the fact of being steady at a particular price, or likely to rise ○ *the firmness of the dollar on foreign exchanges*

'Toronto failed to mirror New York's firmness as a drop in gold shares on a falling bullion price left the market closing on a mixed note' [*Financial Times*]

firm order /ˌfɜːm ˈɔːdə/ *noun* 1. a confirmed order, which the purchaser cannot withdraw 2. an order to a broker to sell or buy on a certain date

firm price /ˌfɜːm ˈpraɪs/ *noun* a price which will not change ○ *They are quoting a firm price of $1.23 a unit.*

firm sale /ˌfɜːm ˈseɪl/ *noun* a sale which does not allow the purchaser to return the goods

first in first out /ˌfɜːst ɪn ˌfɜːst ˈaʊt/ *phrase* 1. a redundancy policy, in which the people who have been working longest are the first to be made redundant 2. an accounting policy in which it is assumed that stocks in hand were purchased last, and that stocks sold during the period were purchased first. Abbreviation **FIFO**. Compare **last in first out**

first option /ˌfɜːst ˈɒpʃən/ *noun* allowing someone to be the first to have the possibility of deciding something

first quarter /ˌfɜːst ˈkwɔːtə/ *noun* the period of three months from January to the end of March ○ *The first quarter's rent is payable in advance.*

fiscal /ˈfɪskəl/ *adjective* referring to tax or to government revenues

fiscal agent /ˈfɪskəl ˌeɪdʒənt/ *noun* a bank which acts as an agent for a eurobond issue

fiscal drag /ˌfɪskəl ˈdræg/ *noun* 1. the effect of inflation on a government's tax revenues. As inflation increases so do prices and wages, and tax revenues rise proportionally. Even if inflation is low, increased earnings will give the government increased revenues anyway. **2.** the negative effect of higher personal taxation on an individual's work performance

fiscal measures /ˌfɪskəl 'meʒəz/ *plural noun* tax changes made by a government to improve the working of the economy

fiscal policy /ˌfɪskəl 'pɒlɪsi/ *noun* the policy of a government regarding taxation and revenues

'…the standard measure of fiscal policy – the public sector borrowing requirement – is kept misleadingly low' [*Economist*]

fiscal year /ˌfɪskəl 'jɪə/ *noun* a twelve-month period on which taxes are calculated. In the UK this is 6th April to 5th April.

'…last fiscal year the chain reported a 116% jump in earnings' [*Barron's*]

Five-Year Plan /ˌfaɪv jɪə 'plæn/ *noun* proposals for running a country's economy over a five-year period

fixation /fɪk'seɪʃ(ə)n/ *noun* the act of stating a price on an options market

fixed /fɪkst/ *adjective* unable to be changed or removed

'…you must offer shippers and importers fixed rates over a reasonable period of time' [*Lloyd's List*]

fixed assets /ˌfɪkst 'æsets/ *plural noun* property or machinery which a company owns and uses, but which the company does not buy or sell as part of its regular trade, including the company's investments in shares of other companies

fixed capital /ˌfɪkst 'kæpɪt(ə)l/ *noun* capital in the form of buildings and machinery

fixed costs /ˌfɪkst 'kɒsts/ *plural noun* business costs which do not change with the quantity of the product made

fixed deposit /ˌfɪkst dɪ'pɒzɪt/ *noun* a deposit which pays a stated interest over a set period

fixed exchange rate /ˌfɪkst ɪks 'tʃeɪndʒ ˌreɪt/ *noun* a rate of exchange of one currency against another which cannot fluctuate, and can only be changed by devaluation or revaluation

fixed expenses /ˌfɪkst ɪk'spensɪz/ *plural noun* expenses which do not vary with different levels of production, e.g. rent, staff salaries and insurance

fixed income /ˌfɪkst 'ɪnkʌm/ *noun* income which does not change from year to year, as from an annuity

fixed-income derivatives /ˌfɪkst ˌɪnkʌm dɪ'rɪvətɪvz/ *plural noun* derivatives which pay a fixed interest at stated dates in the future

fixed-interest /ˌfɪkst 'ɪntrəst/ *adjective* having an interest rate which does not vary

fixed-interest investments /ˌfɪkst ˌɪntrəst ɪn'vestmənts/ *plural noun* investments producing a level of interest which does not change

fixed-interest securities /ˌfɪkst ˌɪntrəst sɪ'kjʊərɪtiz/ *plural noun* securities such as government bonds which produce a level of interest which does not change

fixed-price /ˌfɪkst 'praɪs/ *adjective* having a price which cannot be changed

fixed-price agreement /ˌfɪkst 'praɪs əˌgriːmənt/ *noun* an agreement where a company provides a service or a product at a price which stays the same for the whole period of the agreement

fixed-price offer for sale /fɪkst ˌpraɪs ˌɒfə fə 'seɪl/ *noun* an offer to purchase shares in a new company for a price which has been fixed at flotation, as opposed to tendering

fixed rate /ˌfɪkst 'reɪt/ *noun* a rate, e.g. an exchange rate, which does not change

fixed rate loan /ˌfɪkst reɪt 'ləʊn/ *noun* a loan on which the rate of interest stays the same for the duration of the loan

fixed scale of charges /ˌfɪkst skeɪl əv 'tʃɑːdʒɪz/ *noun* a set of charges that do not vary according to individual circumstances but are applied consistently in all cases of a particular kind

fixed-term /fɪkst 'tɜːm/ *adjective* lasting for a fixed number of years

fixed-term product /ˌfɪkst tɜːm 'prɒdʌkt/ *noun* a financial product, such as a bond, which runs for a fixed number of years

fixed yield /ˌfɪkst 'jiːld/ *noun* a percentage return which does not change

fixer-upper /'fɪksə/ *noun* a person who has a reputation for arranging business deals, often illegally

fixing /'fɪksɪŋ/ *noun* **1.** arranging ○ *the fixing of charges* ○ *the fixing of a mort-*

gage rate **2.** a regular meeting to set a price

fl *abbreviation* guilder

FLA *abbreviation* Finance and Leasing Association

flag /flæg/ *noun* a term used by chartists to refer to a period when prices consolidate a previous advance or fall

flat /flæt/ *adjective* **1.** used to describe market prices which do not fall or rise, because of low demand ○ *The market was flat today.* **2.** not changing in response to different conditions ○ *a flat rate* ■ *noun* a set of rooms for one family in a building with other sets of similar rooms ○ *He has a flat in the centre of town.* ○ *She is buying a flat close to her office.*

'…the government revised its earlier reports for July and August. Originally reported as flat in July and declining by 0.2% in August, industrial production is now seen to have risen by 0.2% and 0.1% respectively in those months' [*Sunday Times*]

flat bed imprinter /ˌflæt bed ɪm ˈprɪntə/ *noun US* same as **imprinter**

flat out /ˌflæt ˈaʊt/ *adverb* working hard or at full speed ○ *The factory worked flat out to complete the order on time.*

flat rate /ˌflæt ˈreɪt/ *noun* a charge which always stays the same ○ *a flat-rate increase of 10%* ○ *We pay a flat rate for electricity each quarter.* ○ *He is paid a flat rate of £2 per thousand.*

flat yield /ˌflæt ˈjiːld/ *noun* an interest rate as a percentage of the price paid for fixed-interest stock

fledgling companies /ˌfledʒlɪŋ ˈkʌmp(ə)niz/ *plural noun* companies which are just starting in business, especially companies listed on the London Stock Exchange with a capitalisation which is too small for them to be included in the FTSE All-Share Index

fleet rental /ˌfliːt ˈrent(ə)l/ *noun* an arrangement to rent all a company's cars from the same company at a special price

flexibility /ˌfleksɪˈbɪlɪti/ *noun* the ability to be easily changed ○ *There is no flexibility in the company's pricing policy.*

'…they calculate interest on their 'flexible' mortgage on an annual basis rather than daily. Charging annual interest makes a nonsense of the whole idea of flexibility which is supposed to help you pay off your

mortgage more quickly' [*Financial Times*]

flexible /ˈfleksɪb(ə)l/ *adjective* possible to alter or change ○ *We try to be flexible where the advertising budget is concerned.* ○ *The company has adopted a flexible pricing policy.*

flexible mortgage /ˌfleksɪb(ə)l ˈmɔːɡɪdʒ/ *noun* a mortgage that gives the borrower the freedom to change the amount and frequency of his or her mortgage payments

flexible working hours /ˌfleksɪb(ə)l ˈwɜːkɪŋ ˌaʊəz/, **flexible work** *plural noun* a system in which employees can start or stop work at different hours of the morning or evening provided that they work a certain number of hours per day or week

Flexible Work Regulations /ˌfleksɪb(ə)l ˈwɜːk regjʊˌleɪʃ(ə)nz/ *plural noun* (*in the UK*) the legal right for a parent with a child under the age of 6, or with a disabled child under the age of 18, to ask that their working hours should be arranged to help them with their responsibilities

flight /flaɪt/ *noun* **1.** a journey by an aircraft, leaving at a regular time ○ *Flight AC 267 is leaving from Gate 46.* ○ *He missed his flight.* ○ *I always take the afternoon flight to Rome.* ○ *If you hurry you will catch the six o'clock flight to Paris.* **2.** a rapid movement of money out of a country because of a lack of confidence in the country's economic future ○ *The flight of capital from Europe into the US* ○ *The flight from the peso into the dollar.* ■ *verb* to arrange a scheduling pattern for something

flight to quality /ˌflaɪt tə ˈkwɒlɪti/ *noun* a tendency of investors to buy safe blue-chip securities when the economic outlook is uncertain

flip side /ˈflɪp saɪd/ *noun* the negative factors (in a proposal)

float /fləʊt/ *noun* **1.** cash taken from a central supply and used for running expenses ○ *The sales reps have a float of £100 each.* **2.** the process of starting a new company by selling shares in it on the stock exchange ○ *The float of the new company was a complete failure.* **3.** the process of allowing a currency to settle at its own exchange rate, without any government intervention ■ *verb* **1.** □ **to float a company** to start a new company by selling shares in it on the stock exchange □ **to float a loan** to raise a loan on the financial market by asking banks and companies to subscribe to it **2.** to let a currency settle at its own exchange rate on the international markets and not be fixed ○ *The government has let sterling float.* ○ *The government has decided to float the pound.*

floater /ˈfləʊtə/ *noun US* a loan with a variable interest rate

floating /ˈfləʊtɪŋ/ *noun* **1.** □ **floating of a company** the act of starting a new company by selling shares in it on the stock exchange **2.** □ **the floating of the pound** letting the pound find its own exchange rate on the international market ■ *adjective* not fixed ○ *floating exchange rates* ○ *the floating pound*

'…in a world of floating exchange rates the dollar is strong because of capital inflows rather than weak because of the nation's trade deficit' [*Duns Business Month*]

floating capital /ˌfləʊtɪŋ ˈkæpɪt(ə)l/ *noun* same as **working capital**

floating charge /ˈfləʊtɪŋ tʃɑːdʒ/ *noun* a charge linked to any of the company's assets in a category, but not to any specific item

floating rate /ˈfləʊtɪŋ reɪt/ *noun* **1.** same as **variable rate 2.** an exchange rate for a currency, which can vary according to market demand, and is not fixed by the government

floating-rate notes /ˌfləʊtɪŋ reɪt ˈnəʊts/ *plural noun* Eurocurrency loans arranged by a bank which are not at a fixed rate of interest. Abbreviation **FRNs**

floor /flɔː/ *noun* **1.** the part of the room which you walk on □ **on the shop floor** in the works, in the factory, among the ordinary workers ○ *The feeling on the shop floor is that the manager does not know his job.* **2.** all the rooms on one level in a building ○ *Her office is on the 26th floor.* (NOTE: In the UK, the floor at street level is the **ground floor**, but in the US it is the **first floor**. Each floor in the USA is one number higher than the same floor in Britain.) **3.** the bottom level of something, e.g. the lowest exchange rate which a government will accept for its currency

or the lower limit imposed on an interest rate ○ *The government will impose a floor on wages to protect the poor.* (NOTE: The opposite is the **ceiling** or **cap**.) □ **to establish a floor at an auction** to fix the bottom price below which the seller will not sell

floor broker /ˈflɔː ˌbrəʊkə/ *noun* a stockbroker who is a member of a brokerage house

floor limit /ˈflɔː ˌlɪmɪt/ *noun* a highest sale through a credit card that a retailer can accept without having to get authorisation from the bank that issued the card

floor price /ˈflɔː praɪs/ *noun* the lowest price, a price which cannot go any lower

floor space /ˈflɔː speɪs/ *noun* an area of floor in an office or warehouse ○ *We have 3,500 square metres of floor space to let.*

floor trader /ˈflɔː ˌtreɪdə/ *noun* an independent trader on a stock exchange, who buys and sells on his or her own account

flop /flɒp/ *noun* a failure, or something which has not been successful ○ *The new model was a flop.* ■ *verb* to fail or not be a success ○ *The launch of the new shampoo flopped badly.* (NOTE: **flopping – flopped**)

flotation /fləʊˈteɪʃ(ə)n/ *noun* □ **the flotation of a new company** the act of starting a new company by selling shares in it

flow /fləʊ/ *noun* **1.** a movement ○ *the flow of capital into a country* ○ *the flow of investments into Japan* **2.** □ **the company is suffering from cash flow problems** cash income is not coming in fast enough to pay for the expenditure going out ■ *verb* to move smoothly ○ *Production is now flowing normally after the strike.*

flow chart /ˈfləʊ tʃɑːt/, **flow diagram** /ˈfləʊ ˌdaɪəgræm/ *noun* a chart which shows the arrangement of work processes in a series

fluctuate /ˈflʌktʃueɪt/ *verb* to move up and down ○ *Prices fluctuated between £1.10 and £1.25.* ○ *The pound fluctuated all day on the foreign exchange markets.*

fluctuating /ˈflʌktʃueɪtɪŋ/ *adjective* moving up and down ○ *fluctuating dollar prices*

fluctuation /ˌflʌktʃuˈeɪʃ(ə)n/ *noun* an up and down movement ○ *the fluctua-*

tions of the yen ○ *the fluctuations of the exchange rate*

FNMA *abbreviation* Federal National Mortgage Association

FOB /'efəʊ'biː/, **f.o.b.** *abbreviation* free on board

FOK *abbreviation* fill or kill

folio /'fəʊliəʊ/ *noun* a page with a number, especially two facing pages in an account book which have the same number ■ *verb* to put a number on a page

foot /fʊt/ *verb* □ **to foot the bill** to pay the costs □ **to foot up an account** *US* to add up a column of numbers

footings /'fʊtɪŋz/ *noun US* the bottom line in a bank's balance sheet (*informal*)

Footsie /'fʊtsi/ *noun* an index based on the prices of 100 leading companies (this is the main London index) (*informal*) Full form **Financial Times-Stock Exchange 100 index**

FOR full form **free on rail**

'Forbes' 500 /,fɔːbz faɪv 'hʌndrəd/ *noun* a list of the largest US corporations, published each year in 'Forbes' magazine

forbid /fə'bɪd/ *verb* to tell someone not to do something, or to say that something must not be done ○ *The contract forbids resale of the goods to the US* ○ *Smoking is forbidden in our offices.* ○ *Staff are forbidden to speak directly to the press.* (NOTE: **forbidding – forbade – forbidden**)

force /fɔːs/ *noun* **1.** strength □ **to be in force** to be operating or working ○ *The rules have been in force since 1986.* □ **to come into force** to start to operate or work ○ *The new regulations will come into force on 1st January.* **2.** a group of people ■ *verb* to make someone do something ○ *Competition has forced the company to lower its prices.* ○ *After the takeover several of the managers were forced to take early retirement.*

    force down *phrasal verb* to make something such as prices become lower □ **to force prices down** to make prices come down ○ *Competition has forced prices down.*

    force up *phrasal verb* to make something become higher □ **to force prices up** to make prices go up ○ *The war forced up the price of oil.*

forced sale /,fɔːst 'seɪl/ *noun* a sale which takes place because a court orders it or because it is the only way to avoid a financial crisis

force majeure /,fɔːs mæ'ʒɜː/ *noun* something which happens which is out of the control of the parties who have signed a contract, e.g. a strike, war, or storm

forecast /'fɔːkɑːst/ *noun* a description or calculation of what will probably happen in the future ○ *The chairman did not believe the sales director's forecast of higher turnover.* ■ *verb* to calculate or to say what will probably happen in the future ○ *She is forecasting sales of £2m.* ○ *Economists have forecast a fall in the exchange rate.* (NOTE: **forecasting – forecast**)

forecast dividend /,fɔːkɑːst 'dɪvɪdend/ *noun* a dividend which a company expects to pay at the end of the current year. Also called **prospective dividend**

forecaster /'fɔːkɑːstə/ *noun* a person who says what he or she thinks will happen in the future

forecasting /'fɔːkɑːstɪŋ/ *noun* the process of calculating what will probably happen in the future ○ *Manpower planning will depend on forecasting the future levels of production.*

foreclose /fɔː'kləʊz/ *verb* **1.** to sell a property because the owner cannot repay money which he or she has borrowed, using the property as security ○ *to foreclose on a mortgaged property* ○ *The bank foreclosed on his farm.* **2.** to acquire a property because the owner cannot repay money which he or she has borrowed (using the property as security)

foreclosure /fɔː'kləʊʒə/ *noun* an act of foreclosing

foreign /'fɒrɪn/ *adjective* not belonging to your own country ○ *Foreign cars have flooded our market.* ○ *We are increasing our trade with foreign countries.* □ **foreign banks** *or* **foreign branches** banks from other countries which have branches in a country

'…a sharp setback in foreign trade accounted for most of the winter slow-down' [*Fortune*]

foreign currency /,fɒrɪn 'kʌrənsi/ *noun* money of another country

foreign currency account /ˌfɒrɪn
'kʌrənsi əˌkaʊnt/ *noun* a bank account
in the currency of another country, e.g. a
dollar account in a UK bank

foreign currency reserves /ˌfɒrɪn
'kʌrənsi rɪˌzɜːvz/ *plural noun* a
country's reserves held in currencies of
other countries. Also called **foreign
exchange reserves, international
reserves**

'…the treasury says it needs the cash to
rebuild its foreign reserves which have
fallen from $19 billion when the govern-
ment took office to $7 billion in August'
[*Economist*]

foreign direct investment /ˌfɒrɪn
ˌdaɪrekt ɪn'vestmənt/ *noun* an investment in a developing country by foreign
companies or governments. Abbreviation
FDI

foreign exchange /ˌfɒrɪn ɪks
'tʃeɪndʒ/ *noun* **1.** the business of
exchanging the money of one country for
that of another **2.** foreign currencies

'…the dollar recovered a little lost ground
on the foreign exchanges yesterday'
[*Financial Times*]

foreign exchange broker /ˌfɒrɪn
ɪks'tʃeɪndʒ ˌbrəʊkə/, **foreign
exchange dealer** /ˌfɒrɪn ɪks'tʃeɪndʒ
ˌdiːlə/ *noun* a person who deals on the
foreign exchange market

foreign exchange dealing /ˌfɒrɪn
ɪks'tʃeɪndʒ ˌdiːlɪŋ/ *noun* the business of
buying and selling foreign currencies

foreign exchange desk /ˌfɒrɪn ɪks
'tʃeɪndʒ desk/ *noun* a section of a bank
which deals with foreign exchange transactions

foreign exchange market /ˌfɒrɪn
ɪks'tʃeɪndʒ ˌmɑːkɪt/ *noun* **1.** a market
where people buy and sell foreign currencies ○ *She trades on the foreign exchange
market.* **2.** dealings in foreign currencies
○ *Foreign exchange markets were very
active after the dollar devalued.*

foreign exchange reserves /ˌfɒrɪn
ɪks'tʃeɪndʒ rɪˌzɜːvz/ *plural noun*
foreign money held by a government to
support its own currency and pay its debts

foreign exchange transaction
/ˌfɒrɪn ɪks'tʃeɪndʒ trænˌzækʃən/ *noun*
a purchase or sale of foreign currency

foreign exchange transfer /ˌfɒrɪn
ɪks'tʃeɪndʒ ˌtrænsfɜː/ *noun* the sending
of money from one country to another

foreign investments /ˌfɒrɪn ɪn
'vestmənts/ *plural noun* money invested
in other countries

foreign money order /ˌfɒrɪn 'mʌni
ˌɔːdə/ *noun* a money order in a foreign
currency which is payable to someone
living in a foreign country

Foreign Office /'fɒrɪn ˌɒfɪs/ *noun* a
ministry dealing with a country's relations with foreign countries

foreign rights /ˌfɒrɪn 'raɪtz/ *plural
noun* a legal entitlement to sell something
in a foreign country, e.g. the right to translate a book into a foreign language

foreign trade /ˌfɒrɪn 'treɪd/ *noun* a
trade with other countries

forex /'fɔːreks/, **Forex** *noun* same as
foreign exchange

'…the amount of reserves sold by the
authorities were not sufficient to move the
$200 billion Forex market permanently'
[*Duns Business Month*]

forfaiting /'fɔːfɪtɪŋ/ *noun* the action of
providing finance for exporters, where an
agent or forfaiter accepts a bill of
exchange from an overseas customer; he
or she buys the bill at a discount, and
collects the payments from the customer
in due course

forfeit /'fɔːfɪt/ *noun* the fact of having
something taken away as a punishment □
the goods were declared forfeit the court
said that the goods had to be taken away
from the person who was holding them ■
verb to have something taken away as a
punishment □ **to forfeit a patent** to lose a
patent because payments have not been
made □ **to forfeit a deposit** to lose a
deposit which was left for an item
because you have decided not to buy that
item

forfeit clause /'fɔːfɪt klɔːz/ *noun* a
clause in a contract which says that goods
or a deposit will be taken away if the
contract is not obeyed

forfeiture /'fɔːfɪtʃə/ *noun* the act of
forfeiting a property

for hire contract /fə 'haɪə ˌkɒntrækt/
noun US a freelance contract

forint /'fɒrɪnt/ *noun* a unit of currency
used in Hungary

form /fɔːm/ *noun* **1.** □ **form of words** words correctly laid out for a legal document □ **receipt in due form** a correctly written receipt **2.** an official printed paper with blank spaces which have to be filled in with information ○ *a pad of order forms* ○ *You have to fill in form A20.* ○ *Each passenger was given a customs declaration form.* ○ *The reps carry pads of order forms.* ■ *verb* to start, create or organise something ○ *The brothers have formed a new company.*

Form 1099 /fɔːm ˌten naɪnti ˈnaɪn/ *noun US* a statement from a bank or stockbroker, giving details of interest payments or dividends received, which a taxpayer sends on to the IRS

forma /ˈfɔːmə/ *noun* ♦ **pro forma**

formal /ˈfɔːm(ə)l/ *adjective* clearly and legally written ○ *to make a formal application* ○ *to send a formal order* ○ *Is this a formal job offer?* ○ *The factory is prepared for the formal inspection by the government inspector.*

formal documents /ˌfɔːm(ə)l ˈdɒkjʊmənts/ *plural noun* documents giving full details of a takeover bid

formality /fɔːˈmælɪti/ *noun* something which has to be done to obey the law

formation /fɔːˈmeɪʃ(ə)n/, **forming** /ˈfɔːmɪŋ/ *noun* the act of organising ○ *the formation of a new company*

form letter /ˈfɔːm ˌletə/ *noun* a letter which can be sent without any change to several correspondents, e.g. a letter chasing payment

formula investing /ˈfɔːmjələ ɪn ˌvestɪŋ/ *noun* a method of investing according to a set plan, such as purchasing a specific value of shares each month or only investing in shares of companies with a capitalisation of less than £25m

fortune /ˈfɔːtʃən/ *noun* a large amount of money ○ *He made a fortune from investing in oil shares.* ○ *She left her fortune to her three children.*

Fortune 500 /ˌfɔːtʃuːn ˌfaɪv ˈhʌndrəd/ *plural noun* (*the 500 largest companies in the USA*) the 500 largest companies in the US, as listed annually in Fortune magazine

forward /ˈfɔːwəd/ *adjective* in advance or to be paid at a later date ■ *adverb* **1.** □ **to date a cheque forward** to put a later date than the present one on a cheque **2.** □ **to sell forward** to sell foreign currency, commodities, etc., for delivery at a later date **3.** □ **balance brought forward, carried forward** balance which is entered in an account at the end of a period and is then taken to be the starting point of the next period

forwardation /ˌfɔːwədˈeɪʃ(ə)n/ *noun* a situation in which the cash price is lower than the forward price (NOTE: The opposite is **backwardation**.)

forward buying /ˌfɔːwəd ˈbaɪɪŋ/ *noun* the act of buying shares, currency, or commodities at today's price for delivery at a later date

forward contract /ˈfɔːwəd ˌkɒntrækt/ *noun* a one-off agreement to buy currency, shares or commodities for delivery at a later date at a specific price

forward cover /ˈfɔːwəd ˌkʌvə/ *noun* an arrangement to cover the risks on a forward contract

forward dealing /ˈfɔːwəd ˌdiːlɪŋ/ *noun* the activity of buying or selling commodities forward

forward delivery /ˌfɔːwəd dɪˈlɪv(ə)ri/ *noun* a delivery at some date in the future which has been agreed between the buyer and seller

forwarder /ˈfɔːwədə/ *noun* a person or company that arranges shipping and customs documents for several shipments from different companies, putting them together to form one large shipment

forwarding /ˈfɔːwədɪŋ/ *noun* the act of arranging shipping and customs documents

forwarding agent /ˈfɔːwədɪŋ ˌeɪdʒənt/ *noun* a person or company which arranges shipping and customs documents

forwarding instructions /ˈfɔːwədɪŋ ɪnˌstrʌkʃənz/ *plural noun* instructions showing how the goods are to be shipped and delivered

forward integration /ˌfɔːwəd ˌɪntə ˈɡreɪʃ(ə)n/ *noun* a process of expansion in which a company becomes its own distributor or takes over a company in the same line of business as itself ○ *Forward integration will give the company greater control over its selling.* ○ *Forward integration has brought the company closer to its consumers and has made it aware of* *their buying habits.* Compare **backward integration**

forward margin /ˌfɔːwəd ˈmɑːdʒɪn/ *noun* the difference between the current price and the forward price

forward market /ˌfɔːwəd ˈmɑːkɪt/ *noun* a market for purchasing foreign currency, oil or commodities for delivery at a later date

forward sales /ˈfɔːwəd seɪlz/ *plural noun* sales of shares, commodities or foreign exchange for delivery at a later date

forward trading /ˈfɔːwəd ˌtreɪdɪŋ/ *noun* the activity of buying or selling commodities for delivery at a later date

foul bill of lading /ˌfaʊl bɪl əv ˈleɪdɪŋ/ *noun* a bill of lading which says that the goods were in bad condition when received by the shipper

founder /ˈfaʊndə/ *noun* a person who starts a company

founder's shares /ˈfaʊndəz ˌʃeəz/ *noun* special shares issued to the person who starts a company

401(k) plan /ˌfɔː əʊ wʌn ˈkeɪ plæn/ *noun US* a personal pension plan arranged by an employer for a member of staff, invested in bonds, mutual funds or stock (the employee contributes a proportion of salary, on which tax is deferred; the employer can also make contributions)

fourth market /fɔːθ ˈmɑːkɪt/ *noun US* trading in securities which is carried between financial institutions, without going through the stock market

fourth quarter /ˌfɔːθ ˈkwɔːtə/ *noun* a period of three months from October 1st to the end of the year

fraction /ˈfrækʃən/ *noun* a very small amount ○ *Only a fraction of the new share issue was subscribed.*

fractional /ˈfrækʃənəl/ *adjective* very small

fractional certificate /ˈfrækʃənəl səˌtɪfɪkət/ *noun* a certificate for part of a share

fractional reserve /ˌfrækʃənəl rɪˈzɜːv/ *noun* a reserve held by a bank which is a small proportion of its total deposits

fragile /ˈfrædʒaɪl/ *adjective* which can be easily broken ○ *There is an extra*

premium for insuring fragile goods in shipment.

fragility /frəˈdʒɪlɪti/ *noun* the fact of being weak or likely to collapse (NOTE: The opposite is **robustness**.) □ **financial fragility** the fact of being in a weak position financially

franc /fræŋk/ *noun* **1.** a former unit of currency in France and Belgium ○ *French francs* or *Belgian francs* **2.** a unit of currency in Switzerland and several other currencies ○ *It costs twenty-five Swiss francs.*

franchise /ˈfræntʃaɪz/ *noun* a licence to trade using a brand name and paying a royalty for it ○ *He's bought a printing franchise* or *a pizza franchise.* ■ *verb* to sell licences for people to trade using a brand name and paying a royalty ○ *His sandwich bar was so successful that he decided to franchise it.*

'…many new types of franchised businesses will join the ranks of the giant chains of fast-food restaurants, hotels and motels and rental car agencies' [*Franchising Opportunities*]

franchisee /ˌfræntʃaɪˈziː/ *noun* a person who runs a franchise

franchiser /ˈfræntʃaɪzə/ *noun* a person who licenses a franchise

franchising /ˈfræntʃaɪzɪŋ/ *noun* the act of selling a licence to trade as a franchise ○ *She runs her sandwich chain as a franchising operation.*

franchising operation /ˈfræntʃaɪzɪŋ ˌɒpəˌreɪʃ(ə)n/ *noun* an operation involving selling licences to trade as a franchise

franchisor /ˈfræntʃaɪzə/ *noun* another spelling of **franchiser**

franco /ˈfræŋkəʊ/ *adverb* free

franc zone /ˈfræŋk zəʊn/ *noun* a currency area consisting of the former French colonies in Africa or in the Pacific, which uses the CFA franc or the CFP franc as unit of currency

Frankfurt /ˈfræŋkfɜːt/ *noun* the main financial centre in Germany

Frankfurter Allgemeine Zeitung *noun* a daily newspaper published in Frankfurt

Frankfurt Interbank Offered Rate /ˌfræŋkfɜːt ɪntəˌbæŋk ˈɒfəd reɪt/ *noun* a rate used for calculating loans on the

Frankfurt money markets. Abbreviation **FIBOR**

fraud /frɔːd/ *noun* the act of making money by making people believe something which is not true ○ *He got possession of the property by fraud.* ○ *She was accused of frauds relating to foreign currency.* □ **to obtain money by fraud** to obtain money by saying or doing something to cheat someone

fraud squad /'frɔːd skwɒd/ *noun* the special police department which investigates frauds

fraudulent /'frɔːdjʊlənt/ *adjective* not honest, or aiming to cheat people ○ *a fraudulent transaction*

fraudulently /'frɔːdjʊləntli/ *adverb* not honestly ○ *goods imported fraudulently*

fraudulent misrepresentation /ˌfrɔːdjʊlənt mɪsˌreprɪzenˈteɪʃ(ə)n/ *noun* the act of making a false statement with the intention of tricking a customer

FRB *abbreviation* **1.** Federal Reserve Bank **2.** Federal Reserve Board

Freddie Mac /ˌfredɪ ˈmæk/ *noun US* same as **Federal Home Loan Mortgage Corporation** (*informal*)

free /friː/ *adjective, adverb* **1.** not costing any money ○ *I have been given a free ticket to the exhibition.* ○ *The price includes free delivery.* ○ *All goods in the store are delivered free.* ○ *A catalogue will be sent free on request.* □ **free of charge** with no payment to be made **2.** with no restrictions □ **free of tax** with no tax having to be paid ○ *Interest is paid free of tax.* □ **free of duty** with no duty to be paid ○ *to import wine free of duty* ■ *verb* to make something available or easy ○ *The government's decision has freed millions of pounds for investment.*

'American business as a whole is increasingly free from heavy dependence on manufacturing' [*Sunday Times*]

free capital /ˌfriː ˈkæpɪt(ə)l/ *noun* an amount of a company's capital in shares which are available for trading on a stock exchange

free collective bargaining /ˌfriː kəˌlektɪv ˈbɑːgɪnɪŋ/ *noun* negotiations between management and trade unions about wage increases and working conditions

free competition /ˌfriː ˌkɒmpəˈtɪʃ(ə)n/ *noun* the fact of being free to compete without government interference

free currency /ˌfriː ˈkʌrənsi/ *noun* a currency which is allowed by the government to be bought and sold without restriction

free enterprise /ˌfriː ˈentəpraɪz/ *noun* a system of business free from government interference

freefall /'friːfɔːl/ *noun* a sudden collapse of prices ○ *On the news of the devaluation the stock market went into freefall.*

freeholder /'friːhəʊldə/ *noun* a person who owns a freehold property

freehold property /'friːhəʊld ˌprɒpəti/ *noun* property which the owner holds for ever and on which no rent is paid

free issue /ˌfriː ˈɪʃuː/ *noun* same as **bonus issue**

free market /ˌfriː ˈmɑːkɪt/ *noun* a market in which there is no government control of supply and demand, and the rights of individuals and organisations to physical and intellectual property are upheld

free market economy /ˌfriː ˌmɑːkɪt ɪˈkɒnəmi/ *noun* an economic system where the government does not interfere in business activity in any way

free on board /ˌfriː ɒn ˈbɔːd/ *adjective* including in the price all the seller's costs until the goods are on the ship for transportation. Abbreviation **f.o.b.**

free online sessions /friː ˌɒnlaɪn ˈseʃ(ə)nz/ *plural noun* the number of times a customer can access his online bank account without paying a charge

free period /friː ˈpɪəriəd/ *noun* the period of grace allowed to credit card holders before payment for credit card purchases is demanded

free port /'friː pɔːt/ *noun* a port where there are no customs duties to be paid

free reserves /ˌfriː rɪˈzɜːvz/ *plural noun* the part of a bank's reserves which are above the statutory level and so can be used for various purposes as the bank wishes

free sample /ˌfriː ˈsɑːmpəl/ *noun* a sample given free to advertise a product

free-standing /friː ˈstændɪŋ/ *adjective* standing separately, not attached to a wall

free-standing additional voluntary contribution /ˌfriː ˌstændɪŋ ə ˌdɪʃ(ə)nəl ˌvɒlənt(ə)ri ˌkɒntrɪ ˈbjuːʃ(ə)n/ *noun* a payment made by an individual into an independent pension fund to supplement an occupational pension scheme. The anticipated benefits from the two schemes together must be less than the maximum permitted under the rules laid down by the Inland Revenue. Abbreviation **FSAVC**

free-standing additional voluntary contributions plan /friː ˌstændɪŋ əˌdɪʃ(ə)nəl ˌvɒlənt(ə)ri ˌkɒntrɪˈbjuːʃ(ə)ns/ *noun* a separate pension plan taken out by an individual in addition to a company pension scheme ○ *additional costs* ○ *additional charges* ○ *additional clauses to a contract* ○ *additional duty will have to be paid*

free trade /ˌfriː ˈtreɪd/ *noun* a system where goods can go from one country to another without any restrictions

free trade area /ˌfriː ˈtreɪd ˌeəriə/ *noun* a group of countries practising free trade

free trader /ˌfriː ˈtreɪdə/ *noun* a person who is in favour of free trade

free trade zone /ˌfriː ˈtreɪd ˌzəʊn/ *noun* an area where there are no customs duties

free trial /ˌfriː ˈtraɪəl/ *noun* an opportunity to test a machine or product with no payment involved

freeze /friːz/ *noun* □ **a freeze on wages and prices** period when wages and prices are not allowed to be increased ■ *verb* to keep something such as money or costs at their present level and not allow them to rise ○ *to freeze wages and prices* ○ *to freeze credits* ○ *to freeze company dividends* ○ *We have frozen expenditure at last year's level.* (NOTE: **freezing – froze – frozen**)

freeze out *phrasal verb* □ **to freeze out the competition** to trade successfully and cheaply and so prevent competitors from operating

freight /freɪt/ *noun* the cost of transporting goods by air, sea, or land ○ *At an auction, the buyer pays the freight.*

freightage /ˈfreɪtɪdʒ/ *noun* the cost of transporting goods

freight charges /ˈfreɪt ˌtʃɑːdʒɪz/ *plural noun* money charged for transporting goods ○ *Freight charges have gone up sharply this year.*

freight costs /ˈfreɪt kɒsts/ *plural noun* money paid to transport goods

freight forward /ˌfreɪt ˈfɔːwəd/ *noun* a deal where the customer pays for transporting the goods

freight forwarder /ˈfreɪt ˌfɔːwədə/ *noun* a person or company that arranges shipping and customs documents for several shipments from different companies, putting them together to form one large shipment

'…the airline will allow freight forwarder customers to track and trace consignments on the airline's website' [*Lloyd's List*]

freight rates /ˈfreɪt reɪts/ *plural noun* charges for transporting goods

friendly society /ˈfrendli səˌsaɪəti/ *noun* a group of people who pay regular subscriptions which are used to help members of the group when they are ill or in financial difficulties

fringe benefit /ˈfrɪndʒ ˌbenɪfɪt/ *noun* an extra item given by a company to employees in addition to a salary, e.g. company cars or private health insurance ○ *The fringe benefits make up for the poor pay.* ○ *Use of the company recreation facilities is one of the fringe benefits of the job.*

FRNs *abbreviation* floating-rate notes

front /frʌnt/ *noun* a business or person used to hide an illegal trade ○ *His restaurant is a front for a drugs organisation.*

front-end /ˌfrʌnt ˈend/ *adjective* referring to the start of an investment or insurance

front-end fee /frʌnt ˈend fiː/ *noun* an initial loading of the management charges into the first premium paid for an insurance

front-end loaded /ˈfrʌnt end ˌləʊdɪd/ *adjective* used to describe an insurance or investment scheme in which most of the management charges are incurred in the first year of the investment or insurance, and are not spread out over the whole period. Compare **back-end loaded**

front man /'frʌnt mæn/ *noun* a person who seems honest but is hiding an illegal trade

front office /ˌfrʌnt 'ɒfɪs/ *noun* the front-line staff and support staff in a financial institution

front-running /frʌnt 'rʌnɪŋ/ *noun US* the act of buying shares or options because you have heard of a large order to purchase which is coming ○ *They were accused of persistent front-running.*

frozen /'frəʊz(ə)n/ *adjective* not allowed to be changed or used ○ *Wages have been frozen at last year's rates.* □ **his assets have been frozen by the court** the court does not allow him to sell his assets. ◊ **freeze**

frozen account /'frəʊz(ə)n əˌkaʊnt/ *noun* a bank account where the money cannot be moved or used because of a court order

frozen assets /ˌfrəʊz(ə)n 'æsets/ *plural noun* a company's assets which by law cannot be sold because someone has a claim against them

frozen credits /ˌfrəʊz(ə)n 'kredɪtz/ *plural noun* credits in an account which cannot be moved

FSA *abbreviation* Financial Services Authority

FSAVC *abbreviation* free-standing additional voluntary contribution

FT *abbreviation* Financial Times

FTASI *abbreviation* FTSE Actuaries Share Indices

FTSE 100 /ˌfʊtsi wʌn 'hʌndrəd/ *noun* an index based on the prices of one hundred leading companies (this is the main London index)

'…the benchmark FTSE 100 index ended the session up 94.3 points' [*Times*]

FTSE 100 index-tracking unit trust /ˌfʊtsi wʌn ˌhʌndrəd ˌindeks ˌtrækɪŋ 'juːnɪt trʌst/ *noun* a unit trust that follows the Footsie 100 index

FTSE 350 Index /ˌfʊtsi θriː 'fɪfti ˌindeks/ *noun* an index based on the market price of 350 companies listed on the London Stock Exchange (it includes the companies on the FTSE 100 Index and FTSE 250 Index)

FTSE Actuaries Share Indices /ˌfʊtsi ˌæktjʊəriz 'ʃeə ˌindɪsiz/ *plural noun* several indices based on prices on the London Stock Exchange, which are calculated by and published in the Financial Times in conjunction with the Actuaries Investment Research Committee. Abbreviation **FTASI**. ◊ **Financial Times**

FTSE All-Share Index /ˌfʊtsi 'ɔːl ʃeə ˌindeks/ *noun* an index based on the market price of about 840 companies listed on the London Stock Exchange (it includes the companies on the FTSE 100 Index, the 250 Index, plus companies in other indices) (NOTE: Also simply called the **All-Share Index**.)

FTSE All-Share tracker /ˌfʊtsi 'ɔːl ʃeə ˌtrækə/ *noun* a fund which tracks the FTSE All-Share index

FTSE All-Small Index /ˌfʊtsi ɔːl 'smɔːl ˌindeks/ *noun* an index covering the FTSE SmallCap companies, plus about 750 fledgling companies which are too small to be included in the All-Share Index

FTSE Eurotop 300 Index /ˌfʊtsi ˌjʊərəʊtɒp θriː 'hʌndrəd ˌindeks/ *noun* an index of 300 leading European shares, quoted in euros

FTSE Mid 250 Share Index /ˌfʊtsi mɪd tuː ˌfɪfti 'ʃeə ˌindeks/ *noun* an index based on the market prices of 250 companies capitalised at between £300m and £2.5bn (this is about 16% of the total stock market capitalisation)

FTSE Small Cap Index /ˌfʊtsi smɔːl 'kæp ˌindeks/ *noun* an index which covers about 500 smaller companies which are too small to be included in the two main indices

fulfil /fʊl'fɪl/ *verb* to complete something in a satisfactory way ○ *The clause regarding payments has not been fulfilled.* (NOTE: **fulfilling- fulfilled.** The US spelling is **fulfill.**) □ **to fulfil an order** to supply the items which have been ordered ○ *We are so understaffed that we cannot fulfil any more orders before Christmas.*

fulfilment /fʊl'fɪlmənt/ *noun* the act of carrying something out in a satisfactory way (NOTE: The US spelling is **fulfillment.**)

full /fʊl/ *adjective* **1.** complete, including everything □ **we are working at full capacity** we are doing as much work as possible □ **in full discharge of a debt** paying a debt completely **2.** □ **in full** completely ○ *a full refund* or *a refund* *paid in full* ○ *Give your full name and address* or *your name and address in full.* ○ *He accepted all our conditions in full.*

'…a tax-free lump sum can be taken partly in lieu of a full pension' [*Investors Chronicle*]

full costs /ˌfʊl ˈkɒsts/ *plural noun* all the costs of manufacturing a product, including both fixed and variable costs

full cover /ˌfʊl ˈkʌvə/ *noun* insurance cover against a wide range of risks

full employment /ˌfʊl ɪmˈplɔɪmənt/ *noun* a situation where all the people who can work have jobs

full listing /ˌfʊl ˈlɪstɪŋ/ *noun* the listing of a company on the London Stock Exchange (as opposed to trading on the USM market)

full price /ˌfʊl ˈpraɪs/ *noun* a price with no discount ○ *She bought a full-price ticket.*

full rate /ˌfʊl ˈreɪt/ *noun* the standard charge for a service, with no special discounts applied

full refund /ˌfʊl ˈriːfʌnd/ *noun* a refund of all the money paid ○ *He got a full refund when he complained about the service.*

full repairing lease /ˌfʊl rɪˈpeərɪŋ ˌliːs/ *noun* a lease where the tenant has to pay for all repairs to the property

full-scale /ˈfʊl skeɪl/ *adjective* complete or very thorough ○ *The MD ordered a full-scale review of credit terms.* ○ *The HR department will start a full-scale review of the present pay structure.*

'…the administration launched a full-scale investigation into maintenance procedures' [*Fortune*]

full-service /fʊl ˈsɜːvɪs/ *adjective* that provides a full service

full-service banking /ˌfʊl ˌsɜːvɪs ˈbæŋkɪŋ/ *noun* banking that offers a whole range of services including mortgages, loans, pensions, etc.

full-service broker /fʊl ˌsɜːvɪs ˈbrəʊkə/ *noun* a broker who manages portfolios for clients, and gives advice on shares and financial questions in general (as opposed to an execution-only broker or discount broker)

full-time /ˈfʊl taɪm/ *adjective, adverb* working all the usual working time, i.e.

about eight hours a day, five days a week ○ *She's in full-time work* or *She works full-time* or *She's in full-time employment.* ○ *He is one of our full-time staff.*

full-time employment /ˌfʊl taɪm ɪmˈplɔɪmənt/ *noun* work for all of a working day ○ *to be in full-time employment*

fully /ˈfʊli/ *adverb* completely □ **the offer was fully subscribed** all the shares on offer were applied for, so the underwriters to the issue were not forced to buy any □ **the shares are fully valued** the market price of the shares is high enough, possibly too high

'…issued and fully paid capital is $100 million' [*Hongkong Standard*]

fully diluted earnings per share /ˌfʊli daɪˌluːtɪd ˌɜːnɪŋz pə ˈʃeə/, **fully diluted EPS** /ˌfʊli ˌdaɪluːtɪd ˌiː piː ˈes/ *plural noun* earnings per share calculated over the whole number of shares assuming that convertible shares have been converted to ordinary shares

fully diluted shares /ˌfʊli daɪˌluːtɪd ˈʃeəz/ *plural noun* total number of shares which includes convertible shares, stock options, etc.

fully-paid shares /ˌfʊli peɪd ˈʃeəz/ *plural noun* shares for which the full face value has been paid

fully paid-up capital /ˌfʊli peɪd ʌp ˈkæpɪt(ə)l/ *noun* all money paid for the issued capital shares

function key /ˈfʌŋkʃən kiː/ *noun* a key switch that has been assigned a particular task or sequence of instructions

fund /fʌnd/ *noun* **1.** money set aside for a special purpose **2.** money invested in an investment trust as part of a unit trust, or given to a financial adviser to invest on behalf of a client. ◊ **funds** ■ *verb* to provide money for a purpose ○ *The company does not have enough resources to fund its expansion programme.* □ **to fund a company** to provide money for a company to operate

'…the S&L funded all borrowers' development costs, including accrued interest' [*Barrons*]

fund accounting /ˈfʌnd əˌkaʊntɪŋ/ *noun* the preparation of financial statements for an entity such as a non-profit-making organisation, in order to show

how money has been spent rather than how much profit has been made

fundamental /ˌfʌndə'ment(ə)l/ *adjective* basic or most important

fundamental issues /ˌfʌndə ment(ə)l 'ɪʃuːz/ *plural noun* matters relating to a company's profits or assets

fundamental research /ˌfʌndə ment(ə)l rɪ'sɜːtʃ/, **fundamental analysis** /ˌfʌndəment(ə)l ə'næləsɪs/ *noun* an examination of the basic factors which affect a market

fundamentals /ˌfʌndə'ment(ə)lz/ *plural noun* the basic realities of a stock market or of a company, e.g. its assets, profitability and dividends

funded /'fʌndɪd/ *adjective* backed by long-term loans ○ *long-term funded capital*

funded debt /ˌfʌndɪd 'det/ *noun* the part of the British National Debt which pays interest, but with no date for repayment of the principal

funding /'fʌndɪŋ/ *noun* **1.** money for spending ○ *The bank is providing the funding for the new product launch.* **2.** the act of changing a short-term debt into a long-term loan ○ *The capital expenditure programme requires long-term funding.*

fund management /'fʌnd ˌmænɪdʒ mənt/ *noun* the business of dealing with the investment of sums of money on behalf of clients

fund manager /'fʌnd ˌmænɪdʒə/ *noun* **1.** a person who invests money on behalf of clients **2.** a person who manages the investments made by a fund in such a way as to fulfill the fund's stated objectives

funds /fʌndz/ *plural noun* money which is available for spending ○ *The company has no funds to pay for the research programme.* ◊ **non-sufficient funds** □ **the company called for extra funds** the company asked for more money □ **to**

convert funds to another purpose to use money for a wrong purpose □ **to convert funds to your own use** to use someone else's money for yourself

'...small innovative companies have been hampered for lack of funds' [*Sunday Times*]

'...the company was set up with funds totalling NorKr 145m' [*Lloyd's List*]

fungibility /ˌfʌndʒə'bɪlɪti/ *noun* a measure of how easily an asset can be exchanged for something similar

fungible /'fʌndʒəb(ə)l/ *adjective* referring to a security which can be exchanged for another of the same type

funny money /'fʌni ˌmʌni/ *noun* an unusual type of financial instrument created by a company

future /'fjuːtʃə/ *adjective* referring to time to come or to something which has not yet happened ■ *noun* the time which has not yet happened ○ *Try to be more careful in future.* ○ *In future all reports must be sent to Australia by air.*

future delivery /ˌfjuːtʃə dɪ'lɪv(ə)ri/ *noun* delivery at a later date

futures /'fjuːtʃəz/ *plural noun* shares, currency or commodities that are bought or sold for now for delivery at a later date ○ *Gold rose 5% on the commodity futures market yesterday.*

'...cocoa futures plummeted in November to their lowest levels in seven years' [*Business in Africa*]

futures contract /'fjuːtʃəz ˌkɒntrækt/ *noun* a contract for the purchase of commodities for delivery at a date in the future

COMMENT: A futures contract is a contract to purchase; if investors are bullish, they will buy a contract, but if they feel the market will go down, they will sell one.

futures exchange /'fjuːtʃəz ɪks ˌtʃeɪndʒ/ *noun* a commodity market which only deals in futures

G

G5 *abbreviation* Group of Five

G7 *abbreviation* Group of Seven

G8 *abbreviation* Group of Eight

G10 *abbreviation* Group of Ten

GAAP *abbreviation* Generally Accepted Accounting Principles

GAB *abbreviation* General Arrangements to Borrow

gain /geɪn/ *noun* **1.** an increase, or the act of becoming larger □ **gain in profitability** the act of becoming more profitable **2.** an increase in profit, price, or value ○ *Oil shares showed gains on the stock exchange.* ○ *Property shares put on gains of 10%-15%.* ■ *verb* **1.** to get or to obtain ○ *She gained some useful experience working in a bank.* □ **to gain control of a business** to buy more than 50% of the shares so that you can direct the business **2.** to rise in value ○ *The dollar gained six points on the foreign exchange markets.*

galloping inflation /ˌgæləpɪŋ ɪn ˈfleɪʃ(ə)n/ *noun* very rapid inflation which is almost impossible to reduce

gamma shares /ˈgæmə ʃeəz/, **gamma securities** /ˈgæmə sɪ ˌkjʊərətiz/, **gamma stocks** /ˈgæmə stɒks/ *plural noun* shares of companies which are not frequently traded on the London Stock Exchange, but which are listed

gap /gæp/ *noun* an empty space □ **gap in the market** an opportunity to make a product or provide a service which is needed but which no one has sold before ○ *to look for* or *to find a gap in the market* ○ *This laptop has filled a real gap in the market.*

'…these savings are still not great enough to overcome the price gap between American products and those of other nations' [*Duns Business Month*]

gap financing /ˈgæp ˌfaɪnænsɪŋ/ *noun* the process of arranging extra loans such as a bridging loan to cover a purchase not covered by an existing loan

garage /ˈgærɪdʒ, ˈgærɑːʒ/ *noun* a part of the trading floor on the New York Stock Exchange ■ *verb* to put assets into another company so as to reduce tax liability

garnish /ˈgɑːnɪʃ/ *verb US* to withhold salary or property because a person has debts or taxes which are unpaid

garnishee /ˌgɑːnɪˈʃiː/ *noun* a person who owes money to a creditor and is ordered by a court to pay that money to a creditor of the creditor, and not to the creditor himself

garnishee order /ˌgɑːnɪˈʃiː ˌɔːdə/ *noun* a court order, making a garnishee pay money not to the debtor, but to a third party

garnishment /ˈgɑːnɪʃmənt/ *noun* same as **garnishee order**

GATT /gæt/ *abbreviation* General Agreement on Tariffs and Trade

gazump /gəˈzʌmp/ *verb* to stop someone buying a property for which he or she has already agreed a price with the seller by offering a higher price

gazumping /gəˈzʌmpɪŋ/ *noun* the practice of offering a higher price for a house than another buyer has already agreed with the seller

GDP *abbreviation* gross domestic product

gear /gɪə/ *verb* to link something to something else □ **salary geared to the cost of living** salary which rises as the cost of living increases

gearing /ˈgɪərɪŋ/ *noun* the act of borrowing money at fixed interest which is then used to produce more money than the interest paid

COMMENT: High gearing (when a company is said to be 'highly geared') indicates that the level of borrowings is high when compared to its ordinary share capital. A lowly-geared company has borrowings which are relatively low. High gearing has the effect of increasing a company's profitability when the company's trading is expanding. If the trading pattern slows down, then the high interest charges associated with gearing will increase the rate of slowdown.

GEB *abbreviation* Guaranteed Equity Bond

geisha bond /ˈɡeɪʃə bɒnd/ *noun* a bond placed by a non-Japanese borrower in Japan, in a currency other than the yen

general /ˈdʒen(ə)rəl/ *adjective* **1.** ordinary or not special **2.** dealing with everything or with everybody

General Agreement on Tariffs and Trade /ˌdʒen(ə)rəl əˌɡriːmənt ɒn ˌθærɪfs ən ˈtreɪd/ *noun* an international agreement to try to reduce restrictions in trade between countries (replaced in 1998 by the World Trade Organization). Abbreviation **GATT**. ◊ **World Trade Organization**

General Arrangements to Borrow /ˌdʒen(ə)rəl əˌreɪndʒmənts tə ˈbɒrəʊ/ *plural noun* an agreement between members of the G10 group of countries, by which members make funds available to the IMF to cover loans which it makes. Abbreviation **GAB**

general audit /ˌdʒen(ə)rəl ˈɔːdɪt/ *noun* the process of examining all the books and accounts of a company

general average /ˌdʒen(ə)rəl ˈæv(ə)rɪdʒ/ *noun* a process by which the cost of lost goods is shared by all parties to an insurance policy, such as in cases where some goods have been lost in an attempt to save the rest of the cargo

general expenses /ˌdʒen(ə)rəl ɪkˈspensɪz/ *plural noun* minor expenses of various kinds incurred in the running of a business

general fund /ˈdʒen(ə)rəl fʌnd/ *noun* a unit trust with investments in a variety of stocks

general insurance /ˌdʒen(ə)rəl ɪnˈʃʊərəns/ *noun* insurance relating to various potential losses, e.g. theft or damage, but excluding life insurance

general ledger /ˈdʒen(ə)rəl ˌledʒə/ *noun* a book which records a company's income and expenditure in general

general lien /ˌdʒen(ə)rəl ˈliːən/ *noun* **1.** a right to hold goods or property until a debt has been paid **2.** a lien against the personal possessions of a borrower, but not against his or her house or land. ◊ **banker's lien**

Generally Accepted Accounting Principles /ˌdʒen(ə)rəli əkˌseptɪd ə ˈkaʊntɪŋ ˌprɪnsɪp(ə)lz/ *plural noun US* a summary of best practice in respect of the form and content of financial statements and auditor's reports, and of accounting policies and disclosures adopted for the preparation of financial information. GAAP does not have any statutory or regulatory authority in the UK, unlike in a number of other countries where the term is in use, such as the US, Canada. Abbreviation **GAAP**

general manager /ˌdʒen(ə)rəl ˈmænɪdʒə/ *noun* a manager in charge of the administration of a company

general meeting /ˌdʒen(ə)rəl ˈmiːtɪŋ/ *noun* a meeting of all the shareholders of a company or of all the members of a society

general obligation bond /ˌdʒen(ə)rəl ˌɒblɪˈɡeɪʃ(ə)n bɒnd/ *noun US* a municipal or state bond issued to finance public undertakings such as roads, but which is repaid out of general funds. Abbreviation **GO bond**

general office /ˈdʒen(ə)rəl ˌɒfɪs/ *noun* the main administrative office of a company

general partner /ˌdʒen(ə)rəl ˈpɑːtnə/ *noun* a partner in a business whose responsibility for its debts is not limited and, therefore, whose personal assets may be at risk if the company's assets are not sufficient to discharge its debts

general partnership /ˌdʒen(ə)rəl ˈpɑːtnəʃɪp/ *noun* the relationship of a general partner to his or her company

general PEP /ˈdʒen(ə)rəl pep/ *noun* a PEP which has shares of several companies in it, as opposed to a single company PEP

general undertaking /ˌdʒen(ə)rəl ˌʌndəˈteɪkɪŋ/ *noun* an undertaking signed by the directors of a company applying for a stock exchange listing, promising to work within the regulations of the stock exchange

generation-skipping transfer tax /ˌdʒenəreɪʃ(ə)n ˌskɪpɪŋ ˈtrænsfɜː tæks/ noun US a tax on property left to grandchildren or great-grandchildren with the intention of avoiding paying estate duties. Abbreviation **GSTT**

gensaki /dʒenˈsɑːki/ noun a Japanese bond market, dealing in bonds issued with agreements to repurchase at less than twelve months' notice

gentleman's agreement /ˈdʒent(ə)l mənz əˌgriːmənt/ noun a verbal agreement between two parties who trust each other

Gesellschaft /gəˈzelʃɑːft/ noun the German word for company

Gesellschaft mit beschränkter Haftung /gəˌzelʃɑːft mɪt bəˌʃreŋktə ˈhɑːftʊŋ/ noun a German private limited company. Abbreviation **GmbH**

get /get/ verb to receive ○ We got a letter from the solicitor this morning. ○ When do you expect to get more stock? ○ He gets £250 a week for doing nothing. ○ She got £5,000 for her car.

get back phrasal verb to receive something which you had before ○ I got my money back after I had complained to the manager. ○ He got his initial investment back in two months.

get out phrasal verb **1.** to produce something ○ The accounts department got out the draft accounts in time for the meeting. **2.** to sell an investment (informal) ○ He didn't like what he read in the company's annual report, so he got out before the company collapsed.

get out of phrasal verb to stop trading in a product or an area ○ The company is getting out of computers. ○ We got out of the South American market.

get round phrasal verb to avoid ○ We tried to get round the embargo by shipping from Canada.

GIB abbreviation Guaranteed Income Bond

gift /gɪft/ noun a thing which is given to someone

gift coupon /ˈgɪft ˌkuːpɒn/, **gift token** /ˈgɪft ˌtəʊkən/, **gift voucher** /ˈgɪft ˌvaʊtʃə/ noun a card that can be used to buy specified goods up to the value printed on it, often issued by chain stores. The person receiving the voucher is able to redeem it in any store in the chain. ○ We gave her a gift token for her birthday.

gift inter vivos /ˌgɪft ɪntə ˈviːvəʊs/ noun a gift given to another living person. Abbreviation **GIV**

gift tax /ˈgɪft tæks/ noun a tax on gifts. Only gifts between husband and wife are exempt.

gilt-edged /ˈgɪlt edʒd/ adjective used to describe an investment which is very safe

gilt-edged securities /ˌgɪlt edʒd sɪ ˈkjʊərɪtiz/ plural noun investments in British government stock

gilt-edged stock /ˌgɪlt edʒd ˈstɒk/ noun same as **government bonds**

gilts /gɪlts/ plural noun same as **government bonds**

Ginnie Mae /ˌdʒɪni ˈmeɪ/ noun same as **GNMA** (informal)

giro /ˈdʒaɪrəʊ/ noun same as **bank giro**

giro system /ˈdʒaɪrəʊ ˌsɪstəm/ noun a banking system in which money can be transferred from one account to another without writing a cheque

GIV abbreviation gift inter vivos

glamour stock /ˈglæmə stɒk/ noun a stock which is very popular with investors because it has risen in value and provided higher than average earnings over a period of time

global /ˈgləʊb(ə)l/ adjective referring to the whole world ○ We offer a 24-hour global delivery service. □ **global economy** the economy of the whole world

globalisation /ˌgləʊbəlaɪˈzeɪʃ(ə)n/, **globalization** noun the process of making something international or worldwide, especially the process of expanding business interests, operations, and strategies to countries all over the world (NOTE: Globalisation is due to technological developments that make global communications possible, political developments such as the fall of communism, and developments in transport that make travelling faster and more frequent. It can benefit companies by opening up new markets, giving access to new raw materials and investment opportunities, and enabling them to take advantage of lower operating costs in other countries.)

GmbH *abbreviation* Gesellschaft mit beschränkter Haftung

GNMA *noun* a US federal organisation which provides backing for mortgages. Full form **Government National Mortgage Association**

gnomes of Zurich /ˌnəʊmz əv ˈzjʊərɪx/ *plural noun* important Swiss international bankers (*informal*)

GNP *abbreviation* gross national product

go /ɡəʊ/ *verb* to be placed ○ *The date goes at the top of the letter.* (NOTE: **going – went – gone**)

go back on *phrasal verb* not to carry out something after you have promised to do it ○ *Two months later they went back on the agreement.*

go into *phrasal verb* to examine something carefully ○ *The bank wants to go into the details of the inter-company loans.*

go into business *phrasal verb* to start in business ○ *He went into business as a car dealer.* ○ *She went into business in partnership with her son.*

go liquid *phrasal verb* to convert as many assets as possible into cash

go out of business *phrasal verb* to stop trading ○ *The firm went out of business last week.*

go-ahead /ˈɡəʊ əˌhed/ *noun* □ **to give something the go-ahead** to approve something or to say that something can be done ○ *My project got a government go-ahead.* ○ *The board refused to give the go-ahead to the expansion plan.* ■ *adjective* energetic or keen to do well ○ *He is a very go-ahead type.* ○ *She works for a go-ahead clothing company.*

GO bond /ɡəʊ bɒnd/ same as **general obligation bond**

go-go fund /ˈɡəʊ ɡəʊ ˌfʌnd/ *noun* a fund which aims to give very high returns because it is invested in speculative stocks

going /ˈɡəʊɪŋ/ *adjective* current

going concern /ˌɡəʊɪŋ kənˈsɜːn/ *noun* a company that is actively trading and making a profit □ **sold as a going concern** sold as an actively trading company □ **to sell a business as a going concern** to sell a business as an actively trading company

going concern value /ˌɡəʊɪŋ kən ˈsɜːn ˌvæljuː/ *noun* the value of a company as it continues trading as opposed to its break-up value

going price /ˌɡəʊɪŋ ˈpraɪs/ *noun* the usual or current price, the price which is being charged now ○ *What is the going price for 1975 Volkswagen Beetles?*

going rate /ˌɡəʊɪŋ ˈreɪt/ *noun* the usual or current rate of payment ○ *We pay the going rate for typists.* ○ *The going rate for offices is £10 per square metre.*

gold /ɡəʊld/ *noun* a very valuable yellow metal ○ *to buy gold* ○ *to deal in gold* ○ *You can buy gold coins at certain Swiss banks.* ○ *He has a licence to deal in gold.*

COMMENT: Gold is the traditional hedge against investment uncertainties. People buy gold in the form of coins or bars, because they think it will maintain its value when other investments such as government bonds, foreign currency, property, etc., may not be so safe. Gold is relatively portable, and small quantities can be taken from country to country if an emergency occurs. This view, which is prevalent when the political situation is uncertain, has not been borne out in recent years, and gold has not maintained its value for some time.

gold bug /ˈɡəʊld bʌɡ/ *noun* a person who believes that gold is the best investment (*informal*)

gold bullion /ˌɡəʊld ˈbʊliən/ *noun* bars of gold

gold card /ˈɡəʊld kɑːd/ *noun* a credit card issued to important customers, i.e., those with a high income, which gives certain privileges such as a higher spending limit than ordinary credit cards

gold-collar worker /ˌɡəʊld ˌkɒlə ˈwɜːkə/ *noun* an employee who earns a very high salary and bonuses

golden /ˈɡəʊld(ə)n/ *adjective* made of gold or like gold

golden handcuffs /ˌɡəʊld(ə)n ˈhændkʌfs/ *plural noun* a contractual arrangement to make sure that a valued member of staff stays in their job, by which they are offered special financial advantages if they stay and heavy penalties if they leave

golden handshake /ˌɡəʊld(ə)n ˈhændʃeɪk/ *noun* a large, usually tax-free, sum of money given to a director who retires from a company before the end of his or her service contract ○ *The retiring director received a golden handshake of £250,000.*

golden hello /ˌgəʊld(ə)n həˈləʊ/ *noun* a cash inducement paid to someone to encourage them to change jobs and move to another company

golden parachute /ˌgəʊld(ə)n ˈpærəʃuːt/, **golden umbrella** /ˌgəʊld(ə)n ʌmˈbrelə/ *noun* a special contract for a director of a company, which gives him advantageous financial terms if he has to resign when the company is taken over

golden share /ˌgəʊld(ə)n ˈʃeə/ *noun* a share in a privatised company which is retained by the government and carries special privileges such as the right to veto foreign takeover bids

gold fixing /ˈgəʊld ˌfɪksɪŋ/ *noun* a system where the world price for gold is set twice a day in US dollars on the London Gold Exchange and in Paris and Zurich

Goldilocks economy /ˈgəʊldilɒks ɪˌkɒnəmi/ *noun* an economy that is neither too hot or too cold, and that sustains moderate economic growth and low inflation, therefore allowing for a market friendly monetary policy

goldmine /ˈgəʊldmaɪn/ *noun* a mine which produces gold □ **that shop is a little goldmine** that shop is a very profitable business

gold point /ˈgəʊld pɔɪnt/ *noun* an amount by which a currency which is linked to gold can vary in price

gold reserves /ˈgəʊld rɪˌzɜːvz/ *plural noun* the country's store of gold kept to pay international debts

gold/silver ratio /ˌgəʊld ˈsɪlvə ˌreɪʃiəʊ/ *noun* a figure calculated as the number of ounces of silver it takes to buy one ounce of gold

gold standard /gəʊld ˈstændəd/ *noun* an arrangement that links the value of a currency to the value of a quantity of gold

go long /gəʊ ˈlɒŋ/ *verb* to buy securities as a long-term investment

good /gʊd/ *adjective* not bad □ **to buy something in good faith** to buy something thinking it is of good quality, that it

has not been stolen or that it is not an imitation ■ *noun* an item which is made and is for sale

good buy /ˌgʊd ˈbaɪ/ *noun* a thing bought which is worth the money paid for it ○ *That watch was a good buy.*

good industrial relations /gʊd ɪn ˌdʌstriəl rɪˈleɪʃ(ə)nz/ *plural noun* a situation where management and employees understand each others' problems and work together for the good of the company

goods /gʊdz/ *plural noun* items which can be moved and are for sale □ **goods in bond** imported goods held by customs until duty is paid

'…profit margins are lower in the industries most exposed to foreign competition – machinery, transportation equipment and electrical goods' [*Sunday Times*]

'…the minister wants people buying goods ranging from washing machines to houses to demand facts on energy costs' [*Times*]

goods and chattels /ˌgʊdz ən ˈtʃæt(ə)lz/ *plural noun* movable personal possessions

Goods and Services Tax /ˌgʊdz ən ˈsɜːvɪsɪz tæks/ *noun* a tax on the sale of goods or the provision of services ins some countries including Canada and Australia, similar to VAT. Abbreviation **GST**

good till cancelled /ˌgʊd tɪl ˈkænsəld/ *noun* an order given to a broker to buy or sell as instructed until the order is cancelled. Abbreviation **GTC**

goodwill /gʊdˈwɪl/ *noun* **1.** good feeling towards someone ○ *To show goodwill, the management increased the terms of the offer.* **2.** the good reputation of a business, which can be calculated as part of a company's asset value, though separate from its tangible asset value ○ *He paid £10,000 for the goodwill of the shop and £4,000 for the stock.* (NOTE: The goodwill can include the trading reputation, the patents, the trade names used, the value of a 'good site', etc., and is very difficult to establish accurately.)

COMMENT: Goodwill can include such things as the trading reputation, the patents, the trade names used and the value of a 'good site' and is very difficult to establish accurately. It is an intangible asset, and so is not shown as an asset in a company's accounts, unless it figures as part of the purchase price paid when acquiring another company.

go private /ˌgəʊ ˈpraɪvət/ *verb* to become a private company again, by concentrating all its shares in the hands of one or a few shareholders and removing its stock exchange listing

go public /ˌgəʊ ˈpʌblɪk/ *phrasal verb* to become a public company by placing some of its shares for sale on the stock market so that anyone can buy them

go short /gəʊ ˈʃɔːt/ *verb* to sell shares now which you have contracted to purchase at a later date, on the assumption that the market will fall further

gourde /gʊəd/ *noun* a unit of currency used in Haiti

govern /ˈgʌv(ə)n/ *verb* to rule a country ○ *The country is governed by a group of military leaders.*

governance /ˈgʌv(ə)nəns/ *noun* the process of managing a company, especially with respect to the soundness or otherwise of its management

'…the chairman has committed the cardinal sin in corporate governance – he acted against the wishes and interests of the shareholders' [*Investors Chronicle*]

'…in two significant decisions, the Securities and Exchange Board of India today allowed trading of shares through the Internet and set a deadline for companies to conform to norms for good corporate governance' [*The Hindu*]

government /ˈgʌv(ə)nmənt/ *noun* an organisation which administers a country ■ *adjective* coming from the government, referring to the government ○ *a government ban on the import of arms* ○ *Government intervention or Intervention by the government helped to solve the dispute.* ○ *Government employees can belong to one of two unions.*

governmental /ˌgʌv(ə)nˈment(ə)l/ *adjective* referring to a government

government-backed /ˈgʌv(ə)nmənt ˌbækt/ *adjective* backed by the government

government bonds /ˌgʌv(ə)nmənt ˈbɒndz/ *plural noun* bonds or other securities issued by the government on a regular basis as a method of borrowing money for government expenditure

government contractor /ˌgʌv(ə)nmənt kənˈtræktə/ *noun* a company which supplies the government with goods by contract

government-controlled /ˈgʌv(ə)nmənt kənˌtrəʊld/ *adjective* under the direct control of the government ○ *Advertisements cannot be placed in the government-controlled newspapers.*

government economic indicators /ˌgʌv(ə)nmənt ˌiːkənɒmɪk ˈɪndɪkeɪtəz/ *plural noun* statistics which show how the country's economy is going to perform in the short or long term

government expenditure /ˌgʌv(ə)nmənt ɪkˈspendɪtʃə/ *noun* also called **government spending**

government loan /ˌgʌv(ə)nmənt ˈləʊn/ *noun* money lent by the government

Government National Mortgage Association /ˌgʌv(ə)nmənt ˌnæʃ(ə)nəl ˈmɔːgɪdʒ əˌsəʊsieɪʃ(ə)n/ *noun* full form of **GNMA**

government organisation /ˌgʌv(ə)n mənt ˌɔːgənaɪˈzeɪʃ(ə)n/ *noun* an official body run by the government

government-regulated /ˈgʌv(ə)nmənt ˌregjʊleɪtɪd/ *adjective* of which the affairs are subject to government regulation

government securities /ˌgʌv(ə)nmənt sɪˈkjʊərɪtɪz/ *plural noun* same as **government bonds**

government-sponsored /ˈgʌv(ə)nmənt ˌspɒnsəd/ *adjective* encouraged by the government and backed by government money ○ *She is working in a government-sponsored scheme to help small businesses.*

government stock /ˌgʌv(ə)nmənt ˈstɒk/ *noun* same as **government bonds**

government support /ˌgʌv(ə)nmənt səˈpɔːt/ *noun* a financial help given by the government ○ *The aircraft industry relies on government support.*

governor /ˈgʌv(ə)nə/ *noun* **1.** a person in charge of an important institution **2.** US one of the members of the Federal Reserve Board

Governor of the Bank of England /ˌgʌv(ə)nə əv ðə ˌbæŋk əv ˈɪŋglənd/

noun a person (nominated by the British government) who is in charge of the Bank of England (NOTE: The US term is **Chairman of the Federal Reserve Board**.)

GPM *abbreviation* graduated payment mortgage

grace /greɪs/ *noun* a favour shown by granting a delay ○ *to give a creditor a period of grace* or *two weeks' grace*

grace period /'greɪs ˌpɪəriəd/ *noun* the time given to a debtor to repay a loan, to pay the amount purchased using a credit card, or to pay an insurance premium

gradual /'grædʒuəl/ *adjective* slow and steady ○ *The company saw a gradual return to profits.* ○ *Her CV describes her gradual rise to the position of company chairman.*

gradually /'grædʒuəli/ *adverb* slowly and steadily ○ *The company has gradually become more profitable.* ○ *She gradually learnt the details of the import-export business.*

graduate *noun* /'grædʒuət/ a person who has obtained a degree ■ *verb* /'grædʒuˌeɪt/ to get a degree ○ *She graduated from Edinburgh university last year.*

graduated /'grædʒueɪtɪd/ *adjective* changing in small regular stages

graduated income tax /ˌgrædʒueɪtɪd 'ɪnkʌm tæks/ *noun* a tax which rises in steps, with those having the highest income paying the highest percentage of tax

graduated payment mortgage /ˌgrædʒueɪtɪd ˌpeɪmənt 'mɔːgɪdʒ/ *noun* a mortgage where the monthly payments gradually rise over the lifetime of the mortgage. Abbreviation **GPM**

graduated pension scheme /ˌgrædʒueɪtɪd 'penʃən skiːm/ *noun* a pension scheme where the benefit is calculated as a percentage of the salary of each person in the scheme

graduated taxation /ˌgrædʒueɪtɪd tæk'seɪʃ(ə)n/ *noun* same as **progressive taxation**

grand /grænd/ *adjective* important □ **grand plan** *or* **grand strategy** a major plan ○ *They explained their grand plan for redeveloping the factory site.* ■ *noun* one thousand pounds or dollars (*informal*) ○ *They offered him fifty grand for the*

information. ○ *She's earning fifty grand plus car and expenses.*

grand total /ˌgrænd 'təʊt(ə)l/ *noun* the final total made by adding several subtotals

Granny Bond /'græni bɒnd/ *noun* a British government bond giving higher interest or tax privileges but restricted in availability to pensioners

grant /grɑːnt/ *noun* money given by the government to help pay for something ○ *The laboratory has a government grant to cover the cost of the development programme.* ○ *The government has allocated grants towards the costs of the scheme.* ■ *verb* to agree to give someone something ○ *to grant someone a loan* or *a subsidy* ○ *to grant someone three weeks' leave of absence* ○ *The local authority granted the company an interest-free loan to start up the new factory.*

'…the budget grants a tax exemption for $500,000 in capital gains' [*Toronto Star*]

grant-aided scheme /ˌgrɑːnt 'eɪdɪd skiːm/ *noun* a scheme which is funded by a government grant

grantee /grɑːn'tiː/ *noun* a person who receives a grant

grantor /grɑːn'tɔː/ *noun* a person who grants a property to another

graph /grɑːf/ *noun* a diagram which shows the relationship between two sets of quantities or values, each of which is represented on an axis ○ *A graph was used to show salary increases in relation to increases in output.* ○ *According to the graph, as average salaries have risen so has absenteeism.* ○ *We need to set out the results of the questionnaire in a graph.*

gratia ♦ **ex gratia**

gratis /'grætɪs/ *adverb* free or not costing anything ○ *We got into the exhibition gratis.*

gratuity /grə'tjuːɪti/ *noun* a tip, money given to someone who has helped you ○ *The staff are instructed not to accept gratuities.*

graveyard /'greɪvjɑːd/ *noun* a market where prices are low and no one is buying because investors prefer to remain liquid (*informal*)

Great Depression /greɪt dɪ 'preʃ(ə)n/ *noun* the world economic crisis of 1929–33

greenback /ˈɡriːnbæk/ *noun US* a dollar bill (*informal*)

'...gold's drop this year is of the same magnitude as the greenback's 8.5% rise' [*Business Week*]

green bond /ˈɡriːn bɒnd/ *noun* a tax-exempt bond issued for the development of brownfield sites i.e. areas of land that are under developed and that sometimes contain low levels of industrial pollution. Green bonds are short-hand for Qualified Green Building and Sustainable Design Project Bonds.

Green Book /ˌɡriːn ˈbʊk/ *noun US* an economic forecast prepared by the staff of the Federal Reserve Board

green card /ˌɡriːn ˈkɑːd/ *noun* **1.** a special British insurance certificate to prove that a car is insured for travel abroad **2.** an identity card and work permit for a person going to live in the US

Green chips /ˈɡriːn tʃɪps/ *plural noun* small companies with potential for growth

green currency /ˌɡriːn ˈkʌrənsiː/ *noun* formerly, a currency used in the EU for calculating agricultural payments. Each country had an exchange rate fixed by the Commission, so there were 'green pounds', 'green francs', 'green marks', etc.

green day /ˈɡriːn deɪ/ *noun US* a profitable day (NOTE: The opposite is a **red day**.)

green fund /ˈɡriːn fʌnd/ *noun* a mutual fund or other investment vehicle that will only invest in companies that are considered socially conscious in their business dealings or directly promote environmental responsibility

green investment /ˌɡriːn ɪnˈvestmənt/ *noun* an investment that focuses on companies or projects that are committed to environmentally conscious business practices

greenmail /ˈɡriːnmeɪl/ *noun* the practice of making a profit by buying a large number of shares in a company, threatening to take the company over, and then selling the shares back to the company at a higher price

'...he proposes that there should be a limit on greenmail, perhaps permitting payment of a 20% premium on a maximum of 8% of the stock' [*Duns Business Month*]

Green Paper /ˌɡriːn ˈpeɪpə/ *noun* a report from the British government on proposals for a new law to be discussed in Parliament. Compare **White Paper**

green shoots /ˌɡriːn ˈʃuːts/ *plural noun* a term used to indicate signs of economic recovery or positive data during an economic downturn

Gresham's Law /ˈɡreʃəmz lɔː/ *noun* the law that 'bad money will drive out good': where two forms of money with the same denomination exist in the same market, the form with the higher metal value will be driven out of circulation because people hoard it and use the lower-rated form to spend (as when paper money and coins of the same denomination exist in the same market)

grey market /ˈɡreɪ ˌmɑːkɪt/ *noun* an unofficial market run by dealers, where new issues of shares are bought and sold before they officially become available for trading on the stock exchange even before the share allocations are known

gross /ɡrəʊs/ *noun* twelve dozen (144) ○ *He ordered four gross of pens.* (NOTE: no plural) ■ *adjective* total, with no deductions ■ *adverb* with no deductions ○ *My salary is paid gross.* ○ *Building society accounts can pay interest gross to non-taxpayers.* ■ *verb* to make as a gross profit or earn as gross income ○ *The group grossed £25m in 1999.* □ **to gross up** to calculate the percentage rate of a net investment as it would be before tax is deducted

'...gross wool receipts for the selling season to end June appear likely to top $2 billion' [*Australian Financial Review*]

gross borrowings /ɡrəʊs ˈbɒrəʊɪŋz/ *plural noun* the total of all monies borrowed by a company such as overdrafts, long-term loans, etc., but without deducting cash in bank accounts and on deposit

gross dividend per share /ɡrəʊs ˌdɪvɪdend pə ˈʃeə/ *noun* the dividend per share paid before tax is deducted

gross domestic product /ˌɡrəʊs də ˌmestɪk ˈprɒdʌkt/ *noun* the annual value of goods sold and services paid for inside a country. Abbreviation **GDP**

gross earnings /ˌɡrəʊs ˈɜːnɪŋz/ *plural noun* total earnings before tax and other deductions

gross income /ˌɡrəʊs ˈɪnkʌm/ *noun* a salary before tax is deducted

gross income yield /ɡrəʊs ˈɪnkʌm jiːld/ *noun* the yield of an investment before tax is deducted

gross margin /ˌɡrəʊs ˈmɑːdʒɪn/ *noun* the percentage difference between the received price and the unit manufacturing cost or purchase price of goods for resale. Abbreviation **GM**

gross national product /ˌɡrəʊs ˌnæʃ(ə)nəl ˈprɒdʌkt/ *noun* the annual value of goods and services in a country including income from other countries. Abbreviation **GNP**

gross negligence /ˌɡrəʊs ˈneɡlɪdʒəns/ *noun* the act of showing very serious neglect of duty towards other people

gross premium /ɡrəʊs ˈpriːmiəm/ *noun* the total premium paid by a policy-holder before any tax relief or discount is taken into account

gross profit /ˌɡrəʊs ˈprɒfɪt/ *noun* a profit calculated as sales income less the cost of the goods sold, i.e. without deducting any other expenses

gross receipts /ˌɡrəʊs rɪˈsiːts/ *plural noun* the total amount of money received before expenses are deducted

gross salary /ˌɡrəʊs ˈsæləri/ *noun* same as **gross income**

gross sales /ˌɡrəʊs ˈseɪlz/ *plural noun* money received from sales before deductions for goods returned, special discounts, etc. ○ *Gross sales are impressive since many buyers seem to be ordering more than they will eventually need.*

gross tonnage /ˌɡrəʊs ˈtʌnɪdʒ/ *noun* the total amount of space in a ship

gross turnover /ˌɡrəʊs ˈtɜːnəʊvə/ *noun* the total turnover including VAT and discounts

gross weight /ˌɡrəʊs ˈweɪt/ *noun* the weight of both the container and its contents

gross yield /ˌɡrəʊs ˈjiːld/ *noun* a profit from investments before tax is deducted

ground landlord /ˈɡraʊnd ˌlændlɔːd/ *noun* a person or company that owns the freehold of a property which is then let

and sublet ○ *Our ground landlord is an insurance company.*

ground rent /ˈɡraʊnd rent/ *noun* a rent paid by the main tenant to the ground landlord

group /ɡruːp/ *noun* **1.** several things or people together ○ *A group of managers has sent a memo to the chairman complaining about noise in the office.* ○ *The respondents were interviewed in groups of three or four, and then singly.* **2.** several companies linked together in the same organisation ○ *the group chairman* or *the chairman of the group* ○ *group turnover* or *turnover for the group* ○ *the Granada Group* ■ *verb* □ **to group together** to put several items together ○ *Sales from six different agencies are grouped together under the heading 'European sales'.*

group balance sheet /ˌɡruːp ˈbæləns ˌʃiːt/ *noun* same as **consolidated balance sheet**

group health insurance /ɡruːp ˈhelθ ɪnˌʃʊərəns/ *noun* a health insurance for a group of people under a single policy, issued to their employer or to an association

group income protection insurance /ɡruːp ˌɪnkʌm prəˈtekʃ(ə)n ɪnˌʃʊərəns/ *noun* insurance for a group of people which gives them a replacement income when they are sick or incapacitated

Group of Eight /ˌɡruːp əv ˈeɪt/ *noun* the G7 expanded to include Russia. Abbreviation **G8**

Group of Five /ˌɡruːp əv ˈfaɪv/ *noun* a central group of major industrial nations (France, Germany, Japan, the UK and the US), now expanded to form the G7. Abbreviation **G5**

Group of Seven /ˌɡruːp əv ˈsev(ə)n/ *noun* a central group of major industrial nations (Canada, France, Germany, Italy, Japan, the UK and the US) who meet regularly to discuss problems of international trade and finance. Abbreviation **G7**

Group of Ten /ˌɡruːp əv ˈten/ *noun* the major world economic powers working within the framework of the IMF: Belgium, Canada, France, Germany, Italy, Japan, Netherlands, Sweden, the UK and the US There are in fact now eleven members, since Switzerland has joined the original ten. It is also called the 'Paris Club', since its first meeting was in Paris. Abbreviation **G10**

group results /ˌgruːp rɪˈzʌlts/ *plural noun* the end-of-year financial statements and accounts of a group of companies

grow /grəʊ/ *verb* to become larger ○ *The company has grown from a small repair shop to a multinational electronics business.* ○ *Turnover is growing at a rate of 15% per annum.* ○ *The computer industry grew very rapidly in the 1980s.* (NOTE: **growing – grew – has grown**)

'…the thrift had grown from $4.7 million in assets to $1.5 billion' [*Barrons*]

growth /grəʊθ/ *noun* **1.** the fact of becoming larger or increasing □ **the company is aiming for growth** the company is aiming to expand rapidly **2.** the second stage in a product life cycle, following the launch, when demand for the product increases rapidly

'…a general price freeze succeeded in slowing the growth in consumer prices' [*Financial Times*]

'…growth in demand is still coming from the private rather than the public sector' [*Lloyd's List*]

'…population growth in the south-west is again reflected by the level of rental values' [*Lloyd's List*]

growth-and-income fund /ˌgrəʊθ ən ˈɪnkʌm fʌnd/ *noun* a fund which aims to provide both capital growth and income

growth company /ˈgrəʊθ ˌkʌmp(ə)ni/ *noun* company whose share price is expected to rise in value

growth fund /ˈgrəʊθ fʌnd/ *noun* a fund which aims at providing capital growth rather than income

growth index /ˈgrəʊθ ˌɪndeks/ *noun* an index showing the growth in a company's revenues, earnings, dividends or other figures

growth industry /ˈgrəʊθ ˌɪndəstri/ *noun* an industry that is expanding or has the potential to expand faster than other industries

growth market /ˈgrəʊθ ˌmɑːkɪt/ *noun* a market where sales are increasing rapidly ○ *We plan to build a factory in the Far East, which is a growth market for our products.*

growth number /ˈgrəʊθ ˌnʌmbə/ *noun* growth expressed as a percentage

growth prospects /ˈgrəʊθ ˌprɒspekts/ *plural noun* potential for growth in a share

growth rate /ˈgrəʊθ reɪt/ *noun* the speed at which something grows

GST *abbreviation* Goods and Services Tax

'…because the GST is applied only to fees for brokerage and appraisal services, the new tax does not appreciably increase the price of a resale home' [*Toronto Globe & Mail*]

GSTT *abbreviation* generation-skipping transfer tax

GTC *abbreviation* good till cancelled

guarani /ˌgwɑːrəˈniː/ *noun* a unit of currency used in Paraguay

guarantee /ˌgærənˈtiː/ *noun* **1.** a legal document in which the producer agrees to compensate the buyer if the product is faulty or becomes faulty before a specific date after purchase ○ *a certificate of guarantee* or *a guarantee certificate* ○ *The guarantee lasts for two years.* ○ *It is sold with a twelve-month guarantee.* □ **the car is still under guarantee** the car is still covered by the maker's guarantee **2.** a promise that someone will pay another person's debts □ **to go guarantee for someone** to act as security for someone's debts **3.** something given as a security ○ *to leave share certificates as a guarantee* ■ *verb* **1.** to give a promise that something will happen □ **to guarantee a debt** to promise to pay another person's debts if he or she should fail to □ **to guarantee an associate company** to promise that an associate company will pay its debts □ **to guarantee a bill of exchange** to promise that the bill will be paid **2.** □ **the product is guaranteed for twelve months** the manufacturer says that the product will work well for twelve months, and will mend it free of charge if it breaks down

Guaranteed Equity Bond /ˌgæərəntiːd ˈekwɪti bɒnd/ *noun* a bond which provides a return linked to one or more stock market indices (such as the FTSE 100 index) and guarantees a minimum return of the original capital invested. Abbreviation **GEB**

Guaranteed Income Bond /ˌgæərəntiːd ˈɪnkʌm bɒnd/ *noun* a bond which guarantees a certain rate of interest over a certain period of time. Abbreviation **GIB**

guaranteed wage /ˌɡærəntiːd ˈweɪdʒ/ noun a wage which a company promises will not fall below a specific figure

guarantor /ˌɡærənˈtɔː/ noun a person who promises to pay another person's debts if he or she should fail to ○ She stood guarantor for her brother.

guaranty /ˈɡær(ə)ntiː/ noun US same as **guarantee**

guess /ges/ noun a calculation made without any real information ○ The forecast of sales is only a guess. □ **an informed guess** a guess which is based on some information □ **it is anyone's guess** no one really knows what is the right answer ■ verb □ **to guess (at) something** to try to calculate something without any information ○ They could only guess at the total loss. ○ The sales director tried to guess the turnover of the Far East division.

guesstimate /ˈɡestɪmət/ noun a rough calculation (informal)

guilder /ˈɡɪldə/ noun a unit of currency used before the euro in the Netherlands (NOTE: Usually written **fl** before or after figures: fl25, 25fl.)

'…the shares, which eased 1.10 guilders to fl49.80 earlier in the session, were suspended during the final hour of trading' [Wall Street Journal]

H

haggle /ˈhæg(ə)l/ *verb* to discuss prices and terms and try to reduce them ○ *to haggle about* or *over the details of a contract* ○ *After two days' haggling the contract was signed.*

haircut /ˈheəkʌt/ *noun US* **1.** the difference between the market value of a security and the amount lent to the owner using the security as collateral **2.** an estimate of possible loss in investments

half /hɑːf/ *noun* one of two equal parts into which something is divided ○ *The first half of the agreement is acceptable.* □ **we share the profits half and half** we share the profits equally ■ *adjective* divided into two parts □ **half a percentage point** 0.5% □ **his commission on the deal is twelve and a half per cent** his commission on the deal is 12.5% □ **to sell goods off at half price** at 50% of the price for which they were sold before

'…economists believe the economy is picking up this quarter and will do better in the second half of the year' [*Sunday Times*]

half-commission man /ˌhɑːf kə ˈmɪʃ(ə)n ˌmæn/ *noun* a dealer who introduces new clients to a stockbroker, and takes half the broker's commission as a fee

half-dollar /ˌhɑːf ˈdɒlə/ *noun US* fifty cents

half-life /ˈhɑːf laɪf/ *noun* the number of years needed to repay half the capital borrowed on mortgage

half-price sale /ˌhɑːf praɪs ˈseɪl/ *noun* a sale of items at half the usual price

half-year /ˌhɑːf ˈjɪə/ *noun* six months of an accounting period

half-yearly /ˌhɑːf ˈjɪəli/ *adjective* happening every six months, or referring to a period of six months ○ *half-yearly*

accounts ○ *half-yearly payment* ○ *half-yearly statement* ○ *a half-yearly meeting* ■ *adverb* every six months ○ *We pay the account half-yearly.*

Hambrecht & Quist Technology Index /ˌhæmbrekt ən ˌkwɪst tek ˈnɒlədʒi ˌɪndeks/ *noun* a US index based on the prices of 275 technology stocks

hammer /ˈhæmə/ *noun* □ **to go under the hammer** to be sold by auction □ **all the stock went under the hammer** all the stock was sold by auction ■ *verb* to hit hard □ **to hammer the competition** to attack and defeat the competition □ **to hammer prices** to reduce prices sharply

hammering /ˈhæmərɪŋ/ *noun* **1.** a beating or severe losses □ **the company took a hammering in Europe** the company had large losses in Europe or lost parts of its European markets □ **we gave them a hammering** we beat them commercially **2.** (*on the London Stock Exchange*) an announcement of the removal of a member firm because it has failed **3.** the massive selling of stock on a stock market

hand /hænd/ *noun* **1.** the part of the body at the end of each arm □ **to shake hands** to hold someone's hand when meeting to show you are pleased to meet them, or to show that an agreement has been reached ○ *The two negotiating teams shook hands and sat down at the conference table.* □ **to shake hands on a deal** to shake hands to show that a deal has been agreed **2.** □ **by hand** using the hands, not a machine ○ *These shoes are made by hand.* □ **to send a letter by hand** to ask someone to carry and deliver a letter personally, not sending it through the post **3.** □ **in hand** kept in reserve ○ *we have £10,000 in hand* □ **balance in hand**, **cash in hand** cash held to pay small debts and running costs □ **work in hand** work which is in progress but not finished **4.** □ **goods left on hand** unsold goods left with the retailer or manufacturer ○ *They were left with half the stock on their hands.* **5.** □ **to hand** here or present □ **I have the invoice to hand** I have the invoice in front of me **6.** □ **to change hands** to be sold to a new owner ○ *The shop changed hands for £100,000.* **7.** □ **in witness whereof, I set my hand** I sign as a witness

> **hand in** *phrasal verb* to deliver a letter by hand □ **he handed in his notice** *or* **resignation** he resigned

handcuffs /ˈhændkʌfs/ *plural noun* ▶ **golden handcuffs**

handle /ˈhænd(ə)l/ *noun* the whole number of a share price quoted

handling charge /ˈhændlɪŋ tʃɑːdʒ/ *noun* money to be paid for packing, invoicing and dealing with goods which are being shipped

handout /ˈhændaʊt/ *noun* money paid to help someone in difficulties

Hang Seng Index /hæŋ ˈseŋ ˌɪndeks/ *noun* an index of main share prices on the Hong Kong stock market

hard /hɑːd/ *adjective* **1.** strong, not weak □ **to take a hard line in trade union negotiations** to refuse to compromise with the other side **2.** difficult ○ *It is hard to get good people to work on low salaries.* **3.** solid **4.** □ **after weeks of hard bargaining** after weeks of difficult discussions

> '…few of the paper millionaires sold out and transformed themselves into hard cash millionaires' [*Investors Chronicle*]

hard bargain /ˌhɑːd ˈbɑːgɪn/ *noun* a bargain with difficult terms □ **to drive a hard bargain** to be a difficult negotiator □ **to strike a hard bargain** to agree a deal where the terms are favourable to you

hard cash /ˌhɑːd ˈkæʃ/ *noun* money in notes and coins, as opposed to cheques or credit cards

hard currency /ˌhɑːd ˈkʌrənsi/ *noun* the currency of a country which has a strong economy, and which can be changed into other currencies easily ○ *to pay for imports in hard currency* ○ *to sell raw materials to earn hard currency* Also called **scarce currency**. Opposite **soft currency**

harden /ˈhɑːd(ə)n/ *verb* to become more fixed or more inflexible ○ *The union's attitude to the management has hardened since the lockout.* □ **prices are hardening** prices are settling at a higher price

hardening /ˈhɑːd(ə)nɪŋ/ *adjective* **1.** (*of a market*) slowly moving upwards **2.** (*of prices*) becoming settled at a higher level

hard landing /ˌhɑːd ˈlændɪŋ/ *noun* a change in economic strategy to counteract inflation which has serious results for the population such as high unemployment, rising interest rates, etc.

hard market /ˌhɑːd ˈmɑːkɪt/ *noun* a market which is strong and not likely to fall

hardness /ˈhɑːdnəs/ *noun* □ **hardness of the market** the state of the market when it is strong and not likely to fall

hard sell /ˌhɑːd ˈsel/ *noun* □ **to give a product the hard sell** to make great efforts to persuade people to buy a product □ **he tried to give me the hard sell** he put a lot of effort into trying to make me buy

harmonisation /ˌhɑːmənaɪˈzeɪʃ(ə)n/, **harmonization** *noun* a standardisation, making things the same in several countries

harmonise /ˈhɑːmənaɪz/, **harmonize** *verb* to make things such as tax rates or VAT rates the same in several countries

harmonised /ˈhɑːmənaɪzd/, **harmonized** *adjective* which has been made standard in several countries

harmonised European index /ˌhɑːmənaɪzd ˌjʊərəpiːən ˈɪndeks/ *noun* a method of calculating inflation which is standard throughout the EU

hatchet man /ˈhætʃɪt mæn/ *noun* a recently appointed manager, whose job is to make staff redundant and reduce expenditure (*informal*)

haven /ˈheɪv(ə)n/ *noun* a safe place

head /hed/ *noun* the most important person ■ *adjective* most important or main ○ *Ask the head waiter for a table.* ■ *verb* to be first ○ *The two largest oil companies head the list of stock market results.*

> **head for** *phrasal verb* to go towards □ **the company is heading for disaster**

the company is going to collapse

head and shoulders /ˌhed ən ˈʃəʊldəz/ *noun* a term used by chartists showing a share price which rises to a peak, then falls slightly, then rises to a much higher peak, then falls sharply and rises to a lower peak before falling again, looking similar to a person's head and shoulders when shown on a graph

head buyer /ˌhed ˈbaɪə/ *noun* the most important buyer in a store

headhunt /ˈhedhʌnt/ *verb* to look for managers and offer them jobs in other companies □ **she was headhunted** she was approached by a headhunter and offered a new job

headhunter /ˈhedhʌntə/ *noun* a person or company whose job is to find suitable top managers to fill jobs in companies

headlease /ˈhedliːs/ *noun* a lease from the freehold owner to a tenant

headline inflation rate /ˌhedlaɪn ɪn ˈfleɪʃ(ə)n ˌreɪt/ *noun* a British inflation figure which includes items such as mortgage interest and local taxes, which are not included in the inflation figures for other countries. Compare **underlying inflation rate**

head of department /ˌhed əv dɪ ˈpɑːtmənt/ *noun* a person in charge of a department

head office /ˌhed ˈɒfɪs/ *noun* an office building where the board of directors works and meets

headquarters /hedˈkwɔːtəz/ *plural noun* the main office, where the board of directors meets and works ○ *The company's headquarters are in New York.* □ **to reduce headquarters staff** to have fewer people working in the main office. Abbreviation **HQ**

heads of agreement /ˌhedz əv ə ˈgriːmənt/ *plural noun* **1.** a draft agreement with not all the details complete **2.** the most important parts of a commercial agreement

head teller /hed ˈtelə/ *noun US* a main teller in a bank

health /helθ/ *noun* **1.** the state of being fit and well, not ill **2.** □ **to give a company a clean bill of health** to report that a company is trading profitably

'…the main US banks have been forced to pull back from international lending as nervousness continues about their financial health' [*Financial Times*]

'…financial health, along with a dose of independence, has largely sheltered Japan's pharmaceutical companies from a global wave of consolidation. Those assets, however, are expected to soon lure foreign suitors too powerful to resist' [*Nikkei Weekly*]

health insurance /ˈhelθ ɪnˌʃʊərəns/ *noun* insurance which pays the cost of treatment for illness, especially when travelling abroad

health warning /ˈhelθ ˌwɔːnɪŋ/ *noun* a warning message printed on advertisements for investments, stating that the value of investments can fall as well as rise. This is a legal requirement in the UK.

healthy /ˈhelθi/ *adjective* □ **a healthy balance sheet** a balance sheet which shows a good profit

heavily /ˈhevɪli/ *adverb* □ **he is heavily in debt** he has many debts □ **they are heavily into property** they have large investments in property □ **the company has had to borrow heavily to repay its debts** the company has had to borrow large sums of money

'…the steel company had spent heavily on new equipment' [*Fortune*]

heavy /ˈhevi/ *adjective* **1.** large or in large quantities ○ *a programme of heavy investment overseas* ○ *He suffered heavy losses on the stock exchange.* ○ *The government imposed a heavy tax on luxury goods.* □ **heavy costs** *or* **heavy expenditure** large sums of money that have to be spent **2.** used to describe a share which has such a high price that small investors are reluctant to buy it (in which case the company may decide to split the shares so as to make them more attractive: in the UK, a share price of £10.00 is considered 'heavy', though many shares have higher prices than this) **3.** having too many investments in the same type of share ○ *His portfolio is heavy in banks.*

'…heavy selling sent many blue chips tumbling in Tokyo yesterday' [*Financial Times*]

heavy industry /ˌhevi ˈɪndəstri/ *noun* an industry which deals in heavy raw materials such as coal or makes large products such as ships or engines

heavy machinery /ˌhevi məˈʃiːnəri/ *noun* large machines

heavy market /ˌhevi ˈmɑːkɪt/ *noun* a stock market where prices are falling

heavy share price /ˌhevi ˈʃeə praɪs/ *noun* a price on the London Stock Exchange which is over £10.00 per share, and so discourages the small investor

hectic /ˈhektɪk/ *adjective* wild, very active ○ *a hectic day on the stock exchange* ○ *After last week's hectic trading, this week has been very calm.*

hedge /hedʒ/ *noun* a protection against a possible loss, which involves taking an action which is the opposite of an action taken earlier □ **a hedge against inflation** investment which should increase in value more than the increase in the rate of inflation ○ *He bought gold as a hedge against exchange losses.* ■ *verb* to protect against the risk of a loss □ **to hedge your bets** to make investments in several areas so as to be protected against loss in one of them □ **to hedge against inflation** to buy investments which will rise in value faster than the increase in the rate of inflation

'…during the 1970s commercial property was regarded by investors as an alternative to equities, with many of the same inflation-hedge qualities' [*Investors Chronicle*]

'…the move saved it from having to pay its creditors an estimated $270 million owed in connection with hedge contracts which began working against the company when the price of gold rose unexpectedly during September' [*Business in Africa*]

hedge fund /ˈhedʒ fʌnd/ *noun* a partnership open to a small number of rich investors, which invests in equities, currency futures and derivatives and may produce high returns but carries a very high risk

'…much of what was described as near hysteria was the hedge funds trying to liquidate bonds to repay bank debts after losing multi-million dollar bets on speculations that the yen would fall against the dollar' [*Times*]

'…hedge funds generally have in common an ability to sell short (that is, sell stocks you do not own), and to increase growth prospects – and risk – by borrowing to

enhance the fund's assets' [*Money Observer*]

'…the stock is a hedge fund – limited by the Securities and Exchange Commission to only wealthy individuals and qualified institutions' [*Smart Money*]

COMMENT: Originally, hedge funds were funds planned to protect equity investments against possible falls on the stock market. Nowadays the term is applied to funds which take speculative positions in financial futures or equities, and are usually highly-geared: in other words, they do nothing to 'hedge' their holdings.

hedging /ˈhedʒɪŋ/ *noun* the act of buying investments at a fixed price for delivery later, so as to protect against possible loss

Helsinki Stock Exchange /hel ˌsɪŋki ˈstɒk ɪksˌtʃeɪndʒ/ *noun* the main stock exchange in Finland. Abbreviation **HEX**

hemline theory /ˈhemlaɪn ˌθɪəri/ *noun* the theory that movements of the stock market reflect the current fashionable length of women's skirts (the shorter the skirt, the more bullish the market)

hereafter /hɪərˈɑːftə/ *adverb* from this time on

hereby /hɪəˈbaɪ/ *adverb* in this way, by this letter ○ *We hereby revoke the agreement of 1st January 1982.*

hereditament /ˌherɪˈdɪtəmənt/ *noun* a property, including land and buildings

herewith /hɪəˈwɪð/ *adverb* together with this letter ○ *Please find the cheque enclosed herewith.*

HEX *abbreviation* Helsinki Stock Exchange

Hex Index /heks ˈɪndeks/ *noun* an index of share prices on the Helsinki Stock Exchange

hidden /ˈhɪd(ə)n/ *adjective* not possible to see

hidden asset /ˌhɪd(ə)n ˈæset/ *noun* an asset which is valued much less in the company's accounts than its true market value

hidden economy /ˌhɪd(ə)n ɪ ˈkɒnəmi/ *noun* same as **black economy**

hidden reserves /ˌhɪd(ə)n rɪˈzɜːvz/ *plural noun* **1.** reserves which are not easy to identify in the company's balance sheet. Reserves which are illegally kept hidden are called 'secret reserves'. **2.**

illegal reserves which are not declared in the company's balance sheet

high /haɪ/ *adjective* **1.** large, not low ○ *High overhead costs increase the unit price.* ○ *High prices put customers off.* ○ *They are budgeting for a high level of expenditure.* ○ *High interest rates are crippling small businesses.* □ **high sales** a large amount of revenue produced by sales □ **high taxation** taxation which imposes large taxes on incomes or profits □ **highest tax bracket** the group which pays the most tax □ **high volume (of sales)** a large number of items sold **2.** □ **the highest bidder** the person who offers the most money at an auction ○ *The tender will be awarded to the highest bidder.* ○ *The property was sold to the highest bidder.* ■ *adverb* □ **prices are running high** prices are above their usual level ■ *noun* a point where prices or sales are very large ○ *Prices have dropped by 10 per cent since the high of 2nd January.* □ **highs and lows on the Stock Exchange** a list of shares which have reached a new high or low price in the previous day's trading □ **sales volume has reached an all-time high** the sales volume has reached the highest point it has ever been at

'American interest rates remain exceptionally high in relation to likely inflation rates' [*Sunday Times*]

'…faster economic growth would tend to push US interest rates, and therefore the dollar, higher' [*Australian Financial Review*]

'…in a leveraged buyout the acquirer raises money by selling high-yielding debentures to private investors' [*Fortune*]

high finance /ˌhaɪ ˈfaɪnæns/ *noun* the lending, investing and borrowing of very large sums of money organised by financiers

high flier /ˌhaɪ ˈflaɪə/ *noun* **1.** a person who is very successful or who is likely to rise to a very important position **2.** a share whose market price is rising rapidly

high gearing /ˌhaɪ ˈɡɪərɪŋ/ *noun* a situation where a company has a high level of borrowing compared to its share price

high-grade bond /ˌhaɪ ɡreɪd ˈbɒnd/ *noun* a bond which has the highest rating

high-income /ˌhaɪ ˈɪnkʌm/ *adjective* used for referring to a fund that yields a high rate of return ○ *high-income shares* ○ *a high-income portfolio*

high-income bond /haɪ ˈɪnkʌm ˌbɒnd/ *noun* bond which aims to produce a high income. Abbreviation **HiB**

highly /ˈhaɪli/ *adverb* very □ **she is highly thought of by the managing director** the managing director thinks she is very competent

highly-geared company /ˌhaɪli ɡɪəd ˈkʌmp(ə)ni/ *noun* a company which has a high proportion of its funds from fixed-interest borrowings

highly-paid /ˌhaɪli ˈpeɪd/ *adjective* earning a large salary

highly-placed /ˌhaɪli ˈpleɪst/ *adjective* occupying an important post ○ *The delegation met a highly-placed official in the Trade Ministry.*

highly-priced /ˌhaɪli ˈpraɪst/ *adjective* with a large price

high pressure /ˌhaɪ ˈpreʃə/ *noun* a strong insistence that somebody should do something □ **working under high pressure** working very hard, with a manager telling you what to do and to do it quickly, or with customers asking for supplies urgently

high-risk /ˌhaɪ ˈrɪsk/ *adjective* which involves more risk than normal

high-risk investment /ˌhaɪ rɪsk ɪnˈvestmənt/ *noun* an investment which carries a higher risk than other investments

high security area /haɪ sɪˈkjʊəriti ˌeəriə/ *noun* a special part of a bank with strong doors where cash can be kept safely

high street /ˈhaɪ striːt/ *noun* the main shopping street in a British town ○ *the high street shops* ○ *a high street bookshop*

High Street banks /ˌhaɪ striːt ˈbæŋks/ *plural noun* the main British banks which accept deposits from individual customers

high-tech /ˌhaɪ ˈtek/ *adjective* used to describe devices and methods that use advanced technology □ **high-tech companies** companies in advanced technological fields, such as computers, telecommunications or scientific research □

high-tech share *or* **stock** a share in a technology sector such as software or biotechnology

high yield /ˌhaɪ ˈjiːld/ *noun* a dividend yield which is higher than is usual for the type of company

high-yield /haɪ ˈjiːld/ *adjective* which gives a very high return on investment

high-yield bond /ˌhaɪ jiːld ˈbɒnd/ *noun* same as **junk bond**

hike /haɪk/ *noun* an increase ■ *verb* to increase

HIPS *abbreviation* Home Information Pack

hire /ˈhaɪə/ *noun* **1.** an arrangement whereby customers pay money to be able to use a car, boat or piece of equipment owned by someone else for a time (NOTE: The more usual term in the US is **rent**) **2.** □ **to work for hire** to work freelance ■ *verb* **1.** to employ someone new to work for you □ **to hire staff** to employ someone new to work for you **2.** □ **to hire out cars** *or* **equipment** *or* **workers** to lend cars, equipment or workers to customers who pay for their use

COMMENT: An agreement to hire a piece of equipment, etc., involves two parties: the hirer and the owner. The equipment remains the property of the owner while the hirer is using it. Under a hire-purchase agreement, the equipment remains the property of the owner until the hirer has complied with the terms of the agreement (i.e., until he or she has paid all monies due).

hire and fire /ˌhaɪər ən ˈfaɪə/ *verb* to employ new staff and dismiss existing staff very frequently

hire purchase /ˌhaɪə ˈpɜːtʃɪs/ *noun* a system of buying something by paying a sum regularly each month ○ *to buy a refrigerator on hire purchase* (NOTE: The US term is **installment credit**, **installment plan** or **installment sale**.)

hire-purchase agreement /ˌhaɪə ˈpɜːtʃɪs əˌgriːmənt/ *noun* a contract to pay for something by instalments □ **to sign a hire-purchase agreement** to sign a contract to pay for something by instalments

hire-purchase company /ˌhaɪə ˈpɜːtʃɪs ˌkʌmp(ə)ni/ *noun* a company which provides money for hire purchase

hiring /ˈhaɪərɪŋ/ *noun* the act of employing new staff ○ *Hiring of new personnel has been stopped.*

histogram /ˈhɪstəgræm/ *noun* same as **bar chart**

historic /hɪˈstɒrɪk/, **historical** /hɪˈstɒrɪk(ə)l/ *adjective* dating back over a period of time

'…the Federal Reserve Board has eased interest rates in the past year, but they are still at historically high levels' [*Sunday Times*]

'…the historic p/e for the FTSE all-share index is 28.3 and the dividend yield is barely 2 per cent. Both indicators suggest that the stock markets are very highly priced' [*Times*]

COMMENT: By tradition, a company's accounts are usually prepared on the historic(al) cost principle, i.e. that assets are costed at their purchase price. With inflation, such assets are undervalued, and current-cost accounting or replacement-cost accounting may be preferred.

historical cost /hɪˌstɒrɪk(ə)l ˈkɒst/, **historic cost** /hɪˌstɒrɪk ˈkɒst/ *noun* the actual cost of purchasing something which was bought some time ago

historical cost accounting /hɪˌstɒrɪk(ə)l ˈkɒst əˌkaʊntɪŋ/ *noun* the preparation of accounts on the basis of historical cost, with assets valued at their original cost of purchase. Compare **current cost accounting**

historical cost depreciation /hɪˌstɒrɪk(ə)l ˈkɒst dɪˌpriːʃieɪʃ(ə)n/ *noun* depreciation based on the original cost of the asset

historical figures /hɪˌstɒrɪk(ə)l ˈfɪgəz/ *plural noun* figures that were correct at the time of purchase or payment, as distinct from, e.g., a current saleable value or market value

historical trading range /hɪˌstɒrɪk(ə)l ˈtreɪdɪŋ reɪndʒ/ *noun* the difference between the highest and lowest price for a share or bond over a period of time

hit /hɪt/ *verb* **1.** to reach something ○ *He hit his head against the table.* ○ *The strong dollar which hit a seven-year high against the yen last week.* **2.** to hurt or to damage someone or something ○ *The company was badly hit by the falling exchange rate.* ○ *Our sales of summer clothes have been hit by the bad weather.*

○ *The new legislation has hit the small companies hardest.* (NOTE: **hitting – hit**)

hive /haɪv/ *verb*

hive off *phrasal verb* to split off part of a large company to form a smaller subsidiary, giving shares in the subsidiary to its existing shareholders ○ *The new managing director hived off the retail sections of the company.*

HM Revenue & Customs /ˌeɪtʃ ˌem ˌrevənjuː ən ˈkʌstəmz/ *noun* **1.** a UK government department which deals with taxes on imports and on products such as alcohol produced in the country. It also deals with VAT and tax credits. Abbreviation **HMRC 2.** an office of this department at a port or airport

hoard /hɔːd/ *verb* **1.** to buy and store goods in case of need **2.** to keep cash instead of investing it

hoarder /ˈhɔːdə/ *noun* a person who buys and stores goods in case of need

hoarding /ˈhɔːdɪŋ/ *noun* □ **hoarding of supplies** the buying of large quantities of goods to keep in case of need

'…as a result of hoarding, rice has become scarce with prices shooting up' [*Business Times (Lagos)*]

hold /həʊld/ *noun* the action of keeping something □ **these shares are a hold** these shares should be kept and not sold ■ *verb* **1.** to own or to keep something ○ *She holds 10% of the company's shares.* **2.** to make something happen ○ *The receiver will hold an auction of the company's assets.* **3.** not to sell ○ *You should hold these shares – they look likely to rise.*

'…as of last night, the bank's shareholders no longer hold any rights to the bank's shares' [*South China Morning Post*]

hold back *phrasal verb* to wait, not to do something at the present time □ **investors are holding back until after the Budget** investors are waiting until they hear the details of the Budget before they decide whether to buy or sell □ **he held back from signing the lease until he had checked the details** he delayed signing the lease until he had checked the details □ **payment will be held back until the contract has been signed** payment will not be made until the contract has been signed

hold down *phrasal verb* **1.** to keep at a low level ○ *We are cutting margins to hold our prices down.* **2.** □ **to hold down a job** to manage to do a difficult job

'…real wages have been held down; they have risen at an annual rate of only 1% in the last two years' [*Sunday Times*]

hold on *phrasal verb* to wait, not to change □ **the company's shareholders should hold on and wait for a better offer** they should keep their shares and not sell them until they are offered a higher price

hold out for *phrasal verb* to wait and ask for something □ **you should hold out for a 10% pay rise** you should not agree to a pay rise of less than 10%

hold to *phrasal verb* not to allow something or someone to change □ **we will try to hold him to the contract** we will try to stop him going against the contract □ **the government hopes to hold wage increases to 5%** the government hopes that wage increases will not be more than 5%

hold up *phrasal verb* **1.** to stay at a high level ○ *Share prices have held up well.* ○ *Sales held up during the tourist season.* **2.** to delay something ○ *The shipment has been held up at customs.* ○ *Payment will be held up until the contract has been signed.* ○ *The strike will hold up dispatch for some weeks.* ○ *The employees are holding up production as a form of protest against poor conditions.*

holdback /ˈhəʊlbæk/ *noun* a part of a loan to a property developer which is not paid until the development is almost finished

holder /ˈhəʊldə/ *noun* **1.** a person who owns or keeps something ○ *holders of government bonds* or *bondholders* ○ *holder of stock* or *of shares in a company* ○ *holder of an insurance policy* or *policy holder* **2.** a thing which keeps something, which protects something

holder in due course /ˌhəʊldə ɪn djuː ˈkɔːs/ *noun* a person who holds a negotiable instrument, such as a bill of exchange, in good faith, without knowing of any other claim against it

holder of record /ˌhəʊldə əv ˈrekɔːd/ *noun* the person who is registered as the owner of shares in a company

holding /ˈhəʊldɪŋ/ *noun* a group of shares owned ○ *She has sold all her holdings in the Far East.* ○ *The company has holdings in German manufacturing companies.*

holding company /ˈhəʊldɪŋ ˌkʌmp(ə)ni/ *noun* **1.** a company which owns more than 50% of the shares in another company. ◊ **subsidiary company 2.** a company which exists only or mainly to own shares in subsidiary companies. ◊ **subsidiary**

hologram /ˈhɒləgræm/ *noun* a three-dimensional picture which is used on credit cards as a means of preventing forgery

home /həʊm/ *noun* the place where a person lives

home address /ˌhəʊm əˈdres/ *noun* the address of a house or flat where a person lives ○ *Please send the documents to my home address.*

home banking /ˌhəʊm ˈbæŋkɪŋ/ *noun* a system of banking using a personal computer in your own home to carry out various financial transactions such as paying invoices or checking your bank account

home equity credit /ˌhəʊm ˈekwɪti ˌkredɪt/ *noun* a loan made to a home-owner against the security of the equity in his or her property (i.e., the value of the property now less the amount outstanding on any mortgage)

home improvement loan /ˌhəʊm ɪmˈpruːvmənt ləʊn/ *noun* a loan made to a homeowner to pay for improvements to his or her home

home income plan /həʊm ˈɪnkʌm plæn/ *noun* a method of releasing equity from an unmortgaged property so that a homeowner has income or cash without actually leaving the property

Home Information Pack /ˌhəʊm ˌɪnfəˈmeɪʃ(ə)n ˌpæk/ *noun* information about a property that, since August 2007, must be provided before a property in England and Wales with three or more bedrooms can be put on the open market for sale with vacant possession. Abbreviation **HIPS**

home loan /ˈhəʊm ləʊn/ *noun* a loan by a bank or building society to help someone buy a house

home market /ˌhəʊm ˈmɑːkɪt/ *noun* the market in the country where the selling company is based ○ *Sales in the home market rose by 22%.*

home office /həʊm ˈɒfɪs/ *noun* an office organised inside your own home

Home Office /ˈhəʊm ˌɒfɪs/ *noun* a ministry dealing with the internal affairs of the country

home trade /ˌhəʊm ˈtreɪd/ *noun* trade in the country where a company is based

honorarium /ˌɒnəˈreəriəm/ *noun* money paid to a professional person such as an accountant or a lawyer when a specific fee has not been requested (NOTE: The plural is **honoraria**.)

honorary /ˈɒnərəri/ *adjective* not paid a salary for the work done for an organisation ○ *He is honorary president of the translators' association.*

honorary secretary /ˌɒnərəri ˈsekrət(ə)ri/ *noun* a person who keeps the minutes and official documents of a committee or club, but is not paid a salary

honorary treasurer /ˌɒnərəri ˈtreʒərə/ *noun* a treasurer who does not receive any fee

honour /ˈɒnə/ *verb* to pay something because it is owed and is correct ○ *to honour a bill* ○ *The bank refused to honour his cheque.* (NOTE: The US spelling is **honor**.) □ **to honour a signature** to pay something because the signature is correct

horizontal integration /ˌhɒrɪzɒnt(ə)l ˌɪntɪˈɡreɪʃ(ə)n/ *noun* the process of joining similar companies or taking over a company in the same line of business as yourself

horizontal spread /ˌhɒrɪzɒnt(ə)l ˈspred/ *noun* the buying and selling of two options at the same price but with different maturity dates

horse trading /ˈhɔːs ˌtreɪdɪŋ/ *noun* hard bargaining which ends with someone giving something in return for a concession from the other side

hostile /ˈhɒstaɪl/ *adjective* unfriendly, showing dislike

hostile bid /ˌhɒstaɪl ˈbɪd/ *noun* same as **contested takeover**

hostile bidder /ˌhɒstaɪl ˈbɪdə/, **hostile suitor** /ˌhɒstaɪl ˈsuːtə/ *noun* a person or company making a hostile bid

hostile takeover bid /ˌhɒstaɪl ˈteɪkəʊvə ˌbɪd/ *noun* a takeover where the board of the company do not recommend it to the shareholders and try to fight it

hot card /hɒt ˈkɑːd/ *noun* a stolen credit card

hot money /ˌhɒt ˈmʌni/ *noun* money which is moved from country to country to get the best returns

hot stock /hɒt ˈstɒk/ *noun* a stock (usually in a new issue) which rises rapidly on the stock exchange because of great demand

hour /aʊə/ *noun* **1.** a period of time lasting sixty minutes □ **to work a thirty-five hour week** to work seven hours a day each weekday □ **we work an eight-hour day** we work for eight hours a day, e.g. from 8.30 to 5.30 with one hour for lunch **2.** sixty minutes of work ○ *She earns £14 an hour.* ○ *We pay £16 an hour.* □ **to pay by the hour** to pay people a fixed amount of money for each hour worked **3.** □ **outside hours** *or* **out of hours** when the office is not open ○ *He worked on the accounts out of hours.*

hourly wage /ˌaʊəli ˈweɪdʒ/ *noun* the amount of money paid for an hour's work

house /haʊs/ *noun* **1.** the building in which someone lives **2.** a company ○ *the largest London finance house* ○ *a brokerage house* ○ *a publishing house*

housecleaning /ˈhaʊsˌkliːnɪŋ/ *noun* a general reorganising of a business ○ *She has mainly been performing house-cleaning measures.*

household goods /ˌhaʊshəʊld ˈɡʊdz/ *plural noun* items which are used in the home

house insurance /ˈhaʊs ɪnˌʃʊərəns/ *noun* insuring a house and its contents against damage

house journal /ˈhaʊs ˌdʒɜːn(ə)l/, **house magazine** /ˈhaʊs mæɡəˌziːn/ *noun* a magazine produced for the employees or shareholders in a company to give them news about the company

house property /ˈhaʊs ˌprɒpəti/ *noun* private houses or flats, not shops, offices, or factories

house starts /ˈhaʊs ˈstɑːts/, **housing starts** /ˈhaʊzɪŋ ˈstɑːts/ *plural noun* the number of new private houses or flats of which the construction has begun during a year

housing authority bond /ˈhaʊzɪŋ ɔː ˌθɒrəti bɒnd/ *noun* a bond issued by a US municipal housing authority to raise money to build dwellings

housing bubble /ˈhaʊzɪŋ ˌbʌb(ə)l/ *noun* an increase in housing prices fuelled by demand and speculation. When demand decreases or stagnates at the same time as supply increases, prices drop sharply causing the bubble to burst.

HP *abbreviation* hire purchase

hryvnia /ˈhrɪvniə/ *noun* a unit of currency used in the Ukraine

human resources department /ˌhjuːmən rɪˈzɔːsɪz dɪˌpɑːtmənt/ *noun* the section of the company which deals with its staff

human resources officer /ˌhjuːmən rɪˈzɔːsɪz ˌɒfɪsə/ *noun* a person who deals with the staff in a company, especially interviewing candidates for new posts

hurdle rate /ˈhɜːd(ə)l reɪt/ *noun* **1.** the rate of growth in a portfolio required to repay the final fixed redemption price of zero dividend preference shares **2.** a minimum rate of return needed by a bank to fund a loan, the rate below which a loan is not profitable for the bank

hyper- /haɪpə/ *prefix* very large

hyperinflation /ˌhaɪpərɪnˈfleɪʃ(ə)n/ *noun* inflation which is at such a high percentage rate that it is almost impossible to reduce

hypothecation /haɪˌpɒθəˈkeɪʃ(ə)n/ *noun* **1.** an arrangement in which property such as securities is used as collateral for a loan but without transferring legal ownership to the lender, as opposed to a mortgage, where the lender holds the title to the property **2.** an action of earmarking money derived from specific sources for related expenditure, as when investing taxes from private cars or petrol sales solely on public transport

I

IBO *abbreviation* institutional buyout

IBRD *abbreviation* International Bank for Reconstruction and Development

ICAEW *abbreviation* Institute of Chartered Accountants in England and Wales

ICAI *abbreviation* Institute of Chartered Accountants in Ireland

Icarus factor /ˈɪkərəs ˌfæktə/ *noun* the tendency of managers or executives to embark on projects which are too ambitious and consequently fail (NOTE: In Greek mythology, Icarus tried to escape from Crete using wings made of wax and feathers, but flew too near the sun and drowned in the sea after the wax melted.)

ICAS *abbreviation* Institute of Chartered Accountants in Scotland

ICCH *abbreviation* International Commodities Clearing House

idle /ˈaɪd(ə)l/ *adjective* not working ○ 2,000 employees were made idle by the recession.

idle capital /ˌaɪd(ə)l ˈkæpɪt(ə)l/ *noun* capital which is not being used productively

IFA *abbreviation* 1. independent financial adviser 2. Institute of Financial Accountants

IFC *abbreviation* International Finance Corporation

IFRIC *abbreviation* International Financial Reporting Interpretations Committee

IFRS *abbreviation* International Financial Reporting Standards

IHT *abbreviation* inheritance tax

illegal /ɪˈliːg(ə)l/ *adjective* not legal or against the law

illegality /ˌɪliːˈgælɪti/ *noun* the fact of being illegal

illegally /ɪˈliːgəli/ *adverb* against the law ○ He was accused of illegally laundering money.

illicit /ɪˈlɪsɪt/ *adjective* not legal or not permitted ○ the illicit sale of alcohol ○ trade in illicit alcohol

illiquid /ɪˈlɪkwɪd/ *adjective* 1. referring to an asset which is not easy to change into cash 2. used to describe a person or business that lacks cash or assets such as securities that can readily be converted into cash

ILO *abbreviation* International Labour Organization

IMF *abbreviation* International Monetary Fund

IMM *abbreviation* International Monetary Market

IMMA *abbreviation* insured money market account

immovable /ɪˈmuːvəb(ə)l/ *adjective* impossible to move

immovable property /ɪˌmuːvəb(ə)l ˈprɒpəti/ *noun* houses and other buildings on land

immunisation /ˌɪmjʊnaɪˈzeɪʃ(ə)n/, **immunization** *noun US* arrangements to protect the income from a portfolio of investments against any risk in a volatile stock market

impact /ˈɪmpækt/ *noun* a shock or strong effect ○ the impact of new technology on the cotton trade ○ The new design has made little impact on the buying public.

impaired /ɪmˈpeəd/ *adjective* not certain, not perfect

impaired credit /ɪmˌpeəd ˈkredɪt/ *noun US* a situation where a person becomes less creditworthy than before

impaired loans /ɪmˌpeəd 'ləʊnz/ *plural noun US* doubtful loans

implement /'ɪmplɪˌment/ *verb* to put into action ○ *to implement an agreement* ○ *to implement a decision*

implementation /ˌɪmplɪmən'teɪʃ(ə)n/ *noun* the process of putting something into action ○ *the implementation of new rules*

import /ɪm'pɔːt/ *verb* to bring goods from abroad into a country for sale ○ *The company imports television sets from Japan.* ○ *This car was imported from France.*

importation /ˌɪmpɔː'teɪʃ(ə)n/ *noun* the act of importing ○ *The importation of arms is forbidden.* ○ *The importation of livestock is subject to very strict controls.*

import ban /'ɪmpɔːt bæn/ *noun* a government order forbidding imports of a particular kind or from a particular country ○ *The government has imposed an import ban on arms.*

import duty /'ɪmpɔːt ˌdjuːti/ *noun* a tax on goods imported into a country

importer /ɪm'pɔːtə/ *noun* a person or company that imports goods ○ *a cigar importer* ○ *The company is a big importer of foreign cars.*

import-export /ˌɪmpɔːt 'ekspɔːt/ *adjective, noun* referring to business which deals with both bringing foreign goods into a country and sending locally made goods abroad ○ *Rotterdam is an important centre for the import-export trade.* ○ *She works in import-export.*

importing /ɪm'pɔːtɪŋ/ *adjective* bringing goods into a country ○ *oil-importing countries* ○ *an importing company* ■ *noun* the act of bringing foreign goods into a country for sale ○ *The importing of arms into the country is illegal.*

import levy /'ɪmpɔːt ˌlevi/ *noun* a tax on imports, especially in the EU a tax on imports of farm produce from outside the EU

import licence /'ɪmpɔːt ˌlaɪs(ə)ns/, **import permit** *noun* an official document which allows goods to be imported

import quota /'ɪmpɔːt ˌkwəʊtə/ *noun* a fixed quantity of a particular type of goods which the government allows to be imported ○ *The government has imposed a import quota on cars.*

import restrictions /'ɪmpɔːt rɪˌstrɪkʃ(ə)nz/ *plural noun* actions taken by a government to reduce the level of imports by imposing quotas, duties, etc.

imports /'ɪmpɔːts/ *plural noun* goods brought into a country from abroad for sale ○ *Imports from Poland have risen to $1m a year.* (NOTE: Usually used in the plural, but the singular is used before a noun.)

import surcharge /'ɪmpɔːt ˌsɜːtʃɑːdʒ/ *noun* the extra duty charged on imported goods, to try to stop them from being imported and to encourage local manufacture

impose /ɪm'pəʊz/ *verb* to give orders for something regarded as unpleasant or unwanted, such as a tax or a ban ○ *to impose a tax on bicycles* ○ *They tried to impose a ban on smoking.* ○ *The government imposed a special duty on oil.*

imposition /ˌɪmpə'zɪʃ(ə)n/ *noun* the act of imposing something

impound /ɪm'paʊnd/ *verb* to take something away and keep it until a tax is paid ○ *Customs impounded the whole cargo.*

impounding /ɪm'paʊndɪŋ/ *noun* an act of taking something and keeping it until a tax is paid

imprest system /'ɪmprest ˌsɪstəm/ *noun* a system of controlling petty cash, where cash is paid out against a written receipt and the receipt is used to get more cash to bring the float to the original level

imprinter /ɪm'prɪntə/ *noun* a hand-operated machine for printing the details of a customer's credit card on a sales voucher

improve /ɪm'pruːv/ *verb* to make something better, or to become better ○ *We are trying to improve our image with a series of TV commercials.* ○ *They hope to improve the company's market share.* ○ *We hope the cash flow position will improve or we will have difficulty in paying our bills.* □ **export trade has improved sharply during the first quarter** export trade has increased suddenly and greatly in the first period of the year

'…we also invest in companies whose growth and profitability could be improved by a management buyout' [*Times*]

improve on *phrasal verb* to do better than □ *she refused to improve on her previous offer* she refused to make a better offer

improved offer /ɪmˌpruːvd ˈɒfə/ *noun* an offer which is larger or has better terms than the previous offer

improvement /ɪmˈpruːvmənt/ *noun* **1.** the process of getting better ○ *There is no improvement in the cash flow situation.* ○ *Sales are showing a sharp improvement over last year.* ○ *Employees have noticed an improvement in the working environment.* **2.** something which is better □ **an improvement on an offer** an act of making a better offer

'…the management says the rate of loss-making has come down and it expects further improvement in the next few years' [*Financial Times*]

impulse /ˈɪmpʌls/ *noun* a sudden decision □ **to do something on impulse** to do something because you have just thought of it, not because it was planned

impulse buyer /ˈɪmpʌls ˌbaɪə/ *noun* a person who buys something on impulse, not because he or she intended to buy it

impulse buying /ˈɪmpʌls ˌbaɪɪŋ/ *noun* the practice of buying items which you have just seen, not because you had planned to buy them

impulse purchase /ˈɪmpʌls ˌpɜːtʃɪs/ *noun* something bought as soon as it is seen

imputation system /ˌɪmpjuː ˈteɪʃ(ə)n ˌsɪstəm/ *noun* a former system of taxation of dividends, where the company paid Advance Corporation Tax on the dividends it paid to its shareholders, and the shareholders paid no tax on the dividends received, assuming that they paid tax at the standard rate

impute /ɪmˈpjuːt/ *verb* to pass the responsibility for something to someone else

imputed value /ɪmˌpjuːtɪd ˈvæljuː/ *noun* a value which is given to figures, for which an accurate value cannot be calculated

IMRO *abbreviation* Investment Management Regulatory Organisation

inactive /ɪnˈæktɪv/ *adjective* not active or not busy

inactive account /ɪnˌæktɪv əˈkaʊnt/ *noun* a bank account which is not used over a period of time

inactive market /ɪnˌæktɪv ˈmɑːkɪt/ *noun* a stock market with few buyers or sellers

Inc *abbreviation US* incorporated

incentive /ɪnˈsentɪv/ *noun* something which encourages a customer to buy, or employees to work better

'…some further profit-taking was seen yesterday as investors continued to lack fresh incentives to renew buying activity' [*Financial Times*]

'…a well-designed plan can help companies retain talented employees and offer enticing performance incentives – all at an affordable cost' [*Fortune*]

'…the right incentives can work when used strategically' [*Management Today*]

'…an additional incentive is that the Japanese are prepared to give rewards where they are due' [*Management Today*]

incentive bonus /ɪnˈsentɪv ˌbəʊnəs/, **incentive payment** /ɪnˈsentɪv ˌpeɪmənt/ *noun* an extra payment offered to employees to make them work better

incentive scheme /ɪnˈsentɪv skiːm/ *noun* a plan to encourage better work by paying higher commission or bonuses ○ *Incentive schemes are boosting production.*

inchoate /ɪnˈkəʊət/ *adjective* referring to an instrument which is incomplete

incidental /ˌɪnsɪˈdent(ə)l/ *adjective* not important, but connected with something else

incidental expenses /ˌɪnsɪdent(ə)l ɪkˈspensɪz/ *plural noun* small amounts of money spent at various times in addition to larger amounts

incidentals /ˌɪnsɪˈdent(ə)lz/ *plural noun* same as **incidental expenses**

include /ɪnˈkluːd/ *verb* to count something along with other things ○ *The charge includes VAT.* ○ *The total is £140 not including insurance and freight.* ○ *The account covers services up to and including the month of June.*

inclusive /ɪnˈkluːsɪv/ *adjective* counting something in with other things ○ *inclusive of tax* ○ *not inclusive of VAT* □ **inclusive of** including ○ *inclusive of tax* ○ *not inclusive of VAT*

inclusive charge /ɪnˌkluːsɪv ˈtʃɑːdʒ/, **inclusive sum** /ɪnˌkluːsɪv ˈsʌm/ *noun* a charge which includes all items or costs

income /ˈɪnkʌm/ *noun* **1.** money which a person receives as salary or dividends □ **lower income bracket, upper income bracket** the groups of people who earn low or high salaries considered for tax purposes **2.** money which an organisation receives as gifts or from investments ○ *The hospital has a large income from gifts.*

'...there is no risk-free way of taking regular income from your money much higher than the rate of inflation' [*Guardian*]

income drawdown /ˈɪnkʌm ˌdrɔːdaʊn/ *noun* an arrangement by which you take smaller amounts on a regular basis out of money accumulating in the pension fund, instead of taking it all at the same time in a lump sum to pay for an annuity

income fund /ˈɪnkʌm fʌnd/ *noun* a fund which aims at providing a high income rather than capital growth

income gearing /ˈɪnkʌm ˌɡɪərɪŋ/ *noun* the ratio of the interest a company pays on its borrowing shown as a percentage of its pretax profits before the interest is paid

income shares /ˈɪnkʌm ʃeəz/ *plural noun* shares in an investment trust that receive income from the investments, but do not benefit from any rise in capital value of the investments

incomes policy /ˈɪnkʌmz ˌpɒlɪsi/ *noun* the government's ideas on how incomes should be controlled

income support /ˈɪnkʌm səˌpɔːt/ *noun* a government benefit paid to low-income earners who are working less than 16 hours per week, provided they can show that they are actively looking for jobs. Abbreviation **IS**

income tax /ˈɪnkʌm tæks/ *noun* **1.** the tax on a person's income, both earned and unearned **2.** the tax on the profits of a corporation

income tax form /ˈɪnkʌm tæks ˌfɔːm/ *noun* a form to be completed which declares all income to the tax office

income tax return /ˈɪnkʌm tæks rɪˌtɜːn/ *noun* a completed tax form, with details of income and allowances. Also called **declaration of income, tax return**

income units /ˈɪnkʌm ˌjuːnɪts/ *plural noun* units in a unit trust, from which the investor receives dividends in the form of income

income yield /ˈɪnkʌm jiːld/ *noun* an actual percentage yield of government stocks, the fixed interest being shown as a percentage of the market price

incoming /ˈɪnkʌmɪŋ/ *adjective* referring to someone who has recently been elected or appointed ○ *the incoming chairman*

inconvertible /ˌɪnkənˈvɜːtəb(ə)l/ *adjective* referring to currency which cannot be easily converted into other currencies

incorporate /ɪnˈkɔːpəreɪt/ *verb* **1.** to bring something in to form part of a main group ○ *Income from the 1998 acquisition is incorporated into the accounts.* **2.** to form a registered company ○ *a company incorporated in the US* ○ *an incorporated company* ○ *J. Doe Incorporated*

COMMENT: A company is incorporated by drawing up a memorandum of association, which is lodged with Companies House. In the UK, a company is either a private limited company (they print Ltd after their name) or a public limited company (they print Plc after their name). A company must be a Plc to obtain a stock exchange listing. In the US, there is no distinction between private and public companies, and all are called 'corporations'; they put Inc. after their name.

incorporation /ɪnˌkɔːpəˈreɪʃ(ə)n/ *noun* an act of incorporating a company

COMMENT: A corporation (a body which is legally separate from its members) is formed in one of three ways: 1) registration under the Companies Act (the normal method for commercial companies); 2) granting of a royal charter; 3) by a special Act of Parliament. A company is incorporated by drawing up a memorandum and articles of association, which are lodged with Companies House.

increase *noun* /ˈɪnkriːs/ **1.** an act of becoming larger ○ *There have been several increases in tax or tax increases in the last few years.* ○ *There is an automatic 5% increase in price or price increase on 1st January.* ○ *Profits showed a 10% increase or an increase of 10% on* *last year.* □ **increase in the cost of living** a rise in the annual cost of living **2.** a higher salary ○ *increase in pay* or *pay increase* ○ *The government hopes to hold salary increases to 3%.* □ **she had two increases last year** her salary went up twice ■ *verb* /ɪnˈkriːs/ **1.** to grow bigger or higher ○ *Profits have increased faster than the increase in the rate of inflation.* ○ *Exports to Africa have increased by more than 25%.* ○ *The price of oil has increased twice in the past week.* □ **to increase in price** to cost more □ **to increase in size** *or* **value** to become larger or more valuable **2.** to make something bigger or higher □ **the company increased her salary to £50,000** the company gave her a rise in salary to £50,000

'…turnover has the potential to be increased to over 1 million dollars with energetic management and very little capital' [*Australian Financial Review*]

'…competition is steadily increasing and could affect profit margins as the company tries to retain its market share' [*Citizen (Ottawa)*]

increment /ˈɪŋkrɪmənt/ *noun* a regular automatic increase in salary ○ *an annual increment* □ **salary which rises in annual increments of £1000** each year the salary is increased by £1000

incremental /ˌɪŋkrɪˈment(ə)l/ *adjective* rising automatically in stages

incremental cost /ˌɪŋkrɪment(ə)l ˈkɒst/ *noun* the cost of making extra units above the number already planned. This may then include further fixed costs.

incremental increase /ˌɪŋkrɪment(ə)l ˈɪŋkriːs/ *noun* an increase in salary according to an agreed annual increment

incremental scale /ˌɪŋkrɪment(ə)l ˈskeɪl/ *noun* a salary scale with regular annual salary increases

incur /ɪnˈkɜː/ *verb* to make yourself liable to something (NOTE: **incurring – incurred**) □ **to incur the risk of a penalty** to make it possible that you risk paying a penalty □ **the company has incurred heavy costs to implement the expansion programme** the company has had to pay large sums of money

'…the company blames fiercely competitive market conditions in Europe for a

£14m operating loss last year, incurred despite a record turnover' [*Financial Times*]

indebted /ɪnˈdetɪd/ *adjective* owing money to someone ○ *to be indebted to a property company*

indemnification /ɪnˌdemnɪfɪˈkeɪʃən/ *noun* payment for damage

indemnify /ɪnˈdemnɪfaɪ/ *verb* to pay for damage ○ *to indemnify someone for a loss*

indemnity /ɪnˈdemnɪti/ *noun* **1.** a guarantee of payment after a loss ○ *She had to pay an indemnity of £100.* **2.** compensation paid after a loss

indemnity insurance /ɪnˈdemnɪti ɪnˌʃʊərəns/ *noun* an insurance policy that protects business owners and employees against claims made in the workplace

indent *noun* /ˈɪndent/ **1.** an order placed by an importer for goods from overseas ○ *They put in an indent for a new stock of soap.* **2.** a line of typing which starts several spaces from the left-hand margin ■ *verb* /ɪnˈdent/ □ **to indent for something** to put in an order for something ○ *The department has indented for a new computer.*

indenture /ɪnˈdentʃə/ *noun* US a formal agreement showing the terms of a bond issue

independent /ˌɪndɪˈpendənt/ *adjective* not under the control or authority of anyone else

independent authenticator /ˌɪndɪ pendənt ɔːˈθentɪkeɪtə/ *noun* a company that has the authority (from the government or the internet controlling body) to issue certificates of authentication when they are sure that a company is who it claims to be

independent company /ˌɪndɪ pendənt ˈkʌmp(ə)ni/ *noun* a company which is not controlled by another company

independent financial adviser /ˌɪndɪpendənt faɪˌnænʃ(ə)l ədˈvaɪzə/ *noun* a person who gives impartial advice on financial matters, who is not connected with any financial institution. Abbreviation **IFA**

independents /ˌɪndɪˈpendənts/ *plural noun* shops or companies which are owned by private individuals or families

'…many independents took advantage of the bank holiday period when the big multiples were closed' [*The Grocer*]

independent trader /ˌɪndɪpendənt ˈtreɪdə/, **independent shop** /ˌɪndɪpendənt ˈʃɒp/ *noun* a shop which is owned by an individual proprietor, not by a chain

index /ˈɪndeks/ *noun* **1.** a list of items classified into groups or put in alphabetical order **2.** a regular statistical report which shows rises and falls in prices, values, or levels **3.** a figure based on the current market price of shares on a stock exchange (NOTE: [all noun senses] The plural is **indexes** or **indices**.) ■ *verb* to link a payment to an index ○ *salaries indexed to the cost of living*

'…the index of industrial production sank 0.2 per cent for the latest month after rising 0.3 per cent in March' [*Financial Times*]

'…an analysis of the consumer price index for the first half of the year shows that the rate of inflation went down by 12.9 per cent' [*Business Times (Lagos)*]

index arbitrage /ˌɪndeks ˈɑːbɪtrɑːʒ/ *noun* buying or selling a basket of stocks against an index option or future

indexation /ˌɪndekˈseɪʃ(ə)n/ *noun* the linking of something to an index

indexation of wage increases /ˌɪndekseɪʃ(ə)n əv ˈweɪdʒ ˌɪnkriːsɪz/ *noun* the linking of wage increases to the percentage rise in the cost of living

indexed portfolio /ˌɪndekst ˈpɔːtfəʊliəʊ/ *noun* a portfolio of shares in all the companies which form the basis of a stock exchange index

index fund /ˈɪndeks fʌnd/ *noun* an investment fund consisting of shares in all the companies which are used to calculate a stock exchange index

index letter /ˈɪndeks ˌletə/ *noun* a letter of an item in an index

index-linked /ˈɪndeks ˌlɪŋkt/ *adjective* rising automatically by the percentage increase in the cost of living ○ *index-linked government bonds* ○ *Inflation did not affect her as she has an index-linked pension.*

'…two-year index-linked savings certificates now pay 3 per cent a year tax free, in addition to index-linking' [*Financial Times*]

index number /ˈɪndeks ˌnʌmbə/ *noun* **1.** a number of something in an index **2.** a number showing the percentage rise of something over a period

index tracker /ˈɪndeks ˌtrækə/ *noun* an investor or fund manager who tracks an index

index-tracking /ˈɪndeks ˌtrækɪŋ/ *adjective* adjusted to follow changes in a particular index, e.g. the Bank of England's base rate

indicate /ˈɪndɪkeɪt/ *verb* to show something ○ *The latest figures indicate a fall in the inflation rate.* ○ *Our sales for last year indicate a move from the home market to exports.*

indicator /ˈɪndɪkeɪtə/ *noun* a factor of a situation that gives an indication of a general trend

'…it reduces this month's growth in the key M3 indicator from about 19% to 12%' [*Sunday Times*]

'…we may expect the US leading economic indicators for April to show faster economic growth' [*Australian Financial Review*]

'…other indicators, such as high real interest rates, suggest that monetary conditions are extremely tight' [*Economist*]

indirect /ˌɪndaɪˈrekt/ *adjective* not direct

indirect costs /ˌɪndaɪrekt ˈkɒsts/, **indirect expenses** /ˌɪndaɪrekt ɪkˈspensɪz/ *plural noun* costs which are not directly related to the making of a product, e.g. cleaning, rent or administration

indirect labour costs /ˌɪndaɪrekt ˈleɪbə ˌkɒsts/ *plural noun* the cost of paying employees not directly involved in making a product, such as cleaners or administrative staff. Such costs cannot be allocated to a cost centre.

indirect loss /ˌɪndaɪrekt ˈlɒs/ *noun* same as **consequential loss**

indirect tax /ˌɪndaɪrekt ˈtæks/ *noun* a tax such as VAT paid to someone who then pays it to the government

indirect taxation /ˌɪndaɪrekt tækˈseɪʃ(ə)n/ *noun* taxes which are not paid direct to the government, e.g. sales tax ○ *The government raises more money by indirect taxation than by direct.*

individual /ˌɪndɪ'vɪdʒuəl/ *noun* one single person ○ *a savings plan tailored to the requirements of the private individual* ■ *adjective* single or belonging to one person ○ *a pension plan designed to meet each person's individual requirements* ○ *We sell individual portions of ice cream.*

Individual Retirement Account /ˌɪndɪvɪdʒuəl rɪ'taɪəmənt ə,kaʊnt/ *noun* US a tax-deferred pension scheme, that allows individuals to make contributions to a personal retirement fund. Abbreviation **IRA**

Individual Savings Account /ˌɪndɪvɪdʒuəl 'seɪvɪŋz ə,kaʊnt/ *noun* a British scheme by which individuals can invest by putting a limited amount of money each year in a tax-free account. Abbreviation **ISA**

inducement /ɪn'djuːsmənt/ *noun* something which helps to persuade someone to do something ○ *They offered her a company car as an inducement to stay.*

industrial /ɪn'dʌstriəl/ *adjective* referring to manufacturing work □ **to take industrial action** to go on strike or go-slow □ **land zoned for light industrial use** land where planning permission has been given to build small factories for light industry

'…indications of renewed weakness in the US economy were contained in figures on industrial production for April' [*Financial Times*]

industrial accident /ɪn,dʌstriəl 'æksɪd(ə)nt/ *noun* an accident which takes place at work

industrial arbitration tribunal /ɪn,dʌstriəl ,ɑːbɪ'treɪʃ(ə)n traɪ,bjuːn(ə)l/ *noun* a court which decides in industrial disputes

industrial bank /ɪn'dʌstriəl bæŋk/ *noun* a finance house which lends to business customers

industrial capacity /ɪn,dʌstriəl kə'pæsɪti/ *noun* the amount of work which can be done in a factory or several factories

industrial centre /ɪn'dʌstriəl ,sentə/ *noun* a large town with many industries

industrial court /ɪn,dʌstriəl 'kɔːt/ *noun* a court which can decide in industrial disputes if both parties agree to ask it to judge between them

industrial debenture /ɪn,dʌstriəl dɪ'bentʃə/ *noun* a debenture raised by an industrial company

industrial development /ɪn,dʌstriəl dɪ'veləpmənt/ *noun* the planning and building of new industries in special areas

industrial espionage /ɪn,dʌstriəl 'espiənɑːʒ/ *noun* the practice of trying to find out the secrets of a competitor's work or products, usually by illegal means

industrial expansion /ɪn,dʌstriəl ɪk'spænʃən/ *noun* the growth of industries in a country or a region

industrial injury /ɪn,dʌstriəl 'ɪndʒəriz/ *noun* an injury to an employee that occurs in the workplace

industrialisation /ɪn,dʌstriəlaɪ'zeɪʃ(ə)n/, **industrialization** *noun* the process of change by which an economy becomes based on industrial production rather than on agriculture

industrialise /ɪn'dʌstriə,laɪz/, **industrialize** *verb* to set up industries in a country which had none before

'…central bank and finance ministry officials of the industrialized countries will continue work on the report' [*Wall Street Journal*]

industrial loan /ɪn,dʌstriəl 'ləʊn/ *noun* a loan raised by an industrial company

industrial processes /ɪn,dʌstriəl 'prəʊsesɪz/ *plural noun* the various stages involved in manufacturing products in factories

industrial property /ɪn,dʌstriəl 'prɒpəti/ *noun* factories or other buildings used for industrial purposes

industrial relations /ɪn,dʌstriəl rɪ'leɪʃ(ə)nz/ *plural noun* relations between management and employees ○ *The company has a history of bad labour relations.*

'Britain's industrial relations climate is changing' [*Personnel Today*]

industrials /ɪn'dʌstriəlz/ *plural noun* shares in manufacturing companies

industrial training /ɪn,dʌstriəl 'treɪnɪŋ/ *noun* the training of new employees to work in an industry

industrial tribunal /ɪn,dʌstriəl traɪ'bjuːn(ə)l/ *noun* a court which can decide in disputes about employment

'ACAS has a legal obligation to try and solve industrial grievances before they reach industrial tribunals' [*Personnel Today*]

industry /ˈɪndəstri/ *noun* **1.** all factories, companies, or processes involved in the manufacturing of products ○ *All sectors of industry have shown rises in output.* **2.** a group of companies making the same type of product or offering the same type of service ○ *the aircraft industry* ○ *the food-processing industry* ○ *the petroleum industry* ○ *the advertising industry*

'…with the present overcapacity in the airline industry, discounting of tickets is widespread' [*Business Traveller*]

ineligible /ɪnˈelɪdʒɪb(ə)l/ *adjective* not eligible

ineligible bill /ɪnˌelɪdʒəb(ə)l ˈbɪl/ *noun* a bill of exchange which cannot be discounted by a central bank

inflate /ɪnˈfleɪt/ *verb* **1.** □ **to inflate prices** to increase prices without any reason **2.** □ **to inflate the economy** to make the economy more active by increasing the money supply

inflated /ɪnˈfleɪtɪd/ *adjective* **1.** □ **inflated prices** prices which are increased without any reason ○ *Tourists don't want to pay inflated London prices.* **2.** □ **inflated currency** currency which is too high in relation to other currencies

inflation /ɪnˈfleɪʃ(ə)n/ *noun* a greater increase in the supply of money or credit than in the production of goods and services, resulting in higher prices and a fall in the purchasing power of money ○ *to take measures to reduce inflation* ○ *High interest rates tend to increase inflation.* □ **we have 3% inflation** *or* **inflation is running at 3%** prices are 3% higher than at the same time last year □ **spiralling inflation** inflation where price rises make workers ask for higher wages which then increase prices again

inflation accounting /ɪnˈfleɪʃ(ə)n əˌkaʊntɪŋ/ *noun* an accounting system in which inflation is taken into account when calculating the value of assets and the preparation of accounts

inflationary /ɪnˈfleɪʃ(ə)n(ə)ri/ *adjective* tending to increase inflation ○ *inflationary trends in the economy* □ **the economy is in an inflationary spiral** the

economy is in a situation where price rises encourage higher wage demands which in turn make prices rise

'…inflationary expectations fell somewhat this month, but remained a long way above the actual inflation rate, according to figures released yesterday. The annual rate of inflation measured by the consumer price index has been below 2 per cent for over 18 months' [*Australian Financial Review*]

inflation-proof /ɪnˈfleɪʃ(ə)n pruːf/ *adjective* referring to a pension, etc. which is index-linked, so that its value is preserved in times of inflation

inflation-proof pension /ɪnˌfleɪʃ(ə)n pruːf ˈpenʃən/ *noun* a pension which will rise to keep pace with inflation

inflation rate /ɪnˈfleɪʃ(ə)n reɪt/ *noun* a figure, in the form of a percentage, which shows the amount by which inflation has increased over a period of time, usually a year. Also called **rate of inflation**

'…the decision by the government to tighten monetary policy will push the annual inflation rate above the year's previous high' [*Financial Times*]

'…when you invest to get a return, you want a 'real' return – above the inflation rate' [*Investors Chronicle*]

'…the retail prices index rose 0.4 per cent in the month, taking the annual headline inflation rate to 1.7 per cent. The underlying inflation rate, which excludes mortgage interest payments, increased to an annual rate of 3.1 per cent' [*Times*]

COMMENT: The inflation rate in the UK is calculated on a series of figures, including prices of consumer items: petrol, gas and electricity, interest rates, etc. This gives the 'underlying' inflation rate which can be compared to that of other countries. The calculation can also include mortgage interest and local taxes which give the 'headline' inflation figure. This is higher than in other countries because of these extra items. Inflation affects businesses, in that as their costs rise, so their profits may fall and it is necessary to take this into account when pricing products.

inflation target /ɪnˈfleɪʃ(ə)n ˌtɑːɡɪt/ *noun* an inflation rate which the government aims to reach at some date in the future

inflow /ˈɪnfləʊ/ *noun* the act of coming in or being brought in □ **inflow of capital**

into the country capital which is coming into a country in order to be invested

'...the dollar is strong because of capital inflows rather than weak because of the trade deficit' [*Duns Business Month*]

influx /ˈɪnflʌks/ *noun* an inflow, especially one where people or things come in in large quantities ○ *an influx of foreign currency into the country* ○ *an influx of cheap labour into the cities*

'...the retail sector will also benefit from the expected influx of tourists' [*Australian Financial Review*]

information officer /ˌɪnfəˈmeɪʃ(ə)n ˌɒfɪsə/ *noun* **1.** a person whose job is to give information about a company, an organisation or a government department to the public **2.** a person whose job is to give information to other departments in the same organisation

infringe /ɪnˈfrɪndʒ/ *verb* to break a law or a right □ **to infringe a patent** to make a product which works in the same way as a patented product and not pay a royalty to the patent holder

infringement of patent /ɪnˌfrɪndʒmənt əv ˈpeɪtənt/ *noun* an act of illegally using, making or selling an invention which is patented, without the permission of the patent holder

ingot /ˈɪŋgət/ *noun* a bar of gold or silver

inherit /ɪnˈherɪt/ *verb* to get something from a person who has died ○ *When her father died she inherited the shop.* ○ *He inherited £10,000 from his grandfather.*

inheritance /ɪnˈherɪt(ə)ns/ *noun* property which is received from a dead person

inheritance tax /ɪnˈherɪt(ə)ns tæks/ *noun* tax payable on wealth or property worth above a certain amount and inherited after the death of someone. The current threshold is £285,000, and the estate is liable for 40% tax on the excess amount. Abbreviation **IHT**. Also called **death duty**

initial /ɪˈnɪʃ(ə)l/ *adjective* first or starting ○ *The initial response to the TV advertising has been very good.* ■ *verb* to write your initials on a document to show you have read it and approved ○ *to initial an amendment to a contract* ○ *Please initial the agreement at the place marked with an X.*

'...the founding group has subscribed NKr 14.5m of the initial NKr 30m share capital' [*Financial Times*]

'...career prospects are excellent for someone with potential, and initial salary is negotiable around $45,000 per annum' [*Australian Financial Review*]

initial capital /ɪˌnɪʃ(ə)l ˈkæpɪt(ə)l/ *noun* capital which is used to start a business

initial public offering /ɪˌnɪʃ(ə)l ˌpʌblɪk ˈɒf(ə)rɪŋ/ *noun US* the process of offering shares in a corporation for sale to the public for the first time. Abbreviation **IPO** (NOTE: The UK term is **offer for sale**.)

initials /ɪˈnɪʃ(ə)lz/ *plural noun* a first letters of the words in a name ○ *What do the initials IMF stand for?* ○ *The chairman wrote his initials by each alteration in the contract he was signing.*

initial sales /ɪˌnɪʃ(ə)l ˈseɪlz/ *plural noun* the first sales of a new product

initial yield /ɪˌnɪʃ(ə)l ˈjiːld/ *noun* the estimated yield of an investment fund at the time when it is launched

initiate /ɪˈnɪʃieɪt/ *verb* to start ○ *to initiate discussions*

initiative /ɪˈnɪʃətɪv/ *noun* the decision to start something □ **to take the initiative** to decide to do something

inject /ɪnˈdʒekt/ *verb* □ **to inject capital into a business** to put money into a business

injection /ɪnˈdʒekʃən/ *noun* □ **a capital injection of £100,000** *or* **an injection of £100,000 capital** putting £100,000 into an existing business

injunction /ɪnˈdʒʌŋkʃ(ə)n/ *noun* a court order telling someone not to do something ○ *He got an injunction preventing the company from selling his car.* ○ *The company applied for an injunction to stop their rival from marketing a similar product.*

inland /ˈɪnlənd/ *adjective* inside a country

inland freight charges /ˌɪnlənd ˈfreɪt ˌtʃɑːdʒɪz/ *plural noun* charges for carrying goods from one part of the country to another

Inland Revenue /ˌɪnlənd ˈrevənjuː/ *noun* a former UK government department which dealt with taxes such as income tax, corporation tax, capital gains tax and inheritance tax, but not duties such as Value Added Tax. It merged with the Customs and Excise to form HM Revenue & Customs in 2005. ○ *He received a letter from the Inland Revenue.* (NOTE: The US term is **Internal Revenue Service** or **IRS**.)

in play /ɪn ˈpleɪ/ *adjective* being obviously up for sale or a possible takeover target

input /ˈɪnpʊt/ *verb* □ **to input information** to put data into a computer

inputs /ˈɪnpʊts/ *plural noun* goods or services bought by a company and which may be liable to VAT

input tax /ˈɪnpʊt tæks/ *noun* VAT which is paid by a company on goods or services bought

inquiry office /ɪnˈkwaɪəri ˌɒfɪs/ *noun* an office which members of the public can go to to have their questions answered

inquorate /ɪnˈkwɔːreɪt/ *adjective* without a quorum

COMMENT: If there is a quorum at a meeting, the meeting is said to be 'quorate'; if there aren't enough people present to make a quorum, the meeting is 'inquorate'.

inside /ɪnˈsaɪd/ *adjective, adverb* in, especially in a company's office or building ○ *We do all our design work inside.* ■ *preposition* in ○ *We have a contact inside our rival's production department who gives us very useful information.*

inside director /ˌɪnsaɪd daɪˈrektə/ *noun* a director who works full-time in a corporation, as opposed to an outside director

inside information /ˌɪnsaɪd ˌɪnfə ˈmeɪʃ(ə)n/ *noun* information which is passed from people working in a company to people outside, and which can be valuable to investors in the company

insider /ɪnˈsaɪdə/ *noun* a person who works in an organisation and therefore knows its secrets

COMMENT: In the US, an insider is an officer or director of a company, or an owner of 10 per cent or more of a class of that company's shares. An insider must report any trade to the SEC by the 10th of the month following the transaction.

insider information /ˌɪnsaɪdə ˌɪnfə ˈmeɪʃ(ə)n/ *noun* same as **inside information**

insider trader /ˌɪnsaɪdə ˈtreɪdə/ *noun* a person who carries out insider dealing, i.e. illegal buying or selling of shares by staff of a company or other persons who have secret information about the company's plans

insider trading /ɪnˌsaɪdə ˈtreɪdɪŋ/, **insider buying** /ˌɪnsaɪdə ˈbaɪɪŋ/, **insider dealing** /ɪnˌsaɪdə ˈdiːlɪŋ/ *noun* the illegal buying or selling of shares by staff of a company or other persons who have secret information about the company's plans

inside worker /ˈɪnsaɪd ˌwɜːkə/ *noun* an employee who works in an office or factory

insolvency /ɪnˈsɒlvənsi/ *noun* the fact of not being able to pay debts. Opposite **solvency** □ **he was in a state of insolvency** he could not pay his debts

'…hundreds of thrifts found themselves on the brink of insolvency after a deregulation programme prompted them to enter dangerous financial waters' [*Times*]

insolvent /ɪnˈsɒlvənt/ *adjective* not able to pay debts ○ *The company was declared insolvent.* (NOTE: see note at **insolvency**) □ **he was declared insolvent** he was officially stated to be insolvent

COMMENT: A company is insolvent when its liabilities are higher than its assets; if this happens it must cease trading.

inspect /ɪnˈspekt/ *verb* to examine in detail ○ *to inspect a machine* or *an installation* ○ *Officials from the DTI have come to inspect the accounts.* □ **to inspect products for defects** to look at products in detail to see if they have any defects

inspection /ɪnˈspekʃ(ə)n/ *noun* the close examination of something ○ *to make an inspection* or *to carry out an inspection of a machine* or *an installation* ○ *the inspection of a product for defects* □ **to carry out a tour of inspection** to visit various places, offices or factories to inspect them □ **to issue an inspection order** to order an official inspection

inspection stamp /ɪnˈspekʃən stæmp/ *noun* a stamp placed on something to show it has been inspected

inspector /ɪn'spektə/ *noun* an official who inspects ○ *The inspectors will soon be round to make sure the building is safe.*

inspectorate /ɪn'spekt(ə)rət/ *noun* an authority to which inspectors are responsible

inspector of taxes /ɪn,spektər əv 'tæksɪz/ *noun* in the UK, an official who reports to HM Revenue & Customs and is responsible for issuing tax returns and assessments, agreeing tax liabilities and conducting appeals on matters of tax

inspector of weights and measures /ɪn,spektər əv ,weɪts ən 'meʒəz/ *noun* a government official who inspects weighing machines and goods sold in shops to see if the quantities and weights are correct

instability /,ɪnstə'bɪlɪti/ *noun* the state of being unstable or moving up and down □ **a period of instability in the money markets** a period when currencies fluctuate rapidly

install /ɪn'stɔːl/ *verb* **1.** to set up a piece of machinery or equipment, e.g. a new computer system, so that it can be used **2.** to configure a new computer program to the existing system requirements

installation /,ɪnstə'leɪʃ(ə)n/ *noun* the act of setting up a piece of equipment

installment plan /ɪn'stɔːlmənt plæn/, **installment sales** /ɪn'stɔːlmənt seɪlz/, **installment buying** /ɪn,stɔːlmənt 'baɪɪŋ/, **installment credit** /ɪn,stɔːlmənt 'kredɪt/ *noun US* same as **hire purchase** ○ *to buy a car on the installment plan*

instalment /ɪn'stɔːlmənt/ *noun* a part of a payment which is paid regularly until the total amount is paid ○ *The first instalment is payable on signature of the agreement.* (NOTE: The US spelling is **installment**.) □ **the final instalment is now due** the last of a series of payments should be paid now □ **to pay £25 down and monthly instalments of £20** to pay a first payment of £25 and the rest in payments of £20 each month □ **to miss an instalment** not to pay an instalment at the right time

instant /'ɪnstənt/ *adjective* immediately available ○ *Instant credit is available to current account holders.*

instant access account /,ɪnstənt 'ækses ə,kaʊnt/ *noun* a deposit account which pays interest and from which you can withdraw money immediately without penalty

Institute of Chartered Accountants in England and Wales /,ɪnstɪtjuːt əv ,tʃɑːtəd ə,kaʊntənts ɪn ,ɪŋglənd ən 'weɪlz/ *noun* the largest professional accountancy body in Europe, providing qualification by examinations, ensuring high standards of education and training, and supervising professional conduct. Abbreviation **ICAEW**

Institute of Chartered Accountants in Ireland /,ɪnstɪtjuːt əv ,tʃɑːtəd ə,kaʊntənts ɪn 'aɪələnd/ *noun* the oldest and largest professional body for accountants in Ireland, founded in 1888 with the aims of in promoting best practice in chartered accountancy and maintaining high standards of professionalism among its members. Abbreviation **ICAI**

Institute of Chartered Accountants in Scotland /,ɪnstɪtjuːt əv ,tʃɑːtəd ə,kaʊntənts ɪn 'skɒtlənd/ *noun* the world's oldest professional body for accountants, based in Edinburgh. Abbreviation **ICAS**

institution /,ɪnstɪ'tjuːʃ(ə)n/ *noun* an organisation or society set up for a particular purpose. ◊ **financial institution**

institutional /,ɪnstɪ'tjuːʃ(ə)n(ə)l/ *adjective* relating to an institution, especially a financial institution

'…during the 1970s commercial property was regarded by big institutional investors as an alternative to equities' [*Investors Chronicle*]

institutional buying /,ɪnstɪ tjuːʃ(ə)n(ə)l 'baɪɪŋ/ *noun* the buying of shares by financial institutions

institutional buyout /,ɪnstɪ tjuːʃ(ə)n(ə)l 'baɪaʊt/ *noun* a takeover of a company by a financial institution, which backs a group of managers who will run it. Abbreviation **IBO**

institutional investor /,ɪnstɪ tjuːʃ(ə)n(ə)l ɪn'vestə/ *noun* **1.** a financial institution which invests money in securities **2.** an organisation (such as a pension fund or insurance company) with large sums of money to invest

institutional selling /ˌɪnstɪˈtjuːʃ(ə)n(ə)l ˈselɪŋ/ *noun* the selling of shares by financial institutions

instruction /ɪnˈstrʌkʃən/ *noun* an order which tells what should be done or how something is to be used ○ *She gave instructions to his stockbroker to sell the shares immediately.* □ **to await instructions** to wait for someone to tell you what to do □ **to issue instructions** to tell people what to do

instrument /ˈɪnstrʊmənt/ *noun* **1.** a tool or piece of equipment **2.** a legal document

insufficient funds /ˌɪnsəfɪʃ(ə)nt ˈfʌndz/ *plural noun US* same as **non-sufficient funds**

insurable /ɪnˈʃʊərəb(ə)l/ *adjective* possible to insure

insurable interest /ɪnˌʃʊərəb(ə)l ˈɪntrəst/ *noun* the value of the thing insured which is attributed to the person who is taking out the insurance

insurance /ɪnˈʃʊərəns/ *noun* an agreement that in return for regular payments called 'premiums', a company will pay compensation for loss, damage, injury or death ○ *to take out insurance* ○ *Repairs will be paid for by the insurance.* □ **to take out an insurance against fire** to pay a premium, so that, if a fire happens, compensation will be paid □ **to take out an insurance on the house** to pay a premium, so that, if the house is damaged, compensation will be paid □ **the damage is covered by the insurance** the insurance company will pay for the damage □ **to pay the insurance on a car** to pay premiums to insure a car

insurance agent /ɪnˈʃʊərəns ˌeɪdʒənt/, **insurance broker** /ɪnˈʃʊərəns ˌbrəʊkə/ *noun* a person who arranges insurance for clients

insurance claim /ɪnˈʃʊərəns kleɪm/ *noun* a request to an insurance company to pay compensation for damage or loss

insurance company /ɪnˈʃʊərəns ˌkʌmp(ə)ni/ *noun* a company whose business is insurance

insurance contract /ɪnˈʃʊərəns ˌkɒntrækt/ *noun* an agreement by an insurance company to insure

insurance cover /ɪnˈʃʊərəns ˌkʌvə/ *noun* protection guaranteed by an insurance policy

insurance policy /ɪnˈʃʊərəns ˌpɒlɪsi/ *noun* a document which shows the conditions of an insurance contract

insurance premium /ɪnˈʃʊərəns ˌpriːmiəm/ *noun* an annual payment made by a person or a company to an insurance company

insurance rates /ɪnˈʃʊərəns reɪts/ *plural noun* the amount of premium which has to be paid per £1000 of insurance

insurance salesman /ɪnˈʃʊərəns ˌseɪlzmən/ *noun* a person who encourages clients to take out insurance policies

insure /ɪnˈʃʊə/ *verb* to have a contract with a company whereby, if regular small payments are made, the company will pay compensation for loss, damage, injury or death ○ *to insure someone's life* ○ *to insure baggage against loss* ○ *to insure against loss of earnings* ○ *She was insured for £100,000.* □ **the insured** the person or organisation that will benefit from an insurance □ **the sum insured** the largest amount of money that an insurer will pay under an insurance policy

insured account /ɪnˌʃʊəd əˈkaʊnt/ *noun* an account with a bank which is insured by the customer's insurance

insured money market account /ɪnˌʃʊəd ˈmʌni ˌmɑːkɪt əˌkaʊnt/ *noun* a high-yield account, in which the investor has to deposit a certain minimum sum, which is insured by the provider against capital loss. Abbreviation **IMMA**

insurer /ɪnˈʃʊərə/ *noun* a company which insures (NOTE: For life insurance, UK English prefers to use **assurer**.)

intangible /ɪnˈtændʒɪb(ə)l/ *adjective* not possible to touch

intangible assets /ɪnˌtændʒɪb(ə)l ˈæsets/, **intangible fixed assets** /ɪnˌtændʒɪb(ə)l fɪkst ˈæsets/, **intangibles** /ɪnˈtændʒɪb(ə)lz/ *plural noun* assets that have a value but which cannot be seen, e.g. goodwill or a trademark

integrate /ˈɪntɪgreɪt/ *verb* to link things together to form one whole group

integration /ˌɪntɪˈgreɪʃ(ə)n/ *noun* the act of bringing several businesses together under a central control

COMMENT: In a case of horizontal integration, a large supermarket might take over another smaller supermarket chain; on the other hand, if a supermarket takes over a food packaging company the integration would be vertical.

intent /ɪnˈtent/ *noun* something that someone plans to do

inter- /ɪntə/ *prefix* between □ **inter-company dealings** dealings between two companies in the same group □ **inter-company comparisons** comparing the results of one company with those of another in the same product area

inter-bank /ˌɪntə ˈbæŋk/ *adjective* between banks □ **inter-bank deposits** money which banks deposit with other banks □ **inter-bank rates** rates of interest charged on inter-bank loans

inter-bank loan /ˌɪntə bæŋk ˈləʊn/ *noun* a loan from one bank to another

inter-bank market /ˌɪntə bæŋk ˈmɑːkɪt/ *noun* a market where banks lend to or borrow from each other

inter-dealer broker /ˌɪntə ˈdiːlə ˌbrəʊkə/ *noun* a broker who acts as an intermediary between dealers in government securities

interest /ˈɪntrəst/ *noun* **1.** payment made by a borrower for the use of money, calculated as a percentage of the capital borrowed **2.** money paid as income on investments or loans ○ *to receive interest at 5%* ○ *deposit which yields* or *gives* or *produces* or *bears 5% interest* ○ *account which earns interest at 10%* or *which earns 10% interest* ○ *The bank pays 10% interest on deposits.* ○ *The loan pays 5% interest.* □ **accrual of interest** the automatic addition of interest to capital **3.** a part of the ownership of something, e.g. if you invest money in a company you acquire a financial share or interest in it □ **to acquire a substantial interest in the company** to buy a large number of shares in a company □ **to declare an interest** to state in public that you own shares in a company being discussed or that you are related to someone who can benefit from your contacts ■ *verb* to attract someone's attention ○ *She tried to interest several companies in her new invention.* ○ *The company is trying to interest a wide range of customers in its products.* □ **interested in** paying attention to ○ *The managing director is interested only in increasing profitability.*

interest-bearing account /ˌɪntrəst ˌbeərɪŋ əˈkaʊnt/ *noun* a bank account which gives interest

interest-bearing deposits /ˌɪntrəst ˌbeərɪŋ dɪˈpɒzɪts/ *plural noun* a deposit of money with a financial institution that pays interest on the deposit

interest charges /ˈɪntrəst ˌtʃɑːdʒɪz/ *plural noun* money paid as interest on a loan

interest cover /ˈɪntrəst ˌkʌvə/ *noun* the ability to pay interest payments on a loan

interested party /ˌɪntrestɪd ˈpɑːti/ *noun* a person or company with a financial interest in a company

interest-free credit /ˌɪntrəst friː ˈkredɪt/ *noun* a credit or loan where no interest is paid by the borrower ○ *The company gives its staff interest-free loans.*

interest rate /ˈɪntrəst reɪt/ *noun* a figure which shows the percentage of the capital sum borrowed or deposited which is to be paid as interest. Also called **rate of interest**

interest rate margin /ˈɪntrəst reɪt ˌmɑːdʒɪn/ *noun* the difference between the interest a bank pays on deposits and the interest it charges on loans

interest rate swap /ˈɪntrəst reɪt ˌswɒp/ *noun* an agreement between two companies to exchange borrowings. A company with fixed-interest borrowings might swap them for variable interest borrowings of another company. Also called **plain vanilla swap**

interest-sensitive purchases /ˌɪntrəst ˌsensətɪv ˈpɜːtʃɪsɪz/ *plural noun* purchases such as houses or items bought on hire-purchase, which are influenced by interest rates

interest yield /ˈɪntrəst jiːld/ *noun* a yield on a fixed-interest investment

interface /ˈɪntəfeɪs/ *noun* a point where two groups of people come into contact

interim /ˈɪntərɪm/ *adjective* made, measured or happening in the middle of a period, such as the financial year, and before the final result for the period is available ■ *noun* a statement of interim profits or dividends □ **in the interim** meanwhile, for the time being

'…the company plans to keep its annual dividend unchanged at 7.5 per share, which includes a 3.75 interim payout' [*Financial Times*]

interim dividend /ˌɪntərɪm ˈdɪvɪdend/ *noun* a dividend paid at the end of a half-year

interim payment /ˌɪntərɪm ˈpeɪmənt/ *noun* a payment of part of a dividend

interim report /ˌɪntərɪm rɪˈpɔːt/, **interim statement** /ˌɪntərɪm ˈsteɪtmənt/ *noun* a report given at the end of a half-year

intermediary /ˌɪntəˈmiːdiəri/ *noun* a person who is the link between people or organisations who do not agree or who are negotiating ○ *He refused to act as an intermediary between the two directors.*

intermediate term /ˌɪntəmiːdiət ˈtɜːm/ *noun* a period of one or two years

intermediation /ˌɪntəmiːdiˈeɪʃ(ə)n/ *noun* the arrangement of finance or insurance by an intermediary

internal /ɪnˈtɜːn(ə)l/ *adjective* **1.** inside a company □ **we decided to make an internal appointment** we decided to appoint an existing member of staff to the post, and not bring someone in from outside the company **2.** inside a country or a region

internal audit /ɪnˌtɜːn(ə)l ˈɔːdɪt/ *noun* an audit carried out by a department inside the company

internal audit department /ɪnˌtɜːn(ə)l ˈɔːdɪt dɪˌpɑːtmənt/ *noun* a department of a company which examines the internal accounting controls of that company

internal auditor /ɪnˌtɜːn(ə)l ˈɔːdɪtə/ *noun* a member of staff who audits a company's accounts

internal control /ɪnˌtɜːn(ə)l kənˈtrəʊl/ *noun* a system set up by the management of a company to monitor and control the company's activities

internal growth /ɪnˌtɜːn(ə)l ˈɡrəʊθ/ *noun* the development of a company by growing its existing business with its own finances, as opposed to acquiring other businesses. Also called **organic growth**. Opposite **external growth**

Internal Market /ɪnˌtɜːn(ə)l ˈmɑːkɪt/ *noun* the EU considered as one single market, with no tariff barriers between its member states

internal rate of return /ɪnˌtɜːn(ə)l reɪt əv rɪˈtɜːn/ *noun* an average annual yield of an investment, where the interest earned over a period of time is the same as the original cost of the investment. Abbreviation **IRR**

Internal Revenue Service /ɪnˌtɜːn(ə)l ˈrevənjuː ˌsɜːvɪs/ *noun* in the US, the branch of the federal government charged with collecting the majority of federal taxes. Abbreviation **IRS**

internal trade /ɪnˌtɜːn(ə)l ˈtreɪd/ *noun* trade between various parts of a country. Opposite **external trade**

international /ˌɪntəˈnæʃ(ə)nəl/ *adjective* working between countries

International Bank for Reconstruction and Development /ˌɪntənæʃ(ə)nəl bæŋk fə ˌriːkən ˈstrʌkʃ(ə)n ən dɪˈveləpmənt/ *noun* the official name of the World Bank. Abbreviation **IBRD**

International Commodities Clearing House /ˌɪntənæʃ(ə)nəl kə ˌmɒdɪtiz ˈklɪərɪŋ haʊs/ *noun* a clearing house which deals in settlements of futures contracts in commodities and financial futures. Abbreviation **ICCH**

International Finance Corporation /ˌɪntənæʃ(ə)nəl ˈfaɪnæns ˌkɔːpə reɪʃ(ə)n/ *noun* a subsidiary of the World Bank which makes loans to private companies. Abbreviation **IFC**

International Labour Organization /ˌɪntənæʃ(ə)nəl ˈleɪbə ˌɔːɡə naɪzeɪʃ(ə)n/ *noun* a section of the United Nations which tries to improve working conditions and workers' pay in member countries. Abbreviation **ILO**

international law /ˌɪntənæʃ(ə)nəl ˈlɔː/ *noun* laws referring to the way countries deal with each other

international lawyer /ˌɪntənæʃ(ə)nəl ˈlɔːjə/ *noun* a person who specialises in international law

International Monetary Fund /ˌɪntənæʃ(ə)nəl ˈmʌnɪt(ə)ri ˌfʌnd/ *noun* a type of bank which is part of the United Nations and helps member states in financial difficulties, gives financial advice to members and encourages world trade. Abbreviation **IMF**

International Monetary Market /ˌɪntənæʃ(ə)nəl 'mʌnɪt(ə)ri ˌmɑːkɪt/ *noun* a part of the Chicago Mercantile Exchange dealing in financial futures. Abbreviation **IMM**

international monetary system /ˌɪntənæʃ(ə)nəl 'mʌnɪt(ə)ri ˌsɪstəm/ *noun* methods of controlling and exchanging currencies between countries

international money markets /ˌɪntənæʃ(ə)nəl 'mʌni ˌmɑːkɪts/ *plural noun* markets such as the Euromarket, the international market for lending or borrowing in Eurocurrencies

international money order /ˌɪntənæʃ(ə)nəl 'mʌni ˌɔːdɪə/ *noun* a money order in a foreign currency which is payable to someone living in a foreign country

International Petroleum Exchange /ˌɪntənæʃ(ə)nəl pə 'trəʊliəm ɪksˌtʃeɪndʒ/ *noun* a London commodity exchange dealing in crude oil and natural gas futures. Abbreviation **IPE**

international reserves /ˌɪntə næʃ(ə)nəl rɪ'zɜːvz/ *plural noun* same as **foreign currency reserves**

international trade /ˌɪntənæʃ(ə)nəl 'treɪd/ *noun* trade between different countries

Internet /'ɪntənet/ *noun* the global, public network of computers and telephone links that houses websites, allows email to be sent, and is accessed with the aid of a modem ○ *Much of our business is done on the Internet.* ○ *Internet sales form an important part of our turnover.*

'…they predict a tenfold increase in sales via internet or TV' [*Investors Chronicle*]

'…in two significant decisions, the Securities and Exchange Board of India today allowed trading of shares through the Internet and set a deadline for companies to conform to norms for good corporate governance' [*The Hindu*]

Internet bank /'ɪntənet bæŋk/ *noun* a bank that allows it customers to havie credit in an account on the Internet, and use it to pay for purchases made on the Internet

Internet banking /ˌɪntənet 'bæŋkɪŋ/ *noun* the operation of a bank account over the Internet

Interstate Commerce Commission /ˌɪntəsteɪt 'kɒmɜːs kəˌmɪʃ(ə)n/ *noun US* a federal agency which regulates business activity involving two or more of the states in the US. Abbreviation **ICC**

intervene /ˌɪntə'viːn/ *verb* to try to make a change in a situation in which you have not been involved before □ **to intervene in a dispute** to try to settle a dispute

intervention /ˌɪntə'venʃən/ *noun* the act of becoming involved in a situation in order to change it ○ *the central bank's intervention in the banking crisis*

intervention mechanism /ˌɪntə 'venʃən ˌmekənɪz(ə)m/ *noun* a method used by central banks in maintaining exchange rate parities, e.g. buying or selling foreign currency

intervention price /ˌɪntə'venʃ(ə)n praɪs/ *noun* a price at which the EU will buy farm produce which farmers cannot sell, in order to keep prices high

inter vivos /ˌɪntə 'viːvəʊs/ *phrase* a Latin phrase, 'between living people'

inter vivos trust /ˌɪntə 'viːvəʊs trʌst/ *noun* a trust set up by one person for another living person

intestate /ɪn'testət/ *adjective* □ **to die intestate** to die without having made a will

COMMENT: When someone dies intestate, the property automatically goes to the parents or siblings of an unmarried person or, if married, to the surviving partner, unless there are children.

intraday /'ɪntrədeɪ/ *adjective* within the day ○ *The stock hit a new record of 86 intraday on Friday.*

intraday liquidity /ˌɪntrədeɪ lɪ 'kwɪdɪti/ *noun* availability of cash in the banking system

intrinsic value /ɪnˌtrɪnsɪk 'væljuː/ *noun* a value which exists as part of something, such as the value of an option (for a call option, it is the difference between the current price and the higher striking price)

introduce /ˌɪntrə'djuːs/ *verb* to make someone get to know somebody or something □ **to introduce a client** to bring in a new client and make them known to someone □ **to introduce a new product on the market** to produce a new product and launch it on the market

introduction /ˌɪntrə'dʌkʃ(ə)n/ *noun* **1.** a letter someone get to know another person ○ *I'll give you an intro-duction to the MD – he is an old friend of mine.* **2.** the act of bringing an established company to the stock exchange (i.e. getting permission for the shares to be traded on the stock exchange, used when a company is formed by a demerger from an existing larger company, and no new shares are being offered for sale)

introductory offer /ˌɪntrədʌkt(ə)ri ˈɒfə/ *noun* a special price offered on a new product to attract customers

invalid /ɪnˈvælɪd/ *adjective* not valid or not legal ○ *This permit is invalid.* ○ *The claim has been declared invalid.*

invalidate /ɪnˈvælɪdeɪt/ *verb* to make something invalid ○ *Because the company has been taken over, the contract has been invalidated.*

invalidation /ɪnˌvælɪˈdeɪʃən/ *noun* the act of making invalid

invalidity /ˌɪnvəˈlɪdɪti/ *noun* the fact of being invalid ○ *the invalidity of the contract*

inventory /ˈɪnvənt(ə)ri/ *noun* **1.** *especially US* all the stock or goods in a ware-house or shop ○ *to carry a high inventory* ○ *to aim to reduce inventory* Also called **stock 2.** a list of the contents of a building such as a house for sale or an office for rent ○ *to draw up an inventory of fixtures and fittings* □ **to agree the inventory** to agree that the inventory is correct ■ *verb* to make a list of stock or contents

inventory control /ˈɪnvənt(ə)ri kənˌtrəʊl/ *noun US* same as **stock control**

inventory financing /ˈɪnvənt(ə)ri ˌfaɪnænsɪŋ/ *noun especially US* the use of money from working capital to purchase stock for resale

inventory turnover /ˈɪnvənt(ə)ri ˌtɜːnəʊvə/ *noun especially US* the total value of stock sold during a year, divided by the value of the goods remaining in stock

invest /ɪnˈvest/ *verb* **1.** to put money into shares, bonds, a building society, etc., hoping that it will produce interest and increase in value ○ *He invested all his money in unit trusts.* ○ *She was advised to invest in real estate* or *in government bonds.* □ **to invest abroad** to put money into shares or bonds in overseas countries

2. to spend money on something which you believe will be useful ○ *to invest money in new machinery* ○ *to invest capital in a new factory*

'…we have substantial venture capital to invest in good projects' [*Times*]

investigate /ɪnˈvestɪɡeɪt/ *verb* to examine something which may be wrong ○ *The Serious Fraud Office has been asked to investigate his share dealings.*

investigation /ɪnˌvestɪˈɡeɪʃ(ə)n/ *noun* an examination to find out what is wrong ○ *They conducted an investigation into petty theft in the office.*

investment /ɪnˈvestmənt/ *noun* **1.** the placing of money so that it will produce interest and increase in value ○ *They called for more government investment in new industries.* ○ *She was advised to make investments in oil companies.* **2.** a share, bond or piece of property bought in the hope that it will produce more money than was used to buy it □ **he is trying to protect his investments** he is trying to make sure that the money he has invested is not lost

'…investment trusts, like unit trusts, consist of portfolios of shares and there-fore provide a spread of investments' [*Investors Chronicle*]

'…investment companies took the view that prices had reached rock bottom and could only go up' [*Lloyd's List*]

investment adviser /ɪnˈvestmənt ədˌvaɪzə/ *noun* a person who advises people on what investments to make

investment bank /ɪnˈvestmənt bæŋk/ *noun US* a bank which deals with the underwriting of new issues, and advises corporations on their financial affairs (NOTE: The UK term is **issuing house**.)

investment environment /ɪnˈvestmənt ɪnˌvaɪrənmənt/ *noun* the general economic situation in which an investment is made

investment fund /ɪnˈvestmənt fʌnd/ *noun* a fund that invests in start-up companies or other new projects

investment grant /ɪnˈvestmənt ɡrɑːnt/ *noun* a government grant to a company to help it to invest in new machinery

investment income /ɪn'vestmənt ˌɪnkʌm/ *noun* income from investments, e.g. interest and dividends. Compare **earned income**

investment magazine /ɪn'vestmənt ˌmæɡəziːn/ *noun* a magazine dealing with shares, unit trusts and other possible investments

Investment Management Regulatory Organisation /ɪnˌvestmənt ˌmænɪdʒmənt 'reɡjʊlət(ə)ri ˌɔːɡənaɪzeɪʃ(ə)n/ *noun* a self-regulatory organisation which regulates managers of investment funds, such as pension funds, now part of the FSA. Abbreviation **IMRO**

investment trust /ɪn'vestmənt trʌst/ *noun* a company whose shares can be bought on the stock exchange and whose business is to make money by buying and selling stocks and shares

investor /ɪn'vestə/ *noun* a person who invests money

investor protection /ɪn'vestə prəˌtekʃ(ə)n/ *noun* legislation to protect small investors from unscrupulous investment brokers and advisers

Investors in Industry /ɪnˌvestəz ɪn 'ɪndəstri/ *plural noun* a finance group partly owned by the big British High Street banks, providing finance especially to smaller companies. Abbreviation **3i**

invisible assets /ɪnˌvɪzɪb(ə)l 'æsets/ *plural noun* US same as **intangible assets**

invisible earnings /ɪnˌvɪzɪb(ə)l 'ɜːnɪŋz/ *plural noun* foreign currency earned by a country by providing services, receiving interests or dividends, but not by selling goods

invisible exports /ɪnˌvɪzɪb(ə)l 'ekspɔːts/ *plural noun* services, e.g. banking, insurance and tourism, that are provided to customers overseas and paid for in foreign currency. Opposite **visible exports**

invisible imports /ɪnˌvɪzɪb(ə)l 'ɪmpɔːts/ *plural noun* services that overseas companies provide to domestic customers who pay for them in local currency. Opposite **visible imports**

invisibles /ɪn'vɪzɪb(ə)lz/ *plural noun* invisible imports and exports

invisible trade /ɪnˌvɪzɪb(ə)l 'treɪd/ *noun* trade involving invisible imports and exports. Opposite **visible trade**

invitation /ˌɪnvɪ'teɪʃ(ə)n/ *noun* an act of asking someone to do something ○ *to issue an invitation to someone to join the board* ○ *They advertised the invitation to tender for a contract.*

invite /ɪn'vaɪt/ *verb* to ask someone to do something, or to ask for something ○ *to invite someone to join the board* ○ *to invite shareholders to subscribe to a new issue* ○ *to invite tenders for a contract*

invoice /'ɪnvɔɪs/ *noun* a note asking for payment for goods or services supplied ○ *your invoice dated November 10th* ○ *to make out an invoice for £250* ○ *to settle* or *to pay an invoice* ○ *They sent in their invoice six weeks late.* □ **the total is payable within thirty days of invoice** the total sum has to be paid within thirty days of the date on the invoice ■ *verb* to send an invoice to someone ○ *to invoice a customer* □ **we invoiced you on November 10th** we sent you the invoice on November 10th

invoice clerk /'ɪnvɔɪs klɑːk/ *noun* an office employee who deals with invoices

invoice discounting /'ɪnvɔɪs ˌdɪskaʊntɪŋ/ *noun* a method of obtaining early payment of invoices by selling them at a discount to a company which will receive payment of the invoices when they are paid. The debtor is not informed of this arrangement, as opposed to factoring, where the debtor is informed.

invoice price /'ɪnvɔɪs praɪs/ *noun* the price as given on an invoice, including any discount and VAT

invoicing /'ɪnvɔɪsɪŋ/ *noun* the work of sending invoices ○ *All our invoicing is done by computer.* □ **invoicing in triplicate** the preparation of three copies of invoices

invoicing department /'ɪnvɔɪsɪŋ dɪˌpɑːtmənt/ *noun* the department in a company which deals with preparing and sending invoices

involuntary /ɪn'vɒlənt(ə)ri/ *adjective* not done willingly or deliberately

involuntary bankruptcy /ɪnˌvɒlənt(ə)ri 'bæŋkrʌptsi/ *noun US* an application by creditors to have a person or corporation made bankrupt (NOTE: The UK term is **compulsory winding up**.)

inward /ˈɪnwəd/ *adjective* towards the home country

inward bill /ˌɪnwəd ˈbɪl/ *noun* a bill of lading for goods arriving in a country

inward investment /ˌɪnwəd ɪnˈvestmənt/ *noun* an investment from outside a country, as when a foreign company decides to set up a new factory there

inward mission /ˌɪnwəd ˈmɪʃ(ə)n/ *noun* a visit to your home country by a group of foreign businesspeople

IOU /ˌaɪ əʊ ˈjuː/ *noun* 'I owe you', a signed document promising that you will pay back money borrowed ○ *to pay a pile of IOUs*

IPE *abbreviation* International Petroleum Exchange

IPO *abbreviation* initial public offering

IRA /ˈaɪrə/ *abbreviation US* Individual Retirement Account

IRR *abbreviation* internal rate of return

irrecoverable /ˌɪrɪˈkʌv(ə)rəb(ə)l/ *adjective* not possible to get back

irrecoverable debt /ɪrɪˌkʌv(ə)rəb(ə)l ˈdet/ *noun* a debt which will never be paid

irredeemable /ɪrɪˈdiːməb(ə)l/ *adjective* not possible to redeem

irredeemable bond /ɪrɪˌdiːməb(ə)l ˈbɒnd/ *noun* a government bond which has no date of maturity and which therefore provides interest but can never be redeemed at full value

irregular /ɪˈregjʊlə/ *adjective* not correct or not done in the correct way ○ ○ *This procedure is highly irregular.*

irregularities /ɪˌregjʊˈlærɪtiz/ *plural noun* things which are not done in the correct way and which are possibly illegal ○ *to investigate irregularities in the share dealings*

'…the group, which asked for its shares to be suspended last week after the discovery of accounting irregularities, is expected to update investors about its financial predicament by the end of this week' [*Times*]

irrevocable /ɪˈrevəkəb(ə)l/ *adjective* unchangeable

irrevocable acceptance /ɪˌrevəkəb(ə)l əkˈseptəns/ *noun* an acceptance which cannot be withdrawn

irrevocable letter of credit /ɪˌrevəkəb(ə)l ˌletər əv ˈkredɪt/ *noun* a letter of credit which cannot be cancelled or changed, except if agreed between the two parties involved

IRS *abbreviation US* Internal Revenue Service

IS *abbreviation* income support

ISA /ˈaɪsə/ *abbreviation* Individual Savings Account

issuance /ˈɪʃuəns/ *noun* an action of issuing new shares or new bonds

issue /ˈɪʃuː/ *noun* an act of offering new shares for sale ■ *verb* to put out or to give out ○ *to issue a letter of credit* ○ *to issue shares in a new company* ○ *to issue a writ against someone*

'…the rights issue should overcome the cash flow problems' [*Investors Chronicle*]

'…the company said that its recent issue of 10.5 per cent convertible preference shares at A\$8.50 a share has been oversubscribed' [*Financial Times*]

issued capital /ˌɪʃuːd ˈkæpɪt(ə)l/ *noun* an amount of capital which is given out as shares to shareholders

issued price /ˌɪʃuːd ˈpraɪs/, **issue price** /ˈɪʃuː praɪs/ *noun* the price of shares in a new company when they are offered for sale for the first time

issuer /ˈɪʃuə/ *noun* a financial institution that issues credit and debit cards and maintains the systems for billing and payment

issuing /ˈɪʃuɪŋ/ *adjective* organising an issue of shares

IT *abbreviation* information technology

item /ˈaɪtəm/ *noun* **1.** something for sale □ **we are holding orders for out-of-stock items** we are holding orders for goods which are not in stock ○ *Please find enclosed an order for the following items from your catalogue.* **2.** a piece of information ○ *items on a balance sheet* □ **item of expenditure** goods or services which have been paid for and appear in the accounts **3.** a point on a list □ **we will now take item four on the agenda** we will now discuss the fourth point on the agenda

itemise /ˈaɪtəmaɪz/, **itemize** *verb* to make a detailed list of things ○ *Itemising the sales figures will take about two days.*

itemised account /ˌaɪtəmaɪzd əˈkaʊnt/ *noun* a detailed record of money paid or owed

itemised invoice /ˌaɪtəmaɪzd ˈɪnvɔɪs/ *noun* an invoice which lists each item separately

itemised statement /ˌaɪtəmaɪzd ˈsteɪtmənt/ *noun* a bank statement where each transaction is recorded in detail

J

J curve /ˈdʒeɪ kɜːv/ *noun* a line on a graph shaped like a letter 'J', with an initial short fall, followed by a longer rise, used to describe the effect of a falling exchange rate on a country's balance of trade

jeep mortgage /ˈdʒiːp ˌmɔːgɪdʒ/ *noun US* same as **graduated payment mortgage** (*informal*)

job /dʒɒb/ *noun* **1.** an order being worked on ○ *We are working on six jobs at the moment.* ○ *The shipyard has a big job starting in August.* **2.** regular paid work ○ *She is looking for a job in the computer industry.* ○ *He lost his job when the factory closed.* ○ *Thousands of jobs will be lost if the factories close down.* □ **to give up your job** to resign or retire from your work □ **to look for a job** to try to find work □ **to retire from your job** to leave work and take a pension □ **to be out of a job** to have no work

'…he insisted that the tax advantages he directed toward small businesses will help create jobs' [*Toronto Star*]

job analysis /ˈdʒɒb əˌnæləsɪs/ *noun* a detailed examination and report on the duties involved in a job

jobber /ˈdʒɒbə/ *noun* **1.** □ (**stock**) **jobber** formerly on the London Stock Exchange, a person who bought and sold shares from other traders **2.** *US* a wholesaler

jobbing /ˈdʒɒbɪŋ/ *noun* □ (**stock**) **jobbing** formerly on the London Stock Exchange, the business of buying and selling shares from other traders

job classification /ˈdʒɒb klæsɪfɪˌkeɪʃ(ə)n/ *noun* the process of describing jobs listed in various groups

job creation scheme /ˌdʒɒb kriˈeɪʃ(ə)n ˌskiːm/ *noun* a government-backed scheme to make work for the unemployed

job cuts /ˈdʒɒb kʌts/ *plural noun* reductions in the number of jobs

job description /ˈdʒɒb dɪˌskrɪpʃən/ *noun* a description of what a job consists of and what skills are needed for it ○ *The letter enclosed an application form and a job description.*

job evaluation /ˈdʒɒb ɪvæljuˌeɪʃ(ə)n/ *noun* the process of examining different jobs within an organisation to see what skills and qualifications are needed to carry them out

jobless /ˈdʒɒbləs/ *plural noun* people with no jobs, the unemployed (NOTE: takes a plural verb)

'…the contradiction between the jobless figures and latest economic review' [*Sunday Times*]

job lot /ˌdʒɒb ˈlɒt/ *noun* **1.** a group of miscellaneous items sold together ○ *They sold the household furniture as a job lot.* **2.** a small parcel of shares traded on a stock exchange

job opportunities /ˈdʒɒb ɒpəˌtjuːnɪtiz/ *plural noun* new jobs which are available ○ *The increase in export orders has created hundreds of job opportunities.*

job performance /ˈdʒɒb pəˌfɔːməns/ *noun* the degree to which a job is done well or badly

job satisfaction /ˈdʒɒb sætɪsˌfækʃən/ *noun* an employee's feeling that he or she is happy at work and pleased with the work he or she does

job security /ˈdʒɒb sɪˌkjʊərɪti/ *noun* **1.** the likelihood that an employee will keep his or her job for a long time or until retirement **2.** an employee's feeling that he has a right to keep his job, or that he will never be made redundant

job specification /'dʒɒb ˌspesɪfɪ keɪʃ(ə)n/ *noun* a very detailed description of what is involved in a job

job title /'dʒɒb ˌtaɪt(ə)l/ *noun* the name given to the person who does a particular job ○ *Her job title is 'Chief Buyer'.*

joint /dʒɔɪnt/ *adjective* **1.** carried out or produced together with others ○ *a joint undertaking* **2.** one of two or more people who work together or who are linked ○ *They are joint beneficiaries of the will.* ○ *She and her brother are joint managing directors.* ○ *The two countries are joint signatories of the treaty.*

joint account /'dʒɔɪnt əˌkaʊnt/ *noun* a bank or building society account shared by two people ○ *Many married couples have joint accounts so that they can pay for household expenses.*

joint-life annuity /'dʒɔɪnt laɪf əˌnjuəti/ *noun* an annuity that continues until both parties have died. They are attractive to married couples as they ensure that the survivor has an income for the rest of his or her life.

jointly /'dʒɔɪntli/ *adverb* together with one or more other people ○ *to own a property jointly* ○ *to manage a company jointly* ○ *They are jointly liable for damages.* □ **jointly and severally liable** liable both as a group and as individuals

joint management /ˌdʒɔɪnt 'mænɪdʒ mənt/ *noun* management done by two or more people

joint ownership /ˌdʒɔɪnt 'əʊnəʃɪp/ *noun* the owning of a property by several owners

joint-stock bank /ˌdʒɔɪnt 'stɒk ˌbæŋk/ *noun* a bank which is a public company quoted on the stock exchange

joint-stock company /'dʒɔɪnt stɒk ˌkʌmp(ə)ni/ *noun* formerly, a public company in the UK whose shares were owned by very many people. Now called a Public Limited Company or Plc.

joint venture /ˌdʒɔɪnt 'ventʃə/ *noun* a situation where two or more companies join together for one specific large business project

journal /'dʒɜːn(ə)l/ *noun* a book with the account of sales and purchases made each day

judge /dʒʌdʒ/ *noun* a person who decides in a legal case ○ *The judge sent him to prison for embezzlement.*

judgement lien /'dʒʌdʒmənt ˌliːən/ *noun* a court order putting a lien on the property of a judgement debtor

judgment /'dʒʌdʒmənt/, **judgement** *noun* a legal decision or official decision of a court

judgment debtor /'dʒʌdʒmənt ˌdetə/ *noun* a debtor who has been ordered by a court to pay a debt

judicial /dʒuːˈdɪʃ(ə)l/ *adjective* referring to the law

judicial processes /dʒuːˌdɪʃ(ə)l 'prəʊsesɪz/ *plural noun* the ways in which the law works

judicial review /dʒuːˌdɪʃ(ə)l rɪˈvjuː/ *noun* **1.** the examination of a case a second time by a higher court because a lower court has acted wrongly **2.** the examination of administrative decisions by a court

jumbo CD /ˌdʒʌmbəʊ ˌsiː 'diː/ *noun* a certificate of deposit for a very large amount of money which is bought as an investment

jump /dʒʌmp/ *noun* a sudden rise ○ *a jump in the cost-of-living index* ○ *There was a jump in unemployment figures in December.* ■ *verb* to go up suddenly ○ *Oil prices have jumped since the war started.* ○ *Share values jumped on the stock exchange.*

jumpy /'dʒʌmpi/ *adjective* nervous or excited □ **the market is jumpy** the stock market is nervous and share prices are likely to fluctuate

junior /'dʒuːniə/ *adjective* less important than something else

junior capital /ˌdʒuːniə 'kæpɪt(ə)l/ *noun* capital in the form of shareholders' equity, which is repaid only after secured loans called 'senior capital' have been paid if the firm goes into liquidation

junior mortgage /ˌdʒuːniə 'mɔːɡɪdʒ/ *noun* a second mortgage

junior partner /ˌdʒuːniə 'pɑːtnə/ *noun* a person who has a small part of the shares in a partnership

junior security /ˌdʒuːniə sɪˈkjʊərɪti/ *noun* a security which is repaid after other securities

junior staff /ˌdʒuːniə ˈstɑːf/ *noun* people in less important positions in a company

junk /dʒʌŋk/ *noun* rubbish, useless items ○ *You should throw away all that junk.*

junk bond /ˈdʒʌŋk bɒnd/ *noun* a high-interest bond raised as a debenture on the security of a company which is the subject of a takeover bid

'…the big US textile company is running deep in the red, its junk bonds are trading as low as 33 cents on the dollar' [*Wall Street Journal*]

jurisdiction /ˌdʒʊərɪsˈdɪkʃən/ *noun* □ **within the jurisdiction of the court** in the legal power of a court

K

K *abbreviation* one thousand □ **'salary: £20K+'** salary more than £20,000 per annum

keen /kiːn/ *adjective* **1.** eager or active □ **keen competition** strong competition ○ *We are facing some keen competition from European manufacturers.* □ **keen demand** wide demand ○ *There is a keen demand for home computers.* **2.** □ **keen prices** prices which are kept low so as to be competitive ○ *Our prices are the keenest on the market.*

keep /kiːp/ *verb* **1.** to do what is necessary for something □ **to keep an appointment** to be there when you said you would be **2.** to hold items for sale or for information □ **to keep someone's name on file** to have someone's name on a list for reference **3.** to hold things at some level ○ *to keep spending to a minimum* ○ *We must keep our mailing list up to date.* ○ *The price of oil has kept the pound at a high level.* ○ *Lack of demand for the product has kept prices down.* (NOTE: **keeping – kept**)

keep back *phrasal verb* to hold on to something which you could give to someone ○ *to keep back information* or *to keep something back from someone* ○ *to keep £10 back from someone's salary*
keep up *phrasal verb* to hold at a certain high level ○ *We must keep up the turnover in spite of the recession.* ○ *She kept up a rate of sixty words per minute for several hours.*

Keogh plan /ˈkiːəʊ ˌplæn/ *noun US* a private pension plan allowing self-employed businesspeople and professionals to set up pension and retirement plans for themselves

kerb market /ˈkɜːb ˌmɑːkɪt/, **kerb trading** /ˈkɜːb ˌtreɪdɪŋ/ *noun* an unoffi-cial after-hours market in shares, bonds or commodities

key /kiː/ *noun* the part of a computer or typewriter which you press with your fingers ○ *There are sixty-four keys on the keyboard.* ■ *adjective* important ○ *a key factor* ○ *key industries* ○ *key personnel* ○ *a key member of our management team* ○ *She has a key post in the organisation.* ○ *We don't want to lose any key staff in the reorganisation.*

'…he gave up the finance job in September to devote more time to his global responsibilities as chairman and to work more closely with key clients' [*Times*]

key holding /ˌkiː ˈhəʊldɪŋ/ *noun* an important block of shares owned by a single investor, which is large enough to influence the decisions of the board of directors

key money /ˈkiː ˌmʌni/ *noun* a premium paid when taking over the keys of a flat or office which you are renting

key-person insurance /ˈkiː pɜːs(ə)n ɪnˌʃʊərəns/ *noun* an insurance policy taken out to cover the costs of replacing an employee who is particularly impor-tant to an organisation if he or she dies or is ill for a long time

key rate /ˈkiː reɪt/ *noun* an interest rate which gives the basic rate on which other rates are calculated, e.g. the former bank base rate in the UK, or the Federal Reserve's discount rate in the USA

kickback /ˈkɪkbæk/ *noun* an illegal commission paid to someone, especially a government official, who helps in a busi-ness deal

kicker /ˈkɪkə/ *noun* a special induce-ment to buy a bond, e.g. making it convertible to shares at a preferential rate (*informal*)

kill /kɪl/ *verb* □ **to kill an order** to stop an order taking place after it has been given (*informal*) ○ *'Kill that order' he shouted, but it was too late.*

killing /ˈkɪlɪŋ/ *noun* a huge profit (*informal*) ○ *He made a killing on the stock market.*

kina /ˈkiːnə/ *noun* a unit of currency used in Papua New Guinea

kind /kaɪnd/ *noun* a sort or type ○ *The printer produces two kinds of printout.* ○ *Our drinks machine has three kinds of cold drinks.* □ **payment in kind** payment made by giving goods or food, but not money

kip /kɪp/ *noun* a unit of currency used in Laos

kite /kaɪt/ *noun* □ **to fly a kite** to put forward a proposal to try to interest people ■ *verb* **1.** *US* to write cheques on one account which may not be able to honour them and deposit them in another, withdrawing money from the second account before the cheques are cleared **2.** *US* to write cheques on one account and deposit them in a second account on the last day of the accounting period, thus showing the amount twice in the company's books, since the sum will not yet have been debited from the first account **3.** *US* to write a cheque for an amount which is higher than the total amount of money in the account, then deposit enough to cover the cheque **4.** to use stolen credit cards or cheque books

kite flier /ˈkaɪt ˌflaɪə/ *noun* a person who tries to impress people by putting forward a proposal

kite-flying /ˈkaɪt ˌflaɪɪŋ/ *noun* the practice of trying to impress people by putting forward grand plans

kitty /ˈkɪti/ *noun* money which has been collected by a group of people to be used later, such as for an office party ○ *We each put £5 into the kitty.*

knock /nɒk/ *verb* □ **to knock the competition** to hit competing firms hard by vigorous selling

knock down *phrasal verb* □ **to knock something down to a bidder** to sell something to somebody at an auction ○ *The furniture was knocked down to him for £100.*

knock off *phrasal verb* to reduce a price by a particular amount ○ *She knocked £10 off the price for cash.*

knockdown price /ˌnɒkdaʊn ˈpraɪs/ *noun* a very low price ○ *He sold me the car at a knockdown price.*

knock for knock /ˌnɒk fə ˈnɒk/ *noun* an arrangement between motor insurance companies where each company pays for its own clients' claims and does not claim against the other company

knock-on effect /ˈnɒk ɒn ɪˌfekt/ *noun* the effect which an action will have on other situations ○ *The strike by customs officers has had a knock-on effect on car production by slowing down exports of cars.*

koruna /kəˈruːnə/ *noun* a unit of currency used in the Czech Republic and Slovakia

krona /ˈkrəʊnə/ *noun* a unit of currency used in Sweden and Iceland

krone /ˈkrəʊnə/ *noun* a unit of currency used in Denmark and Norway

kroon /kruːn/ *noun* a unit of currency used in Estonia (NOTE: The plural is **krooni.**)

krugerrand /ˈkruːgərænd/ *noun* a gold coin weighing one ounce, minted in South Africa

kuna /ˈkuːnə/ *noun* a unit of currency used in Croatia

kwacha /ˈkwɑːtʃə/ *noun* a unit of currency used in Malawi and Zambia

kwanza /ˈkwænzə/ *noun* a unit of currency used in Angola

kyat /kiˈɑːt/ *noun* a unit of currency used in Myanmar (formerly Burma)

L

L *US* a measurement of money supply, calculated as M3 (broad money supply), plus Treasury bills, bonds and commercial paper

labour /'leɪbə/ *noun* **1.** heavy work (NOTE: The US spelling is **labor.**) □ **to charge for materials and labour** to charge for both the materials used in a job and also the hours of work involved □ **labour is charged at £15 an hour** each hour of work costs £15 **2.** workers, the workforce ○ *We will need to employ more labour if production is to be increased.* ○ *The costs of labour are rising in line with inflation.* (NOTE: The US spelling is **labor.**)

'...the possibility that British goods will price themselves back into world markets is doubtful as long as sterling labour costs continue to rise faster than in competitor countries' [*Sunday Times*]

labour costs /'leɪbə kɒsts/ *plural noun* the cost of the employees employed to make a product, not including materials or overheads

labour dispute /'leɪbə dɪ,spjuːt/ *noun* a conflict or disagreement between employer and employees or between the groups who represent them

labour force /'leɪbə fɔːs/ *noun* all the employees in a company or in an area ○ *The management has made an increased offer to the labour force.* ○ *We are opening a new factory in the Far East because of the cheap local labour force.*

'70 per cent of Australia's labour force is employed in service activity' [*Australian Financial Review*]

labour-intensive industry /,leɪbər ɪn,tensɪv 'ɪndəstri/ *noun* an industry which needs large numbers of employees and where labour costs are high in relation to turnover

labour laws /'leɪbə lɔːz/ *plural noun* laws concerning the employment of workers

labour market /'leɪbə ,mɑːkɪt/ *noun* the number of people who are available for work ○ *25,000 school-leavers have just come on to the labour market.*

labour relations /'leɪbə rɪ,leɪʃ(ə)nz/ *plural noun* relations between management and employees ○ *The company has a history of bad labour relations.*

lack /læk/ *noun* the fact of not having enough □ **lack of funds** not enough money ○ *The project was cancelled because of lack of funds.* ■ *verb* not to have enough of something ○ *The company lacks capital.* ○ *The industry lacks skilled staff.*

ladder /'lædə/ *noun* **1.** a series of different levels through which an employee may progress **2.** an investment portfolio consisting of bonds with a series of maturity dates from very short-dated to long-dated

laddering /'lædərɪŋ/ *noun US* **1.** the action of repeatedly buying shares in a newly launched corporation so as to force up the price, then selling the whole investment at a profit **2.** the action of making a series of investments which mature at different times, cashing each one at maturity and then reinvesting the proceeds

lading /'leɪdɪŋ/ *noun* the work of putting goods on a ship

Laffer curve /'læfə kɜːv/ *noun* a chart showing that cuts in tax rates increase output in the economy. Alternatively, increases in tax rates initially produce more revenue and then less as the economy slows down.

lag /læg/ *verb* to be behind or to be slower than something

lagging indicator /'lægɪŋ ˌɪndɪkeɪtə/ *noun* an indicator which shows a change in economic trends later than other indicators, e.g. the gross national product. Opposite **leading indicator**

laissez-faire economy /ˌleseɪ 'feər ɪ ˌkɒnəmɪ/ *noun* an economy where the government does not interfere because it believes it is right to let the economy run itself

lakh /læk/ *noun* (*in India*) one hundred thousand (NOTE: Ten lakh equal one crore.)

lame duck /ˌleɪm 'dʌk/ *noun* a company which is in financial difficulties ○ *The government has refused to help lame duck companies.*

land /lænd/ *noun* an area of earth ■ *verb* **1.** to put goods or passengers on to land after a voyage by sea or by air ○ *The ship landed some goods at Mombasa.* ○ *The plane stopped for thirty minutes at the local airport to land passengers and mail.* **2.** to come down to earth after a flight ○ *The plane landed ten minutes late.*

Land /lɑːnt/ *noun* one of the administrative states in Germany

land agent /'lænd ˌeɪdʒənt/ *noun* a person who runs a farm or a large area of land for the owner

landed costs /ˌlændɪd 'kɒsts/ *plural noun* the costs of goods which have been delivered to a port, unloaded, and passed through customs

Landeszentralbank *noun* the central bank in one of the German states (Länder)

landing /'lændɪŋ/ *noun* the arrival of a plane on land or the arrival of a passenger on land

landing charges /'lændɪŋ ˌtʃɑːdʒɪz/ *plural noun* payments for putting goods on land and paying customs duties

landing order /'lændɪŋ ˌɔːdə/ *noun* a permit which allows goods to be unloaded into a bonded warehouse without paying customs duty

landlord /'lændlɔːd/ *noun* a person or company which owns a property which is let

land register /'lænd ˌredʒɪstə/ *noun* a list of pieces of land, showing who owns each and what buildings are on it

land registration /'lænd redʒɪˌstreɪʃ(ə)n/ *noun* a system of registering land and its owners

land tax /'lænd tæks/ *noun* a tax on the amount of land owned

lapse /læps/ *noun* □ **a lapse of time** a period of time which has passed ■ *verb* to stop being valid, or to stop being active ○ *The guarantee has lapsed.* ○ *The takeover bid was allowed to lapse when only 13% of the shareholders accepted the offer.* □ **to let an offer lapse** to allow time to pass so that an offer is no longer valid

lapsed option /ˌlæpst 'ɒpʃən/ *noun* an option which has not been taken up, and now has expired

lapsed policy /ˌlæpst 'pɒlɪsi/ *noun* an insurance policy which has been terminated because premiums have not been paid

large-sized /'lɑːdʒ saɪzd/ *adjective* big, of a very large size

large-sized company /ˌlɑːdʒ saɪzd 'kʌmp(ə)ni/ *noun* a company which has a turnover of more than £5.75m or employs more than 250 staff

last /lɑːst/ *adjective, adverb* coming at the end of a series ○ *Out of a queue of twenty people, I was served last.* ○ *This is our last board meeting before we move to our new offices.* ○ *We finished the last items in the order just two days before the promised delivery date.*

last in first out /ˌlɑːst ɪn ˌfɜːst 'aʊt/ *phrase* **1.** a redundancy policy using the principle that the people who have been most recently appointed are the first to be made redundant **2.** an accounting method where stock is valued at the price of the earliest purchases. Abbreviation **LIFO.** Compare **first in first out**

last quarter /ˌlɑːst 'kwɔːtə/ *noun* a period of three months at the end of the financial year

last trading day /lɑːst 'treɪdɪŋ/ *adjective, adverb* the last day when stock exchange trading takes place in an account, or the last day when futures trading takes place relating to a certain delivery month

lat /læt/ *noun* a unit of currency used in Latvia

launch /lɔːntʃ/ *verb* to put a company on the stock exchange for the first time ■

noun the act of putting a company on the stock exchange for the first time

launder /'lɔːndə/ *verb* to pass illegal profits, money from selling drugs, money which has not been taxed, etc., into the banking system ○ *to launder money through an offshore bank*

'…it has since emerged that the bank was being used to launder drug money and some of its executives have been given lengthy jail sentences' [*Times*]

law /lɔː/ *noun* a rule governing some aspect of human activity made and enforced by the state □ **(the) law** all the laws that are in force in a country considered as a body or system

lawful /'lɔːf(ə)l/ *adjective* acting within the law □ **lawful practice** action which is permitted by the law □ **lawful trade** trade which is allowed by law

law of diminishing returns /,lɔː əv dɪ,mɪnɪʃɪŋ rɪ'tɜːnz/ *noun* a general rule that as more factors of production such as land, labour, and capital are added to the existing factors, so the amount they produce is proportionately smaller

law of supply and demand /,lɔː əv sə,plaɪ ən dɪ'mɑːnd/ *noun* a general rule that the amount of a product which is available is related to the needs of potential customers

lawsuit /'lɔːsuːt/ *noun* a case brought to a court □ **to bring a lawsuit against someone** to tell someone to appear in court to settle an argument □ **to defend a lawsuit** to appear in court to state your case

lawyer /'lɔːjə/ *noun* a person who has studied law and practises law as a profession

lay off *phrasal verb* **1.** to dismiss employees for a time until more work is available ○ *The factory laid off half its employees because of lack of orders.* **2.** *especially US* to dismiss employees permanently □ **to lay off risks** to protect oneself against risk in one investment by making other investments

'…the company lost $52 million last year, and has laid off close to 2,000 employees' [*Toronto Star*]

lay out *phrasal verb* to spend money ○ *We had to lay out half our cash budget on equipping the new factory.*

LBO *abbreviation* leveraged buyout

L/C *abbreviation* letter of credit

LCE *abbreviation* London Commodity Exchange

LDC *abbreviation* **1.** least developed country **2.** less developed country

LDT *abbreviation* licensed deposit-taker

lead /liːd/ *noun* **1.** information which may lead to a sale ○ *It has been difficult starting selling in this territory with no leads to follow up.* ○ *I was given some useful leads by the sales rep who used to cover this territory.* **2.** a prospective purchaser who is the main decision-maker when buying a product or service ■ *adjective* most important, in the front

lead bank /,liːd 'bæŋk/ *noun* the main bank in a loan syndicate

leader /'liːdə/ *noun* **1.** a product which sells best **2.** an important share, one which is often bought or sold on the stock exchange

leading /'liːdɪŋ/ *adjective* **1.** most important ○ *Leading industrialists feel the end of the recession is near.* ○ *Leading shares rose on the stock exchange.* ○ *Leading shareholders in the company forced a change in management policy.* ○ *They are the leading company in the field.* **2.** which comes first

leading indicator /,liːdɪŋ 'ɪndɪkeɪtə/ *noun* an indicator such as manufacturing order books which shows a change in economic trends earlier than other indicators. Opposite **lagging indicator**

lead manager /,liːd 'mænɪdʒə/ *noun* a person who organises a syndicate of underwriters for a new issue of securities

lead time /'liːd taɪm/ *noun* **1.** the time between deciding to place an order and receiving the product ○ *The lead time on this item is more than six weeks.* **2.** the time between the start of a task and its completion

lead underwriter /,liːd 'ʌndəraɪtə/ *noun* an underwriting firm which organises the underwriting of a share issue (NOTE: The US term is **managing underwriter**.)

Learning and Skills Council /,lɜːnɪŋ ən 'skɪlz ,kaʊnsəl/ *noun* a government organisation responsible for the education and training of people over the age of 16

learning curve /'lɜːnɪŋ kɜːv/ *noun* **1.** a process of learning something that starts slowly and then becomes faster **2.** a line on a graph which shows the relationship between experience in doing something and competence at carrying it out **3.** a diagram or graph that represents the way in which people gain knowledge or experience over time (NOTE: A steep learning curve represents a situation where people learn a great deal in a short time; a shallow curve represents a slower learning process. The curve eventually levels out, representing the time when the knowledge gained is being consolidated.) **4.** the decrease in the effort required to produce each single item when the total number of items produced is doubled (NOTE: The concept of the learning curve has its origin in productivity research in the aircraft industry of the 1930s, when it was discovered that the time and effort needed to assemble an aircraft decreased by 20% each time the total number produced doubled.)

lease /liːs/ *noun* **1.** a written contract for letting or renting a building, a piece of land or a piece of equipment for a period against payment of a fee ○ *to rent office space on a twenty-year lease* □ **the lease expires next year** *or* **the lease runs out next year** the lease comes to an end next year □ **on expiration of the lease** when the lease comes to an end **2.** □ **to hold an oil lease in the North Sea** to have a lease on a section of the North Sea to explore for oil ■ *verb* **1.** to let or rent offices, land or machinery for a period ○ *to lease offices to small firms* ○ *to lease equipment* **2.** to use an office, land or machinery for a time and pay a fee ○ *to lease an office from an insurance company* ○ *All our company cars are leased.*

lease back *phrasal verb* to sell a property or machinery to a company and then take it back on a lease ○ *They sold the office building to raise cash, and then leased it back on a twenty-five year lease.*

lease-back /'liːs bæk/ *noun* an arrangement where property is sold and then taken back on a lease ○ *They sold the office building and then took it back under a lease-back arrangement.*

leasehold /'liːshəʊld/ *noun, adjective* possessing property on a lease, for a fixed time ○ *to buy a property leasehold* ○ *We are currently occupying a leasehold property.* ○ *The company has some valuable leaseholds.*

leaseholder /'liːshəʊldə/ *noun* a person who holds a property on a lease

leasing /'liːsɪŋ/ *noun* the use of a lease or of equipment under a lease ○ *an equipment-leasing company* ○ *The company has branched out into car leasing.* ◊ **lessee**

least developed country /ˌliːst dɪ ˌveləpt 'kʌntri/ *noun* a country in the Third World which is not economically advanced, especially one of those which borrowed heavily from commercial banks in the 1970s and 1980s to finance their industrial development, and so created an international debt crisis. Abbreviation **LDC**

ledger /'ledʒə/ *noun* a book in which accounts are written

ledger balance /'ledʒə ˌbæləns/ *noun* same as **current balance**

left /left/ *adjective* **1.** on the side of the body which usually has the weaker hand, not right ○ *The numbers run down the left side of the page.* ○ *Put the debits in the left column.* **2.** not with others ○ *10m new shares were left with the underwriters when the offer was undersubscribed.*

left-hand /ˌleft 'hænd/ *adjective* belonging to the left side ○ *The debits are in the left-hand column in the accounts.* ○ *He keeps the personnel files in the left-hand drawer of his desk.*

legacy /'legəsi/ *noun* a piece of property given by someone to someone else in a will

legal /'liːg(ə)l/ *adjective* **1.** according to the law or allowed by the law ○ *The company's action in sacking the accountant was completely legal.* **2.** referring to the law □ **to take legal action** to sue someone or to take someone to court □ **to take legal advice** to ask a lawyer to advise about a legal problem

legal adviser /ˌliːg(ə)l əd'vaɪzə/ *noun* a person who advises clients about the law

Legal Aid /ˌliːg(ə)l 'eɪd skiːm/, **Legal Aid scheme** *noun* a British government scheme where a person with very little money can have legal representation and advice paid for by the state

legal charge /ˌliːg(ə)l ˈtʃɑːdʒ/ *noun* a legal document held by the Land Registry showing who has a claim on a property

legal claim /ˈliːg(ə)l kleɪm/ *noun* a statement that someone owns something legally ○ *He has no legal claim to the property.*

legal costs /ˈliːg(ə)l kɒsts/, **legal charges** /ˈliːg(ə)l ˌtʃɑːdʒɪz/, **legal expenses** /ˈliːg(ə)l ɪkˌspensɪz/ *plural noun* money spent on fees to lawyers ○ *The clerk could not afford the legal expenses involved in suing her boss.*

legal currency /ˌliːg(ə)l ˈkʌrənsi/ *noun* money which is legally used in a country

legal department /ˈliːg(ə)l dɪˌpɑːtmənt/ *noun* a section of a company dealing with legal matters

legal expert /ˈliːg(ə)l ˌekspɜːt/ *noun* a person who knows a lot about the law

legal holiday /ˌliːg(ə)l ˈhɒlɪdeɪ/ *noun* a day when banks and other businesses are closed

legalisation /ˌliːgəlaɪˈzeɪʃ(ə)n/, **legalization** *noun* the act of making something legal ○ *the campaign for the legalisation of cannabis*

legalise /ˈliːgəlaɪz/, **legalize** *verb* to make something legal

legal list /ˈliːg(ə)l lɪst/ *noun* a list of blue-chip securities in which banks and financial institutions are allowed to invest by the state in which they are based

legal personality /ˌliːg(ə)l ˌpɜːsəˈnæləti/ *noun* existence in a form that enables something to be affected by the law

legal proceedings /ˈliːg(ə)l prəˌsiːdɪŋz/ *plural noun* legal action or a lawsuit

legal profession /ˈliːg(ə)l prəˌfeʃ(ə)n/ *noun* all qualified lawyers

legal section /ˈliːg(ə)l ˌsekʃ(ə)n/ *noun* a department in a company dealing with legal matters

legal tender /ˌliːg(ə)l ˈtendə/ *noun* coins or notes which can be legally used to pay a debt

legatee /ˌlegəˈtiː/ *noun* a person who receives property from someone who has died

legislation /ˌledʒɪˈsleɪʃ(ə)n/ *noun* laws □ **labour legislation** laws concerning the employment of workers

lek /lek/ *noun* a unit of currency used in Albania

lempira /lemˈpɪərə/ *noun* a unit of currency used in Honduras

lend /lend/ *verb* to allow someone to use something for a period ○ *to lend something to someone* or *to lend someone something* ○ *to lend money against security* ○ *He lent the company money* or *He lent money to the company.* ○ *The bank lent her £50,000 to start her business.* (NOTE: **lending – lent**)

lender /ˈlendə/ *noun* a person who lends money

lender of the last resort /ˌlendə əv ðə ˌlɑːst rɪˈzɔːt/ *noun* a central bank which lends money to commercial banks

lending /ˈlendɪŋ/ *noun* an act of letting someone use money for a time

lending limit /ˈlendɪŋ ˌlɪmɪt/ *noun* a restriction on the amount of money a bank can lend

lending margin /ˈlendɪŋ ˌmɑːdʒɪn/ *noun* an agreed spread for lending, based on the LIBOR

length of service /ˌleŋθ əv ˈsɜːvɪs/ *noun* the number of years someone has worked

leone /liːˈəʊn/ *noun* a unit of currency used in Sierra Leone

less /les/ *adjective* smaller than, of a smaller size or of a smaller value ○ *We do not grant credit for sums of less than £100.* ○ *He sold it for less than he had paid for it.* ■ *preposition* minus, with a sum removed ○ *purchase price less 15% discount* ○ *interest less service charges* ■ *adverb* not as much

less developed country /les dɪˌveləpt ˈkʌntri/ *noun* the former name for a **least developed country** (*dated*) Abbreviation **LDC**

lessee /leˈsiː/ *noun* a person who has a lease or who pays money for a property he or she leases

lessor /leˈsɔː/ *noun* a person who grants a lease on a property

let /let/ *verb* to allow the use of a house, an office or a farm to someone for the payment of rent (NOTE: **letting – let**. The US term is **rent**.) □ **offices to let** offices which are available to be leased by companies ■ *noun* the period of the lease of a property ○ *They took the office on a short let.*

let-out clause /'let aʊt ˌklɔːz/ *noun* a clause which allows someone to avoid doing something in a contract ○ *He added a let-out clause to the effect that the payments would be revised if the exchange rate fell by more than 5%.*

letter /'letə/ *noun* **1.** a piece of writing sent from one person or company to another to ask for or to give information **2.** □ **to acknowledge receipt by letter** to write a letter to say that something has been received **3.** a written or printed sign (such as A, B, C etc.) ○ *Write your name and address in block letters or in capital letters.*

COMMENT: First names are commonly used between business people in the US and UK; they are less often used in other European countries (France and Germany), for example, where business letters tend to be more formal.

letter of acknowledgement /ˌletər əv ək'nɒlɪdʒmənt/ *noun* a letter which says that something has been received

letter of advice /ˌletər əv əd'vaɪs/ *noun* **1.** same as **advice note** ○ *The letter of advice stated that the goods would be at Southampton on the morning of the 6th.* ○ *The letter of advice reminded the customer of the agreed payment terms.* **2.** a letter from one bank to another, advising that a transaction has taken place

letter of application /ˌletər əv æplɪ'keɪʃ(ə)n/ *noun* a letter in which someone applies for a job

letter of appointment /ˌletər əv ə'pɔɪntmənt/ *noun* a letter in which someone is appointed to a job

letter of comfort /ˌletər əv 'kʌmfət/ *noun* a letter supporting someone who is trying to get a loan

letter of credit /ˌletər əv 'kredɪt/ *noun* a document issued by a bank on behalf of a customer authorising payment to a supplier when the conditions specified in the document are met. Abbreviation **L/C**

letter of indemnity /ˌletər əv ɪn'demnɪti/ *noun* a letter promising payment as compensation for a loss

letter of intent /ˌletər əv ɪn'tent/ *noun* a letter which states what a company intends to do if something happens

letter of reference /ˌletər əv 'ref(ə)rəns/ *noun* a letter in which an employer recommends someone for a new job

letter of renunciation /ˌletər əv rɪˌnʌnsi'eɪʃ(ə)n/ *noun* a form sent with new shares, which allows the person who has been allotted the shares to refuse to accept them and so sell them to someone else

letter security /'letə sɪˌkjʊərɪti/, **letter stock** /'letə stɒk/ *noun US* a share which has not been registered with the SEC and therefore can be sold privately, together with a letter of intent, or traded in the normal way if the owner files with the SEC using a Form 144

letters of administration /ˌletəz əv ədˌmɪnɪ'streɪʃ(ə)n/ *plural noun* a letter given by a court to allow someone to deal with the estate of a person who has died

letters patent /ˌletəz 'peɪtənt/ *plural noun* the official term for a patent

letting agency /'letɪŋ ˌeɪdʒənsi/ *noun* an agency which deals in property to let

leu /'leɪjuː/ *noun* a unit of currency used in Romania and Moldova

lev /lev/ *noun* a unit of currency used in Bulgaria

level /'lev(ə)l/ *noun* the position of something compared to others ○ *low levels of productivity* or *low productivity levels* ○ *to raise the level of employee benefits* ○ *to lower the level of borrowings* □ **high level of investment** large amounts of money invested ■ *verb* □ **to level off** *or* **to level out** to stop rising or falling ○ *Profits have levelled off over the last few years.* ○ *Prices are levelling out.* (NOTE: UK English is **levelling** – **levelled**, but the US spelling is **leveling** – **leveled**.)

'…figures from the Fed on industrial production for April show a decline to levels last seen in June 1984' [*Sunday Times*]

'…applications for mortgages are running at a high level' [*Times*]

'…employers having got their staff back up to a reasonable level are waiting until the scope for overtime working is exhausted before hiring' [*Sydney Morning Herald*]

leverage /ˈlevərɪdʒ/ *noun* **1.** same as **gearing 2.** the act of borrowing money at fixed interest which is then used to produce more money than the interest paid

COMMENT: High leverage (or high gearing) has the effect of increasing a company's profitability when trading is expanding; if the company's trading slows down, the effect of high fixed-interest charges is to increase the rate of slowdown.

leveraged /ˈliːvərɪdʒ/ *adjective* borrowing relatively large sums of money in order to finance assets

leveraged buyout /ˌliːvərɪdʒd ˈbaɪaʊt/, **leveraged takeover** /ˌliːvərɪdʒd ˈteɪkəʊvə/ *noun* an act of buying all the shares in a company by borrowing money against the security of the shares to be bought. Abbreviation **LBO**

'…the offer came after management had offered to take the company private through a leveraged buyout for $825 million' [*Fortune*]

leveraged stock /ˈliːvərɪdʒd stɒk/ *noun* stock bought with borrowed money

levy /ˈlevi/ *noun* money which is demanded and collected by the government □ **levies on luxury items** taxes on luxury items ■ *verb* to demand payment of a tax or an extra payment and to collect it ○ *to levy a duty on the import of luxury items* ○ *The government has decided to levy a tax on imported cars.* □ **to levy members for a new club house** to ask members of the club to pay for the new building

'…royalties have been levied at a rate of 12.5% of full production' [*Lloyd's List*]

liabilities /ˌlaɪəˈbɪlɪtiz/ *plural noun* the debts of a business, including dividends owed to shareholders ○ *The balance sheet shows the company's assets and liabilities.* □ **he was not able to meet his liabilities** he could not pay his debts □ **to discharge your liabilities in full** to pay everything which you owe

liability /ˌlaɪəˈbɪliti/ *noun* **1.** a legal responsibility for damage, loss or harm ○ *The two partners took out insurance to cover employers' liability.* □ **to accept liability for something** to agree that you

are responsible for something □ **to refuse liability for something** to refuse to agree that you are responsible for something **2.** responsibility for a payment such as the repayment of a loan

liable /ˈlaɪəb(ə)l/ *adjective* **1.** □ **liable for** legally responsible for ○ *The customer is liable for breakages.* ○ *The chairman was personally liable for the company's debts.* ○ *The garage is liable for damage to customers' cars.* **2.** □ **liable to** which is officially due to be paid ○ *goods which are liable to stamp duty* ○ *Employees' wages are liable to tax.*

LIBID *abbreviation* London Interbank Bid Rate

LIBOR /ˈlaɪbɔː/ *abbreviation* London Interbank Offered Rate

licence /ˈlaɪs(ə)ns/ *noun* an official document which allows someone to do something (NOTE: The US spelling is **license**.) □ **drinks licence, alcohol licence, liquor license** a permit to sell alcohol in a restaurant, etc. □ **goods manufactured under licence** goods made with the permission of the owner of the copyright or patent

license /ˈlaɪs(ə)ns/ *noun* US spelling of **licence** ■ *verb* to give someone official permission to do something for a fee, e.g. when a company allows another company to manufacture its products abroad ○ *licensed to sell beers, wines and spirits* ○ *to license a company to manufacture spare parts* ○ *She is licensed to run an employment agency.*

licensed dealer /ˌlaɪs(ə)nst ˈdiːlə/ *noun* a person who has been licensed by the DTI to buy and sell securities for individual clients

licensed deposit-taker /ˌlaɪs(ə)nst dɪˈpɒzɪt ˌteɪkə/, **licensed institution** /ˌlaɪs(ə)nst ˌɪnstɪˈtjuːʃ(ə)n/ *noun* a deposit-taking institution which is licensed to receive money on deposit from private individuals and to pay interest on it, e.g. a building society, bank or friendly society. Abbreviation **LDT**

licensee /ˌlaɪs(ə)nˈsiː/ *noun* a person who has a licence, especially a licence to sell alcohol or to manufacture something

licensing /ˈlaɪs(ə)nsɪŋ/ *adjective* referring to licences ○ *a licensing agreement* ○ *licensing laws*

lien /ˈliːən/ *noun* the legal right to hold someone's goods and keep them until a debt has been paid

lieu /ljuː/ *noun* □ **in lieu of** instead of □ **she was given two months' salary in lieu of notice** she was given two months' salary and asked to leave immediately

life /laɪf/ *noun* the period of time for which something or someone exists □ **life of a contract** the remaining period of a futures contract before it expires

life assurance /ˈlaɪf əˌʃʊərəns/ *noun* insurance which pays a sum of money when someone dies, or at an agreed date if they are still alive

life assurance company /ˈlaɪf əˌʃɔːrəns ˌkʌmp(ə)ni/ *noun* a company providing life assurance, but usually also providing other services such as investment advice

life assured /ˌlaɪf əˈʃʊəd/ *noun* the person whose life has been covered by a life assurance policy

lifeboat operation /ˌlaɪfˌbəʊt ˌɒpəˈreɪʃ(ə)n/ *noun* actions taken to rescue of a company (especially of a bank) which is in difficulties

life estate /laɪf ɪˈsteɪt/ *noun* same as **life interest**

life expectancy /ˈlaɪf ɪkˌspektənsi/ *noun* the number of years a person is likely to live

life insurance /ˈlaɪf ɪnˌʃʊərəns/ *noun* US same as **life assurance**

life insured /laɪf ɪnˈʃʊəd/ *noun* same as **life assured**

life interest /ˌlaɪf ˈɪntrəst/ *noun* a situation where someone benefits from a property as long as he or she is alive

lifeline account /ˈlaɪflaɪn əˌkaʊnt/ *noun* US a simple bank account for people with low incomes, used for receiving salary payments and offering few services

lifestyle /ˈlaɪfstaɪl/ *noun* the way of living of a particular section of society ○ *These upmarket products appeal to people with an extravagant lifestyle.* ○ *The magazine ran a series of articles on the lifestyles of some successful businessmen.*

lifestyle audit /ˈlaɪfstaɪl ˌɔːdɪt/ *noun* a study of a person's living standards to see if it is consistent with his reported income

Lifetime Individual Savings Account /ˌlaɪftaɪm ˌɪndɪvɪdʒuəl ˈseɪvɪŋz əˌkaʊnt/ *noun* a British scheme by which individuals can invest for their retirement by putting a limited amount of money each year in a tax-free unit trust account. Abbreviation **LISA**. ◊ **ISA**

LIFFE *abbreviation* London International Financial Futures and Options Exchange

LIFO /ˈlaɪfəʊ/ *abbreviation* last in first out

light /laɪt/ *adjective* **1.** not heavy, not very busy or active □ **shares fell back in light trading** shares lost value on a day when there was little business done on the stock exchange **2.** not having enough of a certain type of share in a portfolio ○ *His portfolio is light in banks.*

lighten /ˈlaɪt(ə)n/ *verb* to sell shareholdings if a portfolio is too 'heavy' in a certain type of share

light industry /ˌlaɪt ˈɪndəstri/ *noun* an industry making small products such as clothes, books, or calculators

like-for-like /ˌlaɪk fə ˈlaɪk/ *adjective* □ **on a like-for-like basis** when comparing the same stores over different periods □ **like-for-like store sales** sales for the same stores over an earlier period

lilangeni /ˌliːlæŋˈɡeɪni/ *noun* a unit of currency used in Swaziland

limit /ˈlɪmɪt/ *noun* the point at which something ends or the point where you can go no further □ **he has exceeded his credit limit** he has borrowed more money than he is allowed □ **limit 'up'**, **limit 'down'** upper or lower limits to share price movements which are regulated by some stock exchanges ■ *verb* to stop something from going beyond a specific point, to restrict the number or amount of something □ **the banks have limited their credit** the banks have allowed their customers only a specific amount of credit

'…the biggest surprise of 1999 was the rebound in the price of oil. In the early months of the year commentators were talking about a fall to $5 a barrel but for the first time in two decades, the oil exporting countries got their act together, limited production and succeeded in pushing prices up' [*Financial Times*]

limitation /ˌlɪmɪ'teɪʃ(ə)n/ *noun* the act of allowing only a specific quantity of something ○ *The contract imposes limitations on the number of cars which can be imported.* □ **limitation of liability** the fact of making someone liable for only a part of the damage or loss

limited /'lɪmɪtɪd/ *adjective* restricted

limited company /ˌlɪmɪtɪd 'kʌmp(ə)ni/ *noun* a company in which each shareholder is responsible for the company's debts only to the amount that he or she has invested in the company. Limited companies must be formed by at least two directors. Abbreviation **Ltd**. Also called **limited liability company**

limited liability /ˌlɪmɪtɪd ˌlaɪə'bɪlɪti/ *noun* a situation where someone's liability for debt is limited by law

limited liability company /ˌlɪmɪtɪd ˌlaɪəbɪlɪti 'kʌmp(ə)ni/ *noun* same as **limited company**

limited market /ˌlɪmɪtɪd 'mɑːkɪt/ *noun* a market which can take only a specific quantity of goods

limited partnership /ˌlɪmɪtɪd 'pɑːtnəʃɪp/ *noun* a registered business where the liability of the partners is limited to the amount of capital they have each provided to the business and where the partners may not take part in the running of the business

limiting /'lɪmɪtɪŋ/ *adjective* not allowing something to go beyond a point, restricting ○ *a limiting clause in a contract* ○ *The short holiday season is a limiting factor on the hotel trade.*

limit order /'lɪmɪt ˌɔːdə/ *noun* an order to a broker to sell if a security falls to an agreed price

line /laɪn/ *noun* **1.** a long mark printed or written on paper ○ *paper with thin blue lines* ○ *I prefer notepaper without any lines.* ○ *She drew a thick line before the column of figures.* **2.** a row of letters or figures on a page **3.** a block of shares (traded on a stock exchange)

'…cash paid for overstocked lines, factory seconds, slow sellers, etc.' [*Australian Financial Review*]

line chart /'laɪn tʃɑːt/ *noun* a chart or graph using lines to indicate values

line of credit /ˌlaɪn əv 'kredɪt/ *noun* **1.** the amount of money made available to a customer by a bank as an overdraft □ **to open a line of credit** *or* **a credit line** to make credit available to someone **2.** the borrowing limit on a credit card

line of shares /ˌlaɪn əv 'ʃeəz/ *noun* a large block of shares sold as one deal on the stock exchange

link /lɪŋk/ *verb* to join or to attach to something else ○ *to link pensions to inflation* ○ *to link bonus payments to productivity* ○ *His salary is linked to the cost of living.* ◊ **index-linked**

liquid /'lɪkwɪd/ *adjective* easily converted to cash, or containing a large amount of cash

liquid assets /ˌlɪkwɪd 'æsets/ *plural noun* cash, or investments which can be quickly converted into cash

liquidate /'lɪkwɪdeɪt/ *verb* □ **to liquidate a company** to close a company and sell its assets, usually in order to pay debts □ **to liquidate a debt** to pay a debt in full □ **to liquidate stock** to sell stock to raise cash

liquidation /ˌlɪkwɪ'deɪʃ(ə)n/ *noun* **1.** the sale of assets for cash, usually in order to pay debts □ **liquidation of a debt** payment of a debt **2.** the winding up or closing of a company and selling of its assets □ **on a liquidation basis** at a very low price to encourage buyers □ **the company went into liquidation** the company was closed and its assets sold

liquidator /'lɪkwɪdeɪtə/ *noun* a person named to supervise the closing of a company which is in liquidation

liquidity /lɪ'kwɪdɪti/ *noun* cash, or the fact of having cash or assets which can be changed into cash □ **liquidity crisis** not having enough cash or other liquid assets

liquidity ratio /lɪ'kwɪdɪti ˌreɪʃiəʊ/ *noun* an accounting ratio used to measure an organisation's liquidity. It is calculated by taking the business's current assets, minus its stocks, divided by its current liabilities. Also called **acid test ratio**, **quick ratio**

liquid market /ˌlɪkwɪd 'mɑːkɪt/ *noun* a market in a security where there are enough shares available to allow sales to take place without distorting the price (the opposite is a 'thin' market)

lira /ˈlɪərə/ *noun* **1.** a former unit of currency in Italy ○ *the book cost 2,700 lira or L2,700* (NOTE: **Lira** is usually written **L** before figures: **L2,700**.) **2.** a unit of currency used in Turkey

LISA *abbreviation* Lifetime Individual Savings Account

lis pendens /ˌlɪs ˈpendenz/ *adverb* a Latin phrase meaning 'pending suit'

list /lɪst/ *noun* **1.** several items written one after the other ○ *They have an attractive list of products* or *product list.* ○ *I can't find that item on our stock list.* ○ *Please add this item to the list.* ○ *She crossed the item off her list.* **2.** a catalogue

listed company /ˌlɪstɪd ˈkʌmp(ə)ni/ *noun* a company whose shares can be bought or sold on the stock exchange

listed securities /ˌlɪstɪd sɪˈkjʊərɪtiz/ *plural noun* shares which can be bought or sold on the stock exchange, shares which appear on the official stock exchange list

Listing Agreement /ˈlɪstɪŋ əˌɡriːmənt/ *noun* a document which a company signs when being listed on the stock exchange, in which it promises to abide by stock exchange regulations

listing details /ˈlɪstɪŋ ˌdiːteɪlz/, **listing particulars** *plural noun* **1.** details of a company which are published when the company applies for a stock exchange listing (the US equivalent is the 'registration statement') **2.** details of the institutions which are backing an issue

listing requirements /ˈlɪstɪŋ rɪˌkwaɪəmənts/ *plural noun* the conditions which must be met by a corporation before its stock can be listed on the New York Stock Exchange

list price /ˈlɪst praɪs/ *noun* the price for something as given in a catalogue

litas /ˈliːtɑːs/ *noun* a unit of currency used in Lithuania

litigation /ˌlɪtɪˈɡeɪʃ(ə)n/ *noun* the bringing of a lawsuit against someone

Little Board /ˈlɪt(ə)l bɔːd/ *noun* same as **American Stock Exchange**

lively /ˈlaɪvli/ *adjective* □ **lively market** an active stock market, with many shares being bought or sold

Lloyd's /lɔɪdz/ *noun* the central London insurance market □ **a ship which is A1 at Lloyd's** a ship in very good condition

COMMENT: Lloyd's is an old-established insurance market. The underwriters who form Lloyd's are divided into syndicates, each made up of active underwriters who arrange the business and non-working underwriters (called 'names') who stand surety for any insurance claims which may arise.

Lloyd's broker /ˌlɔɪdz ˈbrəʊkə/ *noun* an agent who represents a client who wants insurance and who arranges this insurance for him through a Lloyd's underwriting syndicate

Lloyd's Register /ˌlɔɪdz ˈredʒɪstə/ *noun* a classified list showing details of all the ships in the world and estimates of their condition

Lloyd's syndicate /ˈlɔɪdz ˌsɪndɪkət/ *noun* a group of underwriters on the Lloyd's insurance market, made up of active underwriters who arrange the business and non-working underwriters (called 'names') who stand surety for any insurance claims which may arise

Lloyd's underwriter /ˌlɔɪdz ˈʌndəraɪtə/ *noun* a member of an insurance group at Lloyd's who accepts to underwrite insurances

LME *abbreviation* London Metal Exchange

load /ləʊd/ *noun* an amount of goods which are transported in a particular vehicle or aircraft ■ *verb* to add extra charges to a price

load factor /ˈləʊd ˌfæktə/ *noun* a number of seats in a bus, plane or train which are occupied by passengers who have paid the full fare

load fund /ˈləʊd fʌnd/ *noun* a fund sold through a broker, with a high initial management charge or commission

loan /ləʊn/ *noun* money which has been lent ■ *verb* to lend something ○ *The truck has been loaned by the local haulage company.*

'…over the last few weeks, companies raising new loans from international banks have been forced to pay more, and an unusually high number of attempts to syndicate loans among banks has failed' [*Financial Times*]

loan capital /ˈləʊn ˌkæpɪt(ə)l/ *noun* a part of a company's capital which is a loan to be repaid at a later date

loan committee /ˈləʊn kəˌmɪti/ *noun* a committee which examines applications for special loans, such as higher loans than normally allowed by a bank

loan/deposit ratio /ˌləʊn dɪˈpɒzɪt ˌreɪʃiəʊ/ *noun* a ratio between the amount of loans made by a bank and the amount it holds on deposit

loan participation /ˈləʊn pɑː ˌtɪsɪpeɪʃ(ə)n/ *noun* an arrangement whereby several banks come together as a group to share a very large loan to one single customer

loan portfolio /ˈləʊn pɔːtˌfəʊliəʊ/ *noun* all the loans which a financial institution has made and which are still outstanding

loan shark /ˈləʊn ʃɑːk/ *noun* a person who lends money at a very high interest rate

loan stock /ˈləʊn stɒk/ *noun* stock issued to an organisation in return for a loan. Loan stock earns interest.

loan to value /ˌləʊn tə ˈvæljuː/ *noun* the amount of a mortgage expressed as a percentage of the value of the property. Abbreviation **LTV**

loan-to-value ratio /ˌləʊn tə ˈvælju: ˌreɪʃiəʊ/ *noun* the amount of a first mortgage lien as a percentage of the total appraised value of real property

local /ˈləʊk(ə)l/ *adjective* referring to a particular area, especially one near where a factory or an office is based ■ *noun* **1.** an independent dealer in futures or options or an independent trader on the LIFFE **2.** *US* a branch of a national trade union

'...each cheque can be made out for the local equivalent of £100 rounded up to a convenient figure' [*Sunday Times*]

'...the business agent for Local 414 of the Store Union said his committee will recommend that the membership ratify the agreement' [*Toronto Star*]

'EC regulations insist that customers can buy cars anywhere in the EC at the local pre-tax price' [*Financial Times*]

local authority /ˌləʊk(ə)l ɔːˈθɒrɪti/ *noun* an elected section of government which runs a small area of the country

local authority bond /ˌləʊk(ə)l ɔː ˈθɒrəti bɒnd/ *noun* a fixed- interest bond, repayable on a specific date, used by a local authority in order to raise a loan and similar to a Treasury bond

local authority deposits /ˌləʊk(ə)l ɔːˈθɒrəti dɪˌpɒzɪts/ *plural noun* money deposited with a local authority to earn interest for the depositor

local call /ˌləʊk(ə)l ˈkɔːl/ *noun* a telephone call to a number on the same exchange as your own or to one on a neighbouring exchange

local government /ˌləʊk(ə)l ˈgʌv(ə)nmənt/ *noun* elected authorities and administrative organisations which deal with the affairs of small areas of a country

local labour /ˌləʊk(ə)l ˈleɪbə/ *noun* workers who are recruited near a factory, and are not brought there from a distance

local press /ˌləʊk(ə)l ˈpres/ *noun* newspapers which are sold in a small area of the country ○ *The product was only advertised in the local press as it was only being distributed in that area of the country.*

lock up /ˌlɒk ˈʌp/ *phrasal verb* □ **to lock up capital** to have capital invested in such a way that it cannot be used for other investments

lockbox /ˈlɒkbɒks/ *noun US* **1.** a box at a post office which can be rented and can be opened only by the person or company renting it **2.** a system where cheques sent to a Post Office box are picked up and deposited in a bank account

locking up /ˌlɒkɪŋ ˈʌp/ *noun* □ **the locking up of money in stock** the act of investing money in stock so that it cannot be used for other, possibly more profitable, investments

lock into /ˌlɒk ˈɪntə/, **lock in** /ˌlɒk ˈɪn/ *verb* to be fixed to an interest rate or exchange rate ○ *By buying francs forward the company is in effect locking itself into a pound-franc exchange rate of 10.06.* □ **to lock in profits** to take profits, to sell investments at a profit to ensure that the profit is realised ○ *The shares had become overpriced – it was time to lock in the profits.*

lodge /lɒdʒ/ *verb* □ **to lodge money with someone** to deposit money with someone □ **to lodge securities as collateral** to put securities into a bank to be used as collateral for a loan

lodgement /ˈlɒdʒmənt/ *noun* the act of depositing money or cheques in an account

Lombard Rate /'lɒmbɑːd reɪt/ *noun* the rate at which the German Bundesbank lends to commercial banks

London Bullion Market /ˌlʌndən 'bʊliən ˌmɑːkɪt/ *noun* an international market dealing in gold and silver bullion and gold coins

London Commodity Exchange /ˌlʌndən kə'mɒdəti ɪks.tʃeɪndʒ/ *noun* a London exchange dealing in commodities such as cotton, coffee, cocoa, etc., but not in metals. Abbreviation **LCE**

London Interbank Bid Rate /ˌlʌndən ˌɪntəbæŋk 'bɪd reɪt/ *noun* the rate at which banks are prepared to borrow from each other. Abbreviation **LIBID**

London Interbank Offered Rate /ˌlʌndən ˌɪntəbæŋk 'ɒfəd reɪt/ *noun* the rate at which banks offer to lend Eurodollars to other banks. Abbreviation **LIBOR**

London International Financial Futures and Options Exchange /ˌlʌndən ˌɪntənæʃ(ə)nəl faɪˌnænʃ(ə)l ˌfjuːtʃəz ən 'ɒpʃənz ɪks.tʃeɪndʒ/ *noun* a market where futures contracts are traded in financial instruments such as gilts, equity options, euroyen, US Treasury bonds, etc. and also commodities such as cocoa, coffee, wheat, potatoes, barley and sugar. Abbreviation **LIFFE**

London Metal Exchange /ˌlʌndən 'met(ə)l ɪks.tʃeɪndʒ/ *noun* a commodity exchange dealing in aluminium, copper, lead, nickel, tin and zinc. Abbreviation **LME**

London Securities and Derivatives Exchange /ˌlʌndən sɪˌkjʊərɪtiz ən dɪ'rɪvətɪvz ɪks.tʃeɪndʒ/ *noun* the London exchange where securities and derivatives are traded. Abbreviation **OMLX**

London Stock Exchange /ˌlʌndən 'stɒk ɪks.tʃeɪndʒ/ *noun* the main British stock exchange where securities are bought and sold. Abbreviation **LSE**

London Traded Options Market /ˌlʌndən ˌtreɪdɪd 'ɒpʃənz ˌmɑːkɪt/ *noun* a market where options are traded. Abbreviation **LTOM**

long /lɒŋ/ *adjective* for a large period of time □ **in the long term** over a long period of time □ **to take the long view** to plan for a long period before current

investment becomes profitable □ **to be long of a stock** *or* **to go long** to buy a share as a long-term investment on the assumption that the price will rise

long bond /'lɒŋ bɒnd/, **long coupon bond** /'lɒŋ ˌkuːpɒn ˌbɒnd/ *noun* a bond which will mature in more than ten years' time

long credit /ˌlɒŋ 'kredɪt/ *noun* credit terms which allow the borrower a long time to pay

long-dated bill /ˌlɒŋ ˌdeɪtɪd 'bɪl/ *noun* a bill which is payable in more than three months' time

long-dated securities /ˌlɒŋ ˌdeɪtɪd sɪ'kjʊərɪtiz/ *plural noun* same as **longs**

long-dated stocks /ˌlɒŋ ˌdeɪtɪd 'stɒks/ *plural noun* same as **longs**

long lease /ˌlɒŋ 'liːs/ *noun* a lease which runs for fifty years or more ○ *to take an office building on a long lease*

long position /ˌlɒŋ pə'zɪʃ(ə)n/ *noun* a situation where an investor sells long, i.e. sells forward shares which he or she owns. Compare **short position**

long-range /ˌlɒŋ 'reɪndʒ/ *adjective* for a long period of time in the future □ **long-range economic forecast** a forecast which covers a period of several years

longs /lɒŋz/ *plural noun* government stocks which will mature in over fifteen years' time. Also called **long-dated stocks**

long-tail business /ˌlɒŋ teɪl 'bɪznɪs/ *noun* insurance business where a claim only arises some years after the insurance contract was taken out

long-term /ˌlɒŋ 'tɜːm/ *adjective* relating to a long time into the future ○ *The management projections are made on a long-term basis.* ○ *Sound long-term planning will give the company more direction.* ○ *It is in the company's long-term interests to have a contented staff.* □ **on a long-term basis** continuing for a long period of time □ **long-term debts** debts which will be repaid many years later □ **long-term forecast** a forecast for a period of over three years □ **long-term loan** a loan to be repaid many years later □ **long-term objectives** aims which will take years to achieve

long-term borrowings /ˌlɒŋ tɜːm 'bɒrəʊɪŋz/ *plural noun* borrowings which do not have to be repaid for some years

long-term security /ˌlɒŋ tɜːm sɪ'kjʊərɪti/ *noun* a security which will mature in more than fifteen years' time

loophole /'luːphəʊl/ *noun* □ **to find a loophole in the law** to find a means of legally avoiding the law □ **to find a tax loophole** to find a means of legally not paying tax

'…because capital gains are not taxed but money taken out in profits is taxed, owners of businesses will be using accountants and tax experts to find loopholes in the law' [*Toronto Star*]

loose change /ˌluːs 'tʃeɪndʒ/ *noun* money in coins

lose /luːz/ *verb* **1.** not to have something any more □ **to lose an order** not to get an order which you were hoping to get ○ *During the strike, the company lost six orders to American competitors.* □ **to lose control of a company** to find that you have less than 50% of the shares and so are no longer able to control the company **2.** to have less money ○ *He lost £25,000 in his father's computer company.* (NOTE: **losing – lost**) **3.** to drop to a lower price ○ *The dollar lost two cents against the yen.* ○ *Gold shares lost 5% on the market yesterday.* (NOTE: **losing – lost**) □ **the pound has lost value** the pound is worth less

loss /lɒs/ *noun* **1.** the state or process of not having something any more □ **loss of customers** not keeping customers because of bad service, high prices, etc. □ **loss of an order** not getting an order which was expected □ **the company suffered a loss of market penetration** the company found it had a smaller share of the market □ **compensation for loss of earnings** payment to someone who has stopped earning money or who is not able to earn money □ **compensation for loss of office** payment to a director who is asked to leave a company before his or her contract ends **2.** the state of having less money than before or of not making a profit □ **the company suffered a loss** the company did not make a profit □ **to report a loss** not to show a profit in the accounts at the end of the year ○ *The company reported a loss of £1m on the first year's trading.* □ **the car was written off as a dead loss** *or* **a total loss**

the car was so badly damaged that the insurers said it had no value □ **at a loss** making a loss, not making any profit ○ *The company is trading at a loss.* ○ *We sold the shop at a loss.* □ **to cut your losses** to stop doing something which is losing money **3.** damage to property or destruction of property, which is then subject to an insurance claim □ **the cargo was written off as a total loss** the cargo was so badly damaged that the insurers said it had no value

'…against losses of FFr 7.7m two years ago, the company made a net profit of FFr 300,000 last year' [*Financial Times*]

loss-leader /'lɒs ˌliːdə/ *noun* an article which is sold at a loss to attract customers ○ *We use these cheap films as a loss-leader.*

'…against losses of FFr 7.7m in 1993, the company made a net profit of FFr 300,000 last year' [*Financial Times*]

loss relief /'lɒs rɪˌliːf/ *noun* an amount of tax not to be paid on one year's profit to offset a loss in the previous year

lot /lɒt/ *noun* **1.** a group of items sold together at an auction ○ *to bid for lot 23* ○ *At the end of the auction half the lots were unsold.* **2.** a group of shares which are sold ○ *to sell a lot of shares* ○ *to sell shares in small lots* **3.** *US* a piece of land, especially one to be used for redevelopment ○ *They bought a lot and built a house.*

lottery /'lɒtəri/ *noun* a game where numbered tickets are sold and prizes given for some of the numbers

low /ləʊ/ *adjective* not high or not much ○ *Low overhead costs keep the unit cost low.* ○ *We try to keep our wages bill low.* ○ *The company offered him a mortgage at a low rate of interest.* ○ *The pound is at a very low rate of exchange against the dollar.* □ **the tender will go to the lowest bidder** the contract will be awarded to the person who offers the best terms ■ *noun* a point where prices or sales are very small ○ *the highs and lows on the stock market* ○ *Sales have reached a new low.* □ **highs and lows on the stock exchange** a list of shares which have reached a new high or low price in the previous day's trading □ **shares have hit an all-time low** shares have reached their lowest price ever

'…after opening at 79.1 the index touched a peak of 79.2 and then drifted to a low of 78.8' [*Financial Times*]

'…the pound which had been as low as $1.02 earlier this year, rose to $1.30' [*Fortune*]

low coupon stocks /ləʊ ˌkuːpɒn ˈstɒks/ *plural noun* government bonds which pay a low rate of interest

lower /ˈləʊə/ *adjective* smaller or less high ○ *a lower rate of interest* ○ *Sales were lower in December than in November.* ■ *verb* to make something smaller or less expensive ○ *to lower prices to secure a larger market share* ○ *Industrialists have asked the bank to lower interest rates.*

'Canadian and European negotiators agreed to a deal under which Canada could keep its quotas but lower its import duties' [*Globe and Mail (Toronto)*]

lowering /ˈləʊərɪŋ/ *noun* the act of making smaller or less expensive ○ *Lowering the prices has resulted in increased sales.* ○ *We hope to achieve low prices with no lowering of quality.*

low gearing /ˌləʊ ˈɡɪərɪŋ/ *noun* the fact of not having much borrowing in proportion to your capital

low-grade /ˈləʊ ɡreɪd/ *adjective* not of very good quality ○ *The car runs best on low-grade petrol.*

low-profile /ləʊ ˈprəʊfaɪl/ *adjective* □ **low-profile company** a company which does not publicise itself much

low yield /ˌləʊ ˈjiːld/ *noun* a yield on the share price which is low for the sector, suggesting that investors anticipate that the company will grow fast, and have pushed up the share price in expectation of growth

loyalty /ˈlɔɪəlti/ *noun* the state of being faithful to someone or something

loyalty bonus /ˈlɔɪəlti ˌbəʊnəs/ *noun* a special privilege given to shareholders who keep their shares for a long period of time, used especially to attract investors to privatisation issues

LSE *abbreviation* London Stock Exchange

Ltd *abbreviation* limited company

LTOM *abbreviation* London Traded Options Market

LTV *abbreviation* loan to value

lull /lʌl/ *noun* a quiet period ○ *After last week's hectic trading this week's lull was welcome.*

lump sum /ˌlʌmp ˈsʌm/ *noun* money paid in one single amount, not in several small sums ○ *When he retired he was given a lump-sum bonus.* ○ *She sold her house and invested the money as a lump sum.*

luxury goods /ˈlʌkʃəri ɡʊdz/, **luxury items** /ˈlʌkʃəri ˌaɪtəmz/ *plural noun* expensive items which are not basic necessities

luxury tax /ˈlʌkʃəri tæks/ *noun* a tax on goods or services that are considered non-essential

M

m *abbreviation* **1.** metre **2.** mile **3.** million

M0 /ˌem ˈnɔːt/ *symbol* the narrowest British measure of money supply, including coins and notes in circulation plus the deposits of commercial banks with the Bank of England

'Bank of England calculations of notes in circulation suggest that the main component of the narrow measure of money supply, M0, is likely to have risen by 0.4 per cent after seasonal adjustments' [*Times*]

M1 /ˌem ˈwʌn/ *symbol* a measure of money supply, including all coins and notes plus personal money in current accounts

M2 /ˌem ˈtuː/ *symbol* a measure of money supply, including coins and notes and personal money in current and deposit accounts

M3 /ˌem ˈθriː/ *symbol* a broad measure of money supply, including M2 and personal money in government deposits and deposits in currencies other than sterling (in the US, it includes time deposits of more than $100,000 and money market funds and Eurodollars held by US residents)

£M3 *symbol* a British measure of sterling money supply, including coins and notes, personal money in current and deposit accounts and government deposits

Maastricht Treaty /ˈmɑːstrɪkt ˌtriːti/ *noun* a treaty signed in 1992 which sets out the principles for a European Union and the convergence criteria for states wishing to join the EMU

macro- /mækrəʊ/ *prefix* very large, covering a wide area

macroeconomics /ˌmækrəʊiːkəˈnɒmɪks/ *plural noun* a study of the economics of a whole area, a whole industry, a whole group of the population or a whole country, in order to help in economic planning. Compare **microeconomics** (NOTE: takes a singular verb)

macro funds /ˈmækrəʊ fʌndz/ *plural noun* large hedge funds which bet on whole economies

macro hedge fund /ˌmækrəʊ ˈhedʒ ˌfʌnd/ *noun* a hedge fund which invests in whole regions

Madam Chairman /ˌmædəm ˈtʃeə mən/, **Madam Chairwoman** /ˌmædəm ˈtʃeəˌwʊmən/ *noun* a way of speaking to a female chairman of a committee or meeting

magazine /ˌmægəˈziːn/ *noun* a special type of newspaper, usually published only weekly or monthly, often with a glossy cover and often devoted to a particular subject

magnetic character reading /mæg ˌnetɪk ˈkærɪktə ˌriːdɪŋ/, **magnetic character recognition** /mæg ˌnetɪk ɪŋk ˌkærɪktə ˌrekəgˈnɪʃ(ə)n/ *noun* a system that recognises characters by sensing magnetic ink used on cheques. Abbreviation **MCR**, **MICR**

magnetic ink /mæg ˌnetɪk ˈɪŋk/ *noun* a special ink with magnetic particles in it, used for printing cheques

magnetic strip /mæg ˌnetɪk ˈstrɪp/, **magnetic stripe** /mæg ˌnetɪk ˈstraɪp/ *noun* a black strip on credit cards and cashpoint cards, on which personal information about the account is recorded

mail /meɪl/ *noun* **1.** a system of sending letters and parcels from one place to another ○ *The cheque was lost in the mail.* ○ *The invoice was put in the mail yesterday.* ○ *Mail to some of the islands in the Pacific can take six weeks.* □ **by mail**

using the postal services, not sending something by hand or by messenger □ **we sent the order by first-class mail** we sent the order by the most expensive mail service, designed to be faster **2.** same as **email** ■ *verb* **1.** to send something by mail **2.** same as **email**

main /meɪn/ *adjective* most important ○ *main office* ○ *main building* ○ *one of our main customers* ○ *The main building houses our admin and finance departments.*

main market /ˌmeɪn ˈmɑːkɪt/ *noun* the London Stock Exchange, as opposed to the AIM market

mainstream corporation tax /ˌmeɪnstriːm ˌkɒpəˈreɪʃ(ə)n tæks/ *noun* the total tax paid by a company on its profits less any advance corporation tax, which a company has already paid when distributing profits to its shareholders in the form of dividends. Abbreviation **MCT**

Main Street /ˈmeɪn striːt/ *noun US* the most important street in a town, where the shops and banks usually are

maintain /meɪnˈteɪn/ *verb* **1.** to keep something going or working ○ *We try to maintain good relations with our customers.* ○ *Her trip aims to maintain contact with her important overseas markets.* **2.** to keep something working at the same level ○ *to maintain an interest rate at 5%* ○ *The company has maintained the same volume of business in spite of the recession.* □ **to maintain a dividend** to pay the same dividend as the previous year

maintenance /ˈmeɪntənəns/ *noun* **1.** the process of keeping things going or working ○ *Maintenance of contacts is important for a sales rep.* ○ *It is essential to ensure the maintenance of supplies to the factory.* **2.** the process of keeping a machine in good working order ○ *We offer a full maintenance service.*

'...responsibilities include the maintenance of large computerized databases' [*Times*]

'...the federal administration launched a full-scale investigation into the airline's maintenance procedures' [*Fortune*]

maintenance contract /ˈmeɪntənəns ˌkɒntrækt/ *noun* a contract by which a company keeps a piece of equipment in good working order

maintenance fee /ˈmeɪntənəns fiː/ *noun* a fee charged for keeping an account or a contract going

majeure /mæˈʒɜː/ ♦ **force majeure**

major /ˈmeɪdʒə/ *adjective* important ○ *There is a major risk of fire.* □ **major shareholder** a shareholder with a large number of shares

'...a client base which includes many major commercial organizations and nationalized industries' [*Times*]

majority /məˈdʒɒrɪti/ *noun* more than half of a group □ **majority of the shareholders** more than 50% of the shareholders □ **the board accepted the proposal by a majority of three to two** three members of the board voted to accept the proposal and two voted against accepting it

majority shareholder /məˌdʒɒrɪti ˈʃeəhəʊldə/ *noun* a person who owns more than half the shares in a company

majority shareholding /məˌdʒɒrɪti ˈʃeəhəʊldɪŋ/ *noun* a group of shares which are more than half the total

majority vote /məˈdʒɒrɪti vəʊt/, **majority decision** /məˈdʒɒrɪti dɪˌsɪʒ(ə)n/ *noun* a decision which represents the wishes of the largest group as shown by a vote

make /meɪk/ *verb* **1.** to do an action (NOTE: **making – made**) □ **to make a bid for something** to offer to buy something □ **to make a payment** to pay □ **to make a deposit** to pay money as a deposit **2.** to earn money ○ *He makes £50,000 a year or £25 an hour.* (NOTE: **making – made**) **3.** to increase in value ○ *The shares made $2.92 in today's trading.* (NOTE: **making – made**) **4.** □ **to make a profit** to have more money after a deal □ **to make a loss** to have less money after a deal □ **to make a killing** to make a very large profit

make out *phrasal verb* to write something ○ *to make out an invoice* ○ *The bill is made out to Smith & Co.* □ **to make out a cheque to someone** to write someone's name on a cheque

make over *phrasal verb* to transfer property legally ○ *to make over the house to your children*

make up *phrasal verb* □ **to make up accounts** to complete the accounts

make up for *phrasal verb* to compensate for something ○ *to make up for a short payment* or *for a late payment*

maker /'meɪkə/ *noun* a person who signs a promissory note in which he or she promises to pay money

maladministration /ˌmæləd̩mɪnɪ'streɪʃ(ə)n/ *noun* incompetent administration

malfeasance /mæl'fiːz(ə)ns/ *noun* an unlawful act

manage /'mænɪdʒ/ *verb* **1.** to direct or to be in charge of something ○ *to manage a branch office* ○ *A competent and motivated person is required to manage an important department in the company.* **2.** □ **to manage property** to look after rented property for the owner □ **to manage a currency** to intervene in the markets to influence a currency's exchange rates

'…the research director will manage and direct a team of graduate business analysts reporting on consumer behaviour throughout the UK' [*Times*]

manageable /'mænɪdʒəb(ə)l/ *adjective* which can be dealt with ○ *The problems which the company faces are too large to be manageable by one person.* ○ *The interest payments, though high, are still manageable.*

managed derivatives fund /ˌmænɪdʒd dɪ'rɪvətɪvz fʌnd/ *noun* a fund which uses mainly futures and options instead of investing in the underlying securities

managed float /'mænɪdʒd fləʊt/ *noun* a process of floating of a currency where the exchange rate is controlled by the central bank. Compare **clean float**. Also called **dirty float**

managed fund /'mænɪdʒd fʌnd/ *noun* a unit trust fund which is invested in specialist funds within the group and can be switched from one specialised investment area to another. Also called **managed unit trust**

managed unit trust /ˌmænɪdʒd 'juːnɪt trʌst/ *noun* same as **managed fund**

management /'mænɪdʒmənt/ *noun* **1.** the process of directing or running a business ○ *a management graduate* or *a graduate in management* ○ *She studied*

management at university.* ○ *Good management* or *efficient management is essential in a large organisation.* ○ *Bad management* or *inefficient management can ruin a business.* **2.** a group of managers or directors ○ *The management has decided to give everyone a pay increase.* (NOTE: Where **management** refers to a group of people it is sometimes followed by a plural verb.) **3.** the process of running a fund or investment portfolio for a client

'…the management says that the rate of loss-making has come down and it expects further improvement in the next few years' [*Financial Times*]

management accountant /'mænɪdʒmənt ə̩kaʊntənt/ *noun* an accountant who prepares financial information for managers so that they can take decisions

management accounts /'mænɪdʒ mənt ə̩kaʊnts/ *plural noun* financial information prepared for a manager so that decisions can be made, including monthly or quarterly financial statements, often in great detail, with analysis of actual performance against the budget

management buyin /ˌmænɪdʒmənt 'baɪɪn/ *noun* the purchase of a subsidiary company by a group of outside directors. Abbreviation **MBI**

management buyout /ˌmænɪdʒ mənt 'baɪaʊt/ *noun* the takeover of a company by a group of employees, usually senior managers and directors. Abbreviation **MBO**

management by objectives /ˌmænɪdʒmənt baɪ əb'dʒektɪvz/ *noun* a way of managing a business by planning work for the managers to do and testing if it is completed correctly and on time

management charge /'mænɪdʒ mənt tʃɑːdʒ/ *noun* same as **annual management charge**

management consultant /'mænɪdʒ mənt kən̩sʌltənt/ *noun* a person who gives advice on how to manage a business

management course /'mænɪdʒ mənt kɔːs/ *noun* a training course for managers

management team /'mænɪdʒmənt tiːm/ *noun* all the managers who work in a particular company

management trainee /ˌmænɪdʒmənt treɪˈniː/ *noun* a young member of staff who is being trained to be a manager

management training /ˌmænɪdʒmənt ˈtreɪnɪŋ/ *noun* the process of training staff to be managers, by making them study problems and work out solutions

manager /ˈmænɪdʒə/ *noun* **1.** the head of a department in a company ○ *She's a department manager in an engineering company.* ○ *Go and see the human resources manager if you have a problem.* ○ *The production manager has been with the company for only two weeks.* ○ *Our sales manager started as a rep in London.* **2.** the person in charge of a branch or shop ○ *Mr Smith is the manager of our local Lloyds Bank.* ○ *The manager of our Lagos branch is in London for a series of meetings.*

'…the No. 1 managerial productivity problem in America is managers who are out of touch with their people and out of touch with their customers' [*Fortune*]

managerial /ˌmænəˈdʒɪəriəl/ *adjective* referring to managers ○ *All the managerial staff are sent for training every year.*

managership /ˈmænɪdʒəʃɪp/ *noun* the job of being a manager ○ *After six years, she was offered the managership of a branch in Scotland.*

managing agent /ˌmænɪdʒɪŋ ˈeɪdʒ(ə)nt/ *noun* the person who runs the day-to-day activities of a Lloyd's syndicate

managing director /ˌmænədʒɪŋ daɪˈrektə/ *noun* the director who is in charge of a whole company. Abbreviation **MD**

managing underwriter /ˌmænɪdʒɪŋ ˈʌndəraɪtə/ *noun US* an underwriting firm which organises the underwriting of a share issue

manat /ˈmænæt/ *noun* a unit of currency used in Turkmenistan

M&A *abbreviation* mergers and acquisitions

mandate /ˈmændeɪt/ *noun* an order which allows something to take place

mandatory /ˈmændət(ə)ri/ *adjective* obligatory ○ *Wearing a suit is mandatory for all managerial staff.* □ **mandatory meeting** a meeting which all staff have to attend

'…the wage talks are focusing on employment issues such as sharing of work among employees and extension of employment beyond the mandatory retirement age of 60 years' [*Nikkei Weekly*]

mandatory bid /ˌmændət(ə)ri ˈbɪd/ *noun* an offer to purchase the shares of a company which has to be made when a shareholder acquires 30% of that company's shares

M&E fee /ˌem ən ˈiː fiː/ *noun* same as **mortality and expense risk charge**

manipulate /məˈnɪpjʊleɪt/ *verb* □ **to manipulate the accounts** to make false accounts so that the company seems profitable □ **to manipulate the market** to work to influence share prices in your favour

manpower forecasting /ˈmænpaʊə ˌfɔːkɑːstɪŋ/ *noun* the process of calculating how many employees will be needed in the future, and how many will actually be available

manpower planning /ˈmænpaʊə ˌplænɪŋ/ *noun* the process of planning to obtain the right number of employees in each job

manufactured goods /ˌmænjuˈfæktʃəd ˈɡʊdz/ *plural noun* items which are made by machine

marché *noun* the French word for market. ◊ **MATIF**

margin /ˈmɑːdʒɪn/ *noun* **1.** the difference between the money received when selling a product and the money paid for it □ **we are cutting our margins very fine** we are reducing our margins to the smallest possible in order to be competitive □ **our margins have been squeezed** profits have been reduced because our margins have to be smaller to stay competitive **2.** extra space or time allowed **3.** the difference between interest paid to depositors and interest charged to borrowers by a bank, building society, etc. **4.** a deposit paid when purchasing a futures contract

'…profit margins in the industries most exposed to foreign competition – machinery, transportation equipment and electrical goods – are significantly worse than usual' [*Australian Financial Review*]

marginal /ˈmɑːdʒɪn(ə)l/ *adjective* **1.** hardly worth the money paid **2.** not very profitable ○ *a marginal return on invest-ment*

marginal cost /ˌmɑːdʒɪn(ə)l ˈkɒst/ *noun* the cost of making a single extra unit above the number already planned

marginal land /ˌmɑːdʒɪn(ə)l ˈlænd/ *noun* land which is almost not worth farming

marginal pricing /ˌmɑːdʒɪn(ə)l ˈpraɪsɪŋ/ *noun* **1.** the practice of basing the selling price of a product on its vari-able costs of production plus a margin, but excluding fixed costs **2.** the practice of making the selling price the same as the cost of a single extra unit above the number already planned

marginal purchase /ˌmɑːdʒɪn(ə)l ˈpɜːtʃɪs/ *noun* something which a buyer feels is only just worth buying

marginal rate of tax /ˌmɑːdʒɪn(ə)l reɪt əv ˈtæks/, **marginal rate of taxa-tion** /ˌmɑːdʒɪn(ə)l reɪt əv tæksˈeɪʃ(ə)n/ *noun* the percentage of tax which a taxpayer pays at the top rate, which he or she therefore pays on every further pound or dollar he or she earns. Also called **marginal tax rate**

'…pensioner groups claim that pensioners have the highest marginal rates of tax. Income earned by pensioners above $30 a week is taxed at 62.5 per cent, more than the highest marginal rate' [*Australian Financial Review*]

marginal revenue /ˌmɑːdʒɪn(ə)l ˈrevɪnjuː/ *noun* the income from selling a single extra unit above the number already sold

marginal tax rate /ˌmɑːdʒɪn(ə)l ˈtæks reɪt/ *noun* same as **marginal rate of tax**

margin call /ˈmɑːdʒɪn kɔːl/ *noun* a request for a purchaser of a futures contract or an option to pay more margin, since the fall in the price of the securities or commodity has removed the value of the original margin deposited

margin of error /ˌmɑːdʒɪn əv ˈerə/ *noun* the number of mistakes which can be accepted in a document or in a calcula-tion

margin of safety /ˌmɑːdʒɪn əv ˈseɪfti/ *noun* the units produced or sales of such units which are above the breakeven point

marine underwriter /məˌriːn ˈʌndəraɪtə/ *noun* a person or company that insures ships and their cargoes

marital /ˈmærɪt(ə)l/ *adjective* referring to a marriage

marital deductions /ˌmærɪt(ə)l dɪˈdʌkʃ(ə)ns/ *plural noun* that part of an estate which is not subject to estate tax because it goes to the dead person's spouse

marital status /ˌmærɪt(ə)l ˈsteɪtəs/ *noun* the condition of being married or not

maritime law /ˌmærɪtaɪm ˈlɔː/ *noun* laws referring to ships, ports, etc.

maritime lawyer /ˌmærɪtaɪm ˈlɔːjə/ *noun* a lawyer who specialises in legal matters concerning ships and cargoes

mark /mɑːk/ *noun* **1.** a sign put on an item to show something **2.** a former unit of currency in Germany ○ *The price was twenty-five marks.* ○ *The mark rose against the dollar.* (NOTE: Usually written **DM** after a figure: 25DM.)

mark down *phrasal verb* to make the price of something lower □ **to mark down a price** to lower the price of something ○ *This range has been marked down to $24.99.* ○ *We have marked all prices down by 30% for the sale.*

mark up *phrasal verb* to make the price of something higher □ **to mark prices up** to increase prices ○ *These prices have been marked up by 10%.*

marka /ˈmɑːkə/, **markka** *noun* a unit of currency used before the euro in Finland (NOTE: written **MK**)

mark-down /ˈmɑːk daʊn/ *noun* **1.** a reduction of the price of something to less than its usual price **2.** the percentage amount by which a price has been lowered ○ *There has been a 30% mark-down on all goods in the sale.*

market /ˈmɑːkɪt/ *noun* **1.** an area where a product might be sold or the group of people who might buy a product ○ *There is no market for this product.* ○ *Our share of the Far eastern market has gone down.* **2.** a place where money or commodities are traded □ **global financial markets** world-wide finance markets ○ *The global financial markets precipitated the Mexican crisis of 1994–95.* **3.** □ **to buy shares in the open market** to buy shares on the stock exchange, not privately □ **to come to the market** (*of a company*) to apply for a stock exchange listing, by offering existing shares for sale, or by floating it as a new company □ **sell at the market** an instruction to stockbroker to sell shares at the best price possible □ **to bring a company to the market** to arrange the flotation of a company's shares on the market □ **to make a market in securities** to offer to buy or sell securities on a selected list at any time **4.** a place where shares are bought and sold ○ *The market in oil shares was very active* or *There was a brisk market in oil shares.* **5.** □ **to go up market, to go down market** to make products which appeal to a wealthy section of the market or to a wider, less wealthy section of the market **6.** □ **to be in the market for secondhand cars** to look for secondhand cars to buy □ **to come on to the market** to start to be sold ○ *This soap has just come on to the market.* □ **to put something on the market** to start to offer something for sale ○ *They put their house on the market.* ○ *I hear the company has been put on the market.* □ **the company has priced itself out of the market** the company has raised its prices so high that its products do not sell ■ *verb* to sell a product, or to present and promote a product in a way which will help to sell it ○ *This product is being marketed in all European countries.*

'…market analysts described the falls in the second half of last week as a technical correction to a market which had been pushed by demand to over the 900 index level' [*Australian Financial Review*]

marketability /ˌmɑːkɪtəˈbɪlɪti/ *noun* the fact of being able to be sold easily ○ *the marketability of shares in electronic companies*

marketable /ˈmɑːkɪtəb(ə)l/ *adjective* easily sold

marketable securities /ˌmɑːkɪtəb(ə)l sɪˈkjʊərɪtiz/ *plural noun* stocks, shares, CDs etc., which can be bought or sold on a stock market

market analysis /ˌmɑːkɪt əˈnæləsɪs/ *noun* the detailed examination and report of a market

market analyst /ˌmɑːkɪt ˈænəlɪst/ *noun* a person who studies the stock market in general

market basket /ˈmɑːkɪt ˌbɑːskɪt/ *noun* same as **shopping basket**

market capitalisation /ˌmɑːkɪt ˌkæpɪtəlaɪˈzeɪʃ(ə)n/ *noun* the total market value of a company, calculated by multiplying the price of its shares on the stock exchange by the number of shares outstanding ○ *company with a £1m capitalisation*

market concentration /ˌmɑːkɪt ˌkɒns(ə)nˈtreɪʃ(ə)n/ *noun* same as **concentration**

market cycle /ˌmɑːkɪt ˈsaɪk(ə)l/ *noun* a period during which a market expands, then slows down and then expands again

market economist /ˌmɑːkɪt ɪˈkɒnəmɪst/ *noun* a person who specialises in the study of financial structures and the return on investments in the stock market

market economy /ˌmɑːkɪt ɪˈkɒnəmi/ *noun* same as **free market economy**

market forces /ˌmɑːkɪt ˈfɔːsɪz/ *plural noun* the influences on the sales of a product which bring about a change in prices

market forecast /ˌmɑːkɪt ˈfɔːkɑːst/ *noun* a forecast of prices on the stock market

marketing /ˈmɑːkɪtɪŋ/ *noun* the business of presenting and promoting goods or services in such a way as to make customers want to buy them

'…reporting to the marketing director, the successful applicant will be responsible for the development of a training programme for the new sales force' [*Times*]

marketing agreement /ˈmɑːkɪtɪŋ əˈɡriːmənt/ *noun* a contract by which one company will market another company's products

marketing department /ˈmɑːkɪtɪŋ dɪˌpɑːtmənt/ *noun* the section of a company dealing with marketing and sales

marketing manager /ˈmɑːkɪtɪŋ ˌmænɪdʒə/ *noun* a person in charge of a marketing department ○ *The marketing manager has decided to start a new advertising campaign.*

market jitters /ˌmɑːkɪt ˈdʒɪtəz/ *plural noun* feelings of nervousness caused by uncertaintyor fear about the current investment environment

market leader /ˌmɑːkɪt ˈliːdə/ *noun* **1.** a product which sells most in a market **2.** the company with the largest market share ○ *We are the market leader in home computers.*

'…market leaders may benefit from scale economies or other cost advantages; they may enjoy a reputation for quality simply by being at the top, or they may actually produce a superior product that gives them both a large market share and high profits' [*Accountancy*]

marketmaker /ˈmɑːkɪtmeɪkə/ *noun* a person or firm that buys and sells shares on the stock market and offers to do so (NOTE: Marketmakers list the securities they are willing to buy or sell and their bid and offer prices. If the prices are met, they immediately buy or sell and make their money by charging a commission on each transaction. Marketmakers play an important part in maintaining an orderly market.)

market neutral funds /ˌmɑːkɪt ˈnjuːtrəl fʌndz/ *plural noun* hedge funds not related to general market movements, but which try to find opportunities to arbitrage temporary slight changes in the relative values of particular financial assets

market operator /ˌmɑːkɪt ˈɒpəreɪtə/ *noun* a person who trades on a stock market or financial market

market opportunity /ˌmɑːkɪt ɒpəˈtjuːnɪti/ *noun* the possibility of going into a market for the first time

market optimism /ˌmɑːkɪt ˈɒptɪˌmɪzəm/ *noun* a feeling that the stock market will rise

market order /ˌmɑːkɪt ˈɔːdə/ *noun* an order to a broker to buy or sell at the current price

market polarisation /ˌmɑːkɪt ˌpəʊləraɪˈzeɪʃ(ə)n/ *noun* a situation where a market is concentrated round a few suppliers or traders

market price /ˈmɑːkɪt praɪs/ *noun* **1.** the price at which a product can be sold **2.** the price at which a share stands in a stock market

market professionals /ˌmɑːkɪt prəˈfeʃ(ə)nəlz/ *plural noun* people who work in a stock market, as brokers, analysts, etc.

market purchases /ˌmɑːkɪt ˈpɜːtʃɪsɪz/ *plural noun* purchases of shares in a company on the normal stock market (by a company planning a takeover bid)

market rate /ˌmɑːkɪt ˈreɪt/ *noun* the usual price in the market ○ *We pay the market rate for temporary staff* or *We pay temporary staff the market rate.*

'…after the prime rate cut yesterday, there was a further fall in short-term market rates' [*Financial Times*]

market research /ˌmɑːkɪt rɪˈsɜːtʃ/ *noun* the process of examining the possible sales of a product and the possible customers for it before it is put on the market

market sentiment /ˌmɑːkɪt ˈsentɪmənt/ *noun* a general feeling among investors or financial analysts on a stock market

market share /ˌmɑːkɪt ˈʃeə/ *noun* the percentage of a total market which the sales of a company's product cover ○ *We hope our new product range will increase our market share.*

market strategist /ˌmɑːkɪt ˈstrætədʒɪst/ *noun* a person who plans how to buy and sell on the stock market

market trends /ˌmɑːkɪt ˈtrendz/ *plural noun* gradual changes taking place in a market

market value /ˌmɑːkɪt ˈvæljuː/ *noun* the value of an asset, a share, a product or a company if sold today

market value added /ˌmɑːkɪt ˌvæljuː ˈædɪd/ *noun* the difference between a company's market value and the amount of its invested capital. Abbreviation **MVA**

market value adjuster /ˌmɑːkɪt ˈvæljuː əˌdʒʌstə/ *noun* a method of calculating the loss in market value of a bond or insurance when it is being surrendered. Abbreviation **MVA**

market watcher /ˈmɑːkɪt ˌwɒtʃə/ *noun* a person who follows stock market trends closely

mark-up /ˈmɑːk ʌp/ *noun* **1.** an increase in price ○ *We put into effect a 10% mark-up of all prices in June.* ○ *Since I was last in the store they have put at least a 5% mark-up on the whole range of items.* **2.** the difference between the cost of a product or service and its selling price (NOTE: Mark-up is often calculated as a percentage of the production and overhead costs, and represents the profit made on the product or service.) □ **we work to a 3.5 times mark-up** *or* **to a 350% mark-up** we take the unit cost and multiply by 3.5 to give the selling price

mass production /ˌmæs prəˈdʌkʃən/ *noun* the manufacture of large quantities of identical products

mass unemployment /ˌmæs ˌʌnɪmˈplɔɪmənt/ *noun* unemployment affecting large numbers of people

MasterCard *noun* an international credit organisation, backed by a group of banks (NOTE: A similar organisation is **Visa International**.)

matched bargains /mætʃd ˈbɑːgɪnz/ *plural noun* sales and purchases of shares which are conducted at the same time, where the buyers and sellers come together to agree on the price (as opposed to the 'quotation' system, where the marketmakers make the selling prices for shares) □ **to trade on a matched bargain basis** to arrange to sell shares for a client and buy them for another client, without having to take a position in the shares

MATIF *noun* the French financial futures market. Full form **marché à terme des instruments financiers**

mature /məˈtʃʊə/ *adjective* □ **mature economy** a fully developed economy ■ *verb* to become due □ **bills which mature in three weeks' time** bills which will be due for payment in three weeks

maturity /məˈtʃʊərɪti/ *noun* **1.** the third stage in a product life cycle when a product is well established in the market though no longer enjoying increasing sales, after which sooner or later it will start to decline **2.** the time at which something becomes due for payment or repayment □ **amount payable on maturity** the amount received by the insured person when a policy matures

maturity date /məˈtʃʊərɪti deɪt/ *noun* a date when a government stock, an assurance policy or a debenture will become due for payment. Also called **date of maturity**

maturity value /məˈtʃʊərɪti ˌvæljuː/ *noun* the amount payable when a bond or other financial instrument matures

maturity yield /məˈtʃʊərɪti jiːld/ *noun* a calculation of the yield on a fixed-interest investment, assuming it is bought at a certain price and held to maturity

maxi ISA /ˈmæksi ˌaɪsə/ *noun* an ISA that offers the opportunity to invest on the stock market, with a limit on combined cash and stock market investments of £7000 per year. ◊ **mini ISA**

maximisation /ˌmæksɪmaɪˈzeɪʃ(ə)n/, **maximization** *noun* the process of making something as large as possible ○ *profit maximisation* or *maximisation of profit*

maximise /ˈmæksɪmaɪz/, **maximize** *verb* to make something as large as possible ○ *Our aim is to maximise profits.* ○ *The cooperation of the workforce will be needed if we are to maximise production.* ○ *She is paid on results, and so has to work flat out to maximise her earnings.*

maximum /ˈmæksɪməm/ *noun* the largest possible number, price or quantity ○ *It is the maximum the insurance company will pay.* (NOTE: The plural is **maxima** or **maximums**.) □ **up to a maximum of £10** no more than £10 □ **to increase exports to the maximum** to increase exports as much as possible ■ *adjective* largest possible ○ *40% is the maximum income tax rate* or *the maximum rate of tax.* ○ *The maximum load for the truck is one ton.* ○ *Maximum production levels were reached last week.* □ **to increase production to the maximum level** to increase it as much as possible

May Day /ˈmeɪ deɪ/ *noun* the change in practices on American Stock Exchanges which took place on 1st May 1975, with the removal of the system of fixed commissions. This allowed cheaper stock trading by brokers who did not offer any investment advice, and ultimately led to computerised financial dealing in general.

MBO *abbreviation* management buyout

MCT *abbreviation* mainstream corporation tax

mean /miːn/ *adjective* average ○ *The mean annual increase in sales is 3.20%.* □ **mean price** the average price of a share in a day's trading ■ *noun* the average or number calculated by adding several quantities together and dividing by the number of quantities added ○ *Unit sales* *are over the mean for the first quarter* or *above the first-quarter mean.*

means /miːnz/ *noun* a way of doing something ○ *Do we have any means of copying all these documents quickly?* ○ *Bank transfer is the easiest means of payment.* (NOTE: The plural is **means**.) ■ *plural noun* money or resources ○ *The company has the means to launch the new product.* ○ *Such a level of investment is beyond the means of a small private company.*

means test /'miːnz test/ *noun* an inquiry into how much money someone earns to see if they are eligible for state benefits

means-test /'miːnz test/ *verb* to find out how much money someone has in savings and assets ○ *All applicants will be means-tested.*

measure /'meʒə/ *noun* **1.** a way of calculating size or quantity □ **as a measure of the company's perform-ance** as a way of judging if the company's results are good or bad **2.** a type of action □ **to take measures to prevent some-thing happening** to act to stop something happening ■ *verb* □ **to measure the government's performance** to judge how well the government is doing

measurement /'meʒəmənt/ *noun* a way of judging something ○ *growth measurement* ○ *performance measure-ment* or *measurement of performance*

measurement of profitability /ˌmeʒəmənt əv ˌprɒfɪtə'bɪliti/ *noun* a way of calculating how profitable some-thing is

mechanic's lien /mɪˌkæniks 'liːən/ *noun US* a lien on buildings or other property which can be enforced by workmen until they have been paid

median /'miːdiən/ *noun* the middle number in a list of numbers

medical insurance /'medɪk(ə)l ɪn ˌʃʊərəns/ *noun* insurance which pays the cost of medical treatment, especially when someone is travelling abroad

medium /'miːdiəm/ *adjective* middle or average ○ *The company is of medium size.*

medium-dated stocks /ˌmiːdiəm ˌdeɪtɪd 'stɒks/ *plural noun* same as **mediums**

mediums /'miːdiəmz/ *plural noun* government stocks which mature in seven to fifteen years' time

medium-sized company /ˌmiːdiəm saɪzd 'kʌmp(ə)ni/ *noun* a company which has an annual turnover of less than £22.8m and does not employ more than 250 staff ○ *a medium-sized engineering company*

medium-term /ˌmiːdiəm 'tɜːm/ *adjective* referring to a point between short term and long term □ **medium-term forecast** a forecast for two or three years □ **medium-term loan** a bank loan for three to five years

medium-term bond /ˌmiːdiəm tɜːm 'bɒnd/ *noun* a bond which matures within five to fifteen years

meet /miːt/ *verb* **1.** to be satisfactory for something ○ *We must have a product which meets our requirements.* □ **we will try to meet your price** we will try to offer a price which is acceptable to you □ **they failed to meet the deadline** they were not able to complete in time **2.** to pay for something ○ *The company will meet your expenses.* ○ *He was unable to meet his mortgage repayments.* (NOTE: **meeting – met**)

meeting /'miːtɪŋ/ *noun* an event at which a group of people come together in order to discuss matters of common interest to them □ **to hold a meeting** to organise a meeting of a group of people ○ *The meeting will be held in the committee room.* □ **to open a meeting** to start a meeting □ **to conduct a meeting** to be in the chair for a meeting □ **to close a meeting** to end a meeting □ **to address a meeting** to speak to a meeting □ **to put a resolution to a meeting** to ask a meeting to vote on a proposal

'…in proportion to your holding you have a stake in every aspect of the company, including a vote in the general meetings' [*Investors Chronicle*]

mega-cap /'megə kæp/ *noun* a share with the very highest capitalisation and growth. ◊ **cap**, **micro-cap**, **mid-cap**, **small-cap**

member /'membə/ *noun* **1.** a person who belongs to a group, society or organ-isation ○ *Committee members voted on the proposal.* ○ *They were elected members of the board.* ○ *Every employer*

is a member of the employers' federation.
2. a shareholder in a company **3.** an organisation which belongs to a larger organisation ○ *the member states of the EU* ○ *the members of the United Nations* ○ *the member companies of a trade association*

'…it will be the first opportunity for party members and trade union members to express their views on the tax package' [*Australian Financial Review*]

member bank /ˌmembə 'bæŋk/ *noun* a bank which is part of the Federal Reserve system

member firm /ˌmembə 'fɜːm/ *noun* a stockbroking firm which is a member of a stock exchange

member's agent /'membəz ˌeɪdʒənt/ *noun* a person who works on behalf of the names in a Lloyd's syndicate

membership /'membəʃɪp/ *noun* all the members of a group ○ *The membership was asked to vote for the new president.*

'…the bargaining committee will recommend that its membership ratify the agreement at a meeting called for June' [*Toronto Star*]

Member States /'membə steɪts/ *plural noun* states which are members of an organisation such as the EU or the UN ○ *the member countries of the EU* ○ *the members of the United Nations* ○ *the member companies of a trade association*

memorandum and articles of association /meməˌrændəm ənd ˌɑːtɪk(ə)lz əv əˌsəʊsiˈeɪʃ(ə)n/, **memorandum of association** /ˌmemə rændəm əv əˌsəʊsiˈeɪʃ(ə)n/ *noun* the legal documents which set up a limited company and give details of its name, aims, authorised share capital, conduct of meetings, appointment of directors and registered office

mentee /men'tiː/ *noun* a less experienced employee who is offered special guidance and support by a respected and trusted person with more experience (a mentor)

mentor /'mentɔː/ *noun* a person who is respected and trusted by a less experienced employee and offers special guidance and support to them

mercantile /'mɜːkəntaɪl/ *adjective* commercial □ **mercantile country** a country which earns income from trade □ **mercantile law** laws relating to business

mercantile agent /'mɜːkəntaɪl ˌeɪdʒənt/ *noun* a person who sells on behalf of a business or another person and earns a commission

mercantile marine /ˌmɜːkəntaɪl mə 'riːn/ *noun* all the commercial ships of a country

merchant /'mɜːtʃənt/ *noun* a company, shop or other business which accepts a credit card for purchases

merchant bank /'mɜːtʃənt bæŋk/ *noun* **1.** a bank which arranges loans to companies, deals in international finance, buys and sells shares and launches new companies on the stock exchange, but does not provide banking services to the general public **2.** *US* a bank which operates a credit card system, accepting payment on credit cards from retailers or 'merchants'

merchant banker /ˌmɜːtʃənt 'bæŋkə/ *noun* a person who has a high position in a merchant bank

merchant marine /ˌmɜːtʃənt mə 'riːn/, **merchant navy** /ˌmɜːtʃənt 'neɪvi/ *noun* all the commercial ships of a country

merchant number /'mɜːtʃənt ˌnʌmbə/ *noun* a number of the merchant, printed at the top of the report slip when depositing credit card payments

merge /mɜːdʒ/ *verb* to join together ○ *The two companies have merged.* ○ *The firm merged with its main competitor.*

merger /'mɜːdʒə/ *noun* the joining together of two or more companies ○ *As a result of the merger, the company is now the largest in the field.*

merger accounting /'mɜːdʒə ə ˌkaʊntɪŋ/ *noun* a way of presenting the accounts of a newly acquired company within the group accounts, so as to show it in the best possible light

merit increase /'merɪt ˌɪnkriːs/ *noun* an increase in pay given to an employee because his or her work is good

merit rating /'merɪt ˌreɪtɪŋ/ *noun* the process of judging how well an employee works, so that payment can be according to merit

metal /'met(ə)l/ *noun* a material (either an element or a compound) which can carry heat and electricity

COMMENT: Only some metals are traded as commodities: these are the base metals aluminium, copper, lead, nickel, tin, zinc (which are traded on the London Metal Exchange) and the precious metals gold, silver, platinum and palladium (which are traded on the London Bullion Market, COMEX, and other exchanges).

method /'meθəd/ *noun* a way of doing something ○ *They devised a new method of sending data.* ○ *What is the best method of payment?* ○ *Her organising methods are out of date.* ○ *Their manufacturing methods* or *production methods are among the most modern in the country.*

metical /'metɪk(ə)l/ *noun* a unit of currency used in Mozambique

mezzanine class stock /ˌmetsəniːn klɑːs 'stɒk/ *noun* a type of common stock rated at a level below the top double-A or triple-A ratings

mezzanine finance /'metsəniːn ˌfaɪnæns/ *noun* finance provided to a company after it has received start-up finance

COMMENT: Mezzanine finance is slightly less risky than start-up finance, since the company has usually already started trading; it is, however, unsecured. This type of finance is aimed at consolidating a company's trading position before it is floated on a stock exchange.

MFN *abbreviation* most favoured nation

Mibtel /'mɪbtel/ *noun* an index of share prices on the Milan Stock Exchange in Italy

micro- /maɪkrəʊ/ *prefix* very small

micro-cap /'maɪkrəʊ kæp/ *noun* a share in a company with very small capitalisation

microeconomics /'maɪkrəʊ iːkə ˌnɒmɪks/ *plural noun* the study of economics of people or single companies. Compare **macroeconomics** (NOTE: takes a singular verb)

micropayments /'maɪkrəʊ ˌpeɪmənts/ *plural noun* a technology developed to allow visitors to spend very small amounts of money (normally for information) on an Internet site

COMMENT: When people are purchasing goods or spending more than £5 on an

Internet site, it is commercially viable for the retailer to accept payment by credit card or any other form of e-money. When people are being charged very small amounts (normally a few pence or cents) for information, it is not worth while collecting the payment from a standard credit card. Micropayments allow the retailer to debit the visitor's e-purse or bank account directly.

mid- /mɪd/ *prefix* middle □ **from mid 2001** from the middle of 2001 ○ *The factory is closed until mid-July.*

mid-cap /'mɪd kæp/, **midcap** *noun* a share in a company with medium-sized capitalisation (on the London Stock Exchange, a capitalisation of between £300m and £2.5bn)

middle /'mɪd(ə)l/ *adjective* in the centre or between two points

middle-income /ˌmɪd(ə)l 'ɪŋkʌm/ *adjective* □ **people in the middle-income bracket** people with average incomes, not very high or very low

middleman /'mɪd(ə)lˌmæn/ *noun* a person who negotiates with large companies on behalf of personal clients

middle management /ˌmɪd(ə)l 'mænɪdʒmənt/ *noun* department managers in a company, who carry out the policy set by the directors and organise the work of a group of employees

middle price /'mɪd(ə)l praɪs/ *noun* a price between the buying and selling price, usually shown in indices

middle rate /'mɪd(ə)l reɪt/ *noun* an exchange rate between the buy and sell rates for a foreign currency

mid-month /ˌmɪd 'mʌnθ/ *adjective* happening in the middle of the month ○ *mid-month accounts*

mid-sized /'mɪd saɪzd/, **midsize** /'mɪdsaɪz/ *adjective* □ **mid-sized company** *US* a company which is larger than a small company but smaller than a large company

mid-week /ˌmɪd 'wiːk/ *adjective* happening in the middle of a week ○ *the mid-week lull in sales*

mill /mɪl/ *noun* one-fifth of a cent

million /'mɪljən/ *noun* the number 1,000,000 ○ *The company lost £10 million in the African market.* ○ *Our turnover has risen to $13.4 million.* ◊ **billion**, **trillion** (NOTE: Can be written **m** after figures: **$5m** (say 'five million dollars.'))

millionaire /ˌmɪljəˈneə/ *noun* a person who has more than one million pounds or dollars

min *abbreviation* **1.** minute **2.** minimum

mini- /mɪni/ *prefix* very small

minibudget /ˌmɪniˈbʌdʒɪt/ *noun* an interim statement about financial plans from a finance minister

mini ISA /ˈmɪni ˌaɪsə/ *noun* an ISA in which either up to £4000 can be invested in stocks and shares, or up to £3000 cash can be invested, in a given year. ◊ **maxi ISA**

mini Madoff /ˌmɪni ˈmædɒf/ *noun* a financial con man who is accused of or has committed crimes similar to those of Bernard Madoff e.g. in pyramid schemes

minimum /ˈmɪnɪməm/ *noun* the smallest possible quantity, price or number ○ *to keep expenses to a minimum* ○ *to reduce the risk of a loss to a minimum* (NOTE: The plural is **minima** or **minimums**.) ■ *adjective* smallest possible □ **minimum dividend** the smallest dividend which is legal and accepted by the shareholders □ **minimum payment** the smallest payment necessary □ **minimum quantity** the smallest quantity which is acceptable

minimum balance /ˌmɪnɪməm ˈbæləns/ *noun* the smallest amount of money which must be kept in an account to qualify for the services provided

Minimum Lending Rate /ˌmɪnɪməm ˈlendɪŋ reɪt/ *noun* formerly, the rate at which the Bank of England used to lend to other banks (now called the 'base rate'). Abbreviation **MLR**

minimum reserves /ˌmɪnɪməm rɪ ˈzɜːvz/ *plural noun* the smallest amount of reserves which a commercial bank must hold with a central bank

minimum wage /ˌmɪnɪməm ˈweɪdʒ/ *noun* the lowest hourly wage which a company can legally pay its employees

mining /ˈmaɪnɪŋ/ ♦ **data mining**

mining concession /ˈmaɪnɪŋ kən ˌseʃ(ə)n/ *noun* the right to dig a mine on a piece of land

minister /ˈmɪnɪstə/ *noun* a member of a government who is in charge of a ministry ○ *a government minister* ○ *the Minister of Trade* or *the Trade Minister* ○ *the Minister of Foreign Affairs* or *the*

Foreign Minister (NOTE: In the UK and US, they are called **secretary**: **the Foreign Secretary**, **Secretary of Commerce**.)

COMMENT: In the US, heads of government departments are called **secretary**: **the Secretary for Commerce**. In the UK, heads of government departments are called **Secretary of State**: **the Secretary of State for Defence**.

ministry /ˈmɪnɪstri/ *noun* a department in the government ○ *a ministry official* or *an official from the ministry* ○ *She works in the Ministry of Finance* or *the Finance Ministry.* ○ *He is in charge of the Ministry of Information* or *of the Information Ministry.* (NOTE: In the UK and the US, important ministries are called **departments**: **the Department of Trade and Industry**, **the Commerce Department**.)

minor /ˈmaɪnə/ *adjective* less important ○ *Items of minor expenditure are not listed separately.* ○ *The minor shareholders voted against the proposal.* ■ *noun* a person less than eighteen years old

minority /maɪˈnɒrɪti/ *noun* **1.** a number or quantity which is less than half of the total ○ *A minority of board members opposed the chairman.* □ **in the minority** being fewer than half ○ *Good salesmen are in the minority in our sales team.* **2.** a section of the population from a specific racial group, which does nor make up the majority of the population

minority interest /maɪˈnɒrəti ˌɪntrəst/ *noun* the nominal value of those shares in a subsidiary company that are held by members other than the parent company or its nominees

minority shareholder /maɪˌnɒrəti ˈʃeəhəʊldə/ *noun* a person who owns a group of shares but less than half of the shares in a company

minority shareholding /maɪˌnɒrəti ˈʃeəhəʊldɪŋ/ *noun* a group of shares which are less than half the total ○ *He acquired a minority shareholding in the company.*

mint /mɪnt/ *noun* a factory where coins are made ■ *verb* to make coins

minus /ˈmaɪnəs/ *preposition, adverb* less, without ○ *Net salary is gross salary minus tax and National Insurance deductions.* ○ *Gross profit is sales minus production costs.* ■ *adjective* □ **the**

accounts show a minus figure the accounts show that more has been spent than has been received ■ *noun* a printed sign (-) showing a loss or decrease ○ *At the end of the day the index showed a series of minuses, with very few pluses.*

minus factor /'maɪnəs ˌfæktə/ *noun* a factor that is unfavourable in some way, e.g. because it reduces profitability ○ *To have lost sales in the best quarter of the year is a minus factor for the sales team.*

MIRAS *abbreviation* mortgage interest relief at source

mirror fund /'mɪrə fʌnd/ *noun* an investment trust where the manager also runs a unit trust with the same objectives

misappropriate /ˌmɪsə'prəʊprieɪt/ *verb* to use illegally money which is not yours, but with which you have been trusted

misappropriation /ˌmɪsəprəʊpri'eɪʃ(ə)n/ *noun* the illegal use of money by someone who is not the owner but who has been trusted to look after it

miscalculate /mɪs'kælkjʊleɪt/ *verb* to calculate wrongly, or to make a mistake in calculating something ○ *The salesman miscalculated the discount, so we hardly broke even on the deal.*

miscalculation /mɪsˌkælkjʊ'leɪʃ(ə)n/ *noun* a mistake in calculating

miscount *noun* /'mɪskaʊnt/ a mistake in counting ■ *verb* /mɪs'kaʊnt/ to count wrongly, or to make a mistake in counting something ○ *The shopkeeper miscounted, so we got twenty-five bars of chocolate instead of two dozen.*

misfeasance /mɪs'fiːz(ə)ns/ *noun* the offence of doing something in an improper way

mismanage /mɪs'mænɪdʒ/ *verb* to manage something badly ○ *The company had been badly mismanaged under the previous MD.*

mismanagement /mɪs'mænɪdʒmənt/ *noun* bad management ○ *The company failed because of the chairman's mismanagement.*

misrepresent /ˌmɪsreprɪ'zent/ *verb* to report facts or what someone says wrongly ○ *Our spokesman was totally misrepresented in the Sunday papers.*

misrepresentation /ˌmɪsˌreprɪzen'teɪʃ(ə)n/ *noun* **1.** the act of making a

wrong statement in order to persuade someone to enter into a contract such as one for buying a product or service **2.** the act of wrongly reporting facts

mistake /mɪ'steɪk/ *noun* an act or decision which is wrong, or something that has been done wrongly ○ *It was a mistake to let him name his own salary.* ○ *There was a mistake in the address.* □ **to make a mistake** to do something wrong ○ *The shop made a mistake and sent the wrong items.* ○ *He made a mistake in addressing the letter.* □ **by mistake** in error, wrongly ○ *They sent the wrong items by mistake.* ○ *She put my letter into an envelope for the chairman by mistake.*

misuse /mɪs'juːs/ *noun* the act of using something, e.g. invested money, for a wrong purpose ○ *the misuse of funds* or *of assets*

Mittelstand *noun* the German word for the sector of medium-sized companies

mixed /mɪkst/ *adjective* **1.** made up of different sorts or of different types of things together **2.** neither good nor bad

'…prices closed on a mixed note after a moderately active trading session' [*Financial Times*]

mixed economy /ˌmɪkst ɪ'kɒnəmi/ *noun* a system which contains both nationalised industries and private enterprise

MMC /ˌem em 'siː/ *abbreviation* Monopolies and Mergers Commission

mobilise /'məʊbɪlaɪz/, **mobilize** *verb* to bring things or people together and prepare them for action, especially to fight □ **to mobilise capital** to collect capital to support something □ **to mobilise resources to defend a takeover bid** to get the support of shareholders, etc., to stop a company being taken over

mode /məʊd/ *noun* a way of doing something □ **mode of payment** the way in which payment is made, e.g. cash or cheque

model /'mɒd(ə)l/ *noun* **1.** a small copy of something made to show what it will look like when finished ○ *They showed us a model of the new office building.* **2.** a style or type of product ○ *This is the latest model.* ○ *The model on display is last year's.* ○ *I drive a 2001 model Range Rover.* **3.** a person whose job is to wear new clothes to show them to possible buyers **4.** something which can be copied ○ *the Swedish model of industrial relations* **5.** a description in the form of mathematical data ■ *adjective* which is a perfect example to be copied ○ *a model agreement* ■ *verb* to wear new clothes to show them to possible buyers ○ *She has decided on a career in modelling.* (NOTE: **modelling – modelled**. The US spelling is **modeling – modeled**.)

model risk /'mɒd(ə)l rɪsk/ *noun* the possibility that a computer model used when investing may have a flaw which makes it function badly in extreme market conditions

modest /'mɒdɪst/ *adjective* small ○ *Oil shares showed modest gains over the week's trading.*

modified accounts /ˌmɒdɪfaɪd ə'kaʊnts/ *plural noun* ⧫ **abbreviated accounts**

momentum /məʊ'mentəm/ *noun* a movement upwards of share prices, suggesting that prices will continue to rise

momentum investor /məʊ'mentəm ɪnˌvestə/ *noun* an investor who buys shares which seem to be moving upwards

monetarism /'mʌnɪtəˌrɪz(ə)m/ *noun* a theory that the amount of money in the economy affects the level of prices, so that inflation can be controlled by regulating money supply

monetarist /'mʌnɪtərɪst/ *noun* a person who believes in monetarism and acts accordingly ■ *adjective* according to monetarism ○ *monetarist theories*

monetary /'mʌnɪt(ə)ri/ *adjective* referring to money or currency

'…the decision by the government to tighten monetary policy will push the annual inflation rate above the year's previous high' [*Financial Times*]

'…it is not surprising that the Fed started to ease monetary policy some months ago' [*Sunday Times*]

'…a draft report on changes in the international monetary system' [*Wall Street Journal*]

monetary assets /ˌmʌnɪt(ə)ri 'æsets/ *plural noun* assets, principally accounts receivable, cash and bank balances, that are realisable at the amount stated in the accounts. Other assets, e.g., facilities and machinery, inventories, and marketable securities will not necessarily realise the sum stated in a business's balance sheet.

monetary base /'mʌnɪt(ə)ri beɪs/ *noun* also called **high-powered money**

monetary control /'mʌnɪt(ə)ri kən ˌtrəʊl/ *noun* control of the money supply

monetary items /ˌmʌnɪt(ə)ri 'aɪtəmz/ *plural noun* monetary assets such as cash or debtors, and monetary liabilities such as an overdraft or creditors, whose values stay the same in spite of inflation

monetary policy /ˌmʌnɪt(ə)ri 'pɒlɪsi/ *noun* the government's policy relating to finance, e.g. bank interest rates, taxes, government expenditure, and borrowing

Monetary Policy Committee /ˌmʌnɪt(ə)ri 'pɒlɪsi kəˌmɪti/ *noun* a committee of the Bank of England, chaired by the Governor of the Bank, which has responsibility for setting interest rates independently of the British government. Its aim is to set rates with a view to keeping inflation at a certain level, and avoiding deflation. Abbreviation **MPC**

'Its Monetary Policy Committee (MPC) gets an opportunity to reveal whether it is still affected by the Christmas spirit when it meets this Wednesday' [*The Times*]

'The Fed next meets to consider interest rates on February 3 and 4, just one day ahead of the February MPC meeting' [*The Times*]

monetary standard /ˌmʌnɪt(ə)ri 'stændəd/ *noun* a fixed exchange rate for a currency

monetary targets /ˌmʌnɪt(ə)ri 'tɑːgɪts/ *plural noun* figures which are given as targets by the government when setting out its budget for the forthcoming year, e.g. the money supply or the PSBR

monetary unit /'mʌnɪt(ə)ri ˌjuːnɪt/ *noun* a main item of currency of a country

money /'mʌni/ *noun* **1.** coins and notes used for buying and selling □ **to earn money** to have a wage or salary □ **to earn good money** to have a large wage or salary □ **to lose money** to make a loss, not to make a profit □ **the company has been losing money for months** the company has been working at a loss for months □ **to get your money back** to make enough profit to cover your original investment □ **to make money** to make a profit □ **to put**

money into the bank to deposit money into a bank account □ **to put money into a business** to invest money in a business ○ *She put all her redundancy money into a shop.* □ **to put money down** to pay cash, especially as a deposit ○ *We put £25 down and paid the rest in instalments.* □ **money up front** payment in advance ○ *They are asking for £10,000 up front before they will consider the deal.* ○ *He had to put money up front before he could clinch the deal.* □ **they are worth a lot of money** they are valuable **2.** □ **in the money** referring to an option to buy at a lower price or to sell at a higher price than the share is currently at □ **out of the money** referring to an option to buy at a higher price or to sell at a lower price than a share is currently trading at

money at call /ˌmʌni ət ˈkɔːl/ *noun* same as **call money**

money at call and short notice /ˌmʌni ət kɔːl ən ʃɔːt ˈnəʊtɪs/ *noun* in the United Kingdom, balances in an account that are either available upon demand (call) or within 14 days (short notice)

money-back guarantee /ˌmʌni ˈbæk gærənˌtiː/, **money-back offer** /ˌmʌni ˈbæk ˌɒfə/ *noun* a guarantee that money will be paid back to customers who are not satisfied with their purchases

moneyback option /ˌmʌniˈbæk ˌɒpʃən/ *noun* an option that guarantees to return the premium if the option is not taken up

money broker /ˈmʌni ˌbrəʊkə/ *noun* a dealer operating in the interbank and foreign exchange markets

money-changer /ˈmʌni ˌtʃeɪndʒə/ *noun* same as **changer**

money laundering /ˈmʌni ˌlɔːndərɪŋ/ *noun* the act of passing illegal money into the banking system

moneylender /ˈmʌniˌlendə/ *noun* a person who lends money at interest

money lying idle /ˌmʌni ˌlaɪɪŋ ˈaɪd(ə)l/ *noun* money which is not being used to produce interest, which is not invested in business

money-making /ˈmʌni ˌmeɪkɪŋ/ *adjective* able to turn over a profit ○ *a money-making plan*

money management /ˈmʌni ˌmænɪdʒmənt/ *noun* same as **fund management**

money market /ˈmʌni ˌmɑːkɪt/ *noun* **1.** a place where large sums of money are lent or borrowed **2.** a market for buying and selling short-term loans or financial instruments such as Treasury bills and CDs, which can be easily converted to cash ○ *The international money markets are nervous.* ◊ **basis**

money market basis /ˈmʌni ˌmɑːkɪt ˌbeɪsɪs/ *noun* □ **on a money market basis** calculated on a year of 365 days

money market fund /ˈmʌni ˌmɑːkɪt fʌnd/ *noun* an investment fund, which only invests in money market instruments

money market instruments /ˈmʌni ˌmɑːkɪt ˌɪnstrʊmənts/ *plural noun* short-term investments which can be easily turned into cash and are traded on the money markets, e.g. CDs

money on call /ˌmʌni ɒn ˈkɔːl/ *noun* same as **call money**

money order /ˈmʌni ˌɔːdə/ *noun* a document which can be bought as a way of sending money through the post

money purchase scheme /ˌmʌni ˈpɜːtʃɪs skiːm/ *noun* any pension scheme to which members make contributions which determine the final pension (as opposed to a 'final salary scheme' where the pension is a percentage of the final salary earned)

money rates /ˈmʌni reɪts/ *plural noun* rates of interest for borrowers or lenders

money-spinner /ˈmʌni ˌspɪnə/ *noun* an item which sells very well or which is very profitable ○ *The home-delivery service has proved to be a real money-spinner.*

money supply /ˈmʌni səˌplaɪ/ *noun* the amount of money in a country's economy, consisting mainly of the money in circulation and that held in savings and cheque accounts

COMMENT: Money supply is believed by some to be at the centre of control of a country's economy. If money supply is tight (i.e. the government restricts the issue of new notes and reduces the possibility of lending) the amount of money available in the economy is reduced and thus may reduce spending. Money supply is calculated in various ways: **M0** (or narrow money supply), including coins and notes in circulation plus the deposits of commercial banks with the Bank of England; **M1**, including all coins and notes plus personal money in current accounts; **M2**, including coins and notes and personal money in current and deposit accounts; **M3**, including coins and notes, personal money in current and deposit accounts, government deposits and deposits in currencies other than sterling (called **£M3** in Britain); **M4**, including M3 plus money on deposit in banks and Treasury bills; **M5**, the broadest measure, which is formed of M4 plus building society accounts and accounts with national savings. In the US, money supply also includes **L**, which is calculated as M3, plus Treasury bills, bonds and commercial paper.

monies /'mʌniz/ *plural noun* sums of money ○ *monies owing to the company* ○ *to collect monies due*

monitor /'mɒnɪtə/ *verb* to check or to examine how something is working ○ *She is monitoring the progress of sales.* ○ *How do you monitor the performance of the sales reps?*

Monopolies and Mergers Commission /mə,nɒpəliz ən 'mɜːdʒəz kə,mɪʃ(ə)n/ *noun* a government organisation which examines takeover bids at the request of the Office of Fair Trading, to see if a successful bid would result in a monopoly and so harm the consumer by reducing competition. Abbreviation **MMC**

monopoly /mə'nɒpəli/ *noun* a situation where one person or company is the only supplier of a particular product or service ○ *to be in a monopoly situation* ○ *The company has the monopoly of imports of Brazilian wine.* ○ *The factory has the absolute monopoly of jobs in the town.*

month /mʌnθ/ *noun* one of twelve periods which make a year ○ *bills due at the end of the current month* ○ *The company pays him £1600 a month.* ○ *She earns £2,000 a month.* □ **paid by the month** paid once each month □ **to give a customer two months' credit** to allow a customer to pay not immediately, but after two months

month end /,mʌnθ 'end/ *noun* the end of a calendar month, when accounts have to be drawn up ○ *The accounts department are working on the month-end accounts.*

monthly /'mʌnθli/ *adjective* happening every month or which is received every month ○ *We get a monthly statement from the bank.* ○ *She makes monthly payments to the credit card company.* ○ *He is paying for his car by monthly instalments.* ○ *My monthly salary cheque is late.* □ **monthly statement** a statement sent to a customer at the end of each month, itemising transactions which have taken place in his or her account ■ *adverb* every month ○ *She asked if she could pay monthly by direct debit.* ○ *The account is credited monthly.*

monthly sales report /,mʌnθli 'seɪlz rɪ,pɔːt/ *noun* a report made every month showing the number of items sold or the amount of money a company has received for selling stock

Moody's Investors Service /,muːdiːz ɪn'vestəz ,sɜːvɪs/ *noun* an American rating organisation, which gives a rating showing the reliability of a debtor organisation (its ratings run from AAA to C). It also issues ratings on municipal bonds, running from MIG1 (the highest rating) to MIG4. ◊ **Standard & Poor's**

moratorium /,mɒrə'tɔːriəm/ *noun* a temporary stop to repayments of interest on loans or capital owed ○ *The banks called for a moratorium on payments.* (NOTE: The plural is **moratoria** or **moratoriums**.)

Morningstar /'mɔːnɪŋstɑː/ *noun US* an agency which gives ratings to mutual funds

mortality and expense risk charge /mɔː,tæliti ən ɪk,spens 'rɪsk tʃɑːdʒ/ *noun* an extra charge to pay on some annuities to guarantee that if the policyholder dies his heirs will receive a benefit, and also that the insurance company will be compensated for an annuitant who lives longer than he or she should according to the mortality tables. Also called **M&E fee**

mortality rate /mɔː'tæləti reɪt/ *noun* the number of deaths occurring during a particular period, shown as a percentage of the total population

mortgage /'mɔːgɪdʒ/ *noun* money lent on the security of a house or other property owned by the borrower, usually in order to enable the borrower to buy the property ○ *to buy a house with a £200,000 mortgage* □ **mortgage payments** money paid each month as interest on a mortgage, plus repayment of a small part of the capital borrowed □ **first mortgage** the main mortgage on a property □ **to pay off a mortgage** to pay back the principal and all the interest on a loan to buy a property □ **mortgage queue** a list of people waiting for mortgages ■ *verb* to use a property as security for a loan ○ *The house is mortgaged to the bank.* ○ *He mortgaged his house to set up in business.* □ **to foreclose on a mortgaged property** to sell a property because the owner cannot repay money which he or she has borrowed, using the property as security

'…mortgage money is becoming tighter. Applications for mortgages are running at a high level and some building societies are introducing quotas' [*Times*]

'…for the first time since mortgage rates began falling a financial institution has raised charges on homeowner loans' [*Globe and Mail (Toronto)*]

mortgage arrears /ˈmɔːgɪdʒ əˌrɪəz/ *plural noun* mortgage payments which are due but have not been paid

mortgage-backed securities /ˌmɔːgɪdʒ bækt sɪˈkjʊərɪtiz/ *plural noun* shares which are backed by the security of a mortgage

mortgage bank /ˈmɔːgɪdʒ bæŋk/ *noun* a bank which lends money to purchasers of properties, on the security of the property

mortgage bond /ˈmɔːgɪdʒ bɒnd/ *noun* a certificate showing that a mortgage exists and that property is security for it

mortgage broker /ˈmɔːgɪdʒ ˌbrəʊkə/ *noun* a person who arranges mortgages, by putting a borrower in touch with a possible lender

mortgage debenture /ˈmɔːgɪdʒ dɪˌbentʃə/ *noun* a debenture where the lender can be repaid by selling the company's property

mortgagee /ˌmɔːgəˈdʒiː/ *noun* a person or company which lends money for someone to buy a property

mortgage famine /ˈmɔːgɪdʒ ˌfæmɪn/ *noun* a situation where there is not enough money available to offer mortgages to house buyers

mortgage interest relief /ˌmɔːgɪdʒ ˈɪntrəst rɪˌliːf/ *noun* a tax benefit which allows people to pay no tax on mortgage interest payments up to a certain level

mortgage interest relief at source /ˌmɔːgɪdʒ ˌɪntrəst rɪˌliːf ət ˈsɔːs/ *noun* a scheme by which the borrower may repay interest on a mortgage less the standard rate tax which he or she would otherwise have to pay on it, i.e. he or she does not pay the full interest and then reclaim the tax. Abbreviation **MIRAS**

mortgage lender /ˈmɔːgɪdʒ ˌlendə/ *noun* a financial institution such as a bank or building society that lends money to people buying property

mortgage portfolio /ˈmɔːgɪdʒ pɔːtˌfəʊliəʊ/ *noun* all the mortgages made by a bank or building society which have not been paid off

mortgager /ˈmɔːgɪdʒə/, **mortgagor** *noun* a person who borrows money to buy a property

mortgage refinancing /ˈmɔːgɪdʒ riːˌfaɪnænsɪŋ/ *noun* the act of arranging to increase a mortgage on a property so as to pay for improvements to the property

mortgage REIT /ˈmɔːgɪdʒ reɪt/ *noun* a trust which provides mortgages to property developers. Full form **mortgage Real Estate Investment Trust**

mortgage relief /ˈmɔːgɪdʒ rɪˌliːf/ *noun* a reduction in tax on interest paid on a mortgage

most favoured nation /ˌməʊst ˌfeɪvəd ˈneɪʃ(ə)n/ *noun* a foreign country to which the home country allows the best trade terms. Abbreviation **MFN**

most-favoured-nation clause /məʊst ˌfeɪvəd ˈneɪʃ(ə)n klɔːz/ *noun* an agreement between two countries that each will offer the best possible terms in commercial contracts

motivation /ˌməʊtɪˈveɪʃ(ə)n/ *noun* eagerness to work well or sell large quantities of a product

mount up *phrasal verb* to increase rapidly ○ *Costs are mounting up.*

mounting /ˈmaʊntɪŋ/ *adjective* increasing ○ *He resigned in the face of mounting pressure from the shareholders.*

○ *The company is faced with mounting debts.*

move /muːv/ *verb* to propose formally that a motion be accepted by a meeting ○ *He moved that the accounts be agreed.* ○ *I move that the meeting should adjourn for ten minutes.*

movement /'muːvmənt/ *noun* an act of changing position or going up or down ○ *movements in the money markets* ○ *cyclical movements of trade*

movement of capital /ˌmuːvmənt əv 'kæpɪt(ə)l/ *noun* same as **capital flow**

mover /'muːvə/ *noun* a person who proposes a motion

moving average /ˌmuːvɪŋ 'æv(ə)rɪdʒ/ *noun* an average of share prices on a stock market, where the calculation is made over a period which moves forward regularly

COMMENT: The commonest are 100-day or 200-day averages, or 10– or 40-week moving averages. The average is calculated as the average figure for the whole period, and moves forward one day or week at a time. These averages are often used by chartists.

MPC /ˌem piː 'siː/ *abbreviation* Monetary Policy Committee

multi- /mʌlti/ *prefix* referring to many things or many of one thing

multicurrency /ˌmʌltɪ'kʌrənsi/ *adjective* in several currencies □ **multicurrency loan** a loan in several currencies

multilateral /ˌmʌlti'læt(ə)rəl/ *adjective* between several organisations or countries ○ *a multilateral agreement* □ **multilateral trade** trade between several countries

Multilateral Investment Guarantee Agency /ˌmʌltiˌlæt(ə)rəl ɪnˌves(t)mənt ˌgærən'tiː/ *noun* abbreviation **MIGA**

multilateral netting /ˌmʌltilæt(ə)rəl 'netɪŋ/ *noun* a method of putting together sums from various sources into one currency, used by groups of banks trading in several currencies at the same time

multi-manager fund /mʌlti 'mænɪdʒə fʌnd/ *noun* a hedge fund which uses a wide portfolio of fund managers to produce a balanced exposure

for relatively small investors. ◊ **hedge fund**, **manager**

multimillion /ˌmʌlti'mɪljən/ *adjective* referring to several million pounds or dollars ○ *They signed a multimillion pound deal.*

multimillionaire /ˌmʌltimɪljə'neə/ *noun* a person who owns property or investments worth several million pounds or dollars

multinational /ˌmʌlti'næʃ(ə)nəl/ *noun, adjective* (a company) which has branches or subsidiary companies in several countries ○ *The company has been bought by one of the big multinationals.* Also called **transnational**

'…the number of multinational firms has mushroomed in the past two decades. As their sweep across the global economy accelerates, multinational firms are posing pressing issues for nations rich and poor, and those in between' [*Australian Financial Review*]

multiple /'mʌltɪp(ə)l/ *adjective* many ■ *noun* **1.** □ **share on a multiple of 5** a share with a P *or* E ratio of 5 (i.e. 5 is the result when dividing the current market price of a share by the earnings per share) **2.** a company with stores in several different towns

'…many independents took advantage of the bank holiday period when the big multiples were closed' [*The Grocer*]

'…the multiple brought the price down to £2.49 in some stores. We had not agreed to this deal and they sold out very rapidly. When they reordered we would not give it to them. This kind of activity is bad for the brand and we cannot afford it' [*The Grocer*]

multiple applications /ˌmʌltɪp(ə)l ˌæplɪ'keɪʃ(ə)nz/ *plural noun* several applications for a new issue of shares, made by the same person, but under different names. In some share issues, people making multiple applications may be prosecuted.

multiple ownership /ˌmʌltɪp(ə)l 'əʊnəʃɪp/ *noun* a situation where something is owned by several parties jointly

multiple store /'mʌltɪp(ə)l stɔː/ *noun* one store in a chain of stores

multiplication /ˌmʌltɪplɪ'keɪʃ(ə)n/ *noun* an act of multiplying

multiplication   sign   /ˌmʌltɪplɪ
ˈkeɪʃ(ə)n saɪn/ *noun* a sign (x) used to
show that a number is being multiplied by
another

multiplier /ˈmʌltɪplaɪə/ *noun* a number
which multiplies another, or a factor
which tends to multiply something, as the
effect of new expenditure on total income
and reserves

multiply /ˈmʌltɪplaɪ/ *verb* **1.** to calculate the sum of various numbers added
together a particular number of times ○ *If
you multiply twelve by three you get
thirty-six.* ○ *Square measurements are
calculated by multiplying length by width.*
2. to grow or to increase ○ *Profits multiplied in the boom years.*

muni /ˈmjuːni/ *noun* same as **municipal bond** (*informal*)

municipal   bond   /mjuːˌnɪsɪp(ə)l
ˈbɒnd/ *noun US* a bond issued by a town
or district (NOTE: The UK term is **local
authority bond**.)

municipal   bond   fund   /mjuː
ˈnɪsɪp(ə)l bɒnd fʌnd/, **muni fund**
/ˈmjuːni fʌnd/ *noun US* a fund invested

in municipal bonds (NOTE: Usually called
munis.)

mutual /ˈmjuːtʃuəl/ *adjective* owned
by members, not by shareholders ■ *noun*
any commercial organisation that is
owned by its members, rather than by
shareholders

mutual association /ˈmjuːtʃuəl ə
ˌsəʊsieɪʃ(ə)n/ *noun US* a form of savings
and loan association which is owned by
its members

mutual   company   /ˈmjuːtʃuəl
ˌkʌmp(ə)ni/ *noun* same as **mutual
insurance company**

mutual fund /ˈmjuːtʃuəl fʌnd/ *noun
US* same as **unit trust**

mutual   insurance   company
/ˈmjuːtʃuəl ˌkʌmp(ə)ni/ *noun* a
company which belongs to insurance
policy holders. Also called **mutual
company**

mutual savings bank /ˌmjuːtʃuəl
ˈseɪvɪŋz bæŋk/ *noun* a savings bank
which is owned by the customers who
have deposits with it

MVA *abbreviation* **1.** market value added
2. market value adjuster

N

N *abbreviation* naira

nail /neɪl/ *noun* □ **to pay on the nail** to pay promptly, to pay rapidly

naira /'naɪrə/ *noun* a unit of currency used in Nigeria (NOTE: no plural; naira is usually written **N** before figures: **N2,000** say 'two thousand naira')

naked /'neɪkɪd/ *adjective* used for describing investment that is not protected from risks inherent in a particular position or market

name /neɪm/ *noun* **1.** the word used for referring to a person, animal, or thing ○ *I cannot remember the name of the managing director of Smith Ltd* ○ *His first name is John, but I am not sure of his other names.* □ **under the name of** using a particular name □ **trading under the name of 'Best Foods'** using the name 'Best Foods' as a commercial name, and not the name of the company **2.** a person who provides security for insurance arranged by a Lloyd's of London syndicate. ↷ **Lloyd's**

named /neɪmd/ *adjective* □ **the person named in the policy** the person whose name is given on an insurance policy as the person insured

narrow market /'nærəʊ 'mɑːkɪt/ *noun* a market in a share where very few shares are available for sale, and where the price can vary sharply

NASDAQ /'næzdæk/ *abbreviation* a system which provides quotations via computer for the US electronic trading market, mainly in high tech stocks, and also for some large corporations listed on the NYSE, and publishes an index of stock price movements. Full form **National Association of Securities Dealers Automated Quotations system** (NOTE: The UK term is **SEAQ**.)

nation /'neɪʃ(ə)n/ *noun* a country and the people living in it

national /'næʃ(ə)nəl/ *adjective* referring to the whole of a particular country

National Association of Securities Dealers Automated Quotations system *noun* full form of **NASDAQ**

national bank /'næʃ(ə)nəl bæŋk/ *noun* in the US, a bank which is chartered by the federal government and is part of the Federal Reserve system. Compare **state bank**

national central bank /ˌnæʃ(ə)nəl ˌsentrəl 'bæŋk/ *noun* one of central banks of the countries which form the eurozone, under the overall European Central Bank. Abbreviation **NCB**

national currency /ˌnæʃ(ə)nəl 'kʌrənsi/ *noun* the official currency of a country, which is legal tender in that country

National Debt /ˌnæʃ(ə)nəl 'det/ *noun* money borrowed by a government

national income /ˌnæʃ(ə)nəl 'ɪnkʌm/ *noun* the value of income from the sales of goods and services in a country

National Insurance contribution /ˌnæʃ(ə)nəl ɪn'ʃʊərəns ˌkɒntrɪˈbjuːʃ(ə)n/ *noun* a proportion of income paid each month by an employee and the employee's company to the National Insurance scheme, which pays for medical care, hospitals, unemployment benefits, etc. Abbreviation **NIC**

nationalisation /ˌnæʃ(ə)nəlaɪˈzeɪʃ(ə)n/, **nationalization** *noun* the taking over of private industry by the state

nationalise /'næʃ(ə)nəlaɪz/, **nationalize** *verb* to put a privately-owned industry under state ownership and control ○ *The government is planning to nationalise the banking system.*

nationalised industry /ˌnæʃ(ə)nə ˌlaɪzd ˈɪndəstri/ *noun* an industry which was privately owned, but is now owned by the state

nationality /ˌnæʃəˈnælɪti/ *noun* the state of being a citizen of a particular country □ **he is of British nationality** he is a British citizen

nationality declaration /ˌnæʃə ˈnæləti ˌdekləreɪʃ(ə)n/ *noun* a declaration on some share application forms of the applicant's nationality

national press /ˌnæʃ(ə)nəl ˈpres/ *noun* newspapers which sell in all parts of the country ○ *The new car has been advertised in the national press.*

National Savings and Investments /ˌnæʃ(ə)nəl ˌseɪvɪŋz ənd ɪn ˈvestmənts/ *noun* a part of the Exchequer, a savings scheme for small investors including savings certificates and premium bonds. Abbreviation **NS&I**

National Savings Bank /ˌnæʃ(ə)nəl ˈseɪvɪŋz ˌbæŋk/ *noun* in the United Kingdom, a savings scheme established in 1861 as the Post Office Savings Bank and now operated by National Savings and Investments. Abbreviation **NSB**

National Savings certificates /ˌnæʃ(ə)nəl ˈseɪvɪŋz səˌtɪfɪkəts/ *plural noun* certificates showing that someone has invested in National Savings and Investments. The NS&I issues certificates with stated interest rates and stated maturity dates, usually five or ten years.

National Savings Stock Register /ˌnæʃ(ə)nəl ˌseɪvɪŋz ˈstɒk ˌredʒɪstə/ *noun* an organisation, run by National Savings and Investments, which gives private individuals the opportunity to buy British government stocks by post without going through a stockbroker

NAV *abbreviation* net asset value

NB *abbreviation* from a Latin phrase meaning 'note (this) well', i.e. pay attention to this. Full form **Nota bene**

NCB *abbreviation* national central bank

NDIP *abbreviation* non-deposit investment product

near-liquid asset /nɪə ˌlɪkwɪd ˈæset/, **near money** /nɪə ˈmʌni/ *noun* an asset which can easily be converted to cash

negative /ˈnegətɪv/ *adjective* meaning 'no' □ **the answer was in the negative** the answer was 'no'

negative carry /ˌnegətɪv ˈkæri/ *noun* a deal where the cost of finance is more than the return on the capital used

negative cash flow /ˌnegətɪv ˈkæʃ fləʊ/ *noun* a situation where more money is going out of a company than is coming in

negative equity /ˌnegətɪv ˈekwɪti/ *noun* a situation where a house bought with a mortgage becomes less valuable than the money borrowed to buy it because of falling house prices

negative yield curve /ˌnegətɪv ˈjiːld kɜːv/ *noun* a situation where the yield on a long-term investment is less than that on a short-term investment

neglected /nɪˈglektɪd/ *adjective* not well looked after □ **neglected shares** shares which are not bought or sold often ○ *Bank shares have been a neglected sector of the market this week.*

neglected business /nɪˌglektɪd ˈbɪznɪs/ *noun* a company which has not been actively run by its owners and could therefore do better

negligence /ˈneglɪdʒəns/ *noun* **1.** a lack of proper care or failure to carry out a duty (with the result that a person or property is harmed) **2.** the act of not doing a job properly when one is capable of doing it

negligible /ˈneglɪdʒɪb(ə)l/ *adjective* very small □ **shares of negligible value** shares which are considered by the income tax to have no value, because the company has ceased to exist. (Companies in receivership are not of negligible value, though they may end up in that category.).

negotiable /nɪˈgəʊʃiəb(ə)l/ *adjective* **1.** transferable from one person to another or exchanged for cash □ **not negotiable** which cannot be exchanged for cash □ **'not negotiable'** words written on a cheque to show that it can be paid only to a specific person □ **negotiable cheque** a cheque made payable to bearer, i.e. to anyone who holds it **2.** which can be discussed so that an agreement is reached ○ *The salary for the job is negotiable.*

'…initial salary is negotiable around $45,000 per annum' [*Australian Financial Review*]

negotiable certificate of deposit /nɪˌɡəʊʃiəb(ə)l səˌtɪfɪkət əv dɪˈpɒzɪt/, **negotiable CD** /nɪˌɡəʊʃiəb(ə)l ˌsiː ˈdiː/ *noun* a receipt issued by a bank for a large sum deposited with the bank, which acts as an interest-bearing deposit

negotiable instrument /nɪˌɡəʊʃiəb(ə)l ˈɪnstrʊmənt/ *noun* a document which can be exchanged for cash, e.g. a bill of exchange or a cheque

negotiable order of withdrawal /nɪˌɡəʊʃiəb(ə)l ˌɔːdə əv wɪðˈdrɔːəl/ *adjective* a cheque written on a NOW account

negotiable order of withdrawal account /nɪˌɡəʊʃiəb(ə)l ˌɔːdə əv wɪð ˈdrɔːəl əˌkaʊnt/ *noun US* full form of **NOW account**

negotiable paper /nɪˌɡəʊʃiəb(ə)l ˈpeɪpə/ *noun* a document which can be transferred from one owner to another for cash

negotiate /nɪˈɡəʊʃieɪt/ *verb* □ to negotiate with someone to discuss a problem or issue formally with someone, so as to reach an agreement ○ *The management refused to negotiate with the union.* □ **to negotiate terms and conditions** *or* **a contract** to discuss and agree the terms of a contract □ **he negotiated a £250,000 loan with the bank** he came to an agreement with the bank for a loan of £250,000

negotiated commission /nɪˌɡəʊʃieɪtɪd kəˈmɪʃ(ə)n/ *noun* a commission agreed with an advertising agency before work starts, and which may be different from standard commissions

negotiation /nɪˌɡəʊʃiˈeɪʃ(ə)n/ *noun* the discussion of terms and conditions in order to reach an agreement □ **contract under negotiation** a contract which is being discussed □ **a matter for negotiation** something which must be discussed before a decision is reached □ **to enter into** *or* **to start negotiations** to start discussing a problem □ **to resume negotiations** to start discussing a problem again, after talks have stopped for a time □ **to break off negotiations** to stop discussing a problem □ **to conduct negotiations** to negotiate □ **negotiations broke down after six hours** discussions stopped because no agreement was possible

'…after three days of tough negotiations, the company reached agreement with its 1,200 unionized workers' [*Toronto Star*]

negotiator /nɪˈɡəʊʃieɪtə/ *noun* **1.** a person who discusses a problem with the aim of achieving agreement between different people or groups of people □ **experienced union negotiator** a member of a union who has a lot of experience of discussing terms of employment with management **2.** a person who works in an estate agency

nest egg /ˈnest eɡ/ *noun* money which someone has saved over a period of time, usually kept in an interest-bearing account and intended for use after retirement

net /net/ *adjective* **1.** referring to a price, weight, pay, etc., after all deductions have been made **2.** □ **terms strictly net** payment has to be the full price, with no discount allowed (NOTE: [all adjective senses] The spelling **nett** is sometimes used on containers.) ■ *verb* to make a true profit ○ *to net a profit of £10,000* (NOTE: **netting – netted**) □ **to net out** to balance debits and credits to give a net result

'…out of its earnings a company will pay a dividend. When shareholders receive this it will be net, that is it will have had tax deducted at 30 per cent' [*Investors Chronicle*]

net asset value per share /ˌnet ˌæset ˌvæljuː pə ˈʃeə/ *noun* the value of a company calculated by dividing the shareholders' funds by the number of shares issued

net book value /ˌnet ˈbʊk ˌvæljuː/ *noun* the historical cost of an asset less any accumulated depreciation or other provision for diminution in value, e.g., reduction to net realisable value, or asset value which has been revalued downwards to reflect market conditions. Abbreviation **NBV**. Also called **written-down value**

net borrowings /ˌnet ˈbɒrəʊɪŋz/ *plural noun* a company's borrowings, less any cash the company is holding in its bank accounts

net cash flow /ˌnet ˈkæʃ ˌfləʊ/ *noun* the difference between the money coming in and the money going out of a firm

net change on the day /net ˌtʃeɪndʒ ɒn ðə ˈdeɪ/ *adjective* the difference between the opening price of a share at the beginning of a day's trading and the closing price at the end

net current assets /ˌnet ˌkʌrənt ˈæsets/ *plural noun* the current assets of a company, i.e. cash and stocks, less any liabilities. Also called **net working capital**

net dividend per share /ˌnet ˌdɪvɪdend pə ˈʃeə/ *noun* the dividend per share after deduction of personal income tax

net earnings /ˌnet ˈɜːnɪŋz/ *plural noun* the total earnings of a business after tax and other deductions

net income /ˌnet ˈɪnkʌm/ *noun* a person's or organisation's income which is left after taking away tax and other deductions

net interest margin /net ˈɪntrəst ˌmɑːdʒɪn/ *noun* the difference between what a bank receives in interest on loans and what it pays out in interest on deposits

net loss /ˌnet ˈlɒs/ *noun* an actual loss, after deducting overheads

net margin /ˌnet ˈmɑːdʒɪn/ *noun* the percentage difference between received price and all costs, including overheads

net price /ˌnet ˈpraɪs/ *noun* the price of goods or services which cannot be reduced by a discount

net profit /ˌnet ˈprɒfɪt/ *noun* the amount by which income from sales is larger than all expenditure. Also called **profit after tax**

net receipts /ˌnet rɪˈsiːts/ *plural noun* receipts after deducting commission, tax, discounts, etc.

net return /ˌnet rɪˈtɜːn/ *noun* a return on an investment after tax has been paid

net salary /ˌnet ˈsæləri/ *noun* the salary which is left after deducting tax and National Insurance contributions

net sales /ˌnet ˈseɪlz/ *plural noun* the total amount of sales less damaged or returned items and discounts to retailers

net weight /ˌnet ˈweɪt/ *noun* the weight of goods after deducting the packing material and container

net working capital /ˌnet ˌwɜːkɪŋ ˈkæpɪt(ə)l/ *noun* same as **net current assets**

net worth /ˌnet ˈwɜːθ/ *noun* the value of all the property of a person or company after taking away what the person or company owes ○ *The upmarket product is targeted at individuals of high net worth.*

net yield /ˌnet ˈjiːld/ *noun* the profit from investments after deduction of tax

neurolinguistic programming /ˌnjʊərəʊlɪŋgwɪstɪk ˈprəʊgræmɪŋ/ *noun* a theory of behaviour and communication based on how people avoid change and how to help them to change. Abbreviation **NLP**

new /njuː/ *adjective* recent or not old □ **under new management** with a new owner

new issue /ˌnjuː ˈɪʃuː/ *noun* an issue of new shares to raise finance for a company

new issue market /ˌnjuː ˈɪʃuː ˌmɑːkɪt/ *noun* a market where companies can raise finance by issuing new shares, or by a flotation

new issue sale /njuː ˈɪʃuː seɪl/ *noun* a sale of a new issue of shares

new issues department /ˌnjuː ˈɪʃuːz dɪˌpɑːtmənt/ *noun* the section of a bank which deals with issues of new shares

new money /njuː ˈmʌni/ *noun* finance provided by a new issue of shares or by the transfer of money from one account to another

news agency /ˈnjuːz ˌeɪdʒənsi/ *noun* an office which distributes news to newspapers and television stations

new time /ˈnjuː taɪm/ *noun* the next account on a stock exchange (where sales in the last few days of the previous account are credited to the following account)

New York Cotton Exchange /ˌnjuː jɔːk ˈkɒtən ɪksˌtʃeɪndʒ/ *noun* a commodity exchange, based in New York, dealing in cotton and other commodities, and also in financial futures through the NYFE. Abbreviation **NYCE**

New York Futures Exchange /ˌnjuː jɔːk ˈfjuːtʃəz ɪksˌtʃeɪndʒ/ *noun* a financial futures and options exchange, based in New York, part of the NYCE. Abbreviation **NYFE**

New York Stock Exchange /ˌnjuː jɔːk 'stɒk ɪksˌtʃeɪndʒ/ noun the main US Stock Exchange, situated on Wall Street in New York. Abbreviation **NYSE**. Also called **Big Board**

ngultrum /əŋ'gʊltrəm/ noun a unit of currency used in Bhutan

NIC abbreviation National Insurance contribution

niche /niːʃ/ noun a special place in a market, occupied by one company (a 'niche company') ○ They seem to have discovered a niche in the market.

niche bank /'niːʃ bæŋk/ noun a specialised bank which deals only with certain types of customers or services

niche company /ˌniːʃ 'kʌmp(ə)ni/ noun company specialising in a particular type of product or service, which occupies a market niche

nickel /'nɪk(ə)l/ noun **1.** a valuable metal traded on commodity exchanges, such as the London Metal Exchange **2.** US a five cent coin

NIF abbreviation note issuance facility

night /naɪt/ noun a period of time from evening to morning

night rate /'naɪt reɪt/ noun a cheap rate for telephone calls at night

night safe /'naɪt seɪf/ noun a safe in the outside wall of a bank, where money and documents can be deposited at night, using a special door

Nikkei Average /nɪ'keɪ ˌæv(ə)rɪdʒ/ an index of prices on the Tokyo Stock Exchange, based on about 200 leading shares

nil /nɪl/ noun zero or nothing ○ The advertising budget has been cut to nil.

nil paid shares /ˌnɪl peɪd 'ʃeəz/ plural noun new shares which have not yet been paid for

nil return /ˌnɪl rɪ'tɜːn/ noun a report showing no sales, income, tax, etc.

NLP abbreviation neurolinguistic programming

No., No abbreviation number

no-claims bonus /ˌnəʊ 'kleɪmz ˌbəʊnəs/ noun a lower premium paid because no claims have been made against the insurance policy

no-load fund /nəʊ 'ləʊd fʌnd/ noun a fund sold directly by the fund company, with low management charges and no commission to a broker

nominal /'nɒmɪn(ə)l/ adjective (of a payment) very small ○ They are paying a nominal rent. ○ The employment agency makes a nominal charge for its services.

nominal capital /ˌnɒmɪn(ə)l 'kæpɪt(ə)l/ noun the total of the face value of all the shares which a company is authorised to issue

nominal interest rate /ˌnɒmɪn(ə)l 'ɪntrəst reɪt/ noun an interest rate expressed as a percentage of the face value of a bond, not on its market value

nominal ledger /ˌnɒmɪn(ə)l 'ledʒə/ noun a book which records a company's transactions in the various accounts

nominal value /ˌnɒmɪn(ə)l 'væljuː/ noun same as **face value**

nominate /'nɒmɪneɪt/ verb to suggest someone for a job □ **to nominate someone to a post** to appoint someone to a post without an election □ **to nominate someone as proxy** to name someone as your proxy

nomination /ˌnɒmɪ'neɪʃ(ə)n/ noun the act of nominating someone for a position

nominee /ˌnɒmɪ'niː/ noun a person who is nominated, especially someone who is appointed to deal with financial matters on your behalf

nominee account /ˌnɒmɪ'niː əˌkaʊnt/ noun an account held on behalf of someone

COMMENT: shares can be purchased and held in nominee accounts so that the identity of the owner of the shares cannot be discovered easily.

non- /nɒn/ prefix not

non-acceptance /ˌnɒn ək'septəns/ noun a situation in which the person who is to pay a bill of exchange does not accept it

non-bank /'nɒn bæŋk/ noun a financial institution which is not a commercial bank according to the official definition (so an institution which only makes loans, and does not take deposits does not fall within the official definition of a bank and is not subject to the same regulations)

noncash items /ˌnɒn kæʃ 'aɪtəmz/ plural noun cheques, drafts and similar items which are not in the form of cash

noncompete agreement /ˌnɒnkəm
'piːt əˌgriːmənt/ *noun US* a type of
contract of employment by which an
employee guarantees that he will not
work for a competing firm after leaving
his or her job

nondeductible /ˌnɒndɪ'dʌktɪb(ə)l/
adjective which cannot be deducted from
income tax

non-delivery /ˌnɒndɪ'lɪv(ə)ri/ *noun*
the failure to deliver goods that have been
ordered

non-deposit investment product
/nɒndɪˌpɒzɪt ɪn'vestmənt ˌprɒdʌkt/
noun US any investment, such as securities or mutual funds, which is not insured
by the FDIC. Abbreviation **NDIP**

non-durables /nɒn'djʊərəb(ə)lz/,
non-durable goods /ˌnɒn 'djʊərəb(ə)l
gʊdz/ *plural noun* goods which are used
up soon after they have been bought, e.g.
food or newspapers

non-exec /ˌnɒn ɪg'zek/ *noun* same as
non-executive director

non-executive director /ˌnɒn ɪg
ˌzekjʊtɪv daɪ'rektə/ *noun* a director
who attends board meetings and gives
advice, but does not work full-time for the
company. Also called **outside director**.
Compare **executive director**

COMMENT: Non-executive directors keep an
eye on the way the company is run, and in
particular make sure that the executive
directors are doing their work properly.
They may also intervene in disputes
between directors, or between shareholders and directors.

non-feasance /ˌnɒn'fiːz(ə)ns/ *noun* a
failure to do something which should be
done by law

non-interest /nɒn'ɪntrəst/ *noun* a
bank's income from fees and charges, as
opposed to income from interest

non-legal /nɒn'liːg(ə)l/ *adjective* not
legal

non-legal investment /nɒnˌliːg(ə)l
ɪn'vestmənt/ *noun US* an investment
which is not on the legal list, and which a
bank cannot invest in

nonmember bank /nɒn'membə
bæŋk/ *noun US* a bank which is not a
member of the Federal Reserve System

non-negotiable instrument /ˌnɒn
nɪˌgəʊʃəb(ə)l 'ɪnstrʊmənt/ *noun* a

document which cannot be exchanged for
cash, e.g. a crossed cheque

non-payment /ˌnɒn 'peɪmənt/ *noun* □
non-payment of a debt the act of not
paying a debt that is due

non-performing loan /ˌnɒn pɜː
ˌfɔːmɪŋ 'ləʊn/ *noun US* a loan where the
borrower is not likely to pay any interest
nor to repay the principal, as in the case of
loans to Third World countries by western
banks

non-profit-making organisation
/ˌnɒn ˌprɒfɪtmeɪkɪŋ ˌɔːgənaɪ'zeɪʃən/,
non-profit organisation /nɒn 'prɒfɪt
ɔːgənaɪˌzeɪʃ(ə)n/ *noun* an organisation
which is not allowed by law to make a
profit ○ *Non-profit-making organisations
are exempted from tax.* (NOTE: Non-profit-
making organisations include charities,
professional associations, trade unions,
and religious, arts, community,
research, and campaigning bodies. The
US term is **nonprofit organization**.)

non-recurring items /ˌnɒn rɪˌkɜːrɪŋ
'aɪtəmz/ *plural noun* items in an income
statement that are unusual in nature or do
not occur regularly

non-refundable /ˌnɒn rɪ'fʌndəb(ə)l/
adjective not refunded in normal circumstances ○ *You will be asked to make a
non-refundable deposit.*

nonregulated /nɒn'regjʊletɪtɪd/
adjective which is not subject to government regulations ○ *a nonregulated
subsidiary that builds and manages
energy projects for industrial customers*
○ *The banking industry was totally
nonregulated in the nineteenth century.*

non-resident /ˌnɒn 'rezɪd(ə)nt/ *noun,
adjective* a person who is not considered
a resident of a country for tax purposes ○
He has a non-resident bank account.

non-statutory /nɒn 'stætʃʊt(ə)ri/
adjective not covered by legislation

non-sufficient funds /ˌnɒn səˌfɪʃənt
'fʌndz/ *noun US* a lack of enough money
in a bank account to pay a cheque drawn
on that account. Abbreviation **NSF**. Also
called **insufficient funds**, **not sufficient funds**

non-taxable /ˌnɒn 'tæksəb(ə)l/ *adjective* not subject to tax ○ *non-taxable
income* ○ *Lottery prizes are non-taxable.*

non-voting shares /ˌnɒn ˌvəʊtɪŋ
'ʃeəz/ *plural noun* shares which do not

allow the shareholder to vote at meetings. ◊ **A shares**

normal working week /ˌnɔːm(ə)l ˈwɜːkɪŋ wiːk/ *noun* the usual number of hours worked per week ○ *Even though she is a freelance, she works a normal working week.*

nostro account /ˈnɒstrəʊ əˌkaʊnt/ *noun* an account which a bank has with a correspondent bank in another country. ◊ **vostro account**

notary public /ˌnəʊtəri ˈpʌblɪk/ *noun* a lawyer who has the authority to witness documents and spoken statements, making them official (NOTE: The plural is **notaries public.**)

note /nəʊt/ *noun* **1.** a short document or piece of writing, or a short piece of information ○ *to send someone a note* ○ *I left a note on her desk.* □ **notes to the accounts** notes attached to a company's accounts by the auditors to explain items in the accounts or to explain the principles of accounting used **2.** same as **banknote** ■ *verb* to notice an advertisement in a publication but not necessarily read or understand it

note issuance facility /ˈnəʊt ˌɪʃuəns fəˌsɪlɪti/ *noun* a credit facility where a company obtains a loan underwritten by banks and can issue a series of short-term Eurocurrency notes to replace others which have expired. Abbreviation **NIF**

note of hand /ˌnəʊt əv ˈhænd/ *noun* a document stating that someone promises to pay an amount of money on an agreed date

notice /ˈnəʊtɪs/ *noun* **1.** a piece of written information ○ *The company secretary pinned up a notice about the pension scheme.* **2.** an official warning that a contract is going to end or that terms are going to be changed □ **until further notice** until different instructions are given ○ *You must pay £200 on the 30th of each month until further notice.* **3.** the time allowed before something takes place ○ *We require three months' notice* □ **at short notice** with very little warning ○ *The bank manager will not see anyone at short notice.* □ **you must give seven days' notice of withdrawal** you must ask to take money out of the account seven days before you want it

notional /ˈnəʊʃ(ə)n(ə)l/ *adjective* probable but not known exactly or not quantifiable

notional income /ˌnəʊʃ(ə)n(ə)l ˈɪnkʌm/ *noun* an invisible benefit which is not money or goods and services

notional rent /ˌnəʊʃ(ə)n(ə)l ˈrent/ *noun* a sum put into accounts as rent where the company owns the building it is occupying and so does not pay an actual rent

not sufficient funds /ˌnɒt sə ˌfɪʃ(ə)nt ˈfʌndz/ *noun US* same as **non-sufficient funds**. Abbreviation **NSF**

nought /nɔːt/ *noun* the figure 0 ○ *A million pounds can be written as '£1m' or as one and six noughts.* (NOTE: **Nought** is commoner in UK English; in US English, **zero** is more usual.)

novation /nəʊˈveɪʃ(ə)n/ *noun* an agreement to change a contract by substituting a third party for one of the two original parties

NOW account /ˈnaʊ əˌkaʊnt/ *noun US* an interest-bearing account with a bank or savings and loan association, on which cheques called 'negotiable orders of withdrawal' can be drawn. Full form **negotiable order of withdrawal account**

NS&I *abbreviation* National Savings and Investments

NSB *abbreviation* National Savings Bank

NSF /ˌen es ˈef/ *abbreviation* not sufficient funds *or* non-sufficient funds

null /nʌl/ *adjective* which cannot legally be enforced □ **the contract was declared null and void** the contract was said to be not valid

number /ˈnʌmbə/ *noun* **1.** a quantity of things or people ○ *The number of persons on the payroll has increased over the last year.* ○ *The number of days lost through strikes has fallen.* **2.** a printed or written figure that identifies a particular thing ○ *Please write your account number on the back of the cheque.* ○ *If you have a complaint to make, always quote the batch number.* ○ *She noted the cheque number in the ledger.* **3.** an amount in figures ■ *verb* to put a figure on a document ○ *to number an order* ○ *I refer to your invoice numbered 1234.*

number cruncher /ˈnʌmbə ˌkrʌntʃə/ noun a person who makes calculations involving large figures (*informal*)

numbered account /ˌnʌmbəd ə ˈkaʊnt/ noun a bank account, usually in Switzerland, which is referred to only by a number, the name of the person holding it being kept secret

numeric /njuːˈmerɪk/, **numerical** /njuːˈmerɪk(ə)l/ adjective referring to numbers

numerical order /njuːˌmerɪk(ə)l ˈɔːdə/ noun an arrangement by numbers ○ *Put these invoices in numerical order.* □ **in numerical order** in the order of figures, e.g. 1 before 2, 33 before 34 ○ *Put these invoices in numerical order.*

numeric data /njuːˌmerɪk ˈdeɪtə/ noun data in the form of figures

NV abbreviation a Dutch private limited company. Full form **naamloze venootschap**

NYCE abbreviation New York Cotton Exchange

NYFE abbreviation New York Futures Exchange

NYSE abbreviation New York Stock Exchange

O

OAC *abbreviation* on approved credit

O & M *abbreviation* organisation and methods

Obamanomics /ˌəʊbɑːməˈnɒmɪks/ *noun* a term describing the economic philosophy of US president Barack Obama i.e. lower tax rates for companies that meet certain criteria, higher taxes for high-income families and investment in education, healthcare and the sciences

objective /əbˈdʒektɪv/ *noun* something which you hope to achieve ○ *The company has achieved its objectives.* ○ *We set the sales forces specific objectives.* ○ *Our recruitment objectives are to have well-qualified and well-placed staff.* □ **long-term** *or* **short-term objective** an aim which you hope to achieve within a few years or a few months ■ *adjective* considered from a general point of view rather than from that of the person involved ○ *You must be objective in assessing the performance of the staff.* ○ *They have been asked to carry out an objective survey of the market.*

obligate /ˈɒblɪgeɪt/ *verb* □ **to be obligated to do something** to have a legal duty to do something

obligation /ˌɒblɪˈgeɪʃ(ə)n/ *noun* **1.** a duty to do something ○ *There is no obligation to help out in another department* ○ *There is no obligation to buy.* □ **two weeks' free trial without obligation** the customer can try the item at home for two weeks without having to buy it at the end of the test □ **to be under an obligation to do something** to feel it is your duty to do something □ **he is under no contractual obligation to buy** he has signed no contract which forces him to buy □ **to fulfil your contractual obligations** to do what is stated in a contract **2.** a debt □ **to meet your obligations** to pay your debts

o.b.o. *abbreviation* or best offer

occupational /ˌɒkjuˈpeɪʃ(ə)nəl/ *adjective* referring to a job

occupational accident /ˌɒkjuˈpeɪʃ(ə)nəl ˈæksɪd(ə)nt/ *noun* an accident which takes place at work

occupational pension /ˌɒkjuˈpeɪʃ(ə)nəl ˈpenʃə/ *noun* a pension which is paid by the company by which an employee has been employed

occupational pension scheme /ˌɒkjupeɪʃ(ə)nəl ˈpenʃən skiːm/ *noun* a pension scheme where the employee gets a pension from a fund set up by the company he or she has worked for, which is related to the salary he or she was earning. Also called **company pension scheme**

occupier /ˈɒkjupaɪə/ *noun* a person who lives in a property

odd /ɒd/ *adjective* □ **a hundred odd** approximately one hundred □ **keep the odd change** keep the small change which is left over

odd lot /ˌɒd ˈlɒt/ *noun* **1.** a group of miscellaneous items for sale at an auction **2.** *US* a group of less than 100 shares of stock bought or sold together

oddments /ˈɒdmənts/ *plural noun* leftover pieces of large items, sold separately

OECD *abbreviation* Organisation for Economic Co-operation and Development

'...calling for a greater correlation between labour market policies, social policies and education and training, the OECD warned that long-term unemployment would remain unacceptably high without a reassessment of labour market trends' [*Australian Financial Review*]

OEIC /ɔɪk/ *abbreviation* open-ended investment company

OFEX *noun* private trading facilities for buying and selling shares in companies which are not quoted on the London Stock Exchange

off /ɒf/ *adverb* **1.** taken away from a price ○ *We give 5% off for quick settlement.* **2.** lower than a previous price ○ *The shares closed 2% off.* ■ *preposition* **1.** subtracted from ○ *to take £25 off the price* ○ *We give 10% off our usual prices.* **2.** not included □ **items off balance sheet** *or* **off balance sheet assets** financial items which do not appear in a company's balance sheet as assets, such as equipment acquired under an operating lease

'...its stock closed Monday at $21.875 a share in NYSE composite trading, off 56% from its high last July' [*Wall Street Journal*]

off-balance-sheet financing /ˌɒf ˈbæləns ʃiːt ˌfaɪnænsɪŋ/ *noun* a way of raising finance through a long-term lease that does not qualify as a capital lease and therefore does not appear on the balance sheet

offer /ˈɒfə/ *noun* **1.** a statement that you are willing to give or do something, especially to pay a specific amount of money to buy something ○ *to make an offer for a company* ○ *We made an offer of £10 a share.* ○ *We made a written offer for the house.* ○ *£1,000 is the best offer I can make.* ○ *We accepted an offer of £1,000 for the car.* □ **the house is under offer** someone has made an offer to buy the house and the offer has been accepted provisionally □ **we are open to offers** we are ready to discuss the price which we are asking □ **or near offer** *US*, **or best offer** or an offer of a price which is slightly less than the price asked (*often shortened to* **o.n.o.** *or* **o.b.o.**) ○ *The car is for sale at £2,000 or near offer.* **2.** a statement that you are willing to sell something □ **on offer** for sale or available **3.** a statement that you are willing to employ someone □ **she received six offers of jobs** *or* **six job offers** six companies told her she could have a job with them **4.** a statement that a company is prepared to buy another company's shares and take the company over ■ *verb* **1.** to say that you are willing to do something ○ *We offered to go with them to the meeting.* □ **to offer someone a job** to tell

someone that they can have a job in your company ○ *She was offered a directorship with Smith Ltd.* **2.** to say that you are willing to pay a specific amount of money for something ○ *to offer someone £500,000 for their house* ○ *She offered £10 a share.* **3.** to say that you are willing to sell something ○ *They are offering special prices on winter holidays in the US* ○ *We offered the house for sale.*

offer document /ˈɒfə ˌdɒkjʊmənt/ *noun* a formal document where a company offers to buy shares at some price as part of a takeover bid

offered market /ˌɒfəd ˈmaːkɪt/ *noun* a market where there are more sellers than buyers

offered price /ˌɒfəd ˈpraɪs/ *noun* a price at which shares are offered for sale by a marketmaker on the stock exchange. The opposite, i.e. the price at which an investor sells shares, is the 'bid price', the difference between the two is the 'spread'.

offered rate /ˌɒfəd ˈreɪt/ *noun* a rate of interest at which banks are prepared to lend each other money

offer for sale /ˌɒfə fə ˈseɪl/ *noun* a situation in which a company advertises new shares for sale to the public as a way of launching itself on the stock exchange (NOTE: The other ways of launching a company are a 'tender' or a 'placing'.)

offer for subscription /ˌɒfə fə səbˈskrɪpʃ(ə)n/ *noun* a similar to an offer for sale, except there is a minimum level of subscription for the shares, and if this is not reached the offer is withdrawn

offering /ˈɒf(ə)rɪŋ/ *noun* an action of stating that you are prepared to sell something at some price

'...shares of newly public companies posted their worst performance of the year last month as a spate of initial public offerings disappointed followers' [*Wall Street Journal*]

'...if the partnership supports a sale, a public offering of shares would be set for as early as the fourth quarter' [*Wall Street Journal*]

offering circular /ˈɒf(ə)rɪŋ ˌsɜːkjʊlə/ *noun* a document which gives information about a company whose shares are being sold to the public for the first time

offer period /ˈɒfə ˌpɪəriəd/ *noun* a time during which a takeover bid for a company is open

offer price /ˈɒfə praɪs/ *noun* the price at which investors buy new shares or units in a unit trust. The opposite, i.e. the selling price, is called the 'bid price', the difference between the two is the 'spread'.

office /ˈɒfɪs/ *noun* **1.** a set of rooms where a company works or where business is done □ **for office use only** something which must only be used in an office **2.** a room where someone works and does business ○ *Come into my office.* ○ *The human resources manager's office is on the third floor.* **3.** a government department **4.** a post or position ○ *She holds or performs the office of treasurer* □ **compensation for loss of office** payment to a director who is asked to leave a company before his contract ends

office hours /ˌɒfɪs ˈaʊəz/ *plural noun* the time when an office is open ○ *Do not make private phone calls during office hours.*

Office of Fair Trading /ˌɒfɪs əv feə ˈtreɪdɪŋ/ *noun* a department of the UK government that protects consumers against unfair or illegal business. Abbreviation **OFT**

Office of Management and Budget /ˌɒfɪs əv ˌmænɪdʒmənt ən ˈbʌdʒɪt/ *noun US* the department of the US government that prepares the federal budget. Abbreviation **OMB**

Office of Thrift Supervision /ˌɒfɪs əv ˈθrɪft suːpəˌvɪʒ(ə)n/ *noun US* a department of the US government which regulates the savings and loan associations. Abbreviation **OTS**

officer /ˈɒfɪsə/ *noun* a person who has an official position, especially an unpaid one in a club or other association ○ *The election of officers takes place next week.*

office staff /ˌɒfɪs ˈstɑːf/ *noun* people who work in offices

official /əˈfɪʃ(ə)l/ *adjective* from a government department or organisation ○ *She went to France on official business.* ○ *He left official documents in his car.* ○ *She received an official letter of explanation.* □ **speaking in an official capacity** speaking officially □ **to go through official channels** to deal with officials, espe-

cially when making a request ■ *noun* a person working in a government department ○ *airport officials inspected the shipment* ○ *Government officials stopped the import licence.* □ **minor official** a person in a low position in a government department ○ *Some minor official tried to stop my request for building permission.*

officialese /əˌfɪʃəˈliːz/ *noun* the language used in government documents which can be difficult to understand

official exchange rate /əˌfɪʃ(ə)l ɪks ˈtʃeɪndʒ ˌreɪt/ *noun* an exchange rate which is imposed by the government ○ *The official exchange rate is ten to the dollar, but you can get fifty on the black market.*

official intervention /əˌfɪʃ(ə)l ˌɪntə ˈvenʃ(ə)n/ *noun* an attempt by a government to influence the exchange rate by buying or selling foreign currency

Official List /əˌfɪʃ(ə)l ˈlɪst/ *noun* a daily publication by the London Stock Exchange of the highest and lowest prices recorded for each share during the trading session

official market /əˌfɪʃ(ə)l ˈmɑːkɪt/ *noun* the market in shares on the London Stock Exchange, as opposed to the grey market

official receiver /əˌfɪʃ(ə)l rɪˈsiːvə/ *noun* a government official who is appointed to run a company which is in financial difficulties, to pay off its debts as far as possible and to close it down ○ *The company is in the hands of the official receiver.* Also called **receiver**

official return /əˌfɪʃ(ə)l rɪˈtɜːn/ *noun* an official report

officio /əˈfɪʃɪəʊ/ ♦ **ex officio**

offload /ɒfˈləʊd/ *verb* to pass something which you do not want to someone else (NOTE: You offload something **from** a thing or person **on to** another thing or person.) □ **to offload excess stock** to try to sell excess stock □ **to offload costs on to a subsidiary company** to try to get a subsidiary company to pay some charges so as to reduce tax

offre publique d'achat *noun* the French word for takeover bid. Abbreviation **OPA**

offset /ɒfˈset/ *verb* to balance one thing against another so that they cancel each other out ○ *to offset losses against tax* ○

Foreign exchange losses more than offset profits in the domestic market. (NOTE: **offsetting – offset**)

offshore /ˈɒfʃɔː/ *adjective, adverb* **1.** on an island or in the sea near to land ○ *an offshore oil field* ○ *an offshore oil platform* **2.** on an island which is a tax haven **3.** based outside a country, especially in a tax haven

offshore account /ˌɒfʃɔː əˈkaʊnt/ *noun* an account in a tax haven

offshore banking /ˌɒfʃɔː ˈbæŋkɪŋ/ *noun* banking in a tax haven

offshore finance subsidiary /ˌɒfʃɔː ˈfaɪnæns səbˌsɪdiəri/ *noun* a company created in another country to handle financial transactions, giving the owning company certain tax and legal advantages in its home country (NOTE: The US term is **offshore financial subsidiary.**)

offshore financial centre /ˌɒfʃɔː faɪˈnænʃəl ˌsentə/ *noun* a country or other political unit that has banking laws intended to attract business from industrialised nations

offshore fund /ˌɒfʃɔː ˈfʌnd/ *noun* a fund that is based overseas, usually in a country that has less strict taxation regulations

offshore investments /ˌɒfʃɔː ɪnˈvestmənts/ *plural noun* investments which are sold and run by companies licensed in an offshore tax haven, such as Jersey, Guernsey or the Isle of Man

off-the-shelf company /ˌɒf ðə ˌʃelf ˈkʌmp(ə)ni/ *noun* a company which has already been registered by an accountant or lawyer, and which is ready for sale to someone who wants to set up a new company quickly

OFT *abbreviation* Office of Fair Trading

oil-exporting country /ˈɔɪl ɪkˌspɔːtɪŋ ˌkʌntri/ *noun* a country which produces oil and sells it to others

oil-importing country /ˌɔɪ lɪmˌpɔːtɪŋ ˈkʌntri/ *noun* a country which imports oil

oil-producing country /ɔɪl prəˌdjuːsɪŋ ˈkʌntri/ *noun* a country which produces oil

oil shares /ˈɔɪl ʃeəz/, **oils** /ɔɪlz/ *plural noun* shares in companies engaged in extracting or selling oil and petrol

Old Lady of Threadneedle Street /əʊld ˌleɪdi əv θredˈniːd(ə)l striːt/ *noun* the Bank of England (*informal*)

oligopoly /ˌɒlɪˈɡɒpəli/ *noun* a situation where only a few sellers control the market ○ *An oligopoly means that prices can be kept high.*

OMB *abbreviation* Office of Management and Budget

ombudsman /ˈɒmbʊdzmən/ *noun* an official who investigates complaints by the public against government departments or other large organisations (NOTE: The plural is **ombudsmen.**)

'…radical changes to the disciplinary system, including appointing an ombudsman to review cases where complainants are not satisfied with the outcome, are proposed in a consultative paper the Institute of Chartered Accountants issued last month' [*Accountancy*]

COMMENT: The main Ombudsman is the Parliamentary Commissioner for Standards, who is a civil servant and investigates complaints against government departments. The Financial Ombudsman Service is an independent body which investigates complaints by the public against banks, financial advisers, building societies, pension funds, or insurance companies. It is regulated by the Financial Services Authority (FSA) and the Office of Fair Trading (OFT).

omission /əʊˈmɪʃ(ə)n/ *noun* a thing which has been omitted, or the act of omitting something

omit /əʊˈmɪt/ *verb* not to do something ○ *He omitted to tell the managing director that he had lost the documents.* (NOTE: **omitting – omitted**) □ **to omit a dividend** *US* to pay no dividend in a certain year. The UK term is **to pass a dividend.**

OMLX *abbreviation* London Securities and Derivatives Exchange

on /ɒn/ *preposition* **1.** being a member of a group ○ *to sit on a committee* ○ *She is on the boards of two companies.* ○ *We have 250 people on the payroll.* ○ *She is on our full-time staff.* **2.** in a certain way ○ *on a commercial basis* ○ *to buy something on approval* ○ *to buy a car on hire-purchase* ○ *to get a mortgage on easy terms* ○ *He is still on probation.* ○ *She is employed on very generous terms.* □ **on the understanding that** on condition that, provided that ○ *We accept the terms* *of the contract, on the understanding that it has to be ratified by our main board.* **3.** at a time ○ *The shop is closed on Wednesday afternoons.* ○ *We work 7 hours a day on weekdays.* ○ *The whole staff has the day off on May 24th.* **4.** doing something ○ *The director is on holiday.* ○ *She is in the States on business.* ○ *The switchboard operator is on duty from 6 to 9.*

on approved credit /ɒn ə,pruːvd 'kredɪt/ *adjective US* showing that a bank loan has been made available to a client who has a good credit history. Abbreviation **OAC**

oncosts /'ɒnkɒsts/ *plural noun* business costs that cannot be charged directly to a particular good or service and must be apportioned across the business

one-man business /,wʌn mæn 'bɪznɪs/, **one-man firm** /,wʌn mæn 'fɜːm/, **one-man company** /,wʌn mæn 'kʌmp(ə)ni/ *noun* a business run by one person alone with no staff or partners

one-off /,wʌn 'ɒf/ *adjective* done or made only once ○ *one-off item* ○ *one-off deal* ○ *one-off payment*

onerous /'əʊnərəs/ *adjective* heavy, needing a lot of effort or money □ **the repayment terms are particularly onerous** the loan is particularly difficult to pay back

one-sided /,wʌn 'saɪdɪd/ *adjective* favouring one side and not the other in a negotiation

one-stop banking /,wʌn stɒp 'bæŋkɪŋ/ *noun* a type of banking where a single organisation offers a whole range of services, including such things as mortgages, loans and pensions

one-stop shopping /'wʌn stɒp/ *noun* the practice of taking a range of financial services from a single organisation, e.g. from a bank which offers loans, mortgages, pensions and insurance as well as the normal personal banking services

one-way trade /,wʌn weɪ 'treɪd/ *noun* a situation in which one country sells to another, but does not buy anything in return

one-year money /,wʌn jɪə 'mʌni/ *noun* money invested for one year

online /ɒn'laɪn/; /'ɒnlaɪn/ *adjective, adverb* linked via a computer directly to another computer, a computer network or, especially, the Internet; on the Internet ○ *The sales office is online to the warehouse.* ○ *We get our data online from the stock control department.*

'…there may be a silver lining for 'clicks-and-mortar' stores that have both an online and a high street presence. Many of these are accepting returns of goods purchased online at their traditional stores. This is a service that may make them more popular as consumers become more experienced online shoppers' [*Financial Times*]

'…a survey found that even among experienced users – those who shop online at least once a month – about 10% abandoned a planned purchase because of annoying online delays and procedures' [*Financial Times*]

'…some online brokers failed to foresee the huge increase in private dealing and had problems coping with the rising volume. It has been the year when private investors were able to trade online quickly, cheaply, and on the whole, with little bother' [*Financial Times*]

online banking /,ɒnlaɪn 'bæŋkɪŋ/ *noun* a system by which customers have bank accounts which they can access direct from their home computers, using the Internet, and can carry out operations such as checking on their account balance, paying invoices and receiving their salaries electronically

online bill paying /,ɒnlaɪn 'bɪl ,peɪɪŋ/ *noun* a system of paying bills directly from an account using the Internet

o.n.o. *abbreviation* or near offer

on the side /,ɒn ðə 'saɪd/ *adverb* separate from your normal work, and hidden from your employer ○ *He works in an accountant's office, but he runs a construction company on the side.* ○ *Her salary is too small to live on, so the family lives on what she can make on the side.*

OPA *abbreviation* offre publique d'achat

OPEC /'əʊpek/ *abbreviation* Organization of Petroleum Exporting Countries

open /'əʊpən/ *adjective* **1.** at work, not closed ○ *The store is open on Sunday mornings.* ○ *Our offices are open from 9 to 6.* ○ *They are open for business every day of the week.* **2.** ready to accept something □ **the job is open to all applicants** anyone can apply for the job □ **open to**

offers ready to accept a reasonable offer □ **the company is open to offers for the empty factory** the company is ready to discuss an offer which is lower than the suggested price ■ *verb* **1.** to start a new business ○ *She has opened a shop in the High Street.* ○ *We have opened a branch in London.* **2.** to start work, to be at work ○ *The office opens at 9 a.m.* ○ *We open for business on Sundays.* **3.** to begin something □ **to open negotiations** to begin negotiating ○ *She opened the discussions with a description of the product.* ○ *The chairman opened the meeting at 10.30.* **4.** to set something up or make something available □ *to open a bank account* ○ *to open a line of credit* ○ *to open a loan* **5.** □ **shares opened lower** share prices were lower at the beginning of the day's trading

'…after opening at 79.1 the index touched a peak of 79.2 and then drifted to a low of 78.8' [*Financial Times*]

open account /ˌəʊpən əˈkaʊnt/ *noun* an account where the supplier offers the purchaser credit without security

open cheque /ˌəʊpən ˈtʃek/ *noun* same as **uncrossed cheque**

open credit /ˌəʊpən ˈkredɪt/ *noun* credit given to good customers without security

open-end /ˌəʊpən ˈend/ *US verb* to make a fund open-ended ■ *adjective* same as **open-ended**

open-ended /ˌəʊpən ˈendɪd/ *adjective* with no fixed limit or with some items not specified ○ *They signed an open-ended agreement.* ○ *The candidate was offered an open-ended contract with a good career plan.* (NOTE: The US term is **open-end**.)

open-ended credit /ˌəʊpən ˌendɪd ˈkredɪt/ *noun* same as **revolving credit**

open-ended fund /ˌəʊpən ˈendɪd ˌfʌnd/ *noun* a fund such as a unit trust where investors buy units, the money paid being invested in a range of securities. This is as opposed to a closed fund, such as an investment trust, where the investor buys shares in the trust company, and receives dividends.

open-ended investment company /ˌəʊpən ˌendɪd ɪnˈvestmənt ˌkʌmp(ə)ni/ *noun* a form of unit trust, in which the investor purchases shares at a

single price, as opposed to the bid-offer pricing system used by ordinary unit trusts. Abbreviation **OEIC**

open-ended management company /ˌəʊpən ˌendɪd ˈmænɪdʒmənt ˌkʌmp(ə)ni/ *noun* a company that sells unit trusts (NOTE: The US term is **open-end management company**.)

open-ended trust /ˌəʊpən ˈendɪd ˌtrʌst/ *noun* a fund in which investors can freely buy and sell units at any time

opening /ˈəʊp(ə)nɪŋ/ *noun* **1.** the act of starting a new business ○ *the opening of a new branch* ○ *the opening of a new market* or *of a new distribution network* **2.** an available job ○ *She's applied for the opening in the sales department.* ■ *adjective* being at the beginning, or the first of several

opening balance /ˈəʊp(ə)nɪŋ ˌbæləns/ *noun* a balance at the beginning of an accounting period

opening bid /ˈəʊp(ə)nɪŋ ˈbɪd/ *noun* the first bid at an auction

opening entry /ˈəʊp(ə)nɪŋ ˌentri/ *noun* the first entry in an account

opening price /ˈəʊp(ə)nɪŋ ˈpraɪs/ *noun* a price at the start of a day's trading

opening stock /ˈəʊp(ə)nɪŋ ˈstɒk/ *noun* on a balance sheet, the closing stock at the end of one accounting period that is transferred forward and becomes the opening stock in the one that follows (NOTE: The US term is **beginning inventory**.)

open market /ˌəʊpən ˈmɑːkɪt/ *noun* a market where anyone can buy or sell

open market operation /ˌəʊpən ˈmɑːkɪt ɒpəˌreɪʃ(ə)n/ *noun* a sale or purchase of government stock by ordinary investors, used by the government as a means of influencing money supply

open outcry system /ˌəʊpən ˈaʊtkraɪ ˌsɪstəm/ *noun* a system of buying and selling used in some exchanges, where the brokers shout prices, offers or orders to each other

open ticket /ˌəʊpən ˈtɪkɪt/ *noun* a ticket which can be used on any date

operate /ˈɒpəreɪt/ *verb* to do business, or to run a business or a machine

'…the company gets valuable restaurant locations which will be converted to the family-style restaurant chain that it operates and franchises throughout most parts of the US' [*Fortune*]

operating /ˈɒpəreɪtɪŋ/ *noun* the general running of a business or of a machine

'…the company blamed over-capacity and competitive market conditions in Europe for a £14m operating loss last year' [*Financial Times*]

operating budget /ˈɒpəreɪtɪŋ ˌbʌdʒɪt/ *noun* a forecast of income and expenditure over a period of time

operating costs /ˈɒpəreɪtɪŋ kɒsts/ *plural noun* the costs of the day-to-day activities of a company. Also called **operating expenses**, **running costs**

operating earnings /ˌɒpəreɪtɪŋ ˈɜːnɪŋz/ *plural noun* same as **operating income**

operating expenses /ˈɒpəreɪtɪŋ ɪkˌspensɪz/ *plural noun* same as **operating costs**

operating income /ˈɒpəreɪtɪŋ ˌɪnkʌm/, **operating profit** /ˈɒpəreɪtɪŋ ˌprɒfɪt/ *noun* the profit made by a company in its usual business. Also called **operating earnings**

operating loss /ˈɒpəreɪtɪŋ lɒs/ *noun* a loss made by a company in its usual business

operation /ˌɒpəˈreɪʃ(ə)n/ *noun* an activity or a piece of work, or the task of running something ○ *the company's operations in West Africa* ○ *He heads up the operations in Northern Europe.*

'…a leading manufacturer of business, industrial and commercial products requires a branch manager to head up its mid-western Canada operations based in Winnipeg' [*Globe and Mail (Toronto)*]

operational /ˌɒpəˈreɪʃ(ə)nəl/ *adjective* referring to the day-to-day activities of a business or to the way in which something is run

operational budget /ˌɒpəreɪʃ(ə)nəl ˈbʌdʒɪt/ *noun* same as **operating budget**

operational costs /ˌɒpəreɪʃ(ə)nəl ˈkɒsts/ *plural noun* the costs of running a business

operational gearing /ˌɒpəreɪʃ(ə)nəl ˈɡɪərɪŋ/ *noun* a situation where a

company has high fixed costs which are funded by borrowings

operational planning /ˌɒpəreɪʃ(ə)nəl ˈplænɪŋ/ *noun* the planning of how a business is to be run

operational research /ˌɒpəreɪʃ(ə)nəl rɪˈsɜːtʃ/ *noun* a study of a company's way of working to see if it can be made more efficient and profitable

operations department /ˌɒpəˈreɪʃ(ə)nz dɪˌpɑːtmənt/ *noun* the general administration department of a company

operations review /ˌɒpəˈreɪʃ(ə)nz rɪˌvjuː/ *noun* an act of examining the way in which a company or department works to see how it can be made more efficient and profitable

operator /ˈɒpəreɪtə/ *noun* **1.** a person who runs a business **2.** (*stock exchange*) a person who buys and sells shares hoping to make a quick profit

'…a number of block bookings by American tour operators have been cancelled' [*Economist*]

OPM *abbreviation* other people's money

opportunity /ˌɒpəˈtjuːnɪti/ *noun* a chance to do something successfully

'…the group is currently undergoing a period of rapid expansion and this has created an exciting opportunity for a qualified accountant' [*Financial Times*]

opportunity cost /ˌɒpəˈtjuːnɪti kɒst/ *noun* **1.** the cost of a business initiative in terms of profits that could have been gained through an alternative plan ○ *It's a good investment plan and we will not be deterred by the opportunity cost.* Also called **alternative cost 2.** the value of another method of investment which could have been used, instead of the one adopted

oppose /əˈpəʊz/ *verb* to try to stop something happening; to vote against something ○ *A minority of board members opposed the motion.* ○ *We are all opposed to the takeover.*

optimal /ˈɒptɪm(ə)l/ *adjective* best

optimism /ˈɒptɪmɪz(ə)m/ *noun* a state of mind in which you are sure that everything will work out well ○ *He has considerable optimism about sales possibilities in the Far East.*

optimistic /ˌɒptɪˈmɪstɪk/ *adjective* feeling sure that everything will work out well □ **he takes an optimistic view of the exchange rate** he expects the exchange rate will go in his favour

optimum /ˈɒptɪməm/ *adjective* best ○ *The market offers optimum conditions for sales.*

option /ˈɒpʃən/ *noun* the opportunity to buy or sell something, such as a security, within a fixed period of time at a fixed price □ **to grant someone a six-month option on a product** to allow someone six months to decide if they want to manufacture the product □ **to take up an option** *or* **to exercise an option** to accept the option which has been offered and to put it into action ○ *They exercised their option* or *they took up their option to acquire sole marketing rights to the product.* □ **I want to leave my options open** I want to be able to decide what to do when the time is right □ **to take the soft option** to decide to do something which involves the least risk, effort or problems

optional /ˈɒpʃ(ə)n(ə)l/ *adjective* able to be done or not done, taken or not taken, as a person chooses ○ *The insurance cover is optional.* ○ *Attendance at staff meetings is optional, although the management encourages employees to attend.*

option contract /ˈɒpʃən ˌkɒntrækt/ *noun* a right to buy or sell a specific number of shares at a fixed price

option dealing /ˈɒpʃən ˌdiːlɪŋ/ *noun* the activity of buying and selling share options

option holder /ˈɒpʃən ˌhəʊldə/ *noun* a person who has bought and holds an option

option to purchase /ˌɒpʃən tə ˈpɜːtʃɪs/ *noun* an option which gives someone the possibility to buy something within a period of time

option to sell /ˌɒpʃən tə ˈsel/ *noun* an option which gives someone the possibility to sell something within a period of time

option trading /ˈɒpʃən ˌtreɪdɪŋ/ *noun* the business of buying and selling share options

oral contract /ˌɔːrəl ˈkɒntrækt/ *noun* a type of business agreement that is spoken, not written down and is legally binding even though the terms of the contract can be difficult to prove in the event of a breach

order /ˈɔːdə/ *noun* **1.** the way in which records such as filing cards or invoices are arranged ○ *in alphabetical or numerical order* **2.** an official request for goods to be supplied ○ *to give someone an order* or *to place an order with someone for twenty filing cabinets* ○ *The management ordered the workforce to leave the factory.* □ **to fill an order, to fulfil an order** to supply items which have been ordered ○ *We are so understaffed we cannot fulfil any more orders before Christmas.* □ **items available to order only** items which will be manufactured only if someone orders them □ **on order** ordered but not delivered ○ *This item is out of stock, but is on order.* **3.** a document which allows money to be paid to someone ○ *She sent us an order on the Chartered Bank.* **4.** (*stock exchange*) an instruction to a broker to buy or sell **5.** □ **pay to Mr Smith or order** pay money to Mr Smith or as he orders □ **pay to the order of Mr Smith** pay money directly to Mr Smith or to his account ■ *verb* to give an official request for something to be done or for something to be supplied ○ *to order twenty filing cabinets to be delivered to the warehouse*

order book /ˈɔːdə bʊk/ *noun* a book which records orders received

order cheque /ˈɔːdə tʃek/ *noun* a cheque which is paid to a named person with the words 'or order' after the payee's name, showing that he or she can endorse it and pass it to someone else if desired

order-driven system /ˈɔːdə ˌdrɪv(ə)n ˌsɪstəm/, **order-driven market** /ˌɔːdə ˌdrɪv(ə)n ˈmɑːkɪt/ *noun* a price system on a stock exchange where prices vary according to the level of orders. Compare **quote-driven system**

order fulfilment /ˈɔːdə fʊlˌfɪlmənt/ *noun* the process of supplying items which have been ordered

order processing /ˈɔːdə ˌprəʊsesɪŋ/ *noun* the work of dealing with orders

ordinary /ˈɔːd(ə)n(ə)ri/ *adjective* not special

ordinary interest /ˌɔːd(ə)n(ə)ri ˈɪntrəst/ *noun* annual interest calculated on the basis of 360 days, as opposed to 'exact interest' which is calculated on 365 days

ordinary member /ˌɔːd(ə)n(ə)ri ˈmembə/ *noun* a person who pays a subscription to belong to a group

ordinary resolution /ˌɔːd(ə)n(ə)ri ˌrezəˈluːʃ(ə)n/ *noun* a resolution put before an AGM, usually referring to some general procedural matter, and which requires a simple majority of votes to be accepted

ordinary share capital /ˌɔːd(ə)n(ə)ri ˈʃeə ˌkæpɪt(ə)l/ *noun* the capital of a company in the form of money paid for ordinary shares

ordinary shareholder /ˌɔːd(ə)n(ə)ri ˈʃeəhəʊldə/ *noun* a person who owns ordinary shares in a company

ordinary shares /ˈɔːd(ə)n(ə)ri ʃeəz/ *plural noun* shares that entitle the holder to receive a dividend after the dividend on preference shares has been paid (NOTE: The US term is **common stock**.)

organic growth /ɔːˌɡænɪk ˈɡrəʊθ/ *noun* same as **internal growth**

organisation /ˌɔːɡənaɪˈzeɪʃ(ə)n/, **organization** *noun* **1.** a way of arranging something so that it works efficiently ○ *the organisation of the head office into departments* ○ *The chairman handles the organisation of the AGM.* ○ *The organisation of the group is too centralised to be efficient.* **2.** a group or institution which is arranged for efficient work

'…working with a client base which includes many major commercial organizations and nationalized industries' [*Times*]

organisational /ˌɔːɡənaɪˈzeɪʃ(ə)n(ə)l/, **organizational** *adjective* referring to the way in which something is organised ○ *The paper gives a diagram of the company's organisational structure.*

organisational chart /ˌɔːɡənaɪˈzeɪʃ(ə)n(ə)l tʃɑːt/ *noun* a chart that shows the relationships of people in an organisation in terms of their areas of authority and responsibility

organisation and methods /ˌɔːɡənaɪzeɪʃ(ə)n ən ˈmeθədz/ *noun* a process of examining how an office works, and suggesting how it can be made more efficient. Abbreviation **O & M**

organisation chart /ˌɔːɡənaɪ ˈzeɪʃ(ə)n tʃɑːt/ *noun* same as **organisational chart**

Organisation for Economic Co-operation and Development /ˌɔːɡənaɪzeɪʃ(ə)n fər iːkəˌnɒmɪk kəʊ ˌɒpəreɪʃ(ə)n ən dɪˈveləpmənt/ *noun* an organisation representing the industrialised countries, aimed at encouraging international trade, wealth and employment in member countries. Abbreviation **OECD**

organise /ˈɔːɡənaɪz/, **organize** *verb* **1.** to set up a system for doing something ○ *The company is organised into six profit centres.* ○ *The group is organised by sales areas.* **2.** to arrange something so that it works

'…we organize a rate with importers who have large orders and guarantee them space at a fixed rate so that they can plan their costs' [*Lloyd's List*]

organised labour /ˌɔːɡənaɪzd ˈleɪbə/ *noun* employees who are members of trade unions

'…governments are coming under increasing pressure from politicians, organized labour and business to stimulate economic growth' [*Duns Business Month*]

Organization of Petroleum Exporting Countries /ˌɔːɡənaɪ zeɪʃ(ə)n əv pəˌtrəʊliəm ekˌspɔːtɪŋ ˈkʌntriz/ *noun* a group of major countries who are producers and exporters of oil. Abbreviation **OPEC**

originating fee /əˈrɪdʒɪneɪtɪŋ fiː/, **origination fee** /əˌrɪdʒɪˈneɪʃ(ə)n fiː/ *noun US* a front-end fee charged to cover the costs of dealing with an application for a loan

orphan stock /ˈɔːf(ə)n stɒk/ *noun* a neglected share, which is not often recommended by market analysts

OTC *abbreviation* over-the-counter

other people's money /ˌʌðə ˌpiːp(ə)lz ˈmʌni/ *noun* money that belongs to customers, clients or shareholders, i.e. not to the people who are using it or investing it. Abbreviation **OPM**

ouguiya /uːˈɡiːjə/ *noun* a unit of currency used in Mauritania

ounce /aʊns/ *noun* a measure of weight (= 28 grams) (NOTE: Usually written **oz** after figures: *25oz.* Note also that the ounce is now no longer officially used in the UK)

out /aʊt/ *adverb* **1.** on strike ○ *The workers have been out on strike for four weeks.* ○ *As soon as the management made the offer, the staff came out.* ○ *The shop stewards called the workforce out.* **2.** □ **to be out** to be wrong in calculating something, or to be wrongly calculated ○ *The balance is £10 out.* □ **we are £20,000 out in our calculations** we have £20,000 too much or too little **3.** *US* away from work because of illness (NOTE: The UK term for this sense is **off**.)

outbid /aʊtˈbɪd/ *verb* to offer a better price than someone else ○ *We offered £100,000 for the warehouse, but another company outbid us.* (NOTE: **outbidding – outbid**)

outflow /ˈaʊtfləʊ/ *noun* □ **outflow of capital from a country** capital which is sent out of a country for investment abroad

outflows /ˈaʊtfləʊz/ *plural noun* money withdrawn from a fund in which it was previously invested

outgoings /ˈaʊtgəʊɪŋz/ *plural noun* money which is paid out

outlay /ˈaʊtleɪ/ *noun* money spent, expenditure □ **for a modest outlay** for a small sum ○ *For a modest outlay he was able to take control of the business.*

outlook /ˈaʊtlʊk/ *noun* a view of what is going to happen in the future ○ *The economic outlook is not good.* ○ *The stock market outlook is worrying.*

'American demand has transformed the profit outlook for many European manufacturers' [*Duns Business Month*]

out-of-date cheque /ˌaʊt əv deɪt ˈtʃek/ *noun* a cheque which has not been cleared because its date is too old, normally more than six months

out-of-favour *adjective*, *adverb* neglected, not liked (NOTE: The US spelling is **out-of-favor**.)

out of pocket /ˌaʊt əv ˈpɒkɪt/ *adjective*, *adverb* having paid out money personally ○ *The deal has left me out of pocket.*

out-of-pocket expenses /ˌaʊt əv ˌpɒkɪt ɪkˈspensɪz/ *plural noun* an amount of money paid back to an employee who has spent his or her personal money on company business

outperform /ˌaʊtpəˈfɔːm/ *verb* to do better than other companies

'…on the fairly safe assumption that there is little to be gained in attempting to find the share or trust that outperforms everything else, there is every reason to buy an index-tracking fund' [*Money Observer*]

outperformance /ˌaʊtpəˈfɔːməns/ *noun* the fact of doing better than other companies

output /ˈaʊtpʊt/ *noun* the amount which a company, person, or machine produces ○ *Output has increased by 10%.* ○ *25% of our output is exported.*

'…crude oil output plunged during the last month and is likely to remain near its present level for the near future' [*Wall Street Journal*]

output per hour /ˌaʊtpʊt pər ˈaʊə/ *noun* the amount of something produced in one hour

output tax /ˈaʊtpʊt tæks/ *noun* VAT charged by a company on goods or services sold, and which the company pays to the government

outright /ˌaʊtˈraɪt/ *adverb*, *adjective* completely

outsell /aʊtˈsel/ *verb* to sell more than someone ○ *The company is easily outselling its competitors.* (NOTE: **outselling – outsold**)

outside /ˈaʊtsaɪd/ *adjective*, *adverb* **1.** not in a company's office or building □ **to send work to be done outside** to send work to be done in other offices **2.** □ **outside office hours** not during office hours, when the office is not open

outside dealer /ˌaʊtsaɪd ˈdiːlə/ *noun* a person who is not a member of the stock exchange but is allowed to trade

outside director /ˌaʊtsaɪd daɪˈrektə/ *noun* same as **non-executive director**

outside office hours /ˌaʊtsaɪd ˈɒfɪs aʊəz/ *adverb* when the office is not open

outside shareholder /ˌaʊtsaɪd ˈʃeəhəʊldə/ same as **minority shareholder**

outside worker /ˈaʊtsaɪd ˌwɜːkə/ *noun* an employee who does not work in a company's offices

outstanding /aʊtˈstændɪŋ/ *adjective* not yet paid or completed □ **outstanding debts** debts which are waiting to be paid □ **outstanding orders** orders received but not yet supplied □ **what is the amount outstanding?** how much money is still owed? □ **matters outstanding from the previous meeting** questions which were not settled at the previous meeting

COMMENT: Note the difference between 'outstanding' and 'overdue'. If a debtor has 30 days credit, then his debts are outstanding until the end of the 30 days, and they only become overdue on the 31st day.

outstanding cheque /aʊtˌstændɪŋ ˈtʃek/ *noun* a cheque which has been written and therefore has been entered in the company's ledgers, but which has not been presented for payment and so has not been debited from the company's bank account

outturn /ˈaʊttɜːn/ *noun* an amount produced by a country or company

outvote /aʊtˈvəʊt/ *verb* to defeat someone in a vote □ **the chairman was outvoted** the majority voted against the chairman

overall /ˌəʊvərˈɔːl/ *adjective* covering or including everything □ **the company reported an overall fall in profits** the company reported a general fall in profits □ **overall plan** a plan which covers everything

overall balance of payments /ˌəʊvərɔːl ˌbæləns əv ˈpeɪmənts/ *noun* the total of current and long-term balance of payments

overborrowed /ˌəʊvəˈbɒrəʊd/ *adjective* referring to a company which has very high borrowings compared to its assets, and has difficulty in meeting its interest payments

overbought /ˌəʊvəˈbɔːt/ *adjective* having bought too much □ **the market is overbought** prices on the stock market are too high, because there have been too many people wanting to buy

'...they said the market was overbought when the index was between 860 and 870 points' [*Australian Financial Review*]

overcapacity /ˌəʊvəkəˈpæsɪti/ *noun* an unused capacity for producing something

'...with the present overcapacity situation in the airline industry the discounting of tickets is widespread' [*Business Traveller*]

overcapitalised /ˌəʊvəˈkæpɪtəlaɪzd/, **overcapitalized** *adjec-*

tive referring to a company with more capital than it needs

overcharge *noun* /ˈəʊvətʃɑːdʒ/ a charge which is higher than it should be ○ *to pay back an overcharge* ■ *verb* /ˌəʊvəˈtʃɑːdʒ/ to ask someone for too much money ○ *They overcharged us for our meals.* ○ *We asked for a refund because we'd been overcharged.*

overdraft /ˈəʊvədrɑːft/ *noun* **1.** an amount of money which a company or person can withdraw from a bank account, with the bank's permission, despite the fact that the account is empty ○ *The bank has allowed me an overdraft of £5,000.* Abbreviation **O/D** (NOTE: The US term is **overdraft protection.**) □ **we have exceeded our overdraft facilities** we have taken out more than the overdraft allowed by the bank **2.** a negative amount of money in an account, i.e. a situation where a cheque is more than the money in the account on which it is drawn

overdraft facilities /ˈəʊvədrɑːft fəˌsɪlɪtiz/ *plural noun* an arrangement with a bank to have an overdraft

overdraft limit /ˈəʊvədrɑːft ˌlɪmɪt/ *noun* a total which is agreed between the bank and a customer as the maximum amount the customer's account may be overdrawn

overdraft protection /ˈəʊvədrɑːft prəˌtekʃ(ə)n/ *noun* a system which protects a customer from overdrawing his account, either by switching money automatically from another account, or by offering a line of credit

overdraw /ˌəʊvəˈdrɔː/ *verb* to take out more money from a bank account than there is in it

overdue /ˌəʊvəˈdjuː/ *adjective* having not been paid on time □ **interest payments are three weeks overdue** interest payments which should have been made three weeks ago

overestimate /ˌəʊvərˈestɪmeɪt/ *verb* to think something is larger or worse than it really is ○ *She overestimated the amount of time needed to fit out the factory.* ○ *They overestimated the costs of moving the offices to central London.*

overexposure /ˌəʊvərɪksˈpəʊʒə/ *noun* the fact of being too exposed to risky loans

overextend /ˌəʊvərɪkˈstend/ *verb* □ **the company overextended itself** the company borrowed more money than its assets would allow

overfunding /ˌəʊvəˈfʌndɪŋ/ *noun* a situation where the government borrows more money than it needs for expenditure, by selling too much government stock

overgeared /ˌəʊvəˈɡɪəd/ *adjective* referring to a company which has high borrowings in comparison to its assets

overhang *noun* /ˈəʊvəhæŋ/ a large quantity of shares or of a commodity or of unsold stock available for sale, which has the effect of depressing the market price ■ *verb* /ˌəʊvəˈhæŋ/ to put downward pressure on share or commodity prices ○ *Major uncertainties about the economy are overhanging the market.* □ **to overhang the market** to be available for sale, and so depress the share price

overhead /ˈəʊvəhed/ *noun US* same as **overheads**

overhead budget /ˌəʊvəhed ˈbʌdʒɪt/ *noun* a plan of probable overhead costs

overhead costs /ˌəʊvəhed ˈkɒsts/, **overhead expenses** /ˌəʊvəhed ɪkˈspensɪz/ *plural noun* same as **overheads**

overheads /ˈəʊvəhedz/ *plural noun* the indirect costs of the day-to-day running of a business, i.e. not money spent of producing goods, but money spent on such things as renting or maintaining buildings and machinery ○ *The sales revenue covers the manufacturing costs but not the overheads.* (NOTE: The US term is **overhead**.)

overheating /ˌəʊvəˈhiːtɪŋ/ *noun* a rise in industrial activity in an economy, leading to a rise in inflation (the economy is then said to be 'overheated')

overnight /ˌəʊvəˈnaɪt/ *adverb* from the evening of one day to the morning of the next

overnight money /ˌəʊvənaɪt ˈmʌni/ *noun* money deposited for less than 24 hours

overnight repo /ˌəʊvənaɪt ˈriːpəʊ/ *noun* a repurchase agreement, where banks sell securities for cash and repurchase them the next day at a higher price (used by central banks as a means of regulating the money markets)

overpaid /ˌəʊvəˈpeɪd/ *adjective* paid too much ○ *Our staff are overpaid and underworked.*

overpay /ˌəʊvəˈpeɪ/ *verb* **1.** to pay too much to someone or for something ○ *We overpaid the invoice by $245.* **2.** to pay an extra amount to reduce the total capital borrowed on a mortgage

overpayment /ˌəʊvəˈpeɪmənt/ *noun* **1.** an act of paying too much **2.** the payment of a lump sum to reduce the capital borrowed on a mortgage

overrated /ˌəʊvəˈreɪtɪd/ *adjective* valued more highly than it should be ○ *The effect of the dollar on European business cannot be overrated.* ○ *Their 'first-class service' is very overrated.*

overrider /ˈəʊvəraɪdə/, **overriding commission** /ˌəʊvəraɪdɪŋ kəˈmɪʃ(ə)n/ *noun* a special extra commission which is above all other commissions

overseas *adjective* /ˈəʊvəsiːz/, *adverb* /ˌəʊvəˈsiːz/ across the sea, or to or in foreign countries ○ *Management trainees knew that they would be sent overseas to learn about the export markets.* ○ *Some workers are going overseas to find new jobs.* ■ *noun* /ˈəʊvəsiːz/; /ˌəʊvəˈsiːz/ foreign countries ○ *The profits from overseas are far higher than those of the home division.*

overseas division /ˌəʊvəsiːz dɪˈvɪʒ(ə)n/ *noun* the section of a company dealing with trade with other countries

overseas funds /ˌəʊvəˈsiːz fʌndz/ *plural noun* investment funds based in other countries

overseas markets /ˌəʊvəsiːz ˈmɑːkɪts/ *plural noun* markets in foreign countries

overseas money order /ˌəʊvəsiːz ˈmʌni ˌɔːdə/ *noun* a money order in a foreign currency which is payable to someone living in a foreign country

overseas trade /ˌəʊvəsiːz ˈtreɪd/ *noun* same as **foreign trade**

oversell /ˌəʊvəˈsel/ *verb* to sell more than you can produce (NOTE: **overselling – oversold**) □ **he is oversold** he has agreed to sell more product than he can produce □ **the market is oversold** stock-market prices are too low, because there have been too many sellers

overspend /ˌəʊvəˈspend/ *verb* to spend too much (NOTE: **overspending –**

overspent) □ **to overspend your budget** to spend more money than is allowed in your budget

overspending /ˌəʊvəˈspendɪŋ/ *noun* the act of spending more than is allowed ○ *The board decided to limit the overspending by the production departments.*

overstock /ˌəʊvəˈstɒk/ *verb* to have a bigger stock of something than is needed □ **to be overstocked with spare parts** to have too many spare parts in stock

'Cash paid for your stock: any quantity, any products, overstocked lines, factory seconds' [*Australian Financial Review*]

overstocks /ˈəʊvəstɒks/ *plural noun US* a surplus of stock ○ *We will have to sell off the overstocks to make room in the warehouse.*

oversubscribe /ˌəʊvəsəbˈskraɪb/ *verb* □ **the share offer was oversubscribed six times** people applied for six times as many new shares as were available

oversubscription /ˌəʊvəsəbˈskrɪpʃ(ə)n/ *noun* a situation where people have subscribed for more shares in a new issue than are being issued

over-the-counter /ˌəʊvə ðə ˈkaʊntə/ *adjective* involving shares that are not listed on the main stock exchange. Abbreviation **OTC**

over-the-counter market /ˌəʊvə ðə ˈkaʊntə ˌmɑːkɪt/ *noun* a secondary market in shares which are not listed on the main stock exchange

over-the-counter sales /ˌəʊvə ðə ˈkaʊntə ˌseɪlz/ *plural noun* the legal selling of shares that are not listed in the official stock exchange list, usually carried out by telephone

overtime /ˈəʊvətaɪm/ *noun* hours worked in addition to your usual working hours ○ *to work six hours' overtime* ○ *The overtime rate is one and a half times normal pay.* ■ *adverb* □ **to work overtime** to work longer hours than stated in the contract of employment

overtime ban /ˈəʊvətaɪm bæn/ *noun* an order by a trade union which forbids overtime work by its members

overtime pay /ˈəʊvətaɪm peɪ/ *noun* pay for extra time worked

overtrading /ˌəʊvəˈtreɪdɪŋ/ *noun* a situation where a company increases sales and production too much and too quickly, so that it runs short of cash

overvalue /ˌəʊvəˈvæljuː/ *verb* to give a higher value to something or someone than is right (NOTE: The opposite is **undervalue.**) □ **these shares are overvalued at £1.25** the shares are worth less than the £1.25 for which they are selling □ **the pound is overvalued against the dollar** the exchange rate gives too many dollars to the pound, considering the strength of the two countries' economies

'…the fact that sterling has been overvalued for the past three years shows that currencies can remain above their fair value for very long periods' [*Investors Chronicle*]

owe /əʊ/ *verb* to have to pay money ○ *He owes the bank £250,000.* □ **they still owe the company for the stock they purchased last year** they have still not paid for the stock

owing /ˈəʊɪŋ/ *adjective* owed ○ *money owing to the directors* ○ *How much is still owing to the company by its debtors?*

own /əʊn/ *verb* to have or to possess ○ *She owns 50% of the shares.*

owner /ˈəʊnə/ *noun* a person who owns something ○ *The owners of a company are its shareholders.* □ **goods sent at owner's risk** a situation where the owner has to insure the goods while they are being transported

owner-occupier /ˌəʊnər ˈɒkjʊpaɪə/ *noun* a person who owns the property in which he or she lives

owners' equity /ˌəʊnəz ˈekwɪti/ *noun* the value of the shares in a company owned by the owners of the company

ownership /ˈəʊnəʃɪp/ *noun* the fact of owning something □ **the ownership of the company has passed to the banks** the banks have become owners of the company

oz *abbreviation* ounce(s)

P

P* *symbol US* a measure of M2 shown as a ratio of the velocity of money, used as an indication of inflation

P45 /ˌpiː ˈfɔːti ˈfaɪv/ *noun* a form given to an employee who leaves a company, showing how much tax has been deducted from his or her salary

p.a. *abbreviation* per annum

pa'anga /ˈpɑːŋgə/ *noun* a unit of currency used in Tonga

Pacific Rim /pəˌsɪfɪk ˈrɪm/ *noun* the countries on the edge of the Pacific Ocean: especially Hong Kong, Japan, Korea, Malaysia, Singapore, Thailand and Taiwan

package /ˈpækɪdʒ/ *noun* a group of different items joined together in one deal

'…airlines offer special stopover rates and hotel packages to attract customers to certain routes' [*Business Traveller*]

'…the remuneration package will include an attractive salary, profit sharing and a company car' [*Times*]

'…airlines will book not only tickets but also hotels and car hire to provide a complete package' [*Business Traveller*]

package deal /ˈpækɪdʒ ˌdiːl/ *noun* an agreement which covers several different things at the same time ○ *They agreed a package deal which involves the construction of the factory, training of staff, and purchase of the product.*

Pac-man /ˈpæk mæn/ *noun* a method of defence against a takeover bid, where the target company threatens to take over the company which is trying to take it over

paid /peɪd/ *adjective* **1.** for which money has been given ○ *The invoice is marked 'paid'.* **2.** □ **paid holidays** holidays where the worker's wages are still paid even though he or she is not working

3. referring to an amount which has been settled ○ *The order was sent carriage paid.* □ **paid bills** bills which have been settled

paid assistant /ˌpeɪd əˈsɪst(ə)nt/ *noun* an assistant who receives a salary

paid-in capital /ˌpeɪd ɪn ˈkæpɪt(ə)l/ *noun* capital in a business which has been provided by its shareholders, usually in the form of payments for shares above their par value

paid-up capital /ˌpeɪd ʌp ˈkæpɪt(ə)l/, **paid-up share capital** /ˌpeɪd ʌp ˈʃeə ˌkæpɪt(ə)l/ *noun* an amount of money paid for the issued capital shares (it does not include called-up capital which has not yet been paid for)

paid-up shares /ˌpeɪd ʌp ˈʃeəz/ *noun* shares which have been completely paid for by the shareholders

palmtop /ˈpɑːmtɒp/ *noun* a very small computer which can be held in your hand and which usually has a character recognition screen instead of a keyboard

PAN *abbreviation* primary account number

P&L *abbreviation* profit and loss

P&L statement /ˌpiː ənd ˈel əˌkaʊnt/ *noun US* same as **profit and loss account**

panel /ˈpæn(ə)l/ *noun* **1.** a flat vertical surface **2.** a group of people who give advice on a problem ○ *a panel of experts*

panic /ˈpænɪk/ *noun* a state of being very frightened □ **panic selling of sterling** a rush to sell sterling at any price because of possible devaluation

panic buying /ˈpænɪk ˌbaɪɪŋ/ *noun* a rush to buy something at any price because stocks may run out

paper /'peɪpə/ *noun* **1.** □ **on paper** in theory ○ *On paper the system is ideal, but we have to see it working before we will sign the contract.* **2.** a document which can represent money, e.g. a bill of exchange or a promissory note **3.** shares in the form of share certificates

paperchase /'peɪpə,tʃeɪs/ *noun* a takeover bid where the purchasing company issues large numbers of new shares to offer in exchange for the shares in the company being bought

paper gain /,peɪpə 'geɪn/ *noun* same as **paper profit**

'…the profits were tax-free and the interest on the loans they incurred qualified for income tax relief; the paper gains were rarely changed into spending money' [*Investors Chronicle*]

paper loss /,peɪpə 'lɒs/ *noun* a loss made when an asset has fallen in value but has not been sold. Also called **unrealised loss**

paper millionaire /,peɪpə ,mɪljə'neə/ *noun* a person who owns shares which, if sold, would be worth one million pounds or dollars

paper money /,peɪpə 'mʌni/ *noun* payments in paper form, e.g., cheques

paper offer /,peɪpə 'ɒfə/ *noun* a takeover bid where the purchasing company offers its shares in exchange for shares in the company being taken over, as opposed to a cash offer

paper profit /,peɪpə 'prɒfɪt/ *noun* a profit on an asset which has increased in price but has not been sold ○ *He is showing a paper profit of £25,000 on his investment.* Also called **paper gain**, **unrealised profit**

paperwork /'peɪpəwɜːk/ *noun* an office work, especially writing memos and filling in forms ○ *Exporting to Russia involves a large amount of paperwork.*

par /pɑː/ *adjective* equal, at the same price □ **shares at par** shares whose market price is the same as their face value

parallel economy /,pærəlel ɪ'kɒnəmi/ *noun* same as **black economy**

parallel loan /,pærəlel 'ləʊn/ *noun* same as **back-to-back loan**

parallel markets /,pærəlel 'mɑːkɪts/ *plural noun* money markets, where institutions such as banks, or organisations such as local authorities, can lend or borrow money without having to go through the main money markets

parameter /pə'ræmɪtə/ *noun* a fixed limit ○ *The budget parameters are fixed by the finance director.* ○ *Spending by each department has to fall within agreed parameters.*

parcel of shares /,pɑːs(ə)l əv 'ʃeəz/ *noun* a fixed number of shares which are sold as a group ○ *The shares are on offer in parcels of 50.*

parcel rate /'pɑːs(ə)l reɪt/ *noun* the postage (calculated by weight) for sending a parcel

parent company /'peərənt ,kʌmp(ə)ni/ *noun* a company which owns more than 50% of the shares of another company

Pareto's Law /pə'riːtəʊ lɔː/, **Pareto Effect** /pə'riːtəʊ ɪ,fekt/ *noun* the theory that incomes are distributed in the same way in all countries, whatever tax regime is in force, and that a small percentage of a total is responsible for a large proportion of value or resources. Also called **eighty/twenty law**

COMMENT: Also called the 80/20 law, because 80/20 is the normal ratio between majority and minority figures: so 20 per cent of accounts produce 80 per cent of turnover; 80 per cent of GDP enriches 20 per cent of the population, etc.

pari passu /,pæri 'pæsuː/ *adverb* a Latin phrase meaning 'equally' ○ *The new shares will rank pari passu with the existing ones.*

Paris Club /'pæris 'klʌb/ *noun* the Group of Ten, the major world economic powers working within the framework of the IMF (there are in fact eleven: Belgium, Canada, France, Germany, Italy, Japan, Netherlands, Sweden, Switzerland, UK and the US It is called the 'Paris Club' because its first meeting was in Paris)

Paris Hilton stock index /,pæris 'hɪlt(ə)n ,ɪndeks/ *noun* a share index comprised of companies associated with the socialite Paris Hilton. Some investors believe her influence on the consumer spending habits of her fans is material enough to give these companies a competitive advantage.

parity /'pærɪti/ *noun* a situation when the price of a commodity, foreign currency or security is the same in different markets

'…the draft report on changes in the international monetary system casts doubt about any return to fixed exchange-rate parities' [*Wall Street Journal*]

Parkinson's law /'pɑːkɪnsənz ˌlɔː/ *noun* a law, based on wide experience, that in business the amount of work increases to fill the time available for it. The principle is named after the book written in 1958 by C. Northcote Parkinson.

part /pɑːt/ *noun* □ **in part** not completely ○ *to contribute in part to the costs* or *to pay the costs in part*

part delivery /pɑːt dɪ'lɪv(ə)ri/ *noun* a delivery that contains only some of the items in an order

part exchange /ˌpɑːt ɪks'tʃeɪndʒ/ *noun* the act of giving an old product as part of the payment for a new one ○ *to take a car in part exchange*

partial /'pɑːʃ(ə)l/ *adjective* not complete □ **partial loss** a situation where only part of the insured property has been damaged or lost □ **he got partial compensation for the damage to his house** he was compensated for part of the damage

participate /pɑː'tɪsɪpeɪt/ *verb* to take part in an activity or enterprise ○ *The staff are encouraged to participate actively in the company's decision-making processes.*

participating preference shares /pɑːˌtɪsɪpeɪtɪŋ 'pref(ə)rəns ˌʃeəz/, **participating preferred stock** /pɑː ˌtɪsɪpeɪtɪŋ prɪˌfɜːd 'stɒk/ *plural noun* preference shares which get an extra bonus dividend if company profits reach a high level

participation /pɑːˌtɪsɪ'peɪʃ(ə)n/ *noun* the act of taking part ○ *The workers are demanding more participation in the company's affairs.* ○ *Participation helps to make an employee feel part of the organisation.*

participation fee /pɑːˌtɪsɪ'peɪʃ(ə)n fiː/ *noun* a fee paid to a bank for taking part in underwriting a loan

participator /pɑː'tɪsɪpeɪtə/ *noun* a person who has an interest in a company,

e.g. an ordinary or preference shareholder, a creditor or the owner of rights to shares

particular average /pəˌtɪkjʊlə 'æv(ə)rɪdʒ/ *noun* a situation in which part of a shipment is lost or damaged and the insurance costs are borne by the owner of the lost goods and not shared among all the owners of the shipment

partly /'pɑːtli/ *adverb* not completely □ **partly-secured creditors** creditors whose debts are not fully covered by the value of the security

partly-paid capital /ˌpɑːtli peɪd 'kæpɪt(ə)l/ *noun* a capital which represents partly-paid shares

partly-paid up shares /ˌpɑːtli peɪd ʌp 'ʃeəz/, **partly-paid shares** /ˌpɑːtli peɪd 'ʃeəz/ *plural noun* shares in which the shareholders have not paid the full face value

partner /'pɑːtnə/ *noun* a person who works in a business and has an equal share in it with other partners ○ *I became a partner in a firm of solicitors.*

partnership /'pɑːtnəʃɪp/ *noun* an unregistered business where two or more people (but not more than twenty) share the risks and profits according to a partnership agreement ○ *to go into partnership with someone* ○ *to join with someone to form a partnership* □ **to offer someone a partnership**, **to take someone into partnership with you** to have a working business and bring someone in to share it with you □ **to dissolve a partnership** to bring a partnership to an end □ **to go into partnership with someone** to join with someone to form a partnership

partnership agreement /'pɑːtnəʃɪp əˌgriːmənt/ *noun* a document setting up a partnership, giving the details of the business and the amount each partner is contributing to it. Also called **articles of partnership**

part order /ˌpɑːt 'ɔːdə/ *noun* same as **part delivery**

part-owner /ˌpɑːt 'əʊnə/ *noun* a person who owns something jointly with one or more other people ○ *I am part-owner of the restaurant.*

part-ownership /ˌpɑːt 'əʊnəʃɪp/ *noun* a situation where two or more persons own the same property

part payment /ˌpɑːt ˈpeɪmənt/ *noun* a partial payment that leaves a balance to pay at some future time ○ *I gave him £250 as part payment for the car.*

part shipment /ˌpɑːt ˈʃɪpmənt/ *noun* same as **part delivery**

part-time /ˌpɑːt ˈtaɪm/ *adjective*, *adverb* not working for the whole working week ○ *a part-time employee* ○ *We are looking for part-time staff for our sales desk.* ○ *She only works part-time as she has small children to look after.*

part-time work /ˌpɑːt taɪm ˈwɜːk/, **part-time employment** /ˌpɑːt taɪm ɪm ˈplɔɪmənt/ *noun* work for part of a working week (officially, between 8 and 16 hours per week) ○ *He is trying to find part-time work when the children are in school.*

party /ˈpɑːti/ *noun* a person or organisation involved in a legal dispute or legal agreement ○ *How many parties are there to the contract?* ○ *The company is not a party to the agreement.*

par value /ˌpɑː ˈvæljuː/ *noun* same as **face value**

pass /pɑːs/ *verb* **1.** □ **to pass a dividend** to pay no dividend in a certain year **2.** to approve something ○ *The finance director has to pass an invoice before it is sent out.* ○ *The loan has been passed by the board.* □ **to pass a resolution** to vote to agree to a resolution ○ *The meeting passed a proposal that salaries should be frozen.* **3.** to be successful in an examination or test ○ *He passed his typing test.* ○ *She has passed all her exams and now is a qualified accountant.*

pass off *phrasal verb* □ **to pass something off as something else** to pretend that something is another thing in order to cheat a customer ○ *She tried to pass off the wine as French, when in fact it came from outside the EU.*

passbook /ˈpɑːsbʊk/ *noun* same as **bank book**

'…instead of customers having transactions recorded in their passbooks, they will present plastic cards and have the transactions printed out on a receipt' [*Australian Financial Review*]

passbook account /ˈpɑːsbʊk əˌkaʊnt/ *noun* an account which carries a passbook

passive /ˈpæsɪv/ *adjective* not taking any action

passive investor /ˌpæsɪv ɪnˈvestə/ *noun* same as **sleeping partner**

passive stake /ˈpæsɪv steɪk/ *noun* a shareholding where the shareholder takes no active part in running the company

password /ˈpɑːswɜːd/ *noun* a special word which a user has to give when carrying out operations on an account by phone

pataca /pəˈtɑːkə/ *noun* a unit of currency used in Macao

patent /ˈpeɪtənt, ˈpætənt/ *noun* an official document showing that a person has the exclusive right to make and sell an invention ○ *to take out a patent for a new type of light bulb* ○ *to apply for a patent for a new invention* □ '**patent applied for**', '**patent pending**' words on a product showing that the inventor has applied for a patent for it □ **to forfeit a patent** to lose a patent because payments have not been made □ **to infringe a patent** to make and sell a product which works in the same way as a patented product and not pay a royalty for it □ **to file a patent application** to apply for a patent ■ *verb* □ **to patent an invention** to register an invention with the patent office to prevent other people from copying it

patent agent /ˈpeɪtənt ˌeɪdʒənt/ *noun* a person who advises on patents and applies for patents on behalf of clients

patented /ˈpeɪtəntɪd, ˈpætəntɪd/ *adjective* which is protected by a patent

patent office /ˈpeɪtənt ˌɒfɪs/ *noun* a government office which grants patents and supervises them

patent rights /ˈpeɪtənt raɪts/ *plural noun* the rights which an inventor holds because of a patent

pathfinder prospectus /ˈpɑːθfaɪndə prəˌspektəs/ *noun* a preliminary prospectus about a company which is going to be launched on the stock exchange, sent to potential major investors before the issue date, giving details of the company's background, but not giving the price at which shares will be sold

pattern /ˈpæt(ə)n/ *noun* the general way in which something usually happens ○ *The pattern of sales* or *The sales pattern is quite different this year.*

pattern of trade /ˌpæt(ə)n əv ˈtreɪd/ *noun* a general way in which trade is carried on ○ *The company's trading pattern shows high export sales in the first quarter and high home sales in the third quarter.*

pawn /pɔːn/ *noun* □ **to put something in pawn** to leave a valuable object with someone in exchange for a loan which has to be repaid if you want to take back the object □ **to take something out of pawn** to repay the loan and so get back the object which has been pawned ■ *verb* □ **to pawn a watch** to leave a watch with a pawnbroker who gives a loan against it

pawnbroker /ˈpɔːnbrəʊkə/ *noun* a person who lends money against the security of valuable objects

pawnshop /ˈpɔːnʃɒp/ *noun* a pawnbroker's shop

pawn ticket /ˈpɔːn ˌtɪkɪt/ *noun* a receipt given by the pawnbroker for an object left in pawn

pay /peɪ/ *noun* a salary or wages, money given to someone for regular work □ **holiday with pay** a holiday which an employee can take by contract and for which he or she is paid ■ *verb* **1.** to give money to buy an item or a service ○ *to pay £1,000 for a car* ○ *How much did you pay to have the office cleaned?* (NOTE: **paying – paid**) □ '**pay cash**' words written on a crossed cheque to show that it can be paid in cash if necessary □ **to pay in advance** to pay before you receive the item bought or before the service has been completed ○ *We had to pay in advance to have the new telephone system installed.* □ **to pay in instalments** to pay for an item by giving small amounts regularly ○ *We are buying the van by paying instalments of £500 a month.* □ **to pay cash** to pay the complete sum in cash □ **to pay by cheque** to pay by giving a cheque, not by using cash or credit card □ **to pay by credit card** to pay using a credit card, not a cheque or cash **2.** to produce or distribute money (NOTE: **paying – paid**) □ **to pay a dividend** to give shareholders a part of the profits of a company ○ *These shares pay a dividend of 1.5p.* □ **to pay interest** to give money as interest on money borrowed or invested ○ *Some building societies pay interest of 5%.* **3.** to give an employee money for work done ○ *The workforce has not been paid for three*

weeks. ○ *We pay good wages for skilled workers.* ○ *How much do they pay you per hour?* (NOTE: **paying – paid**) □ **to be paid by the hour** to get money for each hour worked □ **to be paid at piecework rates** to get money for each piece of work finished **4.** to give money which is owed or which has to be paid ○ *He was late paying the bill.* ○ *We phoned to ask when they were going to pay the invoice.* ○ *You will have to pay duty on these imports.* ○ *She pays tax at the highest rate.* □ **to pay on demand** to pay money when it is asked for, not after a period of credit □ **please pay the sum of £10** please give £10 in cash or by cheque **5.** □ **to pay a cheque into an account** to deposit money in the form of a cheque (NOTE: **paying – paid**)

'…recession encourages communication not because it makes redundancies easier, but because it makes low or zero pay increases easier to accept' [*Economist*]

'…the yield figure means that if you buy the shares at their current price you will be getting 5% before tax on your money if the company pays the same dividend as in its last financial year' [*Investors Chronicle*]

pay back *phrasal verb* to give money back to someone ○ *Banks are warning students not to take out loans which they cannot pay back.* ○ *I lent him £50 and he promised to pay me back in a month.* ○ *She has never paid me back the money she borrowed.*

pay down *phrasal verb* □ **to pay money down** to make a deposit ○ *They paid £50 down and the rest in monthly instalments.*

pay off *phrasal verb* **1.** to finish paying money which is owed for something ○ *He won the lottery and paid off his mortgage.* ○ *She is trying to pay off the loan by monthly instalments.* **2.** to terminate somebody's employment and pay all wages that are due ○ *When the company was taken over the factory was closed and all the employees were paid off.*

pay out *phrasal verb* to give money ○ *The company pays out thousands of pounds in legal fees.* ○ *We have paid out half our profits in dividends.*

pay up *phrasal verb* to give money which is owed ○ *The company only paid up when we sent them a letter from* *our solicitor.* ○ *She finally paid up six months late.*

payable /'peɪəb(ə)l/ *adjective* due to be paid □ **payable in advance** which has to be paid before the goods are delivered □ **payable on delivery** which has to be paid when the goods are delivered □ **payable on demand** which must be paid when payment is asked for □ **payable at sixty days** which has to be paid by sixty days after the date on the invoice □ **cheque made payable to bearer** a cheque which will be paid to the person who has it, not to any particular name written on it □ **shares payable on application** shares which must be paid for when you apply to buy them □ **electricity charges are payable by the tenant** the tenant (and not the landlord) must pay for the electricity

pay as you earn /ˌpeɪ əz jʊ 'ɜːn/ *noun* a tax system, where income tax is deducted from the salary before it is paid to the worker. Abbreviation **PAYE** (NOTE: The US term is **pay-as-you-go**.)

pay-as-you-go /ˌpeɪ əz juː 'gəʊ/ *noun* **1.** same as **pay as you earn 2.** a payment system where the purchaser pays in small instalments as he or she uses the service

payback /'peɪbæk/ *noun* the act of paying back money which has been borrowed

payback clause /'peɪbæk klɔːz/ *noun* a clause in a contract which states the terms for repaying a loan

payback period /'peɪbæk ˌpɪəriəd/ *noun* **1.** a period of time over which a loan is to be repaid or an investment is to pay for itself **2.** the length of time it will take to earn back the money invested in a project

pay-cheque /'peɪ tʃek/ *noun* a monthly cheque by which an employee is paid (NOTE: The US spelling is **paycheck**.)

pay day /'peɪ deɪ/ *noun* a day on which wages are paid to employees

pay desk /'peɪ desk/ *noun* a place in a store where you pay for goods bought

pay differentials /'peɪ dɪfəˌrenʃəlz/ *plural noun* the difference in salary between employees in similar types of jobs. Also called **salary differentials**, **wage differentials**

paydown /'peɪdaʊn/ *noun* a repayment of part of a sum which has been borrowed

PAYE *abbreviation* pay as you earn

payee /peɪ'iː/ *noun* a person who receives money from someone, or the person whose name is on a cheque

payer /'peɪə/ *noun* a person who gives money to someone

payer bank /'peɪə bæŋk/ *noun* a bank which pays a cheque drawn on one of its accounts

pay hike /'peɪ haɪk/ *noun* an increase in salary

paying /'peɪɪŋ/ *adjective* **1.** making a profit ○ *It is a paying business.* □ **it is not a paying proposition** it is not a business which is going to make a profit **2.** producing money, source of money ■ *noun* the act of giving money

paying agent /'peɪɪŋ ˌeɪdʒənt/ *noun* a bank which pays dividend or interest to a bondholder

paying-in book /ˌpeɪɪŋ 'ɪn bʊk/ *noun* a book of forms for paying money into a bank account or a building society account

paying-in slip /ˌpeɪɪŋ 'ɪn slɪp/ *noun* a printed form which is filled in when money is being deposited in a bank (NOTE: The US term is **deposit slip**.)

payment /'peɪmənt/ *noun* **1.** the act of giving money in exchange for goods or a service ○ *We always ask for payment in cash* or *cash payment and not payment by cheque.* ○ *The payment of interest* or *the interest payment should be made on the 22nd of each month.* □ **payment on account** paying part of the money owed □ **payment on invoice** paying money as soon as an invoice is received □ **payment in kind** paying by giving goods or food, but not money □ **payment by results** money given which increases with the amount of work done or goods produced **2.** money paid □ **repayable in easy payments** repayable with small sums regularly

payment date /'peɪmənt deɪt/ *noun* a date when a payment should be or has been made

payment gateway /'peɪmənt ˌgeɪtweɪ/ *noun* software that processes online credit-card payments. It gets authorisation for the payment from the credit-card company and transfers money into the retailer's bank account.

payment holiday /ˈpeɪmənt ˌhɒlɪdeɪ/ noun a period when payments do not need to be made, especially when repaying a debt or a mortgage

payment order /ˈpeɪmənt ˌɔːdə/ noun an order to someone to make a payment

pay negotiations /ˈpeɪ nɪɡəʊʃi ˌeɪʃ(ə)nz/, **pay talks** /ˈpeɪ tɔːks/ plural noun discussions between management and employees about pay increases

payoff /ˈpeɪɒf/ noun money paid to finish paying something which is owed, such as money paid to an employee when his or her employment is terminated

'…the finance director of the group is to receive a payoff of about £300,000 after deciding to leave the company and pursue other business opportunities' [*Times*]

payoff period /ˈpeɪɒf ˌpɪəriəd/ noun same as **payback period**

payout /ˈpeɪaʊt/ noun money paid to help a company or person in difficulties, a subsidy ○ *The company only exists on payouts from the government.*

'…after a period of recession followed by a rapid boost in incomes, many tax payers embarked upon some tax planning to minimize their payouts' [*Australian Financial Review*]

pay package /ˈpeɪ ˌpækɪdʒ/ noun the salary and other benefits offered with a job ○ *The job carries an attractive pay package.*

pay packet /ˈpeɪ ˌpækɪt/ noun wages or salary, or an envelope containing cash wages and a pay slip

PayPal /ˈpeɪˌpæl/ an e-commerce business allowing payments and money transfers to be made through the Internet

pay phone /ˈpeɪ fəʊn/ noun a public telephone which works if you put coins into it

pay restraint /ˈpeɪ rɪˌstreɪnt/ noun the process of keeping increases in wages under control

pay review /ˈpeɪ rɪˌvjuː/ noun an occasion when an employee's salary is considered and usually increased ○ *I'm soon due for a pay review and hope to get a rise.*

pay rise /ˈpeɪ raɪz/ noun an increase in pay

payroll /ˈpeɪrəʊl/ noun **1.** the list of people employed and paid by a company ○ *The company has 250 on the payroll.* **2.** the money paid by a company in salaries ○ *The office has a weekly payroll of £10,000.*

payroll clerk /ˈpeɪrəʊl klɑːk/ noun a person employed to administer the payment of employees. Also called **wages clerk**

payroll ledger /ˈpeɪrəʊl ˌledʒə/ noun a list of staff and their salaries

payroll tax /ˈpeɪrəʊl tæks/ noun a tax on the people employed by a company

pay scale /ˈpeɪ skeɪl/ noun a hierarchy of wage levels, typically varying according to job title, salary or length of service. Also called **salary scale**, **wage scale**

pay slip /ˈpeɪ slɪp/, **pay statement** /ˈpeɪ ˌsteɪtmənt/ noun a piece of paper showing the full amount of an employee's pay, and the money deducted as tax, pension and National Insurance contributions

pay threshold /ˈpeɪ ˌθreʃhəʊld/ noun a point at which pay increases because of a threshold agreement

PCB abbreviation petty cash book

PDA /ˌpiː diː ˈeɪ/ abbreviation personal digital assistant

P/E abbreviation price/earnings

peak /piːk/ noun the highest point ○ *The shares reached their peak in January.* ○ *The share index has fallen 10% since the peak in January.* ○ *Withdrawals from bank accounts reached a peak in the week before Christmas.* ○ *He has reached the peak of his career.* ■ verb to reach the highest point ○ *Productivity peaked in January.* ○ *Shares have peaked and are beginning to slip back.* ○ *He peaked early and never achieved his ambition of becoming managing director.* ○ *Demand peaks in August, after which sales usually decline.*

peak output /ˌpiːk ˈaʊtpʊt/ noun the highest output

peak year /ˌpiːk ˈjɪə/ noun the year when the largest quantity of products was produced or when sales were highest

peanuts /'pi:nʌts/ *plural noun* a small amount of money (*informal*)

pecuniary /pɪ'kju:niəri/ *adjective* referring to money □ **he gained no pecuniary advantage** he made no profit

peddle /'ped(ə)l/ *verb* to sell goods from door to door or in the street

peg /peg/ *verb* to maintain or fix something at a specific level (NOTE: **pegging – pegged**) □ **to peg a currency** to fix an exchange rate for a currency which previously was floating □ **to peg prices** to fix prices to stop them rising □ **to peg wage increases to the cost-of-living index** to limit increases in wages to the increases in the cost-of-living index

P/E multiple /pi:'i: ˌmʌltɪp(ə)l/ *noun US* same as **price/earnings ratio**

penalise /'pi:nəlaɪz/, **penalize** *verb* to punish or fine someone ○ *to penalise a supplier for late deliveries* ○ *They were penalised for bad time-keeping.*

penalty /'pen(ə)lti/ *noun* **1.** a punishment, often a fine, which is imposed if something is not done or is done incorrectly or illegally **2.** an arbitrary prearranged sum that becomes payable if one party breaks a term of a contract or an undertaking. The most common penalty is a high rate of interest on an unauthorised overdraft.

penalty clause /'pen(ə)lti klɔ:z/ *noun* a clause which lists the penalties which will be imposed if the terms of the contract are not fulfilled ○ *The contract contains a penalty clause which fines the company 1% for every week the completion date is late.*

penalty-free /ˌpen(ə)lti 'fri:/ *adjective* without incurring any penalty, without losing any interest on money invested ○ *penalty-free withdrawal*

pence /pens/ *plural noun* ♦ **penny**

penny /'peni/ *noun* **1.** a small coin, of which one hundred make a pound (NOTE: Written **p** after a figure: *26p*. The plural is **pence**.) **2.** *US* a small coin, one cent (*informal*) (NOTE: The plural in US English is **pennies**. In UK English, say 'pee' for the coin, and 'pee' or 'pence' for the amount: **a five 'pee' coin; it costs ten 'pee'** *or* **ten 'pence'**. In US English, say **'pennies'** for coins and **'cents'** for the amount.)

penny share /'peni 'ʃeə/ *noun* a very cheap share, costing about 10p (NOTE: The US term is **penny stock**.)

COMMENT: These shares can be considered as a good speculation, since buying even large numbers of them does not involve a large amount of money, and the share price of some companies can rise dramatically; the price can of course fall, but in the case of penny shares, the loss is not likely to be as much as with shares with a higher market value.

pension /'penʃən/ *noun* money paid regularly to someone who no longer works ■ *verb* □ **to pension someone off** to ask someone to retire and take a pension

pensionable /'penʃənəb(ə)l/ *adjective* able to receive a pension

pensionable age /ˌpenʃənəb(ə)l 'eɪdʒ/ *noun* an age after which someone can stop working and take a pension

pensionable service /ˌpenʃənəb(ə)l 's3:vɪs/ *noun* the period of service used in calculating pension benefits from an occupational pension scheme

pension contributions /'penʃən kɒntrɪˌbju:ʃ(ə)nz/ *plural noun* money paid by a company or employee into a pension fund

pension drawdown /'penʃən ˌdrɔ:daʊn/ *noun* same as **income drawdown**

pension entitlement /'penʃən ɪnˌtaɪt(ə)lmənt/ *noun* the amount of pension which someone has the right to receive when he or she retires

pensioner /'penʃənə/ *noun* a person who receives a pension

pension fund /'penʃən fʌnd/ *noun* a large sum of money made up of contributions from employees and their employer which provides pensions for retired employees

pension funds /'penʃən fʌndz/ *plural noun* investments managed by pension companies to produce pensions for investors

pension scheme /'penʃən ski:m/, **pension plan** /'penʃən plæn/ *noun* an arrangement by which an employer and, usually, an employee pay into a fund that is invested to provide the employee with a pension on retirement

People's Bank of China /ˌpiːp(ə)lz bæŋk əv ˈtʃaɪnə/ *noun* the Central Bank of China

PEP /ˌpiː iː ˈpiː/ *abbreviation* Personal Equity Plan

peppercorn rent /ˌpepəkɔːn ˈrent/ *noun* a very small or nominal rent ○ *to lease a property for* or *at a peppercorn rent* ○ *The charity pays only a peppercorn rent.*

per /pɜː, pə/ *preposition* **1.** □ **as per** according to □ **as per invoice** as stated in the invoice □ **as per sample** as shown in the sample □ **as per previous order** according to the details given in our previous order **2.** for each □ **we pay £10 per hour** we pay £10 for each hour worked □ **the earnings per share** the dividend received for each share □ **the average sales per representative** the average sales achieved by one representative

'…a 100,000 square-foot warehouse generates $600 in sales per square foot of space' [*Duns Business Month*]

PER *abbreviation* price/earnings ratio

per annum /pər ˈænəm/ *adverb* in a year ○ *What is their turnover per annum?* ○ *What is his total income per annum?* ○ *She earns over £100,000 per annum.*

P/E ratio /ˌpiː ˈiː ˌreɪʃiəʊ/ *noun* same as **price/earnings ratio**

per capita /pə ˈkæpɪtə/ *adjective, adverb* for each person □ **average income per capita** *or* **per capita income** average income of one person

per cent /pə ˈsent/ *adjective, adverb* out of each hundred, or for each hundred □ **10 per cent** ten in every hundred ○ *What is the increase per cent?* ○ *Fifty per cent of nothing is still nothing.*

'…this would represent an 18 per cent growth rate – a slight slackening of the 25 per cent turnover rise in the first half' [*Financial Times*]

'…buildings are depreciated at two per cent per annum on the estimated cost of construction' [*Hongkong Standard*]

percentage /pəˈsentɪdʒ/ *noun* an amount shown as part of one hundred

'…state-owned banks cut their prime rates a percentage point to 11%' [*Wall Street Journal*]

'…a good percentage of the excess stock was taken up during the last quarter' [*Australian Financial Review*]

'…the Federal Reserve Board, signalling its concern about the weakening American economy, cut the discount rate by one-half percentage point to 6.5%' [*Wall Street Journal*]

percentage discount /pəˌsentɪdʒ ˈdɪskaʊnt/ *noun* a discount calculated at an amount per hundred

percentage increase /pəˌsentɪdʒ ˈɪnkriːs/ *noun* an increase calculated on the basis of a rate for one hundred

percentile /pəˈsentaɪl/ *noun* one of a series of ninety-nine figures below which a percentage of the total falls

per contra /ˌpɜː ˈkɒntrə/ *adverb* words showing that a contra entry has been made

perform /pəˈfɔːm/ *verb* to do well or badly □ **how did the shares perform?** did the shares go up or down?

performance /pəˈfɔːməns/ *noun* **1.** the way in which someone or something acts ○ *Last year saw a dip in the company's performance.* □ **the poor performance of the shares on the stock market** the fall in the share price on the stock market □ **as a measure of the company's performance** as a way of judging if the company's results are good or bad □ **performance of staff against objectives** how staff have worked, measured against the objectives set **2.** the way in which a share increases in value

'…inflation-adjusted GNP edged up at a 1.3% annual rate, its worst performance since the economic expansion began' [*Fortune*]

performance fund /pəˈfɔːməns fʌnd/ *noun* an investment fund designed to produce a high return, reflected in the higher risk involved

performance incentive /pə ˈfɔːməns ɪnˌsentɪv/ *noun* an extra payment to reward an employee's performance at work

performance-linked bonus /pə ˌfɔːməns ˌlɪŋkt ˈbəʊnəs/ *noun* a bonus calculated according to the performance of a worker or group of workers

performance rating /pəˈfɔːməns ˌreɪtɪŋ/ *noun* a judgment of how well a share or a company has performed

performance review /pəˈfɔːməns rɪˌvjuː/ *noun* a yearly interview between a manager and each employee to discuss how the employee has worked during the year

performance share /pəˈfɔːməns ʃeə/ *noun* a share which is likely to show capital growth, though perhaps not income. These are usually riskier shares than those which provide income.

per head /pə ˈhed/ *adverb* for each person ○ *Allow £15 per head for expenses.* ○ *Representatives cost on average £50,000 per head per annum.*

period /ˈpɪəriəd/ *noun* a length of time ○ *for a period of time* or *for a period of months* or *for a six-year period* ○ *sales over a period of three months* ○ *to deposit money for a fixed period*

periodic /ˌpɪəriˈɒdɪk/, **periodical** /ˌpɪəriˈɒdɪk(ə)l/ *adjective* happening from time to time ○ *a periodic review of the company's performance*

period of account /ˌpɪəriəd əv əˈkaʊnt/ *noun* the period usually covered by a firm's accounts

period of qualification /ˌpɪəriəd əv ˌkwɒlɪfɪˈkeɪʃ(ə)n/ *noun* the time which has to pass before someone qualifies for something

perk /pɜːk/ *noun* an extra item given by a company to employees in addition to their salaries, e.g. company cars or private health insurance (*informal*) ○ *She earns a good salary and in addition has all sorts of perks.*

permanent /ˈpɜːmənənt/ *adjective* which will last for a long time or for ever ○ *the permanent staff and part-timers* ○ *She has found a permanent job.* ○ *She is in permanent employment.*

permanent interest-bearing share /ˌpɜːmənənt ˌɪntrəst ˌbeərɪŋ ˈʃeə/ *noun* a share issued by a building society to attract investment capital. Abbreviation **PIBS**

permit *noun* /ˈpɜːmɪt/ an official document which allows someone to do something ■ *verb* /pəˈmɪt/ to allow someone to do something ○ *This document permits you to export twenty-five computer systems.* ○ *The ticket permits three people to go into the exhibition.* ○ *Will we be permitted to use her name in the advertising copy?* ○ *Smoking is not permitted in the design studio.* (NOTE: **permitting – permitted**)

perpetual inventory /pəˌpetʃuəl ˈɪnvənt(ə)ri/ *noun* a stock recording and valuation system where each item of stock purchased is added to the total and each item sold is deducted, so that the stock figures are always correct and up-to-date

per pro /ˌpɜː ˈprəʊ/ *abbreviation* per procurationem ○ *The secretary signed per pro the manager.*

per procurationem /pə ˌprɒkjʊræsɪˈəʊnəm/ *preposition* 'a Latin phrase meaning 'on behalf of' or 'acting as the representative of''

perquisite /ˈpɜːkwɪzɪt/ *noun* same as **perk**

person /ˈpɜːs(ə)n/ *noun* **1.** a man or a woman ○ *an insurance policy which covers a named person* □ **the persons named in the contract** the people whose names are given in the contract □ **the document should be witnessed by a third person** someone who is not named in the document should witness it **2.** □ **in person** by doing something or going somewhere yourself, not through another person or means □ **this important package is to be delivered to the chairman in person** the package has to be given to the chairman himself (and not to his secretary, assistant, etc.)

personal /ˈpɜːs(ə)n(ə)l/ *adjective* referring to one person □ **apart from the family shares, she has a personal share-holding in the company** apart from shares belonging to her family as a group, she has shares which she owns herself □ **the car is for his personal use** the car is for him to use himself

personal allowance /ˌpɜːs(ə)n(ə)l əˈlaʊəns/ *noun* a part of a person's income which is not taxed

personal assets /ˌpɜːs(ə)n(ə)l ˈæsets/ *plural noun* movable assets which belong to a person

personal banker /ˌpɜːs(ə)nəl ˈbæŋkə/ *noun* a bank employee who looks after a client, and is the one whom the client contacts when there are problems

personal customer /ˌpɜːs(ə)nəl ˈkʌstəmə/ *noun* a private individual who has an account with a bank, as opposed to a business customer

personal digital assistant /ˌpɜːs(ə)n(ə)l ˌdɪdʒɪt(ə)l əˈsɪstənt/ *noun* a portable device which can be used as a mobile phone, personal organiser and can host a web browser to access the Internet ○ *She accessed the latest sales figures on her PDA.* Abbreviation **PDA**

Personal Equity Plan /ˌpɜːs(ə)nəl ˈekwɪti plæn/ *noun* a share-based investment replaced by the ISA in 1999. Abbreviation **PEP**

COMMENT: There are several types of equity PEP: the single company PEP, where only shares in one company are allowed, and the general PEP, where shares in several companies can be held or other types of investment.

Personal Identification Number /ˌpɜːs(ə)n(ə)l aɪˌdentɪfɪˈkeɪʃ(ə)n ˌnʌmbə/ *noun* a unique number allocated to the holder of a cash card or credit card, by which he or she can enter an automatic banking system, as e.g., to withdraw cash from a cash machine or to pay in a store. Abbreviation **PIN**

personal income /ˌpɜːs(ə)n(ə)l ˈɪnkʌm/ *noun* the income received by an individual person before tax is paid

Personal Investment Authority /ˌpɜːs(ə)nəl ɪnˈvestmənt ɔːˌθɒrəti/ *noun* a self-regulatory body which regulates the activities of financial advisers, insurance brokers and others who give financial advice or arrange financial services for small clients. Abbreviation **PIA**

personalised /ˈpɜːs(ə)nəlaɪzd/, **personalized** *adjective* with the name or initials of a person printed on it ○ *She has a personalised briefcase.*

personal loan /ˌpɜːs(ə)nəl ˈləʊn/ *noun* a loan to a person for household or other personal use, not for business use

personal pension plan /ˌpɜːs(ə)n(ə)l ˈpenʃən ˌplæn/ *noun* a pension plan which applies to one employee only, usually a self-employed person, not to a group. Abbreviation **PPP**

personal property /ˌpɜːs(ə)n(ə)l ˈprɒpəti/ *noun* things which belong to a person ○ *The fire caused considerable damage to personal property.*

personal sector /ˈpɜːs(ə)nəl ˌsektə/ *noun* the part of the investment market

which is owned by private investors, as opposed to the corporate or institutional sector

personnel department /ˌpɜːsəˈnel dɪˌpɑːtmənt/ *noun* same as **human resources department**

personnel officer /ˌpɜːsəˈnel ˌɒfɪsə/ *noun* same as **human resources officer**

peseta /pəˈseɪtə/ *noun* a unit of currency used before the euro in Spain (NOTE: Usually written **ptas** after a figure: *2,000ptas.*)

peso /ˈpeɪsəʊ/ *noun* a unit of currency used in Mexico and many other countries such as Argentina, Bolivia, Chile, Colombia, Cuba, the Dominican Republic, the Philippines and Uruguay

pessimism /ˈpesɪmɪz(ə)m/ *noun* a state of mind in which you expect that everything will turn out badly ○ *There is considerable pessimism about job opportunities.*

pessimistic /ˌpesɪˈmɪstɪk/ *adjective* feeling sure that things will work out badly □ **he takes a pessimistic view of the exchange rate** he expects the exchange rate to fall

peter out *phrasal verb* to come to an end gradually

'…economists believe the economy is picking up this quarter and will do better in the second half of the year, but most expect growth to peter out next year' [*Sunday Times*]

Peter principle /ˈpiːtə ˌprɪnsɪp(ə)l/ *noun* a law, based on wide experience, that people are promoted until they occupy positions for which they are incompetent

petrocurrency /ˈpetrəʊkʌrənsi/ *noun* a foreign currency which is earned by exporting oil

petrodollar /ˈpetrəʊdɒlə/ *noun* a dollar earned by a country from exporting oil, then invested outside that country

petroleum /pəˈtrəʊliəm/ *noun* raw natural oil, found in the ground

petroleum industry /pəˈtrəʊliəm ˌɪndəstri/ *noun* an industry which uses petroleum to make other products such as petrol or soap

petroleum products /pəˌtrəʊliəm ˈprɒdʌkts/ *plural noun* products such as petrol, soap and paint which are made from crude petroleum

petroleum revenues /pə'trəʊliəm ˌrevənjuːz/ *plural noun* income from selling oil

petty /'peti/ *adjective* not important

petty cash /ˌpeti 'kæʃ/ *noun* a small amount of money kept in an office to pay small debts. Abbreviation **P/C**

petty cash book /ˌpeti 'kæʃ ˌbʊk/ *noun* a book in which petty cash payments are noted. Abbreviation **PCB**

petty cash box /ˌpeti 'kæʃ bɒks/ *noun* a locked metal box in an office where the petty cash is kept

petty expenses /ˌpeti ɪk'spensɪz/ *plural noun* small sums of money spent

PGP /ˌpiː dʒiː 'piː/ *noun* a method of encrypting information so that only the intended recipient can read the message; often used to send credit card details via electronic mail. Full form **pretty good privacy**

phase /feɪz/ *noun* a period or part of something which takes place ○ *the first phase of the expansion programme*

phase in *phrasal verb* to bring something in gradually ○ *The new invoicing system will be phased in over the next two months.*

'…the budget grants a tax exemption for $500,000 in capital gains, phased in over the next six years' [*Toronto Star*]

phase out *phrasal verb* to remove something gradually ○ *Smith Ltd will be phased out as a supplier of spare parts.*

phoenix company /'fiːnɪks ˌkʌmp(ə)ni/ *noun* a company formed by the directors of a company which has gone into receivership, which trades in the same way as the first company, and in most respects (except its name) seems to be exactly the same as the first company

'…the prosecution follows recent calls for a reform of insolvency legislation to prevent directors from leaving behind a trail of debt while continuing to trade in phoenix companies – businesses which fold only to rise again, often under a slightly different name in the hands of the same directors and management' [*Financial Times*]

physical market /ˌfɪzɪk(ə)l 'mɑːkɪt/ *noun* a commodity market where purchasers actually buy the commodities, as opposed to the futures market, where they buy and sell the right to purchase commodities at a future date

physical price /ˌfɪzɪk(ə)l 'praɪs/ *noun* a current cash price for a commodity for immediate delivery

physicals /'fɪzɪk(ə)lz/ *plural noun* actual commodities which are sold on the current market, as opposed to futures

physical stock check /ˌfɪzɪk(ə)l 'stɒk tʃek/ *noun* an act of counting actual items of stock (and then checking this figure against stock records)

PIA *abbreviation* Personal Investment Authority

PIB *abbreviation* permanent interest-bearing share

pick /pɪk/ *noun* a thing chosen ○ *the former research analyst never before talked to the press about his stock picks* ■ *verb* to choose ○ *The board picked the finance director to succeed the retiring MD.* ○ *The Association has picked Paris for its next meeting.* □ **to pick stocks** to select which shares to buy

pick up *phrasal verb* **1.** to get better or to improve ○ *Business* or *Trade is picking up.* **2.** to fetch something or someone in a vehicle ○ *The company sent a driver to pick him up at the airport.* ○ *We sent a courier to pick up the packet and deliver it to the designer.*

picking /'pɪkɪŋ/ *noun* ♦ **stockpicking**

piece rate /'piːs reɪt/ *noun* a rate of pay calculated as an amount for each product produced or for each piece of work done, and not as an amount for each hour worked ○ *to earn piece rates*

piecework /'piːswɜːk/ *noun* work for which employees are paid in accordance with the number of products produced or pieces of work done and not at an hourly rate

pieceworker /'piːswɜːkə/ *noun* a person who is employed at a piece rate

pie chart /'paɪ tʃɑːt/ *noun* a diagram where information is shown as a circle cut up into sections of different sizes

piggybacking /'pɪgibækɪŋ/ *noun US* the practice of selling existing shares in a company, as well as new shares being offered for sale for the first time

pilot /'paɪlət/ *noun* a test project, undertaken to see whether something is likely to be successful or profitable

PIN /pɪn/ *abbreviation* Personal Identification Number

pink slip /pɪŋk 'slɪp/ *noun US* an official letter of dismissal given to an employee (in place of a final interview)

Pink 'Un /'pɪŋk ən/ *noun* same as **Financial Times** (*informal*)

pit /pɪt/ *noun* the area of a stock exchange or of a commodities exchange where dealers trade

place /pleɪs/ *verb* to put □ **to place money in an account** to deposit money in an account □ **to place a block of shares** to find a buyer for a block of shares □ **to place a contract** to decide that a certain company shall have the contract to do work □ **to place something on file** to file something □ **to place an issue** to find buyers (usually a small number of investors) for all of a new issue of shares

placement /'pleɪsmənt/ *noun* **1.** the act of finding work for someone ○ *The bureau specialises in the placement of former executives.* **2.** *US* the act of finding buyers for an issue of new shares (NOTE: The UK term is **placing**.)

placing /'pleɪsɪŋ/ *noun* the act of finding a single buyer or a group of institutional buyers for a large number of shares in a new company or a company that is going public □ **the placing of a line of shares** finding a purchaser for a block of shares which was overhanging the market

plaintiff /'pleɪntɪf/ *noun* a person who starts an action against someone in the civil courts (NOTE: Since April 1999, this term has been replaced by **claimant**.)

plain vanilla swap /ˌpleɪn vəˌnɪlə 'swɒp/ *noun* same as **interest rate swap**

plan /plæn/ *noun* **1.** an idea of how something should be done, which has been decided on and organised in advance □ **the government's economic plans** the government's proposals for running the country's economy **2.** an organised way of doing something ○ *an investment plan* ○ *a pension plan* ○ *a savings plan* ■ *verb* to organise carefully how something should be done in the future (NOTE: **planning – planned**) □ **to plan for an increase in bank interest charges** to change a way of doing things because you think there will be an increase in bank interest charges □ **to plan investments** to propose how investments should be made

'…the benefits package is attractive and the compensation plan includes base, incentive and car allowance totalling $50,000+' [*Globe and Mail (Toronto)*]

planned economy /ˌplænd ɪ'kɒnəmi/ *noun* a system where the government plans all business activity, regulates supply, sets production targets and itemises work to be done. Also called **command economy, central planning**

planner /'plænə/ *noun* a person who plans □ **the government's economic planners** people who plan the future economy of the country for the government

planning /'plænɪŋ/ *noun* the process of organising how something should be done in the future ○ *Setting up a new incentive scheme with insufficient planning could be a disaster.* ○ *The long-term planning or short-term planning of the project has been completed.*

'…buildings are closely regulated by planning restrictions' [*Investors Chronicle*]

plastic /'plæstɪk/ *noun* credit cards and charge cards (*informal*)

platinum /'plætɪnəm/ *noun* a rare precious metal traded on bullion markets

platinum card /'plætɪnəm kɑːd/ *noun* a special credit card for people with very large incomes

play /pleɪ/ *noun* □ **in play** likely to be the object of a takeover □ **company in play** company which is being targeted by several takeover bids

Plc, PLC, plc *abbreviation* public limited company

pledge /pledʒ/ *noun* an object given to a pawnbroker as security for money borrowed □ **to redeem a pledge** to pay back a loan and interest and so get back the security ■ *verb* □ **to pledge share certificates** to deposit share certificates with a lender as security for money borrowed (the title to the certificates is not transferred and the certificates are returned when the debt is repaid)

pledgee /ˌpledʒ'iː/ *noun* a person who receives an item as a pledge against a loan

pledgor /ˌpledʒˈɔː/ *noun* a person who pledges a piece of his or her property as security for a loan

plenary meeting /ˈpliːnəri ˈmiːtɪŋ/, **plenary session** /ˈpliːnəri ˌseʃ(ə)n/ *noun* a meeting at a conference when all the delegates meet together

plough back *phrasal verb* □ **to plough back profits into the company** to invest the profits in the business (and not pay them out as dividends to the shareholders) by using them to buy new equipment or to create new products (NOTE: The US spelling is **plow back**.)

plug /plʌg/ *verb* to block or to stop ○ *The company is trying to plug the drain on cash reserves.* (NOTE: **plugging – plugged**)

plummet /ˈplʌmɪt/, **plunge** /plʌndʒ/ *verb* to fall sharply ○ *Share prices plummeted* or *plunged on the news of the devaluation.*

'…in the first six months of this year secondhand values of tankers have plummeted by 40%' [*Lloyd's List*]

'…crude oil output plunged during the past month' [*Wall Street Journal*]

plus /plʌs/ *preposition* added to ○ *Her salary plus commission comes to more than £45,000.* ○ *Production costs plus overheads are higher than revenue.* ■ *adverb* more than □ **houses valued at £500,000 plus** houses valued at over £500,000 ■ *adjective* favourable, good and profitable ○ *A plus factor for the company is that the market is much larger than they had originally thought.* □ **the plus side of the account** the credit side of the account □ **on the plus side** this is a favourable point ○ *On the plus side, we must take into account the new product line.* ■ *noun* **1.** a printed sign (+) showing an addition or increase ○ *At the end of the day the index showed a series of pluses, with very few minuses.* **2.** a good or favourable point ○ *To have achieved £1m in new sales in less than six months is certainly a plus for the sales team.* ○ *His marketing experience is a definite plus.*

p.m. /ˌpiː ˈem/ *adverb* in the afternoon or in the evening, after 12 o'clock midday ○ *The train leaves at 6.50 p.m.* ○ *If you phone New York after 6 p.m. the calls are at a cheaper rate.* (NOTE: The US spelling is **P.M.**)

pocket /ˈpɒkɪt/ *noun* □ **to be £25 in pocket** to have made a profit of £25 □ **to be £25 out of pocket** to have lost £25

point /pɔɪnt/ *noun* **1.** a place or position **2.** same as **decimal point 3.** a unit for calculations □ **the dollar gained two points** the dollar increased in value against another currency by two hundredths of a cent □ **the exchange fell ten points** the stock market index fell by ten units

point of sale /ˌpɔɪnt əv ˈseɪl/ *noun* a place where a product is sold, e.g. a shop. Abbreviation **POS**

point-of-sale material /ˌpɔɪnt əv ˈseɪl məˌtɪəriəl/ *noun* a display material to advertise a product where it is being sold, e.g. posters or dump bins. Abbreviation **POS material**

point of sale terminal /ˌpɔɪnt əv ˈseɪl ˌtɜːmɪn(ə)l/ *noun* an electronic cash terminal at a pay desk which records transactions and stock movements automatically when an item is bought. Abbreviation **POS terminal**

poison pill /ˌpɔɪz(ə)n ˈpɪl/ *noun* an action taken by a company to make itself less attractive to a potential takeover bid

COMMENT: In some cases, the officers of a company will vote themselves extremely high redundancy payments if a takeover is successful; or a company will borrow large amounts of money and give it away to the shareholders as dividends, so that the company has an unacceptably high level of borrowing.

polarisation /ˌpəʊləraɪˈzeɪʃ(ə)n/, **polarization** *noun* a provision of the Financial Services Act by which a financial adviser must either be tied to one financial product provider, or completely independent

police record /pəˌliːs ˈrekɔːd/ *noun* a note of previous crimes for which someone has been convicted ○ *He did not say that he had a police record.*

policy /ˈpɒlɪsi/ *noun* **1.** a course of action or set of principles determining the general way of doing something ○ *a company's trading policy* ○ *The country's economic policy seems to lack any direction.* ○ *We have a policy of only hiring qualified staff.* ○ *Our policy is to submit all contracts to the legal department.* □ **company policy** the company's agreed plan of action or the company's way of doing things ○ *What is the company policy on credit?* ○ *It is against company policy to give more than thirty days' credit.* **2.** a contract for insurance □ **to take out a policy** to sign the contract for an insurance and start paying the premiums ○ *She took out a life insurance policy* or *a house insurance policy.*

policyholder /ˈpɒlɪsi ˌhəʊldə/ *noun* a person who is insured by an insurance company

pool /puːl/ *noun* **1.** an unused supply ○ *a pool of unemployed labour* or *of expertise* **2.** *US* a group of mortgages and other collateral used to back a loan ■ *verb* □ **to pool resources** to put all resources together so as to be more powerful or profitable □ **to pool interests** to exchange shares between companies when a merger takes place

poor /pɔː/ *adjective* **1.** without much money ○ *The company tries to help the poorest members of staff with loans.* ○ *It is one of the poorest countries in the world.* **2.** not very good ○ *poor quality* ○ *poor service* ○ *poor performance by office staff* ○ *poor organisation of working methods*

poorly /ˈpɔːli/ *adverb* badly ○ *The offices are poorly laid out.* ○ *The plan was poorly presented.* □ **poorly-paid staff** staff with low wages

population /ˌpɒpjʊˈleɪʃ(ə)n/ *noun* **1.** all the people living in a particular country or area ○ *Paris has a population of over three million.* ○ *Population statistics show a rise in the 18–25 age group.* ○ *Population trends have to be taken into account when drawing up economic plans.* ○ *The working population of the country is getting older.* **2.** the group of items or people in a survey or study

population forecast /ˌpɒpjʊˈleɪʃ(ə)n ˌfɔːkɑːst/ *noun* a calculation of how many people will be living in a country or in a town at some point in the future

pork bellies /ˈpɔːk ˌbeliz/ *plural noun* meat from the underside of pig carcasses used to make bacon, traded as futures on some American exchanges

portability /ˌpɔːtəˈbɪlɪti/ *noun* the fact of being able to be moved around

portable /ˈpɔːtəb(ə)l/ *adjective* possible to carry ○ *a portable computer* ■

noun □ **a portable** a computer or typewriter which can be carried ○ *He keys all his orders on his portable and then emails them to the office.*

portable pension /ˌpɔːtəb(ə)l ˈpenʃən/, **portable pension plan** /ˌpɔːtəb(ə)l ˈpenʃən plæn/ *noun* a pension entitlement which can be moved from one company to another without loss as an employee changes jobs

portfolio /pɔːtˈfəʊliəʊ/ *noun* **1.** □ **a portfolio of shares** all the shares owned by a single investor **2.** a folder containing a selection of samples ○ *The student brought a portfolio of designs to show the design department manager.*

portfolio investments /pɔːtˌfəʊliəʊ ɪnˈvestmənts/ *plural noun* investments in shares and government stocks, etc. as opposed to investments in property, etc.

portfolio management /pɔːtˈfəʊliəʊ ˌmænɪdʒmənt/ *noun* the systematic buying and selling shares in order to make the highest-possible profits for a single investor

portfolio manager /pɔːtˈfəʊliəʊ ˌmænɪdʒə/ *noun* a person who manages a share portfolio

portfolio theory /pɔːtˈfəʊliəʊ ˌθɪəri/ *noun* a basis for managing a portfolio of investments, i.e. a mix of safe stocks and more risky ones

portfolio value /pɔːtˈfəʊliəʊ ˌvæljuː/ *noun* the value of someone's portfolio of investments

POS /pɒz/, **p.o.s.** *abbreviation* point of sale

position /pəˈzɪʃ(ə)n/ *noun* **1.** a situation or state of affairs □ **what is the cash position?** what is the state of the company's current account? □ **to cover a position** to have enough money to pay for a forward purchase **2.** the state of a person's current financial holding in a stock □ **to close a position** to arrange your affairs so that you no longer have any liability to pay (as by selling all your securities or when a purchaser of a futures contract takes on a sales contract for the same amount to offset the risk) □ **to take a bear position** to act on the assumption that the market will fall □ **to take a position in a share** to buy shares on your own account, expecting to sell them later at a profit

positioning /pə'zɪʃ(ə)nɪŋ/ *noun* the promotion of a product in a particular area of a market

position of trust /pə,zɪʃ(ə)n əv 'trʌst/ *noun* a job in which a person is trusted to act correctly and honestly

positive /'pɒzɪtɪv/ *adjective* meaning 'yes' ○ *The board gave a positive reply.*

positive carry /,pɒzɪtɪv 'kæri/ *noun* a situation in which the cost of financing an investment is less than the return obtained from it

positive cash flow /,pɒzɪtɪv 'kæʃ fləʊ/ *noun* a situation in which more money is coming into a company than is going out

positive yield curve /,pɒzɪtɪv 'jiːld ,kɜːv/ *noun* a situation where the yield on a short-term investment is less than that on a long-term investment

POS material /,piː əʊ 'es mə,tɪəriəl/ *noun* same as **point-of-sale material**

possess /pə'zes/ *verb* to own something ○ *The company possesses property in the centre of the town.* ○ *He lost all he possessed in the collapse of his company.* Compare **repossess**

possession /pə'zeʃ(ə)n/ *noun* the fact of owning or having something □ **the documents are in his possession** he is holding the documents

possessions /pə'zeʃ(ə)nz/ *plural noun* property, things owned ○ *They lost all their possessions in the fire.* Compare **repossession**

post /pəʊst/ *noun* a system of sending letters and parcels from one place to another ○ *to send an invoice by post* ○ *He put the letter in the post.* ○ *The cheque was lost in the post.* □ **to send a reply by return of post** to reply to a letter immediately ■ *verb* **1.** to send a letter or parcel by post **2.** to record or enter something □ **to post an entry** to transfer an entry to an account □ **to post up a ledger** to keep a ledger up to date **3.** □ **to post an increase** to let people know that an increase has taken place

'Toronto stocks closed at an all-time high, posting their fifth day of advances in heavy trading' [*Financial Times*]

postal /'pəʊst(ə)l/ *adjective* referring to the post

postal account /'pəʊst(ə)l ə,kaʊnt/ *noun* a bank account where all dealings are done by post, so reducing overhead costs and allowing a higher interest to be paid

postal ballot /'pəʊst(ə)l ,bælət/, **postal vote** /'pəʊst(ə)l vəʊt/ *noun* an election where the voters send their ballot papers by post

postal charges /'pəʊst(ə)l ,tʃɑːdʒɪz/ *plural noun* money to be paid for sending letters or parcels by post ○ *Postal charges are going up by 10% in September.*

postal order /'pəʊst(ə)l ,ɔːdə/ *noun* a document bought at a post office, used as a method of paying small amounts of money by post

post-balance sheet event /,pəʊst ,bæləns ʃiːt ɪ'vent/ *noun* something which happens after the date when the balance sheet is drawn up, and before the time when the balance sheet is officially approved by the directors, which affects a company's financial position

postdate /,pəʊst'deɪt/ *verb* to put a later date on a document ○ *He sent us a postdated cheque.* ○ *Her cheque was postdated to June.*

post-earnings-announcement drift /,pəʊst ,ɜːnɪŋz ə'naʊnsmənt drɪft/ *noun* an unexplained downward movement of shares in companies following announcements that quarterly earnings have exceeded expectations

posting /'pəʊstɪŋ/ *noun* the action of entering transactions in accounts

potential /pə'tenʃəl/ *adjective* possible □ **potential customers** people who could be customers □ **potential market** a market which could be exploited ■ *noun* the possibility of becoming something □ **a share with a growth potential** *or* **with a potential for growth** a share which is likely to increase in value □ **a product with considerable sales potential** a product which is likely to have very large sales □ **to analyse the market potential** to examine the market to see how large it possibly is

'...career prospects are excellent for someone with growth potential' [*Australian Financial Review*]

'...for sale: established general cleaning business; has potential to be increased to over 1 million dollar turnover' [*Australian Financial Review*]

pound /paʊnd/ *noun* **1.** a measure of weight (= 0.45 kilos) ○ *to sell oranges by the pound* ○ *a pound of oranges* ○ *Oranges cost 50p a pound.* (NOTE: Usually written **lb** after a figure: **25lb**. Note also that the pound is now no longer officially used in the UK) **2.** a unit of currency used in the UK and many other countries including Egypt, Lebanon, Malta, Sudan, Syria and, before the euro, Ireland

poundage /'paʊndɪdʒ/ *noun* a rate charged per pound in weight

pound-cost averaging /ˌpaʊnd kɒst 'æv(ə)rɪdʒɪŋ/ *noun* the practice of buying securities at different times, but always spending the same amount of money

pound sterling /ˌpaʊnd 'stɜːlɪŋ/ *noun* the official term for the UK currency

power /'paʊə/ *noun* **1.** strength or ability □ **the power of a consumer group** ability of a group to influence the government or manufacturers **2.** a force or legal right □ **the full power of the law** the full force of the law when applied ○ *We will apply the full power of the law to get possession of our property again.* ○ *There was a power struggle in the boardroom, and the finance director had to resign.*

power of appointment /ˌpaʊər əv ə 'pɔɪntmənt/ *noun* the power of a trustee to dispose of interests in property to another person

power of attorney /ˌpaʊər əv ə'tɜːni/ *noun* a legal document which gives someone the right to act on someone's behalf in legal matters

p.p. *abbreviation* per procurationem ■ *verb* □ **to p.p. a letter** to sign a letter on behalf of someone ○ *Her assistant p.p.'d the letter while the manager was at lunch.*

PPP *abbreviation* personal pension plan

practice /'præktɪs/ *noun* a way of doing things, a custom or habit ○ *Her practice was to arrive at work at 7.30 and start counting the cash.* □ **restrictive practices** ways of working which make people less free (such as when trade unions stop workers from doing certain jobs, or stores do not allow customers a free choice of product)

'…the EC demanded international arbitration over the pricing practices of the provincial boards' [*Globe and Mail (Toronto)*]

preannouncement /ˌpriːə'naʊns mənt/ *noun* an announcement of something earlier than the date on which it should normally be announced

precautionary measure /prɪ 'kɔːʃ(ə)n(ə)ri ˌmeʒə/ *noun* an action taken to prevent something unwanted taking place

precious metals /ˌpreʃəs 'met(ə)lz/ *plural noun* very valuable metals, such as gold and platinum

predator /'predətə/ *noun* an individual (or company) who spends most of the time looking for companies to purchase cheaply

predict /prɪ'dɪkt/ *verb* to say that something will happen in the future

predictability /prɪˌdɪktə'bɪlɪti/ *noun* the ability to be predicted

pre-empt /ˌpriː 'empt/ *verb* to stop something happening or stop someone doing something by taking action quickly before anyone else can ○ *They staged a management buyout to pre-empt a take-over bid.*

pre-emption right /priː'empʃən raɪt/ *noun* the right of an existing shareholder to be first to buy a new stock issue

pre-emptive /ˌpriː 'emptɪv/ *adjective* done before anyone else takes action in order to stop something happening □ **pre-emptive strike against a takeover bid** rapid action taken to prevent a takeover bid

preference /'pref(ə)rəns/ *noun* **1.** a thing which someone prefers ○ *the customers' preference for small corner shops* **2.** a thing which has an advantage over something else

preference shareholder /ˌpref(ə)rəns 'ʃeəhəʊldə/ *noun* an owner of preference shares

preference shares /'pref(ə)rəns ʃeəz/ *plural noun* shares, often with no voting rights, which receive their dividend before all other shares and are repaid first at face value if the company goes into liquidation (NOTE: The US term is **preferred stock**.)

COMMENT: Preference shares, because they have less risk than ordinary shares, normally carry no voting rights.

preferential /ˌprefəˈrenʃəl/ *adjective* showing that something is preferred more than another

preferential creditor /ˌprefərenʃ(ə)l ˈkredɪtə/, **preferred creditor** /prɪˌfɜːd ˈkredɪtə/ *noun* a creditor who must be paid first if a company is in liquidation

preferred shares /prɪˌfɜːd ˈʃeəz/, **preferred stock** /prɪˌfɜːd ˈstɒk/ *plural noun* same as **preference shares**

pre-financing /ˌpriː ˈfaɪnænsɪŋ/ *noun* money paid in advance by customers to help finance a project the future products of which the customer contracts to buy by making additional payments

prelim /ˈpriːlɪm/ *noun* same as **preliminary announcement** (*informal*)

preliminary /prɪˈlɪmɪn(ə)ri/ *adjective* early, happening before anything else

'…preliminary indications of the level of business investment and activity during the March quarter will be available this week' [*Australian Financial Review*]

preliminary announcement /prɪˌlɪmɪn(ə)ri əˈnaʊnsmənt/ *noun* an announcement of a company's full-year results, given out to the press before the detailed annual report is released

preliminary prospectus /prɪˌlɪmɪn(ə)ri prəˈspektəs/ *noun* same as **pathfinder prospectus**

pre-market trading /priː ˌmɑːkɪt ˈtreɪdɪŋ/ *noun* trading that takes place before a stock exchange officially opens in the morning

premium /ˈpriːmiəm/ *noun* **1.** a regular payment made to an insurance company for the protection provided by an insurance policy **2.** an amount to be paid to a landlord or a tenant for the right to take over a lease ○ *flat to let with a premium of £10,000* ○ *annual rent: £8,500, premium: £25,000* **3.** an extra sum of money in addition to a usual charge, wage, price or other amount **4.** a gift, discount or other incentive to encourage someone to buy ■ *adjective* **1.** of very high quality **2.** very high

premium bond /ˈpriːmiəm bɒnd/ *noun* a government bond, part of the National Savings and Investment scheme, which pays no interest, but gives the owner the chance to win a weekly or monthly prize

premium income /ˌpriːmiəm ˈɪnkʌm/ *noun* income which an insurance company derives from premiums paid by insured persons

premium offer /ˈpriːmiəm ˌɒfə/ *noun* a free gift offered to attract more customers

prepaid /priːˈpeɪd/ *adjective* paid in advance

prepay /priːˈpeɪ/ *verb* to pay something in advance (NOTE: **prepaying – prepaid**)

prepayment /priːˈpeɪmənt/ *noun* **1.** a payment in advance, or the act of paying in advance □ **to ask for prepayment of a fee** to ask for the fee to be paid before the work is done **2.** *US* the repayment of the principal of a loan before it is due

prepayment penalty /priːˈpeɪmənt ˌpen(ə)lti/ *noun US* a charge levied on someone who repays a loan such as a mortgage before it is due

present /ˈprez(ə)nt/ *adjective* **1.** happening now ○ *The shares are too expensive at their present price.* ○ *What is the present address of the company?* **2.** being there when something happens ○ *Only six directors were present at the board meeting.* ■ *verb* /prɪˈzent/ to bring or send and show a document □ **to present a bill for acceptance** to present a bill for payment by the person who has accepted it □ **to present a bill for payment** to send a bill to be paid

presentation /ˌprez(ə)nˈteɪʃ(ə)n/ *noun* the showing of a document □ **cheque payable on presentation** a cheque which will be paid when it is presented □ **free admission on presentation of this card** you do not pay to go in if you show this card

presentment /prɪˈzentmənt/ *noun US* same as **presentation**

present value /ˌprez(ə)nt ˈvæljuː/ *noun* **1.** the value something has now ○ *In 1984 the pound was worth five times its present value.* **2.** the value now of a specified sum of money to be received in the future, if invested at current interest rates. Abbreviation **PV 3.** a price which a share must reach in the future to be the equivalent of today's price, taking inflation into account

COMMENT: The present value of a future sum of money is found by discounting that future sum, and can be used to decide how much money to invest now at current interest rates in order to receive the sum you want to have in a given number of years' time.

press /pres/ *noun* newspapers and magazines ○ *We plan to give the product a lot of press publicity.* ○ *There was no mention of the new product in the press.*

press conference /'pres ˌkɒnf(ə)rəns/ *noun* a meeting where newspaper and TV reporters are invited to hear news of something such as a new product or a takeover bid

press coverage /'pres ˌkʌv(ə)rɪdʒ/ *noun* reports about something in newspapers, and magazines and other media ○ *The company had good press coverage for the launch of its new model.*

press cutting /'pres ˌkʌtɪŋ/ *noun* a piece cut out of a newspaper or magazine which refers to an item which you find interesting ○ *We have kept a file of press cuttings about the new car.*

pressing /'presɪŋ/ *adjective* urgent □ **pressing engagements** meetings which have to be attended □ **pressing bills** bills which have to be paid

press recommendation /'pres ˌrekəmenˌdeɪʃ(ə)n/ *noun* a share which has been tipped as a good buy in the financial column of a newspaper

press release /'pres rɪˌliːs/ *noun* a sheet giving news about something which is sent to newspapers and TV and radio stations so that they can use the information ○ *The company sent out a press release about the launch of the new car.*

pressure /'preʃə/ *noun* something which forces you to do something □ **he was under considerable financial pressure** he was forced to act because he owed money □ **to put pressure on someone to do something** to try to force someone to do something ○ *The group tried to put pressure on the government to act.* ○ *The banks put pressure on the company to reduce its borrowings.* □ **working under high pressure** working with customers asking for supplies urgently or with a manager telling you to work faster □ **the pound has come under pressure on the foreign exchanges** many people have been trying to sell pounds,

and this has brought down its exchange rate ○ *The group tried to put pressure on the government to act.* ○ *The banks put pressure on the company to reduce its borrowings.*

pressure group /'preʃə gruːp/ *noun* a group of people who try to influence the government, the local town council or some other organisation

pretax /'priːtæks/, **pre-tax** *adjective* before tax has been deducted or paid

'…the company's goals are a growth in sales of up to 40 per cent, a rise in pre-tax earnings of nearly 35 per cent and a rise in after-tax earnings of more than 25 per cent' [*Citizen (Ottawa)*]

'EC regulations which came into effect in July insist that customers can buy cars anywhere in the EC at the local pre-tax price' [*Financial Times*]

pretax profit /ˌpriːtæks 'prɒfɪt/ *noun* the amount of profit a company makes before taxes are deducted ○ *The dividend paid is equivalent to one quarter of the pretax profit.* Also called **profit before tax**, **profit on ordinary activities before tax**

pretax profit margin /ˌpriːtæks 'prɒfɪt ˌmɑːdʒɪn/ *noun* the pretax profit shown as a percentage of turnover in a profit and loss account

previous /'priːviəs/ *adjective* happening earlier or which existed before ○ *List all previous positions with the salaries earned.*

previous balance /ˌpriːviəs 'bæləns/ *noun* a balance in an account at the end of the accounting period before the current one

prey /preɪ/ *noun* company which is being attacked by another (the 'predator') in a takeover bid

price /praɪs/ *noun* money which has to be paid to buy something □ **asking price** price which the seller is hoping to be paid for the item when it is sold □ **competitive price** a low price aimed to compete with a rival product □ **to sell goods off at half price** to sell goods at half the price at which they were being sold before □ **cars in the £18–19,000 price range** cars of different makes, selling for between £18,000 and £19,000 □ **price ex warehouse** the price for a product which is to be collected from the manufacturer's or agent's warehouse and so does not include delivery □ **to increase in price** to become more expensive ○ *Petrol has increased in price* or *the price of petrol has increased.* □ **to increase prices, to raise prices** to make items more expensive □ **we will try to meet your price** we will try to offer a price which is acceptable to you □ **to cut prices** to reduce prices suddenly □ **to lower prices, to reduce prices** to make items cheaper ■ *verb* to give a price to a product ○ *We have two used cars for sale, both priced at £5,000.* □ **competitively priced** sold at a low price which competes with that of similar goods from other companies □ **the company has priced itself out of the market** the company has raised its prices so high that its products do not sell

price/book ratio /ˌpraɪs ˈbʊk ˌreɪʃiəʊ/ *noun* a ratio of the price of a stock to its book value

price ceiling /ˈpraɪs ˌsiːlɪŋ/ *noun* a limit beyond which prices will not or cannot rise

price change /ˈpraɪs tʃeɪndʒ/ *noun* an amount by which the price of a share moves during a day's trading

price controls /ˈpraɪs kənˌtrəʊlz/ *plural noun* legal measures to prevent prices rising too fast

price cutting /ˈpraɪs ˌkʌtɪŋ/ *noun* a sudden lowering of prices

price-cutting war /ˈpraɪs ˌkʌtɪŋ wɔː/ *noun* same as **price war**

price differential /ˈpraɪs dɪfəˌrenʃəl/ *noun* the difference in price between products in a range

price/earnings ratio /ˌpraɪs ˈɜːnɪŋz ˌreɪʃiəʊ/ *noun* a ratio between the current market price of a share of stock and the earnings per share (the current dividend it produces), calculated by dividing the market price by the earnings per share ○ *These shares sell at a P/E ratio of 7* Also called **P/E ratio**. Abbreviation **PER**

COMMENT: The P/E ratio is an indication of the way investors think a company will perform in the future, as a high market price suggests that investors expect earnings to grow and this gives a high P/E figure; a low P/E figure implies that investors feel that earnings are not likely to rise.

price ex factory /ˌpraɪs eks ˈfækt(ə)ri/, **price ex works** /ˌpraɪs eks

ˈwɜːks/ *noun* a price not including transport from the maker's factory

price fixing /ˈpraɪs ˌfɪksɪŋ/ *noun* an illegal agreement between companies to charge the same price for competing products

price label /ˈpraɪs ˌleɪb(ə)l/ *noun* a label which shows a price

price list /ˈpraɪs lɪst/ *noun* a sheet giving prices of goods for sale

price movement /ˈpraɪs ˌmuːvmənt/ *noun* a change in the prices of shares or commodities

price range /ˈpraɪs reɪndʒ/ *noun* a series of prices for similar products from different suppliers

price-sensitive /ˌpraɪs ˈsensətɪv/ *adjective* referring to a product for which demand will change significantly if its price is increased or decreased

price tag /ˈpraɪs tæg/ *noun* **1.** a label attached to an item being sold that shows its price **2.** the value of a person or thing ○ *The takeover bid put a $2m price tag on the company.*

price war /ˈpraɪs wɔː/ *noun* a competition between companies to get a larger market share by cutting prices. Also called **price-cutting war**

pricing /ˈpraɪsɪŋ/ *noun* the act of giving a price to a product

pricing model /ˈpraɪsɪŋ ˌmɒd(ə)l/ *noun* a computerised system for calculating a price, based on costs, anticipated margins, etc.

pricing policy /ˈpraɪsɪŋ ˌpɒlisi/ *noun* a company's policy in giving prices to its products ○ *Our pricing policy aims at producing a 35% gross margin.*

primary /ˈpraɪməri/ *adjective* **1.** basic **2.** first, most important

'…farmers are convinced that primary industry no longer has the capacity to meet new capital taxes or charges on farm inputs' [*Australian Financial Review*]

primary account number /ˌpraɪməri əˈkaʊnt ˌnʌmbə/ *noun* series of figures on a credit card, which are the number of the issuing bank and the personal number of the account. Abbreviation **PAN**

primary commodities /ˌpraɪməri kə ˈmɒdɪtiz/ *plural noun* farm produce grown in large quantities, e.g. corn, rice or cotton

primary dealer /ˌpraɪməri ˈdiːlə/ noun a marketmaker dealing in government stocks

primary industry /ˌpraɪməri ˈɪndəstri/ noun an industry dealing with basic raw materials such as coal, wood, or farm produce

primary market /ˌpraɪməri ˈmɑːkɪt/ noun a market where new securities or bonds are issued. Also called **new issue market**

primary products /ˌpraɪməri ˈprɒdʌkts/ plural noun products which are basic raw materials, e.g. wood, milk, or fish

prime /praɪm/ adjective **1.** most important **2.** basic ■ noun same as **prime rate**

prime bills /ˌpraɪm ˈbɪlz/ plural noun bills of exchange which do not involve any risk

prime cost /ˌpraɪm ˈkɒst/ noun the cost involved in producing a product, excluding overheads

prime rate /ˈpraɪm reɪt/ noun US the best rate of interest at which a bank lends to its customers. Also called **prime**

prime sites /ˌpraɪm ˈsaɪts/ plural noun the most valuable commercial sites, i.e. in main shopping streets. Compare **secondary sites**

prime time /ˈpraɪm taɪm/ noun the most expensive advertising time for TV commercials ○ We are putting out a series of prime-time commercials.

priming /ˈpraɪmɪŋ/ noun ♦ pump priming

principal /ˈprɪnsɪp(ə)l/ noun **1.** a person or company that is represented by an agent ○ The agent has come to London to see his principals. **2.** a person acting for him or herself, such as a marketmaker buying securities on his or her own account **3.** money invested or borrowed on which interest is paid ○ to repay principal and interest ○ We try to repay part of principal each month. (NOTE: Do not confuse with **principle**.) ■ adjective most important ○ The principal shareholders asked for a meeting. ○ The country's principal products are paper and wood. ○ The company's principal asset is its design staff.

'…the company was set up with funds totalling NorKr 145m with the principal aim of making capital gains on the second-hand market' [Lloyd's List]

principle /ˈprɪnsɪp(ə)l/ noun a basic point or general rule (NOTE: Do not confuse with **principal**.) □ **in principle** in agreement with a general rule □ **agreement in principle** agreement with the basic conditions of a proposal

prior /ˈpraɪə/ adjective earlier □ **prior agreement** an agreement which was reached earlier □ **without prior knowledge** without knowing before

prior-charge capital /ˌpraɪə ˈtʃɑːdʒ ˌkæpɪt(ə)l/ noun a capital in the form of preference shares, which ranks before other capital in terms of distributions of profits and repayment when a company goes into liquidation

priority /praɪˈɒrɪti/ noun □ **to have priority** to have the right to be first □ **to have priority over** or **to take priority over something** to be more important than something ○ Reducing overheads takes priority over increasing turnover. ○ Debenture holders have priority over ordinary shareholders. □ **to give something top priority** to make something the most important item

privacy /ˈprɪvəsi/ noun a method of ensuring that a person's personal or credit card payment details cannot be intercepted and read when transferred over the Internet

private /ˈpraɪvət/ adjective belonging to a single person or to individual people, not to a company or the state □ **a letter marked 'private and confidential'** a letter which must not be opened by anyone other than the person it is addressed to

private bank /ˌpraɪvət ˈbæŋk/ noun **1.** a bank that is owned by a single person or a limited number of private shareholders **2.** a bank that provides banking facilities to high net worth individuals. ◊ **private banking**

private banking /ˌpraɪvət ˈbæŋkɪŋ/ noun a service offered by certain financial institutions to high net worth individuals. In addition to standard banking services, it will typically include portfolio management and advisory services on taxation, including estate planning.

private client stockbroker /ˌpraɪvət ˌklaɪənt ˈstɒkbrəʊkə/ noun a stockbroker who deals on behalf of private investors

private company /ˌpraɪvət ˈkʌmp(ə)ni/ noun a registered company whose shares are not offered for sale to the public

private debt /ˌpraɪvət ˈdet/ noun money owed by individuals and organisations other than governments

private enterprise /ˌpraɪvət ˈentəpraɪz/ noun businesses that are owned privately, not nationalised ○ The project is completely funded by private enterprise.

private income /ˌpraɪvət ˈɪnkʌm/ noun income from dividends, interest or rent which is not part of a salary

private investor /ˌpraɪvət ɪnˈvestə/ noun an ordinary person with money to invest

private limited company /ˌpraɪvət ˌlɪmɪtɪd ˈkʌmp(ə)ni/ noun **1.** a company with a small number of shareholders, whose shares are not traded on the stock exchange **2.** a subsidiary company whose shares are not listed on the stock exchange, while those of its parent company are ▶ abbreviation **Pty Ltd**

private means /ˌpraɪvət ˈmiːnz/ plural noun income from dividends, interest, or rent which is not part of someone's salary

private ownership /ˌpraɪvət ˈəʊnə ʃɪp/ noun a situation in which a company is owned by private shareholders

private placing /ˌpraɪvət ˈpleɪsɪŋ/, **private placement** /ˌpraɪvət ˈpleɪs mənt/ noun the act of placing a new issue of shares with a group of selected financial institutions

private property /ˌpraɪvət ˈprɒpəti/ noun property which belongs to a private person, not to the public

private sector /ˈpraɪvət ˌsektə/ noun one of the parts of the economy of a country, which itself is made up of the corporate sector (firms owned by private shareholders), the personal sector (individuals and their income and expenditure), and the financial sector (banks and other institutions dealing in money) ○ The expansion is completely funded by the private sector. ○ Salaries in the private sector have increased faster than in the public sector.

privatisation /ˌpraɪvətaɪˈzeɪʃ(ə)n/, **privatization** noun the process of selling a nationalised industry to private owners

privatise /ˈpraɪvətaɪz/, **privatize** verb to sell a nationalised industry to private owners

pro /prəʊ/ preposition for

probate /ˈprəʊbeɪt/ noun legal acceptance that a document, especially a will, is valid □ **the executor was granted probate** or **obtained a grant of probate** the executor was told officially that the will was valid

probate court /ˈprəʊbeɪt kɔːt/ noun a court which examines wills to see if they are valid

procedure /prəˈsiːdʒə/ noun a way in which something is done ○ The inquiry found that the company had not followed the approved procedures. □ **this procedure is very irregular** this is not the proper way to do something □ **accounting procedures** set ways of doing the accounts of a company

'…this was a serious breach of disciplinary procedure and the dismissal was unfair' [Personnel Management]

proceed /prəˈsiːd/ verb to go on, to continue ○ The negotiations are proceeding slowly. □ **to proceed against someone** to start a legal action against someone □ **to proceed with something** to go on doing something ○ Shall we proceed with the committee meeting?

proceedings /prəˈsiːdɪŋz/ plural noun □ **to institute proceedings against someone** to start a legal action against someone

proceeds /ˈprəʊsiːdz/ plural noun money received from selling something □ **the proceeds of a sale** money received from a sale after deducting expenses ○ He sold his shop and invested the proceeds in a computer repair business.

process /ˈprəʊses/ noun □ **decision-making processes** ways in which decisions are reached ■ verb **1.** □ **to process figures** to sort out information to make it easily understood ○ The sales figures are being processed by our accounts department. ○ The data is being processed by our computer. **2.** to deal with something in the usual routine way ○ It usually takes at least two weeks to process an insurance claim. ○ Orders are processed in our warehouse.

processing /'prəʊsesɪŋ/ noun **1.** the act of sorting information ○ the processing of information or of statistics by a computer **2.** □ **the processing of a claim for insurance** putting a claim for insurance through the usual office routine in the insurance company

produce noun /'prɒdjuːs/ products from farms and gardens, especially fruit and vegetables ○ home produce ○ agricultural produce ○ farm produce ■ verb /prə'djuːs/ **1.** to bring something out and show it ○ He produced documents to prove his claim. ○ The negotiators produced a new set of figures. ○ The customs officer asked him to produce the relevant documents. **2.** to make or manufacture something ○ The factory produces cars or engines. □ **to mass produce** to make large quantities of a product **3.** to give an interest ○ investments which produce about 10% per annum

producer /prə'djuːsə/ noun a person, company or country that manufactures ○ a country which is a producer of high-quality watches ○ The company is a major car producer. Also called **supplier**

product /'prɒdʌkt/ noun **1.** something which is made or manufactured **2.** a manufactured item for sale

product advertising /'prɒdʌkt ˌædvətaɪzɪŋ/ noun the advertising of a particular named product, not the company which makes it

product analysis /'prɒdʌkt ə ˌnæləsɪs/ noun an examination of each separate product in a company's range to find out why it sells, who buys it, etc.

product design /'prɒdʌkt dɪˌzaɪn/ noun the design of consumer products

product development /'prɒdʌkt dɪ ˌveləpmənt/ noun the process of improving an existing product line to meet the needs of the market

product engineer /ˌprɒdʌkt ˌendʒɪ 'nɪə/ noun an engineer in charge of the equipment for making a product

production /prə'dʌkʃən/ noun **1.** the act of showing something □ **on production of** when something is shown ○ The case will be released by customs on production of the relevant documents. ○

Goods can be exchanged only on production of the sales slip. **2.** the work of making or manufacturing goods for sale ○ We are hoping to speed up production by installing new machinery. ○ Higher production is rewarded with higher pay.

production cost /prə'dʌkʃən kɒst/ noun the cost of making a product

production department /prə 'dʌkʃən dɪˌpɑːtmənt/ noun the section of a company which deals with the making of the company's products

production line /prə'dʌkʃən laɪn/ noun a system of making a product, where each item such as a car moves slowly through the factory with new sections added to it as it goes along ○ He works on the production line. ○ She is a production-line employee.

production manager /prə'dʌkʃən ˌmænɪdʒə/ noun the person in charge of the production department

production rate /prə'dʌkʃ(ə)n reɪt/ noun same as **rate of production**

production target /prə'dʌkʃən ˌtɑːgɪt/ noun the number of units a business is expected to produce

production unit /prə'dʌkʃən ˌjuːnɪt/ noun a separate small group of employees producing a product

productive /prə'dʌktɪv/ adjective producing something, especially something useful □ **productive discussions** useful discussions which lead to an agreement or decision

productive capital /prə,dʌktɪv 'kæpɪt(ə)l/ noun capital which is invested to give interest

productivity /ˌprɒdʌk'tɪvɪti/ noun the rate of output per employee, or per item of equipment, in a business ○ Bonus payments are linked to productivity. ○ The company is aiming to increase productivity. ○ Productivity has fallen or risen since the company was taken over.

'…though there has been productivity growth, the absolute productivity gap between many British firms and their foreign rivals remains' [Sunday Times]

productivity agreement /ˌprɒdʌk 'tɪvɪti əˌgriːmənt/ noun an agreement to pay a productivity bonus

productivity bonus /ˌprɒdʌk'tɪvɪti ˌbəʊnəs/ noun an extra payment made to employees because of increased production per employee

productivity drive /ˌprɒdʌkˈtɪvɪti draɪv/ *noun* an extra effort to increase productivity

product management /ˈprɒdʌkt ˌmænɪdʒmənt/ *noun* the process of overseeing the making and selling of a product as an independent item

product mix /ˈprɒdʌkt mɪks/ *noun* the range of different products which a company has for sale

profession /prəˈfeʃ(ə)n/ *noun* **1.** an occupation for which official qualifications are needed and which is often made a lifelong career ○ *The managing director is an accountant by profession.* ○ *HR management is now more widely recognised as a profession.* **2.** a group of specialised workers ○ *the accounting profession* ○ *the legal profession*

'…one of the key advantages of an accountancy qualification is its worldwide marketability. Other professions are not so lucky: lawyers, for example, are much more limited in where they can work' [*Accountancy*]

professional /prəˈfeʃ(ə)nəl/ *adjective* **1.** referring to one of the professions ○ *The accountant sent in his bill for professional services.* ○ *We had to ask our lawyer for professional advice on the contract.* ○ *The professional institute awards diplomas.* □ **professional man, professional woman** a man or woman who works in one of the professions such as a lawyer, doctor or accountant **2.** doing work for money ○ *a professional tennis player* □ **he is a professional troubleshooter** he makes his living by helping companies to sort out their problems

professional qualification /prəˌfeʃ(ə)nəl ˌkwɒlɪfɪˈkeɪʃ(ə)n/ *noun* a document which shows that someone has successfully finished a course of study which allows him or her to work in one of the professions

profit /ˈprɒfɪt/ *noun* money gained from a sale which is more than the money spent on making the item sold or on providing the service offered □ **to take your profit** to sell shares at a higher price than was paid for them, and so realise the profit, rather than to keep them as an investment □ **to show a profit** to make a profit and

state it in the company accounts ○ *We are showing a small profit for the first quarter.* □ **to make a profit** to have more money as a result of a deal □ **to move into profit** to start to make a profit ○ *The company is breaking even now, and expects to move into profit within the next two months.* □ **to sell at a profit** to sell at a price which gives you a profit □ **healthy profit** quite a large profit

profitability /ˌprɒfɪtəˈbɪlɪti/ *noun* **1.** the ability to make a profit ○ *We doubt the profitability of the project.* **2.** the amount of profit made as a percentage of costs

profitable /ˈprɒfɪtəb(ə)l/ *adjective* making a profit ○ *She runs a very profitable employment agency.*

profitably /ˈprɒfɪtəbli/ *adverb* making a profit ○ *The aim of every company must be to trade profitably.*

profit after tax /ˌprɒfɪt ɑːftə ˈtæks/ *noun* same as **net profit**

profit and loss account /ˌprɒfɪt ənd ˈlɒs əˌkaʊnt/ *noun* the accounts for a company showing expenditure and income over a period of time, usually one calendar year, balanced to show a final profit or loss. Also called **consolidated profit and loss account, P&L statement** (NOTE: The UK term is **consolidated profit and loss account**.)

profit before tax /ˌprɒfɪt bɪfɔː ˈtæks/ *noun* same as **pretax profit**

profit centre /ˈprɒfɪt ˌsentə/ *noun* a person, unit or department within an organisation which is considered separately for the purposes of calculating a profit ○ *We count the kitchen equipment division as a single profit centre.*

profiteer /ˌprɒfɪˈtɪə/ *noun* a person who makes too much profit, especially when goods are rationed or in short supply

profiteering /ˌprɒfɪˈtɪərɪŋ/ *noun* the practice of making too much profit

profit-making /ˈprɒfɪt ˌmeɪkɪŋ/ *adjective* making a profit, or operated with the primary objective of making a profit ○ *The whole project was expected to be profit-making by 2001 but it still hasn't broken even.* ○ *It is hoped to make it into a profit-making concern.*

profit margin /ˈprɒfɪt ˌmɑːdʒɪn/ *noun* the percentage difference between sales income and the cost of sales

profit on ordinary activities before tax /ˌprɒfɪt ɒn ˌɔːd(ə)n(ə)ri æk ˌtɪvɪtiz bɪˌfɔː 'tæks/ *noun* same as **pretax profit**

profit-sharing /'prɒfɪt ˌʃeərɪŋ/ *noun* an arrangement whereby employees get a share of the profits of the company they work for ○ *The company runs a profit-sharing scheme.*

profit squeeze /'prɒfɪt skwiːz/ *noun* a strict control of the amount of profits which companies can pay out as dividend

profits tax /'prɒfɪts tæks/ *noun* a tax to be paid on profits

profit-taker /'prɒfɪt ˌteɪkə/ *noun* a person who sells an investment in order to realise a profit

profit-taking /'prɒfɪt ˌteɪkɪŋ/ *noun* the act of selling investments to realise the profit, rather than keeping them ○ *Share prices fell under continued profit-taking.*

'…some profit-taking was seen yesterday as investors continued to lack fresh incentives to renew buying activity' [*Financial Times*]

pro forma /ˌprəʊ 'fɔːmə/ *adverb* 'for the sake of form' ■ *verb* to issue a pro forma invoice ○ *Can you pro forma this order?* ■ *noun* a document issued before all relevant details are known, usually followed by a final version

pro forma invoice /ˌprəʊ ˌfɔːmə 'ɪnvɔɪs/, **pro forma** /ˌprəʊ 'fɔːmə/ *noun* an invoice sent to a buyer before the goods are sent, so that payment can be made or so that goods can be sent to a consignee who is not the buyer ○ *They sent us a pro forma invoice.* ○ *We only supply that account on pro forma.*

program /'prəʊgræm/ *noun* **1.** US same as **programme 2.** a set of instructions that tell a computer to carry out specific tasks ■ *verb* to write a program for a computer (NOTE: **programming – programmed**) □ **to program a computer** to install a program in a computer ○ *The computer is programmed to print labels.*

programmable /'prəʊgræməb(ə)l/ *adjective* possible to programme

programme /'prəʊgræm/ *noun* a plan of things which will be done ○ *to draw up a programme of investment* or *an investment programme* ○ *She is running the development programme* or *the research*

programme. ○ *The training programme sends all managers for retraining every year.* ○ *We are initiating a new recruitment programme.* (NOTE: The US spelling is **program**.)

programmed trading /ˌprəʊgræmd 'treɪdɪŋ/ *noun* same as **program trading**

program trader /'prəʊgræm ˌtreɪdə/ *noun* a person who buys or sells according to a computer program

program trading /'prəʊgræm ˌtreɪdɪŋ/ *noun* the practice of buying and selling shares according to instructions given by a computer program (the computer is programmed to buy or sell when certain prices are reached or when a certain volume of sales on the market is reached)

progress *noun* /'prəʊgres/ the movement of work towards completion ○ *to report on the progress of the work* or *of the negotiations* □ **to make a progress report** to report how work is going □ **in progress** which is being done but is not finished ○ *negotiations in progress* ○ *work in progress* ■ *verb* /prəʊ'gres/ to move forward, to go ahead ○ *The contract is progressing through various departments.*

progressive /prə'gresɪv/ *adjective* moving forward in stages

progressive taxation /prəˌgresɪv tæk'seɪʃ(ə)n/ *noun* a taxation system where tax levels increase as the income is higher. Also called **graduated taxation**. Compare **regressive taxation**

progress payment /'prəʊgres ˌpeɪmənt/ *noun* a payment made as a particular stage of a contract is completed ○ *The fifth progress payment is due in March.*

prohibitive /prəʊ'hɪbɪtɪv/ *adjective* with a price so high that you cannot afford to pay it ○ *The cost of redesigning the product is prohibitive.*

project /'prɒdʒekt/ *noun* **1.** a plan ○ *She has drawn up a project for developing new markets in Europe.* **2.** a particular job of work which follows a plan ○ *We are just completing an engineering project in North Africa.* ○ *The company will start work on the project next month.*

project analysis /'prɒdʒekt əˌnæləsɪs/ *noun* the examination of all the costs or problems of a project before work on it is started

projected /prə'dʒektɪd/ *adjective* planned or expected □ **projected sales** a forecast of sales ○ *Projected sales in Europe next year should be over £1m.*

project engineer /ˌprɒdʒekt ˌendʒɪ 'nɪə/ *noun* an engineer in charge of a project

projection /prə'dʒekʃən/ *noun* a forecast of something which will happen in the future ○ *Projection of profits for the next three years.* ○ *The sales manager was asked to draw up sales projections for the next three years.*

project manager /ˌprɒdʒekt 'mænɪdʒə/ *noun* the manager in charge of a project

promise /'prɒmɪs/ *noun* an act of saying that you will do something □ **to keep a promise** to do what you said you would do ○ *He says he will pay next week, but he never keeps his promises.* □ **to go back on a promise** not to do what you said you would do ○ *The management went back on its promise to increase salaries across the board.* □ **a promise to pay** a promissory note ■ *verb* to say that you will do something ○ *They promised to pay the last instalment next week.* ○ *The personnel manager promised he would look into the grievances of the office staff.*

promissory note /'prɒmɪsəri ˌnəʊt/ *noun* a document stating that someone promises to pay an amount of money on a specific date

promote /prə'məʊt/ *verb* **1.** to give someone a more important job or to move someone to a higher grade ○ *He was promoted from salesman to sales manager.* **2.** to advertise a product □ **to promote a new product** to increase the sales of a new product by a sales campaign, by TV commercials or free gifts, or by giving discounts **3.** □ **to promote a new company** to organise the setting up of a new company

promotion /prə'məʊʃ(ə)n/ *noun* **1.** the fact of being moved up to a more important job ○ *I ruined my chances of promotion when I argued with the managing director.* ○ *The job offers good promotion chances* or *promotion prospects.* □ **to earn promotion** to work hard and effi-

ciently and so be promoted **2.** all means of conveying the message about a product or service to potential customers, e.g. publicity, a sales campaign, TV commercials or free gifts ○ *Our promotion budget has been doubled.* ○ *The promotion team has put forward plans for the launch.* ○ *We are offering free holidays in France as part of our special in-store promotion.* ○ *We a running a special promotion offering two for the price of one.* **3.** □ **promotion of a company** the setting up of a new company

promotional /prə'məʊʃ(ə)n(ə)l/ *adjective* used in an advertising campaign ○ *The admen are using balloons as promotional material.*

promotional budget /prə ˌməʊʃ(ə)n(ə)l 'bʌdʒɪt/ *noun* a forecast of the cost of promoting a new product

prompt /prɒmpt/ *adjective* rapid or done immediately ○ *We got very prompt service at the complaints desk.* ○ *Thank you for your prompt reply to my letter.* □ **prompt payment** payment made rapidly □ **prompt supplier** a supplier who delivers orders rapidly

prompt date /'prɒmpt deɪt/ *noun* a date for delivery, stated on a futures contract

prompt payer /prɒmpt 'peɪə/ *noun* a company or person that pays bills rapidly

proof /pruːf/ *noun* evidence which shows that something is true

-proof /pruːf/ *suffix* protected from the negative effect of something ○ *a dust-proof cover* ○ *an inflation-proof pension* ○ *a soundproof studio*

property /'prɒpəti/ *noun* **1.** land and buildings ○ *Property taxes are higher in the inner city.* ○ *They are assessing damage to property* or *property damage after the storm.* ○ *The commercial property market is booming.* **2.** a building ○ *We have several properties for sale in the centre of the town.* **3.** things which a person or organisation owns

property bond /'prɒpəti bɒnd/ *noun* an investment in a fund invested in properties or in property companies

property company /'prɒpəti ˌkʌmp(ə)ni/ *noun* a company which buys buildings to lease them

property developer /'prɒpəti dɪ ˌveləpə/ *noun* a person who buys old buildings or empty land and plans and builds new houses or factories for sale or rent

property development /ˈprɒpəti dɪˌveləpmənt/ *noun* the business of renovating old buildings or building new ones on their sites

property portfolio /ˈprɒpəti pɔːtˌfəʊliəʊ/ *noun* all the investment property which belongs to one person or company

property shares /ˈprɒpəti ʃeəz/ *plural noun* shares in property companies

property tax /ˈprɒpəti tæks/ *noun* a tax paid on building or land, such as the council tax in the UK

proportion /prəˈpɔːʃ(ə)n/ *noun* a part of a total ○ *A proportion of the pre-tax profit is set aside for contingencies.* ○ *Only a small proportion of our sales comes from retail shops.* □ **in proportion to** compared to something else, by an amount related to something else ○ *Sales in Europe are small in proportion to those in the US* ○ *Profits went up in proportion to the fall in overhead costs.*

proportional /prəˈpɔːʃ(ə)nəl/ *adjective* increasing or decreasing at the same rate as something else ○ *The increase in profit is proportional to the reduction in overheads.*

proportionally /prəˈpɔːʃ(ə)nəli/ *adverb* in a way that is proportional

proprietary /prəˈpraɪət(ə)ri/ *noun, adjective* a product, e.g. a medicine which is made and owned by a company

proprietary company /prəˌpraɪət(ə)ri ˈkʌmp(ə)ni/ *noun US* a company formed to invest in stock of other companies so as to control them. Abbreviation **pty**

proprietary drug /prəˌpraɪət(ə)ri ˈdrʌg/ *noun* a drug which is made by a particular company and marketed under a brand name

pro rata /ˌprəʊ ˈrɑːtə/ *adjective, adverb* at a rate which varies according to the size or importance of something ○ *When part of the shipment was destroyed we received a pro rata payment.* ○ *The full-time pay is £800 a week and the part-timers are paid pro rata.* □ **dividends are paid pro rata** dividends are paid according to the number of shares held

prospect /ˈprɒspekt/ *noun* a chance or possibility that something will happen in the future □ **her job prospects are good** she is very likely to find a job

prospective /prəˈspektɪv/ *adjective* possibly happening in the future

prospective dividend /prəˌspektɪv ˈdɪvɪdend/ *noun* same as **forecast dividend**

prospective P/E ratio /prəˌspektɪv ˌpiː ˈiː ˌreɪʃiəʊ/ *noun* a P/E ratio expected in the future on the basis of forecast dividends

prospectus /prəˈspektəs/ *noun* a document which gives information to attract buyers or customers ○ *The restaurant has people handing out prospectuses in the street.*

'…when the prospectus emerges, existing shareholders and any prospective new investors can find out more by calling the free share information line; they will be sent a leaflet. Non-shareholders who register in this way will receive a prospectus when it is published; existing shareholders will be sent one automatically' [*Financial Times*]

prosperity /prɒˈsperɪti/ *noun* the state of being rich □ **in times of prosperity** when people are rich

prosperous /ˈprɒsp(ə)rəs/ *adjective* rich ○ *a prosperous shopkeeper* ○ *a prosperous town*

protect /prəˈtekt/ *verb* to defend something against harm ○ *The workers are protected from unfair dismissal by government legislation.* ○ *The cover is supposed to protect the machine from dust.* □ **to protect an industry by imposing tariff barriers** to stop a local industry from being hit by foreign competition by taxing foreign products when they are imported

protection /prəˈtekʃən/ *noun* **1.** a defence against harm ○ *The legislation offers no protection to part-time workers.* ○ *The new equipment offers more protection against noise.* **2.** the imposing of tariffs to protect domestic producers from competition from imports

protectionism /prəˈtekʃənɪz(ə)m/ *noun* the practice of protecting producers in the home country against foreign competitors by banning or taxing imports or by imposing import quotas

protective /prə'tektɪv/ *adjective* which protects

protective tariff /prə,tektɪv 'tærɪf/ *noun* a tariff which tries to ban imports to stop them competing with local products

pro tem /ˌprəʊ 'tem/ *adverb* temporarily, for a time

protest *noun* /'prəʊtest/ **1.** a statement or action to show that you do not approve of something ○ *to make a protest against high prices* **2.** an official document which proves that a bill of exchange has not been paid ■ *verb* /prə'test/ □ **to protest a bill** to draw up a document to prove that a bill of exchange has not been paid

provide /prə'vaɪd/ *verb* **1.** to give or supply something **2.** □ **to provide for** to allow for something which may happen in the future ○ *The contract provides for an annual increase in charges.* ○ *£10,000 of expenses have been provided for in the budget.* **3.** to put money aside in accounts to cover expenditure or loss in the future ○ *£25,000 is provided against bad debts.*

provident /'prɒvɪd(ə)nt/ *adjective* providing benefits in case of illness, old age or other cases of need ○ *a provident fund* ○ *a provident society*

provision /prə'vɪʒ(ə)n/ *noun* **1.** □ **to make provision for** to see that something is allowed for in the future **2.** a legal condition □ **we have made provision to this effect** we have put into the contract terms which will make this work **3.** an amount of money put aside in accounts for anticipated expenditure where the timing or amount of expenditure is uncertain, often for doubtful debts ○ *The bank has made a £2m provision for bad debts* or *a $5bn provision against Third World loans.*

'…landlords can create short lets of dwellings which will be free from the normal security of tenure provisions' [*Times*]

provisional /prə'vɪʒ(ə)n(ə)l/ *adjective* temporary, not final or permanent ○ *The sales department has been asked to make a provisional forecast of sales.* ○ *The provisional budget has been drawn up for each department.* ○ *They faxed their provisional acceptance of the contract.*

provisionally /prə'vɪʒ(ə)nəli/ *adverb* not finally ○ *The contract has been accepted provisionally.*

proxy /'prɒksi/ *noun* **1.** a document which gives someone the power to act on behalf of someone else ○ *to sign by proxy* **2.** a person who acts on behalf of someone else ○ *She asked the chairman to act as proxy for her.*

proxy form /'prɒksi fɔːm/, **proxy card** /'prɒksi kɑːd/ *noun* a form that shareholders receive with their invitations to attend an AGM, and that they fill in if they want to appoint a proxy to vote for them on a resolution

proxy statement /'prɒksi ˌsteɪtmənt/ *noun* a document, filed with the SEC, outlining executive pay packages, option grants and other perks, and also giving details of dealings by executives in shares of the company

proxy vote /'prɒksi vəʊt/ *noun* a vote made on behalf of someone who is not present ○ *The proxy votes were all in favour of the board's recommendation.*

prudent /'pruːdənt/ *adjective* careful, not taking any risks

prudential /pru'denʃ(ə)l/ *adjective* being careful, prudent

prudential ratio /pru,denʃ(ə)l 'reɪʃiəʊ/ *noun* a ratio of capital to assets which a bank feels it is prudent to have, according to EU regulations

prudent man rule /ˌpruːd(ə)nt 'mæn ruːl/ *noun* a rule that trustees who make financial decisions on behalf of other people should act carefully, as an average prudent person would

PSBR *abbreviation* Public Sector Borrowing Requirement

PSDR *abbreviation* Public-Sector Debt Repayment

PSFD *abbreviation* Public-Sector Financial Deficit

PSNCR *abbreviation* Public-Sector Net Cash Requirement

ptas *abbreviation* pesetas

Pte *abbreviation* private limited company

Pty *abbreviation* proprietary company

Pty Ltd *abbreviation* private limited company

public /'pʌblɪk/ *adjective* **1.** referring to all the people in general **2.** referring to the government or the state

public company /ˌpʌblɪk
'kʌmp(ə)ni/ *noun* same as **public
limited company**

public debt /ˌpʌblɪk 'det/ *noun* the
money that a government or a set of
governments owes

public expenditure /ˌpʌblɪk ɪk
'spendɪtʃə/ *noun* money spent by the
local or central government

public finance /ˌpʌblɪk 'faɪnæns/
noun the raising of money by governments by taxes or borrowing, and the
spending of it

public funds /ˌpʌblɪk 'fʌndz/ *plural
noun* government money available for
expenditure

public holiday /ˌpʌblɪk 'hɒlɪdeɪ/
noun a day when all employees are entitled to take a holiday

publicity budget /pʌ'blɪsɪti ˌbʌdʒɪt/
noun money allowed for expenditure on
publicity

public limited company /ˌpʌblɪk
ˌlɪmɪtɪd 'kʌmp(ə)ni/ *noun* a company
whose shares can be bought on the stock
exchange. Abbreviation **Plc, PLC, plc**.
Also called **public company**

public monopoly /ˌpʌblɪk mə
'nɒpəli/ *noun* a situation where an organisation owned and run by the state (e.g.
the Post Office) is the only supplier of a
product or service

public offering /ˌpʌblɪk 'ɒf(ə)rɪŋ/
noun an offering of new shares in a
corporation for sale to the public as a way
of launching the corporation on the stock
exchange

public ownership /ˌpʌblɪk 'əʊnəʃɪp/
noun a situation in which the government
owns a business, i.e. where an industry is
nationalised

public placing /ˌpʌblɪk 'pleɪsɪŋ/,
public placement /ˌpʌblɪk 'pleɪsmənt/
noun an act of offering a new issue of
shares to investing institutions, though
not to private investors in general

public sector /'pʌblɪk ˌsektə/ *noun*
nationalised industries and services ○ *a
report on wage rises in the public sector*
or *on public-sector wage settlements* Also
called **government sector**

**Public Sector Borrowing
Requirement** /ˌpʌblɪk ˌsektə
'bɒrəʊɪŋ rɪˌkwaɪəmənt/ *noun* the

amount of money which a government
has to borrow to pay for its own spending.
Abbreviation **PSBR**

public spending /ˌpʌblɪk 'spendɪŋ/
noun spending by the government or by
local authorities

public-to-private deal /ˌpʌblɪk tə,
tʊ 'praɪvət/ *noun* an arrangement by
which a quoted company leaves the stock
exchange and becomes a privately owned
investment. ◊ **take-private**

public utilities /ˌpʌblɪk juː'tɪlɪtiz/
plural noun companies such as electricity,
gas or transport companies which provide
a service used by the whole community

pula /'puːlə/ *noun* a unit of currency
used in Botswana

pull /pʊl/ *verb* □ **pull the plug on something** to bring something such as a business project to an end, especially by
cutting off its financial support (*informal*)

pull off *phrasal verb* to succeed in
negotiating a deal (*informal*)

pull out *phrasal verb* to stop being part
of a deal or agreement ○ *Our Australian
partners pulled out of the contract.*

pump /pʌmp/ *verb* to put something in
by force ○ *Venture capitalists have been
pumping money into the company to keep
it afloat.*

'...in each of the years 1986 to 1989,
Japan pumped a net sum of the order of
$100bn into foreign securities, notably
into US government bonds' [*Financial
Times Review*]

pump priming /'pʌmp ˌpraɪmɪŋ/
noun government investment in new
projects which it hopes will benefit the
economy

punt /pʌnt/ *noun* **1.** a former unit of
currency in the Republic of Ireland **2.** a
gamble, bet (*informal*) ○ *That stock is
worth a punt.* ○ *He took a punt on the
exchange rate falling.* ■ *verb* to gamble
or to bet (on something)

punter /'pʌntə/ *noun* **1.** a person who
gambles or who hopes to make money on
the stock exchange in the ○ *The share
price shot up as punters rushed to buy.* **2.**
a customer (*informal*) ○ *The product
looks attractive but will the punters like
it?*

'...if punters don't come in for their
regular packet of cigarettes, then they are

unlikely to make any impulse buys'
[*The Grocer*]

purchase /'pɜːtʃɪs/ *noun* a product or
service which has been bought □ **to make
a purchase** to buy something ■ *verb* to
buy something □ **to purchase something
for cash** to pay cash for something

purchase acquisition /ˌpɜːtʃɪs
ˌækwɪ'zɪʃ(ə)n/ *noun* same as **acquisition accounting**

purchase book /'pɜːtʃɪs bʊk/ *noun* a
book in which purchases are recorded

purchase ledger /'pɜːtʃɪs ˌledʒə/
noun a book in which purchases are
recorded

purchase order /'pɜːtʃɪs ˌɔːdə/ *noun*
an official order made out by a purchasing
department for goods which a company
wants to buy ○ *We cannot supply you
without a purchase order number.*

purchase price /'pɜːtʃɪs praɪs/ *noun*
a price paid for something

purchaser /'pɜːtʃɪsə/ *noun* a person or
company that purchases ○ *The company
has found a purchaser for its warehouse.*
□ **the company is looking for a
purchaser** the company is trying to find
someone who will buy it

purchase tax /'pɜːtʃɪs tæks/ *noun* a
tax paid on things which are bought

purchasing /'pɜːtʃɪsɪŋ/ *noun, adjective* buying

purchasing department /'pɜːtʃɪsɪŋ
dɪˌpɑːtmənt/ *noun* the section of a
company which deals with the buying of
stock, raw materials, equipment, etc.

purchasing manager /'pɜːtʃɪsɪŋ
ˌmænɪdʒə/ *noun* the head of a
purchasing department

purchasing officer /'pɜːtʃɪsɪŋ
ˌɒfɪsə/ *noun* a person in a company or
organisation who is responsible for
buying stock, raw materials, equipment,
etc.

purchasing power /'pɜːtʃɪsɪŋ ˌpaʊə/
noun the quantity of goods which can be
bought by a particular group of people or
with a particular sum of money ○ *the
purchasing power of the school market* ○
*The purchasing power of the pound has
fallen over the last five years.*

push /pʊʃ/ *verb* □ **to push a share** to try
to persuade investors to buy a share (using
forceful means)

put /pʊt/ *noun* same as **put option** ■
verb to place or to fix (NOTE: **putting –
put**) □ **the accounts put the stock value
at £10,000** the accounts state that the
value of the stock is £10,000 □ **to put a
proposal to the vote** to ask a meeting to
vote for or against a proposal □ **to put a
proposal to the board** to ask the board to
consider a suggestion

put down *phrasal verb* **1.** to make a
deposit ○ *to put down money on a house*
2. to write an item in a ledger or an
account book ○ *to put down a figure for
expenses*

put in *phrasal verb* □ **to put in a bid
for something** to offer to buy something, usually in writing □ **to put in an
estimate for something** to give
someone a written calculation of the
probable costs of carrying out a job □ **to
put in a claim for damage** to ask an
insurance company to pay for damage □
the union put in a 6% wage claim the
union asked for a 6% increase in wages

put into *phrasal verb* □ **to put money
into a business** to invest money in a
business

put on *phrasal verb* **1.** □ **to put an
item on the agenda** to list an item for
discussion at a meeting □ **to put an
embargo on trade** to forbid trade **2.** □
**property shares put on gains of 10%-
15%** shares in property companies
increased in value by 10%-15%

put out *phrasal verb* to send something
out for other people to work on ○ *We
are planning to put out most of the work
to freelancers.* □ **to put work out to
contract** to decide that work should be
done by a company on a contract, rather
than employ members of staff to do it

put up *phrasal verb* **1.** □ **who put up
the money for the shop?** who provided
the investment money for the shop to
start? □ **to put something up for sale** to
advertise that something is for sale ○
*When he retired he decided to put his
town flat up for sale.* **2.** to increase
something, to make something higher ○
The shop has put up all its prices by 5%.

put option /'pʊt ˌɒpʃən/ *noun* an
option to sell a specified number of shares
at a specified price within a specified
period of time. Also called **put**. Opposite
call option

PV *abbreviation* present value

pyramiding /'pɪrəmɪdɪŋ/ *noun* **1.** the process of building up a major group by acquiring controlling interests in many different companies, each larger than the original company **2.** the illegal practice of using new investors' deposits to pay the interest on the deposits made by existing investors

pyramid scheme /'pɪrəmɪd ˌskiːm/ *noun* a non-sustainable, fraudulent business model that involves the exchange of money primarily for enrolling other people into the scheme, without any product or service being delivered

pyramid selling /'pɪrəmɪd ˌselɪŋ/ *noun* an illegal way of selling goods or investments to the public, where each selling agent pays for the franchise to sell the product or service, and sells that right on to other agents together with stock, so that in the end the person who makes the most money is the original franchiser, and sub-agents or investors may lose all their investments

'…much of the population had committed their life savings to get-rich-quick pyramid investment schemes – where newcomers pay the original investors until the money runs out – which inevitably collapsed' [*Times*]

Q

qty *abbreviation* quantity

quadruplicate /kwɒˈdruːplɪkət/ *noun* □ **in quadruplicate** with the original and three copies ○ *The invoices are printed in quadruplicate.* ○ *The application form should be completed in quadruplicate.*

qualification /ˌkwɒlɪfɪˈkeɪʃ(ə)n/ *noun* a document or some other formal proof of the fact that someone has successfully completed a specialised course of study or has acquired a skill ○ *You must have the right qualifications for the job.* ○ *Job-hunting is difficult if you have no qualifications.*

'…personnel management is not an activity that can ever have just one set of qualifications as a requirement for entry into it' [*Personnel Management*]

qualification of accounts /ˌkwɒlɪfɪ keɪʃ(ə)n əv əˈkaʊnts/ *noun* same as **auditors' qualification**

qualified /ˈkwɒlɪfaɪd/ *adjective* **1.** having passed special examinations in a subject ○ *She is a qualified accountant.* ○ *We have appointed a qualified designer to supervise the decorating of the new reception area.* □ **highly qualified** with very good results in examinations ○ *All our staff are highly qualified.* ○ *They employ twenty-six highly qualified engineers.* **2.** with some reservations or conditions ○ *qualified acceptance of a contract* ○ *The plan received qualified approval from the board.*

'…applicants will be professionally qualified and ideally have a degree in Commerce and postgraduate management qualifications'
[*Australian Financial Review*]

qualified accounts /ˌkwɒlɪfaɪd əˈkaʊnts/ *plural noun* accounts which

have been noted by the auditors because they contain something with which the auditors do not agree

qualify /ˈkwɒlɪfaɪ/ *verb* **1.** □ **to qualify for** to be entitled to something ○ *The company does not qualify for a government grant.* ○ *She qualifies for unemployment benefit.* **2.** □ **to qualify as** to follow a specialised course of study and pass examinations so that you can do a certain job ○ *She has qualified as an accountant.* ○ *He will qualify as a solicitor next year.* **3.** □ **the auditors have qualified the accounts** the auditors have found something in the accounts of the company which has made them unable to agree that they show a 'true and fair' view of the company's financial position (NOTE: [all senses] **qualifies – qualifying – qualified**)

'…federal examiners will also determine which of the privately insured savings and loans qualify for federal insurance' [*Wall Street Journal*]

qualifying distribution /ˌkwɒlɪfaɪɪŋ ˌdɪstrɪˈbjuːʃ(ə)n/ *noun* a payment of a dividend, or other distribution of profits, that was subject, in the UK, to advance corporation tax before it was scrapped in 1999

qualifying period /ˈkwɒlɪfaɪɪŋ ˌpɪəriəd/ *noun* a time which has to pass before something or someone qualifies for something, e.g. a grant or subsidy ○ *There is a six-month qualifying period before you can get a grant from the local authority.*

qualifying ratio /ˈkwɒlɪfaɪɪŋ ˌreɪʃiəʊ/ *noun* a calculation of how much mortgage a borrower can afford, by comparing his monthly incoming against his monthly outgoings

qualifying service /'kwɒlɪfaɪɪŋ ˌsɜːvɪs/ *noun* the period for which an employee must be employed by a company before becoming eligible to join a group pension scheme

qualifying shares /ˌkwɒlɪfaɪɪŋ 'ʃeəz/ *plural noun* the number of shares you need to earn to get a bonus issue or to be a director of the company, etc.

quality control /'kwɒlɪti kənˌtrəʊl/ *noun* the process of making sure that the quality of a product is good

quant funds /'kwɒnt fʌndz/ *plural noun* same as **quantitative funds**

quantifiable /'kwɒntɪfaɪəb(ə)l/ *adjective* possible to quantify ○ *The effect of the change in the discount structure is not quantifiable.*

quantify /'kwɒntɪfaɪ/ *verb* □ **to quantify the effect of something** to show the effect of something in figures ○ *It is impossible to quantify the effect of the new legislation on our turnover.* (NOTE: **quantifies – quantifying – quantified**)

quantitative /'kwɒntɪtətɪv/ *adjective* referring to quantity

'…the collection of consumer behaviour data in the book covers both qualitative and quantitative techniques' [*Quarterly Review of Marketing*]

quantitative funds /'kwɒntɪtətɪv fʌndz/ *plural noun* funds which invest according to the instructions given by a computer model

quantity /'kwɒntɪti/ *noun* an amount, especially a large amount

quantity discount /ˌkwɒntɪti 'dɪskaʊnt/ *noun* a discount given to people who buy large quantities

quantity purchase /'kwɒntɪti ˌpɜːtʃɪs/ *noun* a large quantity of goods bought at one time ○ *The company offers a discount for quantity purchase.*

quantum meruit /ˌkwæntʊm 'meruɪt/ *phrase* a Latin phrase meaning 'as much as has been earned'

quarter /'kwɔːtə/ *noun* **1.** one of four equal parts (25%) ○ *She paid only a quarter of the list price.* □ **a quarter of an hour** 15 minutes **2.** a period of three months ○ *The instalments are payable at the end of each quarter.* **3.** US a 25 cent coin (*informal*)

'…corporate profits for the first quarter showed a 4 per cent drop from last year's final three months' [*Financial Times*]

'…economists believe the economy is picking up this quarter and will do better still in the second half of the year' [*Sunday Times*]

quarter day /'kwɔːtə deɪ/ *noun* a day at the end of a quarter, when rents, fees etc. should be paid

COMMENT: In England, the quarter days are 25th March (Lady Day), 24th June (Midsummer Day), 29th September (Michaelmas Day) and 25th December (Christmas Day).

quarterly /'kwɔːtəli/ *adjective, adverb* happening once every three months ○ *There is a quarterly charge for electricity.* ○ *The bank sends us a quarterly statement.* ○ *We agreed to pay the rent quarterly* or *on a quarterly basis.* ■ *noun* the results of a corporation, produced each quarter

quartile /'kwɔːtaɪl/ *noun* one of a series of three figures below which 25%, 50% or 75% of the total falls

quasi- /kweɪzaɪ/ *prefix* almost or which seems like ○ *a quasi-official body*

quasi-loan /ˌkweɪzaɪ 'ləʊn/ *noun* an agreement between two parties where one agrees to pay the other's debts, provided that the second party agrees to reimburse the first at some later date

quasi-public corporation /ˌkweɪzaɪ ˌpʌblɪk ˌkɔːpə'reɪʃ(ə)n/ *noun* a US institution which is privately owned, but which serves a public function, such as the Federal National Mortgage Association

quetzal /'kets(ə)l/ *noun* a unit of currency used in Guatemala

queue /kjuː/ *noun* **1.** a line of people waiting one behind the other ○ *to form a queue* or *to join a queue* ○ *Queues formed at the doors of the bank when the news spread about its possible collapse.* (NOTE: The US term is **line.**) **2.** a series of documents such as orders or application forms which are dealt with in order □ **his order went to the end of the queue** his order was dealt with last □ **mortgage queue** a list of people waiting for mortgages ■ *verb* to form a line one after the other for something ○ *When food was rationed, people had to queue for bread.* ○ *We queued for hours to get tickets.* ○ *A list of* *companies queueing to be launched on the stock exchange.* ○ *The candidates queued outside the interviewing room.*

quick /kwɪk/ *adjective* fast, not taking much time ○ *The company made a quick recovery.* ○ *He is looking for a quick return on his investments.* ○ *We are hoping for a quick sale.*

quick assets /kwɪk 'æsets/ *plural noun* cash, or bills which can easily be changed into cash

quick ratio /ˌkwɪk 'reɪʃiəʊ/ *noun* same as **liquidity ratio**

quid pro quo /ˌkwɪd prəʊ 'kwəʊ/ *noun* money paid or an action carried out in return for something ○ *She agreed to repay the loan early, and as a quid pro quo the bank released the collateral.*

quitclaim /'kwɪtkleɪm/ *noun* a release of someone from any claim that might exist against him or her or that he or she might have on something

quorum /'kwɔːrəm/ *noun* a minimum number of people who have to be present at a meeting to make it valid □ **to have a quorum** to have enough people present for a meeting to go ahead ○ *Do we have a quorum?*

> COMMENT: If there is a quorum at a meeting, the meeting is said to be 'quorate'; if there aren't enough people present to make a quorum, the meeting is 'inquorate'.

quota /'kwəʊtə/ *noun* a limited amount of something which is allowed to be produced, imported, etc.

> 'Canada agreed to a new duty-free quota of 600,000 tonnes a year' [*Globe and Mail (Toronto)*]

quota system /'kwəʊtə ˌsɪstəm/ *noun* **1.** a system where imports or supplies are regulated by fixed maximum amounts **2.** an arrangement for distribu-

tion which allows each distributor only a specific number of items

quotation /kwəʊ'teɪʃ(ə)n/ *noun* **1.** an estimate of how much something will cost ○ *They sent in their quotation for the job.* ○ *Our quotation was much lower than all the others.* ○ *We accepted the lowest quotation.* **2.** □ **the company is going for a quotation on the stock exchange** the company has applied to the stock exchange to have its shares listed ○ *We are seeking a stock market quotation.*

quote /kwəʊt/ *verb* **1.** to repeat words or a reference number used by someone else ○ *He quoted figures from the annual report.* ○ *In reply please quote this number.* ○ *When making a complaint please quote the batch number printed on the box.* ○ *She replied, quoting the number of the account.* **2.** to estimate what a cost or price is likely to be ○ *to quote a price for supplying stationery* ○ *Their prices are always quoted in dollars.* ○ *He quoted me a price of £1,026.* ○ *Can you quote for supplying 20,000 envelopes?* ■ *noun* an estimate of how much something will cost (*informal*) ○ *to give someone a quote for supplying computers* ○ *We have asked for quotes for refitting the shop.* ○ *Her quote was the lowest of three.* ○ *We accepted the lowest quote.*

quoted company /ˌkwəʊtɪd 'kʌmp(ə)ni/ *noun* a company whose shares can be bought or sold on the stock exchange

quote-driven system /'kwəʊt ˌdrɪv(ə)n ˌsɪstəm/ *noun* a system of working a stock market, where market-makers quote a price for a stock. Compare **order-driven system**

quoted shares /ˌkwəʊtɪd 'ʃeəz/, **quoted stocks** *plural noun* shares which can be bought or sold on the stock exchange

R

racket /ˈrækɪt/ *noun* an illegal deal which makes a lot of money ○ *She runs a cut-price ticket racket.*

racketeer /ˌrækɪˈtɪə/ *noun* a person who runs a racket

racketeering /ˌrækɪˈtɪərɪŋ/ *noun US* the crime of carrying on an illegal business to make money

‘…he was charged with 98 counts of racketeering and securities fraud and went on to serve two years in jail. He was banned for life from the securities industry’ [*Times*]

rack rent /ˈræk rent/ *noun* a very high rent

raid /reɪd/ *noun* a sudden attack

raid alarm /ˈreɪd ə,lɑːm/ *noun* an automatic alarm in a bank which goes off when a robbery is taking place

raider /ˈreɪdə/ *noun* a person or company that buys a stake in another company before making a hostile takeover bid. Also called **corporate raider**

‘…bear raiding involves trying to depress a target company’s share price by heavy selling of its shares, spreading adverse rumours or a combination of the two. As an added refinement, the raiders may sell short. The aim is to push down the price so that the raiders can buy back the shares they sold at a lower price’ [*Guardian*]

raise /reɪz/ *noun US* an increase in salary ○ *He asked the boss for a raise.* ○ *She is pleased – she has had her raise.* ○ *She got her raise last month.* (NOTE: The UK term is **rise**.) ■ *verb* **1.** □ **to raise an invoice** to write out or print out an invoice □ **to raise a cheque** to write out a cheque, either by hand or by machine **2.** to increase or to make higher ○ *The government has raised the tax levels.* ○ *Air fares will be raised on June 1st.* ○ *The company* raised its dividend by 10%. ○ *When the company raised its prices, it lost half of its share of the market.* ○ *The organisation will raise wages if inflation gets worse.* ○ *This increase in production will raise the standard of living in the area.* **3.** to obtain money or to organise a loan ○ *The company is trying to raise the capital to fund its expansion programme.* ○ *The government raises more money by indirect taxation than by direct.* ○ *Where will he raise the money from to start up his business?*

‘…the company said yesterday that its recent share issue has been oversubscribed, raising A$225.5m’ [*Financial Times*]

‘…investment trusts can raise capital, but this has to be done as a company does, by a rights issue of equity’ [*Investors Chronicle*]

‘…over the past few weeks, companies raising new loans from international banks have been forced to pay more’ [*Financial Times*]

raised check /ˌreɪzd ˈtʃek/ *noun* a cheque where the amount has been increased by hand illegally

rake *verb*

rake in *phrasal verb* to gather something together □ **to rake in cash**, **to rake it in** to make a lot of money

rake-off /ˈreɪk ɒf/ *noun* a person’s share of profits from a deal, especially if obtained illegally ○ *The group gets a rake-off on all the company’s sales.* ○ *He got a £100,000 rake-off for introducing the new business.* (NOTE: The plural is **rake-offs**.)

rally /ˈræli/ *noun* a rise in price when the trend has been downwards ○ *Shares staged a rally on the stock exchange.* ○

After a brief rally shares fell back to a new low. ■ *verb* to rise in price, when the trend has been downwards ○ *Shares rallied on the news of the latest government figures.*

'…when Japan rallied, it had no difficulty in surpassing its previous all-time high, and this really stretched the price-earnings ratios into the stratosphere' [*Money Observer*]

'…bad news for the US economy ultimately may have been the cause of a late rally in stock prices yesterday' [*Wall Street Journal*]

ramp /ræmp/ *noun* an act of buying shares in order to force up the price (as when a company buys its own shares illegally during a takeover bid)

rand /rænd/ *noun* a unit of currency used in South Africa

R&D *abbreviation* research and development

random /'rændəm/ *adjective* done without making any special selection

random check /,rændəm 'tʃek/ *noun* a check on items taken from a group without any special selection

random sample /,rændəm 'sɑːmpəl/ *noun* a sample taken without any selection

random sampling /,rændəm 'sɑːmplɪŋ/ *noun* the action of choosing samples for testing without any special selection

random walk /,rændəm 'wɔːk/ *noun* **1.** a sampling technique which allows for random selection within specific limits set up by a non-random technique **2.** a movement which cannot be predicted, used to describe movements in share prices which cannot be forecast

range /reɪndʒ/ *noun* a scale of items from a low point to a high one □ **range of prices** the difference between the highest and lowest price for a share or bond over a period of time

range forward /reɪndʒ 'fɔːwəd/ *noun* a forward currency contract which includes an option to purchase currency futures and so has the effect of limiting potential exchange losses

rank /ræŋk/ *noun* a position in a company or an organisation, especially one which shows how important someone is relative to others ○ *All managers are of*

equal rank. ○ *Promotion means moving up from a lower rank.* □ **in rank order** in order according to position of importance ■ *verb* to classify in order of importance ○ *Candidates are ranked in order of their test results.* **2.** to be in a position ○ *The non-voting shares rank equally with the voting shares.* ○ *Deferred ordinary shares do not rank for dividend.*

rata /'rɑːtə/ ♦ **pro rata**

rate /reɪt/ *noun* **1.** the money charged for time worked or work completed **2.** an amount of money paid, e.g. as interest or dividend, shown as a percentage **3.** the value of one currency against another ○ *What is today's rate* or *the current rate for the dollar?* □ **to calculate costs on a fixed exchange rate** to calculate costs on an exchange rate which does not change **4.** an amount, number or speed compared with something else ○ *the rate of increase in redundancies* ○ *The rate of absenteeism* or *The absenteeism rate always increases in fine weather.*

rateable value /,reɪtəb(ə)l 'væljuː/ *noun* the value of a property as a basis for calculating local taxes

rate of exchange /,reɪt əv ɪks'tʃeɪndʒ/ *noun* same as **exchange rate** ○ *The current rate of exchange is $1.60 to the pound.*

rate of inflation /,reɪt əv ɪn'fleɪʃ(ə)n/ *noun* the percentage increase in prices over a twelve-month period

rate of interest /,reɪt əv 'ɪntrəst/ *noun* same as **interest rate**

rate of production /,reɪt əv prə'dʌkʃən/ *noun* the speed at which items are made. Also called **production rate**

rate of return /,reɪt əv rɪ'tɜːn/ *noun* the amount of interest or dividend which comes from an investment, shown as a percentage of the money invested

rate of sales /,reɪt əv 'seɪlz/ *noun* the speed at which units are sold

rate of unemployment /,reɪt əv ,ʌnɪm'plɔɪmənt/ *noun* same as **unemployment rate**

rates /reɪts/ *plural noun* local UK taxes formerly levied on property in the UK and now replaced by the council tax

rating /'reɪtɪŋ/ *noun* **1.** the act of giving something a value, or the value given **2.** the valuing of property for local taxes. ◊ **ratings**

rating agency /'reɪtɪŋ ˌeɪdʒənsi/ *noun* an organisation which gives a rating to companies or other organisations issuing bonds

rating officer /'reɪtɪŋ ˌɒfɪsə/ *noun* an official in a local authority who decides the rateable value of a commercial property

ratings /'reɪtɪŋz/ *plural noun* the estimated number of people who watch TV programmes ○ *The show is high in the ratings, which means it will attract good publicity.*

ratio /'reɪʃiəʊ/ *noun* a proportion or quantity of something compared to something else ○ *the ratio of successes to failures* ○ *Our product outsells theirs by a ratio of two to one.* ○ *With less manual work available, the ratio of employees to managers is decreasing.*

ratio analysis /'reɪʃiəʊ əˌnæləsɪs/ *noun* a method of analysing the performance of a company by showing the figures in its accounts as ratios and comparing them with those of other companies

raw /rɔː/ *adjective* in the original state or not processed

'...it makes sense for them to produce goods for sale back home in the US from plants in Britain where raw materials are relatively cheap' [*Duns Business Month*]

raw data /ˌrɔː 'deɪtə/ *noun* data as it is put into a computer, without being analysed

raw materials /ˌrɔː məˈtɪəriəlz/ *plural noun* basic materials which have to be treated or processed in some way before they can be used, e.g. wood, iron ore or crude petroleum

RCPC *abbreviation* regional check processing center

R/D *abbreviation* refer to drawer

RDG *abbreviation* regional development grant

re- /riː/ *prefix* again

reach /riːtʃ/ *verb* to get to something □ **to reach an accommodation with creditors** to agree terms for settlement with creditors

react /riˈækt/ *verb* □ **to react to** to do or to say something in reply to what someone has done or said ○ *Shares reacted sharply to the fall in the exchange rate.* ○ *How will the chairman react when we tell him the news?*

reaction /riˈækʃən/ *noun* a change or action in reply to something said or done ○ *the reaction of the shares to the news of the takeover bid* ○ *His immediate reaction was to make half the workforce redundant.*

reader/sorter /ˌriːdə 'sɔːtə/ *noun* a machine in a bank which reads cheques and sorts them automatically

readjust /ˌriːəˈdʒʌst/ *verb* to adjust something again or in a new way, or to change in response to new conditions ○ *to readjust prices to take account of the rise in the costs of raw materials* ○ *to readjust salary scales* ○ *Share prices readjusted quickly to the news of the devaluation.*

readjustment /ˌriːəˈdʒʌstmənt/ *noun* an act of readjusting ○ *a readjustment in pricing* ○ *After the devaluation there was a period of readjustment in the exchange rates.*

ready /'redi/ *adjective* quick □ **these items find a ready sale in the Middle East** these items sell rapidly or easily in the Middle East

ready cash /ˌredi 'kæʃ/ *noun* money which is immediately available for payment

ready money /ˌredi 'mʌni/ *noun* cash or money which is immediately available

real¹ /rɪəl/ *adjective* (*of prices or amounts*) shown in terms of money adjusted for inflation □ **in real terms** actually or really ○ *Salaries have gone up by 3% but with inflation running at 5% that is a fall in real terms.*

'...real wages have been held down dramatically: they have risen as an annual rate of only 1% in the last two years' [*Sunday Times*]

'...sterling M3 rose by 13.5% in the year to August – seven percentage points faster than the rate of inflation and the biggest increase in real terms for years' [*Economist*]

'Japan's gross national product for the April-June quarter dropped 0.4% in real terms from the previous quarter' [*Nikkei Weekly*]

'...the Federal Reserve Board has eased interest rates in the past year, but they are still at historically high levels in real terms' [*Sunday Times*]

real² /rɪəl/ *noun* a unit of currency used in Brazil

real earnings /ˌrɪəl ˈɜːnɪŋz/, **real wages** /ˌrɪəl ˈweɪdʒɪz/ *plural noun* income which is available for spending after tax and other contributions have been deducted, corrected for inflation. Also called **real income**, **real wages**

real estate /ˈrɪəl ɪˌsteɪt/ *noun* property in the form of land or buildings

'…on top of the cost of real estate, the investment in inventory and equipment to open a typical warehouse comes to around $5 million' [*Duns Business Month*]

real estate agent /ˈrɪəl ɪˌsteɪt ˌeɪdʒənt/, **real estate broker** *noun US* a person who sells property for customers

real estate investment trust /ˌrɪəl ɪ ˌsteɪt ɪnˈvestmənt trʌst/ *noun* a public trust company which invests only in property. Abbreviation **REIT**

real income /ˌrɪəl ˈɪnkʌm/ *noun* same as **real earnings**

real interest rate /ˌrɪəl ˈɪntrəst ˌreɪt/ *noun* an interest rate after taking inflation into account

realisable assets /ˌrɪəlaɪzəb(ə)l ˈæsets/ *noun* assets which can be sold for money

realisation /ˌrɪəlaɪˈzeɪʃ(ə)n/, **realization** *noun* the act of making real □ **the realisation of a project** putting a project into action ○ *The plan moved a stage nearer realisation when the contracts were signed.*

realisation of assets /ˌrɪəlaɪzeɪʃ(ə)n əv ˈæsets/ *noun* the act of selling of assets for money

realise /ˈrɪəlaɪz/, **realize** *verb* **1.** to make something become real □ **to realise a project** *or* **a plan** to put a project or a plan into action **2.** to sell for money ○ *The company was running out of cash, so the board decided to realise some property or assets.* ○ *The sale realised £100,000.*

realised profit /ˌrɪəlaɪzd ˈprɒfɪt/ *noun* an actual profit made when something is sold, as opposed to paper profit

real money /rɪəl ˈmʌni/ *noun* cash used for settling debts (as opposed to cheques, drafts, etc.)

real rate of return /ˌrɪəl ˌreɪt əv rɪ ˈtɜːn/ *noun* an actual rate of return, calculated after taking inflation into account

real return after tax /ˌrɪəl rɪˌtɜːn ˌɑːftə ˈtæks/ *noun* the return calculated after deducting tax and inflation

real time /ˈrɪəl taɪm/ *noun* the time when a computer is working on the processing of data while the event to which the data refers is actually taking place ○ *The website allows you to check share prices in real time or gives real time information on share prices.*

real-time gross settlement system /ˌrɪəl taɪm grəʊs ˈset(ə)lmənt ˌsɪstəm/ *noun* an international system for making computerised transfers of money. Abbreviation **RTGS system**

real-time system /ˈrɪəl taɪm ˌsɪstəm/ *noun* a computer system where data is inputted directly into the computer which automatically processes it to produce information which can be used immediately

Realtor™ /ˈrɪəltə/ *trademark US* a trademark, used by a real estate agent or broker who is a member of the National Association of Realtors

realty /ˈrɪəlti/ *noun* property or real estate

real value /ˌrɪəl ˈvæljuː/ *noun* a value of an investment which is kept the same, e.g. by index-linking

real wages /ˌrɪəl ˈweɪdʒɪz/ *plural noun* same as **real earnings**

reasonable /ˈriːz(ə)nəb(ə)l/ *adjective* **1.** sensible, or not annoyed ○ *The manager of the shop was very reasonable when I tried to explain that I had left my credit cards at home.* □ **no reasonable offer refused** we will accept any offer which is not extremely low **2.** moderate or not expensive ○ *The union has decided to put in a reasonable wage claim.*

reassess /ˌriːəˈses/ *verb* to assess again ○ *The manager was asked to reassess the department staff, after the assessments were badly done by the supervisors.*

reassessment /ˌriːəˈsesmənt/ *noun* a new assessment

reassurance /ˌriːəˈʃʊərəns/ *noun* the act of making someone feel less worried

reassure /ˌriːəˈʃʊə/ *verb* **1.** to make someone calm or less worried ○ *The markets were reassured by the government statement on import controls.* ○ *The manager tried to reassure her that she* *would not lose her job.* **2.** to spread the insurance risk, by having another insurance company cover part of it and receive part of the original premium

rebate /ˈriːbeɪt/ *noun* **1.** a reduction in the amount of money to be paid ○ *We are offering a 10% rebate on selected goods.* **2.** money returned to someone because they have paid too much ○ *She got a tax rebate at the end of the year.*

rebound /rɪˈbaʊnd/ *verb* to go back up again quickly ○ *The market rebounded on the news of the government's decision.*

recapitalisation /riːˌkæpɪt(ə)laɪ ˈzeɪʃ(ə)n/ *noun* a change in the capital structure of a company as when new shares are issued, especially when undertaken to avoid the company going into liquidation

recapitalise /riːˈkæpɪt(ə)laɪz/ *verb* to change the capital structure of a company (as by issuing new shares), especially to avoid the company going into liquidation

recd *abbreviation* received

receipt /rɪˈsiːt/ *noun* **1.** a piece of paper showing that money has been paid or that something has been received ○ *He kept the customs receipt to show that he had paid duty on the goods.* ○ *Keep the receipt for items purchased in case you need to change them later.* **2.** the act of receiving something ○ *Goods will be supplied within thirty days of receipt of order.* ○ *Invoices are payable within thirty days of receipt.* ○ *On receipt of the notification, the company lodged an appeal.* □ **to acknowledge receipt of a letter** to write to say that you have received a letter ○ *We acknowledge receipt of your letter of the 15th.* ◊ **receipts** ■ *verb* to stamp or to sign a document to show that it has been received, or to stamp an invoice to show that it has been paid ○ *Receipted invoices are filed in the ring binder.*

receipt book /rɪˈsiːt bʊk/ *noun* a book of blank receipts to be filled in when purchases are made

receipts /rɪˈsiːts/ *plural noun* money taken in sales ○ *to itemise receipts and expenditure* ○ *Receipts are down against the same period of last year.*

'…the public sector borrowing requirement is kept low by treating the receipts from selling public assets as a reduction in borrowing' [*Economist*]

'…gross wool receipts for the selling season to end June appear likely to top $2 billion' [*Australian Financial Review*]

receipts and payments basis /rɪ ˌsiːts ən ˈpeɪmənts ˌbeɪsɪs/ *noun* an accounting method in which receipts and payments are accounted for when the money is actually received or paid out, not necessarily when they are entered in the books. Also called **cash basis**

receivable /rɪˈsiːvəb(ə)l/ *adjective* able to be received

receivables /rɪˈsiːvəb(ə)lz/ *plural noun* money which is owed to a company

receive /rɪˈsiːv/ *verb* to get something which is given or delivered to you ○ *We received the payment ten days ago.* ○ *The employees have not received any salary for six months.* ○ *The goods were received in good condition.* □ **'received with thanks'** words put on an invoice to show that a sum has been paid

receiver /rɪˈsiːvə/ *noun* **1.** a person who receives something ○ *He signed as receiver of the shipment.* **2.** same as **official receiver**

receivership /rɪˈsiːvəʃɪp/ *noun* □ **the company went into receivership** the company was put into the hands of a receiver

'…it suggests a classic case for receivership. There appear to be good businesses to be sold to the right owner within a group that is terminally sick' [*Times*]

receiving /rɪˈsiːvɪŋ/ *noun* an act of getting something which has been delivered

receiving bank /rɪˈsiːvɪŋ bæŋk/ *noun* a bank which receives money via electronic transfer

receiving clerk /rɪˈsiːvɪŋ klɑːk/ *noun* an official who works in a receiving office

receiving department /rɪˈsiːvɪŋ dɪ ˌpɑːtmənt/ *noun* a section of a company which deals with incoming goods or payments

receiving office /rɪˈsiːvɪŋ ˌɒfɪs/ *noun* an office where goods or payments are received

receiving order /rɪˈsiːvɪŋ ˌɔːdə/ *noun* an order from a court appointing an official receiver to a company

recession /rɪˈseʃ(ə)n/ *noun* a period where there is a decline in trade or in the economy ○ *The recession has reduced profits in many companies.* ○ *Several firms have closed factories because of the recession.*

COMMENT: There are various ways of deciding if a recession is taking place: the usual one is when the GNP falls for three consecutive quarters.

reciprocal /rɪ'sɪprək(ə)l/ *adjective* done by one person, company, or country to another one, which does the same thing in return ○ *We signed a reciprocal agreement* or *a reciprocal contract with a Russian company.*

reciprocal holdings /rɪˌsɪprək(ə)l 'həʊldɪŋz/ *plural noun* a situation in which two companies own shares in each other to prevent takeover bids

reciprocal trade /rɪˌsɪprək(ə)l 'treɪd/ *noun* trade between two countries

reciprocate /rɪ'sɪprəkeɪt/ *verb* to do the same thing for someone as that person has done for you ○ *They offered us an exclusive agency for their cars and we reciprocated with an offer of the agency for our buses.*

reckon /'rekən/ *verb* to calculate something ○ *to reckon the costs at £25,000* ○ *We reckon the loss to be over £1m.* ○ *They reckon the insurance costs to be too high.*

reclamation /ˌreklə'meɪʃ(ə)n/ *noun US* the process of recovering money owed by a bank or securities firm to a customer because of an error

recognise /'rekəgnaɪz/ *verb* to record an item in an account or other financial statement □ **to recognise a union** to agree that a union can act on behalf of employees in a company ○ *Although more than half the staff had joined the union, the management refused to recognise it.*

recognised agent /ˌrekəgnaɪzd 'eɪdʒənt/ *noun* an agent who is approved by the company for which they act

recognised investment exchange /ˌrekəgˌnaɪzd ɪn'vestmənt/ *noun* a stock exchange, futures exchange or commodity exchange recognised by the FSA. Abbreviation **RIE**

recognised professional body /ˌrekəgnaɪzd prəˌfeʃ(ə)nəl 'bɒdi/ *noun* a professional body which is in charge of the regulation of the conduct of its

members and is recognised by the FSA. Abbreviation **RPB**

recommended retail price /ˌrekəmendɪd 'riːteɪl ˌpraɪs/ *noun* the price at which a manufacturer suggests a product should be sold on the retail market, though this may be reduced by the retailer. Abbreviation **RRP**. Also called **administered price**

reconcile /'rekənsaɪl/ *verb* to make two financial accounts or statements agree ○ *She is trying to reconcile one account with another* or *to reconcile the two accounts.*

reconciliation /ˌrekənsɪli'eɪʃ(ə)n/, **reconcilement** /'rekənsaɪlmənt/ *noun* the act of making two accounts or statements agree

reconciliation statement /ˌrekənsɪli'eɪʃ(ə)n ˌsteɪtmənt/ *noun* a statement which explains how two accounts can be made to agree

record /'rekɔːd/ *noun* **1.** a report of something which has happened ○ *The chairman signed the minutes as a true record of the last meeting.* ○ *She has a very poor time-keeping record.* □ **for the record** or **to keep the record straight** in order that everyone knows what the real facts of the matter are ○ *For the record, I should like to say that these sales figures have not yet been checked by the sales department.* □ **on record** reported in a published document, e.g. in a newspaper ○ *The chairman is on record as saying that profits are set to rise.* □ **off the record** unofficially, in private ○ *He made some remarks off the record about the disastrous home sales figures.* **2.** a success which is better than anything before ○ *Last year was a record year for the company.* ○ *Our top sales rep has set a new record for sales per call.* □ **record sales, record losses, record profits** sales, losses or profits which are higher than ever before □ **we broke our record for June** we sold more than we have ever sold before in June ○ *Sales last year equalled the record set in 1997.* ■ *verb* /rɪ'kɔːd/ to note or report something ○ *The company has recorded another year of increased sales.*

record book /'rekɔːd bʊk/ *noun* a book in which minutes of meetings are kept

record-breaking /ˈrekɔːd ˌbreɪkɪŋ/ adjective better or worse than anything which has happened before ○ *We are proud of our record-breaking profits in 2000.*

record date /ˈrekɔːd deɪt/ noun same as **date of record**

recording /rɪˈkɔːdɪŋ/ noun the act of making a note of something ○ *the recording of an order* or *of a complaint*

recording of a lien /rɪˌkɔːdɪŋ əv ə ˈliːən/ noun a note in the public records showing a lien on a property (such as a mortgage)

records /ˈrekɔːdz/ plural noun documents which give information ○ *The names of customers are kept in the company's records.* ○ *We find from our records that our invoice number 1234 has not been paid.*

recoup /rɪˈkuːp/ verb □ **to recoup your losses** to get back money which you thought you had lost

recourse /rɪˈkɔːs/ noun a right of a lender to compel a borrower to repay money borrowed □ **to decide to have recourse to the courts to obtain money due** to decide in the end to sue someone to obtain money owed

recover /rɪˈkʌvə/ verb **1.** to get back something which has been lost ○ *to recover damages from the driver of the car* ○ *to start a court action to recover property* ○ *He never recovered his money.* ○ *The initial investment was never recovered.* **2.** to get better, to rise ○ *The market has not recovered from the rise in oil prices.* ○ *The stock market fell in the morning, but recovered during the afternoon.*

recoverable /rɪˈkʌv(ə)rəb(ə)l/ adjective possible to get back

recoverable ACT /rɪˌkʌv(ə)rəb(ə)l eɪ siː ˈtiː/ noun advance corporation tax which can be set against corporation tax payable for the period

recoverable amount /rɪˌkʌv(ə)rə b(ə)l əˈmaʊnt/ noun the value of an asset, either the price it would fetch if sold, or its value to the company when used, whichever is the larger figure

recovery /rɪˈkʌv(ə)ri/ noun **1.** the act of getting back something which has been lost ○ *to start an action for recovery of property* ○ *We are aiming for the*

complete recovery of the money invested. **2.** a movement upwards of shares or of the economy ○ *signs of recovery after a slump* ○ *The economy staged a recovery.*

recovery share /rɪˈkʌv(ə)ri ʃeə/ noun a share which is likely to go up in value because the company's performance is improving

rectify /ˈrektɪfaɪ/ verb to correct something, to make something right ○ *to rectify an entry* (NOTE: **rectifies – rectifying – rectified**)

recurrent /rɪˈkʌrənt/ adjective happening again and again ○ *a recurrent item of expenditure* ○ *There is a recurrent problem in supplying this part.*

recurring /rɪˈkɜːrɪŋ/ adjective which happens again and again

recurring payments /rɪˌkɜːrɪŋ ˈpeɪmənts/ plural noun payments, such as mortgage interest or payments on a hire purchase agreement, which are made each month

recycle /riːˈsaɪk(ə)l/ verb to use money in a different way (as by investing profits from industry in developing environmental resources)

recycling /riːˈsaɪklɪŋ/ noun the action of banks in putting deposits into a bank which is in difficulties, in order to keep it afloat

red /red/ noun the colour of debit or overdrawn balances in some bank statements □ **in the red** showing a debit or loss ○ *My bank account is in the red.* ○ *The company went into the red in 1998.* ○ *The company is out of the red for the first time since 1990.*

Red Book /ˈred bʊk/ noun a document published on Budget Day, with the text of the Chancellor of the Exchequer's financial statement and budget

Red chips /ˈred tʃɪps/ plural noun good risk-free Chinese companies

red clause credit /ˌred klɔːz ˈkredɪt/ noun a letter of credit authorising the holder to receive an advance payment, usually so that he or she can continue trading

red day /ˈred deɪ/ noun US a day which is not profitable (NOTE: The opposite is **green day**.)

redeem /rɪˈdiːm/ verb **1.** to pay off a loan or a debt ○ *to redeem a mortgage* ○

to redeem a debt **2.** □ **to redeem a bond** to sell a bond for cash **3.** to exchange a voucher, coupon, or stamp for a gift or a reduction in price

redeemable /rɪˈdiːməb(ə)l/ *adjective* referring to a bond which can be sold for cash

redeemable government stock /rɪ ˌdiːməb(ə)l ˌgʌv(ə)nmənt ˈstɒk/ *noun* stock which can be redeemed for cash at some time in the future. In the UK, only the War Loan is irredeemable.

redeemable preference share /rɪ ˌdiːməb(ə)l ˈpref(ə)rəns ʃeə/ *noun* a preference share which must be bought back by the company at an agreed date and for an agreed price

redeemable security /rɪˌdiːməb(ə)l sɪˈkjʊərɪti/ *noun* a security which can be redeemed at its face value at a specific date in the future

redemption /rɪˈdempʃ(ə)n/ *noun* **1.** the repayment of a loan □ **redemption before due date** paying back a loan before the date when repayment is due **2.** the repayment of a debt ○ *redemption of a mortgage*

redemption date /rɪˈdempʃən deɪt/ *noun* a date on which a loan or debt is due to be repaid

redemption value /rɪˈdempʃən ˌvæljuː/ *noun* the value of a security when redeemed

redemption yield /rɪˈdempʃən jiːld/ *noun* a yield on a security including interest and its redemption value

red herring /red ˈherɪŋ/ *noun US* a preliminary prospectus, the first prospectus for a new share issue, produced to see the market reaction to the proposed issue, but without giving a price for the new shares. This is similar to the British 'pathfinder prospectus'; called this because the first page has a notice printed in red which states that it is not a full offer.

rediscount /riːˈdɪskaʊnt/ *verb* to discount a bill of exchange which has already been discounted by a commercial bank

redistribute /ˌriːdɪˈstrɪbjuːt/ *verb* to move items, work or money to different areas or people ○ *The government aims to redistribute wealth by taxing the rich and giving grants to the poor.* ○ *The orders*

have been redistributed among the company's factories.

redistribution of risk /ˌriːdɪstrɪbjuːʃən əv ˈrɪsk/ *noun* the process of spreading the risk of an investment or of an insurance among various insurers

redistribution of wealth /ˌriːdɪstrɪbjuːʃən əv ˈwelθ/ *noun* the process of sharing wealth among the whole population

redlining /ˈredlaɪnɪŋ/ *noun* the illegal practice of discriminating against prospective borrowers because of the area of the town in which they live

red tape /ˌred ˈteɪp/ *noun* official paperwork which takes a long time to complete ○ *The start of the new project has been held up by extra checks and government red tape.*

reduce /rɪˈdjuːs/ *verb* **1.** to make something smaller or lower ○ *We must reduce expenditure if we want to stay in business.* ○ *They have reduced prices in all departments.* ○ *We were expecting the government to reduce taxes not to increase them.* ○ *We have made some employees redundant to reduce overstaffing.* ○ *The company reduced output because of a fall in demand.* ○ *The government's policy is to reduce inflation to 5%.* □ **to reduce staff** to make employees redundant in order to have a smaller number of staff **2.** to lower the price of something ○ *Carpets have been reduced from £100 to £50.*

reduced /rɪˈdjuːst/ *adjective* lower ○ *Reduced prices have increased unit sales.* ○ *Prices have fallen due to a reduced demand for the goods.*

reduced rate /rɪˌdjuːst ˈreɪt/ *noun* a specially cheap charge

reducing balance method /rɪ ˌdjuːsɪŋ ˈbæləns ˌmeθəd/ *noun* a method of depreciating assets, where the asset is depreciated at a constant percentage of its cost each year. Also called **declining balance method**

reduction /rɪˈdʌkʃən/ *noun* an act of making something smaller or less ○ *Reduction in demand has led to the cancellation of several new projects.* ○ *The company was forced to make reductions in its advertising budget.* ○ *Price reductions have had no effect on our* *sales.* ○ *Working only part-time will mean a significant reduction in take-home pay.*

redundancy /rɪ'dʌndənsi/ *noun* the dismissal of a person whose job no longer needs to be done

redundancy payment /rɪ'dʌndənsi ˌpeɪmənt/ *noun* a payment made to an employee to compensate for losing his or her job

redundancy rebate /rɪ'dʌndənsi ˌriːbeɪt/ *noun* a payment made to a company to compensate for redundancy payments made

redundant /rɪ'dʌndənt/ *adjective* **1.** more than is needed, useless ○ *a redundant clause in a contract* ○ *The new legislation has made clause 6 redundant.* ○ *Retraining can help employees whose old skills have become redundant.* **2.** □ **to make someone redundant** to dismiss an employee who is not needed any more

redundant staff /rɪˌdʌndənt 'stɑːf/ *noun* staff who have lost their jobs because they are not needed any more

re-export *noun* /riː'ekspɔːt/ the exporting of goods which have been imported ○ *The port is a centre for the re-export trade.* ○ *We import wool for re-export.* ○ *The value of re-exports has increased.* ■ *verb* /ˌriːek'spɔːt/ to export something which has been imported

re-exportation /ˌriː ekspɔː'teɪʃ(ə)n/ *noun* the exporting of goods which have been imported

ref *abbreviation* reference

refer /rɪ'fɜː/ *verb* □ **'refer to drawer'** words written on a cheque which a bank refuses to pay and returns it to the person who wrote it. Abbreviation **R** *or* **D** □ **the bank referred the cheque to drawer** the bank returned the cheque to person who wrote it because there was not enough money in the account to pay it (NOTE: [all senses] **referring – referred**)

reference /'ref(ə)rəns/ *noun* **1.** the process of mentioning or dealing with something ○ *with reference to your letter of May 25th* **2.** a series of numbers or letters which make it possible to find a document which has been filed ○ *our reference: PC/MS 1234* ○ *Thank you for your letter (reference 1234).* ○ *Please quote this reference in all correspondence.* **3.** a written report on someone's character or ability ○ *to write someone a*

reference or *to give someone a reference* ○ *to ask applicants to supply references* □ **to ask a company for trade references** *or* **for bank references** to ask for reports from traders or a bank on the company's financial status and reputation

refinance /ˌriː'faɪnæns/ *verb* to extend a loan by exchanging it for a new one (normally done when the terms of the new loan are better)

refinancing /riː'faɪnænsɪŋ/ *noun* □ **refinancing of a loan** the act of taking out a new loan to pay back a previous loan

'…the refinancing consisted of a two-for-five rights issue, which took place in September this year, to offer 55.8m shares at 2p and raise about £925,000 net of expenses' [*Accountancy*]

reflate /riː'fleɪt/ *verb* □ **to reflate the economy** to stimulate the economy by increasing the money supply or by reducing taxes, often leading to increased inflation ○ *The government's attempts to reflate the economy were not successful.*

reflation /riː'fleɪʃ(ə)n/ *noun* an act of stimulating the economy by increasing the money supply or by reducing taxes

reflationary measures /riː ˌfleɪʃ(ə)n(ə)ri 'meʃəz/ *plural noun* actions which are likely to stimulate the economy

refund *noun* /'riːfʌnd/ money paid back ○ *The shoes don't fit – I'm going to ask for a refund.* ○ *She got a refund after complaining to the manager.* ■ *verb* /rɪ'fʌnd/ to pay back money ○ *to refund the cost of postage* ○ *All money will be refunded if the goods are not satisfactory.*

refundable /rɪ'fʌndəb(ə)l/ *adjective* possible to pay back ○ *We ask for a refundable deposit of £20.* ○ *The entrance fee is refundable if you purchase £5 worth of goods.*

refunding /riː'fʌndɪŋ/ *noun* the process, on the part of a government, of funding a debt again, by issuing new stock to replace stock which is about to mature

region /'riːdʒən/ *noun* a large area of a country ○ *Her territory consists of all the eastern region of the country.*

regional /'riːdʒ(ə)nəl/ *adjective* referring to a region

regional bank /ˈriːdʒ(ə)nəl bæŋk/
noun a bank which services one part of
the country

**regional check processing
center** /ˌriːdʒ(ə)nəl tʃek ˈprəʊsesɪŋ
ˌsentə/ *noun US* a Federal Reserve
clearing centre which clears cheques
from banks within a certain area. Abbreviation **RCPC**

regional development grant
/ˌriːdʒ(ə)nəl dɪˈveləpmənt grɑːnt/
noun a grant given to encourage a business to establish itself in a certain part of
the country. Abbreviation **RDG**

regional planning /ˌriːdʒ(ə)nəl
ˈplænɪŋ/ *noun* the work of planning the
industrial development of a region

regional stock exchange
/ˌriːdʒ(ə)nəl ˈstɒk ɪksˌtʃeɪndʒ/ *noun* a
stock exchange which is not in the main
finance centre (e.g. not in New York or
London)

register /ˈredʒɪstə/ *noun* an official list
○ *to enter something in a register* ○ *to
keep a register up to date* ○ *people on the
register of electors* ■ *verb* **1.** to write
something in an official list ○ *to register
a fall in the numbers of unemployed teen-
agers* ○ *To register a company you must
pay a fee to Companies House.* ○ *When a
property is sold, the sale is registered at
the Land Registry.* **2.** to send a letter by
registered post ○ *I registered the letter,
because it contained some money.*

registered /ˈredʒɪstəd/ *adjective*
having been noted on an official list ○ *a
registered share transaction*

registered cheque /ˌredʒɪstəd
ˈtʃek/ *noun* a cheque written on a bank
account on behalf of a client who does not
have a bank account

registered company /ˌredʒɪstəd
ˈkʌmp(ə)ni/ *noun* a company which has
been officially set up and registered with
the Registrar of Companies

registered office /ˌredʒɪstəd ˈɒfɪs/
noun the office address of a company
which is officially registered with the
Companies' Registrar

registered security /ˌredʒɪstəd sɪ
ˈkjʊərɪti/ *noun* a security such as a share
in a quoted company which is registered
with Companies House and whose holder
is listed in the company's share register

register of directors /ˌredʒɪstər əv
daɪˈrektəz/ *noun* an official list of the
directors of a company which has to be
sent to the Registrar of Companies

register of interests in shares
/ˌredʒɪstə əv ˌɪntrəsts ɪn ˈʃeəz/ *noun* a
list kept by a company of those shareholders who own more than 3% of its
shares

registrar /ˌredʒɪˈstrɑː/ *noun* a person
who keeps official records

Registrar of Companies
/ˌredʒɪstrɑː əv ˈkʌmp(ə)niz/ *noun* a
government official whose duty is to
ensure that companies are properly registered, and that, when registered, they file
accounts and other information correctly

registration /ˌredʒɪˈstreɪʃ(ə)n/ *noun*
the act of having something noted on an
official list ○ *the registration of a trademark* or *of a share transaction*

registration fee /ˌredʒɪˈstreɪʃ(ə)n fiː/
noun **1.** money paid to have something
registered **2.** money paid to attend a
conference

registration number /ˌredʒɪ
ˈstreɪʃ(ə)n ˌnʌmbə/ *noun* an official
number, e.g. the number of a car

registration statement /ˌredʒɪ
ˈstreɪʃ(ə)n ˌsteɪtmənt/ *noun US* a document which gives information about a
company when it is registered and listed
on a stock exchange (NOTE: The UK term
is **listing particulars**.)

regression analysis /rɪˈgreʃ(ə)n ə
ˌnæləsɪs/, **regression model** /rɪ
ˈgreʃ(ə)n ˌmɒd(ə)l/ *noun* a method of
discovering the ratio of one dependent
variable and one or more independent
variables, so as to give a value to the
dependent variable

regressive taxation /rɪˌgresɪv tæk
ˈseɪʃ(ə)n/ *noun* a system of taxation in
which tax gets progressively less as
income rises. Compare **progressive
taxation**

regular /ˈregjʊlə/ *adjective* occurring
at the same time each day, each week,
each month or each year ○ *His regular
train is the 12.45.* ○ *The regular flight to
Athens leaves at 06.00.*

regular income /ˌregjʊlər ˈɪnkʌm/
noun an income which comes in every
week or month ○ *She works freelance so
she does not have a regular income.*

regulate /'regjʊleɪt/ *verb* **1.** to adjust something so that it works well or is correct **2.** to change or maintain something by law □ **prices are regulated by supply and demand** prices are increased or lowered according to supply and demand □ **government-regulated price** a price which is imposed by the government

regulated consumer credit agreement /ˌregjʊleɪtɪd kənˌsjuːmə 'kredɪt əˌgriːmənt/ *noun* a credit agreement as defined by the Consumer Credit Act

regulation /ˌregjʊ'leɪʃ(ə)n/ *noun* **1.** a law or rule ○ *the new government regulations on housing standards* ○ *Fire regulations or Safety regulations were not observed at the restaurant.* ○ *Regulations concerning imports and exports are set out in this leaflet.* **2.** the use of laws or rules stipulated by a government or regulatory body, such as the FSA, to provide orderly procedures and to protect consumers and investors ○ *government regulation of trading practices*

'EC regulations which came into effect in July insist that customers can buy cars anywhere in the EC at the local pre-tax price' [*Financial Times*]

'…a unit trust is established under the regulations of the Department of Trade, with a trustee, a management company and a stock of units' [*Investors Chronicle*]

'…fear of audit regulation, as much as financial pressures, is a major factor behind the increasing number of small accountancy firms deciding to sell their practices or merge with another firm' [*Accountancy*]

regulation agency /ˌregjʊ'leɪʃ(ə)n ˌeɪdʒənsi/ *noun* an organisation which sees that members of an industry follow government regulations

Regulation Q /ˌregjʊleɪʃ(ə)n 'kjuː/ *noun US* a federal regulation which limits the amount of interest banks can pay on deposits

Regulation S-X /ˌregjʊleɪʃ(ə)n es 'eks/ *noun* the rule of the US Securities and Exchange Commission which regulates annual reports from companies

regulator /'regjʊleɪtə/ *noun* a person whose job it is to see that regulations are followed

'…the regulators have sought to protect investors and other market participants from the impact of a firm collapsing' [*Banking Technology*]

regulatory /'regjʊlət(ə)ri/ *adjective* applying regulations

regulatory powers /'regjʊlət(ə)ri ˌpaʊəz/ *noun* powers to enforce government regulations

reimburse /ˌriːɪm'bɜːs/ *verb* □ **to reimburse someone their expenses** to pay someone back for money which they have spent ○ *You will be reimbursed for your expenses* or *Your expenses will be reimbursed.*

reimbursement /ˌriːɪm'bɜːsmənt/ *noun* the act of paying back money ○ *reimbursement of expenses*

reinstatement /ˌriːɪn'steɪtmənt/ *noun* the act of giving a borrower back his or her former credit status after he or she has paid off outstanding debts

reinsurance /ˌriːɪn'ʃʊərəns/ *noun* insurance where a second insurer (the reinsurer) agrees to cover part of the risk insured by the first insurer

reinsure /ˌriːɪn'ʃʊə/ *verb* to spread the insurance risk, by having another insurance company cover part of it and receive part of the original premium

reinsurer /ˌriːɪn'ʃʊərə/ *noun* an insurance company which agrees to insure part of the risk for another insurer

reintermediation /riˌɪntəmiːdi'eɪʃ(ə)n/ *noun* the act of withdrawing funds from investments such as shares or bonds and transferring them into cash deposits in banks (NOTE: The opposite is **disintermediation.**)

reinvest /ˌriːɪn'vest/ *verb* to invest money again ○ *She sold her shares and reinvested the money in government stocks.*

reinvestment /ˌriːɪn'vestmənt/ *noun* **1.** the act of investing money again in the same securities **2.** the act of investing a company's earnings in its own business by using them to create new products for sale

'…many large US corporations offer shareholders the option of reinvesting their cash dividend payments in additional company stock at a discount to the market price. But to some big securities firms these discount reinvestment programs are an opportunity to turn a quick profit' [*Wall Street Journal*]

REIT *abbreviation US* real estate investment trust. ◊ **equity REIT**, **mortgage REIT**

reject *noun* /'riːdʒekt/, *adjective* (something) which has been thrown out because it is not of the usual standard ○ *sale of rejects* or *of reject items* ○ *to sell off reject stock* ■ *verb* /rɪ'dʒekt/ to refuse to accept something, or to say that something is not satisfactory ○ *The board rejected the draft budget.* □ **the company rejected the takeover bid** the directors recommended that the shareholders should not accept the bid

rejection /rɪ'dʒekʃən/ *noun* a refusal to accept something, such as a refusal to give a customer credit ○ *The rejection of the company's offer meant that the negotiations had to start again.* ○ *After the union's rejection of the offer, management came back with new redundancy terms.* ○ *The board recommended rejection of the bid.*

related /rɪ'leɪtɪd/ *adjective* connected or linked ○ *related items on the agenda*

related company /rɪˌleɪtɪd 'kʌmp(ə)ni/ *noun* a company in which another company makes a long-term capital investment in order to gain control or influence

relative strength index /ˌrelətɪv 'streŋθ ˌɪndeks/ *noun* an indicator used to compare the current price of an instrument or market to the price at a previous period. It identifies when a share is overbought or oversold. Abbreviation **RSI**

relative value funds /ˌrelətɪv 'væljuː fʌndz/ *plural noun* hedge funds not related to general market movements, but which try to find opportunities to arbitrage temporary slight changes in the relative values of particular financial assets

release /rɪ'liːs/ *noun* **1.** the act of setting someone free or of making something or someone no longer subject to an obligation or restriction ○ *release from a contract* ○ *the release of goods from customs* ○ *She was offered early release so that she could take up her new job.* **2.** the act of making something public, or a public announcement **3.** the act of putting something on the market, or something put on the market ■ *verb* **1.** to free some-

thing or someone ○ *to release goods from customs* ○ *to release someone from a debt* ○ *Customs released the goods against payment of a fine.* **2.** to make something public ○ *The company released information about the new mine in Australia.* ○ *The government has refused to release figures for the number of unemployed women.* **3.** to put something on the market ○ *They released several new CDs this month.* □ **to release dues** to send off orders which had been piling up while a product was out of stock

'...pressure to ease monetary policy mounted yesterday with the release of a set of pessimistic economic statistics' [*Financial Times*]

'...the national accounts for the March quarter released by the Australian Bureau of Statistics showed a real increase in GDP' [*Australian Financial Review*]

release note /rɪ'liːs nəʊt/ *noun* a note from a bank to say that a bill of exchange has been paid

relevant /'reləv(ə)nt/ *adjective* having to do with what is being discussed or the current situation ○ *Which is the relevant government department?* ○ *Can you give me the relevant papers?* ○ *The new assistant does not have any relevant experience.*

relief /rɪ'liːf/ *noun* help

reminder /rɪ'maɪndə/ *noun* a letter to remind a customer that he or she has not paid an invoice ○ *to send someone a reminder*

remission of taxes /rɪˌmɪʃ(ə)n əv 'tæksɪz/ *noun* a refund of taxes which have been overpaid

remit /rɪ'mɪt/ *verb* to send money ○ *to remit by cheque* (NOTE: **remitting – remitted**)

remittance /rɪ'mɪt(ə)ns/ *noun* money which is sent to pay back a debt or to pay an invoice ○ *The family lives on a weekly remittance from their father in the US* ○ *Please send remittances to the treasurer.*

remittance advice /rɪ'mɪt(ə)ns əd ˌvaɪs/, **remittance slip** /rɪ'mɪt(ə)ns slɪp/ *noun* an advice note sent with payment, showing why it is being made, i.e. quoting the invoice number or a reference number

remitting bank /rɪ'mɪtɪŋ bæŋk/ *verb* a bank into which a person has deposited a cheque, and which has the duty to collect the money from the account of the writer of the cheque

remunerate /rɪˈmjuːnəreɪt/ *verb* to pay someone for doing something ○ *The company refused to remunerate them for their services.*

remuneration /rɪˌmjuːnəˈreɪʃ(ə)n/ *noun* payment for services ○ *The job is interesting but the remuneration is low.* ○ *She receives a small remuneration of £400 a month.* ○ *No one will work hard for such poor remuneration.*

COMMENT: Remuneration can take several forms: e.g. a regular monthly salary cheque, a cheque or cash payment for hours worked or for work completed.

remunerative /rɪˈmjuːnərətɪv/ *adjective* referring to a job which pays well ○ *She is in a highly remunerative job.*

render /ˈrendə/ *verb* □ **to render an account** to send in an account ○ *Please find enclosed payment per account rendered.*

renege /rɪˈneɪg, rɪˈniːg/ *verb* □ **to renege on a promise** not to do something which you had promised to do (*formal*) ○ *I was furious when he reneged on the deal.*

renegotiate /ˌriːnɪˈɡəʊʃieɪt/ *verb* to negotiate something again ○ *The company was forced to renegotiate the terms of the loan.*

renew /rɪˈnjuː/ *verb* to continue something for a further period of time ○ *We have asked the bank to renew the bill of exchange.* ○ *The tenant wants to renew his lease.* ○ *Her contract was renewed for a further three years.* □ **to renew a subscription** to pay a subscription for another year □ **to renew an insurance policy** to pay the premium for another year's insurance

renewal /rɪˈnjuːəl/ *noun* the act of renewing ○ *renewal of a lease* or *of a subscription* or *of a bill* ○ *renewal of a contract* ○ *Her contract is up for renewal* ○ *When is the renewal date of the bill?* □ **to be up for renewal** to be due to be renewed ○ *His contract is up for renewal in January.* ○ *The lease is up for renewal next month.*

renewal notice /rɪˈnjuːəl ˌnəʊtɪs/ *noun* a note sent by an insurance

company asking the insured person to renew the insurance

renewal premium /rɪˈnjuːəl ˌpriːmiəm/ *noun* a premium to be paid to renew an insurance

renminbi /ˈrenmɪnbiː/ *noun* a unit of currency used in China

rent /rent/ *noun* money paid to use an office, house or factory for a period of time □ **the flat is let at an economic rent** at a rent which covers all costs to the landlord □ **nominal rent** a very small rent ■ *verb* **1.** to pay money to hire an office, house, factory or piece of equipment for a period of time ○ *to rent an office* or *a car* ○ *He rents an office in the centre of town.* ○ *They were driving a rented car when they were stopped by the police.* **2.** *US* same as **let** □ **to rent (out)** to own a car, office, etc., and let someone use it for money ○ *We rented part of the building to an American company.*

rental /ˈrent(ə)l/ *noun* money paid to use an office, house, factory, car, piece of equipment, etc., for a period of time ○ *The car rental bill comes to over £1000 a quarter.*

'…top quality office furniture: short or long-term rental 50% cheaper than any other rental company' [*Australian Financial Review*]

'…until the vast acres of empty office space start to fill up with rent-paying tenants, rentals will continue to fall and so will values. Despite the very sluggish economic recovery under way, it is still difficult to see where the new tenants will come from' [*Australian Financial Review*]

rental value /ˈrent(ə)l ˌvæljuː/ *noun* a full value of the rent for a property if it were charged at the current market rate, i.e. calculated between rent reviews

rent control /ˈrent kənˌtrəʊl/ *noun* government regulation of rents

rente *noun* the French word for a government annuity

rent review /ˈrent rɪˌvjuː/ *noun* an increase in rents which is carried out during the term of a lease. Most leases allow for rents to be reviewed every three or five years.

rent tribunal /ˈrent traɪˌbjuːn(ə)l/ *noun* a court which can decide if a rent is too high or low

renunciation /rɪˌnʌnsiˈeɪʃ(ə)n/ *noun* an act of giving up ownership of shares

reorder /riːˈɔːdə/ *noun* a further order for something which has been ordered before ○ *The product has only been on the market ten days and we are already getting reorders.* ■ *verb* to place a new order for something ○ *We must reorder these items because stock is getting low.*

reorder interval /riːˈɔːdə ˌɪntəv(ə)l/ *noun* a period of time before a new order for a stock item is placed

reorder level /riːˈɔːdə ˌlev(ə)l/ *noun* a minimum amount of an item which a company holds in stock, such that, when stock falls to this amount, the item must be reordered

reorganisation /riːˌɔːɡənaɪˈzeɪʃ(ə)n/, **reorganization** *noun* the process of organising a company in a different way, as in the US when a bankrupt company applies to be treated under Chapter 11 to be protected from its creditors while it is being reorganised

reorganise /riːˈɔːɡənaɪz/ *verb* to organise something in a new way ○ *We have reorganised all our reps' territories.*

repatriation /riːˌpætriˈeɪʃ(ə)n/ *noun* the return of foreign investments to the home country of their owner

repay /rɪˈpeɪ/ *verb* to pay something back, or to pay back money to someone ○ *to repay money owed* ○ *The company had to cut back on expenditure in order to repay its debts.* (NOTE: **repaying – repaid**) □ **he repaid me in full** he paid me back all the money he owed me

repayable /rɪˈpeɪəb(ə)l/ *adjective* possible to pay back ○ *loan which is repayable over ten years*

repayment /rɪˈpeɪmənt/ *noun* the act of paying money back or money which is paid back ○ *The loan is due for repayment next year.* □ **he fell behind with his mortgage repayments** he was late in paying back the instalments on his mortgage

repayment mortgage /rɪˈpeɪmənt ˌmɔːɡɪdʒ/ *noun* a mortgage where the borrower pays back both interest and capital over the period of the mortgage. This is opposed to an endowment mortgage, where only the interest is repaid, and an insurance is taken out to repay the capital at the end of the term of the mortgage.

replacement cost accounting /rɪˈpleɪsmənt kɒst əˌkaʊntɪŋ/ *noun* same as **current cost accounting**. Compare **historical cost accounting**

replacement cost depreciation /rɪˈpleɪsmənt kɒst dɪˌpriːʃieɪʃ(ə)n/ *noun* depreciation based on the actual cost of replacing the asset in the current year

replacement price /rɪˈpleɪsmənt praɪs/ *noun* a price at which the replacement for an asset would have to be bought

replacement value /rɪˈpleɪsmənt ˌvæljuː/ *noun* the value of something for insurance purposes if it were to be replaced ○ *The computer is insured at its replacement value.*

reply coupon /rɪˈplaɪ ˌkuːpɒn/ *noun* a form attached to a coupon ad which has to be filled in and returned to the advertiser

repo *noun* same as **repurchase agreement** (*informal*) (NOTE: The plural is **repos**)

report /rɪˈpɔːt/ *noun* **1.** a statement describing what has happened or describing a state of affairs ○ *to make a report* or *to present a report* or *to send in a report on market opportunities in the Far East* ○ *The accountants are drafting a report on salary scales.* ○ *The sales manager reads all the reports from the sales team.* ○ *The chairman has received a report from the insurance company.* □ **the treasurer's report** a document from the honorary treasurer of a society to explain the financial state of the society to its members **2.** an official document from a government committee ○ *The government has issued a report on the credit problems of exporters.* ○ *They reported for work at the usual time.* ■ *verb* **1.** to make a statement describing something ○ *The sales force reported an increased demand for the product.* ○ *He reported the damage to the insurance company.* ○ *We asked the bank to report on his financial status.* **2.** □ **to report to someone** to be responsible to or to be under someone ○ *She reports direct to the managing director.* ○ *The sales force reports to the sales director.* **3.** to publish the results of a company for a period and declare the dividend

'…a draft report on changes in the international monetary system' [*Wall Street Journal*]

'…responsibilities include the production of premium quality business reports' [*Times*]

'…the research director will manage a team of business analysts monitoring and reporting on the latest development in retail distribution' [*Times*]

'…the successful candidate will report to the area director for profit responsibility for sales of leading brands' [*Times*]

reporting season /rɪˈpɔːtɪŋ ˌsiːz(ə)n/ *noun* a period when many large companies declare their dividends

repossess /ˌriːpəˈzes/ *verb* to take back an item which someone is buying under a hire-purchase agreement, or a property which someone is buying under a mortgage, because the purchaser cannot continue the payments

repossession /ˌriːpəˈzeʃ(ə)n/ *noun* an act of repossessing ○ *Repossessions are increasing as people find it difficult to meet mortgage repayments.*

represent /ˌreprɪˈzent/ *verb* **1.** to work for a company, showing goods or services to possible buyers ○ *He represents an American car firm in Europe.* ○ *Our French distributor represents several other competing firms.* **2.** to act on behalf of someone ○ *He sent his solicitor and accountant to represent him at the meeting.* ○ *Three managers represent the workforce in discussions with the directors.*

re-present /ˌriː prɪˈzent/ *verb* to present something again ○ *She re-presented the cheque two weeks later to try to get payment from the bank.*

representation /ˌreprɪzenˈteɪʃ(ə)n/ *noun* **1.** the right to sell goods for a company, or a person or organisation that sells goods on behalf of a company ○ *They have no representation in the US* ○ *We offered them exclusive representation in Europe.* **2.** the fact of having someone to act on your behalf ○ *The minority shareholders want representation on the board.* ○ *The ordinary shop floor workers want representation on the committee.*

representative /ˌreprɪˈzentətɪv/ *adjective* which is an example of what all others are like ○ *We displayed a repre-*

sentative selection of our product range. ○ *The sample chosen was not representative of the whole batch.* ■ *noun* **1.** a company which works for another company, selling their goods ○ *We have appointed Smith & Co our exclusive representatives in Europe.* **2.** a person who acts on someone's behalf ○ *He sent his solicitor and accountant to act as his representatives at the meeting.* ○ *The board refused to meet the representatives of the workforce.*

reprice /riːˈpraɪs/ *verb* to change the price on an item, usually to increase it

repudiate /rɪˈpjuːdieɪt/ *verb* to refuse to accept something

repurchase /riːˈpɜːtʃɪs/ *verb* to buy something again, especially something which you have recently bought and then sold

repurchase agreement /riːˈpɜːtʃɪs əˌɡriːmənt/ *noun* an agreement, where a bank agrees to buy something and sell it back later (in effect, giving a cash loan to the seller; this is used especially to raise short-term finance)

require /rɪˈkwaɪə/ *verb* **1.** to ask for or to demand something ○ *to require a full explanation of expenditure* ○ *The law requires you to submit all income to the tax authorities.* **2.** to need something ○ *The document requires careful study.* ○ *Writing the program requires a specialist knowledge of computers.*

required reserves /rɪˌkwaɪəd rɪˈzɜːvz/ *plural noun* reserves which a US bank is required to hold in cash in its vaults or as deposit with the Federal Reserve

requirement /rɪˈkwaɪəmənt/ *noun* **1.** something which someone wants or needs ○ *We hope the items will meet the customer's requirements.* ○ *If you will supply us with a list of your requirements, we shall see if we can meet them.* **2.** something which is necessary to enable something to be done ○ *Are computing skills a requirement for this job?*

requisition /ˌrekwɪˈzɪʃ(ə)n/ *noun* an official order for something ○ *What is the reference number of your latest requisition?* ■ *verb* to put in an official order for something or to ask for supplies to be sent ○ *We have requisitioned three trucks to move the stock.*

rerate /riːˈreɪt/ *verb* to change the rating of a share on the stock exchange (either upwards or downwards)

rerating /riːˈreɪtɪŋ/ *noun* the act of changing the value of a share on the stock exchange, either upwards or downwards

resale /ˈriːseɪl/ *noun* the selling of goods which have been bought ○ *to purchase something for resale* ○ *The contract forbids resale of the goods to the US*

resale price maintenance /ˌriːseɪl ˈpraɪs ˌmeɪntənəns/ *noun* a system in which the price for an item is fixed by the manufacturer, and the retailer is not allowed to sell it at a lower price. Abbreviation **RPM**

reschedule /riːˈʃedjuːl/ *verb* to arrange new credit terms for the repayment of a loan ○ *Companies which are unable to keep up the interest payments on their loans have asked for their loans to be rescheduled.*

rescind /rɪˈsɪnd/ *verb* to annul or to cancel something ○ *to rescind a contract* or *an agreement*

rescission /rɪˈsɪʒ(ə)n/ *noun* an act of rescinding a contract

rescue /ˈreskjuː/ *noun* the act of saving someone or something from danger ■ *verb* to save someone or something from danger ○ *The company nearly collapsed, but was rescued by the banks.*

rescue operation /ˈreskjuː ɒpə ˌreɪʃ(ə)n/ *noun* an arrangement by a group of people to save a company from collapse ○ *The banks planned a rescue operation for the company.*

research /rɪˈsɜːtʃ/ *noun* the process of trying to find out facts or information ■ *verb* to study or try to find out information about something ○ *They are researching the market for their new product.*

research and development /rɪ ˌsɜːtʃ ən dɪˈveləpmənt/ *noun* **1.** a scientific investigation which leads to making new products or improving existing products ○ *The company spends millions on research and development.* Abbreviation **R&D 2.** activities that are designed to produce new knowledge and ideas and to develop ways in which these can be commercially exploited by a business (NOTE: Research and development

activities are often grouped together to form a separate division or department within an organisation.)

COMMENT: Research costs can be divided into (a) applied research, which is the cost of research leading to a specific aim, and (b) basic, or pure research, which is research carried out without a specific aim in mind: these costs are written off in the year in which they are incurred. Development costs are the costs of making the commercial products based on the research.

research and development expenditure /rɪˌsɜːtʃ ən dɪ ˈveləpmənt ɪkˌspendɪtʃə/ *noun* money spent on R & D

research department /rɪˈsɜːtʃ dɪ ˌpɑːtmənt/ *noun* **1.** the section of a company which carries out research **2.** the section of a broker's office which does research into companies

researcher /rɪˈsɜːtʃə/ *noun* a person who carries out research ○ *Government statistics are a useful source of information for the desk researcher.*

resell /riːˈsel/ *verb* to sell something which has just been bought ○ *The car was sold in June and the buyer resold it to an dealer two months later.* (NOTE: **reselling – resold**)

reseller /riːˈselə/ *noun* somebody in the marketing chain who buys to sell to somebody else, e.g. wholesalers, distributors, and retailers

reserve /rɪˈzɜːv/ *noun* money from profits not paid as dividend but kept back by a company in case it is needed for a special purpose □ **reserve for bad debts** money kept by a company to cover debts which may not be paid

COMMENT: The accumulated profits retained by a company usually form its most important reserve.

reserve asset ratio /rɪˌzɜːv ˈæset/ *noun* also called **reserve ratio**

reserve currency /rɪˈzɜːv ˌkʌrənsi/ *noun* a strong currency used in international finance, held by other countries to support their own weaker currencies

reserved market /rɪˌzɜːvd ˈmɑːkɪt/ *noun* a market in which producers agree not to sell more than a specific amount in order to control competition. Also called **restricted market**

reserve for fluctuations /rɪˌzɜːv fə ˌflʌktʃuˈeɪʃ(ə)nz/ *noun* money set aside to allow for changes in the values of currencies

reserve fund /rɪˈzɜːv fʌnd/ *noun* profits in a business which have not been paid out as dividend but have been ploughed back into the business

reserve price /rɪˈzɜːv praɪs/ *noun* the lowest price which a seller will accept, e.g. at an auction or when selling securities through a broker ○ *The painting was withdrawn when it failed to reach its reserve price.*

reserve requirement /rɪˈzɜːv rɪ ˌkwaɪəmənt/ *noun US* the amount of reserves which an American bank has to hold on deposit with a Federal Reserve Bank

reserves /rɪˈzɜːvz/ *plural noun* **1.** supplies kept in case of need ○ *Our reserves of fuel fell during the winter.* ○ *The country's reserves of gas or gas reserves are very large.* **2.** money from profits not paid as dividend, but kept back by a company in case it is needed for a special purpose

residence /ˈrezɪd(ə)ns/ *noun* **1.** a house or flat where someone lives ○ *He has a country residence where he spends his weekends.* **2.** the fact of living or operating officially in a country

residence permit /ˈrezɪd(ə)ns ˌpɜːmɪt/ *noun* an official document allowing a foreigner to live in a country ○ *He has applied for a residence permit.* ○ *She was granted a residence permit for one year* or *a one-year residence permit.*

resident /ˈrezɪd(ə)nt/ *noun, adjective* a person or company considered to be living or operating in a country for official or tax purposes ○ *The company is resident in France.*

residential property /ˌrezɪdenʃ(ə)l ˈprɒpəti/ *noun* houses or flats owned or occupied by individual residents

residual /rɪˈzɪdjuəl/ *adjective* remaining after everything else has gone

residual value /rɪˌzɪdjuəl ˈvæljuː/ *noun* a value of an asset after it has been depreciated in the company's accounts

residue /ˈrezɪdjuː/ *noun* money left over ○ *After paying various bequests the residue of his estate was split between his children.*

resist /rɪˈzɪst/ *verb* to fight against something, not to give in to something ○ *The chairman resisted all attempts to make him resign.* ○ *The company is resisting the takeover bid.*

resistance /rɪˈzɪstəns/ *noun* opposition felt or shown by people to something ○ *There was a lot of resistance from the team to the new plan.* ○ *The chairman's proposal met with strong resistance from the banks.*

resistance level /rɪˈzɪst(ə)ns ˌlev(ə)l/ *noun* a price or index level which investors feel marks a boundary which they are reluctant to cross, since beyond that boundary the price would be too high or too low

COMMENT: Resistance levels on the stock exchange relate to 'sentiment'; if a share is selling at $2.95, and does not rise, it may be that investors see the price of $3.00 as a point above which they feel the share is overvalued; if the price 'breaks through' the $3.00 barrier, then it may continue to rise rapidly, as the resistance level has been broken. The same applies in reverse: if the pound/dollar exchange rate is $1.65, and the pound becomes weaker, the resistance level of $1.60, when broken, may be the sign of a further slide in the pound's value.

resolution /ˌrezəˈluːʃ(ə)n/ *noun* a decision to be reached at a meeting □ **to put a resolution to a meeting** to ask a meeting to vote on a proposal ○ *The meeting carried* or *adopted a resolution to go on strike.* ○ *The meeting rejected the resolution* or *The resolution was defeated by ten votes to twenty.* ○ *A resolution was passed to raise salaries by six per cent.*

COMMENT: There are three types or resolution which can be put to an AGM: the 'ordinary resolution', usually referring to some general procedural matter, and which requires a simple majority of votes; and the 'extraordinary resolution' and 'special resolution', such as a resolution to change a company's articles of association in some way, both of which need 75 per cent of the votes before they can be carried.

resolve /rɪˈzɒlv/ *verb* to decide to do something ○ *The meeting resolved that a dividend should not be paid.*

resources /rɪˈzɔːsɪz/ *plural noun* **1.** a supply of something **2.** the money available for doing something

restitution /ˌrestɪˈtjuːʃ(ə)n/ *noun* **1.** the act of giving back property ○ *The court ordered the restitution of assets to* *the company.* **2.** compensation or payment for damage or loss

restraint /rɪ'streɪnt/ *noun* control

restraint of trade /rɪ,streɪnt əv 'treɪd/ *noun* **1.** a situation where employees are not allowed to use their knowledge in another company on changing jobs **2.** an attempt by companies to fix prices, create monopolies, or reduce competition, which could affect free trade

restrict /rɪ'strɪkt/ *verb* to limit something or to impose controls on something ○ *to restrict credit* ○ *to restrict the flow of trade* or *to restrict imports* ○ *We are restricted to twenty staff by the size of our offices.* □ **to sell into a restricted market** to sell goods into a market where the supplier has agreed to limit sales to avoid competition

restricted market /rɪ,strɪktɪd 'mɑːkɪt/ *noun* same as **reserved market**

restriction /rɪ'strɪkʃ(ə)n/ *noun* a limit or control ○ *import restrictions* or *restrictions on imports* □ **to impose restrictions on imports** *or* **credit** to start limiting imports or credit □ **to lift credit restrictions** *or* **import restrictions** to allow credit to be given freely or imports to enter the country freely

restrictive /rɪ'strɪktɪv/ *adjective* not allowing something to go beyond a point

restrictive covenant /rɪ,strɪktɪv 'kʌvənənt/ *noun* a clause in a contract which prevents someone from doing something

restrictive endorsement /rɪ ,strɪktɪv ɪn'dɔːsmənt/ *noun* an endorsement on a bill of exchange which restricts the use which can be made of it by the person it is endorsed to

restrictive trade practices /rɪ ,strɪktɪv 'treɪd ,præktɪsɪz/, **restrictive practices** /rɪ,strɪktɪv 'præktɪsɪz/ *plural noun* **1.** an arrangement between companies to fix prices or to share the market in order to restrict trade **2.** ways of working which make people less free (such as trade unions stopping workers from doing certain jobs or companies not allowing customers a free choice of product) ○ *Restrictive practices in industry mean that employers will not be able to afford to take on more labour.*

restructure /riː'strʌktʃə/ *verb* to reorganise the financial basis of a company

restructuring /riː'strʌktʃərɪŋ/ *noun* the process of reorganising the financial basis of a company □ **the restructuring of an economy** reorganising the basic ways in which an economy is set up

result /rɪ'zʌlt/ *noun* **1.** a profit or loss account for a company at the end of a trading period ○ *The company's results for last year were an improvement on those of the previous year.* **2.** something which happens because of something else ○ *What was the result of the price investigation?* ○ *The company doubled its sales force with the result that the sales rose by 26%.* □ **the expansion programme has produced results** has produced increased sales □ **payment by results** being paid for profits or increased sales ■ *verb* **1.** □ **to result from** to happen because of ○ *We have to fill several vacancies resulting from the recent internal promotions* **2.** □ **to result in** to produce as a result ○ *The doubling of the sales force resulted in increased sales.* ○ *The extra orders resulted in overtime work for all the factory staff.*

'…the company has received the backing of a number of oil companies who are willing to pay for the results of the survey' [*Lloyd's List*]

'…some profit-taking was noted, but underlying sentiment remained firm in a steady stream of strong corporate results' [*Financial Times*]

retail /'riːteɪl/ *noun* the sale of small quantities of goods to the general public □ **the goods in stock have a retail value of £1m** the value of the goods if sold to the public is £1m, before discounts and other factors are taken into account ■ *adverb* □ **he buys wholesale and sells retail** he buys goods in bulk at a wholesale discount and sells in small quantities to the public ■ *verb* **1.** □ **to retail goods** to sell goods direct to the public **2.** to sell for a price □ **these items retail at or for £2.50** the retail price of these items is £2.50

retail bank /'riːteɪl bæŋk/ *noun* a bank which provides normal banking services for customers (in the UK, this is done by the main high street banks)

retail banking /'riːteɪl ,bæŋkɪŋ/ *noun* services provided by commercial banks to individuals as opposed to business customers, e.g. current accounts, deposit and savings accounts, as well as credit cards, mortgages and investments. Compare **wholesale banking** (NOTE: In the UK, although this service was traditionally provided by high street banks, separate organisations are now providing Internet and telephone banking services.)

retail dealer /ˈriːteɪl ˌdiːlə/ *noun* a person who sells to the general public

retail deposit /ˈriːteɪl dɪˌpɒzɪt/ *noun* a deposit placed by an individual with a bank

retailer /ˈriːteɪlə/ *noun* a person who runs a retail business, selling goods direct to the public

retailer number /ˈriːteɪlə ˌnʌmbə/ *noun* the number of the retailer, printed at the top of the report slip when depositing credit card payments

retail fund /ˈriːteɪl fʌnd/ *noun* a fund sold direct to private investors

retailing /ˈriːteɪlɪŋ/ *noun* the selling of full-price goods to the public ○ *From car retailing the company branched out into car leasing.*

retail investor /ˈriːteɪl ɪnˌvestə/ *noun* a private investor, as opposed to institutional investors

retail outlet /ˈriːteɪl ˌaʊtlet/ *noun* a shop which sells to the general public

retail price /ˈriːteɪl ˌpraɪs/ *noun* the price at which the retailer sells to the final customer

retail price index /ˌriːteɪl ˈpraɪs ˌɪndeks/, **retail prices index** /ˌriːteɪl ˈpraɪsɪz ˌɪndeks/ *noun* an index which shows how prices of consumer goods have increased or decreased over a period of time. Abbreviation **RPI** (NOTE: The US term is **Consumer Price Index**.)

> COMMENT: In the UK, the RPI is calculated on a group of essential goods and services; it includes both VAT and mortgage interest; the US equivalent is the Consumer Price Index.

retail service provider /ˌriːteɪl ˈsɜːvɪs/, **retail house** /ˈriːteɪl haʊs/ *noun* a large stockbroking company dealing directly with private retail investors. Abbreviation **RSP**

retain /rɪˈteɪn/ *verb* **1.** to keep something or someone ○ *measures to retain experienced staff* ○ *Out of the profits, the company has retained £50,000 as provi-*

sion *against bad debts.* **2.** □ **to retain a lawyer to act for a company** to agree with a lawyer that he or she will act for you (and pay him or her a fee in advance)

retained earnings /rɪˌteɪnd ˈɜːnɪŋz/ *plural noun* an amount of profit after tax which a company does not pay out as dividend to the shareholders, but which is kept to be used for the further development of the business. Also called **retentions**

retained income /rɪˌteɪnd ˈɪnkʌm/, **retained profit** /rɪˌteɪnd ˈprɒfɪt/ *noun* same as **retained earnings**

retainer /rɪˈteɪnə/ *noun* money paid in advance to someone so that they will work for you and not for someone else ○ *We pay them a retainer of £1,000.*

retention /rɪˈtenʃ(ə)n/ *noun* the act of keeping the loyalty of existing customers, as opposed to acquisition, which is the act of acquiring new customers. Both can be aims of advertising campaigns.

'…a systematic approach to human resource planning can play a significant part in reducing recruitment and retention problems' [*Personnel Management*]

retentions /rɪˈtenʃənz/ *plural noun* same as **retained earnings**

retiral /rɪˈtaɪərəl/ *noun* same as **retirement**

retire /rɪˈtaɪə/ *verb* **1.** to stop work and take a pension ○ *She retired with a £15,000 pension.* ○ *The founder of the company retired at the age of 85.* ○ *The shop is owned by a retired policeman.* **2.** to make an employee stop work and take a pension ○ *They decided to retire all staff over 50.* **3.** to come to the end of an elected term of office ○ *The treasurer retires from the council after six years.* ○ *Two retiring directors offer themselves for re-election.*

retirement /rɪˈtaɪəmənt/ *noun* **1.** the act of retiring from work ○ *I am looking forward to my retirement.* ○ *Older staff are planning what they will do in retirement.* □ **to take early retirement** to retire from work before the usual age **2.** the period when a person is retired

retirement age /rɪˈtaɪəmənt eɪdʒ/ *noun* the age at which people retire. In the UK this is usually 65 for men and 60 (but soon to become 65) for women.

retirement pension /rɪ'taɪəmənt
ˌpenʃən/ *noun* a state pension given to a
man who is over 65 or and woman who is
over 60

retrenchment /rɪ'trentʃmənt/ *noun* a
reduction of expenditure or of new plans
○ *The company is in for a period of
retrenchment.*

retroactive /ˌretrəʊ'æktɪv/ *adjective*
which takes effect from a time in the past
○ *They got a pay rise retroactive to last
January.*

'The salary increases, retroactive from
April of the current year, reflect the
marginal rise in private sector salaries'
[*Nikkei Weekly*]

retroactively /ˌretrəʊ'æktɪvli/ *adverb*
going back to a time in the past

return /rɪ'tɜːn/ *noun* **1.** a profit or
income from money invested ○ *We are
buying technology shares because they
bring in a quick return.* ○ *What is the
gross return on this line?* **2.** an official
statement or form that has to be sent in to
the authorities □ **to fill in a VAT return** to
complete the form showing VAT receipts
and expenditure ■ *verb* **1.** to send back ○
to return unsold stock to the wholesaler ○
to return a letter to sender **2.** to make a
statement ○ *to return income of £15,000
to the tax authorities*

'…with interest rates running well above
inflation, investors want something that
offers a return for their money' [*Business
Week*]

'Section 363 of the Companies Act 1985
requires companies to deliver an annual
return to the Companies Registration
Office. Failure to do so before the end of
the period of 28 days after the company's
return could lead to directors and
other officers in default being fined up to
£2000' [*Accountancy*]

return date /rɪ'tɜːn deɪt/ *noun* a date
by which a company's annual return has
to be made to the Registrar of Companies

return on assets /rɪ,tɜːn ɒn 'æsets/,
return on capital employed /rɪ,tɜːn ɒn
ˌkæpɪt(ə)l ɪm'plɔɪd/, **return on equity**
/rɪ,tɜːn ɒn 'ekwɪti/ *noun* a profit shown
as a percentage of the capital or money
invested in a business. Abbreviation
ROA, ROCE, ROE

return on investment /rɪ,tɜːn ɒn ɪn
'vestmənt/ *noun* a ratio of the profit

made in a financial year as a percentage of
an investment. Abbreviation **ROI**

returns /rɪ'tɜːnz/ *plural noun* **1.** profits
or income from investment ○ *The
company is looking for quick returns on
its investment.* **2.** unsold goods, especially
books, newspapers, or magazines, sent
back to the supplier

revaluation /riː,væljʊ'eɪʃən/ *noun* **1.**
an act of revaluing ○ *The balance sheet
takes into account the revaluation of the
company's properties.* **2.** the increasing of
the value of a currency ○ *The revaluation
of the dollar against the euro.*

revalue /riː'væljuː/ *verb* to value something again, usually setting a higher value
on it than before ○ *The company's properties have been revalued.* ○ *The dollar
has been revalued against all world
currencies.*

revenue /'revənjuː/ *noun* **1.** money
received ○ *revenue from advertising* or
advertising revenue ○ *Oil revenues have
risen with the rise in the dollar.* **2.** money
received by a government in tax

revenue account /'revənjuː ə
ˌkaʊnt/ *noun* an accounting system
which records the revenue and expenditure incurred by a company during its
usual business

revenue accounts /'revənjuː ə
ˌkaʊnts/ *plural noun* accounts of a business which record money received as
sales, commission, etc.

revenue expenditure /'revənjuː ɪk
ˌspendɪtʃə/ *noun* expenditure on
purchasing stock but not capital items,
which is then sold during the current
accounting period

revenue officer /'revənjuː ˌɒfɪsə/
noun a person working in the government
tax offices

revenue reserves /'revənjuː rɪ
ˌzɜːvz/ *plural noun* retained earnings
which are shown in the company's
balance sheet as part of the shareholders'
funds. Also called **company reserves**

reversal /rɪ'vɜːs(ə)l/ *noun* **1.** a change
from being profitable to unprofitable ○
*The company suffered a reversal in the
Far East.* **2.** a sudden change in a share
price (either a rise or a fall) ○ *In the event
of a market reversal buyers are rare.*

reverse /rɪ'vɜːs/ *adjective* opposite or
in the opposite direction ■ *verb* to change

a decision to the opposite ○ *The committee reversed its decision on import quotas.*

'…the trade balance sank $17 billion, reversing last fall's brief improvement' [*Fortune*]

reverse bid /rɪˌvɜːs ˈbɪd/ *noun* a bid made by a company which is the target of a takeover bid for the company which is trying to take it over

reverse leverage /rɪˌvɜːs ˈlevərɪdʒ/ *noun* the borrowing of money at a rate of interest higher than the expected rate of return on investing the money borrowed

reverse mortgage /rɪˌvɜːs ˈmɔːgɪdʒ/ *noun* an arrangement where the owner of a property mortgages it to receive a regular income from the mortgage lender (and not vice versa), based on the equity value of the property

reverse takeover /rɪˌvɜːs ˈteɪkəʊvə/ *noun* a takeover in which the company that has been taken over ends up owning the company which has taken it over. The acquiring company's shareholders give up their shares in exchange for shares in the target company.

reverse yield gap /rɪˌvɜːs ˈjiːld ˌgæp/ *noun* the amount by which bond yield exceeds equity yield, or interest rates on loans exceed rental values as a percentage of the costs of properties

reversing entry /rɪˈvɜːsɪŋ ˌentri/ *noun* an entry in a set of accounts which reverses an entry in the preceding accounts

reversion /rɪˈvɜːʃ(ə)n/ *noun* the return of property to its original owner □ **he has the reversion of the estate** he will receive the estate when the present lease ends

reversionary /rɪˈvɜːʃ(ə)n(ə)ri/ *adjective* referring to property which passes to another owner on the death of the present one

reversionary annuity /rɪˌvɜːʃ(ə) n(ə)ri əˈnjuːɪti/ *noun* an annuity paid to someone on the death of another person

reversionary bonus /rɪ ˌvɜːʃ(ə)n(ə)ri ˈbəʊnəs/ *noun* an annual bonus on a life assurance policy, declared by the insurer

review /rɪˈvjuː/ *noun* a general examination ○ *to conduct a review of distributors* □ **she had a salary review last April**

her salary was examined (and increased) in April ○ *The company has decided to review freelance payments in the light of the rising cost of living.* ■ *verb* to examine something generally □ **to review salaries** to look at all salaries in a company to decide on increases ○ *His salary will be reviewed at the end of the year.* □ **to review discounts** to look at discounts offered to decide whether to change them

revise /rɪˈvaɪz/ *verb* to change something which has been calculated or planned ○ *Sales forecasts are revised annually.* ○ *The chairman is revising his speech to the AGM.*

revocable /ˈrevəkəb(ə)l/ *adjective* which can be revoked

revocable trust /ˌrevəkəb(ə)l ˈtrʌst/ *noun* a trust which can be changed or revoked

revocation /ˌrevəʊˈkeɪʃ(ə)n/ *noun* an action of cancelling something which has previously been agreed ○ *the revocation of the bank's licence by the central bank*

revoke /rɪˈvəʊk/ *verb* to cancel something ○ *to revoke a decision* or *a clause in an agreement* ○ *The quota on luxury items has been revoked.*

revolving credit /rɪˌvɒlvɪŋ ˈkredɪt/ *noun* a system where someone can borrow money at any time up to an agreed amount, and continue to borrow while still paying off the original loan. Also called **open-ended credit**

revolving loan /rɪˌvɒlvɪŋ ˈləʊn/ *noun* a loan facility whereby the borrower can choose the number and timing of withdrawals against their bank loan and any money repaid may be reborrowed at a future date. Such loans are available both to businesses and personal customers.

revolving loans /rɪˈvɒlvɪŋ ləʊnz/, **revolving credit** /rɪˈvɒlvɪŋ ləʊnz/ *plural noun* also called **open-ended credit**

rial /riˈɑːl/ *noun* a unit of currency used in Iran and other Middle Eastern countries, such as Oman and North Yemen. ◊ **riyal** □ **oil-rich territory** territory which has valuable oil-deposits

-rich /rɪtʃ/ *suffix* meaning 'which contains or has a large amount of something'

rider /ˈraɪdə/ *noun* an additional clause ○ *to add a rider to a contract*

RIE *abbreviation* recognised investment exchange

riel /'riːəl/ *noun* a unit of currency used in Cambodia

rig /rɪg/ *verb* to arrange illegally or dishonestly for a result to be changed ○ *They tried to rig the election of officers.* □ **to rig the market** to make shares prices go up or down so as to make a profit

right /raɪt/ *adjective* not left ○ *The credits are on the right side of the page.* ■ *noun* a legal entitlement to something ○ *There is no automatic right of renewal to this contract.* ○ *She has a right to the property.* ○ *He has no right to the patent.* ○ *The staff have a right to know how the company is doing.*

rightful claimant /ˌraɪtf(ə)l 'kleɪmənt/ *noun* a person who has a legal claim to something (NOTE: This term has now replaced **plaintiff**. The other side in a case is the **defendant**.)

right-hand /ˌraɪt 'hænd/ *adjective* belonging to the right side ○ *The credit side is the right-hand column in the accounts.* ○ *He keeps the address list in the right-hand drawer of his desk.*

right-hand man /ˌraɪt hænd 'mæn/ *noun* a man who is the main assistant to someone

right of way /ˌraɪt əv 'weɪ/ *noun* a legal title to go across someone's property

rights issue /'raɪts ˌɪʃuː/ *noun* an arrangement which gives shareholders the right to buy more shares at a lower price (NOTE: The US term is **rights offering**.)

right to strike /ˌraɪt tə 'straɪk/ *noun* a legal right of employees to stop working if they have a good reason for it

ring /rɪŋ/ *noun* **1.** a group of people who try to fix prices so as not to compete with each other and still make a large profit **2.** a trading floor on a commodity exchange

ring fence /'rɪŋ fens/ *verb* **1.** to separate valuable assets or profitable businesses from others in a group which are unprofitable and may make the whole group collapse **2.** to identify money from certain sources and only use it in certain areas ○ *The grant has been ring-fenced for use in local authority education projects only.* ◊ **hypothecation**

ringgit /'rɪŋgɪt/ *noun* a unit of currency used in Malaysia (also called the 'Malaysian dollar')

rise /raɪz/ *noun* **1.** an increase ○ *a rise in the price of raw materials* ○ *Oil price rises brought about a recession in world trade.* ○ *There has been a rise in sales of 10%* or *Sales show a rise of 10%.* ○ *Salaries are increasing to keep up with the rises in the cost of living.* ○ *The recent rise in interest rates has made mortgages dearer.* **2.** an increase in pay ○ *She asked her boss for a rise.* ○ *He had a 6% rise in January.* (NOTE: The US term is **raise**.) ■ *verb* to move upwards or to become higher ○ *Prices* or *Salaries are rising faster than inflation.* ○ *Interest rates have risen to 15%.* ○ *Salaries are rising faster than inflation.* (NOTE: **rising – rose – risen**)

rising screen /ˌraɪzɪŋ 'skriːn/ *noun* a panel which moves upwards to protect a cashier in a bank against robbers

risk /rɪsk/ *noun* **1.** possible harm or a chance of danger □ **to run a risk** to be likely to suffer harm □ **to take a risk** to do something which may make you lose money or suffer harm **2.** □ **at owner's risk** a situation where goods shipped or stored are insured by the owner, not by the transport company or the storage company ○ *Goods left here are at owner's risk.* ○ *The shipment was sent at owner's risk.* **3.** loss or damage against which you are insured **4.** □ **he is a good** *or* **bad risk** it is not likely or it is very likely that the insurance company will have to pay out against claims where he is concerned

'…remember, risk isn't volatility. Risk is the chance that a company's earnings power will erode – either because of a change in the industry or a change in the business that will make the company significantly less profitable in the long term' [*Fortune*]

risk-adjusted /rɪsk ə'dʒʌstɪd/ *adjective* calculated after taking risk into account

risk arbitrage /'rɪsk ˌɑːbɪtrɑːʒ/ *noun* the business of buying shares in companies which are likely to be taken over and so rise in price

risk arbitrageur /'rɪsk ˌɑːbɪtrɑːʒɜː/ *noun* a person whose business is risk arbitrage

risk asset ratio /ˌrɪsk ˌæset ˈreɪʃiəʊ/ *noun* a proportion of a bank's capital which is in risk assets

risk assets /rɪsk ˈæsets/ *plural noun* assets of a bank which are in securities or bonds which may fall in value

risk-averse /ˌrɪsk əˈvɜːs/ *adjective* not wanting to take risks

risk-based /ˈrɪsk beɪst/ *adjective* calculated against a risk

risk-based capital /ˌrɪsk beɪst ˈkæpɪt(ə)l/ *noun* an internationally approved system of calculating a bank's capital value by assessing the risk attached to its assets (cash deposits and gold, for example, have no risk, while loans to Third World countries have a high risk)

risk capital /ˈrɪsk ˌkæpɪt(ə)l/ *noun* same as **venture capital**

risk-free /ˌrɪsk ˈfriː/, **riskless** /ˈrɪskləs/ *adjective* with no risk involved ○ *a risk-free investment*

'…there is no risk-free way of taking regular income from your money higher than the rate of inflation and still preserving its value' [*Guardian*]

'…many small investors have also preferred to put their spare cash with risk-free investments such as building societies rather than take chances on the stock market. The returns on a host of risk-free investments have been well into double figures' [*Money Observer*]

riskiness /ˈrɪskinəs/ *noun* the fact of being risky

risk management /ˈrɪsk ˌmænɪdʒ mənt/ *noun* the work of managing a company's exposure to risk from its credit terms or exposure to interest rate or exchange rate fluctuations

risk premium /ˈrɪsk ˌpriːmiəm/ *noun* an extra payment, e.g. increased dividend or higher than usual profits, for taking risks

risk-weighted assets /ˌrɪsk ˌweɪtɪd ˈæsets/ *plural noun* assets which include off-balance sheet items for insurance purposes

risky /ˈrɪski/ *adjective* dangerous or which may cause harm ○ *We lost all our money in some risky ventures in South America.*

'…while the bank has scaled back some of its more risky trading operations, it has retained its status as a top-rate advisory house' [*Times*]

rival /ˈraɪv(ə)l/ *noun* a person or company that competes in the same market ○ *a rival company* ○ *to undercut a rival*

riyal /riˈɑːl/ *noun* a unit of currency used in Saudi Arabia, Qatar and Yemen

ROA *abbreviation* return on assets

robber /ˈrɒbə/ *noun* a person who carries out a robbery

robbery /ˈrɒbəri/ *noun* the offence of stealing something from someone using force, or threatening to use force

robust /rəʊˈbʌst/ *adjective* strong, able to survive in difficult circumstances

robustness /rəʊˈbʌstnəs/ *noun* the fact of being strong (NOTE: The opposite is **fragility**.) □ **financial robustness** the fact of being in a strong position financially

ROCE *abbreviation* return on capital employed

rock /rɒk/ *noun* □ **the company is on the rocks** the company is in great financial difficulties

rock bottom /ˌrɒk ˈbɒtəm/ *noun* □ **sales have reached rock bottom** sales have reached the lowest point possible

'…investment companies took the view that secondhand prices had reached rock bottom and that levels could only go up' [*Lloyd's List*]

rocket /ˈrɒkɪt/ *verb* to rise fast ○ *Investors are rushing to cash in on rocketing share prices.* ○ *Prices have rocketed on the commodity markets.*

ROE *abbreviation* return on equity

ROI *abbreviation* return on investment

roll /rəʊl/ *noun* something which has been turned over and over to wrap round itself ○ *The desk calculator uses a roll of paper.* ○ *We need to order some more rolls of fax paper.* ■ *verb* **1.** to make something go forward by turning it over or pushing it on wheels ○ *They rolled the computer into position.* **2.**

roll over *phrasal verb* □ **to roll over a credit** to make credit available over a continuing period □ **to roll over a debt** to allow a debt to stand after the repayment date

'…at the IMF in Washington, officials are worried that Japanese and US banks might decline to roll over the principal of loans made in the 1980s to Southeast Asian and other developing countries' [*Far Eastern Economic Review*]

roll up /ˌrəʊl ˈʌp/ *phrasal verb* to extend a loan, by adding the interest due to be paid to the capital

rolled-up coupons /ˌrəʊld ʌp ˈkuːpɒnz/ *plural noun* interest coupons on securities, which are not paid out, but added to the capital value of the security

rolling account /ˈrəʊlɪŋ əˌkaʊnt/ *noun US* a system where there are no fixed account days, but stock exchange transactions are paid at a fixed period after each transaction has taken place, as opposed to the UK system, where an account day is fixed each month

rolling budget /ˌrəʊlɪŋ ˈbʌdʒɪt/ *noun* a budget which moves forward on a regular basis, such as a budget covering a twelve-month period which moves forward each month or quarter

rolling plan /ˌrəʊlɪŋ ˈplæn/ *noun* a plan which runs for a period of time and is updated regularly for the same period

rolling settlement /ˌrəʊlɪŋ ˈset(ə)lmənt/ *noun US* same as **rolling account**

rollover /ˈrəʊləʊvə/ *noun* an extension of credit or of the period of a loan, though not necessarily on the same terms as previously

rollover credit /ˌrəʊləʊvə ˈkredɪt/ *noun* credit in the form of a medium-term loan, covered by a series of short-term loans

rollover mortgage /ˌrəʊləʊvə ˈmɔːɡɪdʒ/ *noun* a short-term mortgage which is renegotiated with different terms every five years or so

Romalpa clause /rəʊˈmɒlpə ˌklɔːz/ *noun* a clause in a contract whereby the seller provides that title to the goods does not pass to the buyer until the buyer has paid for them

COMMENT: Called after the case of *Aluminium Industrie Vaassen BV v Romalpa Ltd.*

rotation /rəʊˈteɪʃ(ə)n/ *noun* the act of taking turns □ **to fill the post of chairman by rotation** to let each member of the group act as chairman for a period then give the post to another

member □ **two directors retire by rotation** two directors retire because they have been directors longer than any others, but can offer themselves for re-election

Roth account /ˈrɒθ əˌkaʊnt/, **Roth IRA** /ˈrɒθ ˌaɪrə/ *noun* an individual retirement account in which earnings can be withdrawn tax free at age 59½ provided that they have been invested in the account for more than five years

rouble /ˈruːb(ə)l/ *noun* a unit of currency used in Russia and Belarus (NOTE: The US spelling is **ruble**.)

rough /rʌf/ *adjective* approximate, not very accurate

rough out *phrasal verb* to make a draft or a general design of something, which may be changed later ○ *The finance director roughed out a plan of investment.*

rough calculation /ˌrʌf ˌkælkjʊˈleɪʃ(ə)n/ *noun* a way of working out a mathematical problem approximately, or the approximate result arrived at ○ *I made some rough calculations on the back of an envelope.*

rough draft /ˌrʌf ˈdrɑːft/ *noun* a plan of a document which may have changes made to it before it is complete

rough estimate /ˌrʌf ˈestɪmət/ *noun* a very approximate calculation

round *adjective* □ **in round figures** not totally accurate, but correct to the nearest 10 or 100 ■ *phrasal verb* to make a fractional figure a full figure, by increasing or decreasing it ○ *Some figures have been rounded to the nearest cent.*

round down *phrasal verb* to decrease a fractional figure to the nearest full figure

round up *phrasal verb* to increase a fractional figure to the nearest full figure ○ *to round up the figures to the nearest pound*

'…each cheque can be made out for the local equivalent of £100 rounded up to a convenient figure' [*Sunday Times*]

round-tripping /ˈraʊnd ˌtrɪpɪŋ/ *noun* **1.** the practice of borrowing at one rate of interest and lending the same money short-term at a higher rate (used to borrow on overdraft, when short-term deposit rates are higher) **2.** *US* the practice of buying securities and then selling them quickly

routing /ˈruːtɪŋ/ ◆ **check routing symbol**

royalty /ˈrɔɪəlti/ *noun* money paid to an inventor, writer, or the owner of land for the right to use their property, usually a specific percentage of sales, or a specific amount per sale ○ *The country will benefit from rising oil royalties.* ○ *He is still receiving substantial royalties from his invention.*

RPB *abbreviation* recognised professional body

RPI *abbreviation* retail price index

RPM *abbreviation* resale price maintenance

RRP *abbreviation* recommended retail price

RSP *abbreviation* retail service provider

RTGS *abbreviation* real-time gross settlement

rubber check /ˌrʌbə ˈtʃek/ *noun US* a cheque which cannot be cashed because the person writing it does not have enough money in the account to pay it (NOTE: The UK term is **bouncing cheque**.)

rubber stamp /ˌrʌbə ˈstæmp/ *noun* a stamp with rubber letters or figures on it to put the date or a note on a document ○ *He stamped the invoice with the rubber stamp 'Paid'.* ■ *verb* to agree to something without discussing it ○ *The board simply rubber stamped the agreement.*

rule /ruːl/ *noun* a statement that directs how people should behave ○ *It is a company rule that smoking is not allowed in the offices.* ○ *The rules of the organisation are explained during the induction sessions.* □ **as a rule** usually ○ *As a rule, we do not give discounts over 20%.* ■ *verb* **1.** to give an official decision ○ *The commission of inquiry ruled that the company was in breach of contract.* ○ *The judge ruled that the documents had to be deposited with the court.* **2.** to be in force or to be current ○ *prices which are ruling at the moment* ○ *The current ruling agreement is being redrafted.*

rulebook /ˈruːlbʊk/ *noun* a set of rules by which the members of a self-regulatory organisation must operate

rule of 72 /ˌruːl əv ˌsev(ə)nti ˈtuː/ *noun* a calculation that an investment will double in value at compound interest after a period shown as 72 divided by the interest percentage, so interest at 10% compound will double the capital invested in 7.2 years

ruling /ˈruːlɪŋ/ *adjective* in operation at the moment, current ○ *We will invoice at ruling prices.* ■ *noun* a decision ○ *The inquiry gave a ruling on the case.* ○ *According to the ruling of the court, the contract was illegal.*

run /rʌn/ *noun* **1.** a period of time during which a machine is working □ **a cheque run** a series of cheques processed through a computer **2.** a rush to buy something ○ *The Post Office reported a run on the new stamps.* □ **a run on the bank** a rush by customers to take deposits out of a bank which they think may close down □ **a run on the pound** a rush to sell pounds and buy other currencies ■ *verb* to manage or to organise something ○ *She runs a mail-order business from home.* ○ *They run a staff sports club.* ○ *He is running a multi-million-pound company.* (NOTE: **running – ran – run**) ■ **1.** to be in a particular state or to be taking place in a particular way ○ *The meeting was running late.* **2.** to continue or to last ○ *The lease runs for twenty years.* ○ *The lease has only six months to run.* (NOTE: **running – ran – has run**)

'…applications for mortgages are running at a high level' [*Times*]

'…with interest rates running well above inflation, investors want something that offers a return for their money' [*Business Week*]

run down *phrasal verb* **1.** to reduce a quantity gradually ○ *We decided to run down stocks* or *to let stocks run down at the end of the financial year.* **2.** to slow down the business activities of a company before it is going to be closed ○ *The company is being run down.*

run into *phrasal verb* **1.** □ **to run into debt** to start to have debts **2.** to amount to ○ *Costs have run into thousands of pounds.* □ **he has an income running into five figures** he earns more than £10,000

run out of *phrasal verb* to have nothing left of something, to use up all the stock of something ○ *We have run out of* *headed notepaper.* ○ *The printer has run out of paper.*

run up *phrasal verb* to make debts or costs go up quickly ○ *He quickly ran up a bill for £250.*

runaway inflation /ˌrʌnəweɪ ɪn ˈfleɪʃ(ə)n/ *noun* very rapid inflation, which is almost impossible to reduce

running account credit /ˌrʌnɪŋ ə ˌkaʊnt ˈkredɪt/ *noun* an overdraft facility, credit card or similar system that allows customers to borrow up to a specific limit and reborrow sums previously repaid by either writing a cheque or using their card

running costs /ˈrʌnɪŋ kɒsts/ *plural noun* same as **operating costs**

running total /ˌrʌnɪŋ ˈtəʊt(ə)l/ *noun* the total carried from one column of figures to the next

running yield /ˈrʌnɪŋ jiːld/ *noun* a yield on fixed interest securities, where the interest is shown as a percentage of the price paid

run to settlement /ˌrʌn tə ˈset(ə)l mənt/ *noun* a futures sale which runs until the actual commodity is delivered

rupee /ruːˈpiː/ *noun* a unit of currency used in India, Mauritius, Nepal, Pakistan and Sri Lanka (NOTE: Written **Rs** before the figure: *Rs. 250.*)

rupiah /ruːˈpiə/ *noun* a unit of currency used in Indonesia

Russell index /ˈrʌs(ə)l ˌɪndeks/ *noun* any of various indices published by the Russell Company in Tacoma, Washington

COMMENT: The Russell 3000 Index lists the 3000 largest companies (almost all the companies whose shares are traded in the USA); this index is subdivided into two, the Russell 1000 Index lists the 1000 largest companies in the 3000 Index, and the Russell 2000 Index lists the remainder. There are other indices.

S

SA *abbreviation* société anonyme *or* sociedad anónima

s.a.e. *abbreviation* stamped addressed envelope ○ *Send your application form to the personnel officer, with an s.a.e. for reply.*

safe /seɪf/ *noun* a heavy metal box which cannot be opened easily, in which valuable documents and money can be kept ○ *Put the documents in the safe.* ○ *We keep the petty cash in the safe.* ■ *adjective* out of danger □ **keep the documents in a safe place** in a place where they cannot be stolen or destroyed

safe deposit /seɪf dɪˌpɒzɪt/ *noun* a bank safe where you can leave jewellery or documents

safe deposit box /ˌseɪf dɪˈpɒzɪt ˌbɒks/ *noun* a small box which you can rent to keep jewellery or documents in a bank's safe

safeguard /seɪfɡɑːd/ *verb* to protect something or someone ○ *The duty of the directors is to safeguard the interests of the shareholders.* ■ *noun* something that provides protection

safe investment /ˌseɪf ɪnˈvestmənt/ *noun* something, e.g. a share, which is not likely to fall in value

safe keeping /ˌseɪf ˈkiːpɪŋ/ *noun* the fact of being looked after carefully ○ *We put the documents into the bank for safe keeping.*

safety /seɪfti/ *noun* **1.** the fact of being free from danger or risk □ **to take safety precautions** *or* **safety measures** to act to make sure something is safe **2.** □ **for safety** to make something safe, to be safe ○ *to take a copy of the disk for safety* ○ *Put the documents in the cupboard for safety.*

safety margin /ˈseɪfti ˌmɑːdʒɪn/ *noun* a time or space allowed to make sure that something can be done safely

safety regulations /ˈseɪfti ˌreɡjʊleɪʃ(ə)nz/ *plural noun* rules to make a place of work safe for the employees

SAIF *abbreviation* Savings Association Insurance Fund

salami fraud /səˈlɑːmi frɔːd/ *noun* a fraud where a very small amount of money is removed from each transaction and put into a suspense account (the amounts – 1p or 1c per transaction – are so small that no one notices them, but over a period of time they build up to large sums of money)

salaried /sælərɪd/ *adjective* earning a salary ○ *The company has 250 salaried staff.*

salaried partner /ˌsælərɪd ˈpɑːtnə/ *noun* a partner, often a junior one, who receives a regular salary in accordance with the partnership agreement

salary /sæləri/ *noun* **1.** a regular payment for work done, made to an employee usually as a cheque at the end of each month ○ *The company froze all salaries for a six-month period.* ○ *If I get promoted, my salary will go up.* ○ *The salary may be low, but the fringe benefits attached to the job are good.* ○ *She got a salary increase in June.* □ **scale of salaries** *or* **salary scale** a list of salaries showing different levels of pay in different jobs in the same company **2.** the amount paid to an employee, shown as a monthly, quarterly or yearly total (NOTE: The plural is **salaries**.)

salary cheque /ˈsæləri tʃek/ *noun* a monthly cheque by which an employee is paid

salary cut /'sæləri kʌt/ *noun* a sudden reduction in salary

salary deductions /'sæləri dɪ,dʌkʃənz/ *plural noun* money which a company removes from salaries to pay to the government as tax, National Insurance contributions, etc.

salary differentials /'sæləri dɪfə,renʃəlz/ *plural noun* same as **pay differentials**

salary drift /'sæləri drɪft/ *noun* same as **earnings drift**

salary package /'sæləri ,pækɪdʒ/ *noun* same as **pay package**

salary reduction /'sæləri rɪ,dʌkʃ(ə)n/ *noun* the act of removing money from an employee's salary to put into a pension plan

salary review /'sæləri rɪ,vjuː/ *noun* same as **pay review** ○ *She had a salary review last April* or *Her salary was reviewed last April.*

salary scale /'sæləri skeɪl/ *noun* same as **pay scale** ○ *He was appointed at the top end of the salary scale.*

salary structure /'sæləri ,strʌktʃə/ *noun* the organisation of salaries in a company with different rates of pay for different types of job

'…the union of hotel and personal service workers has demanded a new salary structure and uniform conditions of service for workers in the hotel and catering industry' [*Business Times (Lagos)*]

sale /seɪl/ *noun* **1.** an act of giving an item or doing a service in exchange for money, or for the promise that money will be paid □ **for sale** ready to be sold □ **to offer something for sale** *or* **to put something up for sale** to announce that something is ready to be sold ○ *They put the factory up for sale.* ○ *His shop is for sale.* ○ *These items are not for sale to the general public.* □ **on sale** ready to be sold in a shop ○ *These items are on sale in most chemists.* **2.** an act of selling goods at specially low prices ○ *The shop is having a sale to clear old stock.* ○ *The sale price is 50% of the usual price.*

'…the latest car sales for April show a 1.8 per cent dip from last year's total' [*Investors Chronicle*]

sale and lease-back /,seɪl ən 'liːs bæk/ *noun* the sale of an asset, usually a building, to somebody else who then leases it back to the original owner

sales /seɪlz/ *plural noun* **1.** money received for selling something ○ *Sales have risen over the first quarter.* **2.** items sold, or the number of items sold

sales analysis /'seɪlz ə,næləsɪs/ *noun* an examination of the reports of sales to see why items have or have not sold well

sales book /'seɪlz bʊk/ *noun* a record of sales

sales budget /'seɪlz ,bʌdʒɪt/ *noun* a plan of probable sales

sales chart /'seɪlz tʃɑːt/ *noun* a diagram showing how sales vary from month to month

sales curve /'seɪlz kɜːv/ *noun* a graph showing how sales increase or decrease

sales department /'seɪlz dɪ,pɑːt mənt/ *noun* the section of a company which deals with selling the company's products or services

sales executive /'seɪlz ɪg,zekjʊtɪv/ *noun* a person in a company or department in charge of sales

sales figures /'seɪlz ,fɪgəz/ *plural noun* total sales

sales force /'seɪlz fɔːs/ *noun* a group of sales staff

sales forecast /'seɪlz ,fɔːkɑːst/ *noun* an estimate of future sales

sales invoice /'seɪlz ,ɪnvɔɪs/ *noun* an invoice relating to a sale

sales journal /'seɪlz ,dʒɜːn(ə)l/ *noun* the book in which non-cash sales are recorded with details of customer, invoice, amount and date. These details are later posted to each customer's account in the sales ledger.

sales ledger /'seɪlz ,ledʒə/ *noun* a book in which sales to each customer are entered. Also called **debtors ledger**

sales ledger clerk /'seɪlz ,ledʒə ,klɑːk/ *noun* an office employee who deals with the sales ledger

salesman /'seɪlzmən/ *noun* a man who sells an organisation's products or services to customers, especially to retail shops ○ *He is the head salesman in the carpet department.* ○ *His only experience is as a used-car salesman.* ○ *Salesmen are paid a basic salary plus commission.*

sales manager /'seɪlz ˌmænɪdʒə/ noun a person in charge of a sales department

sales mix /'seɪlz mɪks/ noun the sales and profitability of a wide range of products sold by a single company

sales mix profit variance /ˌseɪlz mɪks 'prɒfɪt ˌveəriəns/ noun the differing profitability of different products within a product range

salesperson /'seɪlzˌpɜːs(ə)n/ noun a person who sells products or services to retail shops on behalf of a company (NOTE: The plural is **salespeople**.)

sales representative /'seɪlz reprɪˌzentətɪv/, **sales rep** /'seɪlz rep/ noun same as **salesperson** ○ We have six sales representatives in Europe. ○ They have vacancies for sales representatives to call on accounts in the north of the country.

sales return /'seɪlz rɪˌtɜːn/ noun a report of sales made each day or week or quarter

sales returns /'seɪlz rɪˌtɜːnz/ plural noun items sold which are returned by the purchaser

sales returns book /seɪls rɪ'tɜːnz bʊk/ noun a ledger giving details of goods returned by purchasers, including invoice number, credit notes, quantities, etc. Abbreviation **SRB**

sales revenue /'seɪlz ˌrevənjuː/ noun US the income from sales of goods or services

sales slip /'seɪlz slɪp/ noun a paper showing that an article was bought at a specific shop ○ Goods can be exchanged only on production of a sales slip.

sales target /'seɪlz ˌtɑːɡɪt/ noun the amount of sales a sales representative is expected to achieve

sales tax /'seɪlz tæks/ noun US same as **VAT**

sales value /'seɪlz ˌvæljuː/ noun the amount of money which would be received if something is sold

sales volume /'seɪlz ˌvɒljuːm/ noun the number of units sold (NOTE: The UK term is **turnover**.)

sales volume profit variance /ˌseɪlz ˌvɒljuːm 'prɒfɪt ˌveəriəns/ noun the difference between the profit on the

number of units actually sold and the forecast figure

saleswoman /'seɪlzwʊmən/ noun a woman who sells an organisation's products or services to customers

salvage /'sælvɪdʒ/ noun **1.** the work of saving a ship or a cargo from being destroyed **2.** goods saved from a wrecked ship, from a fire or from some other accident ○ a sale of flood salvage items (NOTE: no plural) ■ verb **1.** to save goods or a ship from being destroyed ○ We are selling off a warehouse full of salvaged goods. **2.** to save something from loss ○ The company is trying to salvage its reputation after the managing director was sent to prison for fraud. ○ The receiver managed to salvage something from the collapse of the company.

salvage money /'sælvɪdʒ ˌmʌni/ noun payment made by the owner of a ship or a cargo to the person who has saved it

salvage vessel /'sælvɪdʒ ˌves(ə)l/ noun a ship which specialises in saving other ships and their cargoes

same /seɪm/ adjective being or looking exactly alike

'…previously, only orders received by 11 a.m. via the Internet could be delivered the same day, and then only for a limited range of items. With fast packaging and inspection, same-day delivery is now possible anywhere in Tokyo' [Nikkei Weekly]

same-day funds /ˌseɪm deɪ 'fʌndz/ plural noun money which can be withdrawn from an account the same day as it is deposited

same-store sales /ˌseɪm stɔː 'seɪlz/ noun sales for the same stores over an earlier period

'…it led the nation's department stores over the crucial Christmas season with an 11.7% increase in same-store sales' [Fortune]

'…its consistent double-digit same-store sales growth also proves that it is not just adding revenue by adding new locations' [Fortune]

sample /'sɑːmpəl/ noun **1.** a small part of an item which is used to show what the whole item is like ○ Can you provide us with a sample of the cloth or a cloth sample? **2.** a small group which is studied in order to show what a larger group is like ○ *We interviewed a sample of potential customers.* ■ *verb* **1.** to test or to try something by taking a small amount of it ○ *to sample a product before buying it* **2.** to ask a representative group of people questions to find out what the reactions of a much larger group would be ○ *They sampled 2,000 people at random to test the new drink.*

sampling /ˈsɑːmplɪŋ/ *noun* **1.** the testing of a product by taking a small amount ○ *a sampling of European Union produce* **2.** the testing of the reactions of a small group of people to find out the reactions of a larger group of consumers

samurai bond /ˈsæmʊraɪ bɒnd/ *noun* an international bond in yen launched on the Japanese market by a non-Japanese corporation. Compare **bulldog bond, shogun bond, Yankee bond**

S&L *abbreviation* savings and loan

S&P *abbreviation* Standard and Poor's

SARL *abbreviation* société anonyme à responsabilité limitée

save /seɪv/ *verb* to choose not to spend money ○ *He is trying to save money by walking to work.* ○ *She is saving to buy a house.*

> **save up** *phrasal verb* to put money aside for a special purpose ○ *They are saving up for a holiday in the US*

save-as-you-earn /ˌseɪv əz juː ˈɜːn/ *noun* a savings-related scheme set up by an employer that gives employees a right to buy a certain number of shares in the company at a fixed price at a particular time. Abbreviation **SAYE**

saver /ˈseɪvə/ *noun* a person who saves money

savings /ˈseɪvɪŋz/ *plural noun* money saved (i.e. money which is not spent) ○ *She put all her savings into a deposit account.*

savings account /ˈseɪvɪŋz əˌkaʊnt/ *noun* an account where you put money in regularly and which pays interest, often at a higher rate than a deposit account

savings and loan /ˌseɪvɪŋz ən ˈləʊn/, **savings and loan association** /ˌseɪvɪŋz ən ˈləʊn əˌsəʊsieɪʃ(ə)n/ *noun US* same as **building society**

COMMENT: Because of deregulation of interest rates in 1980, many S&Ls found that they were forced to raise interest on

deposits to current market rates in order to secure funds, while at the same time they still were charging low fixed-interest rates on the mortgages granted to borrowers. This created considerable problems and many S&Ls had to be rescued by the Federal government.

Savings Association Insurance Fund /ˌseɪvɪŋz əˌsəʊsieɪʃ(ə)n ɪnˈʃʊərəns fʌnd/ *noun* an insurance fund set up in 1989 to provide insurance to savings and loan associations. Abbreviation **SAIF**

savings bank /ˈseɪvɪŋz bæŋk/ *noun* a bank where you can deposit money and receive interest on it

savings bond /ˈseɪvɪŋz bɒnd/ *noun* in the USA, a document showing that money has been invested in a government savings scheme. Interest on US savings bonds is tax exempt. (NOTE: The UK term is **savings certificate**.)

savings certificate /ˈseɪvɪŋz səˌtɪfɪkət/ *noun* a document showing that you have invested money in a government savings scheme

savings income /ˈseɪvɪŋz ˌɪnkʌm/ *noun* income in the form of interest on deposits with banks and building societies, government bonds, etc., but not income from dividends or rental income from property

savings-related share option scheme /ˌseɪvɪŋz rɪˌleɪtɪd ˈʃeər ˌɒpʃən ˌskiːm/ *noun* a scheme which allows employees of a company to buy shares with money which they have contributed to a savings scheme

SAYE *abbreviation* save-as-you-earn

SBA *abbreviation* Small Business Administration

SBF *abbreviation* Société des Bourses Françaises

scale /skeɪl/ *noun* **1.** a system which is graded into various levels □ **scale of charges** *or* **scale of prices** a list showing various prices □ **scale of salaries** a list of salaries showing different levels of pay in different jobs in the same company **2.** □ **to start in business on a small scale** to start in business with a small staff, few products or little capital

> **scale down** *phrasal verb* to lower something in proportion

COMMENT: If a share issue is oversubscribed, applications may be scaled down;

by doing this, the small investor is protected. So, in a typical case, all applications for 1,000 shares may receive 300; all applications for 2,000 shares may receive 500; applications for 5,000 shares receive 1,000, and applications for more than 5,000 shares will go into a ballot.

scale up *phrasal verb* to increase something in proportion

scalp /skælp/ *verb US* to buy or sell to make a quick profit

scalper /'skælpə/ *noun* **1.** *US* a person who buys and sells something to make a large rapid profit (e.g. by buying and reselling tickets for a popular sporting event) **2.** a trader who buys and sells the same futures on the same day

scam /skæm/ *noun* a fraud, an illegal or dishonest scheme (*informal*) ○ *Many financial scams only come to light by accident.*

scarce currency /ˌskeəs 'kʌrənsi/ *noun* same as **hard currency**

scarcity value /'skeəsɪti ˌvæljuː/ *noun* the value something has because it is rare and there is a large demand for it

scatter diagram /'skætə ˌdaɪəgræm/ *noun* a chart where points are plotted according to two sets of variables to see if a pattern exists

scenario /sɪ'nɑːriəʊ/ *noun* the way in which a situation may develop, or a description or forecast of possible future developments

'...on the upside scenario, the outlook is reasonably optimistic, bankers say, the worst scenario being that a scheme of arrangement cannot be achieved, resulting in liquidation' [*Irish Times*]

schedule /'ʃedjuːl/ *noun* **1.** a timetable, a plan of how time should be spent, drawn up in advance ○ *The managing director has a busy schedule of appointments.* ○ *Her assistant tried to fit us into her schedule.* □ **on schedule** at the time or stage set down in the schedule ○ *The launch took place on schedule.* □ **to be ahead of schedule** to be early ○ *The building was completed ahead of schedule.* □ **to be on schedule** to be on time ○ *The project is on schedule.* ○ *We are on schedule to complete the project at the end of May.* □ **to be behind schedule** to be late ○ *I am sorry to say that we are three months behind schedule.* **2.** a list, especially a list forming an additional

document attached to a contract ○ *the schedule of territories to which a contract applies* ○ *Please find enclosed our schedule of charges.* ○ *See the attached schedule* or *as per the attached schedule.* **3.** a list of interest rates **4.** a form relating to a particular kind of income liable for UK income tax

Schedule A /ˌʃedjuːl 'eɪ/ *noun* a schedule under which tax is charged on income from land or buildings

Schedule B /ˌʃedjuːl 'biː/ *noun* a schedule under which tax was formerly charged on income from woodlands

Schedule C /ˌʃedjuːl 'siː/ *noun* a schedule under which tax is charged on profits from government stock

scheduled /'ʃedʒuːld/ *adjective* listed in a separate schedule

Schedule D /ˌʃedjuːl 'diː/ *noun* a schedule under which tax is charged on income from trades or professions, interest and other earnings not derived from being employed

Schedule E /ˌʃedjuːl 'iː/ *noun* a schedule under which tax is charged on income from salaries, wages or pensions

Schedule F /ˌʃedjuːl 'ef/ *noun* a schedule under which tax is charged on income from dividends

scheme /skiːm/ *noun* a plan, arrangement or way of working ○ *Under the bonus scheme all employees get 10% of their annual pay as a Christmas bonus.* ○ *She has joined the company pension scheme.* ○ *We operate a profit-sharing scheme for managers.* ○ *The new payment scheme is based on reward for individual effort.*

scheme of arrangement /ˌskiːm əv ə'reɪndʒmənt/ *noun* a scheme drawn up by an individual or company to offer ways of paying debts, so as to avoid bankruptcy proceedings. Also called **voluntary arrangement**

schilling /'ʃɪlɪŋ/ *noun* a unit of currency used before the euro in Austria

scorched earth policy /ˌskɔːtʃt 'ɜːθ ˌpɒlɪsi/ *noun* a way of combating a take-over bid, where the target company sells valuable assets or purchases unattractive assets. ◊ **poison pill**

scrap /skræp/ *noun* **1.** material left over after an industrial process, and which still has some value, as opposed to waste, which has no value ○ *to sell a ship for scrap* **2.** pieces of metal to be melted down to make new metal ingots

scrap value /'skræp ˌvæljuː/ *noun* the value of an asset if sold for scrap ○ *Its scrap value is £2,500.*

screen /skriːn/ *noun* **1.** a glass surface on which computer information or TV pictures can be shown ○ *She brought up the information on the screen.* ○ *I'll just call up details of your account on the screen.* **2.** a flat panel which acts as a form of protection ■ *verb* **1.** to examine something carefully to evaluate or assess it **2.** to consider a range of items or people and only select some □ **to screen out** to consider things and remove some

screening /'skriːnɪŋ/ *noun* the act of evaluating or assessing new product ideas ○ *Representatives from each department concerned will take part in the screening process.* ○ *Screening showed the product idea to be unrealistic for our production capacity.*

screen trading /'skriːn ˌtreɪdɪŋ/ *noun* trading using a monitor, as opposed to the old open outcry system

scrip /skrɪp/ *noun* a security, e.g. a share, bond, or the certificate issued to show that someone has been allotted a share or bond

'…under the rule, brokers who fail to deliver stock within four days of a transaction are to be fined 1% of the transaction value for each day of missing scrip' [*Far Eastern Economic Review*]

scrip issue /'skrɪp ˌɪʃuː/ *noun* same as **bonus issue**

scripophily /skrɪ'pɒfɪli/ *noun* the practice of collecting old share certificates and bond certificates as a hobby and investment

SDB *abbreviation* sales day book

Sdn *abbreviation* Sendirian

Sdn berhad *abbreviation* Sendirian berhad (NOTE: This is a Malay term for a private limited company.)

SDRs *abbreviation* special drawing rights

sea freight /'siː freɪt/ *noun* the transportation of goods in ships, or goods sent by sea

seal /siːl/ *noun* **1.** a special symbol, often one stamped on a piece of wax,

which is used to show that a document is officially approved by the organisation that uses the symbol □ **contract under seal** a contract which has been legally approved with the seal of the company **2.** a piece of paper, metal, or wax attached to close something, so that it can be opened only if the paper, metal, or wax is removed or broken ■ *verb* **1.** to close something tightly ○ *The computer disks were sent in a sealed container.* **2.** to attach a seal, to stamp something with a seal ○ *Customs sealed the shipment.*

SEAQ *noun* a computerised information system giving details of current share prices and stock market transactions on the London Stock Exchange. Dealers list their offer and bid prices on SEAQ, and transactions are carried out on the basis of the information shown on the screen and are also recorded on the SEAQ database in case of future disputes. Full form **Stock Exchange Automated Quotations system**

search /sɜːtʃ/ *noun* an examination of records by the lawyer acting for someone who wants to buy a property, to make sure that the vendor has the right to sell it

season /'siːz(ə)n/ *noun* a period of time when some activity usually takes place ○ *the selling season*

seasonal /'siːz(ə)n(ə)l/ *adjective* which lasts for a season or which only happens during a particular season ○ *seasonal variations in sales patterns* ○ *The demand for this item is very seasonal.*

seasonal demand /ˌsiːz(ə)n(ə)l dɪ'maːnd/ *noun* a demand which exists only during the high season

seasonal unemployment /ˌsiːz(ə)nəl ˌʌnɪm'plɔɪmənt/ *noun* unemployment which rises and falls according to the season

seasoned /'siːz(ə)nd/ *adjective US* referring to securities which are reputable or a loan which is safe for the long term

seat /siːt/ *noun* membership of a stock exchange

SEC *abbreviation* Securities and Exchange Commission

second /'sekənd/ *noun, adjective* the thing which comes after the first ■ *verb* **1.** □ **to second a motion** to be the first person to support a proposal put forward by someone else ○ *Mrs Smith seconded* *the motion* or *The motion was seconded by Mrs Smith.* **2.** /sɪˈkɒnd/ to lend a member of staff to another company, organisation or department for a fixed period of time ○ *He was seconded to the Department of Trade for two years.*

secondary /ˈsekənd(ə)ri/ *adjective* second in importance

secondary auditor /ˌsekənd(ə)ri ˈɔːdɪtə/ *noun* an auditor for a subsidiary company who has no connection with the primary auditor who audits the accounts of the main company

secondary bank /ˌsekənd(ə)ri ˈbæŋks/ *noun* a finance company which provides money for hire-purchase deals

secondary industry /ˈsekənd(ə)ri ˌɪndəstri/ *noun* an industry which uses basic raw materials to produce manufactured goods

secondary market /ˈsekənd(ə)ri ˌmɑːkɪt/ *noun* a market where existing securities are bought and sold again and again, as opposed to a primary market, where new issues are launched

secondary mortgage market /ˌsekənd(ə)ri ˈmɔːgɪdʒ ˌmɑːkɪt/ *noun* US a nationwide system organised by various federal mortgage associations for polling mortgages and selling them to investors

secondary products /ˈsekənd(ə)ri ˌprɒdʌkts/ *plural noun* products which have been processed from raw materials (as opposed to primary products)

secondary properties /ˌsekənd(ə)ri ˈprɒpətiz/ *plural noun* commercial properties which are not in prime sites and therefore are not as valuable

secondary sites /ˈsekənd(ə)ri saɪts/ *plural noun* less valuable commercial sites. Compare **prime sites**

second earner /ˌsekənd ˈɜːnə/ *noun* a second person in a household, usually a spouse, who also earns a salary

seconder /ˈsekəndə/ *noun* a person who seconds a proposal ○ *There was no seconder for the motion so it was not put to the vote.*

second half /ˌsekənd ˈhɑːf/ *noun* the period of six months from 1st July to 31st December ○ *The figures for the second half are up on those for the first part of the year.*

second half-year /ˌsekənd ˈhɑːf jɪə/ *noun* the six-month period from July to the end of December

secondment /sɪˈkɒndmənt/ *noun* the fact or period of being seconded to another job for a period ○ *She is on three years' secondment to an Australian college.*

second mortgage /ˌsekənd ˈmɔːgɪdʒ/ *noun* a further mortgage on a property which is already mortgaged

second quarter /ˌsekənd ˈkwɔːtə/ *noun* the period of three months from April to the end of June

second-ranker /ˌsekənd ˈræŋkə/ *noun* a company which occupies the second rank, i.e. not one of the top companies

second round /ˌsekənd ˈraʊnd/ *noun* a new tranche of venture capital raised for a new project after the start-up finance

second-tier /ˌsekənd ˈtɪə/ *adjective* not in the first and most important group

second-tier bank /ˌsekənd tɪə ˈbæŋk/ *noun* a bank which is not as large as the main banks in a country

second-tier market /ˌsekənd tɪə ˈmɑːkɪt/ *noun* a secondary market, such as the AIM, where securities which are not listed on the main stock exchange can be traded

secret /ˈsiːkrət/ *adjective* being deliberately kept hidden from people, or which is not known about by many people ○ *The MD kept the contract secret from the rest of the board.* ○ *The management signed a secret deal with a foreign supplier.* ■ *noun* something which is kept hidden or which is not known about by many people ○ *to keep a secret*

secretariat /ˌsekrɪˈteəriət/ *noun* an important office and the officials who work in it ○ *the United Nations secretariat*

'…a debate has been going on over the establishment of a general secretariat for the G7. Proponents argue that this would give the G7 a sense of direction and continuity' [*Times*]

secretary /ˈsekrət(ə)ri/ *noun* **1.** an official of a company or society whose job is to keep records and write letters **2.** a member of the government in charge of a department ○ *the Trade Secretary* ○ *the*

Foreign Secretary ○ *the Education Secretary*

Secretary of State /ˌsekrət(ə)ri əv ˈsteɪt/ *noun* **1.** a member of the government in charge of a department ○ *the Secretary of State for Trade and Industry* **2.** *US* the US government official and cabinet member who is in charge of foreign affairs (NOTE: The UK term is **Foreign Secretary**.)

Secretary of the Treasury /ˌsekrət(ə)ri əv ðə ˈtreʒəri/ *noun US* a senior member of the government in charge of financial affairs

secret ballot /ˌsiːkrət ˈbælət/ *noun* an election where the voters vote in secret

secret reserves /ˌsiːkrət rɪˈzɜːvz/ *plural noun* reserves which are illegally kept hidden in a company's balance sheet, as opposed to 'hidden reserves' which are simply not easy to identify

section /ˈsekʃən/ *noun* **1.** a part of something ○ *You should read the last section of the report – it is very interesting.* **2.** one of the parts of an Act of Parliament

sector /ˈsektə/ *noun* **1.** a part of the economy or the business organisation of a country ○ *All sectors of the economy suffered from the fall in the exchange rate.* ○ *Technology is a booming sector of the economy.* **2.** a section of a stock market, listing shares in one type of industry such as the banking sector

'…government services form a large part of the tertiary or service sector' [*Sydney Morning Herald*]

'…in the dry cargo sector, a total of 956 dry cargo vessels are laid up – 3% of world dry cargo tonnage' [*Lloyd's List*]

sector fund /ˈsektə fʌnd/ *noun* a fund which is invested in only one sector of the stock market

secure /sɪˈkjʊə/ *adjective* safe, which cannot change □ **secure job** a job from which you are not likely to be made redundant □ **secure investment** an investment where you are not likely to lose money ■ *verb* **1.** □ **to secure a loan** to pledge an asset as a security for a loan **2.** to get something safely into your control ○ *He is visiting several banks in an attempts to secure funds for his project.* ○ *He secured the backing of an Australian group.*

secured /sɪˈkjʊəd/ *adjective* used to describe a type of borrowing such as a mortgage where the lender has a legal right to take over an asset or assets of the borrower, if the borrower does not repay the loan

secured creditor /sɪˌkjʊəd ˈkredɪtə/ *noun* a person who is owed money by someone, and can legally claim the same amount of the borrower's property if the borrower fails to pay back the money owed

secured debt /sɪˌkjʊəd ˈdet/ *noun* a debt which is guaranteed by assets which have been pledged

secured liability /sɪˌkjʊəd ˌlaɪəˈbɪlɪti/ *noun* a loan secured by means of a pledge of assets that can be sold if necessary

secured loan /sɪˌkjʊəd ˈləʊn/ *noun* a loan which is guaranteed by the borrower giving assets as security

secure server /sɪˌkjʊə ˈsɜːvə/ *noun* a combination of hardware and software that makes e-commerce credit card transactions safe by stopping unauthorised people from gaining access to credit card details online

secure sockets layer /sɪˌkjʊə ˈsɒkɪts ˌleɪə/ *noun* full form of **SSL**

secure website /sɪˌkjʊə ˈwebsaɪt/ *noun* a website on the Internet that encrypts the messages between the visitor and the site to ensure that no hacker or eavesdropper can intercept the information

securities /sɪˈkjʊərɪtiz/ *plural noun* **1.** investments in stocks and shares **2.** certificates to show that someone owns stocks and shares

securities account /sɪˌkjʊərɪtiz əˈkaʊnt/ *noun* an account that shows the value of financial assets held by a person or organisation

Securities and Exchange Commission /sɪˌkjʊərɪtiz ən ɪks ˈtʃeɪndʒ kəˌmɪʃ(ə)n/ *noun* the official body which regulates the securities markets in the US. Abbreviation **SEC**

Securities and Futures Authority /sɪˌkjʊərɪtiz ən ˈfjuːtʃəz ɔːˌθɒrəti/ *noun* in the UK, a self-regulatory organisation which supervises the trading in shares and futures, now part of the FSA. Abbreviation **SFA**

Securities and Investments Board /sɪˌkjʊərɪtiz ənd ɪnˈvestmənts ˌbɔːd/ *noun* the former regulatory body which regulated the securities markets in the UK, now superseded by the FSA. Abbreviation **SIB**

securities broker /sɪˈkjʊərɪtiz ˌbrəʊkə/ *noun* same as **securities trader**

securities house /sɪˈkjʊərɪtiz haʊz/ *noun* a firm which buys and sells securities for clients

securities market /sɪˈkjʊərɪtiz ˌmɑːkɪt/ *noun* a stock exchange, a place where stocks and shares can be bought or sold

securities trader /sɪˈkjʊərɪtiz ˌtreɪdə/ *noun* a person whose business is buying and selling stocks and shares

securitisation /sɪˌkjʊərɪtaɪˈzeɪʃ(ə)n/, **securitization** *noun* the process of making a loan or mortgage into a tradeable security by issuing a bill of exchange or other negotiable paper in place of it

securitise /sɪˈkjʊərətaɪz/, **securitize** *verb* to make a loan into a security which can be traded (e.g. by issuing an IOU for a loan)

security /sɪˈkjʊərɪti/ *noun* **1.** the fact of being protected against attack □ **office security** the act of protecting an office against theft **2.** the fact of being kept secret □ **security in this office is nil** nothing can be kept secret in this office **3.** a guarantee that someone will repay money borrowed ○ *to give something as security for a debt* ○ *to use a house as security for a loan* ○ *The bank lent him £20,000 without security.* □ **to stand security for someone** to guarantee that if the person does not repay a loan, you will repay it for him **4.** a stock or share

security of employment /sɪˌkjʊərɪti əv ɪmˈplɔɪmənt/ *noun* a feeling by an employee that he or she will be able to stay in the same job until retirement

security of tenure /sɪˌkjʊərɪti əv ˈtenjə/ *noun* a right to keep a job or rented accommodation provided conditions are met

security printer /sɪˈkjʊərɪti ˌprɪntə/ *noun* a printer who prints material that has to be kept secure, such as paper money, share prospectuses or secret government documents

seedcorn /ˈsiːdkɔːn/, **seed money** /ˈsiːd ˌmʌni/ *noun* venture capital invested when a new project is starting up (and therefore more risky than secondary finance or mezzanine finance) ○ *They had their ranch house to operate out of, a used printer and seed money from friends.*

segment /ˈsegmənt/ *noun* a section of a market defined by certain criteria ■ *verb* /segˈment/ to divide a potential market into different segments

segmentation /ˌsegmənˈteɪʃ(ə)n/ *noun* the division of the market or consumers into categories according to their buying habits

selected personal information /sɪˌlektɪd ˌpɜːs(ə)nəl ɪnfəˈmeɪʃ(ə)n/ *noun* information, such as the post code of your home or the maiden name of your mother, used for identification purposes

self- /self/ *prefix* referring to yourself

self-employed /ˌself ɪmˈplɔɪd/ *adjective* working for yourself or not on the payroll of a company ○ *a self-employed engineer* ○ *He worked for a bank for ten years but is now self-employed.* ■ *plural noun* □ **the self-employed** people who work for themselves (*can be followed by a verb in the plural*)

self-financed /ˌself faɪˈnænst/ *adjective* □ **the project is completely self-financed** the project pays its development costs out of its own revenue, with no subsidies

self-financing /ˌself faɪˈnænsɪŋ/ *noun* the process in which a company finances a project or business activity from its own resources, rather than by applying for external finance ■ *adjective* □ **the company is completely self-financing** the company finances its development costs, capital assets, etc. from its own resources

self-insurance /ˌself ɪnˈʃʊərəns/ *noun* insuring against a probable future loss by putting money aside regularly, rather than by taking out an insurance policy

self-made man /ˌself meɪd ˈmæn/ *noun* a man who is rich and successful because of his own work, not because he inherited money or position

self-regulating organisation /self
ˌreɡjuleɪtɪŋ ˌɔːɡənaɪˈzeɪʃ(ə)n/ *noun*
same as **self-regulatory organisation**

self-regulation /ˌself ˌreɡjʊˈleɪʃ(ə)n/
noun the regulation of an industry by its
own members, usually by means of a
committee that issues guidance and sets
standards that it then enforces (NOTE: For
example, the stock exchange is regulated by the Stock Exchange Council.)

self-regulatory /ˌself ˌreɡjʊˈleɪt(ə)ri/
adjective referring to an organisation
which regulates itself

self-regulatory organisation /ˌself
ˌreɡjʊlət(ə)ri ˌɔːɡənaɪˈzeɪʃ(ə)n/ *noun*
an organisation, such as the Securities and
Futures Authority, which regulates the
way in which its own members carry on
their business. Abbreviation **SRO**

self-select PEP /self sɪˈlekt/ *noun* ▶
Personal Equity Plan

self-service banking /self ˌsɜːvɪs
ˈbæŋkɪŋ/ *noun* a situation where a bank's
customers arrange transactions by themselves, without involving bank staff, e.g.
by using ATMs for cash withdrawals

self-supporting /ˌself səˈpɔːtɪŋ/
adjective which finances itself from its
own resources, with no subsidies

sell *verb* **1.** to exchange something for
money ○ *to sell something on credit* ○
*The shop sells washing machines and
refrigerators.* ○ *They tried to sell their
house for £100,000.* ○ *Their products are
easy to sell.* **2.** to be bought ○ *These items
sell well in the pre-Christmas period.* ○
Those packs sell for £25 a dozen. (NOTE:
selling – sold)

  sell forward *phrasal verb* to sell
foreign currency, commodities, etc. for
delivery at a later date

  sell off *phrasal verb* to sell goods
quickly to get rid of them

  sell out *phrasal verb* to sell your business ○ *They sold out and retired to the
seaside.*

  sell up *phrasal verb* to sell a business
and all the stock ○ *He sold up and
bought a farm.*

seller /ˈselə/ *noun* a person who sells ○
*There were few sellers in the market, so
prices remained high.*

seller's market /ˌseləz ˈmɑːkɪt/ *noun*
a market where the seller can ask high

prices because there is a large demand for
the product. Opposite **buyer's market**

selling costs /ˈselɪŋ kɒsts/, **selling
overhead** /ˈselɪŋ ˌəʊvəhed/ *plural noun*
the amount of money to be paid for the
advertising, reps' commissions, and other
expenses involved in selling something

selling price /ˈselɪŋ praɪs/ *noun* the
price at which someone is willing to sell
something

selling price variance /ˈselɪŋ praɪs
ˌveəriəns/ *noun* the difference between
the actual selling price and the budgeted
selling price

sellout /ˈselaʊt/ *noun* □ **this item has
been a sellout** all the stock of the item has
been sold

semi- /semi/ *prefix* half or part

semiannual /ˌsemiˈænjuəl/ *adjective*
referring to interest paid every six months

semi-fixed cost /ˌsemi fɪkst ˈkɒst/
noun same as **semi-variable cost**

semi-variable cost /ˌsemi
ˌveəriəb(ə)l ˈkɒst/ *noun* the amount of
money paid to produce a product, which
increases, though less than proportionally, with the quantity of the product
made ○ *Stepping up production will mean
an increase in semi-variable costs.* Also
called **semi-fixed cost**

Sendirian /ˌsenˈdɪriən/ *noun* a Malay
term meaning 'limited'

Sendirian berhad *noun* a Malay term
meaning 'private limited company'

senior /ˈsiːniə/ *adjective* **1.** referring to
an employee who is more important **2.**
referring to an employee who is older or
who has been employed longer than
another **3.** referring to a sum which is
repayable before others

senior capital /ˌsiːniə ˈkæpɪt(ə)l/
noun capital in the form of secured loans
to a company. It is repaid before junior
capital, such as shareholders' equity, in
the event of liquidation.

senior debt /ˌsiːniə ˈdet/ *noun* a debt
which must be repaid in preference to
other debts (such as a first mortgage over
a second mortgage)

seniority /ˌsiːniˈɒrɪti/ *noun* **1.** the fact
of being more important ○ *in order of
seniority* **2.** the fact of being older or
having been an employee of the company
longer

senior manager /ˌsiːniə ˈmænɪdʒə/, **senior executive** /ˌsiːniər ɪɡˈzekjʊtɪv/ *noun* a manager or director who has a higher rank than others

senior partner /ˌsiːniə ˈpɑːtnə/ *noun* the most important partner in a firm of solicitors or accountants

sensitive /ˈsensɪtɪv/ *adjective* quick to respond to something ○ *The market is very sensitive to the result of the elections.* ◊ **price-sensitive**

sensitivity analysis /ˌsensəˈtɪvəti əˌnæləsɪs/ *noun* the analysis of the effect of a small change in a calculation on the final result

separable /ˈsep(ə)rəb(ə)l/ *adjective* possible to separate

separable net assets /ˌsep(ə)rəb(ə)l net ˈæsets/ *plural noun* assets which can be separated from the rest of the assets of a business and sold off

separate /ˈsep(ə)rət/ *adjective* not connected with something

separate estate /ˌsep(ə)rət ɪˈsteɪt/ *noun* the property of one of the partners in a partnership, as opposed to the property belonging to the partnership itself

separation /ˌsepəˈreɪʃ(ə)n/ *noun US* the act of leaving a job (resigning, retiring or being fired or made redundant) ○ *The interviewer asked the candidate whether the separation mentioned in his CV was due to resignation, redundancy or dismissal.* ○ *The exit interviews attempted to find out what employees really felt about separation.*

sequester /sɪˈkwestə/, **sequestrate** /ˈsiːkwɪstreɪt, sɪˈkwestreɪt/ *verb* to take and keep a bank account or property because a court has ordered it ○ *The union's funds have been sequestrated.*

sequestration /ˌsiːkweˈstreɪʃ(ə)n/ *noun* the act of taking and keeping property on the order of a court, especially of seizing property from someone who is in contempt of court

sequestrator /ˈsiːkwɪstreɪtə, sɪˈkwestreɪtə/ *noun* a person who takes and keeps property on the order of a court

series /ˈsɪəriːz/ *noun* a group of bonds or savings certificates, issued over a period of time but all bearing the same interest

Serious Fraud Office /ˌsɪəriəs ˈfrɔːd ˌɒfɪs/ *noun* a British government department in charge of investigating major fraud in companies. Abbreviation **SFO**

serve /sɜːv/ *verb* □ **to serve someone with a writ** *or* **to serve a writ on someone** to give someone a writ officially, so that they have to receive it

service /ˈsɜːvɪs/ *noun* **1.** a piece of work done to help someone as a duty or a favour ○ *After a lifetime's service to the company he was rewarded with a generous golden handshake.* **2.** a form of business (e.g. insurance, banking, or transport) that provides help in some form when it is needed, as opposed to making or selling goods **3.** the fact of working for an employer, or the period of time during which an employee has worked for an employer ○ *retiring after twenty years service to the company* ○ *The amount of your pension depends partly on the number of your years of service.* **4.** the work of dealing with customers ○ *The service in that restaurant is extremely slow* **5.** payment for help given to the customer ○ *to add on 10% for service* □ **the bill includes service** the bill includes a charge added for the work involved ○ *The service in that restaurant is extremely slow.* ■ *verb* □ **to service a debt** to pay interest on a debt ○ *The company is having problems in servicing its debts.*

service bureau /ˈsɜːvɪs ˌbjʊərəʊ/ *noun* an office which specialises in helping other offices

service charge /ˈsɜːvɪs tʃɑːdʒ/ *noun* **1.** a charge added to the bill in a restaurant to pay for service **2.** an amount paid by tenants in a block of flats or offices for general maintenance, insurance and cleaning **3.** a charge which a bank or business makes for carrying out work for a customer (NOTE: The UK term is **bank charge**.)

service contract /ˈsɜːvɪs ˌkɒntrækt/ *noun* a contract between a company and a director showing all conditions of work ○ *She worked unofficially with no service contract.*

service cost centre /ˌsɜːvɪs ˈkɒst ˌsentə/, **service centre** /ˈsɜːvɪs ˌsentə/ *noun* a section of a company considered as a cost centre, which provides a service to other parts of the company

service department /ˈsɜːvɪs dɪ
ˌpɑːtmənt/ *noun* **1.** the section of a
company which keeps customers'
machines in good working order **2.** a
department of a company which does not
deal with production or sales, e.g.
accounts or human resources

service industry /ˈsɜːvɪs ˌɪndəstri/
noun an industry which does not produce
raw materials or manufacture products
but offers a service such as banking,
retailing or accountancy

services /ˈsɜːvɪsɪz/ *plural noun* benefits which are sold to customers or clients,
e.g. transport or education ○ *We give
advice to companies on the marketing of
services.* ○ *We must improve the exports
of both goods and services.*

service sector /ˈsɜːvɪs ˌsektə/ *noun*
the part of an economy that consists of
service industries

session /ˈseʃ(ə)n/ *noun* a period of
time spent on a specific activity, especially as part of a larger event ○ *The
morning session* or *the afternoon session
will be held in the conference room.*

'…statistics from the stock exchange
show that customer interest in the equity
market has averaged just under £700m in
recent trading sessions' [*Financial Times*]

set /set/ *adjective* fixed, or which cannot
be changed ○ *There is a set fee for all our
consultants.* ■ *verb* to fix or to arrange
something ○ *We have to set a price for the
new computer.* ○ *The price of the calculator has been set low, so as to achieve
maximum unit sales.* (NOTE: **setting –
set**) □ **the auction set a record for high
prices** the prices at the auction were the
highest ever reached

set against *phrasal verb* to balance
one group of figures against another
group to try to make them cancel each
other out ○ *to set the costs against the
sales revenue* ○ *Can you set the
expenses against tax?*

set aside *phrasal verb* to decide not to
apply a decision ○ *The arbitrator's
award was set aside on appeal.*

set off /ˌset ˈɒf/ *verb* to use a debt
owed by one party to reduce a debt
owed to them

set up *phrasal verb* to begin something, or to organise something new ○
to set up an inquiry or *a working party*

□ **to set up a company** to start a
company legally □ **to set up in business**
to start a new business ○ *She set up in
business as an insurance broker.* ○ *He
set himself up as a freelance representative.*

'…the concern announced that it had
acquired a third large tanker since being
set up' [*Lloyd's List*]

setback /ˈsetbæk/ *noun* something that
stops progress ○ *The company has
suffered a series of setbacks over the past
two years.* ○ *The shares had a setback on
the stock exchange.*

'…a sharp setback in foreign trade
accounted for most of the winter slowdown' [*Fortune*]

SET Index /set ˈɪndeks/ *noun* an index
of share prices on the Bangkok Stock
Exchange

Sets *abbreviation* Stock Exchange Electronic Trading System

settle /ˈset(ə)l/ *verb* **1.** □ **to settle an
account** to pay what is owed **2.** to place a
property in trust

settle on *phrasal verb* to leave property to someone when you die ○ *He
settled his property on his children.*

settled account /ˌset(ə)ld əˈkaʊnt/
noun an arrangement between two parties
who agree the accounts between them

settled property /ˌset(ə)ld ˈprɒpəti/
noun property which is held in trust

settlement /ˈset(ə)lmənt/ *noun* **1.** the
payment of an account □ **we offer an
extra 5% discount for rapid settlement**
we take a further 5% off the price if the
customer pays quickly □ **settlement in
cash** *or* **cash settlement** payment of an
invoice in cash, not by cheque **2.** an agreement after an argument or negotiations ○
a wage settlement □ **to effect a settlement between two parties** to bring two
parties together to make them agree

'…he emphasised that prompt settlement
of all forms of industrial disputes would
guarantee industrial peace in the country
and ensure increased productivity' [*Business Times (Lagos)*]

settlement date /ˈset(ə)lmənt deɪt/
noun a date when a payment has to be
made

settlement day /ˈset(ə)lmənt deɪ/
noun **1.** the day on which shares which
have been bought must be paid for. On the

London Stock Exchange the account period is three business days from the day of trade. (NOTE: The US term is **settlement date**) **2.** in the US, the day on which securities bought actually become the property of the purchaser

settlor /'set(ə)lə/ *noun* a person who settles property on someone

seven-day money /ˌsev(ə)n deɪ 'mʌni/ *noun* an investment in financial instruments which mature in seven days' time

severally /'sev(ə)rəli/ *adverb* separately, not jointly □ **they are jointly and severally liable** they are liable both as a group and as individuals for the total amount

severance pay /'sev(ə)rəns peɪ/ *noun* money paid as compensation to an employee whose job is no longer needed

SFA *abbreviation* Securities and Futures Authority

SFO *abbreviation* Serious Fraud Office

shadow director /ˈʃædəʊ daɪˌrektə/ *noun* a person who is not a director of a company, but who tells the directors of a company how to act

shadow economy /ˌʃædəʊ ɪ'kɒnəmi/ *noun* same as **black economy**

shady /'ʃeɪdi/ *adjective* not honest ○ *The newspapers reported that he had been involved in several shady deals.*

shake /ʃeɪk/ *verb* to move something quickly from side to side □ **to shake hands** to hold someone's hand when meeting to show you are pleased to meet them or to show that an agreement has been reached ○ *The two negotiating teams shook hands and sat down at the conference table.* □ **to shake hands on a deal** to shake hands to show that a deal has been agreed

shakeout /ˈʃeɪk ˈaʊt/ *noun* **1.** a reorganisation in a company, in which some people are left, but others go ○ *a shakeout in the top management* **2.** the process of revising prices on a stock market, usually at the end of a sharp rise or fall

shakeup /ˈʃeɪkʌp/ *noun* a total reorganisation ○ *The managing director ordered a shakeup of the sales departments.*

shaky /'ʃeɪki/ *adjective* not very sure or not very reliable ○ *He only has the shak-*

iest idea of what he should be doing. ○ *The new issue got off to a shaky start on the market.*

share /ʃeə/ *noun* **1.** a part of something that has been divided among several people or groups □ **to have a share in** to take part in or to contribute to ○ *to have a share in management decisions* **2.** one of many equal parts into which a company's capital is divided ○ *He bought a block of shares in Marks and Spencer.* ○ *Shares fell on the London market.* ○ *The company offered 1.8m shares on the market.* □ **to allot shares** to give a certain number of shares to people who have applied to buy them

'...falling profitability means falling share prices' [*Investors Chronicle*]

'...the share of blue-collar occupations declined from 48 per cent to 43 per cent' [*Sydney Morning Herald*]

share account /'ʃeər əˌkaʊnt/ *noun* an account at a building society where the account holder is a member of the society. Building societies usually offer another type of account, a deposit account, where the account holder is not a member. A share account is generally paid a better rate of interest, but in the event of the society going into liquidation, deposit account holders are given preference.

share at par /ˌʃeər ət 'pɑː/ *noun* a share whose value on the stock market is the same as its face value

share buyback /'ʃeə ˌbaɪbæk/ *noun* an arrangement whereby a company buys its own shares on the stock market (NOTE: The US term is **stock buyback**.)

share capital /'ʃeə ˌkæpɪt(ə)l/ *noun* the value of the assets of a company held as shares

share certificate /'ʃeə səˌtɪfɪkət/ *noun* a document proving that you own shares

shareholder /'ʃeəhəʊldə/ *noun* a person who owns shares in a company ○ *to call a shareholders' meeting* (NOTE: The US term is **stockholder**.)

'...as of last night the bank's shareholders no longer hold any rights to the bank's shares' [*South China Morning Post*]

'...the company said that its recent issue of 10.5% convertible preference shares at A$8.50 has been oversubscribed, boosting shareholders' funds to A\$700 million plus' [*Financial Times*]

shareholders' equity /ˌʃeəhəʊldəz 'ekwɪtɪ/ *noun* **1.** the value of a company which is the property of its ordinary shareholders (the company's assets less its liabilities) **2.** a company's capital which is invested by shareholders, who thus become owners of the company

shareholders' funds /ˌʃeəhəʊldəz 'fʌndz/ *plural noun* the capital and reserves of a company

shareholding /ˈʃeəhəʊldɪŋ/ *noun* a group of shares in a company owned by one owner

share incentive scheme /ˌʃeər ɪn 'sentɪv skiːm/ *noun* same as **share option scheme**

share index /ˈʃeər ˌɪndeks/ *noun* an index figure based on the current market price of shares on a stock exchange

share issue /ˈʃeər ˌɪʃuː/ *noun* an act of selling new shares in a company to the public

share option /ˈʃeər ˌɒpʃən/ *noun* a right to buy or sell shares at an agreed price at a time in the future

share option scheme /ˈʃeər ˌɒpʃən skiːm/ *noun* a scheme that gives company employees the right to buy shares in the company which employs them, often at a special price

shareout /ˈʃeəraʊt/ *noun* an act of dividing something among many people ○ *a shareout of the profits*

share premium /ˈʃeə ˌpriːmɪəm/ *noun* an amount to be paid above the nominal value of a share in order to buy it

share premium account /ˈʃeə ˌpriːmɪəm əˌkaʊnt/ *noun* a part of shareholders' funds in a company, formed of the premium paid for new shares sold above par. The par value of the shares is the nominal capital of the company.

share register /ˈʃeə ˌredʒɪstə/ *noun* a list of shareholders in a company with their addresses

share split /ˈʃeə splɪt/ *noun* the act of dividing shares into smaller denominations

share warrant /ˈʃeə ˌwɒrənt/ *noun* a document which says that someone has the right to a number of shares in a company

sharing /ˈʃeərɪŋ/ *noun* the act of dividing up

shark repellent /ˈʃɑːk rɪˌpelənt/ *noun* an action taken by a company to make itself less attractive to takeover bidders

sharp /ʃɑːp/ *adjective* sudden ○ *There was a sharp rally on the stock market.* ○ *Last week's sharp drop in prices has been reversed.*

sharply /ˈʃɑːpli/ *adverb* suddenly ○ *Shares dipped sharply in yesterday's trading.*

sharp practice /ˌʃɑːp ˈpræktɪs/ *noun* a way of doing business which is not honest, but is not illegal

shekel /ˈʃek(ə)l/ *noun* a unit of currency used in Israel

shelf registration /ˈʃelf ˌredʒɪ streɪʃ(ə)n/ *noun* a registration of a corporation with the SEC some time (up to two years is allowed) before it is offered for sale to the public

shell company /ˈʃel ˌkʌmp(ə)ni/ *noun* a company that has ceased to trade but is still registered, especially one sold to enable the buyer to begin trading without having to set up a new company (NOTE: The US term is **shell corporation**.)

'…shell companies, which can be used to hide investors' cash, figure largely throughout the twentieth century' [*Times*]

shelter /ˈʃeltə/ *noun* a protected place ■ *verb* to give someone or something protection

sheriff's sale /ˈʃerɪfs ˌseɪl/ *noun US* a public sale of the goods of a person whose property has been seized by the courts because he has defaulted on payments

shilling /ˈʃɪlɪŋ/ *noun* a unit of currency used in Kenya, Somalia, Tanzania and Uganda

shipment /ˈʃɪpmənt/ *noun* an act of sending goods ○ *We make two shipments a week to France.*

shipping company /ˈʃɪpɪŋ ˌkʌmp(ə)ni/ *noun* a company whose business is in transporting goods or passengers in ships

shogun bond /ˈʃəʊgʌn bɒnd/ *noun* a bond issued in Japan by a non-Japanese company in a currency which is not the yen. Compare **samurai bond**

shoot *verb*

shoot up *phrasal verb* to go up fast ○ *Prices have shot up during the strike.* (NOTE: **shooting – shot**)

shop /ʃɒp/ *noun* **1.** a retail outlet where goods of a certain type are sold ○ *a computer shop* ○ *an electrical goods shop* ○ *All the shops in the centre of town close on Sundays.* ○ *She opened a women's clothes shop.* (NOTE: The usual US term is **store**.) **2.** a workshop, the place in a factory where goods are made ■ *verb* to go to shops to make purchases (NOTE: **shopping – shopped**)

shop around *phrasal verb* to go to various shops or suppliers and compare prices before making a purchase or before placing an order ○ *You should shop around before getting your car serviced.* ○ *He's shopping around for a new computer.* ○ *It pays to shop around when you are planning to get a mortgage.*

shopper /ˈʃɒpə/ *noun* a person who buys goods in a shop ○ *The store stays open to midnight to cater for late-night shoppers.*

shoppers' charter /ˌʃɒpəz ˈtʃɑːtə/ *noun* a law which protects the rights of shoppers against shopkeepers who are not honest or against manufacturers of defective goods

shopping /ˈʃɒpɪŋ/ *noun* **1.** goods bought in a shop ○ *a basket of shopping* **2.** the act of going to shops to buy things ○ *to do your shopping in the local supermarket*

shopping basket /ˈʃɒpɪŋ ˌbɑːskɪt/ *noun* a basket used for carrying shopping (NOTE: Its imaginary contents are used to calculate a consumer price index.)

shopping cart /ˈʃɒpɪŋ kɑːt/ *noun* a software package that records the items that an online buyer selects for purchase together with associated data, e.g. the price of the item and the number of items required

shop price /ˈʃɒp praɪs/ *noun* same as **retail price**

short /ʃɔːt/ *adjective, adverb* **1.** for a small period of time □ **in the short term** in the near future or quite soon □ **to borrow short** to borrow for a short period **2.** less than what is expected or desired ○ *The shipment was three items short.* ○ *My*

change was £2 short. □ **when we cashed up we were £10 short** we had £10 less than we should have had □ **to give short weight** to sell something which is lighter than it should be □ **to be short of a stock** not to have shares which you will need in the future (as opposed to being 'long' of a stock) □ **to sell short, to go short** to agree to sell at a future date something (such as shares) which you do not possess, but which you think you will be able to buy for less before the time comes when you have to sell them ■ *verb* to sell short ○ *He shorted the stock at $35 and continued to short it as the price moved up.*

short bill /ˈʃɔːt bɪl/ *noun* a bill of exchange payable at short notice

short-change /ˌʃɔːt ˈtʃeɪndʒ/ *verb* to give a customer less change than is right, either by mistake or in the hope that it will not be noticed

short credit /ʃɔːt ˈkredɪt/ *noun* terms which allow the customer only a little time to pay

short-dated bill /ˌʃɔːt ˌdeɪtɪd ˈbɪl/ *noun* a bill which is payable within a few days

short-dated gilts /ˌʃɔːt ˌdeɪtɪd ˈɡɪlts/ *plural noun* same as **shorts**

short-dated securities /ˌʃɔːt ˌdeɪtɪd sɪˈkjʊərɪtiz/ *plural noun* same as **shorts**

shorten /ˈʃɔːt(ə)n/ *verb* to make shorter ○ *to shorten credit terms*

shortfall /ˈʃɔːtfɔːl/ *noun* an amount which is missing which would make the total expected sum ○ *We had to borrow money to cover the shortfall between expenditure and revenue.*

short lease /ˌʃɔːt ˈliːs/ *noun* a lease which runs for up to two or three years ○ *We have a short lease on our current premises.*

short position /ˌʃɔːt pəˈzɪʃ(ə)n/ *noun* a situation where an investor sells short, i.e. sells forward shares which he or she does not own. Compare **long position**

short-range forecast /ˌʃɔːt reɪndʒ ˈfɔːkɑːst/ *noun* a forecast which covers a period of a few months

shorts /ʃɔːts/ *plural noun* government stocks which mature in less than five years' time

short sale /ʃɔːt ˈseɪlɪŋ/, **short selling** *noun* the act of arranging to sell something in the future which you think you can buy for less than the agreed selling price

short sellers /ʃɔːt 'seləz/ *plural noun* people who contract to sell a share in the future, expecting the price to fall so that they can it buy more cheaply before they have to close the sale

short-term /ˌʃɔːt 'tɜːm/ *adjective* **1.** for a period of weeks or months ○ *to place money on short-term deposit* ○ *She is employed on a short-term contract.* □ **on a short-term basis** for a short period **2.** for a short period in the future ○ *We need to recruit at once to cover our short-term manpower requirements.*

short-term forecast /ˌʃɔːt tɜːm 'fɔːkɑːst/ *noun* a forecast which covers a period of a few months

short-termism /ˌʃɔːt 'tɜːmɪz(ə)m/ *noun* a type of thinking or planning that concentrates on achieving results in the near future rather than on long-term objectives

short-term loan /ˌʃɔːt tɜːm 'ləʊn/ *noun* a loan which has to be repaid within a few weeks or some years

short-term paper /ˌʃɔːt tɜːm 'peɪpə/ *noun* a promissory note, draft, etc. payable at less than nine months

short-term security /ˌʃɔːt tɜːm sɪ 'kjʊərɪti/ *noun* a security which matures in less than 5 years

short-term support /ˌʃɔːt tɜːm sə 'pɔːt/ *noun* support for a currency in the international market, where the central bank can borrow funds from other central banks for a short period

show of hands /ˌʃəʊ əv 'hændz/ *noun* a vote where people show how they vote by raising their hands ○ *The motion was carried on a show of hands.*

COMMENT: If it is difficult to decide which side has won in a show of hands, a ballot may be taken.

shrink /ʃrɪŋk/ *verb* to get smaller ○ *The market has shrunk by 20%.* ○ *The company is having difficulty selling into a shrinking market.* (NOTE: **shrinking – shrank – has shrunk**)

shrinkage /'ʃrɪŋkɪdʒ/ *noun* **1.** the amount by which something gets smaller ○ *to allow for shrinkage* **2.** losses of stock through theft, especially by the shop's own staff (*informal*)

shroff /ʃrɒf/ *noun* (*in the Far East*) an accountant

SIB *abbreviation* Securities and Investments Board

SICAV *abbreviation* société d'investissement à capital variable

side /saɪd/ *noun* a part of something near the edge

sideline /'saɪdlaɪn/ *noun* a business which is extra to your normal work ○ *He runs a profitable sideline selling postcards to tourists.*

sight /saɪt/ *noun* the act of seeing □ **bill payable at sight** a bill which must be paid when it is presented □ **to buy something sight unseen** to buy something without having inspected it

'…if your company needed a piece of equipment priced at about $50,000, would you buy it sight unseen from a supplier you had never met?' [*Nation's Business*]

sight bill /'saɪt bɪl/ *noun* a bill of exchange which is payable at sight

sight deposit /'saɪt dɪˌpɒzɪt/ *noun* a bank deposit which can be withdrawn on demand

sight draft /'saɪt drɑːft/ *noun* a bill of exchange which is payable when it is presented

sight letter of credit /saɪt ˌletə əv 'kredɪt/ *noun* a letter of credit which is paid when the necessary documents have been presented

sight note /'saɪt nəʊt/ *noun* a demand note, a promissory note which must be paid when it is presented

sign /saɪn/ *verb* to write your name in a special way on a document to show that you have written it or approved it ○ *The letter is signed by the managing director.* ○ *Our company cheques are not valid if they have not been signed by the finance director.* ○ *The new recruit was asked to sign the contract of employment.*

signal /'sɪgn(ə)l/ *noun* a warning message ○ *The Bank of England's move sent signals to the currency markets.* ■ *verb* to send warning messages about something ○ *The resolutions tabled for the AGM signalled the shareholders' lack of confidence in the management of the company.*

signatory /'sɪgnət(ə)ri/ *noun* a person who signs a contract, etc. ○ *You have to* *get the permission of all the signatories to the agreement if you want to change the terms.*

signature /ˈsɪɡnɪtʃə/ *noun* a person's name written by themselves on a cheque, document or letter ○ *She found a pile of cheques on his desk waiting for signature.* ○ *All our company's cheques need two signatures.* ○ *The contract of employment had the personnel director's signature at the bottom.*

signature guarantee /ˌsɪɡnətʃə ˌɡærənˈtiː/ *noun* a guarantee, such as a company stamp, that someone's signature is authorised as correct

silent partner /ˌsaɪlənt ˈpɑːtnə/ *noun US* same as **sleeping partner**

silver /ˈsɪlvə/ *noun* a precious metal traded on commodity markets such as the London Metal Exchange

simple average /ˌsɪmp(ə)l ˈæv(ə)rɪdʒ/ *noun* same as **average 1**

simple interest /ˌsɪmpəl ˈɪntrəst/ *noun* interest calculated on the capital invested only, as distinct from compound interest which is calculated on capital and accumulated interest

single /ˈsɪŋɡ(ə)l/ *adjective* **1.** one alone **2.** □ **in single figures** less than ten ○ *Sales are down to single figures.* ○ *Inflation is now in single figures.* ■ *noun* a person who is not married

single-company PEP /ˌsɪŋɡ(ə)l ˌkʌmp(ə)ni ˈpep/ *noun* a PEP which holds shares in one single company (up to £3,000 can be invested in the shares of just one company and protected from tax in this way)

single-entry bookkeeping /ˌsɪŋɡ(ə)l ˌentri ˈbʊkiːpɪŋ/ *noun* a method of bookkeeping where payments or sales are noted with only one entry per transaction, usually in the cash book

single European market /ˌsɪŋɡ(ə)l ˌjʊərəpiːən ˈmɑːkɪt/, **single market** /ˌsɪŋɡ(ə)l ˈmɑːkɪt/ *noun* the EU considered as one single market, with no tariff barriers between its member states

single-figure inflation /ˌsɪŋɡ(ə)l ˌfɪɡə ɪnˈfleɪʃ(ə)n/ *noun* inflation rising at less than 10% per annum

single filer /ˌsɪŋɡ(ə)l ˈfaɪlə/ *noun US* an unmarried individual who files an income tax return

single-life annuity /ˌsɪŋɡ(ə)l laɪf əˈnjuːɪti/ *noun* an annuity which is paid only to one beneficiary, and stops when he or she dies (as opposed to a 'joint-life annuity')

single premium policy /ˌsɪŋɡ(ə)l ˌpriːmiəm ˈpɒlɪsi/ *noun* an insurance policy where only one premium is paid rather than regular annual premiums

sink /sɪŋk/ *verb* **1.** to go down suddenly ○ *Prices sank at the news of the closure of the factory.* **2.** to invest money into something ○ *He sank all his savings into a car-hire business.* (NOTE: **sinking – sank – sunk**)

sinking fund /ˈsɪŋkɪŋ fʌnd/ *noun* a fund built up out of amounts of money put aside regularly to meet a future need, such as the repayment of a loan

sister company /ˈsɪstə ˌkʌmp(ə)ni/ *noun* a company that is part of the same group as another

sitting tenant /ˌsɪtɪŋ ˈtenənt/ *noun* a tenant who is occupying a building when the freehold or lease is sold ○ *The block of flats is for sale with four flats vacant and two with sitting tenants.*

SKA Index /skɑː ˈɪndeks/ *noun* an index of prices on the Zurich Stock Exchange

slam /slæm/ *verb US* to switch (unlawfully) a customer's telephone service without his or her consent ○ *We suddenly realised we'd been slammed.*

slash /slæʃ/ *verb* to reduce something sharply ○ *We have been forced to slash credit terms.* ○ *Prices have been slashed in all departments.* ○ *The banks have slashed interest rates.*

sleeper /ˈsliːpə/ *noun* a share which has not risen in value for some time, but which may suddenly do so in the future

sleeping partner /ˌsliːpɪŋ ˈpɑːtnə/ *noun* a partner who has a share in the business but does not work in it

slide /slaɪd/ *verb* to move down steadily ○ *Prices slid after the company reported a loss.* (NOTE: **sliding – slid**)

sliding /ˈslaɪdɪŋ/ *adjective* rising in steps

sliding scale /ˌslaɪdɪŋ ˈskeɪl/ *noun* a list of charges which rises gradually according to value, quantity, time, etc.

slight /slaɪt/ *adjective* not very large, not very important ○ *There was a slight improvement in the balance of trade.* ○ *We saw a slight increase in sales in February.*

slightly /'slaɪtli/ *adverb* not very much ○ *Sales fell slightly in the second quarter.* ○ *The Swiss bank is offering slightly better terms.*

slip /slɪp/ *noun* a small piece of paper ■ *verb* to go down and back ○ *Profits slipped to £1.5m.* ○ *Shares slipped back at the close.* (NOTE: **slipping – slipped**)

'…with long-term fundamentals reasonably sound, the question for brokers is when does cheap become cheap enough? The Bangkok and Taipei exchanges offer lower p/e ratios than Jakarta, but if Jakarta p/e ratios slip to the 16–18 range, foreign investors would pay more attention to it' [*Far Eastern Economic Review*]

slip-up /'slɪp ʌp/ *noun* a mistake ○ *There has been a slip-up in the customs documentation.* (NOTE: The plural is **slip-ups.**)

slow /sləʊ/ *adjective* not going fast ○ *The sales got off to a slow start, but picked up later.* ○ *Business is always slow after Christmas.* ○ *They were slow to reply* or *slow in replying to the customer's complaints.* ○ *The board is slow to come to a decision.* ○ *There was a slow improvement in sales in the first half of the year.* ■ *verb* to go less fast

'…cash paid for stock: overstocked lines, factory seconds, slow sellers' [*Australian Financial Review*]

'…a general price freeze succeeded in slowing the growth in consumer prices' [*Financial Times*]

'…the fall in short-term rates suggests a slowing economy' [*Financial Times*]

slow down *phrasal verb* to stop rising, moving or falling, or to make something go more slowly ○ *Inflation is slowing down.* ○ *The fall in the exchange rate is slowing down.* ○ *The management decided to slow down production.*

slowdown /'sləʊdaʊn/ *noun* a reduction in business activity ○ *a slowdown in the company's expansion*

slow payer /ˌsləʊ 'peɪə/ *noun* a person or company that does not pay debts on time ○ *The company is well known as a slow payer.*

sluggish economy /ˌslʌgɪʃ ɪ'kɒnəmi/ *noun* a state in the economy in which the growth is slow, flat or declining ○ *The business decided not to take on more staff in the sluggish economy.*

slump /slʌmp/ *noun* **1.** a rapid fall ○ *the slump in the value of the pound* ○ *We experienced a slump in sales* or *a slump in profits.* ○ *The pound's slump on the foreign exchange markets.* **2.** a period of economic collapse with high unemployment and loss of trade ○ *We are experiencing slump conditions.* ■ *verb* to fall fast ○ *Profits have slumped.* ○ *The pound slumped on the foreign exchange markets.*

slush fund /'slʌʃ fʌnd/ *noun* money kept to one side to give to people to persuade them to do what you want ○ *The government was brought down by the scandal over the slush funds.* ○ *The party was accused of keeping a slush fund to pay foreign businessmen.*

small /smɔːl/ *adjective* not large

small ads /'smɔːl ædz/ *plural noun* short private advertisements in a newspaper, e.g. selling small items or asking for jobs

small business /ˌsmɔːl 'bɪznɪs/ *noun* a company which has an annual turnover of less than £5.6 million and does not employ more than 50 staff

Small Business Administration /ˌsmɔːl 'bɪznɪs ədˌmɪnɪstreɪʃ(ə)n/ *noun US* a federal agency that advises small businesses and helps them obtain loans to finance their businesses. Abbreviation **SBA**

small business incubator /smɔːl 'bɪznɪs ɪŋkjʊˌbeɪtə/ *noun* a centre which provides support for new businesses before they become really viable

small businessman /ˌsmɔːl 'bɪznɪs mæn/ *noun* a man who owns a small business

small-cap /'smɔːl kæp/ *noun* a share in a company with small capitalisation. ◊ **cap, mega-cap, micro-cap, mid-cap**

small change /ˌsmɔːl 'tʃeɪndʒ/ *noun* coins

small claim /ˌsmɔːl 'kleɪm/ *noun* a claim for less than £5000 in the County Court

small claims court /ˌsmɔːl 'kleɪmz ˌkɔːt/ *noun* a court which deals with disputes over small amounts of money

small companies /ˌsmɔːl
ˈkʌmp(ə)niz/ *plural noun* companies
which are quoted on the stock exchange,
but which have a small capitalisation

small company /smɔːl ˈkʌmp(ə)ni/
noun same as **small business**

small investor /ˌsmɔːl ɪnˈvestə/ *noun*
a person with a small sum of money to
invest

small-scale /ˈsmɔːl skeɪl/ *adjective*
working in a small way, with few staff and
not much money

smart card /ˈsmɑːt kɑːd/ *noun* a credit
card with a microchip, used for withdrawing money from ATMs, or for
purchases at EFTPOS terminals

SMI *abbreviation* the stock market index
of the Zurich stock exchange in Switzerland

smokestack industries
/ˈsməʊkstæk ˌɪndəstriz/ *plural noun*
heavy industries, such as steel-making

smurf /smɜːf/ *noun US* a person who
launders money (*informal*)

snake /sneɪk/ *noun* formerly, the group
of currencies within the European
Exchange Rate Mechanism whose
exchange rates were allowed to fluctuate
against each other within certain bands or
limits (*informal*)

snap /snæp/ *verb*

snap up *phrasal verb* to buy something
quickly ○ *to snap up a bargain* ○ *She
snapped up 15% of the company's
shares.* (NOTE: **snapping – snapped**)

snip /snɪp/ *noun* a bargain (*informal*) ○
These printers are a snip at £50.

soar /sɔː/ *verb* to go up rapidly ○ *Share
prices soared on the news of the takeover
bid* or *the news of the takeover bid sent
share prices soaring.* ○ *Food prices
soared during the cold weather.*

social /ˈsəʊʃ(ə)l/ *adjective* referring to
society in general

Social Charter /ˌsəʊʃ(ə)l ˈtʃɑːtə/
noun same as **European Social Charter**

social costs /ˈsəʊʃ(ə)l kɒsts/ *plural
noun* the ways in which something will
affect people

social investing /ˌsəʊʃ(ə)l ɪn
ˈvestɪŋ/ *noun* the practice of investing in
companies that follow ethical practices,
e.g. paying fair wages and protecting the
environment

socially responsible fund
/ˌsəʊʃ(ə)li rɪˌspɒnsəb(ə)l ˈfʌnd/ *noun
US* a fund which only invests in companies that have a good environmental or
employment or social record

social security /ˌsəʊʃ(ə)l sɪ
ˈkjʊərɪti/, **social insurance** /ˌsəʊʃ(ə)l
ɪnˈʃʊərəns/ *noun* a government scheme
where employers, employees, and the
self-employed make regular contributions
to a fund which provides unemployment
pay, sickness pay, or retirement pensions
○ *He gets weekly social security
payments.* ○ *She never worked but lived
on social security for years.*

social system /ˈsəʊʃ(ə)l ˌsɪstəm/
noun the way society is organised

sociedad anónima *noun* the Spanish
word for a public limited company.
Abbreviation **SA**

società per azioni *noun* the Italian
word for a public limited company.
Abbreviation **SpA**

société *noun* the French word for
company

société anonyme *noun* the French
word for a public limited company.
Abbreviation **SA**

**société anonyme à responsa-
bilité limitée** *noun* the French word for
a private limited company. Abbreviation
SARL

Société des Bourses Françaises
noun a company which operates the
French stock exchanges and derivatives
exchanges. Abbreviation **SBF**

**société d'investissement à
capital variable** *noun* the French word
for a unit trust. Abbreviation **SICAV**

society /səˈsaɪəti/ *noun* **1.** the way in
which the people in a country are organised **2.** a club for a group of people with
the same interests ○ *We have joined a
computer society.*

**Society for Worldwide Interbank
Financial Telecommunications**
/səˌsaɪəti fə ˌwɜːldwaɪd ˌɪntəbæŋk
ˌtelikəmjuːnɪˈkeɪʃ(ə)nz/ *noun* an international organisation which makes the
rapid exchange of payments between
banks and stockbrokers possible on a
worldwide scale. Abbreviation **SWIFT**

socio-economic /ˌsəʊʃiəʊ iːkə
ˈnɒmɪk/ *adjective* referring to social and
economic conditions, social classes and

income groups ○ *the socio-economic system in capitalist countries* ○ *We have commissioned a thorough socio-economic analysis of our potential market.*

socio-economic groups /ˌsəʊʃiəʊ iːkəˌnɒmɪk 'gruːps/ *plural noun* groups in society divided according to income and position

COMMENT: The British socio-economic groups are: **A: upper middle class**: senior managers, administrators, civil servants and professional people; **B: middle class**: middle-ranking managers, administrators, civil servants and professional people; **C1: lower middle class**: junior managers and clerical staff; **C2: skilled workers**: workers with special skills and qualifications; **D: working class**: unskilled workers and manual workers; **E: subsistence level**: pensioners, the unemployed and casual manual workers.

soft /sɒft/ *adjective* not hard □ **to take the soft option** to decide to do something which involves least risk, effort or problems

soft commodities /ˌsɒft kə'mɒdɪtiz/ *plural noun* foodstuffs which are traded as commodities (such as rice, coffee, etc.)

soft currency /ˌsɒft 'kʌrənsi/ *noun* the currency of a country with a weak economy, which is cheap to buy and difficult to exchange for other currencies. Opposite **hard currency**

soft dollars /sɒft 'dɒləz/ *plural noun* rebates given by brokers to money management firms in return for funds' transaction business

soft landing /ˌsɒft 'lændɪŋ/ *noun* a change in economic strategy to counteract inflation, which does not cause unemployment or a fall in the standard of living, and has only minor effects on the bulk of the population

soft loan /'sɒft ləʊn/ *noun* a loan from a company to an employee or from one government to another at a very low rate of interest or with no interest payable at all

soft market /ˌsɒft 'mɑːkɪt/ *noun* a market where there is not enough demand, and where prices fall

soft sell /ˌsɒft 'sel/ *noun* the process of persuading people to buy, by encouraging and not forcing them to do so

sol /sɒl/ *noun* a unit of currency used in Peru

sole /səʊl/ *adjective* only

sole agency /ˌsəʊl 'eɪdʒənsi/ *noun* an agreement to be the only person to represent a company or to sell a product in a particular area ○ *He has the sole agency for Ford cars.*

sole agent /ˌsəʊl 'eɪdʒənt/ *noun* a person who has the sole agency for a company in an area ○ *She is the sole agent for Ford cars in the locality.*

sole distributor /ˌsəʊl dɪ'strɪbjʊtə/ *noun* a retailer who is the only one in an area who is allowed to sell a product

sole owner /ˌsəʊl 'əʊnə/ *noun* a person who owns a business on their own, with no partners, and has not formed a company

sole proprietor /ˌsəʊl prə'praɪətə/, **sole trader** /ˌsəʊl 'treɪdə/ *noun* a person who runs a business, usually by him- or herself, but has not registered it as a company

solvency /'sɒlv(ə)nsi/ *noun* the state of being able to pay all debts on due date. Opposite **insolvency**

solvent /'sɒlv(ə)nt/ *adjective* having assets which are more than your liabilities

som /sɒm/ *noun* a unit of currency used in Kyrgystan

sort code /'sɔːt kəʊd/ *noun* a combination of numbers that identifies a bank branch on official documentation, such as bank statements and cheques (NOTE: The US term is **routing number**.)

sorter/reader /ˌsɔːtə 'riːdə/ *noun* a machine in a bank which reads cheques and sorts them automatically

source /sɔːs/ *noun* the place where something comes from ○ *What is the source of her income?* ○ *You must declare income from all sources to the tax office.* □ **income which is taxed at source** income where the tax is removed and paid to the government by the employer before the income is paid to the employee

source and application of funds statement /ˌsɔːs ənd ˌæplɪkeɪʃ(ə)n əv 'fʌndz ˌsteɪtmənt/, **sources and uses of funds statement** /ˌsɔːsɪz ən ˌjuːzɪz əv 'fʌndz ˌsteɪtmənt/ *noun* a statement in a company's annual accounts, showing where new funds came from during the year, and how they were used

sovereign /'sɒvrɪn/ *noun* a British gold coin, with a face value of £1 ■ *adjective* referring to an independent country

sovereign bond /'sɒvrɪn bɒnd/ *noun* a bond issued by a government

sovereign risk /ˌsɒvrɪn 'rɪsk/ *noun* a risk that a government may default on its debts (a government cannot be sued if it defaults)

sovereign state /ˌsɒvrɪn 'steɪt/ *noun* an independent state which governs itself

sovereign wealth fund /ˌsɒvrɪn 'welθ ˌfʌnd/ *noun* an investment fund owned by a government which has very large amounts of money at its disposal

SpA *abbreviation* società per azioni

spare /speə/ *adjective* extra, not being used ○ *He has invested his spare capital in a computer shop.* □ **to use up spare capacity** to make use of time or space which has not been fully used

Sparkasse *noun* the German word for a savings bank

spec /spek/ *noun* same as **specification** □ **to buy something on spec** to buy something without being sure of its value

special /'speʃ(ə)l/ *adjective* **1.** better than usual ○ *He offered us special terms.* ○ *The car is being offered at a special price.* **2.** referring to one particular thing

'…airlines offer special stopover rates and hotel packages to attract customers to certain routes' [*Business Traveller*]

Special Commissioner /ˌspeʃ(ə)l kə'mɪʃ(ə)nə/ *noun* an official appointed by the Treasury to hear cases where a taxpayer is appealing against an income tax assessment

special deposits /ˌspeʃ(ə)l dɪ 'pɒzɪts/ *plural noun* large sums of money which commercial banks have to deposit with the Bank of England

special drawing rights /ˌspeʃ(ə)l 'drɔːɪŋ raɪts/ *plural noun* units of account used by the International Monetary Fund, allocated to each member country for use in loans and other international operations. Their value is calculated daily on the weighted values of a group of currencies shown in dollars. Abbreviation **SDRs**

specialist /'speʃəlɪst/ *noun* **1.** a person or company that deals with one particular type of product or one subject ○ *You should go to a specialist in computers or to a computer specialist for advice.* ○ *We need a manager who can grasp the overall picture rather than a narrow specialist.* **2.** a trader on the NYSE who deals in certain stocks for his own account, selling to or buying from brokers

special mention assets /ˌspeʃ(ə)l 'menʃ(ə)n ˌæsets/ *plural noun* loans made by a bank without the correct documentation

special notice /ˌspeʃ(ə)l 'nəʊtɪs/ *noun* notice of a proposal to be put before a meeting of the shareholders of a company which is made less than 28 days before the meeting

special offer /ˌspeʃ(ə)l 'ɒfə/ *noun* a situation where goods are put on sale at a specially low price ○ *We have a range of men's shirts on special offer.*

special resolution /ˌspeʃ(ə)l ˌrezə 'luːʃ(ə)n/ *noun* a resolution concerning an important matter, such as a change to the company's articles of association which is only valid if it is approved by 75% of the votes cast at a meeting

COMMENT: 21 days' notice must be given for a special resolution to be put to a meeting, as opposed to an 'extraordinary resolution' for which notice must be given, but no minimum period is specified by law. An extraordinary resolution could be a proposal to wind up a company voluntarily, but changes to the articles of association, such as a change of name, or of the objects of the company, or a reduction in share capital, need a special resolution.

specie /'spiːʃiː/ *noun* money in the form of coins

specification /ˌspesɪfɪ'keɪʃ(ə)n/ *noun* detailed information about what or who is needed or about a product to be supplied ○ *to detail the specifications of a computer system* □ **to work to standard specifications** to work to specifications which are acceptable anywhere in an industry □ **the work is not up to specification** *or* **does not meet our specifications** the product is not made in the way which was detailed

specify /'spesɪfaɪ/ *verb* to state clearly what is needed ○ *to specify full details of the goods ordered* ○ *Do not include VAT on the invoice unless specified.* ○ *Candi-*

dates are asked to specify which of the three posts they are applying for. (NOTE: **specifies – specifying – specified**)

specimen /'spesɪmɪn/ *noun* something which is given as a sample □ **to give specimen signatures on a bank mandate** to write the signatures of all the people who can sign cheques for an account so that the bank can recognise them

speculate /'spekjʊleɪt/ *verb* to take a risk in business which you hope will bring you profits □ **to speculate on the stock exchange** to buy shares which you hope will rise in value

speculation /ˌspekjʊ'leɪʃ(ə)n/ *noun* a risky deal which may produce a short-term profit ○ *He bought the company as a speculation.* ○ *She lost all her money in stock exchange speculations.*

speculative share /ˌspekjʊlətɪv 'ʃeə/ *noun* **1.** shares that may go sharply up or down in value **2.** a bond with a low credit rating

speculator /'spekjʊleɪtə/ *noun* a person who buys goods, shares or foreign currency in the hope that it will rise in value ○ *a property speculator* ○ *a currency speculator* ○ *a speculator on the stock exchange* or *a stock exchange speculator*

spend /spend/ *verb* to pay money ○ *They spent all their savings on buying the shop.* ○ *The company spends thousands of pounds on research.* ■ *noun* an amount of money spent ○ *What's the annual spend on marketing?*

spending /'spendɪŋ/ *noun* the act of paying money for goods and services ○ *Both cash spending and credit card spending increase at Christmas.*

spending money /'spendɪŋ ˌmʌni/ *noun* money for ordinary personal expenses

spending power /'spendɪŋ ˌpaʊə/ *noun* **1.** the fact of having money to spend on goods ○ *the spending power of the student market* **2.** the amount of goods which can be bought for a sum of money ○ *The spending power of the pound has fallen over the last ten years.*

spin /spɪn/ *noun* a special meaning given to something

spin off *phrasal verb* □ **to spin off a subsidiary company** to split off part of a large company to form a smaller

subsidiary, giving shares in the subsidiary to the existing shareholders

spin control /'spɪn kənˌtrəʊl/ *noun* the ability to give a special meaning to information

spin doctor /'spɪn ˌdɒktə/ *noun* a person who explains news in a way that makes it flattering to the person or organisation employing him or her (*informal*) ○ *Government spin doctors have been having some difficulty in dealing with the news items about the rise in unemployment.*

spinoff /'spɪnɒf/ *noun* **1.** a useful product developed as a secondary product from a main item ○ *One of the spinoffs of the research programme has been the development of the electric car.* **2.** a corporate reorganisation in which a subsidiary becomes an independent company

spiral /'spaɪrəl/ *noun* something which twists round and round getting higher all the time ■ *verb* to twist round and round, getting higher all the time ○ *a period of spiralling prices* (NOTE: UK English is **spiralling – spiralled**, but the US spelling is **spiraling – spiraled**.) □ **spiralling inflation** inflation where price rises make employees ask for higher wages which then increase prices again

split /splɪt/ *noun* **1.** an act of dividing up □ **the company is proposing a five for one split** the company is proposing that each existing share should be divided into five smaller shares **2.** a lack of agreement ○ *a split in the family shareholders* ■ *verb* **1.** □ **to split shares** to divide shares into smaller denominations □ **the shares were split five for one** five new shares were given for each existing share held **2.** □ **to split the difference** to come to an agreement over a price by dividing the difference between the amount the seller is asking and amount the buyer wants to pay and agreeing on a price between the two (NOTE: [all verb senses] **splitting – split**) ■ *adjective* divided into parts

COMMENT: A company may decide to split its shares if the share price becomes too 'heavy' (i.e. each share is priced at such a high level that small investors may be put off, and trading in the share is restricted). In the UK, a share price of £10.00 is considered 'heavy', though such prices are common on other stock markets.

split-capital trust /ˌsplɪt ˌkæpɪt(ə)l ˈtrʌst/ *noun* same as **split-level investment trust**

split commission /ˌsplɪt kəˈmɪʃ(ə)n/ *noun* commission which is divided between brokers or agents

split-level investment trust /ˌsplɪt ˌlev(ə)l ɪnˈvestmənt ˌtrʌst/ *noun* an investment trust with two categories of shares: income shares which receive income from the investments, but do not benefit from the rise in their capital value, and capital shares, which increase in value as the value of the investments rises, but do not receive any income. Also called **split trust**, **split-capital trust**

split payment /ˌsplɪt ˈpeɪmənt/ *noun* a payment which is divided into small units

split trust /ˌsplɪt ˈtrʌst/ *noun* same as **split-level investment trust**

sponsor /ˈspɒnsə/ *noun* **1.** a company which pays part of the cost of making a TV programme by taking advertising time on the programme **2.** a person or company which pays money to help research or to pay for a business venture **3.** a company which pays to help a sport, in return for advertising rights **4.** an organisation, such as a merchant bank, which backs a new share issue ■ *verb* **1.** to act as a sponsor for something ○ *a government-sponsored trade exhibition* ○ *The company has sponsored the football match.* ○ *Six of the management trainees have been sponsored by their companies.* **2.** *US* to play an active part in something, such as a pension plan for employees ○ *If you're single and not covered by an employer-sponsored retirement plan.*

sponsorship /ˈspɒnsəʃɪp/ *noun* the act of sponsoring ○ *the sponsorship of a season of concerts* ○ *The training course could not be run without the sponsorship of several major companies.*

spot /spɒt/ *noun* **1.** a place **2.** a place for an advertisement on a TV or radio show **3.** the buying of something for immediate delivery ■ *adjective* done immediately

spot cash /ˌspɒt ˈkæʃ/ *noun* cash paid for something bought immediately

spot market /ˈspɒt ˌmɑːkɪt/ *noun* a market that deals in commodities or foreign exchange for immediate rather than future delivery

'…with most of the world's oil now traded on spot markets, Opec's official prices are much less significant than they once were' [*Economist*]

spot price /ˈspɒt praɪs/, **spot rate** /ˈspɒt reɪt/ *noun* a current price or rate for something which is delivered immediately. Also called **cash price**

'…the average spot price of Nigerian light crude oil for the month of July was 27.21 dollars per barrel' [*Business Times (Lagos)*]

spousal /ˈspaʊz(ə)l/ *adjective US* referring to a spouse

spousal IRA /ˌspaʊz(ə)l ˈaɪrə/ *noun US* an IRA set up in the name of a spouse. Full form **spousal Individual Retirement Account**

spouse /spaʊs/ *noun* a husband or wife ○ *All employees and their spouses are invited to the staff party.*

spread /spred/ *noun* **1.** same as **range** **2.** the difference between buying and selling prices, i.e. between the bid and offer prices ■ *verb* to space something out over a period of time ○ *to spread payments over several months* (NOTE: **spreading – spread**) □ **to spread a risk** to make the risk of insurance less great by asking other companies to help cover it

'…dealers said markets were thin, with gaps between trades and wide spreads between bid and ask prices on the currencies' [*Wall Street Journal*]

'…to ensure an average return you should hold a spread of different shares covering a wide cross-section of the market' [*Investors Chronicle*]

spreadsheet /ˈspredʃiːt/ *noun* a computer printout or program that shows a series of columns or rows of figures

square /skweə/ *verb* to balance your position by selling futures to balance purchases

Square Mile /ˌskweə ˈmaɪl/ *noun* the City of London, the British financial centre

squeeze /skwiːz/ *noun* government control carried out by reducing the availability of something ■ *verb* to crush or to press; to make smaller ○ *to squeeze margins* or *profits* or *credit*

'…the real estate boom of the past three years has been based on the availability of easy credit. Today, money is tighter, so property should bear the brunt of the credit squeeze' [*Money Observer*]

SRB *abbreviation* sales returns book

SRO *abbreviation* self-regulatory organisation

SSAPs *abbreviation* Statements of Standard Accounting Practice

SSI *abbreviation* standing settlement instructions

SSL /ˌes es 'el/ *abbreviation* a method of providing a safe channel over the Internet to allow a user's credit card or personal details to be safely transmitted ○ *I only purchase goods from a web site that has SSL security installed.* ○ *The little key logo on my web browser appears when I am connected to a secure site with SSL.* Full form **secure sockets layer**

stabilisation /ˌsteɪbɪlaɪˈzeɪʃ(ə)n/, **stabilization** *noun* the process of making something stable, e.g. preventing sudden changes in prices □ **stabilisation of the economy** keeping the economy stable by preventing inflation from rising, cutting high interest rates and excess money supply

stabilise /ˈsteɪbəlaɪz/, **stabilize** *verb* to become steady, or to make something steady □ **prices have stabilised** prices have stopped moving up or down □ **to have a stabilising effect on the economy** to make the economy more stable

stability /stəˈbɪlɪti/ *noun* the state of being steady or not moving up or down ○ *price stability* ○ *a period of economic stability* ○ *the stability of the currency markets*

stable /ˈsteɪb(ə)l/ *adjective* steady or not moving up or down ○ *stable prices* ○ *a stable exchange rate* ○ *a stable currency* ○ *a stable economy*

staff appraisal /stɑːf əˈpreɪz(ə)l/, **staff assessment** /stɑːf əˈsesmənt/ *noun* a report on how well a member of staff is working

staffer /ˈstɑːfə/ *noun US* a member of the permanent staff

staff incentives /ˌstɑːf ɪnˈsentɪvz/ *plural noun* higher pay and better conditions offered to employees to make them work better

staff training /ˌstɑːf ˈtreɪnɪŋ/ *noun* the process of teaching staff better and more profitable ways of working

stag /stæg/ *noun* **1.** a person who buys new issues of shares and sells them immediately to make a profit **2.** *US* a dealer in stocks who is not a member of a stock exchange ■ *verb* □ **to stag an issue** to buy a new issue of shares not as an investment, but to sell immediately at a profit (NOTE: **stagging – stagged**)

stage /steɪdʒ/ *noun* a period, one of several points in a process of development ○ *the different stages of the production process* □ **the contract is still in the drafting stage** the contract is still being drafted □ **in stages** in different steps ○ *The company has agreed to repay the loan in stages.*

staged payments /ˌsteɪdʒd ˈpeɪmənts/ *plural noun* payments made in stages

stagflation /stægˈfleɪʃ(ə)n/ *noun* inflation and stagnation happening at the same time in an economy

stagger /ˈstægə/ *verb* to arrange holidays or working hours so that they do not all begin and end at the same time ○ *Staggered holidays help the tourist industry.* ○ *We have to stagger the lunch hour so that there is always someone on the switchboard.* ○ *We asked our supplier to stagger deliveries so that the warehouse can cope.*

stagnant /ˈstægnənt/ *adjective* not active, not increasing ○ *Turnover was stagnant for the first half of the year.* ○ *A stagnant economy is not a good sign.*

stagnate /stægˈneɪt/ *verb* not to increase, not to make progress ○ *The economy is stagnating.* ○ *After six hours the talks were stagnating.*

stagnation /stægˈneɪʃ(ə)n/ *noun* the state of not making any progress, especially in economic matters ○ *The country entered a period of stagnation.*

stake /steɪk/ *noun* an amount of money invested □ **to have a stake in a business** to have money invested in a business □ **to acquire a stake in a business** to buy shares in a business ○ *He acquired a 25% stake in the company.* ■ *verb* □ **to stake money on something** to risk money on something

'…her stake, which she bought at $1.45 per share, is now worth nearly $10 million' [*Times*]

'…other investments include a large stake in a Chicago-based insurance company, as well as interests in tobacco products and hotels' [*Lloyd's List*]

stale /steɪl/ *adjective* referring to a cheque which is so old, that the bank will not clear it unless it has been confirmed as correct by the payer

stale bull /steɪl bʊl/ *noun* an investor who bought shares hoping that they would rise, and now finds that they have not risen and wants to sell them

stamp /stæmp/ *noun* a device for making marks on documents; a mark made in this way ○ *The invoice has the stamp 'Received with thanks' on it.* ○ *The customs officer looked at the stamps in her passport.* ■ *verb* **1.** to mark a document with a stamp ○ *to stamp an invoice 'Paid'* ○ *The documents were stamped by the customs officials.* **2.** to put a postage stamp on an envelope or parcel

stamp duty /stæmp ˌdjuːti/ *noun* a tax on legal documents such as those used, e.g., for the sale or purchase of shares or the conveyance of a property to a new owner

standard /ˈstændəd/ *noun* the usual quality or usual conditions which other things are judged against ■ *adjective* normal or usual ○ *a standard model car* ○ *We have a standard charge of £25 for a thirty-minute session.*

standard agreement /ˌstændəd əˈɡriːmənt/, **standard contract** /ˌstændəd ˈkɒntrækt/ *noun* a normal printed contract form

Standard & Poor's /ˌstændəd ən ˈpʊəz/ *noun* an American corporation which rates bonds according to the creditworthiness of the organisations issuing them. Abbreviation **S&P**

> COMMENT: Standard and Poor's also issues several stock market indices: the Standard and Poor's Composite Index (or S&P 500 or Standard & Poor's 500-stock Index) is an index of 500 popular American stocks; other indices are the S&P SmallCap and S&P MidCap.

standard cost /ˌstændəd ˈkɒst/ *noun* a future cost which is calculated in advance and against which estimates are measured

standard deviation /ˌstændəd ˌdiːvi ˈeɪʃ(ə)n/ *noun* the way in which the results of a sample deviate from the mean or average

standard direct labour cost /ˌstændəd daɪˌrekt ˈleɪbə ˌkɒst/ *noun* the cost of labour calculated to produce a product according to specification, used to measure estimates

standard letter /ˌstændəd ˈletə/ *noun* a letter which is sent without change to various correspondents

standard of living /ˌstændəd əv ˈlɪvɪŋ/ *noun* the quality of personal home life (such as amount of food or clothes bought, size of family car, etc.)

standard rate /ˈstændəd reɪt/ *noun* a basic rate of income tax which is paid by most taxpayers

standard risk /ˌstændəd ˈrɪsk/ *noun* a normal risk on a loan which is likely to be repaid on time

standby arrangements /ˈstændbaɪ əˌreɪndʒmənts/ *plural noun* plans for what should be done if an emergency happens, especially money held in reserve in the International Monetary Fund for use by a country in financial difficulties

standby credit /ˈstændbaɪ ˌkredɪt/ *noun* **1.** credit which is available if a company needs it, especially credit guaranteed by a euronote **2.** credit which is available and which can be drawn on if a country needs it, especially credit guaranteed by a lender (a group of banks or the IMF in the case of a member country) and usually in dollars

standby loan /ˈstændbaɪ ləʊn/ *noun* a loan which is available if needed

standing /ˈstændɪŋ/ *noun* a good reputation ○ *The financial standing of a company.* □ **company of good standing** very reputable company

standing order /ˌstændɪŋ ˈɔːdə/ *noun* an order written by a customer asking a bank to pay money regularly to an account ○ *I pay my subscription by standing order.*

standing settlement instructions /ˌstændɪŋ ˈset(ə)lmənt ɪnˌstrʌkʃənz/ *plural noun* instructions given by one bank to other banks as to the procedure to be followed when making payments to it. Abbreviation **SSIs**

standstill agreement /ˈstændstɪl əˌɡriːmənt/ *noun* an agreement between a borrower and a lender that it is better to rengotiate the terms of the loan than for the lender to foreclose on the property used as security

staple commodity /ˌsteɪp(ə)l kə'mɒdɪti/ *noun* a basic food or raw material

start /stɑːt/ *noun* the beginning ■ *verb* to begin to do something □ **to start a business from cold** *or* **from scratch** to begin a new business, with no previous turnover to base it on

starting /'stɑːtɪŋ/ *noun* the act of beginning

starting date /'stɑːtɪŋ deɪt/ *noun* a date on which something starts

starting salary /'stɑːtɪŋ ˌsæləri/ *noun* a salary for an employee when he or she starts work with a company

start-up /'stɑːt ʌp/ *noun* **1.** the beginning of a new company or new product ○ *We went into the red for the first time because of the costs for the start-up of our new subsidiary.* **2.** a new, usually small business that is just beginning its operations, especially a new business supported by venture capital and in a sector where new technologies are used

'It's unusual for a venture capitalist to be focused tightly on a set of companies with a common technology base, and even more unusual for the investment fund manager to be picking start-ups that will be built on a business he's currently running.' [*InformationWeek*]

start-up financing /'stɑːt ʌp ˌfaɪnænsɪŋ/ *noun* the first stage in financing a new project, which is followed by several rounds of investment capital as the project gets under way

state /steɪt/ *noun* **1.** an independent country **2.** a semi-independent section of a federal country such as the US **3.** the government of a country ■ *verb* to say clearly ○ *The document states that all revenue has to be declared to the tax office.*

'...the unions had argued that public sector pay rates had slipped behind rates applying in state and local government areas' [*Australian Financial Review*]

state bank /ˌsteɪt 'bæŋk/ *noun* in the US, a commercial bank licensed by the authorities of a state, and not necessarily a member of the Federal Reserve system. Compare **national bank**

state-controlled /'steɪt kən,trəʊld/ *adjective* run by the state ○ *state-controlled television*

state enterprise /ˌsteɪt 'entəpraɪz/ *noun* a company run by the state

statement /'steɪtmənt/ *noun* **1.** something said or written which describes or explains something clearly □ **to make a false statement** to give wrong details □ **statement of expenses** a detailed list of money spent **2.** □ **statement (of account)** a list of invoices and credits and debits sent by a supplier to a customer at the end of each month □ **monthly** *or* **quarterly statement** a statement which is sent every month or every quarter by the bank □ **statement balance, balance per statement** a balance in an account on a given date as shown in a bank statement

statement of affairs /ˌsteɪtmənt əv ə'feəz/ *noun* a financial statement drawn up when a person is insolvent

Statements of Standard Accounting Practice /ˌsteɪtmənts əv ˌstændəd ə'kaʊntɪŋ ˌpræktɪs/ *plural noun* rules laid down by the Accounting Standards Board for the preparation of financial statements. Abbreviation **SSAPs**

statement stuffer /'steɪtmənt ˌstʌfə/ *noun* an advertising leaflet enclosed with the monthly bank statement

state monopoly /steɪt mə'nɒpəli/ *noun* a situation where the state is the only supplier of a product or service

state of indebtedness /ˌsteɪt əv ɪn'detɪdnəs/ *noun* the fact of being in debt, owing money

state-owned /ˌsteɪt 'əʊnd/ *adjective* owned by the state or by a state

'...state-owned banks cut their prime rates a percentage point to 11%' [*Wall Street Journal*]

state-owned industry /ˌsteɪt əʊnd 'ɪndəstri/ *noun* an industry which is nationalised

state ownership /ˌsteɪt 'əʊnəʃɪp/ *noun* a situation in which an industry is nationalised

statistical /stə'tɪstɪk(ə)l/ *adjective* based on statistics ○ *statistical informa-*

tion ○ *They took two weeks to provide the statistical analysis of the opinion-poll data.*

statistical discrepancy /stə ˌtɪstɪk(ə)l dɪ'skrepənsi/ *noun* the amount by which sets of figures differ

statistician /ˌstætɪ'stɪʃ(ə)n/ *noun* a person who analyses statistics

statistics /stə'tɪstɪks/ *plural noun* **1.** facts or information in the form of figures ○ *to examine the sales statistics for the previous six months* ○ *Government trade statistics show an increase in imports.* ○ *The statistics on unemployment did not take school-leavers into account.* (NOTE: takes a plural verb) **2.** the study of facts in the form of figures (NOTE: takes a singular verb)

status /'steɪtəs/ *noun* **1.** the importance of someone or something relative to others, especially someone's position in society □ **the chairman's car is a status symbol** the size of the car shows how important the chairman is □ **loss of status** the act of becoming less important in a group **2.** □ **legal status** legal position

status inquiry /'steɪtəs ɪnˌkwaɪəri/ *noun* the act of checking on a customer's credit rating

status quo /ˌsteɪtəs 'kwəʊ/ *noun* the state of things as they are now ○ *The contract does not alter the status quo.*

statute /'stætʃuːt/ *noun* an established written law, especially an Act of Parliament. Also called **statute law**

statute-barred /ˌstætʃuːt 'bɑːd/ *adjective* referring to legal action which cannot be pursued because the time limit for it has expired

statute book /'stætʃuːt bʊk/ *noun* all laws passed by Parliament which are still in force

statute law /'stætʃuːt lɔː/ *noun* same as **statute**

statute of limitations /ˌstætʃuːt əv ˌlɪmɪ'teɪʃ(ə)nz/ *noun* a law which allows only a fixed period of time, usually six years, for someone to start legal proceedings to claim property or compensation for damage

statutory /'stætʃʊt(ə)ri/ *adjective* fixed by law ○ *There is a statutory period of probation of thirteen weeks.* ○ *Are all the employees aware of their statutory rights?*

statutory holiday /ˌstætʃʊt(ə)ri 'hɒlɪdeɪ/ *noun* a holiday which is fixed by law ○ *The office is closed for the statutory Christmas holiday.*

statutory regulations /ˌstætʃʊt(ə)ri ˌregjʊ'leɪʃ(ə)nz/ *plural noun* regulations covering financial dealings which are based on Acts of Parliament, such as the Financial Services Act, as opposed to the rules of self-regulatory organisations which are non-statutory

stay of execution /ˌsteɪ əv eksɪ 'kjuːʃ(ə)n/ *noun* the temporary stopping of a legal order ○ *The court granted the company a two-week stay of execution.*

steadily /'stedɪli/ *adverb* in a regular or continuous way ○ *Output increased steadily over the last two quarters.* ○ *The company has steadily increased its market share.*

steadiness /'stedɪnəs/ *noun* the fact of being firm, not fluctuating ○ *The steadiness of the markets is due to the government's intervention.*

steady /'stedi/ *adjective* continuing in a regular way ○ *The company can point to a steady increase in profits.* ○ *The market stayed steady in spite of the collapse of the bank.* ○ *There is a steady demand for computers.* ○ *He has a steady job in the supermarket.* ■ *verb* to become firm, to stop fluctuating ○ *The markets steadied after last week's fluctuations.* ○ *Prices steadied on the commodity markets.* ○ *The government's figures had a steadying influence on the exchange rate.*

steep /stiːp/ *adjective* referring to an increase which is very great and usually sudden or a price which is very high ○ *a steep increase in interest charges* ○ *a steep decline in overseas sales*

step /step/ *noun* a movement forward ○ *Becoming assistant to the MD is a step up the promotion ladder.* □ **in step with** moving at the same rate as ○ *The pound rose in step with the dollar.* □ **out of step with** not moving at the same rate as ○ *The pound was out of step with other European currencies.* ○ *Wages are out of step with the cost of living.*

sterling /'stɜːlɪŋ/ *noun* the standard currency used in the UK ○ *to quote prices in sterling* or *to quote sterling prices*

'…it is doubtful that British goods will price themselves back into world markets as long as sterling labour costs continue to rise faster than in competitor countries' [*Sunday Times*]

sterling area /ˈstɜːlɪŋ ˌeəriə/ *noun* formerly, the area of the world where the pound sterling was the main trading currency

sterling balances /ˌstɜːlɪŋ ˈbælənsɪz/ *plural noun* a country's trade balances expressed in pounds sterling

sterling crisis /ˈstɜːlɪŋ ˌkraɪsɪs/ *noun* a fall in the exchange rate of the pound sterling

sterling index /ˈstɜːlɪŋ ˌɪndeks/ *noun* an index which shows the current value of sterling against a basket of currencies

sterling silver /ˌstɜːlɪŋ ˈsɪlvə/ *noun* an official quality of silver for use in articles made and sold. The current value is 92.5% pure silver.

stimulate /ˈstɪmjʊleɪt/ *verb* to make something or someone become more active ○ *What can the government do to stimulate the economy?* ○ *The aim of the subsidies is to stimulate trade with the Middle East.*

stimulus /ˈstɪmjʊləs/ *noun* a thing which encourages activity (NOTE: The plural is **stimuli**.)

stipulate /ˈstɪpjʊleɪt/ *verb* to state something specifically as a binding condition in a contract ○ *to stipulate that the contract should run for five years* ○ *They found it difficult to pay the stipulated charges.* ○ *The company failed to pay on the date stipulated in the contract.* ○ *The contract stipulates that the seller pays the buyer's legal costs.*

stipulation /ˌstɪpjʊˈleɪʃ(ə)n/ *noun* a condition in a contract ○ *The contract has a stipulation that the new manager has to serve a three-month probationary period.*

stock /stɒk/ *noun* **1.** *especially UK* the quantity of goods for sale in a warehouse or retail outlet. Also called **inventory** □ **to buy a shop with stock at valuation** when buying a shop, to pay a price for the stock which is the same as its value as estimated by the valuer □ **to purchase stock at valuation** to pay the price that stock has been valued at □ **to take stock** to count the items in a warehouse **2.** shares in a company **3.** investments in a company, represented by shares or fixed interest securities

'US crude oil stocks fell last week by nearly 2.5m barrels' [*Financial Times*]

'…the stock rose to over $20 a share, higher than the $18 bid' [*Fortune*]

stockbroker /ˈstɒkbrəʊkə/ *noun* a person who buys or sells shares for clients

stockbroker's commission /stɒk ˌbrəʊkəz kəˈmɪʃ(ə)n/ *noun* the payment to a broker for a deal carried out on behalf of a client

stockbroking /ˈstɒkbrəʊkɪŋ/ *noun* the business of dealing in shares for clients ○ *a stockbroking firm*

stock certificate /ˈstɒk səˌtɪfɪkət/ *noun* a document proving that someone owns stock in a company

stock code /ˈstɒk kəʊd/ *noun* a set of numbers and letters which refer to an item of stock

stock company /ˈstɒk ˌkʌmpəni/ *noun* a company that has its capital divided into shares that are freely tradable

stock control /ˈstɒk kənˌtrəʊl/ *noun* the process of making sure that the correct level of stock is maintained, to be able to meet demand while keeping the costs of holding stock to a minimum

stock controller /ˈstɒk kənˌtrəʊlə/ *noun* a person who notes movements of stock

stock depreciation /ˈstɒk dɪpriːʃi ˌeɪʃ(ə)n/ *noun* a reduction in value of stock which is held in a warehouse for some time

stock dividend /ˈstɒk ˌdɪvɪdend/ *noun US* a dividend paid to a shareholder in the form of additional shares rather than cash

stock exchange[1] /ˈstɒk ɪksˌtʃeɪndʒ/ *noun* same as **stock market**

stock exchange[2] /ˈstɒk ɪksˌtʃeɪndʒ/ *noun* a place where stocks and shares are bought and sold ○ *He works on the stock exchange.* ○ *Shares in the company are traded on the stock exchange.*

'…the news was favourably received on the Sydney Stock Exchange, where the shares gained 40 cents to A$9.80' [*Financial Times*]

Stock Exchange Automated Quotations System /stɒk ɪks ˌtʃeɪndʒ ˌɔːtəmeɪtɪd kwəʊˈteɪʃ(ə)nz ˌsɪstəm/ *noun* full form of **SEAQ**

Stock Exchange Council /ˌstɒk ɪks
ˌtʃeɪndʒ ˈkaʊnsəl/ *noun* a committee
which runs the London International
Stock Exchange and regulates the way in
which its members work

Stock Exchange Electronic Trading System /stɒk ɪks,tʃeɪndʒ
ˌelektrɒnɪk ˈtreɪdɪŋ ˌsɪstəm/ *noun* the
London Stock Exchange's electronic
share trading system in major shares.
Buyers and sellers are automatically
matched by computer. Abbreviation **Sets**

stock exchange listing /ˈstɒk ɪks
ˌtʃeɪndʒ ˌlɪstɪŋ/ *noun* the fact of being
on the official list of shares which can be
bought or sold on the stock exchange ○
*The company is planning to obtain a stock
exchange listing.*

stock exchange operation /ˌstɒk
ɪks,tʃeɪndʒ ˌɒpəˈreɪʃ(ə)n/ *noun* the
activity of buying or selling of shares on
the stock exchange

stock figures /ˈstɒk ˌfɪgəz/ *plural
noun* details of how many goods are in
the warehouse or store

stockholder /ˈstɒkhəʊldə/ *noun US*
same as **shareholder**

stockholding /ˈstɒkhəʊldɪŋ/ *noun*
the shares in a company held by someone

stock-in-trade /ˌstɒk ɪn ˈtreɪd/ *noun*
goods held by a business for sale

stock jobber /ˈstɒk ˌdʒɒbə/ *noun*
formerly, a person who bought and sold
shares from other traders on the stock
exchange

stock jobbing /ˈstɒk ˌdʒɒbɪŋ/ *noun*
formerly, the business of buying and
selling shares from other traders on the
stock exchange

stock level /ˈstɒk ˌlev(ə)l/ *noun* the
quantity of goods kept in stock ○ *We try
to keep stock levels low during the
summer.*

stock market /ˈstɒk ˌmɑːkɪt/ *noun* a
place where shares are bought and sold,
i.e. a stock exchange ○ *stock market price*
or *price on the stock market*

stock market launch /ˈstɒk ˌmɑːkɪt
lɔːntʃ/ *noun* the occasion when shares in
a new company are first sold on the stock
exchange

stock market manipulation /ˈstɒk
ˌmɑːkɪt mə,nɪpjʊleɪʃ(ə)n/ *noun* the
practice of trying to influence the price of

shares by buying or selling in order to
give the impression that the shares are
widely traded

stock market manipulator /ˌstɒk
ˌmɑːkɪt məˈnɪpjʊleɪtə/ *noun* a person
who tries to influence the price of shares
in his or her own favour

stockmarket rating /ˈstɒkmɑːkɪt
ˌreɪtɪŋ/ *noun* the price of a share on the
stock market, which shows how investors
and financial advisers generally consider
the value of the company

stock market valuation /ˌstɒk
ˌmɑːkɪt ˌvæljuˈeɪʃ(ə)n/ *noun* the value
of a company based on the current market
price of its shares

stock mutual funds /stɒk
ˈmjuːtʃuəl fʌndz/ *plural noun* mutual
funds where the money is invested in
corporate stocks as opposed to bonds or
government securities

stock option /ˈstɒk ˌɒpʃən/ *noun US*
same as **share option**

stockout /ˈstɒkaʊt/ *noun* a situation
where an item is out of stock

stock picker /ˈstɒk ˌpɪkə/ *noun* a
person whose job is to choose which
shares to buy

stockpicking /ˈstɒpɪkɪŋ/ *noun* the
task of making a choice as to which
shares to buy (NOTE: The counterpart,
deciding how much money to spend on
shares, is called **asset allocation**.)

stock-purchasing loans /ˈstɒk
ˌpɜːtʃɪsɪŋ ləʊnz/ *plural noun* loans from
a company to members of staff to allow
them to buy shares in the company

stock quote /ˈstɒk kwəʊt/ *noun* a
current price of a share on a stock
exchange

stocks and shares /ˌstɒks ən ˈʃeəz/
plural noun shares in ordinary companies

stocktaking /ˈstɒkteɪkɪŋ/, **stocktake**
/ˈstɒkteɪk/ *noun* the counting of goods in
stock at the end of an accounting period ○
*The warehouse is closed for the annual
stocktaking.*

stocktaking sale /ˈstɒkteɪkɪŋ ˌseɪl/
noun a sale of goods cheaply to clear a
warehouse before stocktaking

stock transfer form /ˌstɒk ˈtrænsfɜː
fɔːm/ *noun* a form to be signed by the
person transferring shares

stock turn /'stɒk tɜːn/, **stock turn-round** /'stɒk ˌtɜːnraʊnd/, **stock turn-over** /'stɒk ˌtɜːnəʊvə/ *noun* the total value of stock sold in a year divided by the average value of goods in stock

stock valuation /ˌstɒk ˌvælju'eɪʃ(ə)n/ *noun* an estimation of the value of stock at the end of an accounting period

stop /stɒp/ *noun* a situation in which someone is not supplying or not paying something □ **account on stop** an account which is not supplied because it has not paid its latest invoices ○ *We put their account on stop and sued them for the money they owed.* □ **to put a stop on a cheque** to tell the bank not to pay a cheque which you have written ■ *verb* **1.** (NOTE: **stopping- stopped**) □ **to stop an account** not to supply an account any more on credit because bills have not been paid □ **to stop payments** not to make any further payments **2.** □ **to stop someone's wages** to take money out of someone's wages ○ *We stopped £25 from his pay because he was late.* (NOTE: **stopping – stopped**)

stop-go /stɒp 'ɡəʊ/ *noun* an economic policy leading to short periods of expansion followed by short periods of squeeze

stop-loss order /ˌstɒp 'lɒs ˌɔːdə/ *noun* an instruction to a stockbroker to sell a share if the price falls to an specified level (NOTE: The US term is **stop order**.)

stoppage /'stɒpɪdʒ/ *noun* a sum of money taken regularly from an employee's wages for insurance, tax, etc.

storage capacity /'stɔːrɪdʒ kə ˌpæsɪti/ *noun* the space available for storage

store card /'stɔː kɑːd/ *noun* a credit card issued by a large department store, which can only be used for purchases in that store

straddle /'stræd(ə)l/ *noun* **1.** a spread, the difference between bid and offer price. **2.** the act of buying a put option and a call option at the same time

straight bonds /'streɪt bɒndz/ *plural noun* normal fixed-interest bonds which can be redeemed at a certain date

straight line depreciation /ˌstreɪt laɪn dɪˌpriːʃi'eɪʃ(ə)n/ *noun* a form of depreciation that divides the cost of a fixed asset evenly over each year of its anticipated lifetime

straight paper /streɪt 'peɪpə/ *noun* same as **straight bonds**

straights /streɪts/ *plural noun* same as **straight bonds**

Straits Times index /streɪts 'taɪmz ˌɪndeks/ an index of prices on the Singapore Stock Exchange

strapped /stræpt/ *adjective* □ **strapped for cash** short of money

street /striːt/ *noun* a road in a town ○ *Their new address is 25 Broad Street.* □ **the Street** *US* Wall Street (*informal*)

street name /'striːt neɪm/ *noun* a nominee name for holding securities

street price /'striːt praɪs/ *noun* same as **retail price**

strength /streŋθ/ *noun* the fact of being strong, or being at a high level ○ *the underlying strength of the market* ○ *The company took advantage of the strength of the demand for mobile phones.* ○ *The strength of the pound increases the possibility of high interest rates.* Opposite **weakness**

strike /straɪk/ *verb* □ **to strike a bargain with someone** to come to an agreement □ **a deal was struck at £25 a unit** we agreed the price of £25 a unit

strike price /'straɪkɪŋ praɪs/, **striking price** *noun* **1.** a price at which a new issue of shares is offered for sale **2.** the lowest selling price when selling a new issue of shares by tender (applicants who tendered at a higher price will get shares; those who tendered at a lower price will not)

strip /strɪp/ *noun* **1.** a band of a colour. ◊ **magnetic strip 2.** *US* an action of separating coupons from a bond

strong /strɒŋ/ *adjective* with a lot of force or strength ○ *This Christmas saw a strong demand for mobile phones.* ○ *The company needs a strong chairman.*

'…everybody blames the strong dollar for US trade problems' [*Duns Business Month*]

'…in a world of floating exchange rates the dollar is strong because of capital inflows rather than weak because of the nation's trade deficit' [*Duns Business Month*]

strongbox /'strɒŋbɒks/ *noun* a heavy metal box which cannot be opened easily, in which valuable documents and money can be kept

strong currency /ˌstrɒŋ ˈkʌrənsi/ noun a currency which has a high value against other currencies

strong market /strɒŋ ˈmɑːkɪt/ noun a market where prices are moving up

strong pound /ˌstrɒŋ ˈpaʊnd/ noun a pound which is high against other currencies

strongroom /ˈstrɒŋruːm/ noun a special room in a bank where valuable documents, money and gold can be kept

structural /ˈstrʌktʃ(ə)rəl/ adjective referring to a structure ○ to make structural changes in a company

structural unemployment /ˌstrʌktʃ(ə)rəl ˌʌnɪmˈplɔɪmənt/ noun unemployment caused by the changing structure of an industry or the economy

structure /ˈstrʌktʃə/ noun the way in which something is organised ○ the price structure in the small car market ○ the career structure within a corporation ○ The paper gives a diagram of the company's organisational structure. ○ The company is reorganising its discount structure. □ **capital structure of a company** way in which a company's capital is set up

stub /stʌb/ noun a slip of paper left after writing a cheque, an invoice or a receipt, as a record of the deal which has taken place

student loan /ˌstjuːd(ə)nt ˈləʊn/ noun a loan made to a student to help him or her through university (the loan is repayable later from earnings)

sub /sʌb/ noun **1.** wages paid in advance **2.** same as **subscription**

sub- /sʌb/ prefix under or less important

sub-account /ˈsʌb əˌkaʊnt/ noun one of several separate investment accounts on which a variable annuity is based. ◊ **annuity**

sub-agency /ˈsʌb ˌeɪdʒənsi/ noun a small agency which is part of a large agency

sub-agent /ˈsʌb ˌeɪdʒənt/ noun a person who is in charge of a sub-agency

subcontract noun /ˈsʌbˌkɒntrækt/ a contract between the main contractor for a whole project and another firm which will do part of the work ○ They have been awarded the subcontract for all the electrical work in the new building. ○ We will put the electrical work out to subcontract. ■ verb /ˌsʌbkənˈtrækt/ (of a main contractor) to agree with a company that they will do part of the work for a project ○ The electrical work has been subcontracted to Smith Ltd

subcontractor /ˈsʌbkənˌtræktə/ noun a company which has a contract to do work for a main contractor

subject to /ˈsʌbdʒɪkt tuː/ adjective **1.** depending on □ **the contract is subject to government approval** the contract will be valid only if it is approved by the government □ **offer subject to availability** the offer is valid only if the goods are available **2.** □ **these articles are subject to import tax** import tax has to be paid on these articles

sublease noun /ˈsʌbliːs/ a lease from a tenant to another tenant ○ They signed a sublease for the property. ■ verb /sʌbˈliːs/ to lease a leased property from another tenant ○ They subleased a small office in the centre of town.

sublessee /ˌsʌbleˈsiː/ noun a person or company that takes a property on a sublease

sublessor /ˌsʌbleˈsɔː/ noun a tenant who leases a leased property to another tenant

sublet /sʌbˈlet/ verb to let a leased property to another tenant ○ We have sublet part of our office to a financial consultancy. (NOTE: **subletting – sublet**)

subordinated loan /səˌbɔːdɪnətɪd ˈləʊn/ noun a loan which ranks after all other borrowings as regards payment of interest or repayment of capital

sub-prime loan /ˌsʌb praɪm ˈləʊn/, **sub-prime credit** /ˌsʌb praɪm ˈkredɪt/ noun a loan offered to borrowers with a tainted or limited credit history using a risk-based pricing system to calculate the terms of the loans, including the interest rate

subscribe /səbˈskraɪb/ verb □ **to subscribe for shares, to subscribe to a share issue** to apply for shares in a new company

subscriber /səbˈskraɪbə/ noun □ **subscriber to a share issue** a person who has applied for shares in a new company

subscription /səb'skrɪpʃən/ *noun* **1.** money paid in advance for a series of issues of a magazine, for membership of a society, or for access to information on a website ○ *Did you remember to pay the subscription to the computer magazine?* ○ *She forgot to renew her club subscription.* **2.** □ **subscription to a new share issue** application to buy shares in a new company

subscription list /səb'skrɪpʃən lɪst/ *noun* a list of subscribers to a new share issue

subscription price /səb'skrɪpʃən praɪs/ *noun* the price at which new shares in an existing company are offered for sale

subsidiary /səb'sɪdiəri/ *adjective* less important ○ *They agreed to most of the conditions in the contract but queried one or two subsidiary items.* ■ *noun* same as **subsidiary company** ○ *Most of the group profit was contributed by the subsidiaries in the Far East.*

subsidiary account /səb,sɪdiəri ə'kaʊnt/ *noun* an account for one of the individual people or organisations that jointly hold another account

subsidiary company /səb,sɪdiəri 'kʌmp(ə)ni/ *noun* a company which is more than 50% owned by a holding company, and where the holding company controls the board of directors

subsidise /'sʌbsɪdaɪz/, **subsidize** *verb* to help by giving money ○ *The government has refused to subsidise the car industry.*

subsidised accommodation /,sʌbsɪdaɪzd ə,kɒmə'deɪʃ(ə)n/ *noun* cheap accommodation which is partly paid for by an employer or a local authority

subsidy /'sʌbsɪdi/ *noun* **1.** money given to help something which is not profitable ○ *The industry exists on government subsidies.* ○ *The government has increased its subsidy to the car industry.* **2.** money given by a government to make something cheaper ○ *the subsidy on rail transport* (NOTE: The plural is **subsidies.**)

substantial /səb'stænʃəl/ *adjective* large or important

subtenancy /sʌb'tenənsi/ *noun* an agreement to sublet a property

subtenant /sʌb'tenənt/ *noun* a person or company to which a property has been sublet

subtotal /'sʌb,təʊt(ə)l/ *noun* the total of one section of a complete set of figures ○ *She added all the subtotals to make a grand total.*

subtract /səb'trækt/ *verb* to take away something from a total ○ *The credit note should be subtracted from the figure for total sales.* ○ *If the profits from the Far Eastern operations are subtracted, you will see that the group has not been profitable in the European market.*

sub-underwriter /,sʌb 'ʌndəraɪtə/ *noun* a company which underwrites an issue, taking shares from the main underwriters

subvention /səb'venʃ(ə)n/ *noun* same as **subsidy**

succeed /sək'siːd/ *verb* **1.** to do well, to be profitable ○ *The company has succeeded best in the overseas markets.* ○ *Her business has succeeded more than she had expected.* **2.** to do what was planned ○ *She succeeded in passing her computing test.* ○ *They succeeded in putting their rivals out of business.*

success /sək'ses/ *noun* **1.** an act of doing something well ○ *The launch of the new model was a great success.* ○ *The company has had great success in the Japanese market.* **2.** an act of doing what was intended ○ *We had no success in trying to sell the lease.* ○ *She has been looking for a job for six months, but with no success.*

suitor /'suːtə/ *noun* a person or company that wants to buy another

sum¹ /sʌm/ *noun* **1.** a quantity of money ○ *A sum of money was stolen from the human resources office.* ○ *He lost large sums on the Stock Exchange.* ○ *She received the sum of £5000 in compensation.* □ **the sum insured** the largest amount which an insurer will pay under the terms of an insurance **2.** the total of a series of figures added together ○ *The sum of the various subtotals is £18,752.*

sum² /sʌm/ *noun* a unit of currency used in Uzbekistan

sums chargeable to the reserve /,sʌmz ,tʃɑːdʒəb(ə)l tə ðə rɪ'zɜːv/ *plural noun* sums which can be debited to a company's reserves

sundries /'sʌndriz/ *plural noun* various small additional items, often of little value, that are not included under any of the main headings in accounts

sundry /'sʌndri/ *adjective* various

sunrise industries /'sʌnraiz ˌindəstriz/ *plural noun* companies in the fields of electronics and other high-tech areas

sunset industries /'sʌnset ˌindəstriz/ *plural noun* old-style industries which are being replaced by new technology

superannuation /ˌsuːpərænjuˈeiʃ(ə)n/ *noun* a pension paid to someone who is too old or ill to work any more

supplementary benefit /ˌsʌpliment(ə)ri 'benifit/ *noun* formerly, payments from the government to people with very low incomes. It was replaced by income support.

supplier /sə'plaiə/ *noun* a person or company that supplies or sells goods or services ○ *We use the same office equipment supplier for all our stationery purchases.* ○ *They are major suppliers of spare parts to the car industry.* Also called **producer**

supply /sə'plai/ *noun* the act of providing something which is needed

supply and demand /sə,plai ən di 'maːnd/ *noun* the amount of a product which is available and the amount which is wanted by customers

Supply Bill /sə'plai bil/ *noun* a bill for providing money for government requirements

supply estimates /sə'plai ,estiməts/ *plural noun* British government expenditure which is voted by Parliament

supply price /sə'plai prais/ *noun* the price at which something is provided

supply shock /sə'plai ʃɒk/ *noun* a sudden rise in productivity which gives higher output and profits without inflation

supply-side economics /sə'plai said iːkə,nɒmiks/ *plural noun* an economic theory that governments should encourage producers and suppliers of goods by cutting taxes, rather than encourage demand by making more money available in the economy (NOTE: takes a singular verb)

support /sə'pɔːt/ *noun* **1.** actions or money intended to help someone or something ○ *The government has provided support to the car industry.* ○ *We have no financial support from the banks.* **2.** agreement or encouragement ○ *The chairman has the support of the committee.* ■ *verb* **1.** to give money to help someone or something ○ *The government is supporting the car industry to the tune of $2m per annum.* ○ *We hope the banks will support us during the expansion period.* □ **to support a share price** to buy shares in order to help the price remain at the current level or even rise **2.** to encourage someone, or to agree with someone ○ *She hopes the other members of the committee will support her.* ○ *The market will not support another price increase.*

support level /sə'pɔːt ,lev(ə)l/ *noun* a level below which a share, a commodity or the stock market will not fall, because of general support from investors

support manager /sə'pɔːt ,mænidʒə/ *noun* a manager of the back office of a securities firm

support point /sə'pɔːt pɔint/ *noun* same as **support level**

support price /sə'pɔːt prais/ *noun* a price in the EU at which a government will buy agricultural produce to stop the price falling

surcharge /'sɜːtʃɑːdʒ/ *noun* an extra charge

surety /'ʃuərəti/ *noun* **1.** a person who guarantees that someone will do something ○ *to stand surety for someone* **2.** deeds, share certificates, etc., deposited as security for a loan

surplus /'sɜːpləs/ *noun* **1.** more of something than is needed **2.** an amount of money remaining after all liabilities have been met □ **to absorb a surplus** to take a surplus into a larger amount ■ *adjective* more than is needed ○ *Profit figures are lower than planned because of surplus labour.* ○ *Some of the machines may have to be sold off as there is surplus production capacity.* ○ *We are proposing to put our surplus staff on short time.*

'Both imports and exports reached record levels in the latest year. This generated a $371 million trade surplus in June, the seventh consecutive monthly surplus and close to market expectations' [*Dominion (Wellington, New Zealand)*]

surrender /sə'rendə/ *noun* the act of giving up of an insurance policy before the contracted date for maturity ■ *verb* □ **to surrender a policy** to give up an insurance policy before the date on which it matures

surrender charge /sə'rendə tʃɑːdʒ/, **surrender fee** /sə'rendə fiː/ *noun* a charge levied when someone withdraws money invested before the date allowed (this is to deter early withdrawals)

surrender value /sə'rendə ˌvæljuː/ *noun* the money which an insurer will pay if an insurance policy is given up

surtax /'sɜːtæks/ *noun* an extra tax on high income

surveillance /sə'veɪləns/ *noun* a careful watch over people or buildings

surveillance camera /sə'veɪləns ˌkæm(ə)rə/ *noun* a camera which takes photographs of people in a bank

sushi bond /'suːʃi bɒnd/ *noun* a bond issued in a foreign currency by a Japanese corporation. ◊ **samurai bond**, **shogun bond**

suspend /sə'spend/ *verb* to stop doing something for a time ○ *We have suspended payments while we are waiting for news from our agent.* ○ *Sailings have been suspended until the weather gets better.* ○ *Work on the construction project has been suspended.* ○ *The management decided to suspend negotiations.*

suspense account /sə'spens ə ˌkaʊnt/ *noun* an account into which payments are put temporarily when the accountant cannot be sure where they should be entered

suspension /sə'spenʃən/ *noun* an act of stopping something for a time ○ *There has been a temporary suspension of payments.* ○ *We are trying to avoid a suspension of deliveries during the strike.*

swap /swɒp/ *noun* an exchange of one thing for another ■ *verb* to exchange one thing for another ○ *He swapped his old car for a new motorcycle.*

swap arrangement /'swɒp ə ˌreɪndʒmənt/ *noun* an arrangement between central banks to allow each other

credit in their respective currencies so as to make currency transactions easier

swaption /'swɒpʃən/ *noun* an option to arrange an interest rate swap at some time in the future

sweetener /'swiːt(ə)nə/ *noun* an incentive offered to help persuade somebody to take a particular course of action (*informal*)

SWIFT *abbreviation* Society for Worldwide Interbank Financial Telecommunications

Swiss franc /ˌswɪs 'fræŋk/ *noun* a unit of currency used in Switzerland and Liechtenstein (normally considered a very stable currency)

switch /swɪtʃ/ *verb* to change, especially to change investment money from one type of investment to another

Switch card /'swɪtʃ kɑːd/ *noun* a card linked to the UK Switch network but, unlike a credit card, when you pay for goods and services with a Switch card, the money leaves your account immediately

syndicate *noun* /'sɪndɪkət/ a group of people or companies working together to make money ○ *a German finance syndicate* ■ *verb* /'sɪndɪkeɪt/ to arrange for a large loan to be underwritten by several international banks

'…over the past few weeks, companies raising new loans from international banks have been forced to pay more, and an unusually high number of attempts to syndicate loans among banks has failed' [*Financial Times*]

synergy /'sɪnədʒi/ *noun* the process of producing greater effects by joining forces than by acting separately ○ *There is considerable synergy between the two companies.*

system /'sɪstəm/ *noun* an arrangement or organisation of things which work together ○ *Our accounting system has worked well in spite of the large increase in orders.* ○ *What system is being used for filing data on personnel?* □ **to operate a quota system** to regulate supplies by fixing quantities which are allowed ○ *We arrange our distribution using a quota system – each agent is allowed only a specific number of units.*

T

tab /tæb/ *noun* same as **tabulator** (*informal*)

table /ˈteɪb(ə)l/ *noun* **1.** a diagram or chart **2.** a list of figures or facts set out in columns ■ *verb* to put items of information on the table before a meeting ○ *The report of the finance committee was tabled.*

Table A /ˌteɪb(ə)l ˈeɪ/ *noun* the model articles of association of a limited company set out in the Companies Act, 1985

Table B /ˌteɪb(ə)l ˈbiː/ *noun* the model memorandum of association of a limited company set out in the Companies Act, 1985

Table C /ˌteɪb(ə)l ˈsiː/ *noun* the model memorandum and articles of association set out in the Companies Act, 1985 for a company limited by guarantee, having no share capital

Table D /ˌteɪb(ə)l ˈdiː/ *noun* the model memorandum and articles of association of a public company with share capital limited by guarantee, set out in the Companies Act, 1985

Table E /ˌteɪb(ə)l ˈiː/ *noun* the model memorandum and articles of association of an unlimited company with share capital, set out in the Companies Act, 1985

table of contents /ˌteɪb(ə)l əv ˈkɒntents/ *noun* a list of contents in a book

tabular /ˈtæbjʊlə/ *adjective* □ **in tabular form** arranged in a table

tabulate /ˈtæbjʊleɪt/ *verb* to set something out in a table

tabulation /ˌtæbjʊˈleɪʃ(ə)n/ *noun* the arrangement of figures in a table

tabulator /ˈtæbjʊleɪtə/ *noun* a feature on a computer which sets words or figures automatically in columns

tael /taɪl/ *noun* a measurement of the weight of gold, used in the Far East (= 1.20oz/38g)

tail /teɪl/ *noun US* **1.** a spread between the bid price and the lowest acceptable price on US Treasury bills **2.** the figures which come after the decimal point (in the quoted price of a bond)

taka /ˈtɑːkə/ *noun* a unit of currency used in Bangladesh

take /teɪk/ *noun* **1.** the money received in a shop ○ *Our weekly take is over £5,000.* **2.** a profit from any sale ■ *verb* **1.** to receive or to get (NOTE: **taking – took – has taken**) □ **the shop takes £2,000 a week** the shop receives £2,000 a week in cash sales □ **she takes home £450 a week** her salary, after deductions for tax, etc. is £450 a week **2.** to perform an action (NOTE: **taking – took – has taken**) □ **to take action** to do something ○ *You must take immediate action if you want to stop thefts.* □ **to take a call** to answer the telephone □ **to take the chair** to be chairman of a meeting ○ *In the absence of the chairman his deputy took the chair.* □ **to take stock** to count the items in a warehouse □ **to take stock of a situation** to examine the state of things before deciding what to do **3.** to need a time or a quantity ○ *It took the factory six weeks* or *The factory took six weeks to clear the backlog of orders.* (NOTE: **taking – took – has taken**)

take away *phrasal verb* to remove one figure from a total ○ *If you take away the home sales, the total turnover is down.*

take off *phrasal verb* **1.** to remove or to

deduct something ○ *He took £25 off the price.* **2.** to start to rise fast ○ *Sales took off after the TV commercials.*

take out *phrasal verb* **1.** to remove something ○ *She's taken all the money out of her account.* **2.** □ **to take out a patent for an invention** to apply for and receive a patent □ **to take out insurance against theft** to pay a premium to an insurance company, so that if a theft takes place the company will pay compensation

'…capital gains are not taxed, but money taken out in profits and dividends is taxed' [*Toronto Star*]

take over *phrasal verb* **1.** to start to do something in place of someone else ○ *Miss Black took over from Mr Jones on May 1st.* ○ *The buyer takes over the company's liabilities.* **2.** □ **to take over a company** to buy a business by offering to buy most of its shares ○ *The company was taken over by a large multinational.*

take up *phrasal verb* □ **to take up an option** to accept an option which has been offered and put into action

take down /ˌteɪk ˈdaʊn/ *verb US* to receive a share allotment

take-home pay /ˈteɪk həʊm ˌpeɪ/ *noun* same as **disposable personal income** ○ *After all the deductions, her take-home pay is only £600 a week.*

take-out /ˈteɪk aʊt/ *noun* the act of removing capital which you had originally invested in a new company by selling your shares

takeover /ˈteɪkəʊvə/ *noun* **1.** an act of buying a controlling interest in a business by buying more than 50% of its shares. Compare **acquisition 2.** the act of starting to do something in place of someone else □ **the take-over period is always difficult** there are always problems during the period when one person is taking over work from another

takeover bid /ˈteɪkəʊvə bɪd/ *noun* an offer to buy all or a majority of the shares in a company so as to control it ○ *They made a takeover bid for the company.* ○ *She had to withdraw her takeover bid when she failed to find any backers.* ○ *Share prices rose sharply on the disclosure of the takeover bid.* □ **to make a takeover bid for a company** to offer to

buy the majority of the shares in a company □ **to withdraw a takeover bid** to say that you no longer offer to buy the shares in a company □ **the company rejected the takeover bid** the directors recommended that the shareholders should not accept the offer ○ *Share prices rose sharply on the disclosure of the takeover bid.*

takeover target /ˈteɪkəʊvə ˌtɑːɡɪt/ *noun* a company which is the object of a takeover bid

takeover timetable /ˈteɪkəʊvə ˌtaɪmteɪb(ə)l/ *noun* a timetable of the various events during a takeover bid

COMMENT: The timetable for a takeover bid is regulated by the London Stock Exchange: the formal documents are sent out by the bidding company some days after it has announced that it is making the bid. From the date of sending out the formal documents, the stock exchange allows the company 60 days in which to try and persuade as many shareholders as possible to accept the offer. If less than 50 per cent accept, then the bidder can extend the offer, or increase of the offer, or simply let the offer lapse. If another company now makes a rival offer, it too has 60 days to try to gain enough acceptances.

take-private /ˌteɪk ˈpraɪvət/ *noun US* an arrangement by which a quoted company leaves the stock exchange and becomes a privately owned investment ○ *The law firm was figuring in six of the seven take-privates last year.* ◊ **public-to-private deal**

taker /ˈteɪkə/ *noun* a person who wants to buy something ○ *There were very few takers for the special offer.*

take up rate /ˈteɪk ʌp ˌreɪt/ *noun* the percentage of acceptances for a rights issue

takings /ˈteɪkɪŋz/ *plural noun* the money received in a shop or a business ○ *The week's takings were stolen from the cash desk.*

tala /ˈtɑːlə/ *noun* a unit of currency used in Samoa

tally /ˈtæli/ *noun* a note of things counted or recorded ○ *to keep a tally of stock movements* or *of expenses* ■ *verb* to agree, to be the same ○ *The invoices do not tally.* ○ *The accounts department tried to make the figures tally.*

tally clerk /ˈtæli klɑːk/ *noun* a person whose job is to note quantities of cargo

tally sheet /ˈtæli ʃiːt/ *noun* a sheet on which quantities are noted

tangible assets /ˌtændʒɪb(ə)l ˈæsets/, **tangible fixed assets** /ˌtændʒɪb(ə)l fɪkst ˈæsets/, **tangible property** /ˌtændʒɪb(ə)l ˈprɒpəti/ *plural noun* assets that are physical, such as buildings, cash and stock. Leases and securities, although not physical in themselves, are classed as tangible assets because the underlying assets are physical.

tangible asset value /ˌtændʒəb(ə)l ˈæset ˌvæljuː/, **tangible net worth** /ˌtændʒəb(ə)l net ˈwɜːθ/ *noun* the value of all the assets of a company less its intangible assets, e.g. goodwill, shown as a value per share

TAO *abbreviation* Taxpayer Assistance Order

tap /tæp/ *noun* same as **tap stock** ■ *verb* to get finance by borrowing from investors, lenders, etc.

taper /ˈteɪpə/, **tapering relief** /ˌteɪpərɪŋ rɪˈliːf/ *noun* a new system of reducing capital gains tax payable when shares are sold, according to the length of time the shares have been held

tap stock /ˈtæp stɒk/ *noun* a government stock issued direct to the Bank of England for sale to investors

COMMENT: Government stocks are normally issued in tranches for sale by tender, but small amounts are kept as 'tap stock' for direct sale to investors; the term is applied to any government stocks sold in this way.

target /ˈtɑːgɪt/ *noun* something to aim for ○ *performance targets* □ **to be on target** to be heading towards the target that has been set □ **to set targets** to fix amounts or quantities which employees have to produce or reach □ **to meet a target** to produce the quantity of goods or sales which are expected □ **to miss a target** not to produce the amount of goods or sales which are expected ○ *They missed the target figure of £2m turnover.* ■ *verb* to aim something at someone, or to take someone or something as a target ○ *a campaign that targets the over-50s*

'…he believes that increased competition could keep inflation below the 2.5 per cent target' [*Investors Chronicle*]

'…the minister is persuading the oil, gas, electricity and coal industries to target their advertising towards energy efficiency' [*Times*]

Target /ˈtɑːgɪt/, **TARGET** *noun* a system set up by the European Central Bank to deal with cross-border payments between member states of the EU. Full form **Trans-European Automated Real-time Gross settlement Express Transfer**. ◊ **real-time gross settlement system**

target company /ˌtɑːgɪt ˈkʌmp(ə)ni/ *noun* same as **takeover target**

'…in a normal leveraged buyout the acquirer raises money by borrowing against the assets of the target company' [*Fortune*]

target market /ˈtɑːgɪt ˌmɑːkɪt/ *noun* the market in which a company is planning to sell its goods

target price /ˈtɑːgɪt praɪs/ *noun* a wholesale price within the EU for certain products, such as wheat, which market management is intended to achieve; it is linked to the intervention price

COMMENT: Target prices are set in terms of fixed agricultural units of account, which are converted into different national currencies using adjusted exchange rates known as 'green rates' (in the UK, the 'green pound'). A system of levies on non-EU agricultural imports is used to protect target prices when they are set above the general level of world prices. In addition, the EU has established an internal price support system based on a set of intervention prices set slightly below the target price. If the level of supply is in excess of what is needed to clear the market at the target price, the excess supply is bought by the Community at the intervention price, thereby preventing overproduction from depressing the common price level as would normally happen in a free market.

tariff /ˈtærɪf/ *noun* a rate of charging for something such as electricity, hotel rooms, or train tickets

tariff barrier /ˈtærɪf ˌbæriə/ *noun* the customs duty intended to make imports more difficult ○ *to impose tariff barriers on* or *to lift tariff barriers from a product*

tax /tæks/ *noun* an amount of money charged by government as part of a person's income or on goods bought □ **basic tax** income tax paid at the normal rate □ **to lift a tax** to remove a tax ○ *The tax on fuel charges has been lifted.* ○ *The tax on company profits has been lifted.* □ **tax deducted at source** tax which is removed from a salary or interest before the money is paid out ∎ *verb* to make someone pay a tax, to impose a tax on something ○ *Businesses are taxed at 40%.* ○ *Income is taxed at 35%.* ○ *Luxury items are heavily taxed.* ○ *The government is proposing to tax businesses at 50%.*

tax abatement /'tæks ə,beɪtmənt/ *noun* a reduction of tax

taxable /'tæksəb(ə)l/ *adjective* able to be taxed

taxable income /,tæksəb(ə)l 'ɪnkʌm/ *noun* income on which a person has to pay tax

taxable items /'tæksəb(ə)l ,aɪtəmz/ *plural noun* items on which a tax has to be paid

taxable supply /,tæksəb(ə)l sə'plaɪ/ *noun* a supply of goods which are subject to VAT

tax adjustments /'tæks ə,dʒʌstmənts/ *plural noun* changes made to tax

tax adviser /'tæks əd,vaɪzə/, **tax consultant** /'tæks kən,sʌltənt/ *noun* a person who gives advice on tax issues and problems

tax allowance /'tæks ə,laʊəns/ *noun* part of the income which a person is allowed to earn and not pay tax on

tax assessment /'tæks ə,sesmənt/ *noun* a calculation by a tax inspector of the amount of tax a person owes

taxation /tæk'seɪʃ(ə)n/ *noun* the system of raising revenue for public funding by taxing individuals and organisations, or the amount of revenue raised

tax avoidance /'tæks ə,vɔɪd(ə)ns/ *noun* the practice of legally trying to pay as little tax as possible

tax bill /'tæks bɪl/ *noun* an amount of tax (to be) paid

tax bracket /'tæks ,brækɪt/ *noun* the section of people paying a particular level of income tax

tax break /'tæks breɪk/ *noun* an allowance which can be set off against tax

tax code /'tæks kəʊd/ *noun* a number given to indicate the amount of tax allowance a person has

tax concession /'tæks kən,seʃ(ə)n/ *noun* an act of allowing less tax to be paid

tax court /'tæks kɔːt/ *noun US* a court which deals with disputes between taxpayers and the Internal Revenue Service

tax credit /'tæks ,kredɪt/ *noun* **1.** a sum of money which can be offset against tax **2.** the part of a dividend on which the company has already paid tax, so that the shareholder is not taxed on it

tax-deductible /,tæks dɪ'dʌktɪb(ə)l/ *adjective* possible to deduct from an income before tax is calculated □ **these expenses are not tax-deductible** tax has to be paid on these expenses

tax deductions /'tæks dɪ,dʌkʃənz/ *plural noun* **1.** money removed from a salary to pay tax **2.** *US* business expenses which can be claimed against tax

tax-deferred /tæks dɪ'fɜːd/ *adjective US* not taxable until a later time, often after retirement

tax-deferred retirement plan /tæks dɪ,fɜːd rɪ'taɪəmənt plæn/, **tax-deferred savings plan** /tæks dɪ,fɜːd 'seɪvɪŋz plæn/ *noun US* a savings plan into which a person can regularly put a certain proportion of income, with tax only being payable on retirement

tax deposit certificate /'tæks dɪ ,pɒzɪt sə,tɪfɪkət/ *noun* a certificate showing that a taxpayer has deposited money in advance of a tax payment. The money earns interest while on deposit.

tax-efficient /tæks ɪ'fɪʃ(ə)nt/ *adjective* referring to an investment which helps avoid tax

tax evasion /'tæks ɪ,veɪʒ(ə)n/ *noun* the practice of illegally trying to not pay tax

tax-exempt /,tæks ɪg'zempt/ *adjective* **1.** referring to a person or organisation not required to pay tax **2.** not subject to tax

tax exemption /'tæks ɪg,zempʃən/ *noun* **1.** the fact of being free from payment of tax **2.** *US* the part of income which a person is allowed to earn and not pay tax on

tax-exempt special savings account /,tæks ɪg,zempt ,speʃ(ə)l 'seɪvɪŋz ə,kaʊnt/ *noun* a now-discontinued form of interest-free savings account largely superseded by the ISA. Abbreviation **TESSA**

tax-favoured investment /,tæks ,feɪvəd ɪn'vestmənt/ *noun* an investment which offers tax-reducing incentives

tax-filing program /ˈtæks ˌfaɪlɪŋ ˌprəʊɡræm/ *noun* computer software to help draw up your income tax return

tax form /ˈtæks fɔːm/ *noun* a blank form to be filled in with details of income and allowances and sent to the tax office each year

tax-free /ˌtæks ˈfriː/ *adjective* with no tax having to be paid ○ *tax-free goods*

tax haven /ˈtæks ˌheɪv(ə)n/ *noun* a country or area where taxes are low, encouraging companies to set up their main offices there

tax holiday /ˈtæks ˌhɒlɪdeɪ/ *noun* a period when a new business is exempted from paying tax

tax inspector /ˈtæks ɪnˌspektə/ *noun* a government employee who investigates taxpayers' declarations

tax loophole /ˈtæks ˌluːphəʊl/ *noun* a legal means of not paying tax

taxpayer /ˈtækspeɪə/ *noun* a person or company that has to pay tax ○ *basic taxpayer* or *taxpayer at the basic rate* ○ *Corporate taxpayers are being targeted by the government.*

taxpayer advocate /ˌtækspeɪə ˈædvəkət/ *noun* a government official whose duty is to adjudicate in cases where ordinary taxpayers complain of treatment by the tax authorities

Taxpayer Assistance Order /ˌtækspeɪə əˈsɪst(ə)ns ˌɔːdə/ *noun* a court order allowing a company to recover debts from a taxpayer's salary before tax is paid ○ *basic taxpayer* or *taxpayer at the basic rate* Abbreviation **TAO**

tax planning /ˈtæks ˌplænɪŋ/ *noun* planning how to avoid paying too much tax, by investing in, e.g., tax-exempt savings schemes or offshore trusts

tax relief /ˈtæks rɪˌliːf/ *noun* reductions in tax liability that are allowed in line with necessary business expenditure

tax return /ˈtæks rɪˌtɜːn/ *noun* a completed tax form, with details of income and allowances

tax schedules /ˈtæks ˌʃedjuːlz/ *plural noun* six types of income as classified for tax. See Comment at **schedule**

tax shelter /ˈtæks ˌʃeltə/ *noun* a financial arrangement such as a pension scheme where investments can be made without tax

tax threshold /ˈtæks ˌθreʃhəʊld/ *noun* a point at which another percentage of tax is payable ○ *The government has raised the minimum tax threshold from £4,000 to £4,500.*

tax year /ˈtæks ˌjɪə/ *noun* a twelve month period on which taxes are calculated. In the UK this is 6th April to 5th April of the following year.

T-bill /ˈtiː bɪl/ *US* same as **Treasury bill** (*informal*)

T-bond /ˈtiː bɒnd/ *noun* same as **Treasury bond**

teaser /ˈtiːzə/, **teaser ad** /ˈtiːzər æd/ *noun* an advertisement that gives a little information about a product in order to attract customers by making them curious to know more

teaser rate /ˈtiːzə reɪt/ *noun* a specially good interest rate on a new product, used to encourage savers to switch funds to that product. It is replaced by a normal rate when enough subscribers have invested in it.

technical /ˈteknɪk(ə)l/ *adjective* **1.** referring to a particular machine or process ○ *The document gives all the technical details on the new computer.* **2.** referring to influences inside a market, e.g. volumes traded and forecasts based on market analysis, as opposed to external factors such as oil-price rises, wars, etc.

'…market analysts described the falls in the second half of last week as a technical correction' [*Australian Financial Review*]

'…at the end of the day, it was clear the Fed had not loosened the monetary reins, and Fed Funds forged ahead on the back of technical demand' [*Financial Times*]

technical analysis /ˌteknɪk(ə)l əˈnæləsɪs/ *noun* a study of the price movements and volumes traded on a stock exchange

technical correction /ˌteknɪk(ə)l kəˈrekʃ(ə)n/ *noun* an adjustment to the price of a share or the value of a currency

technical decline /ˌteknɪk(ə)l dɪˈklaɪn/ *noun* a fall in share prices because of technical analysis

technology stocks /tek'nɒlədʒi stɒks/, **tech stocks** /'tek stɒks/ *plural noun* shares in companies specialising in electronics, communications, etc.

telebanking /'teli,bæŋkɪŋ/ *noun* same as **telephone banking**

telegraphic transfer /,telɪgræfɪk 'trɑːnsfə/ *noun* a transfer of money from one account to another by telegraph

telephone banking /,telɪfəun 'bæŋkɪŋ/ *noun* a service by which a bank customer can carry out transactions over the phone using a password. It may involve direct contact with a bank representative or may be automated using the phone's keypad.

telephone order /'telɪfəun ,ɔːdə/ *noun* an order received by telephone ○ *Since we mailed the catalogue we have received a large number of telephone orders.*

teller /'telə/ *noun* a person who takes cash from or pays cash to customers at a bank

tem /tem/ ♦ **pro tem**

tenancy /'tenənsi/ *noun* an agreement by which a tenant can occupy a property

tenant /'tenənt/ *noun* a person or company which rents a house, flat or office to live or work in ○ *The tenant is liable for repairs.*

tender /'tendə/ *noun* an offer to do something for a specific price ○ *a successful tender* ○ *an unsuccessful tender* (NOTE: The US term is **bid**.) □ **to put a project out to tender, to ask for** *or* **invite tenders for a project** to ask contractors to give written estimates for a job □ **to put in** *or* **submit a tender** to make an estimate for a job □ **to sell shares by tender** to ask people to offer in writing a price for shares ■ *verb* **1.** *US* to sell shares, usually at a price above the current price, in response to a tender offer **2.** to offer money ○ *please tender the correct fare* □ **to tender for a contract** to put forward an estimate of cost for work to be carried out under contract ○ *to tender for the construction of a hospital*

tenderer /'tendərə/ *noun* a person or company that puts forward an estimate of cost ○ *The company was the successful tenderer for the project.* (NOTE: The US term is **bidder**.)

tendering /'tendərɪŋ/ *noun* the act of putting forward an estimate of cost ○ *To be successful, you must follow the tendering procedure as laid out in the documents.* (NOTE: The US term is **bidding**.)

tender offer /'tendər ,ɒfə/ *noun* a method of selling new securities or bonds by asking investors to make offers for them, and accepting the highest offers

tenge /'teŋgeɪ/ *noun* a unit of currency used in Kazakhstan

tenor /'tenə/ *noun* the life of a financial instrument, between the time it is taken out and the maturity date

term /tɜːm/ *noun* **1.** a period of time when something is legally valid ○ *during his term of office as chairman* ○ *the term of a lease* ○ *We have renewed her contract for a term of six months.* ○ *The term of the loan is fifteen years.* **2.** a part of a legal or university year

term account /'tɜːm ə,kaunt/ *noun* same as **term deposit**

term assurance /'tɜːm ə,ʃuərəns/ *noun* a life assurance which covers a person's life for a period of time. At the end of the period, if the person is still alive he receives nothing from the insurance.

term CD /'tɜːm siː ,diː/ *noun* a certificate of deposit which matures in more than twelve months

term deposit /'tɜːm dɪ,pɒzɪt/ *noun* money invested for a fixed period at a higher rate of interest

terminal bonus /,tɜːmɪn(ə)l 'bəunəs/ *noun* a bonus received when an insurance comes to an end

termination clause /,tɜːmɪ'neɪʃ(ə)n klɔːz/ *noun* a clause which explains how and when a contract can be terminated

term insurance /'tɜːm ɪn,ʃuərəns/ *noun US* same as **term assurance**

term loan /'tɜːm ləun/ *noun* a loan for a fixed period of time

terms /tɜːmz/ *plural noun* the conditions or duties which have to be carried out as part of a contract, or the arrangements which have to be agreed before a contract is valid ○ *to negotiate for better terms* ○ *She refused to agree to some of the terms of the contract.* ○ *By* or *Under the terms of the contract, the company is* *responsible for all damage to the property.*

'…companies have been improving communications, often as part of deals to cut down demarcation and to give everybody the same terms of employment' [*Economist*]

'…the Federal Reserve Board has eased interest rates in the past year, but they are still at historically high levels in real terms' [*Sunday Times*]

term shares /ˈtɜːm ʃeəz/ *plural noun* a type of building society deposit that offers a comparatively high rate of interest for a fixed period of time

terms of payment /ˌtɜːmz əv ˈpeɪmənt/ *plural noun* the conditions for paying something

terms of reference /ˌtɜːmz əv ˈref(ə)rəns/ *plural noun* the specific areas which a committee or an inspector can deal with ○ *Under the terms of reference of the committee, it cannot investigate complaints from the public.* ○ *The committee's terms of reference do not cover exports.*

terms of sale /ˌtɜːmz əv ˈseɪl/ *plural noun* the conditions attached to a sale

terms of trade /ˌtɜːmz əv ˈtreɪd/ *plural noun* the ratio of a country's import prices to export prices

tertiary industry /ˌtɜːʃəri ˈɪndəstri/ *noun* an industry which does not produce raw materials or manufacture products but offers a service such as banking, retailing, or accountancy

TESSA /ˈtesə/ *abbreviation* tax-exempt special savings account

thin market /θɪn ˈmɑːkɪt/ *noun* a market where there are not many shares available for sale, so the price is distorted (NOTE: The opposite is a **liquid market**.)

thin trading /θɪn ˈtreɪdɪŋ/ *noun* a day's trading where not many shares are offered for sale, so few bargains are made (NOTE: The opposite is a **liquid market**.)

third /θɜːd/ *noun* one part of something which is divided into three □ **to sell everything at one third off** to sell everything at a discount of 33% □ **the company has two thirds of the total market** the company has 66% of the total market

Third Market /θɜːd ˈmɑːkɪt/ *noun* same as **over-the-counter market**

third party /ˌθɜːd ˈpɑːti/ *noun* a person other than the two main parties involved in a contract, e.g., in an insurance contract, anyone who is not the insurance company nor the person who is insured □ **the case is in the hands of a third party** the case is being dealt with by someone who is not one of the main interested parties

third party insurance /ˌθɜːd pɑːti ɪn ˈʃʊərəns/ *noun* insurance to cover damage to any person who is not one of the people named in the insurance contract (that is, not the insured person nor the insurance company)

third quarter /ˌθɜːd ˈkwɔːtə/ *noun* the period of three months from July to September

Threadneedle Street /ˈθredniːd(ə)l striːt/ *noun* a street in the City of London where the Bank of England is situated. ◊ **Old Lady of Threadneedle Street**

3–6–3 rule /ˌθriː sɪks ˈθriː ˌruːl/ *noun* a rule that alludes to how banks lend out money at a higher rate than what it is paying out to its depositors i.e. that bankers give three per cent interest on depositors' accounts, lend the depositors money at six per cent interest and are playing golf at three pm

3i *abbreviation* Investors in Industry

three quarters /ˌθriː ˈkwɔːtəz/ *noun* 75% ○ *Three quarters of the staff are less than thirty years old.*

threshold /ˈθreʃhəʊld/ *noun* the point at which something changes

threshold agreement /ˈθreʃhəʊld ə ˌɡriːmənt/ *noun* a contract which says that if the cost of living goes up by more than an agreed amount, pay will go up to match it

threshold price /ˈθreʃhəʊld praɪs/ *noun* in the EU, the lowest price at which farm produce imported into the EU can be sold

thrift /θrɪft/ *noun* **1.** a careful attitude towards money, shown by saving or spending it wisely **2.** *US* a private local bank, savings and loan association or credit union, which accepts and pays interest on deposits from small investors

'…the thrift, which had grown from $4.7 million in assets in 1980 to 1.5 billion this year, has ended in liquidation' [*Barrons*]

'…some thrifts came to grief on speculative property deals, some in the high-risk junk bond market, others simply by lending too much to too many people' [*Times*]

thrifty /'θrɪfti/ *adjective* careful not to spend too much money

tick /tɪk/ *noun* **1.** credit (*informal*) ○ *All the furniture in the house is bought on tick.* **2.** a mark on paper to show that something is correct or that something is approved ○ *Put a tick in the box marked 'R'.* (NOTE: The US term is **check** in this meaning.) **3.** one step (up or down) in the price of a government bond or of financial futures ■ *phrasal verb* to mark with a sign to show that something is correct ○ *Tick the box marked 'R' if you require a receipt.* (NOTE: The US term is **check** in this meaning.)

ticker /'tɪkə/ *noun US* a machine (operated by telegraph) which prints details of shares prices and transactions rapidly (formerly printed on paper tape called 'ticker tape', but is now shown online on computer terminals)

ticker symbol /'tɪkə ˌsɪmb(ə)l/ *noun US* a letter used to identify a stock on the ticker tape system

COMMENT: All securities listed on the US stock exchanges are identified by letter symbols on ticker tape. So shares in Hilton are referred to as HLT, Texaco as TX, Xerox as XRX, etc.

tie /taɪ/ *verb* to attach or to link something to something ○ *The interest rate is tied to the RPI.*

tie in *phrasal verb* to link an insurance policy to a mortgage

tie up *phrasal verb* **1.** to attach or to fasten something tightly ○ *The parcel is tied up with string.* ○ *The ship was tied up to the quay.* **2.** to invest money in one way, so that it cannot be used for other investments ○ *He has £100,000 tied up in long-dated gilts.* ○ *The company has £250,000 tied up in stock which no one wants to buy.*

'…a lot of speculator money is said to be tied up in sterling because of the interest-rate differential between US and British rates' [*Australian Financial Review*]

tied loan /taɪd 'ləʊn/ *noun* a loan which involves a guarantee by the borrower to buy supplies from the lender

tier /tɪə/ *noun* a level

COMMENT: The British stock market is said to have two tiers: the first is the London Stock Exchange, with its listed securities. The second tier (which is linked to the first) is the Alternative Investment Market (AIM) which has less strict criteria for admitting securities, and is often used as a first stage in obtaining a main stock exchange quotation.

Tier One /ˌtɪə 'wʌn/ *noun* a first level of core capital which banks have (covering basic equity capital and disclosed reserves) to conform to the guidelines of the Basle Agreement

Tier Two /ˌtɪə 'tuː/ *noun* a second level of capital which banks have (this applies to undisclosed debts, and provisions against bad debts) to conform with the guidelines of the Basle Agreement

tie-up /'taɪ ʌp/ *noun* a link or connection ○ *The company has a tie-up with a German distributor.* (NOTE: The plural is **tie-ups**.)

tight /taɪt/ *adjective* which is controlled, which does not allow any movement ○ *The manager has a very tight schedule today – she cannot fit in any more appointments.* ○ *Expenses are kept under tight control.*

'…mortgage money is becoming tighter' [*Times*]

'…a tight monetary policy by the central bank has pushed up interest rates and drawn discretionary funds into bank deposits' [*Far Eastern Economic Review*]

'…the UK economy is at the uncomfortable stage in the cycle where the two years of tight money are having the desired effect on demand' [*Sunday Times*]

tighten /'taɪt(ə)n/ *verb* to make something tight, to control something ○ *The accounts department is tightening its control over departmental budgets.*

'…the decision by the government to tighten monetary policy will push the annual inflation rate above the previous high' [*Financial Times*]

tighten up on *phrasal verb* to control something more strictly ○ *The government is tightening up on tax evasion.* ○ *We must tighten up on the reps' expenses.*

tight market /taɪt 'mɑːkɪt/ *noun* a market where there is only a small spread between bid and offer prices

tight money /ˌtaɪt ˈmʌni/ *noun* same as **dear money**

tight money policy /ˌtaɪt ˈmʌni ˌpɒlɪsi/ *noun* a government policy to restrict money supply

till /tɪl/ *noun* a drawer for keeping cash in a shop

till float /ˈtɪl fləʊt/ *noun* cash put into the cash box at the beginning of the day to allow business to start

till money /ˈtɪl ˌmʌni/ *noun* cash held by banks

time /taɪm/ *noun* **1.** a period during which something takes place, e.g. one hour, two days, or fifty minutes **2.** the number of hours worked **3.** a period before something happens □ **to keep within the time limits** *or* **within the time schedule** to complete work by the time stated

time and method study /ˌtaɪm ən ˈmeθəd ˌstʌdi/ *noun* a process of examining the way in which something is done to see if a cheaper or quicker way can be found

time and motion expert /ˌtaɪm ən ˈməʊʃ(ə)n ˌekspɜːt/ *noun* a person who analyses time and motion studies and suggests changes in the way work is done

time and motion study /ˌtaɪm ən ˈməʊʃ(ə)n ˌstʌdi/ *noun* a study that seeks to improve efficiency and productivity in an office or factory

time bill /ˈtaɪm bɪl/ *noun* a bill of exchange which is payable at a specific time after acceptance

time deposit /ˈtaɪm dɪˌpɒzɪt/ *noun* a deposit of money for a fixed period, during which it cannot be withdrawn

time limit /ˈtaɪm ˌlɪmɪt/ *noun* the maximum time which can be taken to do something ○ *to set a time limit for acceptance of the offer* ○ *The work was finished within the time limit allowed.* ○ *The time limit on applications to the industrial tribunal is three months.*

time limitation /ˈtaɪm lɪmɪˌteɪʃ(ə)n/ *noun* the restriction of the amount of time available

time of peak demand /ˌtaɪm əv ˌpiːk dɪˈmɑːnd/ *noun* the time when something is being used most

time rate /ˈtaɪm reɪt/ *noun* a rate for work which is calculated as money per hour or per week, and not money for work completed

times /taɪmz/ *preposition* indicating the number of times something is multiplied by another □ **shares selling at 10 times earnings** shares selling at a P *or* E ratio of 10

timescale /ˈtaɪmskeɪl/ *noun* the time which be taken to complete work ○ *Our timescale is that all work should be completed by the end of August.* ○ *He is working to a strict timescale.*

time share /ˈtaɪm ʃeə/ *noun* a system where several people each own part of a property (such as a holiday flat), each being able to use it for a certain period each year

time-sharing /ˈtaɪm ˌʃeərɪŋ/ *noun* **1.** same as **time share 2.** an arrangement for sharing a computer system, with different users using different terminals

timetable /ˈtaɪmteɪb(ə)l/ *noun* a list of appointments or events ○ *The manager has a very full timetable, so I doubt if he will be able to see you today.* ◊ **takeover timetable**

tin /tɪn/ *noun* a valuable metal, formerly traded on commodity markets at an artificially high international price managed by the International Tin Council to protect tin producers from swings in the price

tip /tɪp/ *noun* **1.** money given to someone who has helped you ○ *The staff are not allowed to accept tips.* **2.** a piece of advice on buying or doing something which could be profitable ○ *The newspaper gave several stock market tips.* ○ *She gave me a tip about a share which was likely to rise because of a takeover bid.* ■ *verb* **1.** to give money to someone who has helped you ○ *He tipped the receptionist £5.* **2.** to say that something is likely to happen or that something might be profitable ○ *He is tipped to become the next chairman.* ○ *Two shares were tipped in the business section of the paper.* (NOTE: [all verb senses] **tipping – tipped**)

tip sheet /ˈtɪp ʃiːt/ *noun* a newspaper which gives information about shares which should be bought or sold

title /ˈtaɪt(ə)l/ *noun* a right to own a property ○ *She has no title to the property.* ○ *He has a good title to the property.*

title deeds /ˈtaɪt(ə)l ˌdiːdz/ *plural noun* a document showing who is the owner of a property

TOISA *abbreviation* an ISA into which the capital from a matured TESSA can be put. Full form **TESSA-only ISA**

token /ˈtəʊkən/ *noun* something which acts as a sign or symbol

token charge /ˌtəʊkən ˈtʃɑːdʒ/ *noun* a small charge which does not cover the real costs ○ *A token charge is made for heating.*

token payment /ˈtəʊkən ˌpeɪmənt/ *noun* a small payment to show that a payment is being made

token rent /ˌtəʊkən ˈrent/ *noun* a very low rent payment to show that some rent is being asked

tolar /ˈtəʊlɑː/ *noun* a unit of currency used in Slovenia

toll /təʊl/ *noun* a payment for using a service, usually a bridge or a road ○ *We had to cross a toll bridge to get to the island.* ○ *You have to pay a toll to cross the bridge.*

toll call /ˈtəʊl kɔːl/ *noun US* a long-distance telephone call

toll free /ˌtəʊl ˈfriː/ *adverb, adjective US* without having to pay a charge for a long-distance telephone call ○ *to call someone toll free* ○ *a toll-free number*

COMMENT: Toll-free numbers usually start with the digits 800.

tombstone /ˈtuːmstəʊn/ *noun* an official announcement in a newspaper showing that a major loan or a bond issue has been subscribed, giving details of the banks which have underwritten it (*informal*)

top /tɒp/ *noun* the highest point or most important place ○ *She rose to the top of her profession.* ■ *adjective* highest or most important □ **to give something top priority** to make something the most important item, so that it is done very fast

'…the base lending rate, or prime rate, is the rate at which banks lend to their top corporate borrowers' [*Wall Street Journal*]

'…gross wool receipts for the selling season appear likely to top $2 billion' [*Australian Financial Review*]

top up *phrasal verb* to add to something to make it more complete ○ *He topped up his pension contributions to make sure he received the maximum allowable pension when he retired.*

top-flight /ˌtɒp ˈflaɪt/ *adjective* in the most important position ○ *Top-flight managers can earn very high salaries.* Also called **top-ranking**

top-hat pension /ˌtɒp hæt ˈpenʃən/ *noun* a special extra pension for senior managers

top management /ˌtɒp ˈmænɪdʒmənt/ *noun* the main directors of a company

top official /ˌtɒp əˈfɪʃ(ə)l/ *noun* a very important person in a government department

top-ranking /ˌtɒp ˈræŋkɪŋ/ *adjective* same as **top-flight**

top-slicing /ˈtɒp ˌslaɪsɪŋ/ *noun* the practice of selling part of a holding in a share which is equivalent to the original cost of the investment, leaving another part still held which represents the gain made

tort /tɔːt/ *noun* harm done to a person or property which can be the basis of a civil lawsuit

total /ˈtəʊt(ə)l/ *adjective* complete, or with everything added together ○ *The company has total assets of over £1bn* ○ *The total amount owed is now £1000.* ○ *The total cost was much more than expected.* ○ *Total expenditure on publicity is twice that of last year.* ○ *Our total income from exports rose last year.* □ **the cargo was written off as a total loss** the cargo was so badly damaged that the insurers said it had no value □ **total income** all income from all sources ■ *noun* an amount which is complete, with everything added up ○ *The total of the charges comes to more than £1,000.* ■ *verb* to add up to ○ *costs totalling more than £25,000* (NOTE: **totalling – totalled**. The US spelling is **totaling – totaled**.)

Total Index /ˈtəʊt(ə)l ˌɪndeks/ *noun* an index of share prices on the Oslo Stock Exchange

total invoice value /ˌtəʊt(ə)l ˈɪnvɔɪs ˌvæljuː/ *noun* the total amount on an invoice, including transport, VAT, etc.

total return /ˌtəʊt(ə)l rɪˈtɜːn/ *noun* the total percentage change in the value of an investment over a specified time period, including capital gains, dividends and the investment's appreciation or depreciation

touch /tʌtʃ/ *noun* the narrowest spread between the buy and sell prices of a share

tour /tʊːə/ *noun* a (holiday) journey to various places, coming back in the end to the place the journey started from ○ *The group went on a tour of Italy.* ○ *The minister went on a fact-finding tour of the region.* □ **to carry out a tour of inspection** to visit various places, such as offices or factories, to inspect them

tout /taʊt/ *noun* a person who sells tickets (to games or shows) for more than the price printed on them ■ *verb* □ **to tout for custom** to try to attract customers

toxic debt /ˌtɒksɪk 'det/ *noun* debt that is toxic to the person or institution that will receive the payments as it has a lower chance of being repaid with interest

track /træk/ *verb* to follow someone or something; to follow how something develops, such as one of the stock market indices ○ *This fund tracks the Footsie Index.*

'…tracking the stock market is a good way of providing for the long term, if you're prepared to ride the ups and downs' [*Investors Chronicle*]

tracker fund /'trækə fʌnd/ *noun* a fund which tracks one of the stock market indices, such as the FTSE

tracker PEP /'trækə pep/ *noun* a PEP invested in funds which track a stock market index

tracking /'trækɪŋ/ *noun* the process of following a stock market closely

tracking unit trust /ˌtrækɪŋ 'juːnɪt trʌst/ *noun* a trust which follows closely one of the stock market indices

track record /'træk ˌrekɔːd/ *noun* the success or failure of a company or salesperson in the past ○ *He has a good track record as a secondhand car salesman.* ○ *The company has no track record in the computer market.* ○ *We are looking for someone with a track record in the computer market.*

trade /treɪd/ *noun* **1.** the business of buying and selling □ **adverse balance of trade** situation when a country imports more than it exports ○ *The country had an adverse balance of trade for the second month running.* □ **to do a good trade in a range of products** to sell a large number

of a range of products **2.** a particular type of business, or people or companies dealing in the same type of product ○ *He's in the secondhand car trade.* ○ *She's very well known in the clothing trade.* □ **to ask a company to supply trade references** to ask a company to give names of traders who can report on the company's financial situation and reputation ■ *verb* to buy and sell, to carry on a business ○ *We trade with all the countries of the EU.* ○ *She trades on the stock exchange.* ○ *The company has stopped trading.* ○ *The company trades under the name 'Eeziphitt'.*

'…a sharp setback in foreign trade accounted for most of the winter slowdown. The trade balance sank $17 billion' [*Fortune*]

'…at its last traded price, the bank was capitalized around $1.05 billion' [*South China Morning Post*]

'…with most of the world's oil now traded on spot markets, Opec's official prices are much less significant than they once were' [*Economist*]

'…the London Stock Exchange said that the value of domestic UK equities traded during the year was £1.4066 trillion, more than the capitalization of the entire London market and an increase of 36 per cent compared with previous year's total of £1.037 trillion' [*Times*]

'…trade between Britain and other countries which comprise the Economic Community has risen steadily from 33% of exports to 50% last year' [*Sales & Marketing Management*]

trade in *phrasal verb* to give in an old item as part of the payment for a new one ○ *The chairman traded in his old Rolls Royce for a new model.*

trade agreement /'treɪd əˌɡriːmənt/ *noun* an international agreement between countries over general terms of trade

trade association /'treɪd əˌsəʊsieɪʃ(ə)n/ *noun* a group which links together companies in the same trade

trade balance /treɪd 'bæləns/ *noun* same as **balance of trade**

trade barrier /'treɪd ˌbæriə/ *noun* a limitation imposed by a government on the free exchange of goods between countries. ◊ **import restrictions** (NOTE: NTBs, safety standards, and tariffs are typical trade barriers.)

trade bill /'treɪd bɪl/ *noun* a bill of exchange between two companies who are trading partners. It is issued by one company and endorsed by the other.

trade bureau /'treɪd ˌbjʊərəʊ/ *noun* an office which specialises in commercial inquiries

trade commission /'treɪd kəˌmɪʃ(ə)n/ *noun* same as **broker's commission**

trade counter /'treɪd ˌkaʊntə/ *noun* a shop in a factory or warehouse where goods are sold to retailers

trade credit /'treɪd ˌkredɪt/ *noun* the provision of goods or services to another company with an agreement to invoice them later, which is a major source of capital for many businesses

trade creditors /'treɪd ˌkredɪtəz/ *plural noun* companies which are owed money by a company. The amount owed to trade creditors is shown in the annual accounts.

trade cycle /'treɪd ˌsaɪk(ə)l/ *noun* a period during which trade expands, then slows down, then expands again

trade deficit /'treɪd ˌdefɪsɪt/ *noun* the difference in value between a country's low exports and higher imports. Also called **balance of payments deficit**, **trade gap**

trade description /ˌtreɪd dɪ'skrɪpʃən/ *noun* a description of a product to attract customers

Trade Descriptions Act /ˌtreɪd dɪ'skrɪpʃənz ækt/ *noun* an act which limits the way in which products can be described so as to protect customers from wrong descriptions made by manufacturers

trade directory /'treɪd daɪˌrekt(ə)ri/ *noun* a book which lists all the businesses and business people in a town

trade discount /ˌtreɪd 'dɪskaʊnt/ *noun* a reduction in price given to a customer in the same trade

traded options /ˌtreɪdɪd 'ɒpʃənz/ *plural noun* options to buy or sell shares at a specific price on a specific date in the future, which themselves can be bought or sold

trade fair /'treɪd feə/ *noun* a large exhibition and meeting for advertising and selling a specific type of product ○ *There*

are two trade fairs running in London at the same time – the carpet manufacturers' and the mobile telephone companies'.

trade gap /'treɪd gæp/ *noun* same as **trade deficit**

trade-in /'treɪd ɪn/ *noun US* same as **part exchange**

trademark /'treɪdmɑːk/, **trade name** /'treɪd neɪm/ *verb* to register something as a trademark ○ *They trademarked the name after the family dispute.* ○ *You should trademark the design.*

trade mission /'treɪd ˌmɪʃ(ə)n/ *noun* a visit by a group of businesspeople to discuss trade ○ *He led a trade mission to China.*

trade-off /'treɪd ɒf/ *noun* an act of exchanging one thing for another as part of a business deal (NOTE: The plural is **trade-offs**.)

trade price /'treɪd praɪs/ *noun* a special wholesale price paid by a retailer to the manufacturer or wholesaler

trader /'treɪdə/ *noun* **1.** a person who does business **2.** a person who buys or sells stocks, shares, and options

trade surplus /'treɪd ˌsɜːpləs/ *noun* the difference in value between a country's high exports and lower imports

'Brazil's trade surplus is vulnerable both to a slowdown in the American economy and a pick-up in its own' [*Economist*]

trade terms /'treɪd tɜːmz/ *plural noun* a special discount for people in the same trade

trade-weighted index /'treɪd ˌweɪtɪd ˌɪndeks/ *noun* an index of the value of a currency calculated against a basket of currencies

trading /'treɪdɪŋ/ *noun* **1.** the business of buying and selling □ **adverse trading conditions** bad conditions for trade **2.** an area of a brokerage firm where dealing in securities is carried out by phone, using monitors to display current prices and stock exchange transactions

trading account /'treɪdɪŋ əˌkaʊnt/ *noun* a company bank account administered by an investment dealer and used for managing trading activity, rather than for investment purposes

trading area /'treɪdɪŋ ˌeəriə/ *noun* a group of countries which trade with each other

trading company /ˈtreɪdɪŋ ˌkʌmp(ə)ni/ *noun* a company which specialises in buying and selling goods

trading currency /ˌtreɪdɪŋ ˈkʌrənsi/ *noun* also called **vehicle currency**

trading estate /ˈtreɪdɪŋ ɪˌsteɪt/ *noun* an area of land near a town specially for building factories and warehouses

trading financial assets /ˌtreɪdɪŋ faɪˌnænʃəl ˈæsets/ *plural noun* financial assets acquired or held in order to produce profit from short term changes in price

trading firm /ˈtreɪdɪŋ fɜːm/ *noun* a stockbroking house

trading floor /ˈtreɪdɪŋ flɔː/ *noun* same as **dealing floor**

trading for the account /ˌtreɪdɪŋ fə ðiː əˈkaʊnt/ *noun* same as **account trading**

trading limit /ˈtreɪdɪŋ ˌlɪmɪt/ *noun* the maximum amount of something which can be traded by a single trader

trading loss /ˌtreɪdɪŋ ˈlɒs/ *noun* a situation where a company's receipts are less than its expenditure

trading partner /ˈtreɪdɪŋ ˌpɑːtnə/ *noun* a company or country which trades with another

trading pattern /ˌtreɪdɪŋ ˈpæt(ə)n/ *noun* a general way in which trade is carried on ○ *The company's trading pattern shows high export sales in the first quarter and high home sales in the third quarter.*

trading post /ˈtreɪdɪŋ pəʊst/ *noun* a position on the trading floor of the New York Stock Exchange, where specialist traders operate

trading profit /ˈtreɪdɪŋ ˌprɒfɪt/ *noun* a result where the company' receipts are higher than its expenditure

trading range /ˈtreɪdɪŋ reɪndʒ/ *noun* same as **historical trading range**

trading screens /ˈtreɪdɪŋ skriːnz/ *plural noun* computer monitors listing stock market prices

trading session /ˈtreɪdɪŋ ˌseʃ(ə)n/ *noun* one period (usually a day) during which trading takes place on a stock exchange

trading stamp /ˈtreɪdɪŋ stæmp/ *noun* a special stamp given away by a shop, which the customer can collect and exchange later for free goods

trailing spouse /ˌtreɪlɪŋ ˈspaʊs/ *noun* US a successful working spouse of someone who works abroad (one of the two has to commute at weekends)

trainee /treɪˈniː/ *noun* a person who is learning how to do something ○ *We employ an additional trainee accountant at peak periods.*

traineeship /treɪˈniːʃɪp/ *noun* a post as a trainee

training /ˈtreɪnɪŋ/ *noun* the process of being taught how to do something ○ *There is a ten-week training period for new staff.*

tranche /trɑːnʃ/ *noun* one of a series of instalments, used when referring to loans to companies, government securities which are issued over a period of time, or money withdrawn by a country from the IMF ○ *The second tranche of interest on the loan is now due for payment.*

tranchette /trɑːnˈʃet/ *noun* a small amount of government stock put on to the market for sale to investors

transact /trænˈzækt/ *verb* □ **to transact business** to carry out a piece of business

transaction /trænˈzækʃən/ *noun* an instance of doing business, e.g. a purchase in a shop or a withdrawal of money from savings □ **a transaction on the stock exchange** a purchase or sale of shares on the stock exchange ○ *The paper publishes a daily list of stock exchange transactions.* □ **fraudulent transaction** a transaction which aims to cheat someone

'…the Japan Financial Intelligence Office will receive reports on suspected criminal transactions from financial institutions, determine where a probe should be launched and provide information to investigators' [*Nikkei Weekly*]

transfer *noun* /ˈtrænsfɜː/ an act of moving an employee to another job in the same organisation ○ *She applied for a transfer to our branch in Scotland.* ■ *verb* /trænsˈfɜː/ to move someone or something to a different place, or to move someone to another job in the same organisation ○ *The accountant was transferred to our Scottish branch.* ○ *He transferred his shares to a family trust.* ○ *She transferred her money to a deposit account.*

transferable /trænsˈfɜːrəb(ə)l/ *adjective* possible to pass to someone else ■ *noun* a document such as a bearer bond which can be passed to someone else

transfer of property /ˌtrænsfɜːr əv ˈprɒpəti/, **transfer of shares** /ˌtrænsfɜːr əv ˈʃeəz/ *noun* the act of moving the ownership of property or shares of stock from one person to another

transferred charge call /trænsˌfɜːd ˈtʃɑːdʒ kɔːl/ *noun* a phone call where the person receiving the call agrees to pay for it

transfer value /ˈtrænsfɜː ˌvæljuː/ *noun* the value of a pension when it is moved from one scheme to another

transit /ˈtrænzɪt/ *noun* the movement of passengers or goods on the way to a destination ○ *Some of the goods were damaged in transit.*

transit letter /ˈtrænzɪt ˌletə/ *noun* a letter sent with cheques or drafts, listing what is being sent

translate /trænsˈleɪt/ *verb* to change something into another form

transnational /trænzˈnæʃ(ə)nəl/ *noun* same as **multinational**

transparency /trænsˈpærənsi/ *noun* the fact of being clear about making decisions and being open to the public about how decisions are reached

traveller's cheques /ˈtræv(ə)ləz tʃeks/ *plural noun* cheques bought by a traveller which can be cashed in a foreign country

travelling expenses /ˈtræv(ə)lɪŋ ek ˌspensɪz/ *plural noun* money spent on travelling and hotels for business purposes

treasurer /ˈtreʒərə/ *noun* **1.** a person who looks after the money or finances of a club or society, etc. **2.** a company official responsible for finding new finance for the company and using its existing financial resources in the best possible way **3.** *US* the main financial officer of a company **4.** (*in Australia*) the finance minister in a government

treasurer's account /ˌtreʒərəz ə ˈkaʊnt/ *noun* an account of a club or society with a bank

Treasuries /ˈtreʒəriz/ *plural noun US* treasury bonds and bills (*informal*)

Treasury /ˈtreʒəri/ *noun* **1.** a government department which deals with the country's finance (NOTE: The term is used in both the UK and the US; in most other countries this department is called the **Ministry of Finance**.) **2.** the department of a company or corporation that deals with all financial matters **3.** *US* a Treasury bond, bill, or note issued by the US Treasury

Treasury bill /ˈtreʒəri bɪl/ *noun* a short-term financial instrument which does not give any interest and is sold by the government at a discount through the central bank. In the UK, their term varies from three to six months, in the US, they are for 91 or 182 days, or for 52 weeks. (NOTE: In the US they are also called a **T-bill**)

Treasury bond /ˈtreʒəri bɒnd/ *noun* a long-term bond issued by the British or US government. Also called **T-bond**

treasury management /ˈtreʒəri ˌmænɪdʒmənt/ *noun* an entity's method of dealing of its financial matters, including growing funds for business, maintaining cash flows and currencies, and managing currencies and cash flows

Treasury note /ˈtreʒəri nəʊt/ *noun* a medium-term bond issued by the US government

treasury products /ˌtreʒəri ˈprɒdʌkts/ *plural noun* any financial items produced by a government for sale, such as bonds

Treasury Secretary /ˈtreʒəri ˌsekrət(ə)ri/ *noun* same as **Secretary of the Treasury**

Treasury stocks /ˈtreʒəri stɒkz/ *plural noun* stocks issued by the British government. Also called **Exchequer stocks**

treble /ˈtreb(ə)l/ *verb* to increase three times, or to make something three times larger ○ *The company's borrowings have trebled.* ○ *The acquisition of the chain of stores has trebled the group's turnover.* ■ *adverb* three times ○ *Our borrowings are treble what they were last year.*

trend /trend/ *noun* a general way in which things are developing ○ *a downward trend in investment* ○ *There is a trend away from old-established food stores.* ○ *The report points to inflationary trends in the economy.* ○ *We notice a* *general trend towards selling to the student market.* ○ *We have noticed an upward trend in sales.*

'…the quality of building design and ease of accessibility will become increasingly important, adding to the trend towards out-of-town office development' [*Lloyd's List*]

trend line /'trend laɪn/ *noun* a line on a graph or chart which shows which way a trend is going

trial /'traɪəl/ *noun* **1.** a court case to judge a person accused of a crime ○ *He is on trial* or *is standing trial for embezzlement.* **2.** a test to see if something is good ■ *verb* to test a product to see how good it is (NOTE: **trialling – trialled**)

trial balance /'traɪəl ˌbæləns/ *noun* the draft calculation of debits and credits to see if they balance

tribunal /traɪ'bjuːn(ə)l/ *noun* an official court which examines special problems and makes judgments

trigger /'trɪɡə/ *noun* a thing which starts a process ■ *verb* to start a process

'…the recovery is led by significant declines in short-term interest rates, which are forecast to be roughly 250 basis points below their previous peak. This should trigger a rebound in the housing markets and consumer spending on durables' [*Toronto Globe & Mail*]

trigger point /'trɪɡə pɔɪnt/ *noun* a point in acquiring shares in a company where the purchaser has to declare an interest or to take certain action

COMMENT: If an individual or a company buys five per cent of a company's shares, this shareholding must be declared to the company. If 15 per cent is acquired it is assumed that a takeover bid will be made, and no more shares can be acquired for seven days to give the target company time to respond. There is no obligation to make a bid at this stage, but if the holding is increased to 30 per cent, then a takeover bid must be made for the remaining 70 per cent. If 90 per cent of shares are owned, then the owner can purchase all outstanding shares compulsorily. These trigger points are often not crossed, and it is common to see that a company has acquired 14.9% or 29.9% of another company's shares.

trillion /'trɪljən/ *noun* one million millions (NOTE: In the UK, trillion now has the same meaning as in the US; formerly in UK English it meant one

million million millions, and it is still sometimes used with this meaning; see also the note at **billion**.)

'…if land is assessed at roughly half its current market value, the new tax could yield up to ¥10 trillion annually' [*Far Eastern Economic Review*]

'…behind the decline was a 6.1% fall in exports to ¥47.55 trillion, the second year of falls. Automobiles and steel were among categories showing particularly conspicuous drops' [*Nikkei Weekly*]

'…the London Stock Exchange said that the value of domestic UK equities traded during the year was £1.4066 trillion, more than the capitalization of the entire London market and an increase of 36 per cent compared with previous year's total of £1.037 trillion' [*Times*]

triple /'trɪp(ə)l/ *verb* to become three times larger, or to multiply something three times ○ *The company's debts tripled in twelve months.* ○ *The acquisition of the chain of stores has tripled the group's turnover.* ■ *adjective* three times as much ○ *The cost of airfreighting the goods is triple their manufacturing cost.*

triple A rated /ˌtrɪp(ə)l 'eɪ ˌreɪtɪd/ *adjective* referring to a bond or corporation which has the highest credit rating according to Standard & Poor's or Moody's (so called, because the rating is 'AAA')

triple witching hour /ˌtrɪp(ə)l 'wɪtʃɪŋ aʊə/ *noun* a day when three major types of futures contract fall due at the same time

COMMENT: In the USA, this is the last hour of trading on the third Friday of the months of March, June, September and December, when futures contracts on the Stock Exchange Index, options on these futures contracts, and ordinary stock option contracts all fall due; in the UK, it is a day when euro-options, Footsie options and Footsie futures contracts all expire at the same time. It is normally a day when stock market prices show greater volatility than usual.

triplicate /'trɪplɪkət/ *noun* □ **in triplicate** with an original and two copies ○ *The invoices are printed in triplicate.* ○ *The application form should be completed in triplicate.* □ **invoicing in triplicate** the preparing of three copies of invoices

trophy hunter /'trəʊfi ˌhʌntə/ *noun* an investor who looks for cheap shares

troubled /'trʌb(ə)ld/ *adjective* in a difficult financial position

troubleshooter /'trʌb(ə)lˌʃuːtə/ *noun* a person whose job is to solve problems in a company ○ *They brought in a troubleshooter to try to sort out the management problems.*

trough /trɒf/ *noun* a low point in the economic cycle

troy ounce /ˌtrɔɪ 'aʊns/ *noun* a measurement of weight (= 31.10 grams) (NOTE: In writing, often shortened to **troy oz**. after figures: **25.2 troy oz**.)

troy weight /ˌtrɔɪ 'weɪt/ *noun* a system of measurement of weight used for gold and other metals, such as silver and platinum

COMMENT: Troy weight is divided into grains, pennyweights (24 grains = 1 pennyweight), ounces (20 pennyweights = 1 ounce) and pounds (12 troy ounces = 1 pound). Troy weights are slightly less than their avoirdupois equivalents; the troy pound equals 0.37kg or 0.82lb avoirdupois; see also **avoirdupois**.

true /truː/ *adjective* correct or accurate

true and fair view /ˌtruː ən feə 'vjuː/ *noun* a correct statement of a company's financial position as shown in its accounts and confirmed by the auditors

true copy /ˌtruː 'kɒpi/ *noun* an exact copy of a legal document, as attested by a notary public ○ *I certify that this is a true copy.* ○ *It is certified as a true copy.*

truncate /trʌŋ'keɪt/ *verb* to operate a simplified banking system by not returning physical cheques to the paying bank

truncation /trʌŋ'keɪʃ(ə)n/ *noun* a simplified banking system, where actual cheques are not sent to the paying bank, but held in the receiving bank which notifies the paying bank by computer of the details of cheques received

trust /trʌst/ *noun* **1.** the fact of being confident that something is correct or will work □ **we took his statement on trust** we accepted his statement without examining it to see if it was correct **2.** a legal arrangement to pass goods, money or valuables to someone who will look after them well ○ *She left his property in trust for her grandchildren.* **3.** the management

of money or property for someone ○ *They set up a family trust for their grandchildren.* **4.** *US* a small group of companies which control the supply of a product ■ *verb* □ **to trust someone with something** to give something to someone to look after ○ *Can he be trusted with all that cash?*

trustbusting /'trʌstbʌstɪŋ/ *noun US* the breaking up of monopolies to encourage competition

trust company /'trʌst ˌkʌmp(ə)ni/ *noun US* an organisation which supervises the financial affairs of private trusts, executes wills, and acts as a bank to a limited number of customers

trust deed /'trʌst diːd/ *noun* a document which sets out the details of a private trust

trustee /trʌ'stiː/ *noun* a person who has charge of money in trust ○ *the trustees of the pension fund*

trust fund /'trʌst fʌnd/ *noun* assets such as money, securities or property held in trust for someone

Truth in Lending Act /ˌtruːθ ɪn 'lendɪŋ ækt/ *noun* a US Act of 1969, which requires lenders to state the full terms of their interest rates to borrowers

tugrik /'tuːgrɪk/ *noun* a unit of currency used in the Mongolian Republic

tune /tjuːn/ *noun* □ **the bank is backing him to the tune of £10,000** the bank is helping him with a loan of £10,000

turkey /'tɜːki/ *noun* a bad investment, an investment which has turned out to be worthless (*informal*)

turn /tɜːn/ *noun* **1.** a movement in a circle, or a change of direction **2.** a profit or commission ○ *She makes a turn on everything he sells.*

turn down *phrasal verb* to refuse something ○ *The bank turned down their request for a loan.* ○ *The application for a licence was turned down.* ○ *He turned down the job he was offered.* ○ *The board turned down the proposal.*

turn over *phrasal verb* **1.** to have a specific amount of sales ○ *We turn over £2,000 a week.* **2.** *US* to pass something to someone ○ *She turned over the documents to the lawyer.* (NOTE: In this meaning, the usual UK term is **hand over**.)

turn round *phrasal verb* to make a company change from making a loss to becoming profitable □ **they turned the company round in less than a year** they made the company profitable in less than a year

turnaround /'tɜːnəˌraʊnd/ *noun especially US* same as **turnround**

turnkey operation /'tɜːnkiː ɒpəˌreɪʃ(ə)n/ *noun* a deal where a company takes all responsibility for constructing, fitting and staffing a building (such as a school, hospital or factory) so that it is completely ready for the purchaser to take over

turnover /'tɜːnəʊvə/ *noun* **1.** the amount of sales of goods or services by a company ○ *The company's turnover has increased by 235%.* ○ *We based our calculations on the forecast turnover.* **2.** the number of times something is used or sold in a period, usually one year, expressed as a percentage of a total

turnover of shares /ˌtɜːnəʊvə əv 'ʃeəz/ *noun* the total value of shares bought and sold on the stock exchange during the year

turnover tax /'tɜːnəʊvə tæks/ *noun* same as **VAT**

turnround /'tɜːnraʊnd/ *noun* **1.** the value of goods sold during a year divided by the average value of goods held in stock **2.** the action of emptying a ship, plane, etc., and getting it ready for another commercial journey **3.** the act of making a company profitable again (NOTE: [all senses] The US term is **turn-around**.)

24-hour banking /ˌtwentifɔːr aʊə 'bæŋkiŋ/ *noun* a banking service provided during the whole day (e.g. by cash dispensers in the street and online services)

24-hour service /ˌtwenti fɔːr aʊə 'sɜːvɪs/ *noun* help which is available for the whole day

24-hour trading /ˌtwenti fɔːr aʊə 'treɪdɪŋ/ trading in bonds, securities and currencies during the whole day

COMMENT: 24-hour trading is now possible because of instant communication to stock exchanges in different time zones; the Tokyo Stock Exchange closes about two hours before the London Stock Exchange opens; the New York Stock Exchange opens at the same time as the London one closes.

two-tier market /ˌtuː tɪə 'mɑːkɪt/ *noun* an exchange market where two rates apply (usually one for tourists and a commercial rate for businesses)

two-way market /ˌtuː weɪ 'mɑːkɪt/ *noun* a market where there is active buying and selling

tycoon /taɪ'kuːn/ *noun* an important businessman

U

UBR *abbreviation* uniform business rate

ultimatum /ˌʌltɪˈmeɪtəm/ *noun* a statement to someone that unless they do something within a period of time, action will be taken against them ○ *The union officials argued among themselves over the best way to deal with the ultimatum from the management.* ○ *The banks issued an ultimatum to their largest borrowers.* (NOTE: The plural is **ultimatums** or **ultimata**.)

umbrella organisation /ʌmˈbrelə ˌɔːɡənaɪzeɪʃ(ə)n/ *noun* a large organisation which includes several smaller ones

unacceptable /ˌʌnəkˈseptəb(ə)l/ *adjective* which cannot be accepted ○ *The terms of the contract are quite unacceptable.*

unaccounted for /ˌʌnəˈkaʊntɪd fɔː/ *adjective* lost without any explanation ○ *Several thousand units are unaccounted for in the stocktaking.*

unanimous /juːˈnænɪməs/ *adjective* where everyone agrees or votes in the same way ○ *There was a unanimous vote against the proposal.* ○ *They reached unanimous agreement.*

unanimously /juːˈnænɪməsli/ *adverb* with everyone agreeing ○ *The proposals were adopted unanimously.*

unaudited /ʌnˈɔːdɪtɪd/ *adjective* having not been audited ○ *unaudited accounts*

unauthorised /ʌnˈɔːθəraɪzd/, **unauthorized** *adjective* not permitted ○ *unauthorised access to the company's records* ○ *unauthorised expenditure* ○ *No unauthorised persons are allowed into the laboratory.* ○ *The bank charges 26.8% interest on unauthorised overdrafts.*

unauthorised unit trust /ʌn ˌɔːθəraɪzd ˈjuːnɪt trʌst/ *noun* a private unit trust operated by a stockbroking firm for its clients

unbalanced /ʌnˈbæ_lənst/ *adjective* referring to a budget which does not balance or which is in deficit

unbanked /ʌnˈbæŋkt/ *adjective* **1.** referring to a person who does not have a bank account **2.** referring to a cheque which has not been deposited in a bank account

unbundling /ʌnˈbʌnd(ə)lɪŋ/ *noun* **1.** the process of separating companies from a conglomerate (the companies were independent in the past, and have been acquired by the conglomerate over a period of time) **2.** *US* the practice of charging separately for each different service provided

uncalled /ʌnˈkɔːld/ *adjective* referring to capital which a company is authorised to raise and has been issued but for which payment has not yet been requested

uncashed /ʌnˈkæʃt/ *adjective* having not been cashed ○ *uncashed cheques*

unchanged /ʌnˈtʃeɪndʒd/ *adjective* which has not changed

'…the dividend is unchanged at L90 per ordinary share' [*Financial Times*]

unchecked /ʌnˈtʃekt/ *adjective* which has not been checked ○ *unchecked figures*

uncollected /ˌʌnkəˈlektɪd/ *adjective* which has not been collected ○ *uncollected subscriptions* ○ *uncollected taxes*

uncollected funds /ˌʌnkəlektɪd ˈfʌndz/ *plural noun* deposits which have not yet cleared through the clearing system and so cannot be drawn on

unconditional /ˌʌnkənˈdɪʃ(ə)nəl/ *adjective* with no conditions or provisions attached ○ *unconditional acceptance of the offer by the board* ○ *After the interview he got an unconditional offer of* *a job.* □ **the offer went unconditional last Thursday** the takeover bid was accepted by the majority of the shareholders and therefore the conditions attached to it no longer apply

COMMENT: A takeover bid will become unconditional if more than 50 per cent of shareholders accept it.

unconditionally /ˌʌnkən'dɪʃ(ə)n(ə)li/ *adverb* without imposing any conditions ○ *The offer was accepted unconditionally by the trade union.*

uncontrollable /ˌʌnkən'trəʊləb(ə)l/ *adjective* not possible to control ○ *uncontrollable inflation*

uncovered bear /ˌʌnkʌvəd 'beə/ *noun* a person who sells stock which he or she does not hold, hoping to be able to buy stock later at a lower price when the debt needs to be settled

uncrossed cheque /ˌʌnkrɒst 'tʃek/ *noun* a cheque which does not have two lines across it, and can be cashed anywhere (NOTE: They are no longer used in the UK, but are still found in other countries.)

undated /ʌn'deɪtɪd/ *adjective* with no date indicated or written ○ *She tried to cash an undated cheque.*

COMMENT: The only British government stocks which are undated are the War Loan.

undated bond /ʌnˌdeɪtɪd 'bɒnd/ *noun* a bond with no maturity date

under /'ʌndə/ *preposition* **1.** lower than or less than ○ *The interest rate is under 10%.* ○ *Under half of the shareholders accepted the offer.* **2.** controlled by, according to ○ *Under the terms of the agreement, the goods should be delivered in October.* ○ *He is acting under rule 23 of the union constitution.*

under- /ʌndə/ *prefix* less important than or lower than

underbid /ˌʌndə'bɪd/ *verb* to bid less than someone (NOTE: **underbidding – underbid**)

underbidder /'ʌndəbɪdə/ *noun* a person who bids less than the person who buys at an auction

undercapitalised /ˌʌndə'kæpɪtəlaɪzd/, **undercapitalized** *adjective* without enough capital ○ *The company is severely undercapitalised.*

undercharge /ˌʌndə'tʃɑːdʒ/ *verb* to ask someone for too little money ○ *She undercharged us by £25.*

undercut /ˌʌndə'kʌt/ *verb* to offer something at a lower price than someone else ○ *They increased their market share by undercutting their competitors.* (NOTE: **undercutting – undercut**)

underemployed /ˌʌndərɪm'plɔɪd/ *adjective* with not enough work ○ *The staff is underemployed because of the cutback in production.*

underemployed capital /ˌʌndərɪm plɔɪd 'kæpɪt(ə)l/ *noun* capital which is not producing enough interest

underestimate *noun* /ˌʌndər 'estɪmət/ an estimate which is less than the actual figure ○ *The figure of £50,000 in turnover was a considerable underestimate.* ■ *verb* /ˌʌndər'estɪmeɪt/ to think that something is smaller or not as bad as it really is ○ *They underestimated the effects of the strike on their sales.* ○ *He underestimated the amount of time needed to finish the work.*

underlease /'ʌndəliːs/ *noun* a lease from a tenant to another tenant

underlying inflation rate /ˌʌndəlaɪɪŋ ɪn'fleɪʃ(ə)n reɪt/ *noun* the basic inflation rate calculated on a series of prices of consumer items, petrol, gas and electricity, and interest rates. Compare **headline inflation rate**

underlying value /ˌʌndəlaɪɪŋ 'væljuː/ *noun* the basic value of a company, including its assets, goodwill, etc.

undermentioned /ˌʌndə'menʃ(ə)nd/ *adjective* mentioned lower down in a document ○ *See the undermentioned list of countries to which these terms apply.*

underperform /ˌʌndəpə'fɔːm/ *verb* □ **to underperform the market** to perform worse than the rest of the market ○ *The hotel group has underperformed the sector this year.*

underperformance /ˌʌndəpə'fɔːməns/ *noun* the fact of performing worse than others ○ *The underperformance of the shares has worried investors.*

'Australia has been declining again. Because it has had such a long period of underperfomance, it is now not as vulnerable as other markets' [*Money Observer*]

underrate /ˌʌndəˈreɪt/ *verb* to value someone or something less highly than they should be ○ *Do not underrate the strength of the competition in the European market.* ○ *The power of the yen is underrated.*

underreact /ˌʌndəriˈækt/ *verb* not to react strongly enough to a situation ○ *The markets underreacted to the oil crisis.*

undersell /ˌʌndəˈsel/ *verb* to sell more cheaply than someone ○ *to undersell a competitor* (NOTE: **underselling – undersold**) □ **the company is never undersold** no other company sells goods as cheaply as this one

undersigned /ˌʌndəˈsaɪnd/ *noun* a person who has signed a letter (NOTE: can be followed by a plural verb) □ **we, the undersigned** we, the people who have signed below

underspend /ˌʌndəˈspend/ *verb* to spend less than you should have spent or were allowed to spend (NOTE: **underspending – underspent**) □ **he has underspent his budget** he has spent less than was allowed in the budget

understanding /ˌʌndəˈstændɪŋ/ *noun* a private agreement ○ *to come to an understanding about the divisions of the market*

understate /ˌʌndəˈsteɪt/ *verb* to enter in an account a figure that is lower than the actual figure ○ *The company accounts understate the real profit.*

undersubscribed /ˌʌndəsʌbˈskraɪbd/ *adjective* referring to a share issue in which applications are not made for all the shares on offer, and part of the issue remains with the underwriters

undertake /ˌʌndəˈteɪk/ *verb* to agree to do something ○ *We asked the research unit to undertake an investigation of the market.* ○ *They have undertaken not to sell into our territory.* (NOTE: **undertaking – undertook – undertaken**)

undertaking /ˈʌndəteɪkɪŋ/ *noun* **1.** a business ○ *He is the MD of a large commercial undertaking.* **2.** a promise, especially a legally binding one ○ *They have given us a written undertaking not to sell their products in competition with ours.*

undervaluation /ˌʌndəvæljʊˈeɪʃ(ə)n/ *noun* the state of being valued, or the act of valuing something, at less than the true worth

undervalued /ˌʌndəˈvæljuːd/ *adjective* not valued highly enough ○ *The dollar is undervalued on the foreign exchanges.* ○ *The properties are undervalued on the company's balance sheet.*

'…in terms of purchasing power, the dollar is considerably undervalued, while the US trade deficit is declining month by month' [*Financial Weekly*]

underwater /ˌʌndəˈwɔːtə/ *adjective* which has lost value

underwater loan /ˌʌndəˈwɔːtə ləʊn/ *noun* a loan which is worth less than its book value, as when an item bought with a loan loses its value on the market

underwater option /ˌʌndəˈwɔːtə ˌɒpʃən/ *noun* an option which has no value

underweight /ˌʌndəˈweɪt/ *adjective* not heavy enough □ **the pack is twenty grams underweight** the pack weighs twenty grams less than it should

underwrite /ˌʌndəˈraɪt/ *verb* **1.** to accept responsibility for something □ **to underwrite a share issue** to guarantee that a share issue will be sold by agreeing to buy all shares which are not subscribed ○ *The issue was underwritten by three underwriting companies.* **2.** to insure, to cover a risk ○ *to underwrite an insurance policy* **3.** to agree to pay for costs ○ *The government has underwritten the development costs of the project.* (NOTE: **underwriting – underwrote – has underwritten**)

'…under the new program, mortgage brokers are allowed to underwrite mortgages and get a much higher fee' [*Forbes Magazine*]

underwriter /ˈʌndəraɪtə/ *noun* a person or company that underwrites a share issue or an insurance

COMMENT: When a major company flotation or share issue or loan is prepared, a group of companies (such as merchant banks) will form a syndicate to underwrite the flotation: the syndicate will be organised by the 'lead underwriter', together with a group of main underwriters; these in turn will ask others ('sub-underwriters') to share in the underwriting.

underwriting /ˈʌndəraɪtɪŋ/ *noun* the action of guaranteeing to purchase shares in a new issue if no one purchases them

underwriting fee /ˈʌndəraɪtɪŋ fiː/ noun a fee paid by a company to the underwriters for guaranteeing the purchase of new shares in that company

underwriting syndicate /ˈʌndə raɪtɪŋ ˌsɪndɪkət/ noun a group of underwriters who insure a large risk

undischarged bankrupt /ˌʌndɪs tʃɑːdʒd ˈbæŋkrʌpt/ noun a person who has been declared bankrupt and has not been released from that state

undistributable reserves /ˌʌndɪs trɪbjuːtəb(ə)l rɪˈzɜːvz/ plural noun same as **capital reserves**

undistributed profit /ˌʌndɪstrɪ bjuːtɪd ˈprɒfɪt/ noun profit which has not been distributed as dividends to shareholders

unearned income /ˌʌnɜːnd ˈɪnkʌm/ noun same as **investment income**

uneconomic /ˌʌniːkəˈnɒmɪk/ adjective which does not make a commercial profit □ **it is an uneconomic proposition** it will not be commercially profitable

uneconomic rent /ˌʌniːkənɒmɪk ˈrent/ noun a rent which is not enough to cover costs

unemployed /ˌʌnɪmˈplɔɪd/ adjective not having any paid work ■ noun □ **the unemployed** the people without any jobs

unemployment /ˌʌnɪmˈplɔɪmənt/ noun the state of not having any work

'…tax advantages directed toward small businesses will help create jobs and reduce the unemployment rate' [*Toronto Star*]

unemployment benefit /ˌʌnɪm ˈplɔɪmənt ˌbenɪfɪt/ noun a payment from the government made to someone who is unemployed (NOTE: The US term is **unemployment compensation**.)

unemployment pay /ˌʌnɪm ˈplɔɪmənt peɪ/ noun money given by the government to someone who is unemployed

unemployment rate /ˌʌnɪmˈplɔɪ mənt reɪt/ noun the number of people out of work, shown as a percentage of the total number of people available for work. Also called **rate of unemployment**

unencumbered /ˌʌnɪnˈkʌmbəd/ adjective referring to property which is not mortgaged

unfair competition /ˌʌnfeə ˌkɒmpə ˈtɪʃ(ə)n/ noun the practice of trying to do better than another company by using techniques such as importing foreign goods at very low prices or by wrongly criticising a competitor's products

unfavourable /ʌnˈfeɪv(ə)rəb(ə)l/ adjective not favourable (NOTE: The US spelling is **unfavorable**.) □ **unfavourable balance of trade** a situation where a country imports more than it exports □ **unfavourable exchange rate** an exchange rate which gives an amount of foreign currency for the home currency which is not good for trade ○ *The unfavourable exchange rate hit the country's exports.*

unfulfilled orders /ˌʌnfʊlfɪld ˈɔːdəz/ plural noun orders received in the past and not yet supplied

ungeared /ʌnˈɡɪəd/ adjective with no borrowings

uniform business rate /ˌjuːnɪfɔːm ˈbɪznɪs ˌreɪt/ noun a tax levied on business property which is the same percentage for the whole country. Abbreviation **UBR** (NOTE: The uniform business rate is then multiplied by the **rateable value** of the property to give the total rates to be paid in that year.)

unincorporated /ˌʌnɪnˈkɔːpəreɪtɪd/ adjective referring to a business which has not been made into a company, i.e. which is operating as a partnership or a sole trader

unissued capital /ˌʌnɪʃuːd ˈkæpɪt(ə)l/ noun capital which a company is authorised to issue but has not issued as shares

unit /ˈjuːnɪt/ noun **1.** a single product for sale **2.** a single share in a unit trust

unitary regulator /ˌjuːnɪt(ə)ri ˈreɡjʊleɪtə/ noun a single regulator, where before there were several

Unitas index an index of prices on the Helsinki Stock Exchange

unit cost /ˈjuːnɪt kɒst/ noun the cost of one item, i.e. the total product costs divided by the number of units produced

unitise /ˈjuːnɪtaɪz/, **unitize** verb to form investments into units which are sold to the public

unit-linked insurance /ˌjuːnɪt lɪŋkd ɪnˈʃʊərəns/ noun an insurance policy which is linked to the security of units in a unit trust or fund

unit of account /ˌjuːnɪt əv əˈkaʊnt/ *noun* a standard unit used in financial transactions among members of a group, e.g. SDRs in the IMF

unit price /ˈjuːnɪt praɪs/ *noun* the price of one item

unit trust /ˈjuːnɪt trʌst/ *noun* an organisation which takes money from small investors and invests it in stocks and shares for them under a trust deed, the investment being in the form of shares (or units) in the trust (NOTE: The US term is **mutual fund**.)

COMMENT: Unit trusts have to be authorised by the Department of Trade and Industry before they can offer units for sale to the public, although unauthorised private unit trusts exist.

unlawful /ʌnˈlɔːf(ə)l/ *adjective* against the law, not legal

unlimited /ʌnˈlɪmɪtɪd/ *adjective* with no limits ○ *The bank offered him unlimited credit.*

unlimited liability /ʌnˌlɪmɪtɪd ˌlaɪəˈbɪlɪti/ *noun* a situation where a sole trader or each partner is responsible for all a firm's debts with no limit on the amount each may have to pay

unlisted company /ʌnˌlɪstɪd ˈkʌmp(ə)ni/ *noun* a company whose shares are not listed on the stock exchange

unlisted securities /ʌnˌlɪstɪd sɪˈkjʊərɪtiz/ *plural noun* shares that are not listed on the stock exchange

Unlisted Securities Market /ʌn ˌlɪstɪd sɪˈkjʊərɪtiz ˌmɑːkɪt/ *noun* formerly, the market for buying and selling shares which were not listed on the main stock exchange, now replaced by the Alternative Investment Market (AIM). Abbreviation **USM**

unload /ʌnˈləʊd/ *verb* **1.** to take goods off a ship, lorry etc. ○ *The ship is unloading at Hamburg.* ○ *We need a fork-lift truck to unload the lorry.* ○ *We unloaded the spare parts at Lagos.* ○ *There are no unloading facilities for container ships.* **2.** to sell shares which do not seem attractive ○ *We tried to unload our shareholding as soon as the company published its accounts.*

unlock /ʌnˈlɒk/ *verb* □ **to unlock value** to sell undervalued assets and so increase the value of a company to its shareholders

unpaid /ʌnˈpeɪd/ *adjective* not paid

unpaid balance /ʌnˌpeɪd ˈbæləns/ *noun* a balance of a loan or invoice which still has to be paid after a part payment or instalment payment has been made

unpaid cheque /ʌnˌpeɪd ˈtʃek/ *noun* a cheque which has been deposited but which is bounced by the bank on which it is written, so the account of the person who should receive is not credited

unpaid invoices /ʌnˌpeɪd ˈɪnvɔɪsɪz/ *plural noun* invoices which have not been paid

unprofitable /ʌnˈprɒfɪtəb(ə)l/ *adjective* not profitable

unquoted shares /ˌʌnkwəʊtɪd ˈʃeəz/ *plural noun* shares that have no stock exchange quotation

unrealised /ʌnˈrɪəlaɪzd/, **unrealized** *adjective* not sold to make a profit

unrealised capital gain /ˌʌnrɪəlaɪzd ˌkæpɪt(ə)l ˈɡeɪn/ *noun* an investment which is showing a profit but has not been sold

unrealised loss /ˌʌnrɪəlaɪzd ˈlɒs/ *noun* same as **paper loss**

unrealised profit /ʌnˌrɪəlaɪzd ˈprɒfɪt/ *noun* same as **paper profit**

unredeemed pledge /ˌʌnrɪdiːmd ˈpledʒ/ *noun* a pledge which the borrower has not claimed back because he or she has not paid back the loan

unregistered /ʌnˈredʒɪstəd/ *adjective* used for describing a company that has not been registered on the official list of companies held, in the UK, at Companies House

unsecured creditor /ˌʌnsɪkjʊəd ˈkredɪtə/ *noun* a creditor who is owed money, but has no security from the debtor for the debt

unsecured debt /ˌʌnsɪkjʊəd ˈdet/ *noun* a debt which is not guaranteed by a charge on assets or by any collateral

unsecured loan /ˌʌnsɪkjʊəd ˈləʊn/ *noun* a loan made with no security

unseen /ʌnˈsiːn/ *adverb* not seen □ **to buy something sight unseen** to buy something without having inspected it

unsettled /ʌnˈset(ə)ld/ *adjective* which changes often or which is upset

unstable /ʌnˈsteɪb(ə)l/ *adjective* not stable, changing frequently ○ *unstable exchange rates*

unsubsidised /ʌnˈsʌbsɪdaɪzd/, **unsubsidized** *adjective* with no subsidy

unsuccessful /ˌʌnsəkˈsesf(ə)l/ *adjective* not successful ○ *an unsuccessful businessman* ○ *The project was expensive and unsuccessful.* ○ *He made six unsuccessful job applications before he finally got a job.*

unsuccessfully /ˌʌnsəkˈsesf(ə)li/ *adverb* with no success ○ *The company unsuccessfully tried to break into the South American market.*

unweighted /ʌnˈweɪtɪd/ *adjective* without giving any extra value to a certain factor

up /ʌp/ *adverb, preposition* in or to a higher position ○ *The inflation rate is going up steadily.* ○ *Shares were up slightly at the end of the day.*

upcoming /ˈʌpkʌmɪŋ/ *adjective* which will come in the near future ○ *The company is banking on its upcoming new drug to treat strokes.*

update /ʌpˈdeɪt/ *verb* to revise something so that it is always up to date ○ *The figures are updated annually.*

up front /ˌʌp ˈfrʌnt/ *adverb* in advance

uplift /ˈʌplɪft/ *noun* an increase ○ *The contract provides for an annual uplift of charges.*

up market /ˌʌpˈmɑːkɪt/ *noun* a stock market which is rising or is at its highest level ○ *How your emerging growth fund performs in a down market is just as important as in an up market.*

upmarket /ˌʌpˈmɑːkɪt/ *adverb, adjective* more expensive or appealing to a wealthy section of the population (NOTE: The opposite is **down market**.) □ **the company has decided to move upmarket** the company has decided to start to produce more luxury items

upscale /ˈʌpskeɪl/ *adjective* aimed at customers at the top end of the socio-economic ladder, who are well-educated and have higher incomes

upset price /ˈʌpset praɪs/ *noun* the lowest price which the seller will accept at an auction

upside potential /ˈʌpsaɪd pəˌtenʃəl/ *noun* the possibility for a share to

increase in value. Opposite **downside risk**

upstream /ˌʌpˈstriːm/ *adjective* referring to the operations of a company at the beginning of a process (as drilling for oil as an operation of a petroleum company). Compare **downstream**

upswing /ˈʌpswɪŋ/ *noun* an upward movement of share prices (NOTE: The opposite is **downswing**.)

uptick /ˈʌptɪk/ *noun US* a price of a share sold, which is higher than the previous price

up to /ˈʌp tuː/ *preposition* as far as, as high as ○ *We will buy at prices up to £25.*

upturn /ˈʌptɜːn/ *noun* a movement towards higher sales or profits ○ *an upturn in the economy* ○ *an upturn in the market*

upward /ˈʌpwəd/ *adjective* towards a higher position ○ *an upward movement*

upwards /ˈʌpwədz/ *adverb* towards a higher position ○ *The market moved upwards after the news of the budget.* (NOTE: In the USA, **upward** is used as both adjective and adverb.)

use *noun* /juːs/ a way in which something can be used □ **directions for use** instructions on how to run a machine □ **to make use of something** to use something □ **in use** being worked ○ *The computer is in use twenty-four hours a day.* □ **items for personal use** items which a person will use for himself, not on behalf of the company □ **he has the use of a company car** he has a company car which he uses privately ■ *verb* /juːz/ to take something, e.g. a machine, a company or a process, and work with it ○ *We use airmail for all our overseas correspondence.* ○ *They use freelancers for most of their work.*

user /ˈjuːzə/ *noun* a person who uses something

user-friendly /ˌjuːzə ˈfrendli/ *adjective* which a user finds easy to work ○ *These programs are really user-friendly.*

USM *abbreviation* Unlisted Securities Market

US Treasury bonds /ˌjuː es ˈtreʒəri bɒndz/ *plural noun* bonds issued by the US Treasury

usual /ˈjuːʒʊəl/ *adjective* normal or ordinary ○ *Our usual terms* or *usual* *conditions are thirty days' credit. ○ The usual practice is to have the contract signed by the MD. ○ The usual hours of work are from 9.30 to 5.30.*

usurious /juˈzjʊəriəs/ *adjective* referring to usury ○ *a usurious rate of interest*

usury /ˈjuːʒəri/ *noun* the lending of money at high interest

utilisation /ˌjuːtɪlaɪˈzeɪʃ(ə)n/, **utilization** *noun* the act of making use of something

'...control permits the manufacturer to react to changing conditions on the plant floor and to keep people and machines at a high level of utilization' [*Duns Business Month*]

utilise /ˈjuːtɪlaɪz/, **utilize** *verb* to use something

utility /juːˈtɪlɪti/ *noun* a public service company, such as one that supplies water, gas or electricity or runs public transport ○ *Shares in utility companies* or *utilities offer good dividends.*

V

vacant possession /ˌveɪkənt pə
ˈzeʃ(ə)n/ *adjective* being able to occupy a
property immediately after buying it
because it is empty ○ *The property is to
be sold with vacant possession.*

valorem /vəˈlɔːrəm/ *noun* ♦ **ad
valorem duty**

valuable /ˈvæljʊəb(ə)l/ *adjective*
which is worth a lot of money

valuation /ˌvæljuˈeɪʃ(ə)n/ *noun* an
estimate of how much something is worth
○ *to ask for a valuation of a property
before making an offer for it* □ **to buy a
shop with stock at valuation** when
buying a shop, to pay a price for the stock
which is equal to the value as estimated
by the valuer □ **to purchase stock at
valuation** to pay the price for stock which
it is valued at

value /ˈvæljuː/ *noun* the amount of
money which something is worth ○ *the
fall in the value of sterling* ○ *She
imported goods to the value of £2500.* ○
*The valuer put the value of the stock at
£25,000.* □ **good value (for money)** a
bargain, something which is worth the
price paid for it ○ *That restaurant gives
value for money.* ○ *Buy that computer
now – it is very good value.* ○ *Holidays in
Italy are good value because of the
exchange rate.* □ **to rise** *or* **fall in value** to
be worth more or less ■ *verb* to estimate
how much money something is worth ○
He valued the stock at £25,000. ○ *We are
having the jewellery valued for insurance.*

value added /ˌvæljuː ˈædɪd/ *noun* the
amount added to the value of a product or
service, being the difference between its
cost and the amount received when it is
sold. Also called **net output**

Value Added Tax /ˌvæljuː ædɪd
ˈtæks/ *noun* full form of **VAT**

value investing /ˈvæljuː ɪnˌvestɪŋ/
noun basing investment strategy on the
value of a company rather than simply on
its share price

value investor /ˈvæljuː ɪnˌvestə/
noun a person who buys shares for the
value of the company

value-priced goods /ˌvæljuː praɪst
ˈɡʊdz/ *noun* goods which are good value
for money

valuer /ˈvæljʊə/ *noun* a person who
estimates how much money something is
worth

value stocks /ˈvæljuː stɒks/ *plural
noun* shares which provide a good return
on investment

variable /ˈveəriəb(ə)l/ *adjective*
changeable ■ *noun* something which
varies

variable annuity /ˌveəriəb(ə)l ə
ˈnjuːəti/ *noun* an annuity based on funds
invested in common stock, which varies
with the value of the stock, as opposed to
a fixed annuity

variable costs /ˌveəriəb(ə)l ˈkɒsts/
plural noun production costs which
increase with the quantity of the product
made, e.g. wages or raw materials

variable rate /ˌveəriəb(ə)l ˈreɪt/ *noun*
a rate of interest on a loan which is not
fixed, but can change with the current
bank interest rates. Also called **floating
rate**

variable redemption bond
/ˌveəriəb(ə)l rɪˈdempʃən bɒnd/ *noun* a
bond where the money to be repaid is
linked to a variable, such as the price of
gold at the time of payment

variance /ˈveəriəns/ *noun* the discrepancy between the actual cost of an asset or
business activity and the standard or
expected cost □ **at variance with** not in

agreement with ○ *The actual sales are at variance with the sales reported by the reps.*

variation /ˌveəriˈeɪʃ(ə)n/ *noun* the amount by which something changes □ **seasonal variations** variations which take place at different times of the year ○ *seasonal variations in buying patterns* ○ *There are marked seasonal variations in unemployment in the hotel industry.*

VAT /ˌviː eɪ ˈtiː, væt/ *noun* a tax on goods and services, added as a percentage to the invoiced sales price ○ *The invoice includes VAT at 17.5%.* ○ *The government is proposing to increase VAT to 22%.* ○ *Some items (such as books) are zero-rated for VAT.* ○ *He does not charge VAT because he asks for payment in cash.* Full form **Value Added Tax**

'…the directive means that the services of stockbrokers and managers of authorized unit trusts are now exempt from VAT; previously they were liable to VAT at the standard rate. Zero-rating for stockbrokers' services is still available as before, but only where the recipient of the service belongs outside the EC' [*Accountancy*]

COMMENT: In the UK, VAT is organised by HM Customs and Excise, and not by the Treasury. It is applied at each stage in the process of making or selling a product or service. Company 'A' charges VAT for their work, which is bought by Company 'B', and pays the VAT collected from 'B' to the Customs and Excise; Company 'B' can reclaim the VAT element in Company 'A''s invoice from the Customs and Excise, but will charge VAT on their work in their invoice to Company 'C'. Each company along the line charges VAT and pays it to the Customs and Excise, but claims back any VAT charged to them. The final consumer pays a price which includes VAT, and which is the final VAT revenue paid to the Customs and Excise. Any company or individual should register for VAT if their annual turnover or income is above a certain level.

VAT declaration /ˈvæt deklə ˌreɪʃ(ə)n/ *noun* a statement declaring VAT income to the VAT office

VAT inspection /ˈvæt ɪnˌspekʃ(ə)n/ *noun* a visit by officials of HM Revenue and Customs to see if a company is correctly reporting its VAT

VAT inspector /ˈvæt ɪnˌspektə/ *noun* a government official who examines VAT returns and checks that VAT is being paid

VAT invoice /ˈvæt ˌɪnvɔɪs/ *noun* an invoice which includes VAT

VAT invoicing /ˈvæt ˌɪnvɔɪsɪŋ/ *noun* the sending of an invoice including VAT

VATman /ˈvætmæn/, **vatman** *noun* a VAT inspector (*informal*)

VAT office /ˈvæt ˌɒfɪs/ *noun* the government office dealing with the collection of VAT in an area

vatu /ˈvɑːtuː/ *noun* a unit of currency used in Vanuatu

vault /vɔːlt/ *noun* a strongroom in a bank, usually underground, where valuables can be deposited

vault cash /ˈvɔːlt kæʃ/ *noun* cash held by a bank in its vaults, used for day-to-day needs

VC *abbreviation* venture capitalist

VCT *abbreviation* venture capital trust

velocity of money /vəˌlɒsɪti əv ˈmʌni/ *noun* the rate at which money circulates in the economy, usually calculated as the GNP shown as a percentage of the stock of money supply

vending /ˈvendɪŋ/ *noun* selling

vendor /ˈvendə/ *noun* **1.** a person who sells something, especially a property ○ *the solicitor acting on behalf of the vendor* **2.** a company selling its shares on a stock market for the first time

vendor placing /ˈvendə ˌpleɪsɪŋ/ *noun* the act of arranging for an issue of new shares to be bought by institutions, as a means of financing the purchase of another company

venture /ˈventʃə/ *noun* a commercial deal which involves a risk ○ *They lost money on several import ventures.* ○ *She's started a new venture – a computer shop.* ■ *verb* to risk money

venture capital /ˌventʃə ˈkæpɪt(ə)l/ *noun* capital for investment which may easily be lost in risky projects, but can also provide high returns. Also called **risk capital**

venture capital fund /ˌventʃə ˈkæpɪt(ə)l fʌnd/ *noun* a fund which invests in finance houses providing venture capital

'…the Securities and Exchange Board of India allowed new companies to enter the primary market provided venture capital funds took up 10 per cent of the equity. At present, new companies are allowed to make initial public offerings provided their projects have been appraised by banks or financial institutions which take up 10 per cent of the equity' [*The Hindu*]

venture capitalist /ˌventʃə ˈkæpɪt(ə)lɪst/ *noun* a finance house or private individual specialising in providing venture capital. Abbreviation **VC**

'…along with the stock market boom of the 1980s, the venture capitalists piled more and more funds into the buyout business, backing bigger and bigger deals with ever more extravagant financing structures' [*Guardian*]

venture capital trust /ˌventʃə ˈkæpɪt(ə)l trʌst/ *noun* a trust which invests in smaller firms which need capital to grow. Abbreviation **VCT**

verification /ˌverɪfɪˈkeɪʃ(ə)n/ *noun* the process of checking if something is correct ○ *The shipment was allowed into the country after verification of the documents by customs.*

verify /ˈverɪfaɪ/ *verb* to check to see if something is correct

vertical /ˈvɜːtɪk(ə)l/ *adjective* upright, straight up or down

vertical communication /ˌvɜːtɪk(ə)l kəˌmjuːnɪˈkeɪʃ(ə)n/ *noun* communication between senior managers via the middle management to the workforce

vertical integration /ˌvɜːtɪk(ə)l ˌɪntɪˈɡreɪʃ(ə)n/ *noun* the extent to which supply-chain activities are controlled within an organisation

vested interest /ˌvestɪd ˈɪntrəst/ *noun* a special interest in keeping an existing state of affairs □ **she has a vested interest in keeping the business working** she wants to keep the business working because she will make more money if it does

vesting day /ˈvestɪŋ deɪ/ *noun* a day when a formerly nationalised industry becomes owned by its new shareholders

vet /vet/ *verb* to examine something carefully ○ *All candidates have to be vetted by the managing director.* ○ *The contract has been sent to the legal department for vetting.* (NOTE: **vetting** – **vetted**)

viability /ˌvaɪəˈbɪlɪti/ *noun* the fact of being viable or being able to make a profit

viable /ˈvaɪəb(ə)l/ *adjective* which can work in practice □ **not commercially viable** not likely to make a profit

videoconference /ˈvɪdiəʊˌkɒnf(ə)rəns/ *noun* a system linking video, audio and computer signals from different locations so that distant people can talk and see each other, as if in the same conference room

view /vjuː/ *noun* a way of thinking about something ○ *We asked the sales manager for his views on the reorganisation of the reps' territories.* ○ *The chairman takes the view that credit should never be longer than thirty days.* □ **to take the long view** to plan for a long period before your current investment will become profitable □ **in view of** because of ○ *In view of the falling exchange rate, we have redrafted our sales forecasts.*

viewdata /ˈvjuːdeɪtə/ *noun* a service on TV which gives share prices. Some services also allow trading over the phone.

virement /ˈvaɪəmənt/ *noun* a transfer of money from one account to another or from one section of a budget to another

virtual credit card /ˌvɜːtʃʊəl ˈkredɪt ˌkɑːd/ *noun* a technology that allows a user to set up a new credit account with a bank on the Internet and then use this account number to purchase goods, also on the Internet

virtual tokens /ˌvɜːtʃʊəl ˈtəʊkənz/ *plural noun* banking technology that allows a user to transfer money from their normal bank to an Internet bank and then use this credit to purchase goods on the Internet

VISA™ /ˈviːzə/ *trademark* a trademark for an international credit card system

visible /ˈvɪzɪb(ə)l/ *adjective* referring to real products which are imported or exported

visible exports /ˌvɪzɪb(ə)l ˈekspɔːts/ *plural noun* real products which are exported, as opposed to services

visible imports /ˌvɪzɪb(ə)l ˈɪmpɔːts/ *plural noun* real products which are imported, as opposed to services

visible trade /ˌvɪzɪb(ə)l ˈtreɪd/ *noun* trade involving visible imports and exports

vivos /ˈvaɪvəʊs/ ♦ **inter vivos**

voicemail /ˈvɔɪsmeɪl/ *noun* an electronic communications system which stores digitised recordings of telephone messages for later playback

void /vɔɪd/ *adjective* not legally valid □ **the contract was declared null and void** the contract was said to be no longer valid ■ *verb* □ **to void a contract** to make a contract invalid

voidable /ˈvɔɪdəb(ə)l/ *adjective* referring to a contract which can be annulled

volatile /ˈvɒlətaɪl/ *adjective* referring to a market or price which is not stable, but which rises and falls sharply ○ *The share has been very volatile since it was launched.*

'…blue chip stocks are the least volatile while smaller stocks are the most volatile' [*The Times*]

'…the investment markets appear to have become ever more volatile, with interest rates moving at times to extreme levels, and the stock market veering wildly from boom to slump and back again' [*Financial Times Review*]

'…the FTSE 100 Index ended another volatile session a net 96.3 easier at 6027' [*Financial Times*]

volatility /ˌvɒləˈtɪlɪti/ *noun* the fact of being volatile ○ *Investors are recommended to keep their money in building society accounts because the increasing volatility of the stock market.*

'…while the technology sector has certainly captured the imagination of private investors, the enthusiasm it has aroused among them is likely to cause extreme share price volatility in the short term' [*Financial Times*]

volatility rating /ˌvɒləˈtɪlɪti ˌreɪtɪŋ/ *noun* a calculation of how volatile a share is, by calculating how much its performance is different from the normal pattern

volume /ˈvɒljuːm/ *noun* 1. a quantity of items 2. the quantity of shares traded on a stock market ○ *average daily volume: 130,000 shares*

volume discount /ˈvɒljuːm ˌdɪskaʊnt/ *noun* the discount given to a customer who buys a large quantity of goods

volume of business /ˌvɒljuːm əv ˈbɪznɪs/ *noun* the number of items sold, or the number of shares sold on the stock exchange during a day's trading ○ *The company has maintained the same volume of business in spite of the recession.*

volume of output /ˌvɒljuːm əv ˈaʊtpʊt/ *noun* the number of items produced

volume of sales /ˌvɒljuːm əv ˈseɪlz/ *noun* 1. the number of items sold □ **low or high volume of sales** a small or large number of items sold 2. *US* an amount of money produced by sales (NOTE: The UK term is **turnover**.)

volume of trade /ˌvɒljuːm əv ˈtreɪd/ *noun* same as **volume of business**

volume-weighted prices /ˌvɒljuːm ˌweɪtɪd ˈpraɪsɪz/ *plural noun* prices which are calculated according to the volume of turnover

voluntarily /ˈvɒlənt(ə)rəli/ *adverb* without being forced or paid

voluntary /ˈvɒlənt(ə)ri/ *adjective* 1. done freely without anyone forcing you to act 2. done without being paid

voluntary arrangement /ˌvɒlənt(ə)ri əˈreɪndʒmənt/ *noun* same as **scheme of arrangement**

voluntary liquidation /ˌvɒlənt(ə)ri ˌlɪkwɪˈdeɪʃ(ə)n/ *noun* a situation where a company itself decides it must close and sell its assets

voluntary organisation /ˈvɒlənt(ə)ri ˌɔːɡənaɪzeɪʃ(ə)n/ *noun* an organisation which has no paid staff

voluntary redundancy /ˌvɒlənt(ə)ri rɪˈdʌndənsi/ *noun* a situation where the employee asks to be made redundant, usually in return for a large payment

vostro account /ˈvɒstrəʊ əˌkaʊnt/ *noun* an account held by a correspondent bank for a foreign bank. ◊ **nostro account**

vote /vəʊt/ *noun* the act of marking a paper or holding up your hand, to show your opinion or to show who you want to be elected □ **to take a vote on a proposal, to put a proposal to the vote** to ask people present at a meeting to say if they do or do not agree with the proposal ■ *verb* to show an opinion by marking a paper or by holding up your hand at a meeting ○ *The meeting voted to close the factory.* ○ *52% of the members voted for Mr Smith as chairman.* ○ *Most of the staff voted for a strike.* □ **to vote for or against a proposal** to say that you agree or do not agree with a proposal □ **two directors were voted off the board at the AGM** the AGM voted to dismiss two directors □ **she was voted on to the committee** she was elected a member of the committee

voter /ˈvəʊtə/ *noun* a person who votes

voting /ˈvəʊtɪŋ/ *noun* the act of making a vote

voting paper /ˈvəʊtɪŋ ˌpeɪpə/ *noun* a paper on which the voter puts a cross to show for whom he or she wants to vote

voting rights /ˈvəʊtɪŋ raɪts/ *plural noun* the rights of shareholders to vote at company meetings

voting shares /ˈvəʊtɪŋ ʃeəz/ *plural noun* shares which give the holder the right to vote at company meetings

voucher /ˈvaʊtʃə/ *noun* **1.** a piece of paper which is given instead of money **2.** a written document from an auditor to show that the accounts are correct or that money has really been paid

W

wage /weɪdʒ/ *noun* the money paid to an employee in return for work done, especially when it is paid weekly and in cash ○ *She is earning a good wage* or *good wages for a young person.* (NOTE: The plural **wages** is more usual when referring to the money earned, but **wage** is used before other nouns.)

'European economies are being held back by rigid labor markets and wage structures' [*Duns Business Month*]

'…real wages have been held down dramatically: they have risen at an annual rate of only 1% in the last two years' [*Sunday Times*]

COMMENT: The term 'wages' refers to weekly or hourly pay for workers, usually paid in cash. For employees paid by a monthly cheque, the term used is 'salary'.

wage adjustments /weɪdʒ əˈdʒʌstmənts/ *plural noun* changes made to wages

wage claim /weɪdʒ kleɪm/ *noun* an act of asking for an increase in wages

wage differentials /weɪdʒ dɪfəˈrenʃəlz/ *plural noun* same as **pay differentials**

wage drift /weɪdʒ drɪft/ *noun* same as **earnings drift**

wage-earner /weɪdʒ ˌɜːnə/ *noun* a person who earns a wage

wage-earning /weɪdʒ ˌɜːnɪŋ/ *adjective* □ **the wage-earning population** people who have jobs and earn money

wage indexation /weɪdʒ ˌɪndekseɪʃ(ə)n/ *noun* the linking of increases to the percentage rise in the cost of living

wage negotiations /weɪdʒ nɪɡəʊʃiˌeɪʃ(ə)nz/ *plural noun* same as **pay negotiations**

wage packet /weɪdʒ ˌpækɪt/ *noun* same as **pay packet**

wage-price spiral /ˌweɪdʒ ˈpraɪs ˌspaɪərəl/ *noun* a situation where price rises encourage higher wage demands which in turn make prices rise

wage restraint /weɪdʒ rɪˌstreɪnt/ *noun* the act of keeping increases in wages under control

wages and prices freeze /ˌweɪdʒɪz ən ˈpraɪsɪz friːz/ *noun* a period when wages and prices are not allowed to be increased

wage scale /weɪdʒ skeɪl/ *noun* same as **pay scale**

wages clerk /weɪdʒɪz klɑːk/ *noun* same as **payroll clerk**

wages drift /weɪdʒs drɪft/ *noun* same as **earnings drift**

wages policy /weɪdʒɪz ˌpɒlisi/ *noun* a government policy on what percentage increases should be paid to workers

waive /weɪv/ *verb* to give up a right ○ *He waived his claim to the estate.* □ **to waive a payment** to say that payment is not necessary

waiver /weɪvə/ *noun* an act of giving up a right or removing the conditions of a rule ○ *If you want to work without a permit, you will have to apply for a waiver.*

waiver clause /weɪvə klɔːz/ *noun* a clause in a contract giving the conditions under which the rights in the contract can be given up

walk-in /wɔːk ɪn/ *noun* a person who approaches an organisation for a job, without knowing if any jobs are available (NOTE: The plural is **walk-ins**.)

wall of money /ˌwɔːl əv ˈmʌni/ *noun* a large amount of money ready to be invested on the stock market (especially, money from new investment funds, or foreign investors) (NOTE: Similar to the **weight of money**.)

wallpaper /ˈwɔːlpeɪpə/ noun shares issued in large numbers during a takeover bid where the purchasing company offers them in exchange for the shares in the company being bought

wall safe /ˈwɔːl seɪf/ noun a safe installed in a wall

Wall Street /ˈwɔːl striːt/ noun **1.** a street in New York where the New York Stock Exchange is situated **2.** the US financial centre ○ *Wall Street analysts predict a rise in interest rates.* ○ *She writes the Wall Street column in the newspaper.*

warehouse /ˈweəhaʊs/ noun a large building where goods are stored

warehouse capacity /ˈweəhaʊs kə ˌpæsɪti/ noun the space available in a warehouse

warehousing /ˈweəhaʊzɪŋ/ noun **1.** the act of storing goods in a warehouse ○ *Warehousing costs are rising rapidly.* **2.** an illegal act where someone buys shares in a company on behalf of another company and holds them in readiness to be surrendered when the second company makes a takeover bid

War Loan /ˈwɔː ləʊn/ noun a government loan issued in time of war

warning /ˈwɔːnɪŋ/ noun a notice of possible danger ○ *Warning notices were put up around the construction site.*

warrant /ˈwɒrənt/ noun **1.** an official document which allows someone to do something **2.** ♦ **share warrant**

'…the rights issue will grant shareholders free warrants to subscribe for further new shares' [*Financial Times*]

warrantee /ˌwɒrənˈtiː/ noun a person who is given a warranty

warrant holder /ˈwɒrənt ˌhəʊldə/ noun a person who holds a warrant for shares

warrantor /ˌwɒrənˈtɔː/ noun a person who gives a warranty

warrant premium /ˈwɒrənt ˌpriːmiəm/ noun a premium paid to buy share warrants, above the price of the shares it entitles you to

warranty /ˈwɒrənti/ noun **1.** a legal document which promises that a machine will work properly or that an item is of good quality ○ *The car is sold with a twelve-month warranty.* ○ *The warranty covers spare parts but not labour costs.* **2.** a promise in a contract **3.** a statement made by an insured person which declares that the facts stated by him are true

washing /ˈwɒʃɪŋ/ noun US the practice of selling and buying back the same security, so as to reduce tax liability, or to increase trading volume. ◊ **bond-washing**

wash sale /ˈwɒʃ seɪl/ noun US the sale and then repurchase of a block of shares similar to the British 'bed-and-breakfast deal'. In the US it may also be used as a means of creating fictitious trading volume.

waste /weɪst/ noun material left over from a production process which is of no value and is thrown away ■ verb to use more than is needed ○ *to waste money* or *paper* or *electricity* or *time* ○ *The MD does not like people wasting her time with minor details.* ○ *We turned off all the heating so as not to waste energy.*

COMMENT: Industrial waste has no value, as opposed to scrap which may be sold to a scrap dealer.

wasting asset /ˈweɪstɪŋ ˌæsɪt/ noun an asset which becomes gradually less valuable as time goes by, e.g. a short lease on a property

watchdog /ˈwɒtʃdɒg/ noun an independent person or organisation whose task is to police a particular industry, ensuring that member companies do not act illegally □ **the City watchdog** the Financial Services Authority (FSA), which supervises the financial institutions

water down /ˌwɔːtə ˈdaʊn/ verb to make something less strong ○ *The family's holdings have been watered down by the creation of the new shares.*

watered stock /ˈwɔːtəd stɒk/ noun shares that are worth less than the total capital invested in the company

weak /wiːk/ adjective not strong, not active □ **share prices remained weak** share prices did not rise

weak currency /wiːk ˈkʌrənsi/ noun a currency which is trading at a low level against other currencies

weaken /ˈwiːkən/ verb to become weak □ **the market weakened** share prices fell

'…the Fed started to ease monetary policy months ago as the first stories appeared about weakening demand in manufacturing industry' [*Sunday Times*]

weak market /ˌwiːk ˈmɑːkɪt/ *noun* a share market in which prices tend to fall because there are no buyers

weakness /ˈwiːknəs/ *noun* the fact of being weak or at a low level

'…indications of weakness in the US economy were contained in figures from the Fed on industrial production' [*Financial Times*]

wealth tax /ˈwelθ tæks/ *noun* a tax on money, property or investments owned by a person

website /ˈwebsaɪt/ *noun* a position on the web, which is created by a company, organisation or individual, and which anyone can visit ○ *How many hits did we have on our website last week?*

Wechsel *noun* the German word for foreign exchange

weekend effect /ˈwiːkˈend ɪˌfekt/ *noun* a phenomenon in financial markets in which stock returns on a Monday are lower than those of the preceding Friday, possibly due to bad news being delivered on Friday after the markets close

weight /weɪt/ *noun* a measurement of how heavy something is □ **to sell fruit by weight** the price is per pound or per kilo of the fruit □ **to give short weight** to give less than you should ■ *verb* to give an extra value to a factor

weighted average /ˌweɪtɪd ˈæv(ə)rɪdʒ/ *noun* an average which is calculated taking several factors into account, giving some more value than others

weighted index /ˌweɪtɪd ˈɪndeks/ *noun* an index where some important items are given more value than less important ones

weighting /ˈweɪtɪŋ/ *noun* an additional salary or wages paid to compensate for living in an expensive part of the country ○ *The salary is £15,000 plus London weighting.*

weight of money /ˌweɪt əv ˈmʌni/ *noun* a large amount of money ready to be invested on the stock market, especially cash available in pension funds

wheeler-dealer /ˌwiːlə ˈdiːlə/ *noun* a person who lives on money from a series of profitable business deals

whisper number /ˈwɪspə ˌnʌmbə/ *noun* a figure which is mentioned as a rumour

whistleblower /ˈwɪs(ə)lˌbləʊə/ *noun* a person who reveals dishonest practices (*informal*)

white-collar /ˌwaɪt ˈkɒlə/ *adjective* referring to office workers

'…the share of white-collar occupations in total employment rose from 44 per cent to 49 per cent' [*Sydney Morning Herald*]

white-collar crime /ˌwaɪt ˌkɒlə ˈkraɪm/ *noun* crimes committed by business people or office workers (such as embezzlement, computer fraud or insider dealing)

white-collar job /ˌwaɪt ˈkɒlə dʒɒb/ *noun* a job in an office

white-collar union /ˌwaɪt ˌkɒlə ˈjuːnjən/ *noun* a trade union formed of white-collar workers

white-collar worker /ˌwaɪt ˌkɒlə ˈwɜːkə/ *noun* a worker in an office, not in a factory

white elephant /ˌwaɪt ˈelɪfənt/ *noun* an investment that nobody wants because it is unprofitable

white knight /ˌwaɪt ˈnaɪt/ *noun* a person or company which rescues a firm in financial difficulties, especially one which saves a firm from being taken over by an unacceptable purchaser

White Paper /ˌwaɪt ˈpeɪpə/ *noun* a report issued by the UK government as a statement of government policy on a particular problem. Compare **Green Paper**

whizz-kid /ˈwɪz kɪd/ *noun* a brilliant young person who quickly becomes successful in business ○ *She was a whizz-kid who reached head of department in five years.*

whole-life insurance /ˌhəʊl ˈlaɪf ɪn ˌʃʊərəns/, **whole-life policy** /ˌhəʊl ˈlaɪf ˌpɒlɪsi/ *noun* an insurance policy where the insured person pays a fixed premium each year and the insurance company pays a sum when he or she dies. Also called **whole-of-life assurance**

wholesale /ˈhəʊlseɪl/ *adjective, adverb* referring to the business of buying goods from manufacturers and selling them in large quantities to traders (retailers) who then sell in smaller quantities to the general public ○ *I persuaded him to give us a wholesale discount.* □ **he buys wholesale and sells retail** he buys goods in bulk at a wholesale discount and then sells in small quantities to the public

wholesale banking /ˌhəʊlseɪl ˈbæŋkɪŋ/ *noun* banking services between merchant banks and other financial institutions, as opposed to retail banking

wholesale dealer /ˈhəʊlseɪl ˌdiːlə/ *noun* a person who buys in bulk from manufacturers and sells to retailers

wholesale market /ˈhəʊlseɪl ˌmɑːkɪt/ *noun* an interbank money market, where banks and other financial institutions deal with each other

wholesale price /ˈhəʊlseɪl praɪs/ *noun* the price charged to customers who buy goods in large quantities in order to resell them in smaller quantities to others

wholesale price index /ˌhəʊlseɪl ˈpraɪs ˌɪndeks/ *noun* an index showing the rises and falls of prices of manufactured goods as they leave the factory

wholesaler /ˈhəʊlseɪlə/ *noun* a person who buys goods in bulk from manufacturers and sells them to retailers

wholly-owned subsidiary /ˌhəʊli əʊnd səbˈsɪdjəri/ *noun* a subsidiary which belongs completely to the parent company

will /wɪl/ *noun* a legal document where someone says what should happen to his or her property when he or she dies ○ *He wrote his will in 1984.* ○ *According to her will, all her property is left to her children.*

COMMENT: A will should best be drawn up by a solicitor; it can also be written on a form which can be bought from a stationery shop. To be valid, a will must be dated and witnessed by a third party (i.e. by someone who is not mentioned in the will).

wind *verb*

wind up *phrasal verb* **1.** to end a meeting, or to close down a business or organisation and sell its assets ○ *She wound up the meeting with a vote of thanks to the committee.* **2.** □ **to wind up a company** to put a company into liquidation ○ *The court ordered the company to be wound up.*

windfall /ˈwɪndfɔːl/ *noun* a sudden winning of money or a sudden profit which is not expected

windfall profit /ˈwɪndfɔːl ˌprɒfɪt/ *noun* a sudden profit which is not expected

windfall profits tax /ˈwɪndfɔːl ˌprɒfɪts tæks/, **windfall tax** /ˈwɪndfɔːl tæks/ *noun* a tax on companies that have made large profits because of circumstances outside their usual trading activities. A windfall tax was imposed on the privatised utility companies in 1997.

windfall wealth /ˈwɪndfɔːl welθ/ *noun* wealth which comes from a windfall

winding up /ˌwaɪndɪŋ ˈʌp/ *noun* liquidation, the act of closing a company and selling its assets □ **a compulsory winding up order** an order from a court saying that a company must be wound up

windmill /ˈwɪndmɪl/ *noun* same as **accommodation bill** (*informal*)

window /ˈwɪndəʊ/ *noun* a short period when something is available or possible

window dressing /ˈwɪndəʊ ˌdresɪŋ/ *noun* **1.** the practice of putting goods on display in a shop window, so that they attract customers **2.** the practice of putting on a display to make a business seem better or more profitable or more efficient than it really is

window of opportunity /ˌwɪndəʊ əv ɒpəˈtjuːnɪti/ *noun* a short period which allows an action to take place

window shopping /ˈwɪndəʊ ˌʃɒpɪŋ/ *noun* the practice of looking at goods in shop windows, without buying anything

WIP *abbreviation* work in progress

wipe off /ˌwaɪp ˈɒf/ *verb* to remove something completely

wire transfer /ˈwaɪə ˌtrænsfɜː/ *noun* a transfer of money from one account to another by telegraph

witching hour /ˈwɪtʃɪŋ aʊə/ *noun* a critical moment on a stock exchange, where several options expire at the same time

withdraw /wɪðˈdrɔː/ *verb* **1.** to take money out of an account ○ *to withdraw money from the bank or from your account* ○ *You can withdraw up to £50 from any cash machine by using your card.* (NOTE: **withdrawing – withdrew –**

has withdrawn) 2. to take back an offer ○ *When he found out more about the candidate, the HR manager withdrew the offer of a job.* ○ *When the employees went on strike, the company withdrew its revised pay offer.* (NOTE: **withdrawing – withdrew – has withdrawn**) □ **one of the company's backers has withdrawn** he or she stopped supporting the company financially ○ *We expect they will withdraw their takeover bid.* ○ *The chairman asked him to withdraw the remarks he has made about the finance director.*

withdrawal /wɪð'drɔːəl/ *noun* the act of removing money from an account ○ *to give seven days' notice of withdrawal* ○ *Withdrawals from bank accounts reached a peak in the week before Christmas.* □ **withdrawal without penalty at seven days' notice** money can be taken out of a deposit account, without losing any interest, provided that seven days' notice has been given

withholding tax /wɪð'həʊldɪŋ ˌtæks/ *noun US* a tax which removes money from interest or dividends before they are paid to the investor, usually applied to non-resident investors

with-profit bond /ˌwɪð 'prɒfɪt ˌbɒnd/ *noun* a bond which guarantees a capital return plus the profits which have accumulated during its lifetime

with profits /ˌwɪð 'prɒfɪts/ *adverb* used to describe an insurance policy which guarantees the policyholder a share in the profits of the fund in which the premiums are invested

won /wʌn/ *noun* a unit of currency used in North and South Korea

work /wɜːk/ *noun* **1.** things done using the hands or brain **2.** a job, something done to earn money ○ *It is not the work itself that the employees are complaining about* ○ *He goes to work by bus.* ○ *She never gets home from work before 8 p.m.* ○ *His work involves a lot of travelling.* ○ *He is still looking for work.* ○ *She has been out of work for six months.*

'…the quality of the work environment demanded by employers and employees alike' [*Lloyd's List*]

work out *phrasal verb* to calculate ○ *He worked out the costs on the back of an envelope.* ○ *He worked out the discount at 15%.* ○ *She worked out the*

discount on her calculator.

worker /'wɜːkə/ *noun* a person who is employed □ **worker representation on the board** the fact of having a representative of the workers as a director of the company

worker director /ˌwɜːkə daɪ'rektə/ *noun* a director of a company who is a representative of the workforce

workforce /'wɜːkfɔːs/ *noun* the total number of employees in an organisation, industry or country

working /'wɜːkɪŋ/ *adjective* **1.** referring to work **2.** □ **working control of a company** having enough shares in a company to be able to control all its actions (usually, this means 51% of shares)

working capital /'wɜːkɪŋ ˌkæpɪt(ə)l/ *noun* capital in the form of cash, stocks, and debtors but not creditors, used by a company in its day-to-day operations. Also called **circulating capital, floating capital, net current assets**

working conditions /'wɜːkɪŋ kən ˌdɪʃ(ə)nz/ *plural noun* the general state of the place where people work, e.g. whether it is hot, noisy, dark or dangerous

working partner /'wɜːkɪŋ ˌpɑːtnə/ *noun* a partner who works in a partnership

working-time directive /ˌwɜːkɪŋ 'taɪm daɪˌrektɪv/ *noun* a directive concerning the maximum number of hours an employee can work in the EU

working underwriter /ˌwɜːkɪŋ 'ʌndəraɪtə/ *noun* a member of a Lloyd's syndicate who actively generates business, as opposed to the 'names' who put up the security

working week /ˌwɜːkɪŋ 'wiːk/ *noun* the usual number of hours worked per week ○ *Even though he is a freelance, he works a normal working week.*

work in progress /ˌwɜːk ɪn 'prəʊgres/ *noun* the value of goods being manufactured which are not complete at the end of an accounting period ○ *Our current assets are made up of stock, goodwill and work in progress.* Abbreviation **WIP** (NOTE: The US term is **work in process.**)

workload /'wɜːkləʊd/ *noun* the amount of work which a person has to do

○ *He has difficulty in coping with his heavy workload.*

work permit /'wɜːk ˌpɜːmɪt/ *noun* an official document which allows someone who is not a citizen to work in a country

works /wɜːks/ *noun* a factory ○ *There is a small engineering works in the same street as our office.* ○ *The steel works is expanding.* (NOTE: takes a singular or plural verb)

works committee /'wɜːks kəˌmɪti/, **works council** /'wɜːks ˌkaʊnsəl/ *noun* a committee of employees and management which discusses the organisation of work in a factory

work-sharing /'wɜːk ˌʃeərɪŋ/ *noun* a system that allows two or more part-timers to share one job, each doing part of the work for part of the pay

works manager /'wɜːks ˌmænɪdʒə/ *noun* a person in charge of a works

workspace /'wɜːkspeɪs/ *noun* the memory or space available on a computer for temporary work

workstation /'wɜːkˌsteɪʃ(ə)n/ *noun* a desk, usually with a computer terminal, printer, telephone and other office items at which an employee in an office works

world /wɜːld/ *noun* **1.** the Earth □ **the world market for steel** the possible sales of steel throughout the world **2.** the people in a specific business or people with a special interest ○ *the world of big business* ○ *the world of lawyers* or *the legal world*

World Bank /ˌwɜːld 'bæŋk/ *noun* a central bank, controlled by the United Nations, whose funds come from the member states of the UN and which lends money to member states

world rights /ˌwɜːld 'raɪts/ *plural noun* the right to sell the product anywhere in the world

World Trade Organization /wɜːld 'treɪd ɔːɡənaɪˌzeɪʃ(ə)n/ *noun* an international organisation set up with the aim of reducing restrictions in trade between countries. Abbreviation **WTO**

worldwide /'wɜːldwaɪd/; /wɜːld 'waɪd/ *adjective, adverb* everywhere in the world ○ *The company has a worldwide network of distributors.* ○ *World-wide sales* or *Sales worldwide have topped two million units.* ○ *This make of computer is available worldwide.*

worth /wɜːθ/ *adjective* having a value or a price ○ *Don't get it repaired – it's worth only £25.* ○ *The car is worth £6,000 on the secondhand market.* (NOTE: always follows the verb **to be**) □ **he is worth £10m** he owns property, investments, etc., which would sell for £10m □ **what are ten pounds worth in dollars?** what is the equivalent of £10 in dollars? ■ *noun* a value □ **give me ten pounds' worth of petrol** give me as much petrol as £10 will buy

worthless /'wɜːθləs/ *adjective* having no value ○ *The cheque is worthless if it is not signed.*

wraparound mortgage /'ræpəraʊnd ˌmɔːɡɪdʒ/ *noun US* a type of second mortgage where the borrower pays interest only to the second lender (who then pays the interest payments on the first mortgage to the first lender)

wreck /rek/ *noun* **1.** a ship which has sunk, which has been badly damaged and cannot float ○ *They saved the cargo from the wreck.* ○ *Oil poured out of the wreck of the tanker.* **2.** the fact of collapsing, or a company which has collapsed ○ *He managed to save some of his investment from the wreck of the company.* ○ *Investors lost thousands of pounds in the wreck of the investment trust.* ■ *verb* to damage something badly or to ruin it ○ *They are trying to salvage the wrecked tanker.* ○ *The negotiations were wrecked by the unions.*

writ /ˌrɪt əv 'sʌmənz/, **writ of summons** *noun* a legal document which begins an action in the High Court ○ *The court issued a writ to prevent the trade union from going on strike.* ○ *The company obtained a writ to prevent the trade union from going on strike.* □ **to serve someone with a writ, to serve a writ on someone** to give someone a writ officially, so that he or she has to defend it

write /raɪt/ *verb*

write down *phrasal verb* to note an asset at a lower value than previously ○ *written down value* ○ *The car is written down in the company's books.*

write off *phrasal verb* to cancel a debt, or to remove an asset from the accounts as having no value ○ *We had to write off £20,000 in bad debts.* □ **two cars were written off after the accident** the insurance company considered that both cars were a total loss □ **the cargo was written off as a total loss** the cargo was so badly damaged that the insurers said it had no value

'$30 million from usual company borrowings will either be amortized or written off in one sum' [*Australian Financial Review*]

write out *phrasal verb* to write something in full ○ *She wrote out the minutes of the meeting from her notes.* □ **to write out a cheque** to write the words and figures on a cheque and then sign it

writedown /'raɪtdaʊn/ *noun* a reduction in the recorded value of an asset to comply with the concept of prudence. The valuation of stock at the lower of cost or net realisable value may require the values of some stock to be written down.

'...the holding company has seen its earnings suffer from big writedowns in conjunction with its $1 billion loan portfolio' [*Duns Business Month*]

write-down allowance /'raɪt daʊn ə ˌlaʊəns/ *noun* an allowance for the depreciation of an asset over a period of years

write-off /'raɪt ɒf/ *noun* **1.** the total loss or cancellation of a bad debt, or the removal of an asset's value from a company's accounts ○ *to allow for write-offs in the yearly accounts* **2.** something which is so badly damaged that it cannot be repaired (*informal*) ○ *The car was a write-off.*

writer /'raɪtə/ *noun* a person who writes a cheque □ **writer of an option** person who sells an option

writing /'raɪtɪŋ/ *noun* something which has been written ○ *to put the agreement in writing*

written-down value /ˌrɪt(ə)n daʊn 'væljuː/ *noun* same as **net book value**

WTO *abbreviation* World Trade Organization

XYZ

xa *abbreviation* ex-all

xc *abbreviation* ex-capitalisation

xd *abbreviation* ex dividend

xr *abbreviation* ex-rights

Yankee bank /ˈjæŋki bæŋk/ *noun* a foreign bank trading in the US

Yankee bond /ˈjæŋki bɒnd/ *noun* a dollar bond issued in the American market by a non-US company. Compare **bulldog bond**, **samurai bond**

year /jɪə/ *noun* a period of twelve months

year end /ˌjɪər ˈend/ *noun* the end of the financial year, when a company's accounts are prepared ○ *The accounts department has started work on the year-end accounts.*

yearling bond /ˈjɪəlɪŋ bɒnd/ *noun* a local authority bond which matures in 12 months

yearly /ˈjɪəli/ *adjective* happening once a year ○ *We make a yearly payment of £1000.* ○ *For the past few years she has had a yearly pay rise of 10%.*

Yellow Book /ˈjeləʊ bʊk/ *noun* a publication by the London Stock Exchange which gives details of the regulations covering the listing of companies on the exchange

yen /jen/ *noun* a unit of currency used in Japan (NOTE: It is usually written as ¥ before a figure: **¥2,700** (say two thousand seven hundred yen).)

yield /jiːld/ *noun* the money produced as a return on an investment, shown as a percentage of the money invested ■ *verb* to produce an amount or percentage as interest or dividend ○ *government stocks which yield a small interest* ○ *shares which yield 10%*

'…if you wish to cut your risks you should go for shares with yields higher than average' [*Investors Chronicle*]

COMMENT: To work out the yield on an investment, take the gross dividend per annum, multiply it by 100 and divide by the price you paid for it (in pence): an investment paying a dividend of 20p per share and costing £3.00, is yielding 6.66%.

yield curve /ˈjiːld kɜːv/ *noun* a graph showing the yields on different types of investment

yield to maturity /ˌjiːld tə məˈtʃʊərɪti/ *noun* a calculation of the yield on a fixed-interest investment, assuming it is bought at a certain price and held to maturity

yuan /juˈɑːn/ *noun* a unit of currency used in China

ZDP *abbreviation* zero dividend preference share

zero /ˈzɪərəʊ/ *noun* **1.** nought, the number 0 ○ *The code for international calls is zero zero (00).* **2.** same as **zero dividend preference share**

zero-coupon bond /ˌzɪərəʊ ˈkuːpɒn bɒnd/ *noun* a bond which carries no interest, but which is issued at a discount and so provides a capital gain when it is redeemed at face value

zero dividend preference share /ˌzɪərəʊ ˌdɪvɪdend ˈpref(ə)rəns ʃeəz/ *noun* a bond which pays no dividend, but has a fixed term and a fixed redemption price, which is a little higher than the redemption price on similar gilts though the redemption price is not in fact guaranteed. Abbreviation **ZDPS**. Also called **zero**

zero inflation /ˌzɪərəʊ ɪnˈfleɪʃ(ə)n/ *noun* inflation at 0%

zero-rated /ˌzɪərəʊ ˈreɪtɪd/ *adjective* referring to an item which has a VAT rate of 0%

zero-rated bond /ˈzɪərəʊ ˌreɪtɪd bɒnd/ *noun* same as **zero-coupon bond**

zero-rating /ˈzɪərəʊ ˌreɪtɪŋ/ *noun* the rating of a product or service at 0% VAT

zinc /zɪŋk/ *noun* a metal which is traded on commodity markets, such as the London Metal Exchange

zloty /ˈzlɒti/ *noun* a unit of currency used in Poland

zone /zəʊn/ *noun* an area of a town or country for administrative purposes ■ *verb* to divide a town into different areas for planning and development purposes □ **land zoned for light industrial use** land where planning permission has been given to build small factories for light industry

SUPPLEMENT

Central Banks

Afghanistan	da Afghanistan Bank, Kabul
Albania	Bank of Albania, Tirana
Algeria	Banque d'Algérie, Algiers
Angola	Banco Nacional de Angola, Luanda
Argentina	Banco Central de la República Argentina, Buenos Aires
Armenia	Central Bank of Armenia, Yerevan
Aruba	Centrale Bank Van Aruba, Oranjestad
Australia	Reserve Bank of Australia, Sydney
Austria	Oesterreichische Nationalbank, Vienna
Azerbaijan	Central Bank of Azerbaijan, Baku
Bahamas	Central Bank of the Bahamas, Nassau
Bahrain	Central Bank of Bahrain, Manama
Bangladesh	Bangladesh Bank, Dhaka
Barbados	Central Bank of Barbados, Bridgetown
Belarus	National Bank of the Republic of Belarus, Minsk
Belgium	Banque Nationale de Belgique, Brussels
Benin	Banque Centrale des Etats de l'Afrique de l'Ouest
Bermuda	Bermuda Monetary Authority, Hamilton
Bhutan	Royal Monetary Authority, Thimphu
Bolivia	Banco Central de Bolivia, La Paz
Bosnia & Herzegovina	Centralna Banka Bosne i Hercegovine, Sarajevo
Botswana	Bank of Botswana, Gaborone
Brazil	Banco Central do Brasil, Brasilia
Brunei	Brunei Currency Board
Bulgaria	Bulgarian National Bank, Sofia
Burkina Faso	Banque Centrale des Etats de l'Afrique de l'Ouest
Burundi	Banque de la République du Burundi, Bujumbura
Cambodia	National Bank of Cambodia, Phnom Penh
Cameroon	Banque des Etats de l'Afrique Centrale, Yaoundé
Canada	Bank of Canada, Ottawa
Central African Republic	Banque des Etats de l'Afrique Centrale, Bangui
Chad	Banque des Etats de l'Afrique Centrale, N'Djamena
Chile	Banco Central de Chile, Santiago
China	People's Bank of China, Beijing
Colombia	Banco de la República de Colombia, Bogotá
Comoros	Banque Centrale des Comoros, Moroni
Congo (Republic of)	Banque des Etats de l'Afrique Centrale, Brazzaville
Congo (Democratic Republic of)	Banque Centrale du Congo, Kinshasa
Costa Rica	Banco Central de Costa Rica, San José
Côte d'Ivoire	Banque Centrale des Etats de l'Afrique de l'Ouest, Abidjan
Croatia	Hrvatska Narodna Banka, Zagreb
Cuba	Banco Central de Cuba, Havana
Cyprus	Central Bank of Cyprus, Nicosia
Czech Republic	Ceská Národní Banka, Prague
Denmark	Danmarks Nationalbank, Copenhagen
Dominican Republic	Banco Central de la República Dominicana, Santo Domingo
Ecuador	Banco Central del Ecuador, Quito
Egypt	Central Bank of Egypt, Cairo
El Salvador	Banco Central de Reserva de El Salvador, San Salvador
Equatorial Guinea	Bank of Central African States, Conakry
Estonia	Eesti Pank, Tallinn
Ethiopia	National Bank of Ethiopia, Addis Ababa

Central Banks *continued*

European Union	European Central Bank, Frankfurt
Fiji	Reserve Bank of Fiji, Suva
Finland	Suomen Pankki, Helsinki
France	Banque de France, Paris
Gabon	Banque des Etats de l'Afrique Centrale, Libreville
The Gambia	Central Bank of the Gambia, Banjul
Georgia	National Bank of Georgia, Tbilisi
Germany	Deutsche Bundesbank, Frankfurt
Ghana	Bank of Ghana, Accra
Greece	Bank of Greece, Athens
Guatemala	Banco de Guatemala, Guatemala City
Guinea-Bissau	Banque Centrale des Etats de l'Afrique de l'Ouest, Bissau
Guyana	Bank of Guyana, Georgetown
Haiti	Banque de la République d'Haïti, Port-au-Prince
Honduras	Banco Central de Honduras, Tegucigalpa
Hong Kong	Hong Kong Monetary Authority, Hong Kong
Hungary	Magyar Nemzeti Bank, Budapest
Iceland	Sedlabanki Islands, Reykjavik
India	Reserve Bank of India, Mumbai
Indonesia	Bank Indonesia, Jakarta
Iran	Central Bank of the Islamic Republic of Iran, Teheran
Iraq	Central Bank of Iraq, Baghdad
Ireland	Central Bank and Financial Services Authority of Irleand, Dublin
Israel	Bank of Israel, Jerusalem
Italy	Banca d'Italia, Rome
Jamaica	Bank of Jamaica, Kingston
Japan	Bank of Japan, Tokyo
Jordan	Central Bank of Jordan, Amman
Kazakhstan	National Bank of Kazakhstan, Almaty
Kenya	Central Bank of Kenya, Nairobi
Korea (North)	Central Bank of the Democratic People's Republic of Korea, Pyongyang
Korea (South)	Bank of Korea, Seoul
Kuwait	Central Bank of Kuwait, Kuwait City
Kyrgyzstan	National Bank of the Kyrgyz Republic, Bishkek
Laos	Bank of the Lao People's Democratic Republic, Vientiane
Latvia	Latvijas Banka, Riga
Lebanon	Banque du Liban, Beirut
Lesotho	Central Bank of Lesotho, Maseru
Liberia	National Bank of Liberia, Monrovia
Libya	Central Bank of Libya, Tripoli
Liechtenstein	Liechtensteinische Landesbank
Lithuania	Lietuvos Bankas, Vilnius
Luxembourg	Banque Centrale du Luxembourg
Macedonia	National Bank of the Republic of Macedonia, Skopje
Macao	Monetary Authority of Macao, Macao
Madagascar	Banque Centrale du Madagascar, Antananarivo
Malawi	Reserve Bank of Malawi, Lilongwe
Malaysia	Bank Negara Malaysia, Kuala Lumpur

Central Banks *continued*

Mali	Banque Centrale des Etats de l'Afrique de l'Ouest, Bamako
Malta	Central Bank of Malta, Valletta
Mauritania	Banque Centrale de Mauritanie, Nouakchott
Mauritius	Bank of Mauritius, Port Louis
Mexico	Banco de Mexico, Mexico
Moldova	National Bank of Moldova, Chisinau
Mongolia	Bank of Mongolia, Ulaanbaatar
Montenegro	Central Bank of Montenegro, Podgorica
Morocco	Banque al-Maghrib, Rabat
Mozambique	Banco de Moçambique, Maputo
Myanmar	Central Bank of Myanmar, Yangon
Namibia	Bank of Namibia, Windhoek
Nepal	Nepal Rastra Bank, Kathmandu
Netherlands	De Nederlandsche Bank, Amsterdam
New Zealand	Reserve Bank of New Zealand, Wellington
Nicaragua	Banco Central de Nicaragua, Managua
Niger	Banque Centrale des Etats de l'Afrique de l'Ouest, Niamey
Nigeria	Central Bank of Nigeria, Abuja
Norway	Norges Bank, Oslo
Oman	Central Bank of Oman, Muscat
Pakistan	State Bank of Pakistan, Karachi
Panama	Banco Nacional de Panamá, Panama
Papua New Guinea	Bank of Papua New Guinea, Port Moresby
Paraguay	Banco Central Del Paraguay, Asuncion
Peru	Banco Central de Reserva del Perú, Lima
Philippines	Bangko Sentral ng Pilipinas, Manila
Poland	Narodowy Bank Polski, Warsaw
Portugal	Banco de Portugal, Lisbon
Qatar	Qatar Central Bank, Doha
Romania	National Bank of Romania, Bucharest
Russia	Central Bank of the Russian Federation, Moscow
Rwanda	Banque Nationale du Rwanda, Kigali
Saudi Arabia	Saudi Arabian Monetary Agency, Riyadh
Samoa	Central Bank of Samoa
Senegal	Banque Centrale des Etats de l'Afrique de l'Ouest, Dakar
Serbia	National Bank of Serbia, Belgrade
Seychelles	Central Bank of the Seychelles, Victoria
Sierra Leone	Bank of Sierra Leone, Freetown
Singapore	Monetary Authority of Singapore
Slovakia	Národná Banka Slovenska, Bratislava
Slovenia	Banka Slovenije, Ljubljana
Solomon Islands	Central Bank of Solomon Islands, Honiara
Somalia	Baanka Somaliland, Mogadishu
South Africa	South African Reserve Bank, Pretoria
Spain	Banco de España, Madrid
Sri Lanka	Central Bank of Sri Lanka, Colombo
Sudan	Bank of Sudan, Khartoum
Suriname	Centrale Bank van Suriname, Paramaribo
Sweden	Sveriges Riksbank, Stockholm
Swaziland	Central Bank of Swaziland, Mbabane

Central Banks *continued*

Switzerland	Schweizerische Nationalbank, Banque Nationale Suisse, Berne
Syria	Central Bank of Syria, Damascus
Taiwan	Central Bank of China, Taipei
Tanzania	Bank of Tanzania, Dar es Salaam
Thailand	Bank of Thailand, Bangkok
Tajikistan	National Bank of Tajikistan, Dushanbe
Togo	Banque Centrale des Etats de l'Afrique de l'Ouest, Lomé
Tonga	National Reserve Bank of Tonga, Nuku'alofa
Trinidad and Tobago	Central Bank of Trinidad and Tobago, Port of Spain
Tunisia	Banque Centrale de Tunisie, Tunis
Turkey	Türkiye Cumhuriyet Merkez Bankasi, Ankara
Uganda	Bank of Uganda, Kampala
Ukraine	National Bank of Ukraine, Kiev
United Arab Emirates	Central Bank of the United Arab Emirates, Abu Dhabi
United Kingdom	Bank of England, London
United States of America	Federal Reserve System, Washington
Uruguay	Banco Central del Uruguay, Montevideo
Uzbekistan	Central Bank of the Republic of Uzbekistan, Tashkent
Venezuela	Banco Central de Venezuela, Caracas
Vietnam	State Bank of Vietnam, Hanoi
Yemen	Central Bank of Yemen, Sana'a
Zambia	Bank of Zambia, Lusaka
Zimbabwe	Reserve Bank of Zimbabwe, Harare

World Stock Exchanges

Argentina	Bolsa de Comercio de Buenos Aires
Armenia	Armenian Stock Exchange
Australia	Australian Securities Exchange
Austria	Wiener Börse AG, Vienna
Azerbaijan	Baku Stock Exchange
Bahamas	Bahama & Internationa Stock Exchange
Bahrain	Bahrain Stock Exchange
Bangladesh	Dhaka Stock Exchange
Barbados	Barbados International Securities Exchange, Bridgetown
Belgium	Euronext Brussels
Bermuda	Bermuda Stock Exchange
Bolivia	Bolsa Bolivia de Valores
Botswana	Botswana Stock Exchange
Bosnia Herzogovina	Sarajevo Stock Exchange
Brazil	Bolsa de Valores do Rio de Janeiro
	Bolsa de Valores de São Paulo
Bulgaria	Bulgarian Stock Exchange, Sofia
Cameroon	Douala Stock Exchange
Canada	Montreal Stock Exchange
	Toronto Stock Exchange
	TSX Venture Exchange
	Winnipeg Stock Exchange
Cape Verde	Bolsa de Valores de Cabo Verde
Chile	Santiago Stock Exchange
China	Shanghai Stock Exchange
	Shenzhen Stock Exchange
Colombia	Bolsa de Valores de Colombia
Costa Rica	Bolsa Nacional de Valores, San José
Croatia	Zagreb Stock Exchange
Cyprus	Cyprus Stock Exchange
Czech Republic	Prague Stock Exchange
Denmark	Copenhagen Stock Exchange
Dominican Republic	Bolsa de Valores de la Republic Dominicana
Ecuador	Bolsa de Valores de Guayquil
Egypt	Cairo Stock Exchange
	Alexandria Stock Exchange
El Salvador	Bolsa de Valores de El Salvador
Estonia	Talinn Stock Exchange
Europe	Euronext
	OMX Exchanges
Finland	Helsinki Stock Exchange
	Nordic Stock Exchange Group
Fiji	South Pacific Stock Exchange
France	Euronext Paris
Germany	Deutsche Börse
	Börse Berlin-Bremer
	Börse Düsseldorf
	BÖAG Börse AG, Hamburg/Hanover
	Börse-Stuttgart
	Frankfurt Stock Exchange
Georgia	Georgia Stock Exchange
Greece	Athens Stock Exchange
Guyana	Guyana Stock Exchange
Honduras	Bolsa Centroamericana de Valores

World Stock Exchanges *continued*

Hong Kong	Hong Kong Stock Exchange
Hungary	Budapest Stock Exchange
India	National Stock Exchange of India
	Bombay Stock Exchange
	Calcutta Stock Exchange
	Delhi Stock Exchange
	Madras Stock Exchange
Indonesia	Indonesia Stock Exchange
Iran	Teheran Stock Exchange
Iraq	Iraq Stock Exchange
Ireland	Irish Stock Exchange
Israel	Tel Aviv Stock Exchange
Italy	Borsa Italiana
Jamaica	Jamaica Stock Exchange
Japan	Fukuoka Stock Exchange
	Hiroshima Stock Exchange
	Nagoya Stock Exchange
	Osaka Stock Exchange
	Sapporo Stock Exchange
	Tokyo Stock Exchange
Jordan	Amman Stock Exchange
Kazakhstan	Kazakhstan Stock Exchange
Kenya	Nairobi Stock Exchange
Korea	Korea Exchange
Kuwait	Kuwait Stock Exchange
Kyrgyzstan	Kyrgyz Stock Exchange
Latvia	Riga Stock Exchange
Lebanon	Beirut Stock Exchange
Lithuania	Vilinus Stock Exchange
Luxembourg	Bourse de Luxembourg
Macedonia	Macedonian Stock Exchange
Malawi	Malawi Stock Exchange
Malaysia	Bursa Malaysia Stock Exchange
Maldives	Maldives Stock Exchange
Malta	Malta Stock Exchange
Mauritius	Stock Exchange of Mauritis
Mexico	Bolsa Mexicana de Valores
Moldova	Moldova Stock Exchange
Mongolia	Mongolian Stock Exchange
Montenegro	Montenegro Stock Exchange
Morocco	La Bourse de Casablanca
Mozambique	Bolsa de Valores de Mozambique
Namibia	Namibian Stock Exchange
Nepal	Lima Stock Exchange
Netherlands	Euronext Amsterdam
New Zealand	New Zealand Stock Exchange
Nicuragua	Bolsa de Valores de Nicuragua
Nigeria	Nigerian Stock Exchange, Lagos
Norway	Oslo Børs
Oman	Muscat Securities Market
Pakistan	Karachi Stock Exchange
	Lahore Stock Exchange
Palestine	Palestine Securities Exchange

World Stock Exchanges *continued*

Panama	Bolsa de Valores de Panamá
Peru	Bolsa de Valores de Lima
Philippines	Philippine Stock Exchange
Poland	Warsaw Stock Exchange
Portugal	Euronext Lisbon
Romania	Bucharest Stock Exchange
Russia	Moscow Interbank Currency Exchange
Rwanda	Rwanda Over the Counter Exchange
Saudi Arabia	Tadawul
Serbia	Belgrade Stock Exchange
Singapore	Singapore Exchange
Slovakia	Bratislava Stock Exchange
Slovenia	Ljubljana Stock Exchange
South Africa	Johannesburg Stock Exchange
Spain	Bolsa de Bilbao
	Bolsa de Madrid
	Bolsa de Barcelona
	Bolsa de Valencia
Sri Lanka	Colombo Stock Exchange
Sudan	Khartoum Stock Exchange
Sweden	Stockholmbörsen
	Nordic Stock Exchange Group
Swaziland	Swaziland Stock Exchange
Switzerland	Swiss Exchange
Taiwan	Taiwan Stock Exchange
Tanzania	Dar es Salaam Stock Exchange
Thailand	Stock Exchange of Thailand
Trinidad and Tobago	Trinidad and Tobago Stock Exchange, Port of Spain
Tunisia	Bourse de Tunis
Turkey	Istanbul Menkul Kiymetler Borsasi
Uganda	Uganda Securities Exchange
Ukraine	PFTS Ukraine Stock Exchange
United Arab Emirates	NASDAQ Dubai
United Kingdom	London Stock Exchange
	Channel Islands Stock Exchange
United States	American Stock Exchange, New York
	NASDAQ
	Boston Stock Exchange
	Chicago Stock Exchange
	New York Stock Exchange
	Pacific Exchange, Los Angeles and New York
	Philadelphia Stock Exchange
Uruguay	Bolsa de Valores de Montevideo
Uzbekistan	Tashkent Stock Exchange
Venezuela	Bolsa de Valores de Caracas
Vietnam	Ho Chi Minh Stock Exchange
West Africa	Bourse Regionale des Valeurs Mobilieres, SA (serves Benir, Burkina Faso, Guinea Bissau, Cote d'Ivoire, Mali, Niger, Senegal, Togo)
Zambia	Lusaka Stock Exchange
Zimbabwe	Zimbabwe Stock Exchange, Harare

Money

In the list of world currencies that follows, words (*) usually have no plural: e.g. 1 kyat (one kyat), 200 kyat (two hundred kyat), etc.

Country	Currency	Divided into	Abbreviation
Afghanistan	Afghani*	puli	Af or Afs
Albania	Lek*	qindraka	Lk
Algeria	Algerian dinar	centimes	DA
Andorra	Euro	cents	€
Angola	Kwanza*	lwei	Kzrl
Antigua	East Caribbean dollar	cents	EC$
Argentina	Argentinian peso	australes	
Australia	Australian dollar	cents	A$
Austria	Euro	cents	€
Bahamas	Bahamian dollar	cents	B$
Bahrain	Bahraini dinar	fils	BD
Bangladesh	Taka*	poisha	Tk
Barbados	Barbados dollar	cents	Bd$ or BD$
Belarus	Rouble	kopeks	BYR
Belgium	Euro	cents	€
Belize	Belize dollar	cents	BZ$
Benin	CFA franc	centimes	CFA Fr
Bermuda	Bermuda dollar	cents	Bda$
Bhutan	Ngultrum*	chetrum	N
Bolivia	Boliviano	centavos	$b
Bosnia Herzegovina	Marka		
Botswana	Pula	thebe	P
Brazil	Real	centavos	R$
Brunei	Brunei dollar	sen	B$
Bulgaria	Lev*	stotinki	Lv
Burkina Faso	CFA franc	centimes	CFA Fr
Burundi	Burundi franc	centimes	Bur Fr or FrBr
Cambodia	Riel*	sen	RI
Cameroon	CFA franc	centimes	CFA Fr
Canada	Canadian dollar	cents	Can$ or C$
Cape Verde Islands	Escudo Caboverdiano	centavos	CV esc
Cayman Islands	Cayman Island dollar	cents	CI$
Central African Republic	CFA franc	centimes	CFA Fr
Chad	CFA franc	centimes	CFA Fr
Chile	Chilean peso	centavos	Ch$
China	Yuan* or renminbi*	fen	Y
Colombia	Colombian peso	centavos	Col$
Comoros	CFA franc	centimes	CFA Fr
Congo (Republic of)	CFA franc	centimes	CFA Fr
Congo (Democratic Republic of)	Congolese franc	centimes	
Costa Rica	Colón*	centimos	₡
Croatia	Kuna	lipas	
Cuba	Cuban peso	centavos	Cub$
Cyprus	Cyprus pound	cents	£C or C£
Czech Republic	Koruna	Euro cents	€
Denmark	Krone	öre	DKr or DKK

Money *continued*

Country	Currency	Divided into	Abbreviation
Djibouti	Djibouti franc	centimes	Dj Fr
Dominica	East Caribbean dollar	cents	EC$
Dominican Republic	Dominican peso	centavos	DR$
East Timor	Dollar	cents	$ *or* US $
Ecuador	US Dollars	centavos	$
Egypt	Egyptian pound	piastres	£E *or* E£
El Salvador	US Dollars	centavos	$
Equatorial Guinea	CFA franc	centimes	CFA Fr
Estonia	Kroon	sents	
Ethiopia	Birr* *or* Ethiopian dollar	cents	EB
Fiji	Fiji dollar	cents	$F *or* F$
Finland	Euro	cents	€
France	Euro	cents	€
French Guiana	Euro	cents	€
Gabon	CFA franc	centimes	CFA Fr
Gambia, The	Dalasi*	butut	Di
Germany	Euro	cents	€
Ghana	Cedi*	pesewas	¢
Georgia	Lari	tetri	
Greece	Euro	cents	€
Grenada	East Caribbean dollar	cents	EC$
Guatemala	Quetzal	centavos	Q
Guinea	Guinea franc	centimes	
Guinea-Bissau	CFA franc	centimes	CFA Fr
Guyana	Guyana dollar	cents	G$
Haiti	Gourde*	centimes	Gde
Honduras	Lempira*	centavos	La
Hong Kong	Hong Kong dollar	cents	HK$
Hungary	Forint	filler	Ft
Iceland	Króna	aurar	Ikr
India	Rupee	paisa	R *or* Re *or* R$
Indonesia	Rupiah*	sen	representative
Iran	Rial*	dinars	RI
Iraq	New Iraqi dinar	fils	NID
Irish Republic	Euro	cents	€
Israel	Shekel	agora	IS
Italy	Euro	cents	€
Ivory Coast	CFA franc	centimes	CFA Fr
Jamaica	Jamaican dollar	cents	J$
Japan	Yen*	sen	Y *or* ¥
Jordan	Jordanian Dinar	fils	JD
Kazakhstan	Tenge		
Kenya	Kenya shilling	cents	KSh *or* Sh
Korea (North)	North Korean won*	chon	NK W
Korea (South)	South Korean won*	jeon	SK W
Kuwait	Kuwaiti dinar	fils	KD
Kyrgystan	Som	tyin	
Laos	Kip*	at	K *or* Kp

Money *continued*

Country	Currency	Divided into	Abbreviation
Latvia	Lat	santims	
Lebanon	Lebanese pound	piastres	£Leb *or* L£
Lesotho	Loti*	lisente	L
Liberia	Liberian dollar	cents	L$
Libya	Libyan dinar	dirhams	LD
Liechtenstein	Swiss franc	centimes	SFr *or* FS
Lithuania	Lita		
Luxembourg	Euro	cents	€
Maca	Pataca*	avos	P *or* $
Macedonia	Dinar	paras	
Madagascar	Ariary	iraimbilanja	MGA
Madeira	Euro	cents	€
Malawi	Kwacha*	tambala	K *or* MK
Malaysia	Ringgit *or* Malaysian Dollar	sen	M$
Maldives	Rufiyaa	laaris	MvRe
Mali	CFA franc	cents	CFA Fr
Malta	Euro	cents	€
Mauritania	Ouguiya*	khoums	U
Mauritius	Mauritius rupee	cents	Mau Rs *or* R
Mexico	Peso	centavos	Mex$
Moldova	Leu		
Monaco	Euro	cents	€
Mongolian Republic	Tugrik*	möngös	Tug
Montenegro	Euro	cents	€
Montserrat East	Caribbean dollar	cents	EC$
Morocco	Dirham	centimes	DH
Mozambique	New Metical*	centavos	M
Myanmar	Kyat*	pyas	Kt
Namibia	Namibian dollar	cents	
Nauru	Australian dollar	cents	A$
Nepal	Nepalese rupee	paisa	NR *or* Nre
Netherlands	Euro	cents	€
New Zealand	New Zealand dollar	cents	NZ$
Nicaragua	Córdoba	centavos	C$ *or* C
Niger	CFA franc	centimes	CFA Fr
Nigeria	Naira*	kobo	N *or* ₦
Norway	Krone	ore	NKr
Oman	Rial Omani	baizas	RO
Pakistan	Pakistan rupee	paisa	R *or* Pak Re
Panama	Balboa	centesimos	Ba
Papua New Guinea	Kina*	toea	Ka *or* K
Paraguay	Guarani*	centimos	G
Peru	New Sol	cents	S
Philippines	Philippine peso	centavos	P
Poland	Zloty	groszy	Zl
Portugal	Euro	cents	€
Puerto Rico	US dollar	cents	$ *or* US$
Qatar	Qatar Riyal	dirhams	QR
Reunion	CFA franc	centimes	CFA Fr
Romania	New Leu*	bani	L *or* l
Rwanda	Rwanda franc	centimes	Rw Fr

Money *continued*

Country	Currency	Divided into	Abbreviation
Russia	Rouble	kopeks	Rub
San Marino	Euro	cents	€
St Lucia	East Caribbean dollar	cents	EC$
St Vincent	East Caribbean dollar	cents	EC$
Samoa	Tala	sene	
Saudi Arabia	Saudi riyal *or* rial	halala	SA R
Senegal	CFA franc	centimes	CFA Fr
Serbia & Montenegro	Dinar	paras	DN
Seychelles	Seychelles rupee	cents	Sre *or* R
Sierra Leone	Leone	cents	Le
Singapore	Singapore dollar	cents	S$
Slovakia	Euro	cents	€
Slovenia	Euro	cents	€
Solomon Islands	Solomon Island dollar	cents	SI$
Somalia	Somali shilling	cents	Som Sh
South Africa	Rand*	cents	R
Spain	Euro	cents	€
Sri Lanka	Sri Lankan rupee	cents	SC Re
Sudan	Sudanese pound	piastres	SDG
Suriname	Suriname dollar	cents	$
Swaziland	Lilangeni*	cents	Li *or* E
Sweden	Krona	örer	SKr
Syria	Syrian pound	piastres	S£
Taiwan	New Taiwan dollar	cents	T$ *or* NT$
Tanzania	Tanzanian shilling	cents	TSh
Thailand	Baht*	satang	Bt
Togo	CFA franc	centimes	CFA Fr
Tonga	Pa'anga	seniti	
Trinidad & Tobago	Trinidad & Tobago dollar	cents	TT$
Tunisia	Tunisian dinar	millimes	TD
Turkey	New Turkish lira	kurus	TL
Turkmenistan	Manat	tenesi	
Tuvalu	Australian dollar	cents	$A
Uganda	Uganda Shilling	cents	Ush
Ukraine	Hryvna	kopiykas	
United Arab Emirates	UAE dirham	fils	UAE Dh *or* UD
United Kingdom	Pound sterling	pence	£ *or* £Stg
USA	Dollar	cents	$ *or* US$
Uruguay	Uruguayan peso	centesimos	N$
Uzbekistan	Sum	tiyin	
Vanuatu	Vatu	centimes	
Venezuela	Bolívar	centimos	BS
Vietnam	Dong*	xu	D
Virgin Islands	US dollar	cents	US$
Yemen	Riyal	fils	YR
Zambia	Kwacha*	ngwee	K
Zimbabwe	Zimbabwe dollar	cents	Z$